The Presence of Śiva

Published in cooperation with the
Philadelphia Museum of Art

The Presence of Śiva

STELLA KRAMRISCH

PHOTOGRAPHY BY PRAFUL C. PATEL

PRINCETON UNIVERSITY PRESS

Published by Princeton University Press, Princeton, New Jersey
In the United Kingdom:
Princeton University Press, Guildford, Surrey

Library of Congress Cataloging in Publication Data will be found on the last printed page of this book

This book has been composed in V-I-P Baskerville

Clothbound editions of Princeton University Press books are printed on acid-free paper, and binding materials are chosen for strength and durability

Printed in the United States of America by
Princeton University Press, Princeton, New Jersey

CONTENTS

LIST OF ILLUSTRATIONS

Ellora

ACKNOWLEDGMENTS

This book took shape over about ten years and I am grateful to those who read various drafts of the manuscript, edited the English, and checked the references to Sanskrit texts. Paul Todd Makler, Dorothy Norman, and Svatantra Kumar Pidara gave their unstinting help during the earlier phases. Guy Welbon made valuable suggestions concerning the substance of the text; Darrel Sewell added constructive comments to the Appendix. Susan Oleksiw painstakingly revised in its final form the language and accuracy of the manuscript with regard to its sources. To her in particular, to all those who helped, and to the authorities of the Philadelphia Museum of Art who facilitated my work, I am indebted forever.

Grateful acknowledgment is due to the Archaeological Survey of India for granting permission and facilities to Praful C. Patel to take photographs at Ajanta and Ellora.

GUIDE TO PRONUNCIATION

Vowels should be pronounced as in Italian; a lengthening sign as in ā indicates a long vowel; e and o are always long; ṛ in Sanskrit is a vowel and should be pronounced similar to the ri in ring; c should be pronounced as in church, j as in joy; ś and ṣ similar to sh in ship; h after a consonant should be pronounced distinctly as the th in hot-house.

The Presence of Śiva

I

THE PRIMORDIAL SCENE

1. Raudra Brahman

His name is not uttered. It must not be mentioned; only indirectly is He to be referred to (*AB*.3.34).

A hymn of the *Ṛg Veda* (*RV*.10.61), the most sacred and most ancient work of Indian religious tradition, begins by calling itself a "wild creation" or "a poem about the Wild God" (*raudra brahman*) (*RV*.10.61.1). The hymn knows whom it evokes by these words, for His presence is in these words. In the lucid frenzy of the images of the hymn He arises and abides.

It is when time is about to begin. In the dawn of the world, when the black cow of cosmic night lies with the ruddy cows of morning (*RV*.10.61.4), two figures appear, the Father and the virgin daughter, his own daughter. They are the two actors in the primordial scene. The Father makes love to the daughter. Suddenly he pulls back, his seed falls down to earth, the place of sacrifice (*RV*.10.61.5-7). "In their concern the gods created a poem, a word of power (*brahman*) and out of this they gave shape to Vāstoṣpati, the guardian of the dwelling, the guardian of sacred order (*vratapā*)" (*RV*.10.61.7). "Like a raging bull did the Father foam, running this way and that way and away with scant understanding. Like one rejected she sped south" (*RV*.10.61.8), into cosmic night. In spite of this mishap or on account of it, soon the patter was heard on earth of the progeny of the Father (*RV*.10.61.9).[1]

Creation is an act of violence that infringes upon the Uncreate, the

[1] Different interpretations of this hymn have been proposed. Cf. *Ṛg Veda Saṃhitā (RV)*, tr. Geldner, 1951, 3:225-28.

undifferentiated wholeness that is before the beginning of things. And yet another act of violence is hinted at, and this act is kept secret in these wild and portentous *mantras*. He is implied, for it is He who is invoked in this hymn. He, the most powerful, who with the arrow in his hand hit the target (*RV*.10.61.3). The Father was made to pull back from the creative act that was to be prevented or undone by Him, yet lead to the existence of life on earth. Without revealing their source, sparks of meaning flare up in tense brevity in the *raudra brahman*.

A hymn to Agni, the Fire (*RV*.1.71), sheds light on His nature whose name the *raudra brahman* withholds. This hymn celebrates Agni, who had prepared the seed for Father Heaven. But when Agni noticed the lust of the Father for his daughter, this hunter crept along, then boldly shot his arrow at the Father just when he was quenching his desire in his daughter. The hunter had aimed at the creative act itself. Father Heaven shed his seed. It fell to earth. Agni, the Fire, brought to life the Father's progeny, the benevolent host of immaculate Fire-youths (*RV*.1.71.5, 8).

Fire is a hunter. The flame creeps along, lashes out, it hits the victim with its dart. The arrow of Agni strikes the Father in his passionate embrace of the daughter. But Agni's heat had also ripened the seed in the Father. Foaming in hot fury when he is struck by the fiery arrow, the Father spills his seed on the earth, the site of sacrifice, where it will sprout in the splendor of the immaculate and benevolent Fire-youths, the host of the Aṅgirases, Agni's priests.

The ambiguity of Agni is the ambiguity of fire itself, which both sustains and destroys life. But inasmuch as the Father is the object of this ambiguity, Agni is the name of the hunter who is but a mask of Him whose name is withheld and to whom the gods, the celestial intelligence, in compassionate insight give shape as Vāstoṣpati, the guardian of the dwelling, the guardian of divine law (*vratapā*). They carved (*atakṣan*)[2]—this is the literal translation—this shape out of the poem (*brahman*) while they created it (*RV*.10.61.7). By their wording of the sacred *mantra* His shape arose in its meter, and the vision took form in the rhythm of the words of this *raudra brahman*, this wild, fierce hymn of the god whose name it hides while he is seen as he

[2] M. Mayrhofer, *Concise Etymological Sanskrit Dictionary*, *s.v. takṣati*.

arises in his unfathomable nature and paradoxical shape as guardian of sacred order, lord of *vāstu*.

The mystery of creation in this simultaneity of manifestations begins with a fateful shot, the wound it inflicts on the Father, the loss of his seed, its fall to earth, and the birth of the poem and of mankind to be. In the beginning is the word sung by the gods, the celestial intelligence, compassionate witnesses of primal passion and of the deed of the hunter. The mystery of the *raudra brahman* embraces the cosmic creative act together with the form-engendering creation of the poem. The *brahman* tells of the mystery and at the same time tells of its mode of telling. It shrouds and at the same time conveys His name in the form it gives to him by calling itself a *raudra brahman*, a wild creation, or Rudraic creation, for this poem and the creation are of Rudra, the Wild God. *Raudra*, an adjective from Rudra, means wild, of Rudra nature.[3] Rudra as the name of the god would signify "the Wild One" or "the Fierce God." According to later Vedic tradition, however, the word Rudra is derived from *rud*, to cry, howl (*TS*.1.5.1.1; *MS*.4.2.12; *ŚB*.6.1.3.10). While the words of the *mantras* conjure up the primordial action and evoke the entire myth, they also carry the effect of this action on the gods, that is, on the evoking consciousness. Reflected in that consciousness, the action acquires the form of the poem. In this transmutation the main actor, whose name is withheld because his action and its effect on his victim fully identify him, arises not as Fire, not as Wild Archer, but as Vāstoṣpati, guardian of the dwelling and guardian of sacred order (*vratapā*). In this shape he emerges from the poem of magic power, the *brahman*. Poetry in the sacred order of its meters is his domain. Therein the fire of the Wild Archer sustains the form. Vāstoṣpati, created by the gods, the celestial intelligence, is the guardian of his domain, the world of sacred order—a rhythmic structure that is art, a cosmos. These are *vāstu*, the house that he guards.

Thus His world comes about. The double meaning of the word *raudra* is intentional: the poem is about Rudra, the wild, formidable god, and it is itself a fiercely wild creation charged with many meanings. They emerge from other hymns, are made more explicit in later texts, and are basic to the cosmos of Rudra, which has its image in myths

[3] *Ibid., s.v. rudra*.

and the visual arts. In these two modes of form the mystery of this god has left its imprint over the millennia on the resilient matrix of the Indian mind. The unnamed god evoked in the scene of violence and awe in the primordial moment of the creation of man—when time was about to begin—is the main actor, although he does not figure in the scene. The gods, the collective celestial intelligence, watch the scene and in their concern they turn it into a mantric poem from which the unnamed god arises as Vāstoṣpati, the guardian of sacred order (*vratapā*). Vāstoṣpati means guardian of the *vāstu*, and *vāstu* means both site and dwelling or house.[4]

The Wild Hunter in the precosmic wilderness is Rudra. In the form of their poem, a magic creation (*brahman*), the gods give shape to him as Vāstoṣpati. The *vāstu* that he guards is the cosmos, the site that is his domain is the site of the sacrifice. The sacred order of the cosmos is enacted on the site of the sacrifice in the rhythm of rites and hymns. They are analogous to the rhythms that pervade the cosmos.

2. The Lord of Animals

The primordial, paradigmatic myth of Rudra is told in the *Maitrāyaṇī Saṃhitā* of the *Black Yajurveda*. Father Heaven, henceforth acting under the name of Prajāpati, Lord of Generation, desired his daughter Uṣas, the Dawn. She became a female antelope, he became an antelope[5] and pursued her. While he was taking his perverse pleasure in her, he suddenly turned around toward one who was aiming his arrow at him. Addressing the Archer, Prajāpati in fear exclaimed: "I make you Lord of the Animals (*paśūnāṃ pati*)." "Leave me." Thus his name is Paśupati, Lord of Animals. The first seed that fell was surrounded by fire produced by Agni (*MS*.4.2.12) (cf. Paśupā: *RV*. 1.114.9; cf. *TS*.3.1.5.1).

Thus he came to be, and everything in existence. When he ap-

[4] V. S. Apte, *The Practical Sanskrit-English Dictionary, s.v.*

[5] The animals are *ṛśya* and *rohiṇī*. *Ṛśya* is the male of a species of antelope. *Rohiṇī* connotes a red cow or "a young girl in whom menstruation has just commenced" (Apte, *The Practical Sanskrit-English Dictionary, s.v.*). The *Aitareya Brāhmaṇa* (*AB*.3.33) speaks of *mṛga* and *rohiṇī*. *Mṛga* denotes a wild animal, deer, or antelope. The ritual significance of the black antelope (*kṛṣṇamṛga*) suggests that it was this animal whose shape Prajāpati had taken (Ch. X.A.2.d). The shape of Uṣas, the Dawn, would be that of a female antelope.

proached shooting, he howled (*arodīt*). Hence his name is Rudra, the roarer, according to popular etymology (*MS*.4.2.12). He has two natures or two "names": the one, cruel and wild (*rudra*), the other kind (*śiva*) and tranquil (*śānta*). These he assumes at will (*MS*.4.2.12). They are interconnected, springing from the same root hidden deep in this god. Rudra is *śiva* (*RV*.10.92.9). The *rudra-śiva* polarity of the god is carried by his Rudra-Agni nature.

Agni, the Fire, prepares the seed for the Father, but Rudra himself is Agni. Their shapes overlap. The connection of Rudra and Agni circles a point of identity. Agni is Rudra. This homology, stated again and again in sacred scripture (*RV*.1.27.10; 2.1.6; 3.2.5; 4.3.1; 8.61.3; *TS*.1.3.14.1; 1.5.1.1; 2.6.6.6; 5.4.3.1; 5.4.10.5; 5.5.7.4; *ŚB*.1.7.3.8; 6.1.3.10; 9.1.1.1; *MBh*.3.218.27), is one of nature, not of person. Inasmuch as his nature is that of fire, Rudra is Agni. Rudra prepares the fiery seed of Prajāpati; but Rudra is also the fire that pursues and frightens him when, having intercourse with Uṣas, the Dawn, the antelope, his daughter, he sees the flaming arrow of Rudra, the cruel hunter, the avenger, aimed at him. Prajāpati is the target of Rudra. When his seed falls on earth, it is surrounded by Agni. Moreover, the stages of the drama are simultaneous. Time did not yet exist. Time was just about to begin from out of timeless simultaneity in that first early morning of the world.

Rudra, the Fire, prepares the seed for the Father; Rudra the Archer aims at the Father, hot with passion, who lets fall the seed on earth. Rudra is not a person, not a power confined in one single shape. And he is the cause and also that effect on which again he acts. He prepares the seed for the Father. The seed sends forth the Father's heat of passion. The consummation of passion is being shot at by Rudra. Inasmuch as he is Agni, he prepares the seed. Inasmuch as he is Rudra, he is intent on the destruction of the effect that he has caused. He incites toward creation, and when it takes its course he lets fly his arrow against it. The sequence of contradictory actions is far from self-defeating. It is of the very nature of Rudra, who creates in order to destroy, for he will create again in an inexhaustible renewal of life on earth, where creation is the aeviternal answer to destruction, and both have their ground and antithesis in the Uncreate. This is the course that Rudra set. More truly than any other god he could have said of himself: "I am not a puzzled-out book, I am a god with his contradictions."[6] His contradictions, his polarities operate on all levels of his ambience, radiating from his center.

When the terror of the moment of creation seized the gods, that celestial intelligence made of it a poem, a word of power, a riddle, posed by and solved by Rudra, the *raudra brahman*.

The Rudra-Śiva tension as it is expressed in the *Maitrāyaṇī Saṃhitā* operates on a lower level of realization than that of the *raudra brahman*. In the *mantras* of the *raudra brahman* the tension is between the unnamed god and Vāstoṣpati, guardian of the dwelling, guardian of divine law. By alluding to the act while withholding the name of the actor, the *mantras* make his presence loom over the entire scene. It extends into the creation by the gods, into the measured rhythm of the poem from which the figure of Vāstoṣpati emerges.

Here there are two forms of the unnamed god. One is the appalling Hunter who aims "against nature," against the primordial act of Father Heaven that he as Agni had instigated, against procreation, by which mankind was to come about. The other form is that of Vāstoṣpati, created by the gods, the celestial intelligence, the creativeness itself of mind. The two forms imply the tension between life and its negation on the one side, the wild untamed world, the wilderness in man and nature, and on the other side the world of art and cosmic order. Both are his domain. In the one he acts as the Wild Hunter. In the other he manifests as guardian of the dwelling, as guardian of the sacred cosmic order. The dwelling that he guards and the sacred order that he guards are forms in which—in the poem by the gods—his presence arises out of and on the strength of his fierceness. Vāstoṣpati is the guardian of the sacred order of the cosmos; he watches over all rhythms and rites of life.

The myth of the origin of mankind and the mystery of creation in the cosmos and in art are in the magic words of the *raudra brahman*.

Life on earth began with the shot at the Father in the procreative moment. The seed fell to earth from Father Heaven. The arrow was shot against the Father, against the emission of seed. The arrow hit its target. Dawn ran away from her mate, from her father, into cosmic night—to arise in another aeon. What made the Hunter let fly his arrow so that it hit the Father at the procreative moment?

[6] Paraphrasing C. F. Meyer, *Huttens Letzte Tage, Eine Dichtung*, 8th ed., 1891, p. 1, "ich bin kein ausgeklügelt Buch, Ich bin ein Mensch mit seinem Widerspruch."

The *raudra brahman* is called the fire-storm chant (*āgnimāruta uktha*) in the *Brāhmaṇa of a Hundred Paths* (*ŚB*.1.7.4.4). The *Aitareya Brāhmaṇa* speaks of the *raudra brahman* as a wonder-work of the gods: "There are such wonder-works of the gods, and the arts in this world are to be understood as an imitation thereof" (*AB*.6.27).[7] In this archetypal work of art created by the compassionate gods, that is, by divine insight, Rudra-Vāstoṣpati and his world come to exist. The gods create this wonder-work when mankind is about to begin. And man's works of art will imitate or reflect the primordial works of art of the gods.

In the *Ṛg Veda* myth of Rudra, the origin of mankind, beginning with the Aṅgirases, the mythic Fire-youths, is interwoven with the creation of poetry, the archetypal act of art *in divinis*. Although in this myth man is not created in the image of god, the art of man is in conformable imitation of the wonder-works of gods. Works of art are substantiations of divine prototypes. They are their audible, visible, tangible, concrete form. In rhythms and rites, the guardian of sacred order, Vratapā, surveys his domain.

Even the gods do not always maintain the same high level of creativity. A version of the same myth shows them reacting differently to Prajāpati's desire for his daughter. Because Prajāpati was doing something that was not done before, they made a god to punish Prajāpati. They did not find one horrendous enough for the task, and so they put together the most appalling shapes. This aggregate became the avenger (*AB*.3.33). The gods here were far from benevolent, and were unconcerned with rhythms and rites. Prompted as they were by their fear and horror, they asked the dread aggregate who had become "that god" (*eṣa devaḥ*) to pierce what was going on between Father and daughter, two antelopes, and were glad to grant "that god" the boon that he had asked, namely, lordship over the animals (*paśuman*) (*AB*.3.33; cf. *ŚB*.1.7.4.3). As a fiercely horrendous conglomerate and their agent, the Lord of Animals, Paśuman or Pásupati earned this name as a reward granted by the frightened gods.

The unnamed god of the *Ṛg Veda* hymn was made Lord of Animals by Prajāpati. This title was given to the Wild Archer by the Lord of Generation in his predicament, so that he might be spared by him. This is what the *Maitrāyaṇī Saṃhitā* (*MS*.4.2.12) knows. The *Aitareya*

[7] *Aitareya Brāhmaṇa (AB)*, ed. & tr. M. Haug, 1863, 2:288.

Brāhmaṇa, however, tells of the same situation in a different spirit. Here it is not the Lord of Generation—persecuted animal that he is—who asks a boon from the Wild Hunter, and rewards him by making him Lord of Animals. It is the gods who create a god by combining all the most dreadful shapes in order to avenge the intercourse of Prajāpati with his daughter. This symplegma of horror they reward by making him, at his request, Lord of Animals. Obviously these gods did not like "that god," a projection of their own reactions. They did not have the eye to see what the gods of the *Ṛg Veda* hymn intuited who created the unnamed god, the guardian of the site, the guardian of sacred rites, Vāstoṣpati.

The hunter, the unnamed god, was made Lord of Animals or Paśupati by the Lord of Generation for sparing his life. Or the gods created a horrendous being—"that god"—whom they made Lord of Animals for piercing the Lord of Generation. But whether Paśupati acted mercifully or in fierceness, the seed of the Lord of Generation had fallen down on earth. Why did Rudra aim his arrow at Prajāpati engaged in the procreative act?

3. The Lord of Yoga

The answer comes from far back in historical time. On a seal (seal 420) of the Harappan age of about the last part of the third millennium B.C., a male figure is seen seated, enthroned in a particular yoga posture (*siddha āsana*), the feet crossed below the erect penis (*ūrdhvaliṅga*). Buffalo horns are the most conspicuous part of his headgear. Four animals surround this central figure.[8] Other smaller reliefs also (between ¾ in. and 1½ in. square), though less rich and precise in detail, show the seated yogi as the main or only figure. The throne or dais, in some of the reliefs, rests on bovine legs.[9] While the yogic posture (*āsana*) in each instance is indisputable, the specific *siddha āsana*,

[8] Sir John Marshall, *Mohenjo-Daro and the Indus Civilization*, 1931, vol. 1, pl. XII, no. 17. Also, E.J.H. Mackay, *Further Excavations at Mohenjo-Daro*, 1937, vol. 2, pl. XCIV, no. 420.

[9] Mackay, *Further Excavations at Mohenjo-Daro*, pl. LXXXVII, nos. 222 & 235; and pl. CII, no. 9; and Marshall, *Mohenjo-Daro and the Indus Civilization*, vol. 3, pl. cxviii, no. 11, show a yogi figure flanked by kneeling worshipers and serpents. Cf. W. A. Fairservis, Jr., *The Roots of Ancient India*, 2nd ed., 1971, p. 276, figs. 16-18. Also see D. Srinivasan, "The So-Called Proto-Śiva Seal from Mohenjo-Daro: An Iconological Assessment," p. 55, fig. 13.

in which the crossed heels touch the testicles, is rendered in detail on the large seal only.[10] It is also on the large seal only that a disproportionately large face sits on narrow shoulders covered by a striated pectoral.

Whom this enigmatic figure represents cannot be ascertained. The other Harappan yogi figures have small faces with recognizably human features; bovine traits have possibly been integrated into the face of the large seal.[11] Although the enthroned figure with its large head and sex organ defies identification, it is like the other unidentified figures shown in a yoga posture. On either side of the enthroned yogi and above his arms, a tiger and an elephant are on his right, a rhinoceros and buffalo on his left, and two antelopes are below, that is, in front of his throne. The composition of this steatite relief is hieratic. The horn-crowned and enthroned yogi figure forms an isosceles triangle whose axis connects the middle of the bifurcating horns,[12] the long nose, and the erect phallus of the deity.

About two thousand years lie between the Harappan civilization and the formulation of the yoga system in the *Yogasūtra* of Patañjali in the second century B.C. A similar time interval lies between the Harappan reliefs and those of early Buddhist art, which embody motifs and principles of Harappa.[13]

Although seal 420 cannot be identified as a "proto-Śiva," it shows one of several Harappan yogi representations. Bovine features are conspicuous in these reliefs. In later Indian art, Śiva's particular cognizance as a yogi is the *ūrdhvaliṅga*.[14] The phallus or *liṅga* pointing upward and pressing against the abdomen is a visual convention rendering the concept of *ūrdhvaretas* or the ascent of the semen (cf. Sāyaṇa on *TA*.10.12; *MBh*.13.17.45). The *ūrdhvaliṅga* is exclusively and almost universally characteristic of images of Śiva through the two

[10] A. Hiltebeitel, "The Indus Valley 'Proto-Śiva' Reexamined through Reflections on the Goddess, the Buffalo and the Symbolism of the *Vāhanas*," 1978, p. 769.

[11] D. Srinivasan, "The So-Called Proto-Śiva Seal from Mohenjo-Daro," pp. 47-58.

[12] W. A. Fairservis, Jr., *Excavations at Allahdino*, 1976, p. 14 and fig. 19a; A. Hiltebeitel, "The Indus Valley 'Proto-Śiva,'" (p. 771 n. 13) and others identified the horns as those of a buffalo and not of a bull.

[13] S. Kramrisch, *Indian Sculpture*, 1933, pp. 4, 5-7, pls. 1, 2.

[14] J. C. Harle, *Gupta Sculpture: Indian Sculpture of the Fourth to the Sixth Centuries, A.D.*, 1974, pls. 53, 54, from Kausambi, 3rd-4th centuries; A. de Lippe, *Indian Medieval Sculpture*, 1978, pl. 127; P. Pal, *The Sensuous Immortals: A Selection of Sculptures from the Pan-Asian Collection*, 1978, pl. 43; J. N. Banerjea, *The Development of Hindu Iconography*, 2nd ed., 1956, pl. 39: 1, 2.

millennia of the present era. It implies that no semen is allowed to leave the body; by controlling sexual power the semen held within is absorbed in the body. "Control of the seminal fluid is thought to entail control of all passions and the achievement of desirelessness."[15] This yoga discipline, practiced to this day, and leading to supreme mystical cognition (*samādhi*) would seem to underlie the pictorial symbol of the diminutive relief of the seal from Mohenjo-daro, a surviving token of a no doubt living Indian discipline of making the psycho-physical organism of man the place of metaphysical realization. The harnessing of the sexual urge and the mastery over its working have their image in Śiva, lord of yogis, with the *ūrdhvaliṅga* as his cognizance. Assuming that seal 420 shows the *ūrdhvaliṅga*, a clay figure from Mohenjo-daro, though not in yoga posture, may be mentioned.[16] The figurine, modeled in the round, shows the male sex parts, although not the *ūrdhvaliṅga*, with similar distinction of treatment as in seal 420. This figurine is hermaphroditic; its rounded breasts show it to be female. It is the only surviving example of a bisexual kind. Sex symbolism links this figurine to the seated divinity of the seal, whose penis pointing upward shows that the god has controlled sex. The standing figurine, on the other hand, includes both sexes in its appearance, as do Hindu images of Śiva Ardhanārīśvara more than two thousand years later, though these latter exhibit an altogether different mode of unifying division, in which the right half of the entire figure is male and the left half is female. It would seem, however, that a preoccupation with the signs of sex as carriers of meanings beyond their sexual function had its place in the imagery of Harappan art. The freedom in grafting male and female parts on one figurine is akin to the meaningful spontaneity in which anthropomorphic and theriomorphic parts are coalesced. The god in yoga posture carries mighty buffalo horns on his head above a large face that is striated, as are the horns and their connecting central headgear, the arms, and the triangular pectoral. The parallel ridges are elements of form. The uncannily grooved, large face, with its large long nose, emphasizes the vertical axis of the figure, which is also the vertical axis of the entire hieratic configuration of the seal. The grooves and ridges evolve a pattern of their own, while following the contour of the mask-like face.

Harappan art dematerializes volume by translating it into complex

[15] A. Bharati, *The Tantric Tradition*, 1970, p. 294.

[16] J. Marshall, *Mohenjo-Daro and the Indus Civilization*, vol. 3, pl. 94, fig. 11.

linear patterns of ridged parallels. These are formal idioms, not thematic motifs.

The buffalo horns gracing the head of this figure and other figures in human shape in Harappan art impart bovine grandeur and significance to their appearance. The bull is one of the noblest and most frequently represented animals on the seals, often occupying the entire seal but for its inscription. Other animals, however, are given the same distinction. And some of these—elephant and tiger, buffalo and rhino—also are shown in small size to the right and left of the majestic image of the enthroned buffalo-horned yogi. Two antelopes in front of but shown below the throne seat prefigure the two deer frequently carved on steles from the Gupta age, couchant in front of the throne seat of another yogi, the Buddha. The yogi seals are part of the repertory of Harappan seals, which often portray the animal as the main figure. The combination, moreover, of man and animal in the representation of deities belongs to Harappan art as much as the consorting of gods who are envisioned in the shape of animals belongs to Vedic thought.

About a millennium separates the Vedic from the Harappan age. Though the collection of the hymns of the *Ṛg Veda* was not completed before 1,000 B.C., some of its myths originated in a far remote past. In the *Ṛg Veda* the bovine species, whether as buffalo or bull, lends its glamor to the evocation of the gods. Agni, Indra, Soma, and Varuṇa, the principal Vedic gods, are invoked as buffaloes. Much less frequently are they invoked as bulls. Indra is once praised as a buffalo great in "bull powers" (*RV*.3.46.2), the buffalo obviously taking precedence over the bull. The difference is one not only of power but also of quality. The arch-god *manifesting* is the bull Asura (*RV*.3.38.4). He is bull and cow (*RV*.3.38.7). He is Viśvarūpa or omniform (*RV*.3.38.4). Prior to manifestation he had no name. Agni, the Fire, is a bull when fully manifest; he is a buffalo in the lap of the waters (*RV*.10.8.1) before he rises from them; there buffaloes made him grow (*RV*.10.45.3), and he is freed from this shape in which he dwelt in the depths (*RV*.1.141.3). The buffalo is Agni's shape in the waters, hidden in his power. When he rises from the waters, his bull's roar is heard (*RV*.10.8.1). Soma, too, while in the water striving to acquire his final clarified state, is a buffalo (*RV*.9.96.18-19; 9.97.40-41). The buffalo is power in potentiality, the bull is the power in act, in manifestation. The buffalo stands for hidden potentiality; he is near to the source (cf. *RV*.10.5.7). In the hymn to Rudra that sings his praises as the most glorious in glory of all that is born and the strongest of the strong (*RV*.2.33.3), he is invoked as bull (*RV*.2.33.15). But regardless of whether or not buffalo and bull signify different qualities of power, both bovines stand for power and the horns are its symbol. The buffalo horns of the yogic god of Mohenjo-daro, high on his head, are on either side of the central crest of the figure's headgear and of the vertical axis that refers this tripartite device to the triune shape of the deity's sex organ through which it passes. Animal power and sex controlled by yoga are coalesced in a pattern that renders the enigmatic likeness of the god of the Mohenjo-daro seal.

Though animals as vehicles of deity are to be found neither in Harappan imagery nor in Vedic visions, in Hindu India Śiva's vehicle (*vāhana*) is the bull. The bull conveys the presence of Śiva. The bull, particularly the Indian zebu, figures prominently in the iconography of Rudra. Śiva is shown in anthropomorphic shape in front of the bull on one of the earliest unmistakably identifiable representations of Rudra-Śiva.[17] The Great God (*Mahādeva*) is praised in the *Mahābhārata* as the one who has the bull for his sign, the pride of a bull, the lord of bulls, represented by the horns of the bull, bull of bulls, who has the mark of the bull, and so on (*MBh*.7.173.30-31). In Hindu India, the bull is Śiva's animal. Lying contentedly and attentively, the bull as the image of Nandin, "delight," faces the temple of Śiva. In South India, bulls have their stations on the corners of every story of the sanctuary of a Śiva temple, or as in Mahabalipuram in the eighth century, they are arrayed on top of the surrounding wall of the Shore Temple. The bull, disciplined in its power, represents dharma (*VDhP*.3.48.18). Dharma is cosmic order and righteous performance of one's duty. As such, the bull would belong to Śiva/Rudra, whom the *raudra brahman* knew as Vāstoṣpati, the lord of sacred ordinance (*vratapā*).

By whatever name the central figure of the Harappan seal was called, it embodies yoga power in its posture. The axis of its erect body is marked by the crossed feet below the *ūrdhvaliṅga*. Thence it ascends and carries the wide curves of the horns. Bovine power and yoga power are united in the hieratic form of the figure that dominates the field.

[17] Cf. coins of the Kuṣāṇa ruler, Vima Kadphises, 1st century A.D., J. M. Rosenfield, *The Dynastic Arts of the Kushans*, 1967, p. 22, pl. I, coin 17; pl. II, 19, 21, 23, 26-27, 29.

4. RUDRA, THE FIRE

Lord of Animals—Lord of Yoga—only Rudra has these names and powers. No other god is known in such seemingly disparate majesty. In each of these forms Rudra is fully present. They are more than aspects, more than modes of his being. He has many aspects, many modes, many names—a hundred, a thousand.

Of ruddy brown complexion, he shines in many colors (*RV*.2.33.8-9) like fire (Agni). Indeed, Rudra is Agni and Agni is Rudra (*TS*.2.2.10.4; 3.5.5.2; 5.5.7.4; cf. *MBh*.13.146.1-2). They are one in nature, though not in intensity. Rudra is the terrible, frightening, quintessential Agni. He is the fury of Fire (*TS*.2.2.2.3). Like fire, but fiercer and even more luminous, wild, tremendous Rudra is fire, lightning, and the sun (*MBh*.13.146.4). Fire is the power of illumination and is concentrated in him. He burns; he is atrocious, and full of heat; like fire he devours flesh, blood, and marrow (*MBh*.13.146.7). The Wild God—the essence of fire—is in the fire, in the waters, in the plants; he has entered all beings (*KāS*.40.5; *TS*.5.5.9.3; cf. *AV*.7.87.1). Inwardly he marks them with his signature. "The names of the different manifestations of Rudra . . . should be contemplated as written in fire inside the different parts of the body" (cf. *AP*.293.43-47).[18] Moreover, while Rudra is Agni, he also has other identities and acts under their names. These names, like Agni, conform with his essence. They are Paśupati, Lord of Animals; Śarva, the Archer; and Bhava, Existence. "These names, other than Agni, are full of stress (*aśānta*). Agni is his most gentle (*śāntatama*) name" (*ŚB*.1.7.3.8).

Rudra is Agni; he is the fierce essence of fire. Agni is Rudra's mildest form. Fierce, all-pervading, all-enlivening, all-consuming, Rudra holds the world in his power. He does not serve it, as does Agni—the fire of the hearth and of the altar.

Agni himself had not wanted to serve gods and man as their chief priest in the sacrifice. He was reluctant to be yoked, tied to this office, as were his brothers formerly (*RV*.10.51.4, 6). Secretly he went away and entered the waters and the plants. Yet his splendor was seen shining in the waters by Yama, mortal man, and Agni yielded to the rewards and privileges that the gods held out for him. He took over the high office to which the three thousand three hundred thirty-nine gods had called him (*RV*.10.51.3, 7-9; 10.52.6). Agni allowed himself

[18] *Agni Purāṇa (AP)*, tr. M. N. Dutt, 1903-1904, p. 1086.

to be tamed. Serving gods and man and becoming the sacrificial fire, he sacrificed his freedom. His sense of freedom had not carried him farther than into one abortive flight. In more than one sense is Agni the sacrifice (*RV*.10.88.9).

In his sacrificial role, however, Agni was to play a part analogous, though transposed into the orbit of the sacrifice, to that of Rudra, the fierce archer. Agni himself is an archer. His arrows glow with heat (*RV*.4.4.1), but in his office as priest he has no use for them. On the contrary, absorbed in sacred thought centered in his knowledge of cosmic order (*ṛta*) in its aeviternal truth, he concurred with the Father when the latter, benefaction in mind, offered up his seed in his daughter (*RV*.3.31.1). Then the Aṅgirases were born (cf. *RV*.3.31.3).

Agni is here the primordial, paradigmatic flame arising as the sacred fire. Agni knows the cosmic order (*ṛta*), for he is its first-born in the earliest aeon (*RV*.10.5.7). In this cosmically and sacrificially ordered universe-to-be, Agni and the Father are cooperating powers. The Father inseminating his daughter performs a cosmogonic rite to which the Aṅgirases and ultimately man owe their position in an ordered world. No god is horrified in this case by the intercourse of the Father and his daughter. On the contrary, their intercourse is the essential rite of this paradigmatic sacrifice, a sacrifice enacted in conformity with cosmic order in the presence of Agni, the primordial priest.

Fire as Agni and Fire as Rudra play contradictory and consistent roles. The Wild God defends the Uncreate, the transcendental integrity before the beginning of things. Agni, officiating in the sacrifice of which the cosmos is one counterpart and the ordered life of man-to-be the other, celebrates the primordial rite that will lead to the creation of man.

Agni celebrates the union of the Father and his daughter. The target of Rudra-Agni, the Wild Archer, is the incontinence of the Father that makes him shed into creation the substance of the Uncreate. Rudra avenges the violation, that is the rupture, of the Uncreate. Rudra—Fire and Archer—is Rudra Lord of Yoga and Guardian of the Uncreate. But the Lord of Generation's seed fell down on the earth.

The congress of Father and daughter is essential to the primordial scene, whether it is staged in a sacrificial setting or in the wilderness of the first dawn of the world. In its sacrificial setting the question of incest as something done anomalously and indecorously does not arise. Quite the contrary, the intercourse of Father and daughter is the very core of the rite that is for the good of the world. Agni, the sacrificial fire, had in view mankind and its life in this world. Agni-Rudra, on the other hand, was outraged. He aimed his arrow of fire at the Father, not because it is his daughter with whom he has intercourse but because it is the substance itself of the Uncreate that he is spending into procreation. Rudra acted as guardian and avenger of the Uncreate and metaphysical wholeness; Agni is the guardian of *ṛta*, of cosmic order in creation and of human life lived in accordance with it. Though one in nature, Agni and Rudra face in opposite directions: Agni's concern is the life of man, and Rudra's concern is man's freedom from the contingencies of life, his reintegration into the absolute as it was and is from before creation.

If Agni is the first-born of *ṛta* in the first world age (*RV*.10.5.7), he is also "born from the belly of the Asura" (*RV*.3.29.14),[19] the ancient godhead. Agni has many births (*RV*.10.45.1-2; *RV*.10.5.1), though in truth he "is always the child of himself," in that fire is born from fire. The fire-genealogy, a continuum in time, is spread through all forms of life. Using anthropomorphic terms, it gives Agni three mothers (*RV*.10.45.1), the three worlds of heaven, earth, and midair.[20] They are his places of origin, or rather of manifestation. Rudra, similarly, is Tryambaka, "having three mothers" (*RV*.7.59.12; *VS*.3.58, 60; *ŚB*.2.6.2.14). He is manifest throughout the universe. Family and sex relations furnish spontaneously available metaphors. They evoke biologically potent and particularly cogent images. If Agni is the son of three mothers, he is also "born from the belly of the Asura." The latter place of origin, more abstruse, more recondite than the maternal one, lies beyond the triple world. Or Agni is the father of the gods, though he is their son (*RV*.1.69.1), the gods here confirming by their intermediacy that Agni is always the child of himself. These multiple relationships are without sociological reference or moral overtones. They are conveyed as much by anthropomorphic as by theriomorphic figures. The intercourse of the creator with his hypostasis, the daughter, has the intimacy of fulfillment on either level. If the imagery is theriomorphic, two antelopes act with creaturely assurance in their

[19] A. A. Macdonell, *Vedic Mythology*, 1897, p. 90.

[20] *Ibid.*, p. 12: "The space in which a thing is contained or produced is its father or mother."

own state of grace. While in this universe of discourse Agni is genealogically his own child, ontically and in his theriomorphic image he is the "bull who is also the cow" (*RV*.10.5.7). Agni is complete in simultaneous male-female duality, and in this wholeness of being Agni is nearest to the perfection of the indefinable state of integrity before Agni or anything else was born or became manifest.

The symbol of the bull who is also a cow is one of the ultimate metaphors at the very limit of thought and image whence the ineffable realm beyond creation has its measureless extent (*RV*.10.5.7). Bisexual Agni, aeviternally child of himself, renews himself in each spark, in whatsoever form of life, from aeon to aeon.

Only one at a time of the ultimate metaphors is beheld by the seer, at the end of his field of vision (cf. *RV*.10.5.6). In that sign the mystery of creation unfolds. Each sign at the edge of the world of thought and image is a key and a password to an insight from the limen into the cosmos. Used intellectually, the sign of Agni shines with the light of the first-born of cosmic order (*ṛta*). This sign reflects into the world the principle of order as it works in the universe and in man. Experienced holistically, the ultimate sign of Agni rises in the image of the bull-cow, a bisexual whole of cognitive and vital totality, self-sufficient, impregnated with the possibilities of generation.

In the ongoing myth of Rudra-Śiva, the bull-cow, a theriomorph of Agni, looms in the background of Śiva Ardhanārīśvara, the androgyne (Ch. VII, n. 15; Ch. VIII.2). In this anthropomorphic androgynous image the shape is recast less formidably as a symbol of wholeness based on the polarity of sex. The androgynous image remains an ultimate symbol of the creative fire as it lives in the myth of Rudra-Śiva.

The fire myth of Rudra-Śiva plays on the whole gamut of fire, valuing all its potentialities and phases, from conflagration to illumination. Of Agni and Rudra, cooperating powers to the point of identity, Agni is the first-born, and their roles are not always reversible. Agni acts in Rudra and Rudra exceeds him in intensity. He is Agni's incandescence. As such, Rudra is "king of the sacrifice" (*RV*.4.3.1), "priest of both worlds" (*TS*.1.3.14.1), and "fulfiller of the sacrifice" (*RV*. 1.114.4). Rudra, for not playing Agni's sacerdotal role, is overcompensated and raised above Agni, the high priest. Paradoxically, Agni is praised as the Rudra of sacrifices (*RV*.3.2.5). Rudra did not maintain this exalted position, and the story of his humiliation or self-abasement and even exclusion from the sacrifice is longer and more varied than these lauds in the *Ṛg Veda*.

The gods put all their faith and also all their trust in Agni. Once, when they anticipated a conflict with the Asuras—as they always had reason to—they deposited all their wealth with Agni. Having defeated the Asuras, they wanted back their wealth, but Agni had gone away with it. They pursued him, meaning to take it by force. Agni cried (*arodīt*). Hence Agni's name is Rudra (*TS*.1.5.1.1). By the same popular etymology, but in an altogether different context, Rudra got this name for himself. He cried as a newborn child because, being unnamed, he was not free from evil; hence he was given a name (*ŚB*.6.1.3.9-10). Or simply Rudra got his name because he roared (*arodīt; BD*.2.34).

The *Taittirīya Saṃhitā* story (1.5.1.1) has focused on Agni in one of his weak moments. His escape on this occasion was not the pardonable flight from the monotony of his office, but rather the flight of a thief. He betrayed the trust of the gods and found no better way to disarm them than to cry. In this way he got the name of, and became, Rudra. Rudra appears here as a humiliated Agni, or as Agni absolved from his humiliation, whereas elsewhere he is extolled above Agni. The light of tradition flickers in the assessment of the greatness of these two practically cognate gods. Agni, the Fire, here does not have the incandescence of the fierce Wild God who is Rudra, the frightful form of Agni (*TS*.2.2.2.3).

5. The Avenger

Rudra in the Vedic myth of the primordial hunter and avenger showed himself in his yoga power. He let his arrow fly against the course of events in the cosmic drama that he as Fire had directed, having prepared seed for the Father and having inflamed the Father with sexual passion. When Father Heaven vaulted over the first dawn of the world and his seed started to flow, the wholeness that was before the beginning of things was ruptured. Eternity flowed as time into a world of contingency, where blushing Dawn witnessed the seed of Prajāpati as it fell on earth when he drew back from her. As the seed touched the earth, creatures were to arise from the primordial and partly frustrated embrace of Father Heaven. When the semen of the Lord of Generation touched the earth, it became a lake of fire (*MS*.4.2.12).

The Father played a precarious role. Frightened by the hunter, he begged Rudra to spare him, and made Rudra Lord of Animals (Paśupati) (*MS*.4.2.12). The Father had broken the state of wholeness that existed before the fall of the seed. This state is beyond words. It is indescribable and inaccessible to the senses. It is "neither nonbeing nor being" (*RV*.10.129.1). But if that much can be said about it, it has also been said that it is "nonbeing and being" (*RV*.10.5.7), and that out of nonbeing came being in the first age of the gods (*RV*.10.72.2). It is then that the indefinable wholeness of the total absence or the total presence of both nonbeing and being appears to recede and to set up the screen on which are seen the large figures of gods and their actions. This state of "neither nonbeing nor being," or simultaneously "nonbeing and being," is not within the range of thought. It is a plenum that defies definition, for it has no limits. Yet it is not chaos, the "darkness covered by darkness," said to have existed before the beginning of the ordered universe (*RV*.10.129.3). In its precosmic, preconscious totality, everything is contained, including consciousness and nothingness. Metaphysically, it did not cease when the cosmos came into existence, for it is not subject to time. Mythically, its wholeness had been injured. Mystically, its nameless plenum is inaccessible except in the state of *samādhi*, the final stage of yoga leading to *mokṣa*, the total release from all contingencies. Words like plenum, totality, and wholeness are used here merely as symbols of the Uncreate.

Rudra, the guardian of the Uncreate, an indefinable transcendental plenum, avenged the infringement of that wholeness. He became the avenger of the descent of its substance, the semen, the "heavenly Soma,"[21] into the cosmos. The arrow in his hand threatened the coming into existence of life, and it disturbed the procreative act of the Father, the Lord of Generation, an act of incontinence *sub specie aeternitatis*. Rudra, the avenger, is the Lord of Yoga and of self-containment.

Rudra, the fierce god, is an avenger whose arrow never misses its target. Creation as procreation destroys the integrity, the wholeness,

[21] A. Bergaigne, *La Religion védique*, 2nd ed., 1963, 2:112. Bergaigne early identified these two, Soma and semen. For a later variation on this theme, cf. *SP*.61.68-69.

that was before the beginning of life. The Wild Archer stalks his prey. As the Great Yogi, he is the consciousness and conscience of the Uncreate whole. Thus he is cruel and wild—Rudra; at peace within himself and kind—Śiva. Thus he acts in manifestation. Within his being lie fierceness and grace at opposite ends of one diameter. They radiate from the center of his being. While he manifests himself in specific shapes or actions, it is he in his total being who is present. While he is the Hunter and Avenger, he is also the Great Yogi and Lord of Animals. The animals, the wild creatures in the forest of life, are at his mercy. Within man the microcosm, the animals are the passions. Rudra, the archer, aims at Father Heaven, and inasmuch as the Father embracing the daughter acts according to his passionate nature, the Father is Rudra's prey. Śiva, the Great Yogi, tames and subdues the animals that are the passions. On the Mohenjo-daro seal the Lord of Yoga is enthroned. Peacefully and calmly the forest animals are stationed around him.

The Wild Hunter is Rudra, the raging flame, lashing out, letting the arrow fly at the critical moment. Yet he neither prevented nor did he undo the act of the Father. Only in part did he frustrate it; or was he himself part of it? Rudra is Agni. The fire flames in him. The fire within Rudra is also his *tapas*, the ardor of the ascetic discipline of yoga, of which he is the lord. Rudra is a fierce hunter (*astṛ*). This word connotes one who throws a weapon. It does not refer to the bow. Similarly, the word for archer is *iṣvāsa*, one who throws an arrow. With his arrow Rudra hits his target, the Father at the moment of his begetting life-to-be, spending himself into creation, an act whereby he ravages the self-contained integrity of the state before being came to be. Rudra caused the seed of the Father to fall down to earth. But did not the avenger also avenge his own action? He himself as Agni, in his own fervor, had prepared the seed for the Father. He now lashes out toward the Father and attacks him. The *Aitareya Brāhmaṇa* sees the seed that fell profusely, forming a lake surrounded and consumed by Agni. At that moment "that god" of dread, fashioned by the gods, claimed as his own all that was left on the site of the conflagration (*AB*.3.33-34). "That god," Rudra, claims what belongs to him as Paśupati *and* as Vāstoṣpati. As guardian and lord of the site, he claims what was left on the site. It is his. It was he who had caused the seed to fall. The events follow one upon the other. They lie ready in the meaning of the *Ṛg Veda mantras*, and are assigned their place much as in the visual arts, when by means of "continuous" or "unilocal" narrative, one relief or painting shows the various incidents or phases of a story. As part of the story they are laid out one next to the other. Their simultaneous presence shows forth the entire story, and each verbal version makes more explicit one or the other part of the myth.

Rudra is Agni, the Fire that heats the first passion in the cosmos and turns upon itself, burning to consume its action, avenging itself on itself. Father Heaven is only the locus of its consuming intensity. Whatever fire remains in him is that of rage.

In late Vedic and contemporary understanding, this creation myth of man is considered to have the incest of Father and daughter for its theme. In the beginning of things, however, when there was only the Father and the daughter created or hypostasized out of himself, one can hardly speak of incest. Besides, a condemnation of incest requires a society within which, if incest is committed, it would be judged according to that society's values. The Rudraic myth of creation is not an apotheosis or judgment of social conventions. The gods of the *raudra brahman* did not offer moral criticism. On the contrary, at this occurrence, this infringement of pre-existential wholeness, the gods in their concern made a magically potent poem, and out of the fabric of this creation they gave shape to the lord of the dwelling, Vāstoṣpati, that guardian of sacred order. The seed had fallen to earth, the place of sacrifice whence man and gods by means of the sacrifice ascend to heaven.

In the *Matsya Purāṇa*, compiled midway between the Vedic and our present age, in the third to fifth centuries after the beginning of the present era, a king muses over the Creator's passion for his daughter. "Tell me why he was not regarded as having committed a fearful sin[?]" (*MP*.4.1).[22] The answer is that only men have such doubts, for they have physical bodies, and it is very difficult for them with their gross bodies to understand the primeval creation that is celestial and mysterious. A more than human mind caused it. Only those whose minds are of the same kind can understand its great secret. The gods know no code of prohibition, while beings with physical bodies must not think of doing the same thing (*MP*.4.3-6).

The *Matsya Purāṇa* removes imputed guilt from the Creator's embrace. The transgression of the Creator, however, is not his violation

[22] *Matsya Purāṇa (MP)*, tr. "A Taluqdar of Oudh," 1916, part I, p. 12.

of his daughter. The divine mating of Father and daughter is a symbol of ontic truth. Elsewhere, primal being, nearest to the wholeness of the Uncreate, is male and female in one. Agni is a "bull-cow" (*RV*.10.5.7), two opposites in one, a bisexual fiery deity as large as the cosmos. "Dakṣa is born from Aditi, Aditi from Dakṣa" (*RV*.10.72.4). Words denoting genitals, sex relations, and sex acts are as obvious in their connotation as they are mysterious in their implications; they are universally intelligible symbols of creation in process. Sexual union, engendering, or birth-giving, in this context, are metaphors that evoke situations beyond what is possible or sanctioned among mortals. Such metaphors shock because they touch the springs of life in configurations that are unknown, even unacceptable, to mortals. Lifted from human bodies and transferred to those of animal symbols or to unembodied entities, they enter into combinations whose truths play on strings of meaning of deepest resonance.

Superhuman powers fecundate and generate one another in the cosmos, just as ideas do in the world of man. Aditi, "boundless" and all-embracing femininity, and Dakṣa, "competent," male potency efficient throughout Aditi's realm, give birth to one another. Fire burns in either sex, and unites male and female in the gigantic image of the cosmic bull-cow, who is stationed on that frontier of human understanding beyond which words and images do not reach (cf. *RV*.10.5.6-7). The daughter with whom the Father cohabits is a hypostasis of the Father himself. She was one with him before he knew her. Ardhanārīśvara, Lord Śiva, is male on the right side and female on the left. As the *Purāṇas* know him, Śiva is one who divides himself into god and goddess, Śiva and Śivā. Then, for a thousand years he did not cease in his ardent love making to Śivā (cf. *ŚP*.2.4.1.27-28). Their love has not been considered incestuous by anyone.

Myths of creation in the *Ṛg Veda* had a long past before Vedic seers sang of them. Not all the subsequent narrators who retold them, however, were equal in understanding. The tabu of incest plagued and diverted those who could not dare or were unable to face the Uncreate, the metaphysical plenum. They were compelled to stop before one of the "seven barriers" (*RV*.10.5.6) at the end of the way of human understanding.

According to the *Aitareya Brāhmaṇa*, the gods were manifestly horrified by the close contact of Prajāpati with his own daughter (*AB*.3.33). Their shock can be understood on metaphysical—and, by transfer, also on astronomical—grounds. Prajāpati, pierced, sprang up and became the constellation Mṛga (the antelope; Orion). He who had shot him became the constellation Mṛgavyādha ("the Hunter of the Antelope"; Sirius); Prajāpati's daughter became the constellation Rohiṇī (Aldebaran). The arrow became the constellation Trikāṇḍa (the belt of Orion) (*AB*.3.33; cf. below, Ch. II.4). The story is "written in the stars," for the movement of Prajāpati toward his daughter was observed in the sky when the sun was about to rise.

The gods of the *Ṛg Veda* responded to the love-making of father and daughter and to the seed that was shed by making a poem. It was only much later that the gods of the *Brāhmaṇas* were shocked by what they had seen (*AB*.3.33; *ŚB*.1.7.4.1-2; cf. *TmB*.8.2.10). In the *Ṛg Veda* (*RV*.3.31.1-3), the intercourse of the father with his daughter was the center of a sacred rite conducted by Agni. If the gods of the *Aitareya Brāhmaṇa* were shocked by what they saw, they judged by social standards of human behavior. These, however, were not the only ones, even in the *Aitareya Brāhmaṇa*. Dawn had been created by the Father and he united with her. No mother is known to have given birth to her. Uṣas appeared before Father Heaven as the dawn of a first morning. Father Heaven covered this blushing maiden, part of himself, discernible and other from himself, only to be united with himself. They are not two persons but one self-begotten, begetting entity. Before Uṣas appeared she was in the Father, now the Father is in her. Their mythical sex contact is of a kind that the *Aitareya Brāhmaṇa*—in another context—assigns even to the human condition when it speaks of the son who mounts his mother and his sister (*AB*.7.13). Paradoxically, no incest is implied. The ambience of this seemingly incestuous relationship is different, wider, and at the same time more unified than that of four persons forming a family of father, son, mother, and sister. Their physical relationship serves here as a symbol of the continuous transmission of the substance of the Uncreate. "The father entereth the wife, / Having become a germ (he entereth) the mother, / In her becoming renewed, / He is born. . . . The gods said to men / "This is your mother again." / . . . Therefore a son his mother / and his sister mounteth. / This is the broad and auspicious path / Along which men with sons fare free from sorrow" (*AB*.7.13).[23] Less provocatively, is it said in the *Mahābhārata* that a man entering his wife is

[23] *Aitareya Brāhmaṇa (AB)*, tr. A. B. Keith, 1920, p. 300.

again born therefrom (*MBh*.1.68.36). This reciprocal position is vividly described in the *Yogatattva Upaniṣad*: "the breast he once sucked he now presses and derives pleasure from, delighting now in the genitals from which he was born. She who was his mother is now his wife, and she who was his wife is now his mother. He who is now the father will again be the son, and he who is now the son will be the father again" (*YUp*.131-33).

Procreation, the continuity of life, is not an ever-renewed incest committed with her whom "the gods and the seers brought together as great brilliance" (*AB*.7.13).[24] She arose in that first morning when the Father, seeing her next to himself, mounted her to become his son. It was then that the seed was shed—the immortal substance out of the Uncreate that had been ruptured.

Within a holistic experience of life, sex assigns reciprocal roles to the infant at the mother's breast and to her lover, while in the beginning the Creator embraced his daughter, a hypostasis from within himself in which he asserts himself. To this act of self-love, the emission of seed is biologically a sequel and metaphorically a jolt to the unassailable and undiminished metaphysical plenum. The intercourse of the Creator with his daughter is the two-faced symbol of the rupture of pre-existential wholeness and of the descent to earth of its immortal substance, the seed of life.

This portentous act at the dawn of the world, before the beginning of man's life on earth, is the infringement of the Uncreate and pre-existential wholeness, a spurt from self-contained fullness, the loss of integrity of the absolute. The state before creation is beyond the polarity of opposites. It is as vast as chaos, but having no qualities whatsoever, it lacks disorder. It is known in later Indian mystical realization as *brahman*; it is realized through *samādhi* (at-onement) as *mokṣa* (release), *nirvāṇa* (extinction of the flame of life), *śūnyatā* (emptiness). These names apply to an inner realization of that state beyond the last frontiers of thought (cf. *RV*.10.5.6-7). The archer, whose arrow hits the Father at the very moment when the Father is spending himself into creation, acts as avenging consciousness and guardian of the Uncreate in defense of its integrity. The arrow and the shot of the archer are decisive symbols in the myth, though they were only partly effectual in the course of its events. Indeed, the arrow hit just a fraction of

[24] *Ibid*.

a moment too late. Meant to prevent the act, the flowing of the seed, the shot failed to prevent its consequences. The failure in timing at the dawn of the world was due to time itself, for the latter had not set in as yet; it was just about to begin. The transition from an integer without dimension of space and time into existence is a danger zone between eternity and the passing moment. It lies between metaphysics and myth. Had the timing been perfect, the flying arrow of Rudra would have prevented the coming into existence of man and the flowing down on the earth of the substance of the Uncreate.

II

THE ARCHER

1. The Archer Kṛśānu

Another archer of similar mission did not do better. His name is Kṛśānu (*RV*.4.27.3). Kṛśānu was a Gandharva (*TA*.1.9.3). The Gandharvas were the guardians of Soma (*RV*.9.83.4; *ŚB*.3.6.2.9, 17), the elixir of immortality, the elixir of inspiration. A falcon had stolen the Soma from the eternal abode of the Gandharva (*RV*.1.22.14; 4.27.3). The falcon was Indra himself (*RV*.4.26.3-7), the creator of (his) cosmos. As the falcon winged from heaven to bring Soma to Manu, to man, the sacrificer (*RV*.4.26.4), fear seized Indra of Kṛśānu, the archer (*RV*.4.27.3; 9.77.2), Soma's wondrous (*adbhuta*) warden in the beyond (*RV*.9.83.4). Indra was afraid of Kṛśānu. When the sun-horse had been born, rising from the ocean, and Indra had mounted it, the Gandharva took the reins (*RV*.1.163.1-2). Even so, Kṛśānu's arrow only grazed the flying falcon and a feather of his wing fell down to the earth (*RV*.4.27.3-4).

The Gandharva's station is beyond the gods. "The gods are this side of the creation" (*RV*.10.129.6).[1] The Gandharva precedes creation; he is the creative Soma-inspiration within the seer in sacred secrecy, when Soma himself is about to speak from within the seer, when "the seer makes surge the wave from the ocean" (*RV*.10.123.2) of his heart, and on its crest, Soma, the Gandharva, is born (cf. *RV*.9.86.36), the radiant Sun (*RV*.9.86.29). The Gandharvas were the guardians of Soma, the self-defense within creativity lest it be disturbed and squandered before the Gandharva rises, directed hitherwards, carrying his

[1] W. N. Brown, "Theories of Creation in the Rig Veda," 1965, p. 34.

multicolored weapons, clad in fragrant raiments, looking like the sun and making manifest his names (*RV*.10.123.7). The Gandharva Kṛśānu, like other Gandharvas, was the Guardian of Soma, of inspiration—prior to finding words, prior to acquiring form, at the instant before its *status nascendi*. Unlike Rudra, the Asura of heaven (*RV*. 2.1.6), the Gandharva is not the guardian of the Uncreate, but of the state between the Uncreate and creation. For this reason, it is the Gandharva who guards the virgin. She belongs first to Soma, then to the Gandharva, then to Agni, the Fire (*RV*.10.85.40-44); but it is the Gandharva who is invoked to cede her to her husband (*RV*.10.85.21-22). The role of the Gandharva as the guardian of the virgin, though short—before Agni takes possession of the bride—belongs to the borderland between the state of integrity as it was before creation and its loss in creation.

Rudra, the Asura of heaven, the Great Yogi who withholds his seed, and the Gandharva, Kṛśānu, both aimed well, though not quite on time, and they were not fated to carry out their intent fully. Soma was stolen from its place of origin on high, and was brought by the falcon down to earth, the place of sacrifice where also fell the seed of Father Heaven. Both archers, ill-fated guardians of the integrity of a superhuman, deathless state, were defending the already lost cause of an all-inclusive, homogeneous totality. Henceforward metaphysical reality vaults over and is the ground and background of a cosmogony that occupies and animates the stage contiguous with, but this side of, transcendency.

Of Kṛśānu, the celestial archer and guardian of Soma, the Elixir of immortality, nothing more was heard. His arrow became a serpent, its vehemence a second serpent, and its flash a third (*AB*.3.26). Like lightning and falling stars, these serpents shot across and vanished from the firmament. After Kṛśānu's failure, their light, like that of extinguished stars, did not flare up again. But the flaming arrows of Rudra dart across the mythic cosmos. Again and again their fire consumes a world, and life arises in a new aeon in a renewed mode. It was Agni, the Fire, the savage hunter, who is Rudra, the Wild God, who made ready the seed for the Father, who made passion flare up in him. Outraged with pain, the Father, the Lord of Generation, foamed. Insensate with pain he tottered, the dart sticking in his wound. That hurt bit of flesh was to trouble the minds of generations of priests and bards, from the accounts of the *Brāhmaṇas* to the stories told in the *Purāṇas*. It had to be atoned for in myth and rites. There was a debt to be paid for it by creation, to be expiated by sacrifices. This primordial assault on Prajāpati, the Lord of Generation, who himself had violated pre-existential totality, was the bond *in* creation between the abiding and paradoxically inviolate pre-existential integrity, the fire of creation, and the agony of the Lord of Generation, that foaming bull, the primordial sacrificial victim. Had Agni-Rudra, the avenger of the shed seed of creation, and Kṛśānu, the guardian of the elixir of immortality,[2] timed their intervention more accurately than they did, creation would not have come about, and once it had, mankind would have been deprived of the elixir of immortality. But each guardian of the Uncreate was overtaken by time, by that split second that had escaped from eternity at its rupture, when the falcon raped the Soma plant and when Agni-Rudra, the creative Fire, made ready the seed for the Father. Overtaken by time, Rudra aimed at the Father the burning arrow of his wrath.

Kṛśānu, the Gandharva, had meant to prevent the descent of Soma to gods and man from within the plenum whence a falcon had stolen it. The other archer, Rudra, the Wild God, had meant to prevent an outflow of semen from that very plenum into creation. Neither succeeded, but while Kṛśānu, the archer, is not remembered (except for his defense as guardian of Soma, and for his defiance of the cosmos as it was meant to be—partaking in exalted moments of the plenum that was and is before creation), Rudra the archer renews his assault on the Creator from aeon to aeon.

In addition to Rudra, the god, and Kṛśānu, the Gandharva, both archers, the nameless, formless plenum had a third formidable guardian. He was not an archer. He was Vṛtra, the cosmic serpent. Vṛtra moved coiling around the as yet unmanifest cosmos; the serpent kept its rivers enclosed and thereby prevented their flowing down to earth. These three guardians of the Uncreate, containing the life-giving moisture irradiated by a light unrevealed, failed in their mission. A falcon brought Soma for gods and mortals to drink; the Father, the Lord of Generation, let flow the semen for mortals to continue existence on earth. Indra, the creator of the universe of an earlier aeon, smote the serpent Vṛtra.[3]

[2] A. Bergaigne, *La Religion védique*, 3:32-33, pointed out the resemblance of Rudra and Kṛśānu as archers guarding Soma.

[3] B. G. Tilak, *The Orion or Researches into the Antiquity of the Vedas*, 1955, pp. 123, 124,

Indra killed Vṛtra, and the waters of heaven flowed down to the sea (*RV*.1.32.2). The body of dead Vṛtra lies at the foot of the waters (*RV*.1.32.8), in the abyss, the body of his mother Dānu recumbent on him (*RV*.1.32.9). Over the dead bodies of mother and son the universe came to be, and the sun rose for the first time (cf. *RV*.2.19.3; 1.51.4). Indra, by killing Vṛtra, a brahmin, brought on himself the heinous sin of brahminicide (*BhP*.6.13.4). According to later texts, while Indra made flow into the world the waters that Vṛtra had held captive, by slaying Vṛtra he brought forth brahminicide, causing terror and fear in this world (*MBh*.12.273.10; *BhP*.6.13.7-12, 19-20). Fear seized him (*RV*.1.32.14).

In the presence of the dimensionless plenum or absolute, the drama of creation was enacted. Creation departs from the perfection of the unconditioned state. Thus it is flawed from the moment of its origin. In the precarious beginning, as swift as thought, the gods, as the seed of the Father was falling, compassionately filled the scene with the magic of their poem. Out of its substance they shaped Vāstoṣpati, the guardian of sacred order. "Vāstoṣpati is Rudra" (*TS*. 3.4.10.3). Rudra, the archer, the avenger, arose at the violation of pre-existential wholeness that he failed to prevent, having ambivalently even provoked that violation. Now, irreversibly, within creation, the integrity that was before the beginning had been ruptured. Rudra was created by the gods in the poem of Rudra, the *raudra brahman*, as Vāstoṣpati, Vratapā, the guardian of sacred order. The shape of Vāstoṣpati has been given to him by the rhythms of the *mantras*. Vāstoṣpati, the guardian of the *vāstu*, arises as the guardian of sacred order here on earth. He is Rudra, the avenger of the rupture of the absolute, but he is also Rudra-Agni, who himself has caused that rupture by having prepared the seed for the Father. The seed fell when Rudra threatened to let fly the arrow, lashing out against the Father, the Lord of Generation, who made Rudra Lord of Animals, Paśupati. Paśupati and Vāstoṣpati both denote Rudra. They are his titles from the beginning. Creation was flawed from the start, yet was redeemed at the same time by the intervention of the gods, who out of the substance and rhythm of their magic words fashioned Vāstoṣpati. In that poem Rudra, the fierce god, the guardian of the Uncreate, arose him-

---

assigns on astronomical grounds the decapitation of Vṛtra by Indra to a time when the vernal equinox was in Orion, that is, ca. 4,500 B.C.

self as the protector of sacred order—the guardian of cosmic rhythms and human rites. The *raudra brahman*, the poem of Rudra, is the primordial word of power sustained by the reality of Rudra that it evokes.

The arrow that Rudra had aimed at Prajāpati remained in the wound of the Lord of Generation, Prajāpati, who is the sacrifice (*ŚB*.1.7.4.4) and the primordial sacrificial victim. The arrow in the flesh of Prajāpati was not extracted: the bit had to be cut out (*ŚB*.1.7.4.4-5). Even so, the potency of the cut-out bit of flesh did not diminish in the continuing myth of Rudra. It wreaked havoc among the gods when it was offered to them at the sacrifice (*ŚB*.1.7.4.6-8; *TS*.2.6.8.3-7).

The primordial discharge of Rudra's arrow against the Father marked the direction of his operation in the cosmos. The arrow aimed at the act of generation. It flew in the opposite direction of the generative emission of the father. Its countermovement is consonant with that of yogic and tantric discipline, according to which the drawing up of the seed (*ūrdhvaretas*; cf. Sāyaṇa on *TA*.10.12; *MBh.* 13.17.45) has its mystical psychosomatic equivalent in the upward flow of the sex power. Its phases are realized as it ascends through the subtle centers (*cakras*) of the body, including the highest center of mind, which it fecundates, being itself transubstantiated into the nectar that contributes to the state of *samādhi*, where integration, oneness is realized. The cosmic equivalent of the realization of this state of oneness is the Uncreate that was and is before the beginning of things. The arrow of Rudra was directed into the cosmic scene of the myth, while yoga is effected within the body of the yogi. Rudra-Śiva is the lord of yogis and the Lord of Yoga. Later Vedic traditions concentrated on the wound inflicted by the arrow of Rudra, on the continued potency of his dart within the flesh of the victim, on the magic of its devastating power.

Rudra, the Wild God, the Archer fierce as fire, is the guardian of the Uncreate. Rudra-Paśupati is the Lord of Animals, of creatures wild and tame. The creaturely world of which man is part is his domain. Rudra-Vāstoṣpati is the guardian of the dwelling that is the cosmos. He is at the same time the guardian and lord of the site on earth, the site of the sacrifice. As Vratapā he guards the order of the cosmos in the rhythms of the rites, in the rhythms of all art.

Soma is the elixir of immortality. It was brought to gods and men from afar, where it had been raped by a falcon. The arrow of Kṛśānu, the archer, grazed the falcon but could not prevent the coming down of Soma. Kṛśānu's target was the falcon, who was Indra himself. Rudra's target was Prajāpati, the Lord of Generation, the Father who poured down on earth the semen, a liquid as precious as Soma. By rape and incontinence, powers of creation and procreation came down to earth from the Uncreate. It had never been tapped before, nor depleted. Henceforward it would be known in its fulness by a return to it in the state of *samādhi* or in moments of creative intuition.

2. Śarva, the Archer

Rudra is Śarva (*VS*.16.28; *AV*.6.93.1, 2). The word Śarva is derived from *śaru*, "arrow." The arrow is the essential attribute of Rudra; it has three parts and is joined with Kālāgni, the fire of destruction (*MBh*.7.173.47-48). Śarva was born out of what was cruel in the gods (*JB*.3.262). He is the archer who stalks his prey and is made Paśupati, Lord of Animals. It is this fiery self of his that Rudra injected into the Father. The cruelty of Śarva is the highest degree of Rudra's intensity. The arrow weapon and metaphor of Rudra's power is charged with it. Agni-Rudra-Śarva are of one essence; they are names of degrees of the same power. The Father, the Lord of Generation, Prajāpati, is its essential target. Subsequently, when living beings have come to be, they are exposed to the fatal arrows of the god. Agni is "like a fierce archer" (*RV*.6.16.39),[4] but Rudra is the archer who lets fly the piercing arrow (*RV*.2.33.10, 14; 5.42.11; 6.28.7; 7.46.1; 10.125.6; *VS*.3.61; 16.1, 3, 9, 18, 20, 21, 22-23 in particular, 50, 52, 53; *AV*.4.28.2; 6.93.1; 10.1.23) from his yellow, golden bow (*AV*.11.2.12). The primordial target of the arrow was the procreative act of the Father. Only after this fateful scene could the arrow be directed toward creatures. As Śarva, Rudra hunts in this our world.

The great hymn of the *Yajur Veda* addressed to Rudra of a hundred shapes, known as the *Śatarudriya*, in its opening verse pays homage to the wrath and to the arrow of Rudra (*VS*.16.1; *TS*.4.5.1.1). The arrow now flies downward from heaven to earth (*RV*.7.46.3). It is Śarva who hurls the shaft of lightning (*AV*.10.1.23), the visible cosmic equivalent

[4] *Ṛg Veda Saṃhitā (RV)*, tr. M. N. Dutt, 1906, p. 1021.

of the fiery wrath of Rudra. It is also said of Rudra, though once only (*RV*.2.33.3), that he wields the thunderbolt (*vajra*), which is Indra's (*RV*.1.32.2) and Bṛhaspati's (*RV*.1.40.8; *AV*.11.10.13) weapon. Thunder and lightning are evocative symbols. They manifest the power of a god that is neither confined nor defined by them. They are its signs and have their verbal and visual figures in art: the arrow of Rudra and the *vajra* of Indra and Bṛhaspati. (Inasmuch as Rudra is Agni and Agni is the twin brother of Indra [*RV*.6.59.2], Indra and Agni-Rudra are twin brothers.) In the myth of Rudra it is Prajāpati who plays the role of the Father, while in the *Purāṇas* this role is played by Brahmā. Each of these celestial actors plays in his own way the paradigmatic role of the Father.

Unlike Rudra, Indra severed his bond with the Father. Indra slew him and made his mother a widow (*RV*.4.18.12). Rudra's assault on the Father was both an act of revolt and an act of involvement. As Agni, he prepared the seed for the Father and made his passion flare up. Turning against his own commitment, Agni-Rudra then directed the arrow against the Father, and the passion of his interrupted embrace turned into fury. All the gods abandoned Prajāpati except one, Manyu, "Wrath" (*ŚB*.9.1.1.6).

It is Agni, the creative fire, who prepares the seed and inflames the Father toward the creative act. It is Rudra whose arrow hits the Father and interrupts the creative act. The arrow is aimed toward the origin and against the emission of the seed. Moreover, as Agni prepares the seed, he is the primeval agent who acts on the Father. As Agni-Rudra he is the protagonist of the drama of creation, leading into it and lashing back, letting the arrow fly against it.

His arrow will be set flying in the cosmos in the myth of Rudra at the sacrifice of Dakṣa, and it will pierce the triple city of the demons, the Asuras. This arrow too will be set flying by Rudra within man, in inner realization. Then "the syllable *AUM* is the bow, the *ātman* (self) is indeed the arrow; *brahman* (ultimate reality) is its target; carefully should it be pierced. Thus one becomes united with it like the arrow (with its target)" (*MUp*.2.2.4; *RHUp*.38). At the inception of creation, however, nothing less formidable than the violation of the absolute, ultimate reality, the Uncreate, was the target of Rudra's arrow.

Rudra, the avenger of the violation, has the fierceness of Śarva, the archer. He destroys like a terrible wild animal (*RV*.2.33.11). His arrows bring death. "Whatever destroys any existing thing, movable or stationary, at any time, is . . . Rudra" (*VP*.1.22.39).[5] His power is deadly. Like a gourd from its stalk, he cuts off life or spares it (cf. *RV*.7.59.12). As Paśupati, he spared the life of animals. The archer has the power over life and death. He may avert or restrain his arrow. This is the grace by which he frees from death. He is the liberator.

Though in the *Ṛg Veda* the Wild Hunter is not called Śarva, his arrow (*śaru*), unlike that of any other god, not only makes precarious the life of man and beast, it is a particular threat to the yet unborn, and to the seed itself. In a hymn to Agni, the singer inquires of Agni, the sacrificial fire and messenger between the sacrificer and the gods, what Agni will say to Rudra, the killer of man. Which seed will Agni commend to wide-striding Viṣṇu, which seed will he expose to the great arrow (of Rudra) (*RV*.4.3.6-7)?[6] Rudra's piercing arrow is directed toward the seed, toward nascent life, which lies protected within the span of Viṣṇu's three footsteps, from the earth to the empyrean (cf. *RV*.1.154.2-5; 1.155.3-5). Rudra in his most cruel form is Śarva. His single-pointed arrow traverses the security of Viṣṇu's domain, unless Rudra in his grace (*mīḍhvas*) (*RV*.1.114.3) unstrings his bow. "In the later Vedas the comparative and superlative of this word [*mīḍhvas*] have only been found in connection with Rudra."[7] His extreme fierceness is offset by his extreme grace. Rudra is Śarva as much as he is Śiva. He is the Asura of heaven (*RV*.2.1.6), the ruler (*īśāna*) of this great world (*RV*.2.33.9).

His is the arrow (*ŚB*.2.6.2.3), the power of death. For this reason the *tryambaka* offerings belong to Rudra (1, 3). They consist of rice cakes. *Tryambaka* offerings were made to protect from Rudra's arrows the descendants, born and unborn, of the sacrificer, one cake for each descendant and one more for the issue not yet born. The cakes would deliver each of the descendants from Rudra's power. The rite took place on a crossroad, for the crossroad was Rudra's favorite haunt. A piece was cut out of each cake, except the cake for the yet unborn child, and offered to Rudra (*ŚB*.2.6.2.3-9). That additional cake was buried in a mole hill with the words, "This is your share, O Rudra, the mole is your animal" (*ŚB*.2.6.2.10). The cake was buried and con-

[5] *Viṣṇu Purāṇa (VP)*, tr. H. H. Wilson, 1961, p. 127.

[6] Cf. *Ṛg Veda Saṃhitā (RV)*, tr. Geldner, 1951, 1:420 and nn. 7c, 7d.

[7] A. A. Macdonell, *Vedic Mythology*, p. 75.

cealed, for an embryo is concealed. By this offering, the unborn descendants were delivered from the power of Rudra.

Rudra's arrow is directed toward the seed and the embryo. For the yet unborn a special offering was made, larger by Rudra's part than the cakes offered for the welfare of the living descendants. Moreover, the cake for the embryo had to be buried in a mole hill and concealed—Rudra was given no part of it; instead, the mole became Rudra's victim. The mole was Rudra's share. Rudra would not claim the embryo, though Rudra is greedy like a jackal for embryo flesh (*VāP.*30.212). However, the rest of the cakes for the living descendants were offered to Rudra. They were put in a basket, then attached to a tree or post or a bamboo pole or an ant hill. These were Rudra's provision to take with him beyond Mount Mūjavat, with his bow unstrung (*ŚB*.2.6.2.17). The embryo, the seed, procreation itself, was the special target of Rudra's arrow. He first had let it fly against the procreating Father.

Śarva, as a name and form of Rudra, is invoked together with Yama, the god of death, and with Death itself (Mṛtyu; *AV*.6.93.1), but more frequently he is invoked together with Bhava (existence) (*VāP*.30.188). Śarva the archer and Bhava the king (*AV*.6.93.2) are aspects of Rudra's power here on earth. For this reason, once Rudra is born on earth, the first name given to him by his father, Prajāpati, is Bhava, according to one tradition (*KB*.6.2), and it is Rudra, with Śarva as the second name, according to another (*ŚB*.6.1.3.10-11). Inasmuch as the hunter and king are aspects of Rudra, the arrow is their weapon, and homage is paid to Bhava, to Rudra, and to Śarva (*VS*.16.28). King Bhava is Rudra, the lord of heaven and earth, the spacious atmosphere, and all directions (*AV*.11.2.27); he as much as Śarva hurls his weapon against evil-doers and sorcerers (*AV*.10.1.23). Ethical discrimination would be the prerogative of Bhava the king; Śarva by himself would be less selective in choosing his victim. King and hunter, however, are one in Rudra, and both together are invoked to be gracious, grant happiness, remove sins, and lengthen life (*AV*.8.2.7). Within the totality of Rudra they are Fire (Śarva) and Water (Bhava) (*KB*.6.2-3). Primarily however, it was the eastern people who called Agni Śarva, whereas the Bāhīkas, a people of the western Panjab (?), called him Bhava (*SB*.1.7.3.8). Agni flames up in many tongues. Inasmuch as Rudra is Agni, both gods are invoked by names they have in common, while none of the names by itself comprises the totality that is Rudra.

In the beginning, at the moment of horror, the gods put together their most dreadful shapes and created "that god" (*AB*.3.33). According to the *Jaiminīya Brāhmaṇa*, they put what was cruel in themselves into two earthen bowls (*śarāva*). Because he is born from two earthen bowls (*śarāva*), therefore is he so called (i.e., Śarva) (*JB*.3.262). The earthen bowls to which Śarva here is said, by popular etymology, to owe his name guard the unspeakable horror of that god.

3. Rudra, the Healer

Dreadful are the arrows of Rudra in creation. He takes aim, with a thousand eyes and a thousand arrows (cf. *KB*.6.1), toward men and beasts, and is invoked to spare them. He may refrain from hunting his devotees or heal the wounds that he has inflicted, for he carries in his hands not only fiery arrows and the bow (*RV*.2.33.10, 14; *VS*.16.3), but also healing remedies (*RV*.1.43.4; 1.114.5; 2.33.2; 2.33.4; 2.33.7; 5.42.11 in particular; 6.74.3; 7.35.6; 8.29.5; *AV*.2.27.6; 7.42.2; 6.57.1-2), plants, and the water of life (possibly [cow's] urine),[8] for Rudra is the kind (*śiva*) god (*RV*.10.92.9; cf. *VS*.16.2; *ŚUp*.3.5-6); as such he is Śiva. How could he heal were there no wounds? How could he be God if he, cause of all causes, did not inflict them? He has a thousand remedies (*RV*.7.46.3). Rudra is the best of healers (*RV*.2.33.4; *VS*.3.59; 16.5, 49). He places his merciful hand—which holds the remedy *jalāṣa* (*RV*.2.33.7)—on suffering. The medicine and the arrow are held in the hands of the god who, when he faces life on earth, is archer and healer in one—Rudra, the wild god, and Śiva, the kind god. But he is Rudra when he faces the Father. The touch of his healing hand is withheld from the Father. The burning arrow remains stuck in the

[8] M. Bloomfield, in "Contributions to the Interpretation of the Veda," 1891, pp. 425-29, has examined the use of the terms *jalāṣaḥ, jalāṣabheṣajaḥ, jalāṣam*, and *jālāṣam*, and concluded that they refer to urine as the special remedy of Rudra. Bloomfield discusses the specific application of the remedy in his notes to the translation; cf. *AV*.6.57, tr. M. Bloomfield, 1964, pp. 488-89. A small "waterpot," however, is held in the left hand by images carved from the first to the third century in Mathura and Ahicchatra. They represent Indra (dated A.D. 82), Maitreya, a *yakṣī*, a Nāgarāja, and Śiva (see P. Pal, "A Kushān Indra and Some Related Sculptures," 1979, pp. 212-26, figs. 1, 2, 6, 18, 19, and 16, respectively). Each of these divinities holds the same kind of small round vessel containing the water of life.

wound of Prajāpati. The initial rupture of pre-existent wholeness was not healed. It was avenged but not redeemed by Rudra, the archer. But it is Rudra, Lord of Yoga, who restores the wholeness of the absolute. Rudra heals the ills of mortals with the remedies that he himself created in the waters into which he plunged when Brahmā had asked him to create mortals. Rather than creating mortals, fallible by nature and prone to disease, he chose to do *tapas* and create the herbs and plants that would be their medicine (*MBh*.10.17.10-25). The waters themselves have healing power; they were irradiated by his presence (*AV*.7.87.1; *RV*.10.9.6-7). The waters heal (*RV*.1.23.19-21; *VS*.9.6; *KB*.16.7).

Rudra holds the arrow in one hand and a plant or a water vessel in the other. He holds the destructive power of the fiery arrow that wounds and kills, and the vitalizing fire that pulsates in water and plants and heals. It was Soma himself, Soma who is god, plant, and elixir of life, who revealed to a *Ṛg Veda* poet (*RV*.10.9.6) the healing power of the waters and the plants. Soma, the elixir of life, the drink of immortality, was pressed from a plant. Soma the god arose from the drink and inspired the poet-seers. From far away, the plant was brought to man by a falcon (cf. *RV*.4.26.6). Kṛśānu, the archer, by an infinitesimal fraction of time had failed to pierce with his arrow the falcon who had raped the Soma and who, with the Soma plant clutched in his claw, precipitated himself toward the world of man. Kṛśānu could not prevent the immortal god from coming within the reach of those who would witness his presence on earth by their songs, which he inspired. Nor could he prevent the balm of Soma from healing mortal ills. The elixir of life inspires the seers, heals the sick, and assuages the ills of life. Soma and Rudra are healers. Rudra heals with the remedies that he has created for the ills that he has inflicted on man. These medicines heal the ills of mortals whose coming into existence Rudra failed to prevent.

Kṛśānu, ineffectual guardian of the plant of immortality, was forgotten. He had no further mission. Rudra as the avenging god faces the results of his ineffectual effort to preserve the integrity of the preexistential wholeness by which life that was vulnerable and needed to be healed and redeemed came about on earth.

Soma and Rudra are invoked together in one and the same hymn of the *Ṛg Veda* (*RV*.6.74). They are dual divinities, cooperative powers. No other god is ever associated with or takes part on equal terms in Rudra's being and domain. "Soma is the bestower of seed, Agni is the begetter of offspring" (*TS*.2.2.10.3).[9] Inasmuch as Rudra is Agni, they cooperate in the very field that Rudra, the Wild Hunter, meant to be nonexistent. Whereas life has come into existence, Rudra and Soma conjointly heal the ills of the body, and free it from guilt. Sickness is only a consequence of sin.

The archer Rudra plays his momentous part in the primordial world of man. Man did come into being, and with him the memory of the primordial scene. The archer Kṛśānu, however, was defeated. In the prologue to the life of man on earth, two leading parts are played by archers. In the flight of their arrows time plays a crucial role. Time did not exist before the primordial dawn. Now it intervenes between intent and act, between the discharge of the arrow and its hitting the target. But for that fraction of a second, mankind and life on earth would not have come about. And, mankind having come into existence, but for the fraction of another second (when the arrow of Kṛśānu just grazed the falcon, causing a feather of it to fall but not injuring the bird nor preventing it from bringing down the plant of immortality), the drink of divine inspiration would not have come to man.

Soma, the elixir of immortality, is the hidden essence of Tvaṣṭṛ (*RV*.1.117.22). Tvaṣṭṛ is a name of the Father. He does not create *per generationem* but *per artem*. He is the Father as *deus faber*. Soma, the elixir of immortality, is stored in a wondrous container, the moon (cf. *RV*.1.84.15).[10] The moon vessel goes on changing its shape cyclically, within its own limits. The changes measure time, from the shape of the crescent to the full disc that dwindles, disappears, and shows again as crescent, repeating the same sequence of shapes time after time. The moon is a mystic container, a vessel from which the gods and the dead, the ancestors, drink Soma, the ever-refilling water of life, of immortality (*ŚB*.2.4.4.15; *ChUp*.5.10.4). On his head Śiva carries the crescent moon, symbol of the renewal of vegetative life, of recurrent time, and the abode of the dead (cf. *M*.1.66). Thus the moon is the lord of plants (*MBh*.12.52.33), luminous vessel of Soma and one with Soma, who himself from ancient times is their king.[11]

The cool liquid light of the moon, the water, and the healing plants

[9] *Taittirīya Saṃhitā (TS)*, tr. A. B. Keith, 1914, p. 158.

[10] A. Daniélou, *Hindu Polytheism*, 1964, pp. 98-99.

[11] *Ibid.*

are attributes of the figure of Śiva. He carries them on his head and in his hands. They belong to him, the gracious god who as Rudra aims his arrow. It flies across space, it hits at a particular moment. That moment became fixed in time. It marked the beginning of Time itself, when the arrow hit the Father. Thus life of man began on earth, from the Aṅgirases, the archetypal fire priests, down to the people born as links in the chain of life and death. The arrow and the healing plant are held in cooperative antagonism, in the hands of Rudra. In some of the earliest known sculptures of Śiva the god holds a small vessel in his hand. It could well be a medicine bottle.[12] A water pot is held by Śiva images of the third and fourth century A.D.[13] Was it meant to hold *jalāṣa* (urine), Vedic Rudra's specific medicine?[14]

Rudra heals the wounds he inflicts. When he frees the body of man from sickness, it is guilt from which he liberates him. Sickness is seen as a consequence of sin. Rudra-Soma, the healers of the ills of the body, also free the mind from the concerns of the body (*AV*.7.42.1-2). Soma, the drink of immortality, transports the seer into the regions of the gods, where he sees them face to face. Rudra, the thousand-eyed god, puts into the right hand of the seer an herb that makes him see everything—the three heavens, the three earths, and all existences down to the sorcerers and the ghouls (*AV*.4.20.1-9).

In South Indian images and paintings of Śiva Bhikṣāṭana, the right hand of Śiva, who is represented as a penitent beggar, is extended neither to a sick person nor to a seer. The right hand of Śiva Bhikṣāṭana, holding a plant in *kaṭaka* gesture, is lowered toward an antelope. In his left hand rests a bowl, the skull of Brahmā.[15]

Prajāpati, the Lord of Generation, in the shape of an antelope cohabited with his daughter. Rudra hunted the antelope. In the evolving myth of Śiva, spanning thousands of years, the narrative of the myth proceeds in its own reality. In some instances it perpetuates its figures by throwing them not only on the screen of memory but on the vault of heaven, where they shine as stars.

The primordial, paradigmatic myth cast in analogous shape was en-

[12] N. P. Joshi, "A Unique Figure of Śiva from Musanagar," 1969, pp. 25 f. The date of the sculpture is 50 B.C.-A.D. 50. See n. 8 above.

[13] Cf. also J. C. Harle, *Gupta Sculpture*, pls. 53, 54, 128; A. de Lippe, *Indian Medieval Sculpture*, pl. 7; C. Sivaramamurti, *The Art of India*, 1977, p. 350, fig. 319.

[14] Cf. Ch. II n. 8.

[15] D. Barrett, *Early Cola Bronzes*, 1965, pls. 41, 42.

acted in another aeon when the Sacrifice, pursued by Rudra the hunter, fled to heaven (Ch. X.A.2), where to this day the hunter, the antelope, and the arrow shine at night as constellations in the sky.[16] Has relentless, unforgettingly creative memory allowed for an image of Śiva profoundly connected with the assault on Prajāpati to extend to the antelope a (healing) plant?

4. The Hunter of the Antelope and the Hound of Heaven

a. *The Hunter of the Antelope*

The Gandharva Kṛśānu aimed his arrow from on high so as to prevent the Soma, which had been raped by the falcon, from being brought down to man on earth. Rudra let fly his arrow against the Father, who was engaged in the procreative act. Rudra avenged the infringement of pre-existential wholeness, but did not prevent the seed of the Father from falling down to earth. Soma and semen had the same fate and destination. The semen of the Father was to bring about the life of man on earth and its continuity. Soma was to raise man to a level of inspiration so high that from it the fated descent of Soma and that of the semen of Father Heaven could be intuited. From the high peaks of vision would appear a panorama of many paths of ascent, by sacrifices to be performed and by inner realizations expressed in hymns and other works of art. Kṛśānu by his failure was instrumental in letting Soma and inspiration come to man; Rudra, in a time-caused reverse effect of his intention, brought the life itself of mankind to this earth, and with it he brought time. At the first dawn of the world he rose, the fiery archer.

He assumed, tradition tells, the shape of a star, shooting dazzling arrows of light. Its name is Mṛgavyādha, or "the Hunter of the antelope." Mṛgavyādha, to this day, is the name of the star Sirius.

In transferring to the stars the primordial deed of Rudra, the *Aitareya Brāhmaṇa* (*AB*.3.33) confirmed by the visible movement and stations of the luminaries a mythical reality beyond time and enacted before the sun had ever risen in the sky.

Rudra, the heavenly archer, is invoked in the *Ṛg Veda* together with Kṛśānu and Tiṣya, the archer (*RV*.10.64.8). Who is Tiṣya?

[16] Cf. B. G. Tilak, *The Orion*, p. 100. The three stars of the belt of Orion.

"Tiṣya is Rudra" (*TS*.2.2.10.1-2). The constellation Tiṣya, however, is one of the twenty-seven mansions of the moon. Mṛgavyādha is the star Sirius. The discrepancy between the astronomical facts and the irrefutable identification of Sirius as "Hunter of the Antelope," the star figure of Rudra, on the one hand, and the identification of Tiṣya and Rudra on the other is puzzling, particularly in the light of the *Avesta*.

There is a brilliant star that is called Tištrya in the *Avesta*.[17] Although the phonetic similarity of Tištrya and Tiṣya hardly implies a derivation of the Vedic from the Avestan name, both could perhaps be derived from the same root.[18] In the *Avesta*, the splendid, brilliant Tištrya, which soars rapidly like the arrow, quick as lightning, is the name of the star Sirius.[19] The word Tiṣya is formed from *tviṣ*, which means to shine brilliantly.[20]

Vedic Mṛgavyādha (Sirius) is Rudra. Avestan Tištrya is Sirius,[21] but the Vedic asterism Tiṣya is almost certainly the same as the later Puṣya,[22] and this star, in the Indian astronomical texts (such as the *Sūryasiddhānta* [*SSi*]), the system therein developing its present form in the fifth and sixth centuries A.D.,[23] is given coordinates that clearly identify it as E Cancri.[24] Sirius, at the present state of our knowledge, sheds none of its light on the relation of Tištrya (Sirius), Rudra (Sirius), and Tiṣya (Rudra).

The myth of Rudra, the hunter of the antelope, Prajāpati, the antelope, and Rohiṇī, his daughter, and their catasterism as Mṛgavyādha (Sirius), as Mṛga or Mṛgaśiras (Orion), and as Rohiṇī (Aldebaran) has been told already (Ch. I. 5).

The gods—or their priests—watched the drama of Rudra, Prajāpati, and his daughter as it was enacted in the sky by the sun and the stars.[25] The Vedic sacrificial year began in the spring, at the vernal

[17] H. Lommel, tr., *Die Yäšt's des Awesta*, 1927, pp. 50, 52 (*Yäšt* 8.6 and 16). Cf. G. de Santillana and H. von Dechend, *Hamlet's Mill*, 1968, pp. 52, 215.

[18] A. Scherer, *Gestirnnamen bei den Indogermanischen Völkern*, 1953, pp. 88, 113, 150.

[19] *Ibid.*, p. 113; H. Lommel, tr., *Die Yäšt's des Awesta*, p. 50 (*Yäšt* 8.5-6); Cf. M. Mayrhofer, *Concise Etymological Sanskrit Dictionary, s.v. tiṣyaḥ*.

[20] M. Mayrhofer, *Concise Etymological Sanskrit Dictionary, s.v. tveṣati*.

[21] A. Scherer, *Gestirnnamen bei den Indogermanischen Völkern*, p. 113.

[22] *Ibid.*, pp. 155-56.

[23] *Sūryasiddhānta (SSi)*, tr. E. Burgess, 1860, p. 331; cf. A. Scherer, *Gestirnnamen bei den Indogermanischen Völkern*, p. 150.

[24] *Sūryasiddhānta (SSi)*, tr. E. Burgess, p. 475.

[25] Cf. B. G. Tilak, *The Orion*, pp. 19, 213.

equinox. On that day the rising of the sun was announced by a star that appeared at dawn, just before sunrise, and immediately became invisible in the rays of the rising sun. This was the "auspicious" star for the sacrifice to begin (*TB*.1.5.2.1 and commentary), for the year to begin, a new year in the appointed order of its seasons and their rites. With the unaided eye, over the years, over millennia, the auspicious star of the vernal equinox heralding or supporting the rising sun was awaited. This star was Orion, until it was observed that another star was rising at the vernal equinox and "supported" the sun at the beginning of the year. This star was Aldebaran. The sun was no longer rising in Orion. The beginning of the year had moved from Orion to Aldebaran. This momentous conclusion was based on long observation.

The motion of the vernal equinox, of the beginning of the year, of all rites on which life depended and which were enacted in the sacrifice, had its myth in the figures of Prajāpati and his daughter. The realization that the sun, which had always appeared rising in Orion, had slowly left that station to rise in another star was startling. It appeared anomalous—it came as a shock. The beginning of the year had moved from Orion toward Aldebaran.

The year had its mythical figure in Prajāpati. "Prajāpati is the year" (*ŚB*.3.2.2.4; 5.2.1.2; 10.4.2.1, 2). Prajāpati, the year, experienced and expressed ritually, marked by its beginning at the vernal equinox, had moved toward Rohiṇī, his daughter. The movement of the sun was expressed mythically according to its observed stations, from Orion to Aldebaran. The sun of the vernal equinox, the beginning of the year—the year being Prajāpati—was seen to have left its station (Orion), and the beginning of the year, Prajāpati, had moved toward Rohiṇī (Aldebaran), his daughter. The unexplained anomaly, the shock of this momentous observation, was contracted in the myth of Prajāpati and his daughter, with Rudra as the avenger of this seemingly unprecedented phenomenon. The priests and the gods experienced by observation the startling phenomenon of the precession of the equinoxes.[26] They did not call it by that name; they conveyed

[26] *Ibid.*, pp. 96-100, 124, 125; H. Jacobi, "Der Vedische Kalender und das Alter des Veda," 1895, pp. 218-23. J. Deppert, in a remarkable book, *Rudras Geburt: Systematische Untersuchungen zum Inzest in der Mythologie der Brāhmaṇas*, 1977, p. 189, that came to my notice after *The Presence of Śiva* had gone to press, agrees with Tilak and assigns the era Rohiṇī from c. 3400 B.C. to 2210 B.C., when the vernal equinox was in the Pleiades. The

their observations and their reaction to them through the myth of Rudra, the Hunter of the Antelope, aiming his arrow at the antelope Prajāpati and his daughter.

The observation of the seemingly anomalous movement of the beginning of the year must have been made when the sun of the vernal equinox moved from Orion to Aldebaran, during the fourth millennium B.C.

Vedic myths had a long past before they were collected in the *Ṛg Veda*. Their meaning surfaced in versions and commentaries of succeeding ages, and their images became implanted in the creative mind of India. The *Mahimnastava*, composed about or before the ninth century A.D., mythically and mundanely addresses itself to Śiva: "O lord, the lord of creatures (Brahmā), who in a stag's form had been violently and lustfully pursuing his own daughter / transformed into a doe, while he was obsessed with desire to enjoy her, / and who had fled from you with bow in your hand until he reached the sky—him yonder, pierced by your arrow up to the feathering, / fear-stricken as he is, your ardor for the chase does not release even to this day."[27] (*MSt*.22).

Sirius, however, is the star form not only of Rudra, the Hunter of the Antelope, but also of another mythical image: the hound or dog of heaven. Ṛṣi Vasiṣṭha, the son of god Varuṇa, called him by his name: Vāstoṣpati (*RV*.7.55.1).

b. *The Hound of Heaven*

In the sky, Sirius, the Dog Star, glitters in his formidable shape. "He flies through the atmosphere, looking down upon all existences";[28] his birth is in the waters (*AV*.6.80.1, 3) of the nether world. He is the "hound of heaven." Another luminary of the night sky, the moon, is also called the heavenly dog (*ŚB*.11.1.5.1). This heavenly dog is one of the Sārameyas or the sons of Saramā (*RV*.10.14.10-12; *AV*.18.2.11-

---

battle of Indra with Vṛtra in its most ancient version is assigned to the era of Orion (c. 4500 B.C., p. 200). Sirius is considered to have been the vernal equinoctial point prior to Orion (p. 203).

[27] Cf. *Mahimnastava (MSt)*, ed. & tr. W. N. Brown, 1965, p. 15. The "stag" or deer appealed more to former translators of the word *ṛśya* than did the antelope, just as in another context, the swan instead of the wild gander was thought to be a more romantic way of rendering the word *haṃsa* (cf. Ch. VII.2).

[28] *Atharva Veda Saṃhitā (AV)*, tr. W. D. Whitney, 1962, p. 341.

12). Saramā, the bitch of heaven, the bitch of Indra, undertook a perilous, pioneering journey to the Paṇis,[29] the demons in the dark nether world (*RV*.10.108.1-2). Both sun and moon are dogs of heaven, sons of Saramā.[30] These two are watchdogs and they devour, that is shorten, the life of man. Sirius, the fixed star, preeminent in fame amongst all others, is the bright star-son of Saramā. This "silver-golden son of Saramā" is a fierce watchdog at the gate of the nether world, his teeth glistening like darts (*RV*.7.55.2). In the mythology of heavenly dogs, his role is different from that of sun and moon, the other sons of Saramā. He is the guardian of the house of Varuṇa; his name is Vāstoṣpati (*RV*.7.55.1, 2). Vāstoṣpati is Rudra. The gods had created Vāstoṣpati, the guardian of sacred ordinance (*vratapā*), out of their poem, the *raudra brahman*. In the sky Vāstoṣpati assumes the shape of the dog of heaven.

The names and forms of Rudra interlace. Their total pattern is an inexhaustible concatenation of evocations locked together by his innumerable qualities and actions in the cosmos from aeon to aeon, and anchored in his immutable being beyond manifestation.

Rudra in the sky is Sirius, star of stars, most exalted among them. In the morning dawn, before sunrise, when the red dawn-cows gather, Sirius is the "fire-colored boar of heaven," impetuous, fiery Rudra himself (*RV*.1.114.4, 5) risen from the waters of the nether world. At night he is the silver-golden watchdog of the sky. Other star figures play their own parts in the ongoing myth of Rudra-Śiva: the great bear (*ṛkṣa*) comprising the seven sages or seers (*ṛṣayaḥ*), and the Pleiades, the Kṛttikās, who were to nurse Kārttikeya, sprung from Rudra's seed.[31] However, what is seen in these last-named stars belongs to a later aeon and the later story of Rudra / Śiva. In his most ancient figure he was the Dog Star, the hound of heaven, gnashing his formidably bright teeth. When the sun of the vernal equinox rose in Rohiṇī, he was the star Mṛgavyādha, the archer, the hunter of the antelope shooting forth the arrows of his rays. The dog or hound of heaven is Vāstoṣpati, the Guardian of the Dwelling. The figures of the hunter of the antelope and of the hound were not envisioned simul-

[29] S. Kramrisch, "The Indian Great Goddess," 1975, pp. 240-42.

[30] M. Bloomfield, "The Two Dogs of Yama in a New Role," 1893, p. 167; and A. A. Macdonell, *Vedic Mythology*, pp. 172-73.

[31] Cf. A. Scherer, *Gestirnnamen bei den Indogermanischen Völkern*, pp. 134, 141.

taneously.[32] Only one of them was seen or thought of at a time. They are figures of Rudra, who has more than one form and name.

The invocation of Vāstoṣpati is repeated thrice in a hymn (*RV*.7.54) preceding one that is addressed to the god and protector of the homestead. There, a poet, the seer Vasiṣṭha, begins his hymn with an invocation (*RV*.7.55.1): "Vāstoṣpati, who chases away sickness and assumes all shapes, be our gracious friend." Ṛṣi Vasiṣṭha continues in the next verse (*RV*.7.55.2): "When you, silver-golden son of Saramā, gnash your teeth they shine like darts in your snapping jaws. Fall asleep!" The ṛṣi then admonishes this son of Saramā to bark at a thief or robber, but not at him, a poet; and he repeats his spell: "Fall asleep" (*RV*.7.55.3), and continues: "Attack the boar or the boar will attack you. You bark at Indra's poets. Why do you threaten us? Fall asleep" (*RV*.7.55.4). Rudra, the hound of heaven, is also the boar of heaven. The ruddy boar of heaven, of glittering appearance, his hair coiled up on his head (*kapardin*), holding medicines in his hand, is once again invoked in a hymn to Rudra (*RV*.1.114.5). Typically, Rudra wears his hair coiled up like a conch (*kaparda*).

Ṛṣi Vasiṣṭha, having taunted the hound of heaven, continues his spell. "The mother shall sleep, the father shall sleep, the dog shall sleep, the lord of the manor shall sleep. All relatives shall sleep, all these people everywhere shall sleep. Who sits and who walks and whoever sees us, their eyes we close as we close this firm dwelling" (*RV*.7.55.5-6). "The women who lie on the bench, who lie on the couch, who lie in bed, the scented women, we lull them all to sleep" (*RV*.7.55.8).

This lullaby is said to have been sung by the seer, the Ṛṣi Vasiṣṭha, son of Varuṇa, the all-encompassing god and king who ordained the laws of the universe. Vasiṣṭha, in a dream, had entered at night the house of Varuṇa (*BD*.6.11-12), a lofty structure of a thousand gates (*RV*.7.88.5). There he lulled to sleep the dog who attacked him, he lulled to sleep everyone (*BD*.6.12-13), and then closed the house. Before Vasiṣṭha had this dream, and before he had incurred the wrath of Varuṇa, his father, Varuṇa had chosen to take Vasiṣṭha on his boat, the sun, and let him see into the marvels of the cosmos, swinging

[32] The "hound of heaven" refers to a more remote era than the "hunter of the antelope." B. G. Tilak, *The Orion*, p. 108, assigns it to the vernal equinox in Orion, while J. Deppert, *Rudras Geburt*, considers an even more remote sunrise (see above, n. 26).

along the crests of the waves of the celestial ocean, from the high vault of heaven into the abyss where the sun is imprisoned in darkness (*RV*.7.88.2-3).[33] However, the seer Vasiṣṭha once, on his own—so he dreamed—stealthily went into the house of Varuṇa (*BD*.6.11-12). It was not in the hope of seeing there things even more wondrous than those Varuṇa had already shown him. Varuṇa had opened Vasiṣṭha's vision and let him see deep into the miracles of creation. He conferred on Vasiṣṭha the power to convey his vision in the words of his songs. Varuṇa had made Vasiṣṭha a seer and poet (*RV*.7.88.4). But Vasiṣṭha entered on his own, at night—so he dreamed—the house of god Varuṇa to close the eyes of everyone in the dwelling and to close the house itself. He lulled everyone to sleep, so that behind the closed lids of dream and sleep this world would fade away. Vasiṣṭha, the poet and seer, finally closed the house itself, the mansion of Varuṇa, the universe. He closed and left the house of Varuṇa behind him.

While the "thousand-horned bull" (*RV*.7.55.7) was rising from the ocean and everyone fell asleep,[34] Vasiṣṭha left the mansion of Varuṇa, the cosmos, and entered the radiant light beyond and above the vault of heaven. By himself he found his way as poet and seer into transcendency out of the house of Varuṇa, out of the spectacle of the cosmos whose marvels Varuṇa had shown to him during their voyage in the sun boat along the vault of the sun's course up to the zenith and down to the nadir.

For this daring deed Vasiṣṭha invoked Vāstoṣpati to be his "very dear friend." Vāstoṣpati "chases away sickness and assumes all shapes" (*RV*.7.55.1), for Vāstoṣpati indeed is Rudra, and Rudra, the healer, carries remedies in his healing hand for all ills (*RV*.1.114.5; *RV*.2.33.2, 4, 7). Vasiṣṭha invoked the god who knows how to heal. He felt that Varuṇa would be vengeful, would punish Vasiṣṭha with sickness for his deviousness, as indeed he did: he smote Vasiṣṭha with dropsy (*RV*.7.89.2-4; 7.86.4).[35]

[33] A. Bergaigne, *La Religion védique*, 1:51-52, has identified the sea in *RV*.7.88.4 as the "celestial sea" that is crossed by Vasiṣṭha.

[34] *Ṛg Veda Saṃhitā (RV)*, tr. K. F. Geldner, 1951, 2:230, considers the "thousand-horned bull" to be the moon. In *RV*.5.1.8, the "thousand-horned bull" is Agni. The image appears to be more applicable to the sun than to the moon. (Cf. Sāyaṇa on *RV*.7.55.7). If *RV*.7.55 is taken to be a lullaby, sung in the diurnal night, Geldner's interpretation would be suitable, but neither the image of the thousand-horned bull nor the awakening of the ṛbhus supports Geldner's view.

[35] Cf. Sāyaṇa on *RV*.7.89.4.

Bhṛgu, another son of Varuṇa, thinking himself superior in knowledge to his father, was sent by him in the four directions, one after the other. There he saw scenes of dismemberment and cannibalism, hellish retributions for injuries done in this world (*ŚB*.11.6.1.1-7). Varuṇa had a different punishment for each of his sons.

Vasiṣṭha invoked the god who has the remedies that heal. Addressing himself to Vāstoṣpati Rudra, the healer, Vasiṣṭha invoked the god who assumes all shapes. The shape in which he was seen by Vasiṣṭha was that of the watchdog of his father's house. The dog had formidable teeth. They shot darts of light. The dog was the first whom Vasiṣṭha would lull to sleep, for this watchdog, the guardian of Varuṇa's house, attacked the intruder Vasiṣṭha, the seer and poet. Indignant, Vasiṣṭha taunted the dog: he should have attacked a thief or burglar, not a poet; and, better still, he should have attacked the boar, or the boar would attack him.

But would that silver-golden hound of heaven, gnashing his teeth, attack the fire-colored boar of heaven?[36] In fact, they are one and the same star, and their animal shapes are somehow interchangeable. The fiery boar of heaven (*RV*.1.114.5)—an image of Rudra in his wrath—appears on the sky for but a short while when the star rises before the sun; the star, however, as his alter ego, is the dog of heaven when at the beginning of the night it emerges from the dark waters of the nether world to guard the house of Varuṇa. In his exhortation of the watchdog, the poet, in rhetorical whimsy, eggs the dog on against himself, but the dog has other things to do. He watches over this mansion, the cosmos.

In this capacity, at the proper moment he has to awaken the ṛbhus from sleep (*RV*.1.161.13). These are divine artificers of the vehicles

[36] Cf. *RV*.10.86.4, the dog's eagerness for the boar. The star Sirius is the dog, the Guardian of the House (Vāstoṣpati). In the annual course of the sun, the dog guards the two gates of the house. The one gate marks the sun's entrance from the nether world, the region of Yama (death), the world of the Fathers, into the Devayāna, the path that the gods take (B. G. Tilak, *The Orion*, p. 26, 108). Sirius rose before the sun at the vernal equinox of a remote age and disappeared shortly, as the sun rose in the sky. It is the same star, Sirius, the Dog Star of the night and the Boar (Star) who rises before sunrise. At the rising of Sirius, darkness prevailed and the teeth of the dog glittered. Then, in the dawn, just before sunrise, the star was the ruddy boar who pushed up the sun from the waters of darkness—and disappeared into the sun's light. Sirius, the dog who awakened the ṛbhus at the beginning of the year, is the same star in his capacity as dog, who as a ruddy boar pushed the sun up on the sky in the morning of the spring equinox of a remote aeon.

and receptacles of time (*RV*.1.111.1; 4.34.9). The ṛbhus had been men, and by their creative work they were made immortal (*RV*. 1.110.3-4). Having completed their work during the year, they rest for twelve days, slumbering in the house of Savitṛ, the Impeller of the sun, before starting another year's work at the beginning of the year (*RV*.4.33.7). The dog awakens them.

The dog of heaven watches over all existences in this mansion, the world, where everything has its place and everything its time. It is he who makes the ṛbhus wake from their sleep of twelve days at the end of the year, so that they begin shaping their wondrous works afresh in the new year.

Sirius, the hound—and boar—of heaven, is the same star as Mṛgavyādha, Rudra, the archer. His arrows are star rays, and so are the gleaming teeth of his animal shape. Frighteningly fierce, they command order. Fierceness informs the power of the brilliant star, the watchful hound of heaven, who watches over the mansion of Varuṇa so that everything is kept in order, the order of time in the world, our dwelling. From the tight grip of this order of the world under the stars, the seer poet dreams that he knows how to escape. He lulls to sleep the barking dog, the entire family of man, all their obligations, all the fragrant women, all the seductions, so that he may be free.

As Vāstoṣpati, the guardian of this house—the world—has been fashioned by the gods—the celestial intelligence—out of their poem, so it is within the power of the poet-seer to lull to sleep this creation, close and leave the house for the limitless realm beyond this world.

Rudra, the Wild Archer, by his first shot not only failed to prevent the coming into existence of human beings; he was instrumental in bringing the fire seed of life to earth. As Śarva, the archer, he makes life on earth precarious, yet Rudra the healer has all the remedies to cure the ills of life. Above this earthly condition flies the hound of heaven. Gnashing his teeth, he is the guardian of the house, the fiery star Sirius shooting his rays. He is Vāstoṣpati, the glittering guardian of Varuṇa's house.

Sirius, the hound of heaven, the star form of Rudra, the Wild God, is mythically the most eminent of all stars.[37] Before the sun the fire-colored boar of heaven arises from the dark waters of the nether world. When the sun has set, the hound of heaven shoots silver-

[37] G. de Santillana and H. von Dechend, *Hamlet's Mill*, p. 285, call Sirius "the first star of Heaven" and the "king pin" of archaic astronomy.

golden darts. Barking, he bares his teeth as he keeps watch over those who live under the starry dome of the world-mansion.

In his dream, Vasiṣṭha, the poet of transcendent peace, leaves the house of Varuṇa. The house sleeps and he has locked its door. But in this universe of revolving time he is to suffer for his transgression. "May Vāstoṣpati-Rudra who chases away sickness be Vasiṣṭha's gracious friend!" (*RV*.7.55.1).

Sirius, having risen like an arrow quick as lightning from the dark waters of the nether world,[38] in his ascent before the sunrise, has been figured as the fire-colored boar of heaven (*RV*.1.114.5). The same star guards the night when the sun descends toward the dark midnight, whence it will rise again in the east.

The arrows of Rudra shoot across existence. His first target was Prajāpati. The story is recorded by the stars in the sky. Rudra, having aimed at Prajāpati, the Lord of Generation (the Father), pierced him. Him they call the antelope. The piercer of the antelope is called by that name. The female antelope is Rohiṇī[39] (*AB*.3.33). Prajāpati, who in the shape of the antelope cohabited with his daughter, when pierced by the arrow of Rudra flew up to the sky, where he has his station as the constellation Mṛga, "the antelope," or Orion. The hunter of the antelope is the star Mṛgavyādha or Sirius. The female antelope is the star Rohiṇī (Aldebaran) (*AB*.3.33). Mṛgavyādha, the archer, the sparkling star, is Rudra the Archer. His primordial deed is seen written in the stars. The victimized Prajāpati is the sacrificial victim, and he is the sacrifice (*ŚB*.1.7.4.4; 3.2.2.4; 5.1.1.2; 5.2.1.2; 11.1.1.1; *TS*.2.6.8.3-4). The star Mṛgavyādha tells the myth of Rudra, the avenger of wholeness as it was before the beginning.[40]

It was this undifferentiated wholeness that the poet-seer Vasiṣṭha entered on having closed the house of Varuṇa, having lulled to sleep the hound of heaven, the fierce guardian of the order of time.

Rudra, the archer, let his arrow fly in the dawn of the world against the procreative act of the Father. Paradoxically, Rudra causes the beginning of life, the beginning of mankind on earth. The arrows of

[38] Cf. H. Lommel, tr., *Die Yäšt's des Awesta*, p. 50 (*Yäšt* 8.5-6).

[39] *Aitareya Brāhmaṇa (AB)*, tr. A. B. Keith, 1920, p. 185.

[40] Mythically, the beginning means the beginning of time itself; astronomically, it refers to the beginning of a world age, a new world when the spring equinox was in Rohiṇī. The figure of the "hound of heaven" or heavenly watchdog denotes the star Sirius of an earlier cosmic beginning with a new year, when the ṛbhus were awakened by the dog (cf. B. G. Tilak, *The Orion*, p. 170; and above, n. 26).

Śarva, the archer, threaten or spare man and beast; they have power over life and death. Mṛgavyādha—the star Sirius—rises on the vault of heaven at the appointed time in this ordered universe.

Sirius the dog star is twice and even thrice the star shape of Rudra. He is the star shape of Vāstoṣpati, the guardian of the House of Varuṇa; as such he is the hound of heaven; he is also the boar of heaven. He is Rudra, the Archer, the hunter of the antelope (Mṛgavyādha). To both these roles of his in the *raudra brahman* does Rudra send his light from Sirius. This mighty star is the sidereal equivalent of the *Ṛg Veda* word of power, the *raudra brahman*. It is the star symbol of the Wild Hunter and of the guardian of order, the dog. The star does not bear the name Vāstoṣpati; it is in the myth of Vasiṣṭha that he is so identified.

The Wild Archer, the hunter of the antelope, is Rudra; Vāstoṣpati is Rudra; each dazzlingly corroborates the coincidence of their separate entities in Rudra.

III

VĀSTOṢPATI, THE LORD OF THE DWELLING

Vāstoṣpati is the guardian of the House of Varuṇa, the universe, its dome the starry sky. The brilliant hound of heaven, whose other name is Mṛgavyādha, "the hunter of the antelope," watches over safety and order in this mansion with its thousand gates that lead in and out of the cosmos. There should be no trespass and no escape. He is on perennial duty; rising before the sun, he heralds the beginning of the year in a most distant world age of Rudra's myth.

At a new beginning of the world, the gods made Vāstoṣpati. The substance they made him from was a *brahman*, a "word of power," a mantric poem, uttered by them when the seed of the Creator fell on the earth: the *raudra brahman*. They gave the god his name, making him the Guardian of the House, and of sacred order (*vratapā*). The occasion was the horror of the primordial dawn. The gods' poem could neither undo the violence of that morning, nor mitigate it, but served as a counterweight to balance the disruption of wholeness and of the avenging violence in its wake. They created Vāstoṣpati, the guardian of cosmic order, a multiform counterpart of Paśupati. Vāstoṣpati is Paśupati's alter ego; Rudra comprises both and is each.

The gods created a *brahman* and made Vāstoṣpati as Prajāpati's seed was falling on the earth (*RV*.10.61.7). Prajāpati made the Wild Hunter desist from his murderous intention, and made him Lord of Animals, Paśupati (*MS*.4.2.12); or the horrified gods made "that god" out of their most fearful shapes in order to punish Prajāpati. "That god" thereupon demanded to be given the lordship over animals (*AB*.3.33).

Rudra was born neither as Vāstoṣpati nor as Paśupati. These distinctions were conferred on the Wild Hunter who *was* before he aimed at the Father. As Agni, he had prepared the seed for the Father (*RV*.1.71.5), and that fell on the earth. Thus the seed was shed from which Rudra was to be born, in a world over which the sun as yet had not risen. The primordial scene was enacted before the first sunrise. It is a prelude to the birth of Rudra.

1. The Remainder at the Site of the Lake of Sperm

However the gods vary in their level of creative intuition, they depend on their spokesmen. What the *Ṛg Veda* seer of the *raudra brahman* beheld is seen in another light by the gods, according to the account in the *Aitareya Brāhmaṇa* (*AB*.3.33-34). There they saw the mating of Prajāpati, the antelope, with his daughter. That these beautiful animals should cohabit and that they were father and daughter would not have surprised anyone, but the gods saw more; they perceived this first sexual congress for what it signified, knowing that eternity would never be the same again. It would be set off by beings brought to live and to die. In their horror and fear, the gods assembled the most dread shapes: the forms of their own fright. They asked this awful conglomerate to pierce Prajāpati, the antelope. The dread conglomerate demanded a boon, the overlordship over animals. They granted it to him, and his name became Paśupati, Lord of Animals.

In the account of the *Maitrāyaṇī Saṃhitā* (*MS*.4.2.12), however, the Lord of Animals was not invested with his power by the gods. There it was Prajāpati himself who gave this title to the Wild Hunter, not for piercing him, but rather to make him desist.

The traditions, unanimous in their horror at the primordial scene, differently distribute the roles played by its participants. When the seed of the Father fell on the earth, the gods of the *Ṛg Veda* created a *brahman* and shaped Vāstoṣpati, whereas the gods of the *Aitareya Brāhmaṇa* produced most terrifying shapes of their own, and these awful shapes coalesced into Paśupati.

As soon as they had granted the frightful being the overlordship over animals, it pierced Prajāpati, the antelope, who flew upward and became the star called Mṛga, the "antelope." The pursuer became the star Mṛgavyādha. The tripartite arrow and the daughter became constellations. She became the star Rohiṇī. This happened at that primordial moment as the seed emitted by Prajāpati rained down on earth and became a lake. The gods were concerned that the seed should not be wasted or spoil, for they knew that somehow in the future mankind would come about from that seed. They knew intuitively that out of their wish that the seed should not spoil (*māduṣa*), man (*manu*) would eventually come into existence (*mānuṣa*). Their knowledge was worded cryptically, for the gods love the mysterious (*AB*.3.33). To preserve the seed so that mankind should come to exist, they surrounded with fire the lake of heavenly seed (*AB*.3.34). The flames of Agni rose through the seed of heaven (*RV*.5.17.3); sparks blazed from it. The first spark became the sun and the second became Bhṛgu (*AB*.3.34), which "is the name given to the inner fire of the subtle centers of the body, which burns to ashes the water or semen."[1] The following sparks became the Ādityas, the twelve sovereign gods who rule the universe. The charred residue became dark animals; the earth baked by the fire turned into red animals. The ashes that were left were scattered in all directions in the shape of bovine and antelope-like animals, camel, ass, and ruddy beasts (*AB*.3.34). Indeed, Prajāpati made all the animals out of that seed (*TmB*.8.2.10). Just then "that god" appeared and claimed the animals as belonging to him (*AB*.3.34; cf. *RV*.10.90.8). Although his name is not to be uttered, so as to lessen the terror that would arise from pronouncing that name (*AB*.3.34), it was the Lord of Animals who showed himself to the animals in the shape of terror that the gods had given him together with the name of Paśupati, Lord of Animals (*AB*.3.33). He was "that god." "That god" said to the gods, "mine is this; mine is what is left on the site (*vāstu*)." "That god," however, was made to resign his claim by the recitation of a *mantra* to him (*AB*.3.34). The *mantra* (*RV*.2.33.1), which invokes Rudra, is to be altered, according to the *Aitareya Brāhmaṇa*, in such a way as to omit the name Rudra. In this way, as in the *raudra brahman*, the terror that would have arisen from the pronunciation of the actual word Rudra could be diminished (*AB*.3.34). The *mantra* (*RV*.2.33.1) was a humble prayer to Rudra for life not to be cut off from the light of the sun, and for progeny.

The gods themselves in cosmic fright make mankind their concern. When he comes into existence, man will be vulnerable from the beginning because of the gruesome power of the terrifying shape that the gods had created.

[1] A. Daniélou, *Hindu Polytheism*, p. 218.

Hearing the *mantra*, Rudra desisted from his claim to the remainder on the site where the seed of the Lord of Generation had fallen, where he had spent himself into creation—himself the victim of passion, the sacrificial animal, the sacrifice. "Prajāpati is the sacrifice" (*ŚB*.1.7.4.4; cf. *TS*.2.6.8.3-4). "That god" had not claimed more than what, indeed, belonged to him. What remained on the site were the ashes and burnt residue of Prajāpati's seed. Rudra-Agni had prepared the seed for the Father. Rudra by his shot had caused it to fall down on earth. It was his prey. Rudra had aimed his arrow at the Father to prevent the emission of the seed. Frightened by the hunter, the Father let fall some seed on the earth. Rudra-Agni prevailed over Rudra the avenger. Rudra became Lord of Animals at his own request, granted to him by the procreator god, himself in animal shape, a victim of passion. The lordship over the animals was granted also to Rudra by the gods, the celestial intelligence. By their creative power they formed Vāstoṣpati when the seed of the Father had fallen on earth.

The several versions of the myth carry forward the power immanent in the *Ṛg Veda* vision. They give shape to the consciousness of the loss of pre-existential wholeness in the figure of Rudra, the Wild God. He is the Fire, the Hunter, and Lord of Animals, he is "that god" who claims as his own all that was left on earth, all that was left after the conflagration on the site (*vāstu*) on which the seed had fallen. As Agni, Fire, he had prepared the seed, and as Fire he set the lake of sperm aflame. From it sparks had risen. Its residue stayed on earth, in a disturbed cosmic dawn at the beginning of things, the site where man would have his being. Henceforward Rudra desisted from his claim. The gods had feared that "that god" of their own creation would destroy what was left on earth of the seed of Prajāpati. Though Rudra had claimed it, he spared it. Kind (*śiva*) and tranquil (*śānta*), he showed his grace.

2. The Residue at the Site of the Sacrifice

a. *The First Gift*

On another occasion Rudra repeated his claim to what had remained at the site (*AB*.5.14; cf. however also *TS*.3.1.9.4-6; cf. *MS*.1.5.8). But what remained on the site this time was not the residue of the fire of the lake of semen that had become animals, wild and tame. In this instance he claimed the thousand pieces of cattle of the Aṅgirases, the fire priests. Once again, the site was the site of a sacrifice, but not the primordial sacrifice in which the Lord of Generation offered his substance consumed in the fire for the sake of creation of mankind on earth. Rather, this site was that of a sacrifice held by the Aṅgirases, the primordial fire priests. They were unsuccessful; they could not find the way to heaven, which the sacrifice should have opened to them. On the sixth day of their futile efforts, Nābhānediṣṭha, a student, and the youngest son of Manu (cf. *RV*.10.62.1),[2] offered his help at the suggestion of his father.[3]

Manu had divided his property among his sons, but nothing was left for his youngest son. He advised his son to proceed to the sacrifice of the Aṅgirases. He should communicate to them a certain sacred formula, a spell, a *brahman* (*TS*.3.1.9.4-5).[4] With its help the Aṅgirases would go to heaven, and in return for having shown them the way they would give to Nābhānediṣṭha the thousand pieces of cattle that were left from the sacrifice. The Aṅgirases, then, by means of the *brahman*, went to heaven, leaving their cattle to Nābhānediṣṭha (*AB*.5.14).

He was just collecting the cattle when a large man from the north, clothed in black, stopped him, saying, "this is mine; mine is what is left at the site." The Aṅgirases did not have the power to dispose of the cattle. Nābhānediṣṭha acknowledged the man's claim, but told him how he had come to own the cattle. Nābhānediṣṭha questioned his father on the stranger's claim, and was told by him that the claim was true. Nābhānediṣṭha returned and told the stranger. On ascertaining that Nābhānediṣṭha had spoken the truth, the stranger relinquished his claim and gave the cattle to Nābhānediṣṭha for having spoken the truth (*AB*.5.14).

Manu, "Man" is the first ancestor of mankind, and ruler of the earth. He gave his youngest son a very special patrimony. He made

[2] *Ṛg Veda Saṃhitā (RV)*, tr. R.T.H. Griffith, 1973, p. 576 n. 1 (on *RV*.10.62.1) and Sāyaṇa on 10.62.1.

[3] In the version of the story found in the *Bhāgavata Purāṇa*, the youngest son is called Nābhāga, son of Nabhaga (cf. *BhP*.9.4.1). Although this version varies from others in some details, the essential features of the story are the same (*BhP*.9.4.1-12).

[4] *Brahman*, from the root *bṛh*, "to increase," conveys a heightened state of inspiration. It is the mystic power of creativity. Cf. L. Renou, "Sur la notion de '*brahman*,'" 1949, p. 10; J. Gonda, *Notes on Brahman*, 1950, pp. 18ff., 67. P. Thieme, "*Brahman*," 1952, pp. 113, 117-21, 125-27, deriving *brahman* from another root, arrives at the meaning of formation, formulation; a sacred formula.

him earn it by communicating his knowledge in the form of certain *mantras*, and receiving in return a thousand pieces of cattle from the fire priests, whom he had enabled to go to heaven. But Nābhānediṣṭha's right to the cattle was disputed by an ominous-looking stranger who claimed them as his own, for they had been left on the site, and what is left on the site belonged to him. Nābhānediṣṭha, however, was allowed by the stranger to retain the cattle because he spoke the truth. He acknowledged the claim of the man dressed in black. Twice did Nābhānediṣṭha speak truth; he had not lied, but the other truth is of a different nature. He had acknowledged the claim of Rudra, for it had been revealed to him, implied as it was in the *raudra brahman*, in the *mantras* of the hymn that he had imparted to the Aṅgirases. Without it the Aṅgirases could not have gone to heaven.

The dark-clad stranger identified himself by defining his possessions. They comprise "what remains on the site of the sacrifice." By the same proclamation that what remained on the site of the sacrifice belonged to him, he had introduced himself to the animals, the transformed residue of the burnt-up lake of Prajāpati's semen. Rudra had resigned his claim to the animals as an act of grace. He resigned his claim to Nābhānediṣṭha in recognition of the truth that Nābhānediṣṭha had spoken. Rudra verified the truth that the cattle—which are his who is their lord—were actually given to the youngest son of Manu. He also knew that Nābhānediṣṭha had given the true *brahman* to the fire priests, or else they could not have gone to heaven. Rudra moreover recognized himself in that *brahman*; for the potent *brahman* that Nābhānediṣṭha had given to the fire priests was the *raudra brahman* itself.

As Paśupati, the horrendous Lord of Animals, Rudra showed them his grace. In his guise as a man in dark attire from the north, he recognized himself in the *raudra brahman*. He made doubly sure that Nābhānediṣṭha was a speaker of truth, for Nābhānediṣṭha helped the fire priests to ascend to heaven by means of the same *raudra brahman* in which the Wild God revealed himself to Nābhānediṣṭha, his singer and seer.

Two hymns of the *Ṛg Veda* (*RV*.10.61, 62), one of which is the *raudra brahman*, are traditionally assigned to Nābhānediṣṭha. The word *nābhānediṣṭha* means "nearest relative."[5] The *raudra brahman* is known

[5] M. Mayrhofer, *Concise Etymological Sanskrit Dictionary*, *s.v.* *nābhānediṣṭhaḥ*.

as the hymn of Nābhānediṣṭha, or the song of the seed (*AB*.6.27; cf. *ŚP*.3.29.1-59; *BhP*.9.4.1-12).

Nābhānediṣṭha received the gift of a thousand cows. It was, at the same time, the gift of Manu, the gift of the Aṅgirases, and the gift of Rudra himself to the singer. It was the gift by the god himself to the seer who had seen him. This gift (*dakṣiṇā*) was the first ever given to an inspired seer. It was the prototype for every *dakṣiṇā* or present given to a priest at the completion of a sacrifice. It could have been considered a heavy burden on the recipient, an obligation (cf. *AB*.4.25).

In his image called Dakṣiṇāmūrti, Indian art has celebrated over the millennia Rudra-Śiva as the giver of the first gift to his poet.[6]

In South India the image of Śiva Dakṣiṇāmūrti is enshrined in a niche on the south (*dakṣiṇa*) wall of the main sanctuary of a temple, whether Śaiva or Vaiṣṇava. "Because Śiva was seated facing south when he taught the *ṛishis yoga* and *jñāna* he came to be known as Dakṣiṇāmūrti."[7] This is the accepted view based on the meaning of the word *dakṣiṇā(a)*, which signifies "gift" as well as "south."

The South is the region of death. Śiva as Dakṣiṇāmūrti is the master of gnosis, yoga, music, and other sciences.[8] He teaches the ṛṣis the means of overcoming death, the mortal condition. To the devotee facing Dakṣiṇāmūrti, the image is in the north, where Śiva resides on a mountain, under a banyan or fig tree, the tree of knowledge. In its shade, the ṛṣis have gathered to whom Śiva Dakṣiṇāmūrti imparts or gives the knowledge of transcendency as Jñāna Dakṣiṇāmūrti, of yoga as Yoga Dakṣiṇāmūrti, or of music and the arts as Vīṇādhara Dakṣiṇāmūrti, and as the source and expounder of all the sciences as Vyākhyāna Dakṣiṇāmūrti.[9] In his images as Dakṣiṇāmūrti, Śiva imparts to the sages the gnosis that was his gift to Nābhānediṣṭha.

[6] A very early example of Śiva as Vīṇādhara Dakṣiṇāmūrti can be found in C. Sivaramamurti, *Naṭarāja in Art, Thought, and Literature*, 1976, p. 169, fig. 4, a terracotta image of the Śuṅga period, 2nd century B.C. A much later example, fig. 95 on p. 243, from the early Cola period, illustrates the image in its consolidated iconography.

[7] T. A. Gopinatha Rao, *Elements of Hindu Iconography*, 1968, vol. 2, pt. 1, p. 273.

[8] *Ibid*.

[9] *Ibid*., pp. 274, 276, 273. According to the *Dakṣiṇāmūrti Upaniṣad*, understanding or wisdom (*śemuṣi*) is called *dakṣiṇā*, and since Śiva is gazed upon by *dakṣiṇā*, he is called *dakṣiṇābhimukha* (*DMUp*.31). The *Sūtasaṃhitā* describes the worship of *Dakṣiṇāmūrti*, and describes Śiva in this form as giving *svātmavijñāna*, "understanding of one's Self" (*SS*.3.4.45-51).

b. *Abasement and Recognition of Rudra*

Although Rudra demands "what has been left on the site" as his own, he does not take the animals. He spared the animals on the day of their creation, and he turns over his claim as a gift to Nābhānediṣṭha. However, another account of the outcome of the meeting of Rudra and Nābhānediṣṭha is given in the *Taittirīya Saṃhitā* (*TS.* 3.1.9.4-6). Here Rudra is not the munificent giver of all that has remained on the site (*vāstu*). On the contrary, he becomes the recipient of the remnant (*vāstu*) of the milk and barley offered at the sacrifice of the Aṅgirases, in exchange for relinquishing his claim to the cattle left on the site. Rudra, having challenged the right of the Aṅgirases to leave their cattle to Nābhānediṣṭha, made a counterproposal that he would desist claiming the cattle if he were to receive as libation what was left over from the sacrifice (*TS.*3.1.9.4-6). The exchange was all important to Rudra, for he had been excluded from the sacrifice after his arrow had pierced Prajāpati.

Rudra had resigned his claim to the animals, the converted ashes left after the conflagration of Prajāpati's seed. He would spare them. Rudra, an aggregate of the dread of the gods at the primordial drama, assured those animals of the safety of their lives. Paśupati, Lord of Animals, in his grace would not harm those he rules, and whose existence he as Agni initially had caused. The land around the burnt-out lake of Prajāpati's semen was the first site (*vāstu*) where Rudra Paśupati, the Fierce Hunter, unconditionally resigned his claim to what was left on the site.

On the second occasion, the site was the place of a sacrifice of the Aṅgirases, the fire-youths. They had been enabled to go to heaven on the strength of the *raudra brahman* that Nābhānediṣṭha had revealed to them. Their sacrificial cattle were the reward they left for Nābhānediṣṭha on the site. Rudra appeared in the guise of an uncanny stranger, claiming once again as his own what had been left on the site. He gave up this claim in recognition of the words spoken by Nābhānediṣṭha, who knew Rudra when Rudra had revealed himself to Nābhānediṣṭha in his *brahman*. Rudra gave the young priest the gift of a thousand—of all—the cattle that the fire priests had left for him on the site.

The gift of life to the animals at the site of the burnt-up lake, the gift of mutual recognition of the god and his seer—the first *dakṣiṇā*, witness the grace of Rudra, his Śiva nature within the dread shape of Paśupati and within the dark aspect of the man from the north (*AB*.5.14). However, the encounter of the god and the young seer and priest is told with a different ending in another version (*TS*.3.1.9.4-6). As before, Nābhānediṣṭha is left the cattle, but not unconditionally. In return, Rudra demands and receives remnants of the oblation for which he had asked (*TS*.3.1.9.6). Rudra, who by a covenant with Prajāpati in the first dawn of creation had become the Lord of Animals, and who, although he had the power over their lives, spared this remnant of the burnt-out lake of Prajāpati's seed, is now satisfied with the remnants of the libation offered to him by the seer Nābhānediṣṭha in exchange for relinquishing his claim to the cattle. Nābhānediṣṭha knows the secret of Rudra, the awesome archer whose target was the Father. Rudra let Nābhānediṣṭha take his cattle in even exchange for the remnant of the sacrifice. The remnant of the sacrifice had a special significance for Rudra. His arrow sent against Prajāpati remained in Prajāpati's wound. It was the arrow shot by Rudra, who was made Paśupati in the primordial scene.

The gods held in thrall by the primordial scene compensated for its horror by creating a *brahman* as the seed of the Father was falling, and out of it they gave shape to Vāstoṣpati. According to another tradition, they shaped their own combined horror into a monstrously frightening aggregate, namely, Paśupati. Hence the gods never felt at ease with Paśupati-Rudra. "When the anger of the gods subsided, they cured Prajāpati and cut out that dart of this (Rudra); for Prajāpati, doubtless, is this sacrifice" (*ŚB*.1.7.4.4; cf. *TS*.2.6.8.3-4).[10] That small bit of Prajāpati's flesh that had primordially been pierced by Rudra's arrow, when cut out, proved to be charged with devastating power. When offered as a small portion of the sacrifice to the gods, it blinded one god, knocked out the teeth of another (*ŚB*.1.7.4.5-7), and similarly maimed and injured the other gods to whom it was offered (*KB*.6.13). The effect of this morsel was to become paradigmatic for the havoc created at another sacrifice in another aeon (Ch. X.A.2).

The gods, as the *Brāhmaṇas* tell, obviously dreaded and loathed Rudra. They did not want to share their privilege with the Wild God; they excluded him from the sacrifice. He was not entitled to it. Had he not aimed his arrow at Prajāpati, the Sacrifice, the Lord of Generation?

[10] *Śatapatha Brāhmaṇa (ŚB)* tr. J. Eggeling, 1963, part I, p. 210.

Nābhānediṣṭha, the priest who knew the secret of Rudra and had voiced it as the *raudra brahman*, gave Rudra the remainder of the libation in return for the gift of Rudra's cattle. However, the gods did not want Rudra to have any part in the sacrifice. "Now by means of the sacrifice the gods ascended to heaven. But the god who rules over the cattle was left behind here: hence they call him Vāstavya, for he was then left behind on the (sacrificial) site (*vāstu*)" (*ŚB*.1.7.3.1).[11]

The gods abhorred Rudra, the Wild God. He had let fly the arrow against the Father; his arrows threatened man and beast (*RV*.1.114.7, 8, 10); the power over life and death was in his hands. The *Rudra mantra* (*RV*.7.59.12) invokes Rudra Tryambaka that he may not cut off the life of man like a gourd from its stalk, that he may liberate from death and give a full life span, the nearest thing for mortal bodies to immortality. Rudra the liberator is called the "king of the sacrifice" (*RV*.4.3.1). But the gods would not admit him to the sacrifice. They feared him (*ŚB*.9.1.1.1). They appeased him with the awesome Śatarudriya offering of "a hundred oblations," and with the exultancy of the words of the accompanying hymn to Rudra hundredfold (*TS*.4.5.1-11; *VS*.16.1-66). They made him immortal (*ŚB*.9.1.1.1-2)—who himself held in his hands the power over life and death. They offered the Śatarudriya on completion of the altar for the Soma sacrifice—and they beheld Rudra: he stood flaming on the altar (*ŚB*.9.1.1.1). They were afraid lest he hurt them with his arrows ready in the hundred quivers that he carried, longing for his oblations, longing for food. They appeased him—"the lord of the Soma plant" (*ŚB*.9.1.1.24). By the hymns and oblations of the Śatarudriya sacrifice, preparatory to the Soma sacrifice, the gods made Rudra cast off his pain, his evil (*ŚB*.9.1.2.10, 12, 13, 20).

Besides, they let him have other sacrifices entirely to himself, far from the site of the Soma sacrifice, in the forest or on haunted crossroads. On a road or at a crossroads, rice cakes would be sacrificed to him (*ŚB*.2.6.2.7) and, later, additional rice cakes would be hung in a basket from a tree (*ŚB*.2.6.2.17). He is invoked as Tryambaka (*ŚB*.2.6.2.11-12), for his three mothers are heaven, earth, and air,[12] and his *mantra*, the *Mahāmṛtyuñjaya mantra*, is that of the Great Liberator, the conquerer of death (*RV*.7.59.12; *MS*.1.10.4). Still, he is asked

[11] *Ibid*., pp. 199-200.

[12] Cf. A. A. Macdonell, *Vedic Mythology*, p. 74.

to take with him the offered rice cakes and go away to the north, where he is at home, beyond Mount Mūjavat (*ŚB*.2.6.2.17; cf. *TS*.1.8.6).

He also accepts libations unfit for other gods (*KŚS*.25.2.2-4), and has to be content with the leavings of the sacrifice (*TS*.3.1.9.6). From the beginning he had chosen a lowly guise, that of a hunter. Those in the wilderness of life, the lowly and rejected, can address themselves to him. They know him, for he lives in them (*TS*.4.5.3, 4). He will accept their offerings, and fulfill the needs of those who know him.

He is clad in the skins of animals of the hunt, the tiger and black antelope (*TS*.1.8.6; *MBh*.13.15.11; 13.14.152). One can smell them, and invoke Rudra in his *mantra* as the "scented one" (*RV*.7.59.12; *TS*.1.8.6.2). The offerings made to him range from refuse (*TS*.3.1.9.6) to rice cakes (*ŚB*.2.6.2.8), and from cattle (*ŚŚS*.4.17.1-3) to human lives (*TS*.2.2.2.3-5), even royal blood. The *Mahābhārata* tells of King Jarāsandha, who had planned to offer as a sacrifice to Rudra the princes he had defeated and captured in battle (*MBh*.2.20.8-10). And once Rudra offered himself in a sacrifice, a universal sacrifice (*sarva-medha*) of his own. He poured into it all creatures, and then he offered himself (*MBh*.12.8.36).

Rudra, "king of the sacrifice," accepts the humble offering of rice cakes as in the Tryambaka sacrifice, or even the foam of cooked rice (*GGS*.1.4.31), and he is offered human, even royal sacrificial victims. He accepts all these sacrifices, and offers himself together with everything else as a sacrifice.

In the sequel to the primordial scene, the residue of the conflagration on the site of the lake of semen, namely, the burnt cinder, the earth and ashes that had turned into animals, was claimed as his share by Rudra-Paśupati (*AB*.3.34). Then, on the sacrificial site of the Aṅgirases, Rudra again put forth his claim to what was left on the sacrificial site (*vāstu*) (*AB*.5.14). At yet another sacrifice, he himself was left on the sacrificial site (*vāstu*). Rudra, excluded from the sacrifice and left on the site, went after the gods, threatening them with his arrow (*ŚB*.1.7.3.3). So that he would not hurt them, the gods conceded to him a share in the sacrifice (*ŚB*.1.7.3.4). But already they had all received their offerings. Nothing but the leftover remnants were now there to be made into the offering for Rudra. "This then is the reason why he (Rudra) is called Vāstavya, for a remainder (vāstu) is that part of the sacrifice which (is left) after the oblations have been made" (*ŚB*.1.7.3.7).[13]

The relation of Paśupati-Rudra and the *vāstu* is very close. The *vāstu* itself, the sacred site on which the sacrificial animals had been left, and whatever had been left behind or left over (*vāstu*) on the site (*vāstu*), are both Rudra's. Indeed, he himself had been left behind on the site.

His position is dismal. He is at the bottom and cannot rise. There is something ominous about him; he shows it in the way he is dressed in black, a color most unbecoming for the occasion when he confronts Nābhānediṣṭha at the place of the sacrifice. He now demeans himself when he thinks it necessary to resort to threats, intending to throw his arrow at the gods unless they let him rise with them. This is indeed Rudra, "king of the sacrifice" (*RV*.4.3.1; *TS*.1.3.14.1).

The gods had given him a shape of dread, an aggregate of their own horror and fear. Later, Rudra, wearing a dark garment, appeared in the shape of man; he looked ominous. He now shows himself in an abject state, humiliated by the gods. Or is it in self-humiliation that he plays this role? It was only in his state of power that he appeared as a hunter.

Rudra's acceptance of humiliation was an act of asceticism, a gesture of detachment of the Great Yogi. Centuries later his followers, known as Pāśupatas, strove for the contempt of society as the path to happiness and *mokṣa*.[14] They too thought that abusive treatment should be regarded as a coronation (*PS*.3.5 and commentary).[15] The asceticism of humiliation, and of self-humiliation in particular, is an exercise of the power of Rudra. The Great Yogi displayed it at the place of offering and sacrifice.

Rudra had established his claim on earth. He did it when he claimed as his own the animals that had come to be after the conflagration of the lake of Prajāpati's seed. Nothing else had been left on the site. He was entitled twice over to his claim, for he was the cause of the lake of sperm, not only by having caused the Father to let fall

[13] *Śatapatha Brāhmaṇa (ŚB)*, tr. J. Eggeling, 1963, part I, p. 201.

[14] An excellent discussion of the tenets of the Pāśupata cult is given by D.H.H. Ingalls in his article, "Cynics and Pāśupatas: The Seeking of Dishonor," 1962, pp. 281-98.

[15] *Pāśupata Sūtras (PS)*, ed. R. Ananthakrishna Sastri, 1940, Introduction, p. 9, summarizes the rules by which the disciples were expected to live in the second stage of training: "They had to court disagreeable experiences from the public to show that they had lost pride and other egotistical tendencies."

his seed, but by his preparation of the seed. When the seed fell on the earth, the gods created a rune and fashioned Vāstoṣpati. As Agni, he had also caused the conflagration of that lake. Furthermore, the Father in his role as Prajāpati, Lord of Generation—or the gods—had made him Lord of Animals. However, the gods made him desist from his claim (*AB*.3.34). He spared the animals and gave them the span of their life.

This was Paśupati's first action on earth, according to one version of his myth. Paśupati, Lord of Animals, was the status conferred by Prajāpati himself on the threatening archer for sparing him. At that moment of horror—the Uncreate had been violated—the violator, the Father himself, was about to be shot at. The gods, in the other version of the myth, saw Paśupati, the very image of their horror, and made him into such an image. In this shape, "that god" appeared on earth. The myth does not end here. Its theme repeats itself in another form, on this earth, at the place of sacrifice. When, at that time, Paśupati-Rudra was seen on earth, his guise and appearance were those of an outsider, come from the north. He was clad in black and was uncanny. The scene was the place of the sacrifice of the Aṅgirases. Although the cattle left at the place of the sacrifice were his share, he accepted in their stead the remnant of the offering.

Still, by the offering, though a remnant only, he was admitted to the sacrifice. His dark looming presence had seemed forbidding. He seemed a stranger. He had come from the north, which is Rudra's direction (*ŚB*.1.7.3.3, 20; *TS*.2.6.6.5-6). He came from his Himālayan mountain residence beyond Mount Mūjavat. That was his dwelling in the wilderness on earth. But the north is also the cosmic North, the Zenith. The other gods have the east as their direction.[16]

Rudra in the primordial scene appeared from nowhere; his background was the Uncreate. Though his dreaded name could not be uttered, he was seen as an archer aiming at his prey. If, in the raw crepuscule of the first morning to which man was to owe his existence, the unnamed god could be seen as a hunter, he might well be credited with having come from somewhere here on earth, while his presence could also be felt high up in the sky, where he rose with the sun. His numinous presence is not confined to any location; he can appear in the shape he chooses and in several shapes in one place. In his lowly

[16] A. A. Macdonell, *Vedic Mythology*, p. 76.

guise as a wild hunter or as a man from the north, the god assumed credible shapes in accordance with the significance of his respective role.

His first deed on earth when he confronted his animals was an act of grace. He let them live, he gave them the gift of life. His second deed, on the sacrificial site of the Aṅgirases where Nābhānediṣṭha met him, is told differently in the two versions of this myth. According to one, Rudra graciously gave his reward to his seer, and according to the other he entered into an exchange with the seer. He gave his cattle and received the remnants of the offering. This could almost be seen as a slight, but Rudra was wont to accept any offering, even the most humble. At another sacrifice the gods had not let him have any oblation, and without it he could not rise with them to heaven. He had resorted to force. Indeed, he had sunk low and could not rise with the other gods.

This was the time when, as a rule, an offering was made to Agni the Fire after all the other offerings had been made (cf. *ŚB*.1.7.3.7). When Rudra was left behind on the site, the gods yielded, though they were embarrassed, as all the oblations had been made (*ŚB*.1.7.3.4-5). They contrived a ritually acceptable offering out of the remnants of the oblations made to them, on dishes made ritually fit for the oblation to "that god" (*ŚB*.1.7.3.6-7). It was but a concession. Then the sacrificing priest offered this remnant into Agni, the Fire (*ŚB*.1.7.3.7). This was the end of Rudra's low state. For "Agni [the Fire] is that god;—his are these names": Śarva, Bhava, Paśupati, Rudra, Agni (*ŚB*.1.7.3.8).[17] They are Rudra's names: Śarva, the archer, Paśupati, Lord of Animals, Rudra, and Agni. Bhava's name is added to them. Bhava means existence. *The Brāhmaṇa of a Hundred Paths* explains, however, that this is the name by which the Bāhīkas call him, whereas the eastern people call him Śarva (*ŚB*.1.7.3.8). Whoever the Bāhīkas were, they called Rudra by an essential name, just as Śarva designates Rudra, the thrower of the arrow (*śaru*). But Bhava too is an archer (*AV*.15.5.1).

When Rudra could not rise to heaven, he himself was derelict, left behind by the gods. At the last minute they changed their minds, contrived a mode by which an offering could be put together for him, and offered it not to Rudra, but into the fire, to Agni. The gods, the

[17] *Śatapatha Brāhmaṇa (ŚB)*, tr. J. Eggeling, 1963, part I, p. 201.

celestial intelligence, were well aware of the identity not in person but in essence of Rudra and Agni; they also remembered Rudra's arrow and his target, as well as the shape of horror that they had given him. The gods were ambivalent in their attitude toward Rudra. Indeed, we are told once that when they excluded Rudra from the sacrifice, he pierced the sacrifice with his arrow—Prajāpati is the paradigmatic sacrifice (*TS*.2.6.8.3; *ŚB*.1.7.4.3-4). The gods propitiated Rudra (*TS*. 2.6.8.3). Nonetheless, the wound had been inflicted; the arrow was well aimed, as it had been at the beginning of things. This had never been forgotten. In fact, this story is an echo of the primordial drama in reverse. And the gods relived this scene at the sacrifice of Dakṣa. When the sacrificing priest offered into the fire the share that the gods had contrived for Rudra, Agni the Fire rose heavenward, and Rudra found his way to heaven.

When the Vedic gods in their divine insight in that first dawn fashioned Vāstoṣpati, it was out of the magic words of their poem, the *raudra brahman*, that they "carved" or gave shape to him. That shape of the unnamed god was made of *mantra*, the potent creative word. It counterbalanced the anthropomorphic shape evoked by the action of the fierce archer. Rudra became Vāstoṣpati, lord and guardian of the *vāstu*. *Vāstu* is the key word in the mystery of the transformation of Rudra Paśupati, Lord of Animals, into Vāstoṣpati. Fashioned by the gods out of mantric words, he guards the meanings of *vāstu*.

3. Residence and Residue

Rudra-Paśupati became Vāstavya because he was left behind on the site (*vāstu*) (*ŚB*.1.7.3.1). "(Rudra) [Vāstoṣpati] is called Vāstavya, for a remainder (vāstu) is that part of the sacrifice which (is left) after the oblations have been made" (*ŚB*.1.7.3.7).[18]

Rudra Paśupati becomes and is Vāstavya with regard to the site on which he was left, and also with regard to the leftover portion of the sacrifice. Both site and remnant belong to him in his abject state; there is nothing else that belongs to him. Moreover, when he is left on the *vāstu* as Vāstavya, he dwells in the *vāstu*, the site. The *vāstu* is his residence. There the residue (*vāstu*) of the sacrifice will belong to him. These are his possessions. They are all that he possesses, and he is

[18] *Ibid.*

their lord, Vāstupa (cf. *MS*.2.9.7). Paśupati becomes Rudra-Vāstoṣpati, the lord and guardian of the *vāstu*. It did not take the gods of the *raudra brahman* long to transform the Wild Hunter Paśupati into Vāstoṣpati. They were blessed with creative intuition.

The gods of the *Śatapatha Brāhmaṇa* were less gifted. They were sustained by rites whose proper observance was their concern. They judged the Wild God Rudra by conventional standards. Nothing but the remainder from the sacrifice was considered by the gods to be fit for Rudra. The gods implied a slight, while yet accepting him. The remainder from the sacrifice was superfluous—the sacrifice had been achieved, the rites had been performed. Yet a new oblation was offered to Rudra by the will of the gods from the reconsecrated remnants. Had nothing been left, there would have been an end. There would have been nothing to offer to Rudra. This would have been fatal. "Now Vāstoṣpati is Rudra. If he [the sacrificer] were to go on without offering to Vāstoṣpati, the Fire becoming Rudra would leap after him and slay him" (*TS*.3.4.10.3).[19] The residue of the sacrifice is a potent substance.

4. The Potency of the Residue

A hymn of the *Atharva Veda* (*AV*.11.7) is addressed to the residue. The word there employed referring to the leavings of the sacrifice for the remnant is *ucchiṣṭa*. In the *ucchiṣṭa* are deposited essence (*nāma*) and form; the whole world is deposited in it, heaven and earth and all beings, being and nonbeing, death and Prajāpati. *Ucchiṣṭa* is the father of the progenitor (*AV*.11.7.1-3, 16). The hymn exuberantly extends the potency of the residue throughout manifestation and beyond, to the unmanifest creative principle. Jubilant, it sings of the birth of joys, of delights, and of all the gods in the heavens from the *ucchiṣṭa*.

Fire, ashes, leftovers are all part of the sacrifice, whether it is performed on the sacrificial site of the earth or, at the same time, within the heart of man and in his own house. Fire, ashes, and leftovers are part of the ritual of living. Vāstoṣpati is the lord of the *vāstu*, the site of the sacrifice, and the site of the house.[20] He is the guardian of the dwelling of man, and protects it. As protector of the dwelling, Vās-

[19] *Taittirīya Saṃhitā (TS)*, tr. A. B. Keith, 1914, p. 275.

[20] *Somaśambhupaddhati (SŚp)*, tr. and ed. H. Brunner-Lachaux, 1963, part 1, p. 98 n. 3, succinctly defines *vāstu* as "the site, the building, and its content."

toṣpati is invoked in the *Vedas* (*RV*.7.54.1; 7.55.1; *AV*.6.73.3; cf. *TS*.4.5.7.2), *Brāhmaṇas* (*TB*.3.7.9.7; *JB*.3.120), *Śrautasūtras* (*ĀpŚS*. 6.8.28.8; *BŚS*.14.19; *MŚS*.1.6.3.1; *ŚŚS*.2.16.1-3) and in the *Gṛhyasūtras* (*ĀGS*.2.9.9; *PGS*.3.4.7; *ŚGS*.3.4) in the domestic ritual for building a house.

Vāstu, the "remainder," is doubly potent in its meaning. It is what is left on the site, and it is the site itself. The site, which was a wasteland after the conflagration of the lake of seed, is this earth, the ground of existence. On it the seed of Prajāpati had fallen. The sun rose first from the flaming seed. Animal life arose from its ashes, and from the still-glowing coals the fire priests and Bṛhaspati, the great master and teacher of the gods, came into existence (*AB*.3.34). This earth in its sacral aspect is the site of the sacrifice, the *vedi* (cf. *RV*.1.164.35; 10.110.4). It is regulated by the cyclical movements of the luminaries in the sky, by sunrise and sunset, by the solstitial and equinoctial points, by the movement and meetings of sun and moon, their marriage. Thus in the myth of Cyavana the mystical marriage is recounted of the old decrepit Cyavana, who was left behind on the *vāstu*, where his youth and potency were restored, and he became young again.[21] He knew the *brāhmaṇa* of Vāstupa (*JB*.3.120-28). Knowledge of the *mantra* of Vāstupa, "the lord of the leavings of the sacrifice,"[22] rescues Cyavana, abandoned by his kin in the "wasteland" (*vāstu*); Vāstupa is "the lord of one who is left or deserted."[23] Vāstupa, the guardian of *vāstu*, is none other than Vāstoṣpati, lord of the *vāstu*, the sustainer of man (*RV*.5.41.8). He is Vāstavya, the resident in the residue, the *vāstu* and its lord. Vāstavya and Vāstupa, each is Rudra (*MS*.2.9.7).

As Vāstoṣpati, the guardian of sacred order (*vratapā*), the unnamed god arose in and from the *raudra brahman*, the word of power of the gods when the seed of the Father fell on earth. Lord of the residue (*vāstu*), the potent substance, lord of the site (*vāstu*), the ordered field of power and its numinous guardian, Rudra, the Wild God, arose as Vāstoṣpati, guardian of the order of the cosmos and of the house built by man. It is Rudra who is skilled in art, the best of all artists, and the originator of all arts (*MBh*.12, app. 1, no. 28, line 310). "Because he

[21] The legend of Cyavana / Cyavāna is discussed by E. W. Hopkins in "The Fountain of Youth," *JAOS* 1905, pp. 45-67.

[22] *Ibid*., p. 61.

[23] *Ibid*.

grants an abode to the world and protects it, therefore he is called Vāstoṣpati" (*BD*.2.44; cf. *N*.10.16). He is the Lord of the Dwelling. In its plan and orientation, the house built by man conforms with the laws of the cosmos. It has for its model the house of the cosmos, the House of Varuṇa. In the shape of a fierce, fiery star, Vāstoṣpati, the hound of heaven, is its guardian.

5. The Architect's Myth of Vāstupa

Myth is transmitted verbally, and when it is given concrete form in works of art, also visually. Vāstoṣpati lived in the consciousness of the Indian architects who built the great stone temples about two millennia after the hymns to Vāstoṣpati were first sung. These temples as they stand today arose out of a living tradition. The myth of Vāstupa-Vāstoṣpati, as the builders knew it, is told in textbooks on architecture of the first and second millennium A.D.[24]

In the myth of Rudra-Śiva as the architects knew it, Śiva and Vāstupa play two different roles. Rudra assumes many shapes; some have been named here already. He dwells in each, and each acts out his presence. He assumes these shapes at will. In the *Maitrāyaṇī Saṃhitā* (2.9.7), homage is offered to the many forms of Rudra from the bowman (*niṣaṅgin*) to the lord of the site (*vāstupa*), illustrating not only the variety of forms in which Rudra appears, but also their reference to the center that they have in common, and from which the bowman or archer and the lord of the site are equivalent, at opposite ends of the same diameter. According to the situation that is alive with his presence, he manifests like lightning in an atmosphere charged with electricity. Suddenly he is beheld in one form or another, not necessarily in any visible shape or in any of his known roles, though always unmistakable, whether as a concept or figure that bears the cognizance of Rudra. His names and forms are the actualizations of his presence, which exceeds while it sustains each of them. Excessive, he plays more than one role at a time. Thus he might confront himself. In the myth that the architects knew, Śiva is the Great God, and Vāstupa is a goat-headed Asura or demon. This goat-headed demon came into existence at a sacrifice by Bhārgava, son of Bhṛgu, the priest of the Asuras. His proper name was Kāvya Uśanas. Bhṛgu him-

[24] S. Kramrisch, *The Hindu Temple*, 1977, pp. 75-77; esp. p. 75 n. 34.

self had sprung from the flaming seed of the Lord of Generation (*AB*.3.34).

Bhārgava, the son of Bhṛgu, was enraged because the demons had been defeated by the gods. To overcome this defeat, Bhārgava offered a sacrifice. Heated by the sacrificial fire and by his fury, he let a drop of sweat fall from his brow onto the fire while he sacrificed a goat. The goat became a goat-headed demon, growing until it filled heaven and earth. It left no room anywhere; the gods had nowhere to go. They took refuge in Śiva. The fire from Śiva's third eye burned the goat demon. Bhārgava fled through the three worlds, but he found no refuge. He entered Śiva's ear and wandered through Śiva's body. Bhārgava left Śiva's body through the semen passage. Thus he became Śiva's seed (*śukra*) and son (*ŚRa*.1.7.1-15; *ĪPad*.3.26.93-110; cf. *VmP*.43.26-44). He also became the planet Śukra (semen) (*BhP*. 5.22.11-12). As the morning star, its name is Lucifer.[25] Śukra then asked Śiva, who in his grace had given him asylum, to grant a boon to the disembodied goat-headed demon. The boon that the phantom demon asked for was to dwell (*vas*) on earth together with the gods. Śiva granted him a residence (*vāstu*) on earth, and gave him the name Vāstupa. Whoever builds a house for gods or men should first worship Vāstupa (*ŚRa*.1.7.16-23; *VVi*.4.46-47 and commentary, *ĪPad*.3.26.110-25).

Bhārgava, the Asura priest, having entered Śiva's body, leaves it as Śiva's semen (*śukra*) and becomes his son (*VmP*.43.26-44). He also becomes a star named Śukra (Venus) (*BhP*.5.22.12).[26] Elsewhere, Śukra, son of Bhṛgu, is said to have arisen in the sign of Tiṣya (*VāP*.53.106); Tiṣya is Rudra (*TS*.2.2.10.1-2). As son of Śiva, Śukra mediates between Śiva and the goat demon born of Bhārgava's sweat, and thus his son. The goat, as a sacrificial animal, ritually belongs to Agni and is Agni's animal. Rudra-Śiva, granting a boon to the goat demon whom he had burned, acts in accordance with his gracious nature, that is, as Śiva. He gives to the dimensionless demonic phantom, tenuously though intimately related to himself, a name of its own, Vāstupa, and allots to this being the plan of the sacred sites on earth, the temples and the houses, as residence. On it the gods will have their appointed stations. They will dwell on earth in the sacred geometry

[25] A. Scherer, *Gestirnnamen bei den Indogermanischen Völkern*, pp. 78-79.

[26] *Ibid*., pp. 86-87.

of the *vāstu-maṇḍala*, the magic diagram and form of the fallen demon, the symbolic architectural plan.[27]

The myth of the "birth" of Śukra from Śiva was integrated into the architectural myth from another context dwelt on in the *Mahābhārata* (*Mbh*.12.278.2-37; below, Ch. VI.4). In one version of the architectural myth, in the *Matsya Purāṇa*, the demonic being fallen to the ground is born from the sweat of Śiva himself as it dropped from the forehead of the god fighting the demon Andhaka (*MP*.252.5-7). No less demonical than the goat demon, the being born in direct filiation from Śiva has divine status, being called Vāstu-deva or Vāstu god, the deity of the site (*MP*.252.13-14). God or demon, the fallen being, laid out on earth, partakes of Śiva's nature inasmuch as *tamas*, darkness, belongs to him. On this demonic substratum all the gods find their apportioned stations (*MP*.252.13-14). Together, the underlying demon and the gods distributed over his extended form constitute the paradigmatic ground plan of Indian architecture, which has its origin in Śiva.

[27] Cf. S. Kramrisch, *The Hindu Temple*, p. 67.

IV

MANIFESTATIONS AND REALIZATIONS OF RUDRA

1. Śatarudriya: The Hundred Forms and the Host of Rudras

Unnamed he appears on the cosmic scene in the first dawn of the world, a hunter sure of his target: the sexual embrace of the Father and his daughter. At this moment he revealed the terror of his identity to the Vedic ṛṣi who guarded his secret.

The picture is clear and sharply focused, a close-up on the vast horizon of a yet unpeopled world. The actors, an archer and the copulating antelopes, are, however, not what they seem. They are anthropomorphic and theriomorphic symbols of deity. There was nobody to see the scene except the gods, and when they saw it, it was immediately transformed in different ways. Whatever their attitude, it was the hunter who had all their attention, and now they saw him quite unlike his fierce, fleet figure. It was not so much that the gods saw him in a different shape; it was more sensing than seeing when they carved him as Vāstoṣpati. Though he had no features and did not resemble man or animal, they knew he was the lord who had shown himself, who had stirred them when the hunter took aim at the defenseless creatures absorbed in their vital need. Moved, they gave shape to all that the scene before their eyes called up in them. They carved its counterpoise out of the rhythmic words of the hymn (*RV*.10.61.7) as the Father's seed was falling. Other gods who had witnessed the scene were seized by horror, and they put all their fright—all their most terrible shapes—together, and made it the shape of "that god" whose name the *raudra brahman* does not utter (*AB*.3.33). A conglomerate of shapes of terror is what these gods of the *Aitareya Brāhmaṇa* made out of the figure of the hunter in the primordial scene.

Seen by the gods as a hunter, he was shaped by the gods of the *Ṛg Veda* in the *mantra's* order of rhythms, rites, and laws. This is how the gods with their divine eye saw the frenzied archer. Other gods in later texts, however, were less inspired than overcome by emotion. They combined the dread shapes of their fear and horror in one body, and this conglomerate of divine frightfulness at once asserted its existence. Such was the shape of him who claimed as his own the residue on the wasteland of this earth.

Later, he was seen by man as the great and dreadful archer, of many shapes (*TS*.4.5.1.1). Had not the different hosts of gods already seen him in altogether different shapes? The cowherds saw him, as did the women who carried home water from pond or well (*VS*.16.7; *TS*.4.5.1.3). And others saw him bearing a hundred quivers, and looking at them with a thousand eyes, his color glowing in red hues of fire, and his neck deep blue (*TS*.4.5.1.3-4; *VS*.16.7, 8, 13). The *Śatarudriya*, a hymn of the *Yajur Veda* (*TS*.4.5.1-11; *VS*.16.1-66) to Rudra of a hundred and more shapes, begins with an antiphonal praise to the wrath of Rudra; it offers praise to his arrow and bow, praise also to his kind arrow and kind bow that spare man and beast, and praise to the healer (*TS*.4.5.1.1; *VS*.16.1-5) and hail to him, the pursuer, "dread and destructive like a fierce wild beast" (*TS*.4.5.10.4; cf. *RV*.2.33.11)[1] himself wearing a garment made of skin (*TS*.4.5.10.4); hail to the slayer (*TS*.4.5.8.1).

To this god of dread and bliss, the *Śatarudriya*, a paean incomparable in its compelling immediacy, gives praise. It celebrates Rudra the archer whose flying arrow brings death, whose arrow averted or at rest gives life. From the eleven sections of the hymn in the *Taittirīya Saṃhitā*, Rudra arises throughout the universe and beyond. Ingredients of his being are assembled from many domains and many levels. Their blending evokes his presence. The following extracts compacted from the *Śatarudriya* may give some of the flavor of the juxtapositions set closely in the rich texture of the hymn.[2]

[1] *Taittirīya Saṃhitā (TS)*, tr. A. B. Keith, 1914, p. 361.

[2] For a recent, full, and free translation of the entire hymn, see C. Sivaramamurti, *Śatarudrīya: Vibhūti of Śiva's Iconography*, 1976, pp. 13-32.

Hail to the lord of creatures, hail to the lord of paths, hail to the guardian of fields, hail to the architect, hail to the lord of herbs. Hail to him who loudly roars, hail to the protector of warriors (*TS*.4.5.2).

Hail to the lord of thieves, hail to the archer, hail to the leader of the robbers, to the untrustworthy, to the leader of pilferers, hail to the destructive ones armed with spears, hail to the lord of plunderers. Hail to the archers, to those who stretch the bow string, and to those who take aim. Hail to those sleeping or waking, hail to those standing and running, hail to the horses and lords of horses (*TS*.4.5.3).

Hail to the ill-formed, hail to those of all forms, hail to the high and the low, to the charioteers and those without chariots, to the lords of chariots, hail to the carpenters, hail to the potters and metalworkers, hail to fishermen. Hail to the hunters, hail to the dogs (*TS*.4.5.4).

Hail to Bhava, the lord who is existence, hail to the principal one, to the first, to the quick one, to the swift one, to him in the flux of the waves, hail to the roaring one, hail to him of the island (*TS*.4.5.5).

Hail to the highest and hail to the lowest, hail to the worst one and hail to the one in the depth, hail to him in the world of the living, hail to him in the world of the dead, hail to him who gives peace, hail to sound and to echo (*TS*.4.5.6).

Hail to him of the drum, hail to him of the drum stick, hail to the courageous and to the cautious, to him on the footpath, hail to him of the pond, and to the rivulet, hail to him of the lake. Hail to him of the well. Hail to him of the rain, hail to him of the cloud, hail to him of the sunshine and to him of the storm. Hail to him of the dwelling and to the guardian of the dwelling (*TS*.4.5.7).

Hail to the copper-colored and to the ruddy, hail to him who gives happiness and hail to the lord of sentient creatures, hail to the terrible and to the fearful, hail to the slayer near and far, hail to the trees with green tresses, hail to the liberator. Hail to him of the sacred site and to him of the river bank, hail to him on the farthest shore, hail to him who crosses over and hail to him who crosses

> back. Hail to him of young grass and to him in the foam, hail to him in the sands and in the streams (*TS*.4.5.8).

> Hail to him of the desert and hail to him in the dwelling place, hail to him in the cow pen, and to him in the house, hail to him of the cot and of the palace, hail to him in soil and in air. Hail to him of the wide space, hail to him in the leaves and in the fallen leaves (*TS*.4.5.9).

Furtively the hunter drew near the Father; thus the laud goes to those of furtive pursuits and low standing. They are forms of Rudra; he dwells in those outside the pale, just as he dwells in the abnormal and deformed. He is the healer of all ills and the architect of the universe, and he works through the hands of the craftsmen. He is Rudra, thousand-eyed and of many colors (*TS*.4.5.1.2-3). Rudra looks out of every man and everything. The lord of creatures, Paśupati, the lord of sentient beings, sees himself in them. Throughout the laud of the *Śatarudriya* his protection is invoked.

The protection that is invoked is twofold: that his arrow be averted and his bow unstrung. Yet, though he may not even release the arrow, though the bow be unstrung, the awareness of the arrow by his creatures is a taut bond. The bow of Rudra has a wide span. Pināka or Ajagāva bends along the vault of the firmament and the course of the sun.

When the cowherds saw him, and the women who carried home pots of water on their heads from the pond, and all the world of the living saw him (cf. *TS*.4.5.1.3), they saw his blue throat (*TS*.4.5.1.3) gleaming like that of the peacock. It was a permanent mark on his body. He had acquired it when, at the churning of the cosmic ocean, he drank the world poison and thereby saved all living creatures and the gods. The poison did not harm Rudra. It only left its mark on his throat. Whoever sees it will feel protected by Rudra and strengthened when Śarva, the fierce archer, takes an arrow from his quiver.

The universe resounds with Rudra's presence; he *is* sound and echo, intangible vibration and infinitesimal substance, too, of every particle of dust and foam. His presence is immanent in verdant trees and the soft green grass. He is in the rustling, withered leaves and the silent dead. Unmistakably, the healthy and the afflicted are hallowed by his sign, while his innumerable arrows flit across the universe. At certain spots his presence is acutely felt. These are fords (*tīrtha*), and at them he is the ferryman. He ferries across to the other shore, into the far beyond of which he is the guardian. He is the liberator, but—paradoxically—he is also the ferryman from death to life. The fierce guardian of the Uncreate, at the inception of life on earth, having entered into the created world, is the ferryman who leads to the other shore. In *this* created world his images representing part of his energy are carved in stone on the Sun Temple of Konarak overlooking the ocean, from the thirteenth century to this day. The images are those of the Ghaṇṭākarṇa Bhairavas, two on each side of the temple; one image peaceful, the other wrathful. Each of these large figures dances in a small boat, the "world-boat." It forms the pedestal of the Bhairava. They protect the temple.[3] The world is Rudra's boat; it is also his hunting ground. When the archer hangs his weapon on the highest tree and approaches man, holding only the spear (*TS*.4.5.10.4), then the god gives happiness (Śambhu) here on earth and peace (Śaṅkara) (*TS*.4.5.8.1). In his grace he is Śiva, the giver of happiness (*TS*.4.5.8.1) and of pain (cf. *TS*.4.5.9.1). He keeps in abeyance the innumerable thousands of Rudras, resting in the trees, blue-necked, white-throated, golden and deep red, who unless propitiated and invoked to unstring their bows would pierce man in his food and his cup as he drinks. With propitiation they hold back their arrows and receive within their jaws the enemy of the propitiator (cf. *TS*.4.5.11.1-2). Such is the insecurity of life as it came to be when Agni-Rudra prepared the seed for the Father.

Hundredfold, thousand-eyed Rudra has innumerable faces (cf. *ŚUp*.3.16). He has each and everyone's face. Everything human is in him, for he is in every man. The interchange between god and man is swift and intimate. He is in the faces, heads, and throats of all; he dwells in the heart of all beings. He is the Lord, the all-pervading, omnipresent Śiva (*ŚUp*.3.11). Because he is in the face of man, man sees him with His eyes, tastes him with His tongue; all the senses of man are readied by Śiva for Śiva, and he knows Him in whatever shape. He is woman, man, young man, and young girl; he is the old man. He is the deep blue bird and the green parrot with red eyes; he is the cloud with lightning and the seasons and the seas (*ŚUp*.4.3-4). He has entered them and they vibrate with his intensity. He overwhelms and supports, he haunts, he grips and liberates. A potent fragrance ema-

[3] A. Boner and S. R. Śarma, *New Light on the Sun Temple at Koṇārka*, 1972, pp. 225-26 and pl. 74.

nates from him in terror as well as in glory (*RV*.7.59.12; *TS*.1.8.6.2). He is the one who cuts, pierces, and assails (*MBh*.12, app. 1, no. 28, line 278). He is all anxieties, diseases, the destroyer of disease, and disease itself (*MBh*.12, app. 1, no. 28, line 331). Wherever life is felt most acutely, *that* is Rudra. He is lust; he is subtle, he is gross; he is the golden seed; he is fond of garlands made of Karṇikāra flowers (lines 320, 323). He is shadow and sunshine (line 213). He has the color of the rising sun and the form of a child and of a child's toy (lines 231-32). He is food, its eater, its giver, the eating of it itself, as well as the creator of it (lines 255-56). And he is the Rudras who dwell in and animate all creatures and dwell throughout the universe (lines 368-80). Swiftly he travels from without to within as so many Rudras who are the uncounted, uncountable forms of his presence. He is one, he is eleven,[4] he is the numberless intensity that identifies each Rudra. He leaps into the mouth of man from food and drink; he does not enter through eye and ear alone. All the senses are his doors, by which he goes in and out. The Rudras, hundreds and millions of them (*AP*.18.44), carry arrows; they hit vulnerable, receptive goals on solid ground, in water and air, in every component of life, in the cosmos and in man. They act out His presence. They are the angels, messengers of His awareness springing from every part of His imperceptible body. When Rudra reaches out from within man he recognizes himself in the lowly and abject, in tender grass and the fall of leaves.

The Rudras are an ancient group of gods. They are invoked in the *Ṛg Veda* together with Rudra (*RV*.7.35.6; 7.10.4). Their number is given as eleven (*ŚB*.4.5.7.2) in a tripartite universe of thirty-three gods (*RV*.8.35.3), or they are said to be thirty-three in number (*TS*.1.4.11.1), or many more in a triadic system in which the number of the gods is thirty-three but also three thousand three hundred and thirty-nine (*RV*.3.9.9; 10.52.6). The number eleven remained their numerical cognizance throughout the myth of Śiva, though their host cannot be counted.

[4] G. Dumézil, *Mythe et épopée*, 1968, pp. 247, 248, juxtaposing the Ṛg Vedic decomposition of the thirty-three gods into three groups of eleven gods with the decomposition more frequently found in the *Brāhmaṇas* and Epics into the three groups of eight Vasus, eleven Rudras, and twelve Ādityas, points out the three functions of the respective groups, the Ādityas being the sovereign gods, and the Rudras occupying the second level. That the number eleven of the Rudras remains the same in both kinds of subdivision appears pivotal, though the significance of the number eleven is not accounted for.

Rudra is manifestation itself, together with its consciousness of the absolute. Before the creation of man in the cosmic dawn, he appeared in the guise of an archer, an avenger in defense of the unrevealed absolute, whose substance spurted into creation at the first embrace of the Creator and his self-begotten daughter. Rudra as the consciousness of the absolute had failed to preserve its integrity. He came too late by the fraction of time that the newly rising sun had placed between his bow and his target.

The world of Rudra resounds with repercussions and resonances of his presence. They surround him in throngs and groups, and are his companions. Thus in the *Mahābhārata*, when Aśvatthāman faced the guardian of the gate to the camp of the Pāṇḍavas, this gigantic, inimical figure adopted by Rudra-Śiva to dissimulate his presence, his mouth ablaze with fire (*MBh*.10.6.1-5), was suddenly joined by mighty beings with blazing mouths and eyes and many feet, heads, and arms. They looked like elephants, like mountains. They had the shapes of dogs, boars, and camels, and the faces of horses, jackals, cows, bears, cats, tigers, panthers, crows, frogs, and parrots. Some had the heads of mighty serpents, others those of different birds, tortoises, crocodiles, porpoises, whales, and lions. Some had ears on their hands, a thousand eyes, no flesh, or no heads. They had blazing eyes and tongues and faces of fire. Some were like conches, had faces like conches, or ears like conches. Some wore garlands and girdles of conches, and the voices of some resembled the blare of conches. Some had matted locks and some were bald; some wore diadems. Some had beautiful faces, some had head ornaments of lotuses, some wore white waterlilies. They numbered hundreds and thousands. Some had weapons of various kinds. Some were covered with dust or smeared with mud; all were dressed in white. Some had dark blue limbs and others light red. The excited retinue played upon drums and conches. Some sang, some danced, some leapt and skipped, fleet and fierce, their hair waving in the wind. They were terrible, frightful. Some had large genitals. They were fearless, masters of speech, astonishing the Great God by their worship. They adored him in thought, word, and deed, and he protected them as his legitimate sons (*MBh*.10.7.15-42). These tribes of mighty beings partook of the nature of the Great God. Aśvatthāman saw them all. He felt no fear when he offered himself as a sacrifice into the Great God (49-50).

Rambunctious groups and troops of imaginary beings surrounding

Rudra-Śiva agitated his ambience and made bearable the fierceness, the terror, of his splendor. They flashed across it in frolicsome frightfulness and sprinkled tensions with blood-curdling wit. Reverberations of and commentary to Rudra's presence, their host—lit up by leaping flames—gamboled worshipfully in his light.

Like Rudra himself, the Rudras keep astir their field of action, the ambience of Rudra, seen in a vision, experienced in nature, or felt in the heart. "Abiding in bodies, they do not cry but make the embodied beings cry; they gladden but themselves are not glad" (*MBh.*12, app. 1, no. 28, lines 369-70). "Their number, measure, and form are not known" (line 379). Fitted with any form or having no form, the Rudras activate sentiency, tingle sensibility, tease and sharpen awareness. They predispose creativity for its moment of collection and immediacy of insight. They are the tensions that draw together subject and object; nerves are the strings of their bows.

Unnamed and alone, Rudra had appeared on the cosmic scene in its first dawn, a hunter sure of his target. The exaltation of the *Śatarudriya* and the extravagances of lesser works are but adumbrations of the incommensurable intensity that is Rudra. Exceeding the conscious limits of thought, his being comes to a point at the flaming tip of his arrow. As an archer Rudra appears on the primordial horizon. As Agni he had prepared the seed of life for the Father and thus compelled him toward procreation, toward becoming Prajāpati, the Lord of Generation. As Rudra he lashes out backward against the Father's violation of the hitherto inviolate plenum. The Father rages at the interruption of his embrace. All this violence is but a refraction of the mystery of procreation. Rudra is its avenger and at the same time he is its cause. The Wild God, the hunter, by turning against the first embrace turns against himself who caused this transgression—the rupture of the Uncreate—by the Father. Rudra is Agni; he is the inseminating fire that rages in the fury of sex that he had instigated in the Father who, mounting his daughter, violated the integrity of the pre-existential plenum. The animal form of intercourse of the Father with the daughter, neither a paradigm of incest nor of bestiality, is an image—spontaneous as nature is—of a metaphysical situation, the rupture of the integrity of the pre-existential plenum and of its discharge into existence. In front of the mating pair rises ominously the Wild God Rudra who is Lord of Animals, who is Agni aflame. His body is made of "the fire of yoga" (*ŚUp.*2.12). In this yoga body of fire the wild, fierce god acts at the dawn of creation. His appearance is that of an archer. On the Harappan seal a god in his majesty is enthroned in a yoga posture.

Rudra has two natures, the one wild and fierce, the other calm and kind; but these are only one pair of the extremes that are in him. In the first dawn he acts in his Fire nature, inflaming the Father by preparing for him the seed that holds the spark of life, while as Rudra he counters the consequence of his part in the creative-procreative process. Rudra, the archer, while avenging the leak or opening up of the plenum, like Kṛśānu, and even like Vṛtra, the precosmic serpent, acts counter to creation. These defenders of the integrity of the unmanifest plenum are overcome or only partly successful; in one case due to the Soma powers of Indra, the dragon slayer, in the other case due to Time. Kṛśānu's arrow just grazed the flying falcon and did not prevent his bringing the Soma to man. But neither Vṛtra nor Kṛśānu incited or was the ultimate cause of the violation of the precosmic plenum, or of the rape of its most precious substance. It was Rudra alone who got ready that very substance for Father Heaven and, having given it to him and having avenged the violation, brought guilt on himself.

The fierce Wild God then was given a shape of conglomerate horror for his appearance in the wasteland of this earth. When at another time he came to the place of the sacrifice of the Aṅgirases, the fire-youths who had just ascended to heaven, he looked a stranger, ominously dark. When he was given no share in the Soma sacrifice, he had to accept lesser offerings, not on hallowed ground but away from it at the roadside or the haunted crossroads (*ŚB*.2.6.2.7). Those who had served him felt it necessary to wash their hands lest they become polluted by their contact with him (*ŚB*.2.6.2.18).[5] He had taken on himself this part and played it so well that the down-and-out, the petty criminals, the homicides, the devious and deformed had faith in him, their god. He was real to them in the darkness of life where they have their place.

2. The God of Darkness

The cosmos in Vedic tradition is seen as a fabric woven by the gods in warp and woof (*RV*.6.9.2; 10.130.1). The threads form a grid in

[5] *Śatapatha Brāhmaṇa (ŚB)*, tr. J. Eggeling, 1963, part I, pp. 443 and 2 n. 2.

which everyone has his place. This Vedic symbol of the web, signifying the inherent order of the phenomenal world, is complemented by another symbol that is concerned not with the completed fabric but with the nature of the threads that make the closely woven grid. The symbol is that of the *guṇas* or strands of which the thread is twisted. This symbol is ontological; it applies to the quality of the texture of the fabric, depending as it does on that of the strands or fibers of which the thread is made. Each thread of the cosmic fabric, according to Sāṁkhya,[6] a later Vedic and subsequent mode of seeing or philosophical approach, consists of three strands. They are called *sattva, rajas*, and *tamas*. They are the three constituents of the cosmic "substance" (*prakṛti*), the imperceptible substratum of the manifest world. Ontologically, *prakṛti* is prematter. Each strand of *prakṛti* has a potentiality or tendency of its own: *sattva* is seen ascending and luminous, *tamas* descending and dark, *rajas* twirling and red.[7] *Tamas* is the tendency in the process of manifestation that belongs to Śiva (*LP*.1.65.129). *Sattva* and *rajas* belong to Viṣṇu and Brahmā, respectively (*MaUp*.5.2). In the ongoing myth of Śiva, Brahmā [i.e., Prajāpati or the Father] plays a leading part from the beginning. Viṣṇu appears only later on the scene of Śiva's myth. The three tendencies or *guṇas*, however, are of equal importance in the reification and experience of becoming concrete of the manifesting universe. Looked at ontologically rather than mythically, a state of prematter or "preaction" (*prakṛti*) is postulated. It is not the "Uncreate." If a position could be assigned to *prakṛti* in mythical terms, this would be prior to the very beginning of cosmic dawn, just before Agni-Rudra was about to get the seed ready for the Father. But *prakṛti* is quiescent, motionless in a state of potentiality, though each of the constituents of *prakṛti*—each of the three *guṇas*—has its intrinsic movement. However, the three *guṇas* are in a state of balance and do not interact prior to the initial stress of creation. Then *prakṛti* evolves into *mahat*, the Great Principle, the cosmic will-to-be, or the ordering intelligence of the cosmos; *prakṛti* evolves furthermore into *ahaṁkāra*, the individuating

[6] The following is a general discussion of the Sāṁkhya system of philosophy according to the *Sāṅkhyakārikā of Īśvara Kṛṣṇa*, ed. and tr. S. S. Suryanarayana Sastri, 1973; S. S. Suryanaryana Sastri, "The Philosophy of Śaivism," in H. Bhattacharyya, ed., *The Cultural Heritage of India*, 2nd ed., 1953, 3:387-99.

[7] Cf. S. Radhakrishnan, *Indian Philosophy*, 1927, 2:262-63 and 263 n. 5; cf. *Viṣṇu Purāṇa (VP)*, tr. H. H. Wilson, 1961, p. 30 n. 1.

principle, and also into *manas*, the principle of cognition. Hence the five sense powers (*indriya*) come forth, as do the five subtle elements (*tanmātras*). The sense powers are those of cognition (*jñāna*) and of action (*karma*). They are the powers to hear, feel, see, taste, and smell. The subtle elements are their correlates. They are the essence of sound, touch, form, flavor, and odor. The five powers of action are the power to speak, the power to procreate, the power to excrete, the power to grasp, and the power to move. All these powers are capacities inherent in *manas*, the principle of cognition. The subtle elements, the *tanmātras*, have no magnitude. Throughout this ontology all the three *guṇas* interact, though they are variously dominant at different stages. *Tamas* increasingly exerts its downward pull on the *tanmātras* that become concrete as the five elements (*mahābhūta*): ether, air, fire, water, and earth, perceived through the sense organs.

The Sāṁkhya way of looking (*darśana*) at the becoming or concretization of the perceptible world, the mode of contact of the *tanmātras* with the corresponding faculties of the perceiver, postulates the three *guṇas* or constituents in the evolving prematter (*prakṛti*) out of which things condense. These constituents or tendencies remain unchanged in their potentiality, though the degree of activity of each varies from stage to stage in the process of evolving from prematter to matter with its five elements. *Tamas* is darkness; when this *guṇa* increases its activity, the darkness becomes deeper, denser, and heavier, and by its weight tends to obstruct the other two *guṇas*. It can be considered the first efficient cause of physical manifestation or of the five elements of which the cosmos is composed. It leads the descent from prematter into matter. The descent into matter—beyond which the cooperation of the three *guṇas* does not extend—would end with the dissolution of matter: Rudra, to whom *tamas* belongs, would annihilate the constituents of the cosmos and dissolve them in darkness, steeped in its own density. In it all the fivefold categories of existence and the three *guṇas* are dissolved together with their numbers, Five and Three, Śiva's sacred numbers.

It was as a darkly attired uncanny stranger from the north that Rudra appeared to Nābhānediṣṭha at the place of that sacrifice by which the Aṅgirases had risen to heaven. At another sacrifice Rudra was left behind here below, when he was unable to ascend with the gods. Like a dead weight he was left behind, heavy with misgivings. There is much darkness in Rudra. When he sinks low and into the abyss of his own being, he draws the world with him into the cosmic night of dissolution. *Tamas* is the heavy downward pull into disintegration. *Tamas* is the dark ground of Rudra's being, whence the flame of destruction leaps upward. It ends physical existence and liberates from *ahaṁkāra*, from individuation and the ego. When the thousands and thousands of arrows ready in the hands of Rudra (*TS*.4.5.10.5) have hit their targets, Rudra is seen as Śambhu, the cause of tranquillity, Śaṅkara, the giver of bliss, Śiva, the liberator (*TS*.4.5.8.1). As liberator and giver of happiness, Śiva is in all beings, their indwelling potential of freedom and peace. He also dwells in a blade of grass, a mote of dust, in sound and echo, in all that is manifest in the world of the senses. He pervades the fivefold ontological hierarchy formulated by Sāṁkhya and Yoga philosophy. The *Śvetāśvatara Upaniṣad* meditates on Śiva, the Lord (Īśvara) of and in the manifested world, as a river of five currents, which are the five sense powers (*indriya*), and fed from five sources (the elements) and with five whirlpools (the sense objects), an impetuous flood of five pains (*ŚUp*.1.5 and commentary).[8]

The metaphors and images of the *Śvetāśvatara Upaniṣad* are situated in the microcosm, the universe of meditative introspection. The river of the Lord flows through a world of anguish into a darkness hidden in its waves. It flows down in the direction of *tamas*, into that limitless pool of indistinction, the abyss in which Śiva absorbs all the worlds at the end of time (*ŚUp*.3.2), for in him all dissolves at the end (*ŚUp*.4.11).

The metaphors and images of the *Upaniṣad* correspond to Sāṁkhya categories. The fearful river cascades downward ineluctably, as relentless as the pull of the *tamo guṇa*, the strand of darkness in the web of the cosmic fabric. It was there from the beginning of time. *Tamas*, the strand of darkness in its descending tendency, helped to extend the cosmic fabric in manifestation; the strand of *sattva* with its ascending tendency exerts its counterpull; and *rajas* firmly twists each thread. *Tamas*, the dark, descending, disintegrating tendency, pulls down the fabric of the cosmos out of existence into darkness. This descending tendency, however, also helps to unfold the fabric in existence so that its three-colored structure, the black *tamas*, the white *sattva*, the red *rajas*, upholds the manifold patterns of the multicolored web.

[8] *Śvetāśvatara Upaniṣad (SUp)*, tr. R. F. Hume, 1951, p. 395.

Tamas, beheld from on high, draws into creation as it also pulls out of it. It inheres in all that is manifest. In creation *tamas*, counteracted by the two other *guṇas*, toward the end gains momentum and density, and its weight pulls out of existence the fabric of the universe.

The interaction of the three *guṇas* has its image in divinity. Hinduism knows *rajas* preponderating in Brahmā—for the creation of the Universe; *tamas* preponderating in Śiva—for the destruction of the Universe; and *sattva* predominantly in Viṣṇu—for the welfare of people. The extinction at the end of creation is not a return to, but only a symbol of, the Uncreate. This darkness appears periodically at the end of a world and before the creation of the next cosmos. Within the cosmic fabric the *tamo guṇa* belongs to Rudra as Kāla, the black one, the power of Time and Death in the cosmic process.

At the beginning of creation Rudra in the guise of a Wild Hunter avenged the integrity of the absolute. His arrow hit the Father Prajāpati, the Lord of Generation, cohabiting with his daughter; seed fell down on earth, the very seed that Rudra-Agni had prepared for the Father. Rudra thereafter was born from Prajāpati, and he entered into creation (Ch. V.1).

A seemingly unresolved contradiction links Rudra the Fire with Rudra the Archer. He entered creation and played both these roles, carrying into creation the ambivalence that was at the very beginning of things.

In creation the ambivalence that is in Rudra informs the roles he plays. As the dread archer he dispenses death. If he averts his arrows or does not let them fly, he redeems from death the fear-stricken creature and bestows on it the gift of life. The *Mahāmṛtyuñjaya mantra* invokes Rudra, the conqueror of death, who has the power to inflict or to withhold death (*RV*.7.59.12).

When at the end of days Śiva in his *tamas* nature draws the cosmos into dissolution, it disintegrates into the darkness of nonbeing. It is without shapes, an indefinable continuum, yet unlike the Uncreate. Disintegration of the cosmos prefigures reintegration into the integrity of the Uncreate.

Śiva, the destroyer who leads out of the cosmos, is the Great Yogi who within himself annihilates the world of experience; he is the ferryman and the ferry leading from this world to the other shore (*TS*.4.5.8.2), to a nameless beyond to which the darkness of dissolution is only an allusion. "When there is no darkness, there is neither day nor night, neither being nor nonbeing, only the one (Śiva) alone" (*ŚUp*.4.18). Śiva in absolute transcendency, Śiva in manifestation and its destroyer, Śiva in the darkness of dissolution is at the same time the lord of sentient beings, Paśupati, Lord of Animals, their fierce hunter of a hundred shapes.

3. Encounters with Rudra

a. *The Drink with Keśin, the Ascetic*

The whole world is the place where Rudra is felt to be manifest; at the time of the dissolution of the cosmos, Rudra is also manifest. Within a beginningless and endless pillar of flame he reveals himself to the gods in the darkness of the flood (Ch. VII.2). The extent and existence of the cosmos as well as its nonexistence are the perennial stage of his play seen by gods and man.

He has another place, too, more intimate and hidden within the heart of man the microcosm. When he enters it, everything else is closed out in the mystic realization of his presence. Entranced, the mystic upholds heaven and earth; weightless, he soars with the wind; heated, he glows with the sun. His asceticism sweeps him into ecstasy, his body has no limit, he has drunk poison out of one cup with his god. He is a muni, moved to his depth and carried away in his transport.

One such muni was Keśin, "long hair." He was clad in faded yellow, all that distinguished him in the eye of mortals, who saw only his mortal body, though he carried fire, poison, heaven, and earth (*RV*.10.136.1-3). The long-haired one was called the sun's light (*RV*.10.136.1). Girt with the wind, this entranced, long-haired ascetic rode with the rush of the storm where the god entered him (*RV*.10.136.2). Ecstatic with ascetic rapture he mounted the gale (*RV*.10.136.3). Keśin flew through the air beholding all the shapes below (*RV*.10.136.4). This entranced muni was at home by both the oceans, in the east and in the west (*RV*.10.136.5). Moving with the movement of Apsarases, the ethereal nymphs, their consorts, and the untamed beasts, Long-hair knew their minds and was their sweet, most enchanting companion (*RV*.10.136.6). The wind had stirred it, Kunaṃnama prepared it, and together with Rudra Long-hair drank the poison from a cup (*RV*.10.136.7).

An uncanny power emanates from the unnamed poison prepared

by Kunaṃnama, whose name possibly means the "indomitable." In wind-swept ecstasy, the muni drank the poison out of one cup with Rudra. By this "sacrament" the god entered him. Transcending space, the muni soared, holding in his hands the cup and the fire of Rudra. The muni glided with the wind. The muni, like the Lord of Animals, infused his movements with the grace of the wild beasts, akin to those of the celestial spirits.

The Rudra realization of Keśin is that of a shaman or yogi. Keśin flew in the glow of the fire in him, and which he held in his hand. His elation and ascension were caused by the drink of communion. Like a fiery river, Keśin's long hair traced his swift flight from east to west, high above. While he saw all the world below him, and knew the minds of animals and celestials and that they loved him, weightless he carried heaven and earth to the light of the sun that illumines him.

Rudra had entered the muni. His rapture lifted him together with his god to the sun. He brought it his cup and flame, his knowledge and love. In his ecstasy, the muni had left below the weight of his body and its limits. Rudra had entered him. Keśin soared, filled with the unearthly fire of the god. To Keśin, Rudra revealed himself by entering him, flying with him in the still core of the transport of the long-haired one.

The realization of Rudra by the muni is given form in the wake of a long tradition of shamanistic yoga practice. Its ecstasy glows with the fire and the drink of Rudra. At another time it was not an unknown ascetic but a formidable warrior whom the god entered.

b. *Rudra Enters Aśvatthāman, the Warrior*

His name was Aśvatthāman. The *Mahābhārata* tells of Droṇa, the commander-in-chief of the Kauravas in their war with the Pāṇḍavas, who could not be defeated unless he failed to defend himself. Droṇa was slain by the enemy through a ruse of Kṛṣṇa. Hearing in the midst of a battle the false news that his son Aśvatthāman was dead, Droṇa lost his resolve (*MBh*.7.164.68-77). Defenseless, he was decapitated by the enemy (*MBh*.7.165.38-53), and Aśvatthāman became the commander of the Kauravas. Torn by grief and revenge, he set out in insensate rage, straining to slaughter the Pāṇḍavas, not in battle but during their sleep (*MBh*.10.1.53-64). When he came near their camp a gigantic being, effulgent like the sun, stood at the entrance. His loins were girt with a tiger skin, his upper garment was a black antelope skin. A large serpent was his sacred thread, his long arms wielded weapons. Flames of fire blazed from his open, terrible mouth. His thousands of beautiful eyes shot forth flames. Fire issued from his nose and ears. From those flames hundreds and thousands of Viṣṇus issued, equipped with conch, discus, and mace (*MBh*.10.6.2-9).

Fearlessly, Aśvatthāman hurled his weapons against the blazing being, who devoured them all, while the firmament was crowded with images of Viṣṇu. Finally, Aśvatthāman stood unarmed before the flaming being who had absorbed in fire all his weapons (*MBh*.10.6.10-18). Helplessly, Aśvatthāman took refuge in Rudra, whom he had not recognized in front of him, but who would dispel the being that appeared as a dreadful rod of divine punishment (*MBh*.10.6.32-34). He offered himself to Rudra, ready to sacrifice his body to him. Instantaneously a golden altar appeared before Aśvatthāman, upon it a blazing fire. Hosts of monstrous beings, companions of Rudra, swarmed around Aśvatthāman. Fearlessly, Aśvatthāman asked Rudra to accept him as a sacrificial oblation, ascended the altar, and entered the fire. There he stood immobile with arms raised, and Rudra entered his body, having given him a shining sword. Filled with divine energy, Aśvatthāman became greater in battle (*MBh*.10.7.49-65).

Driven mad by grief and revenge, Aśvatthāman the warrior was to become a murderer. In his rage, he had not recognized Rudra when the god barred his way to the camp of the sleeping enemy. The air had become filled with Viṣṇus that had emanated from the flames of Rudra.[9] He should have recognized him, for the god showed himself in his cosmic, thousand-eyed, flaming glory, attired in raiments that distinguish Rudra alone: the black antelope skin of the ascetic, the lion skin of the hunter, and the serpents that are Rudra's sacred thread and ornaments. When the weapons that Aśvatthāman had hurled against the gigantic fiery body were consumed by the blazing flames issuing from mouth, nose, ears, and all the thousands of eyes, the looming fiery giant contracted into one mighty blazing rod that spelled his punishment to the warrior now unarmed. His own weapons that he had hurled against Rudra now seemed to confront him,

[9] G. Dumézil, *Mythe et épopée*, takes the Viṣṇu images in the sky to prove that the phantasmagoria was produced by Viṣṇu, the protector of the Pāṇḍavas. It seems, however, that Śiva, the Great God, is seen here emanating to the furthest horizon his Viṣṇu power. The many Viṣṇus in the sky contributed to Aśvatthāman's bewilderment, and he did not immediately recognize the Great God—who up to that time had favored Kṛṣṇa, and had been with the Pāñcālas in the enemy's camp, vol. I, p. 214.

fused to the height of the god himself at the core of the fiery shape. The blazing rod appeared to Aśvatthāman as his rod of punishment for his intent of surreptitious murder of the Pāṇḍavas. At this moment Aśvatthāman sought refuge in Rudra, praised the god, and offered his body to him. Aśvatthāman entered the blazing fire on the golden altar that had appeared before him. Motionless he stood in it, himself like a rod with arms raised. He offered himself in his maximal measure with arms extended upward (*MBh*.10.7.59). This is the gesture of the sacrificer by which he exceeds the height of his body and symbolically shows himself as consecrated (cf. *MS*.3.2.4; *ŚB*.10.2.2.6). Within the blazing fire, Rudra gave to Aśvatthāman a shining sword, and entered the warrior's body. The stainless shiny sword forged in that fire would make Aśvatthāman achieve his end.

Inner realization prompted Aśvatthāman's self-sacrifice. It had come out of a haze of grief, rage, and guilt. Unrecognized, Rudra had stood in front of Aśvatthāman. The warrior recognized Rudra when the god was felt by him as the fire of the avenging rod; Aśvatthāman entered the sacrificial fire on the altar, and in its flames he received from the god his shining sword.

Rudra, in his blazing shape of power in front of the camp of the sleeping enemy whom Aśvatthāman was about to murder, was the fire that threatened, enveloped, empowered, and entered the warrior Aśvatthāman. It was Rudra, the dread and terrible slayer, the killer who causes intense pain, the protector of warriors (cf. *TS*.4.5.2; 4.5.8, 9). Beside himself, swept and degraded by his rage, Aśvatthāman was not aware that he was born from a mixture of Mahādeva (Śiva), Antaka (The Ender), Krodha (Wrath), and Kāma (Desire), combined into a unity (*MBh*.1.61.66-67).

Only when Aśvatthāman had spent all his weapons and had made himself defenseless did he recognize the god in him. At that moment, Śiva entered him and filled his being with divine energy. He entered Aśvatthāman as the Destroyer. Aśvatthāman had to bring about destruction like Rudra himself at the end of a yuga. He compared himself to Rudra when he related his plan for slaughtering the enemy (*MBh*.10.3.29). Rage (*krodha*) possessed Aśvatthāman, and the desire for vengeance for Droṇa killed by Kṛṣṇa's ruse and righteous Yudhiṣṭhira's lie, in order to save the Pāṇḍavas from being destroyed by Droṇa. Kṛṣṇa said, "In such circumstances falsehood is better than truth. There is no sin in untruth if it saves life" (*MBh*.7.164.99).

Droṇa was killed when he laid down his weapons on hearing the false message of Aśvatthāman's death, and was hence defenseless against his enemy.

Grief, revenge, and rage drove Aśvatthāman to the night massacre of the sleeping Pāṇḍavas. In a mire of treachery and guilt, the shining sword that Śiva had given to Aśvatthāman was bathed in blood, while the fire of Rudra, the Destroyer, blazed in Aśvatthāman. The time of the lives of the Pāṇḍavas had run out, and like the Lord Mahādeva himself, Aśvatthāman entered the camp of the Pāṇḍavas (*MBh.* 10.7.63-66). The swarms of frightful beings accompanied Aśvatthāman as he entered the camp of the enemy, as though he were Śiva himself penetrating into the Pāṇḍava camp (*MBh.*10.7.66).

The drink, the ecstasy, the flight of the long-haired muni who carried fire, and the grief, rage, and guilt of the warrior were situations in which Rudra came to those whom he had chosen.

c. *The Transfiguration of a Vrātya*

An entire book of the *Atharva Veda* (Book XV) is dedicated to a Vrātya and his transfiguration. The Vrātyas were a host of consecrated people within the Vedic tradition.[10] Little is known about them apart from Book Fifteen of the *Atharva Veda*. They were clad in black, fringed garments; the black color distinguished their attire, as it did that of Rudra when he appeared on the site of the sacrifice by the Aṅgirases. The Vrātyas wore a turban and carried lance and bow (*AV*.15.2.1). Their name is derived from *vrāta*, a host, which in turn may be derived from *vrata*, a vow or observance of a sacred ordinance.[11] In the *Śatarudriya* hymn to the hundred forms and powers of Rudra, the leaders of hosts (Vrātapati, *TS*.4.5.4.1) are invoked. This ecstatic litany imbued with the presence of the god opens with a homage to his wrath, to his arrow, to his bow (*TS*.4.5.1.1). Is he who is Vrātapati, the leader or lord of a consecrated host (*vrāta*), one with Vratapā, the guardian of vow and ordinance (*vrata*) whom the *raudra brahman* lauds (*RV*.10.61.1; 10.61.7)? In that *mantra*, Vāstoṣpati who is Vratapā was created by the gods in the magically ordered sequence of its words and sounds. Vratapā, the guardian of sacred order, as Vrātapati, leads those committed by their vow (*vrata*) to its observance. Vratapā is Rudra emerging out of the making of poesy, out of

[10] J. C. Heesterman, "Vrātya and Sacrifice," 1962, pp. 18, 36.

[11] M. Mayrhofer, *Concise Etymological Sanskrit Dictionary, s.v. vrātaḥ*.

the enacting of his myth audibly, in measured, worded sound. It was created and participated in by the gods, the celestial intelligence.

The book of the Vrātya begins by telling of a roaming Vrātya: "he stirred up Prajāpati. He, Prajāpati, saw in himself gold . . . ; he generated that."[12] It turned into a being with a mark on the forehead and became great, assumed powerful form, passion, and reality. Thus his progeny came about. The being grew; it became the Great God (Mahādeva), it became the Lord (Īśāna). "He became the Sole Vrātya; he took to himself a bow; that was Indra's bow" (*AV*.15.1.1-6).[13] The Vrātya, swayed by his enthusiasm, that is, by the god within him, acted as creative momentum. He stirred the Creator himself so that Prajāpati became aware of the gold that he carried within himself. Prajāpati then emitted that gold from himself. The gold turned into Mahādeva, the Great God whom Prajāpati had engendered. The Great God was marked by the third eye on his forehead. He was the Lord by whom the Vrātya was swayed, and whom he now saw before him as the Sole Vrātya, his god, his reality.

The creation of the Sole Vrātya who is Mahādeva and the transfiguration of the Vrātya has three phases: the birth of a god, the vision of that god, and the building of his monument.

The myth of the Vrātya conveys the ecstasy of an ascetic that stirred Prajāpati into awareness of the gold that the Lord of Generation carried within him. He shed this gold like seed and it became Mahādeva, the Great God, with the mark of the third eye on his forehead. The Vrātya had been the instrument and witness of the taking shape of his god.

The Vrātya surpassed Muni Longhair in his relation to Rudra. Muni Keśin was on one level with Rudra when he drank poison out of one cup with the god. The Vrātya, however, was the instrument that stirred and moved Prajāpati to manifest the "gold" within him in the shape of Mahādeva himself as the Sole Vrātya.

Aside from the myth of the Vrātya, the birth of Rudra from Prajāpati was caused only in an excitement of Prajāpati in which no human agent had part (Ch. V.1).

The Vrātya, a roving ascetic, was roaming about and stirred Prajāpati, the Lord of Generation. The Vrātya stirred him toward the act of generation. As an ascetic, the Vrātya had magic power and acted

[12] *Atharva Veda Saṃhitā (AV)*, tr. W. D. Whitney, 1962, p. 773.

[13] *Ibid.*

not unlike Agni, the Fire, who had prepared the seed for the Father. The Father became sexually excited, and was about to emit the seed into his self-created daughter, but some of the seed fell down on earth. Prajāpati, stirred by the Vrātya, was similarly impelled toward generation. He became aware of the gold that he carried within him; he became aware that he himself held the golden germ (*AV*.15.1.1-2; cf. *hiraṇyagarbha*: *RV*.10.121.1, 10).[14] It was this gold that Prajāpati brought forth. He did it without the intervention of a female partner. Prajāpati shed the gold that he had held within him. At once it turned into the One with a mark on his forehead. This mark was of the shape of a third eye. The Being grew in greatness, full of creative power, full of *tapas* and truth; it went on growing and became Mahādeva, the Great God, who is Śiva, the Lord. He became the Sole Vrātya (*AV*.15.1.1-6).

The crescendo in the transmutation of the gold generated from within himself by Prajāpati reached its climax when the divine progeny had become Īśāna, the Lord who is Śiva, the Great God (Mahādeva)—having a mark on his forehead, Śiva's third eye.

Like Rudra-Agni, who had prepared the seed for the Father, the Vrātya caused great commotion within the progenitor or Prajāpati. It made him shed the immortal substance, the semen or gold. The semen is the immortal seed of creation out of the Uncreate. Gold is the imperishable substance known in creation. Prajāpati as Hiraṇyagarbha is their storehouse.

The Vrātya, a yogi, had magic power, and like Agni himself he aroused Prajāpati. He stirred the Lord of Generation into awareness of himself; he incited and illumined him. This Vrātya was one of the elect among the other Vrātyas. His transforming vision came to him when he was just walking along—and faced Prajāpati. At once Prajāpati saw the gold within himself and became aware of stirrings within himself caused by the Vrātya. Then that golden radiance generated by Prajāpati in instantaneous succession turned into the Great God.

Rudra-Śiva emerged from Prajāpati. He was his son by the agency of the Vrātya. The birth of Rudra is told as it happened in the rapture of the Vrātya. When he knew that he had stirred Prajāpati, he identified himself with his action and with the outcome of his action. When the Vrātya saw Mahādeva, the Lord born from Prajāpati, he

[14] Cf. F. Max Müller, tr., *Vedic Hymns*, *SBE* 32, 1964, part I, pp. 6, 10-13.

saw him become the Sole Vrātya, the one and only Vrātya, the principal Vrātya, the ultimate form in which the ecstatic ascetic recognized as one the Great God and his own true Vrātya being. The Sole Vrātya comprised Rudra in a crescendo of his form, together with the Self of the Vrātya deified in his enthusiasm, whereby he dwelt in God who had moved him while he stirred Prajāpati.

In mystic realization the Vrātya brings about the birth of Rudra from Prajāpati and recognizes in Rudra his own divinity. The miraculous generation of Rudra as son of Prajāpati is the mythical aspect of the mystic realization of the Sole Vrātya.

Now the Sole Vrātya took up a bow. "That was Indra's bow. Blue its belly, red (its) back" (*AV*.15.1.6-7).[15]

i. The Bow of Rudra

Rudra's essential weapon is the arrow, the fire-tipped missile (*TS*.6.2.3.1-2) that hits and inserts itself into his target. The shape of the arrow is that of unilinear flight, while the power of the bow, stored in its curve, vaults over a field of action. The bow that the Sole Vrātya took up was hallowed by long practice. It was Indra's bow. Indra, king of gods, as soon as born took up his bow, asking his mother who were his enemies (*RV*.8.45.4). The bow was to protect Indra from the moment of his birth. His weapon of attack, however, was the *vajra*, the thunderbolt. With it Indra fought Vṛtra, the ancient serpent and guardian of the Uncreate. When Vṛtra's dead body sank into the abyss, the waters of life that had been held captive by him began to flow into the cosmos under the light of the sun (cf. *RV*.1.32.4-9). That was in an earlier aeon. That aeon had Indra for its creator, and his bow—as golden as the sun at first (cf. p. 32)—became the rainbow (*Indrāyudha*; cf. *MBh*.13.14.122), vaulting over his domain in all the colors of the spectrum summarily seen from blue to red. This bow the Sole Vrātya takes up. The newborn god takes over the rule of what had been Indra's domain: the cosmos.

When the Vrātya sees his god taking up the bow in the radiance of his vision, does he see the light shining from the god born of Prajāpati's gold, refracted in the colors of the bow, and does he also see them on the body of the god? In the terse juxtaposition of the words of the hymn lie both meanings.

[15] *Atharva Veda Saṃhitā (AV)*, tr. W. D. Whitney, 1962, p. 773.

The red god with the blue throat was seen by the cowherds and those who carried water (*TS*.4.5.1.3). Nīla-Lohita, the "blue and red," is one of the most common names of Rudra in the *Purāṇas*. Nīla-Lohita is Rudra in manifestation. In these colors, as Nīla-Lohita, he entered the universe (cf. *VāP*.27.1-6).

The Ekavrātya realization by the Vrātya is now filled with colors. They cast their meaning over the god and his domain protected by his bow. Pināka, which means bow, is particularly the bow of Rudra-Śiva; it is also known as Ajagava (*MP*.23.37). Ajagava is the southern part of the path of the sun, where it shines in the midnight of the year, in the darkness of the abyss, in the cosmic South, the realm of death.[16] This other, frightening, aspect of Nīla-Lohita is as much within Rudra's being as it is within the words *nīla-lohita* themselves. *Lohita* means red, it means blood. The blood of the bridal night leaves its dark stain on the bridal garment; darkness has blue (*nīla*) for its color; it is the death color of the red blood. Together, the colors *nīla-lohita* incarnate the life-death magic of blood by which the bride bewitches the groom. This is what the *Ṛg Veda* marriage hymn celebrates: it literally "sets afoot" the magic (*kṛtyā*) of blood (*RV*.10.85.28-29). The power of the blood magic of *nīla-lohita* gets its color signature from sex. Witchcraft lurks in it, life and decay. Over this fatality of the human condition vaults Nīla-Lohita, the bow of Rudra, in the colors of Rudra. The Wild God himself, as soon as born, is Nīla-Lohita, comprising the color spectrum of the flames of fire.

From Indra, king of gods, the rule had passed to the Sole Vrātya. The bow here is the symbol of lordship over the cosmos. While Indra's bow is the rainbow, the bow of the Sole Vrātya has no name. The bow Pināka is indeed the bow of Rudra, called Ajagava in later texts. However, the piercing arrow is more intimately Rudra's weapon. Once pointed it hits its target, whereas the arc of the bow comprises a wide domain. The dart or arrow is the weapon particularly of Rudra-Śarva, who owes his name to his missile, *śaru*, the "arrow." The straight line of the pointed arrow is the symbol of centrifugal aggressive fatal power; the bow, charged with tension, is akin in its curve to that of the vault of heaven. The bow is a symbol of cosmic supremacy. It is a symbol of Rudra, Īśāna, the Lord, one in essence with Rudra

[16] V. S. Apte, *The Practical Sanskrit-English Dictionary, s.v. ajagāva*.

Nīla-Lohita, in whom the light of the sun is refracted in the colors of the blood magic of life and death.

The bow of Rudra / Īśāna is a status symbol of the Lord, the ruler of the universe, whereas the arrow symbolizes Rudra, the Wild God, the hunter in action. It is by their actions that the figures of myth manifest their being.

ii. The Drive into the Cosmos

The mystical transport of the Vrātya, having turned into a color vision of the Sole Vrātya, now lets him see the god in action. The Sole Vrātya arises in his greatness. He moves out on his vehicle, the mind, first toward the east, then toward the south, toward the west, and finally toward the north. He is clad in discernment (*vijñāna*). His hair is night. Day rests on it as his turban (*AV*.15.2.1). Mind is his vehicle. In each of the four directions his retinue is formed by different gods and by different songs. The sacrifice, the sacrificer, and the cattle are with him when he moves toward the south. A harlot and a bard accompany him as he moves out in each of the four directions (*AV*.15.2.2-4). The couples of harlot and bard are not the same in each direction. Faith and friendship[17] are the bard and harlot who go with him toward the east (*AV*.15.2.1); dawn and incantation (*mantra*) to the south (*AV*. 15.2.2); cheer and laughter to the west (*AV*.15.2.3); lightning and thunder northwards (*AV*.15.2.4). His two footmen are "what is" and "what is to be"; the new and full moon; day and night; and "what is heard" (here) and "what is heard abroad,"[18] respectively, for each quarter (*AV*.15.2.1-4).

Moving out from himself as the center, on the chariot of the mind, the Sole Vrātya incorporates into his presence the four directions of the extended universe. They are filled by his retinue.

Having driven out in each of the four directions from his center, he stands still. "He stood a year erect" (*AV*.15.3.1).[19] Carrying day and night on his head, he had moved with them to the four orients in choreographed time, with a *maṇḍala* for a pattern. Now he stands still,

[17] R. Roth's and W. D. Whitney's edition reads *śraddhā puṃścalī mantro māgadho* (*AV*.15.2.1); *mantro* is to be corrected to *mitro*. Cf. *Atharva Veda Saṃhitā (AV)*, tr. W. D. Whitney, 1962, pp. 774-76.

[18] *Atharva Veda Saṃhitā (AV)*, tr. W. D. Whitney, 1962, pp. 774-76.

[19] *Ibid*., p. 776.

erect for one year, the unit of time in its revolving cycles. He orders a throne to be brought to him (*AV*.15.3.2). After he ascends the throne, all beings wait on him (*AV*.15.3.10). His guardians, the months of the year, not only are stationed in the four directions of the extended earth but also protect him in the fixed center and from on high, two guardians in each direction (*AV*.15.4.1-6). This is how the twelve months of the year are distributed.

In the intermediate directions, the attendants of the Sole Vrātya take their stand. All of them are archers, each bearing a name by which Rudra, the primordial archer, had become known. They are Bhava, Śarva, Paśupati, and Ugra, the ferocious (*AV*.15.5.1-4). Rudra is the archer "from the intermediate direction of the fixed quarter" (*AV*.15.5.5),[20] that is, of the center. Mahādeva, the Great God, is the archer in the intermediate direction of the upward point (*AV*.15.5.6). Moreover, the archer Īśāna, the ruler, attends the Sole Vrātya from all directions (*AV*.15.5.7).

When the Sole Vrātya drove out in his chariot, the mind, he took possession of the extent of the earth in the four directions. Time accompanied him on his way. He carried it on his head in his night-black hair and his day-light turban. He established his rule over the earth and over time in its movement. Then he stood still for a year, a firm pillar of the universe, enthroned in the center of the manifest cosmos. All beings waited on him, their central support and ruler. He surrounded his position between heaven and earth in the center of the cosmos by assigning stations to the months of the year. He stood still for a year and then he gathered it around him. He saw to the defense of his position by stationing archers, projections of himself, near to himself. He assigned the central position to the archer Rudra, the Wild God. Īśāna, the ruler, became the archer in all the intermediate directions. The ambience of the Sole Vrātya is safeguarded twice over by the directional extent of the position of each archer, as well as by that of Īśāna in every direction. If the spectacle of the Sole Vrātya taking possession of the earth has the pattern of a *maṇḍala*, his cosmic extent is a monument of time arising with the power of the archer. A fixed (*dhruva*) position is allotted to the archer Rudra. It is the central, quintessential position with reference to the four directions, and the central place on earth below the zenith. One could see in this *dhruva*

[20] *Ibid*., p. 779.

diś or central region a prognostic reflex on earth of Dhruva, the Pole Star, the cosmic North Pole.[21]

In one line, along the central pillar of the Sole Vrātya, the archer Mahādeva is his attendant in the upward quarter. The archer Īśāna, being stationed in each of the six intermediate directional points, is active also next to Rudra and next to Mahādeva, on each critical point of the Vrātya-pyramid or cosmic mountain, an ordered space-time compact, the cosmos of the Sole Vrātya.

iii. The Transcending Monument of Ekavrātya

The movement of the Sole Vrātya exceeds the vertical extent of the visible cosmos, upward beyond the fixed region, beyond also the upward region to the "highest region," thence to the "great region," and further to the "most distant region," and beyond it to the "region without direction," and finally to the "region without return." The Sole Vrātya extends himself into transcendency, encompassing seven levels, seven spheres, in his transcosmic presence, which is built up from the fixed, basic, central position, the domain of Rudra-Īśāna (*AV*.15.5.5; 15.6.1-7).

The Sole Vrātya is a choreographed monument of deity built up by the words of hymns. They set up a structural cosmos whose upward direction, exceeding the height of the cosmic mountain, ends beyond the empyrean, in the region without return. It is reached in one straight line from the fixed quintessential center of the monument, the domain of Rudra-Īśāna, the archer. Īśāna, the archer, is in attendance in each direction. His power rules the cosmos.

In his ecstasy, the Vrātya sees himself born anew through Prajāpati from the immortal substance within the lord of progeny. He sees himself reborn into greatness; he sees himself with a mark (blazing) on his forehead. He has become Mahādeva, the Great God, Īśāna, the Lord: the Sole Vrātya.

Rudra guards the fixed quintessential position in the cosmic structure of the Sole Vrātya. All the archers are multiples of Rudra. They differ in name, for they occupy different positions, equal in value. The transfigured ecstatic Vrātya has been reborn. He is the Sole Vrātya who is Mahādeva, the Great God.

The Vrātya has become an apotheosis of cosmic dimension and

[21] A. Scherer, *Gestirnnamen bei den Indogermanischen Völkern*, p. 117.

transcendental direction. Eliade speaks of the "cosmic structure of the *vrātyas*' 'mystical' experiences."[22] On the level of this earth, the Sole Vrātya, clad in discernment, drove out to the four orients in his chariot, the mind, carrying the light of day in his headgear and night in his dark hair. Wherever he drove, the appropriate gods and songs accompanied him, as well as a couple composed of a bard and a harlot. They are a different couple in each direction of space, amicably matched and of related natures. Faith and friendship, cheer and laughter, lightning and thunder, dawn and *mantra*; they are human, natural, spontaneous, and potent. In a joyous procession, the Sole Vrātya moves out in the four directions of space with the accompaniment of songs, amid the uttering of *mantras*, rumbling thunder, and peals of laughter. The rhythms rest on feelings of faith and friendship. Bard and harlot change costumes and expressions as they enliven the fourfold excursions of the Sole Vrātya extending to east and south, to west and north, bringing the gift of day and night with the assurance of their conjunction in the basic sequential rhythms.

After this prelude, the Sole Vrātya stands still in the center for one full year, drawing into and encompassing within himself his fourfold movement. He stands guarded by time in a space that his movement has traversed. He stands with the majesty he has gathered in himself and for which a throne is needed. The months are appointed guardians of the throne throughout the year, and the four seasons are its legs (*AV*.15.3.4). The Sole Vrātya now arises as lord of the space-time universe, himself the central pillar of a four-sided pyramid, his attendants in the intermediate directions. Each of these attendants is an archer. They are Bhava, Śarva, Paśupati, Ugra, Rudra, and Mahādeva. Rudra is the attendant archer of the fixed point; Mahādeva, the Great God, the attendant of the upper region. Moreover, the archer Īśāna, the Ruler, attends from all directions. All these seven are archers and thus of Rudra nature. They are distinguishable by their names. Bhava means existence and also origin; Śarva is the essential archer; Paśupati the Lord of Animals; Ugra the ferocious; Rudra the Wild God; Mahādeva the Great God, and Īśāna the ruler or Lord. All of them together are the Sole Vrātya, god in manifestation. Yet he exceeds these forms. Unattended by any archers, he extends beyond the upward region through yet higher spheres, of which the last is the

[22] M. Eliade, *Yoga: Immortality and Freedom*, 1958, p. 105.

region of no return. His retinue diminishes as he moves upward from plane to plane. When he comes to that of no return, none but four Great Goddesses follow him (cf. *AV*.15.6.7). Rudra's presence on the firm ground of this earth stands guard, while the Sole Vrātya extracts from it the power to ascend into the empyrean. He is Rudra's transcendency.

In his "enthusiasm"—a state of being in god and of god being in him—a roving ascetic, a Vrātya, realized the birth of his god and his own rebirth in that god. He caused and saw his god being born, he saw him in his majesty on earth and rarefied in his ascent, extending himself into a vanishing point in the beyond.

The metaphysical pyramid of the Sole Vrātya, a construct of inner vision and realization, rises above rites and processions and joyous crowds, protected by the presence of Rudra, the archer. The Sole Vrātya is a realization from here below into the beyond; it is a form that cannot be measured, and in which a Vrātya, one of a roving band, set a monument to Rudra in and beyond the cosmos.[23]

The Vrātyas are classed in the *Mahābhārata* with those low on the social scale, such as Soma vendors, arrow makers, astrologers, poisoners, and the like (*MBh*.5.35.39-41). The Vrātya, whatever his social status may have been, was close to Rudra. That Vrātya, "just going about,"[24] felt in himself the power to stir the creator (*AV*.15.1.1), and he built a metaphysical monument to the Sole Vrātya. It rested on Rudra.

[23] *Atharva Veda Saṃhitā (AV)*, tr. W. D. Whitney, 1962, p. 769.

[24] *Ibid.*, p. 773.

V

THE BIRTH OF RUDRA

1. The Birth from Prajāpati

a. *The Ancient Names*

When Rudra claimed as his own the animals into which the ashes of Prajāpati's fiery lake had turned, his shape was indescribably gruesome and his name was Paśupati. The gods had given him both form and name; they had made him Lord of Animals; they had made him Vāstoṣpati, lord of the *vāstu*. Another time, Rudra claimed the animals as his own, those found not on a wasteland but on a sacrificial site where the animals had been left. Then he appeared as a man darkly clad, a man whose identity was revealed by his claim. As Paśupati, their lord, the cattle belonged to him. They had remained on the site, and what is left over (*vāstu*) on the site (*vāstu*) belongs to Rudra. Paśupati, Lord of Animals, shades over into Vāstoṣpati, lord of the *vāstu* in both its meanings. In the wasteland as well as on the sacrificial site he relinquished his claim. Gruesome and uncanny he looked. This Rudra, the fierce god, acted as Śiva the gracious. Rudra assumes one shape or the other; he is both. As fire and as archer he was the determining presence in the primordial scene; the arrow, his fiery sign, shines to this day in the sky.

The first target of the archer was the Father, Prajāpati, the Lord of Generation. So formidable was the archer, the guardian of the transcendental wholeness, that his name could not be mentioned. Prajāpati, who at that time had the shape of an antelope, in order to arrest the arrow of the archer made that Wild Hunter Lord of Animals, Paśupati. This is the ancient account (*MS*.4.2.12). Did Prajāpati the antelope, investing the Wild Hunter with lordship over animals, implicitly acknowledge him as his Lord? The later version in the *Aitareya Brāhmaṇa* recounts that the gods created this god's shape of terror out of their own horror at Rudra's formidable deed (*AB*.3.33). At that time—or in that version—the gods were swayed by emotion, by their own fears, whereas in their creative inspiration they gave to that god the shape of Vāstoṣpati.

Vāstoṣpati, Paśupati, and also Prajāpati are titles more than names. They designate the particular mode in which a god operates. It is by their actions that the gods are known. They have cognizances but are without stereotyped shape, though Paśupati was created by the gods as a symplegma of horror. Rudra, the savage god, too horrendous even for his name to be said aloud, the primordial guardian of the absolute, becomes the guardian and Lord of Animals as well as the guardian and lord of the *vāstu*. The domains over which he rules are the state of nature and the state of art, the passionate and the creative self of man. While Rudra assumed this double lordship, the semen of Prajāpati, the Lord of Generation, had fallen down on earth. Rudra-Agni had prepared it for Prajāpati, the Father. While it was being shed, the gods created Vāstoṣpati. Agni, the Fire, consumed its copious downpour, and Rudra claimed the cinders and ashes as his own. These turned into animals. Paśupati, Lord of Animals, rules over these creatures of Prajāpati's passion that he had caused to flare up. The formidable guardian of the absolute played an ambiguous, inevitable role. As guardian of the substance of immortality, he entrusted the seed of creation and readied it for the Father, and, too late, attempted to prevent its fall to earth. The involvement of Rudra and Prajāpati is frightening. A straight line leads from the preparation of the seed by Rudra / Agni to its being shed by the Father and to the gods' creation of Vāstoṣpati. This line is crossed by the flight of an arrow.[1] The point of intersection lies in the Father. Rudra carries the action and responsibility, as carrier of the fire seed on the one hand, and as archer and guardian of the Uncreate on the other. Prajāpati is his target and victim. However, the myth of Rudra flows on through new situations prefigured before the sun had risen on the first morning.

Among them his birth is preeminent. In the *Ṛg Veda* and the *Maitrāyaṇī Saṃhitā* Rudra appears full-fledged on the scene, preeminently

[1] The three stars of the belt of Orion are said to correspond to Rudra's tripartite arrow. Cf. B. G. Tilak, *The Orion*, p. 100.

as a hunter. His different forms or designations, Vāstoṣpati and Paśupati, were created by Prajāpati himself, and by the gods according to their own intuition or emotional reaction. The *Brāhmaṇas* and the *Atharva Veda*, on the other hand, deal with the birth of Rudra, child of Prajāpati.

The birth of Rudra from Prajāpati was adumbrated by the falling of the seed and the gods' creation of a *brahman* from which they formed Vāstoṣpati. The mystery of the seed proceeds from its being made ready for the Father by Agni / Rudra to its being shed by the Father, "conceived" by the gods in their *brahman*, and given form as Vāstoṣpati. The cosubstantiality with Rudra of the seed prepared by Agni / Rudra for the Father and emitted by the Father is part of the genealogy of Agni. Rudra, like Agni, is the son of himself (*tanūnapāt*, cf. *RV*.1.13.2). His birth as a crying or self-assertive child, moreover, came about in more than one way, though the father is the same whether he is called Prajāpati or, as is the case subsequently in the *Purāṇas*, Brahmā.

Before Rudra was born, in the myths of the *Brāhmaṇas* he was the god whom the *Śatarudriya* extols and whom the *Ṛg Veda* (*RV*.2.33.11) sees in fierceness enthroned on the high seat of his chariot the world. The birth of the god as a mode of his manifestation introduces the element of time, and henceforth actions of Rudra will be laid out sequentially, though more in a causal than an historical order. They will be the consequences or the transpositions of paradigmatic themes, and their reality will be that of perennial symbols. They will form a framework in the narrative of Śiva, which will be filled by many other myths, so that his being emerges from their total inexhaustible accounts.

b. *The Golden Bowl and the Wrath of Prajāpati*

Prajāpati wished to procreate. He practiced austerities, he exerted himself. Fire, Wind, Sun, Moon, and Dawn were born from him. The four sons of Prajāpati also practiced austerities, and seeing lovely Dawn, their sister, the four sons became excited in holy passion and they shed seed. Prajāpati gathered the sperm in a golden bowl. From this arose the god of a thousand eyes, a thousand feet, a thousand arrows (*KB*.6.1).

This story, obviously an after-image of the primordial myth, makes

Rudra by indirection the son of Prajāpati. Seed is shed as it had been in the primordial scene. However, it was not shed by Prajāpati but by his sons, moved by the appearance of their sister Dawn. They did not have congress with her, the daughter of Prajāpati, nor was there any disturbance; they got excited and were incontinent. Prajāpati collected their sperm in a golden bowl; its height and width were measured by an arrow's flight (*KB*.6.1). Prajāpati took to himself the sperm of his own sons. He held it in a vessel of gold, the incorruptible, immortal substance. Prajāpati carried this precious bowl as if it were his womb and he became the parent of the Archer who holds a thousand arrows, his thousand eyes fastened on his target and carried forth by a thousand feet. In this magnificat, the newborn is Puruṣa or Cosmic Man, hymned in the *Ṛg Veda* (*RV*.10.90). Puruṣa is this whole world (*RV*.10.90.2). He is beheld in the figure of man, but he is immeasurably greater. Puruṣa has a thousand heads, a thousand eyes, and a thousand feet (*RV*.10.90.1).[2] A thousand here is not a numeral, but a symbol of immensity. While he is this whole world, Puruṣa exceeds it. Cosmic Man of the *Ṛg Veda* has no attributes, he has nothing but his body—while the god arisen from the bowl of Prajāpati holds a thousand arrows. Immediately the overpowering figure of this newborn god grasps his father and demands to be given a name (*KB*.6.2). Before, when he appeared, an archer in the early dawn of creation, the terror he aroused was in his action, by his aiming at the very act of creation-procreation. None would dare to utter the name of that god. But now he insists upon being named.

He aims at his father Prajāpati, who asks him, "Why do you shoot at me?" The newborn one demands, "Give me a name; without having a name I shall not eat food here." Prajāpati gives him the name Bhava, Existence. But a second time he aims at Prajāpati. He wants a second name, for with only one name he will not eat any food. Prajāpati gives him his second name, Śarva. A third time he aims at his father, repeats his demand, and receives his third name, Paśupati. Still, he will not eat unless he receives one more name. He aims at his father five times more until he has received five more names: Ugradeva, the formidable god; Mahādeva, the Great God; Rudra; Īśāna,

[2] Puruṣa, Cosmic Man, is the prototype of all Indian images of deity showing proliferation of limbs and body parts. Cf. D. Srinivasan, "The Religious Significance of Multiple Bodily Parts to Denote the Divine Findings from the Rig Veda," 1975, 137-79.

the Lord; and Aśani, lightning (*KB*.6.2-9), eight names in all. Each one of the names implies a cosmic reality or domain, such as the sun, moon, water, and fire.

What food in the world will sustain this avid being of a thousand eyes and a thousand feet unless it be this entire world? The hunger of Rudra newly born is that of existence. He aims at his father and does not let him go until he has been given by him the eighth name. He held him in his power until he, "eating the food he desires, assuming the forms he desires" (*TUp*.3.105),[3] receives name after name. When his indwelling power was confirmed by each new name, only then did he relax his hold. He has received his identity and sustenance. He was relentless in his demand and hunger to assimilate, to convert into his own being, to take into himself the entire creation. This is the food by which he lives, and which, as Agni, he consumes. He is now confirmed in this world—his sustenance and substance. He is Cosmic Man, Puruṣa: "Purusa alone is this entire world, both past and future; he is also the lord of immortality when he mounts above . . . through food" (*RV*.10.90.2).[4] The newborn god takes into himself the whole world. He encompasses the entire earth and exceeds it (*ŚUp*.3.14).

The birth of "that god" from Prajāpati presaged in the *raudra brahman* took place from Prajāpati in more than one manner. An unknown ascetic, a Vrātya swayed by the god within him, stirred the Lord of Generation into consciousness of that gold, the semen in his body; he stirred the Lord of Generation, who then emitted that gold. It turned into a being with a mark on the forehead. The being so marked grew by his innate power and asceticism and became what his "birthmark," the third eye, prognostically showed—the Great God Rudra, the Lord, the one and only Vrātya, Ekavrātya, the Vrātya in excelsis. The unknown Vrātya had made him manifest by means of the mind and body of the Lord of Generation. By an organic alchemy *in divinis*, Rudra, the Lord, Īśāna, was born from Prajāpati. The shining gold from within Prajāpati became Īśāna the Lord. Immediately, Ekavrātya took up a bow, the bow of Indra, as a token that the power of Indra, king of gods, had passed on to him. Ekavrātya with a "mark" on his forehead is as formidable as Rudra risen from the golden bowl of Prajāpati.

[3] J. M. van Boetzelaer, tr., *Sureśvara's Taittīriyopaniṣadbhāsyavārtikam* 1971, p. 193.

[4] W. N. Brown, "The Sources and Nature of *puruṣa* in the Puruṣasūkta (Rigveda 10.90)," 1931, p. 115. Cf. *Ṛg Veda Saṃhitā (RV)*, tr. K. F. Geldner, 1951, 3:287.

If Prajāpati in the *Kauṣītaki Brāhmaṇa* appears a somewhat feminine character carrying the golden bowl in which the seed shed by his sons was gathered, Prajāpati in the book of the Vrātya in the *Atharva Veda* is the male creator whose seed is imperishable radiance in gold (*AV*.15.1.1-2). Hiraṇyagarbha, the "golden germ," generates by its own power. The birth of Mahādeva, the Great God, takes place by autarky of the Lord of Generation. No female element plays any part whatsoever in this nativity. This is also true of another account of the birth of Rudra from Prajāpati given in the *Śatapatha Brāhmaṇa*. Here it is said that when Prajāpati spent himself into creation, all the gods abandoned him except Manyu, Fury, who sparkled like Fire (*ŚB*.9.1.1.6; cf. *RV*.10.84.2). Manyu, creative fury, and *tapas*, creative heat, are as close to each other as are Manyu and Kāma, creative desire (cf. *AV*.9.2.23). They are degrees and aspects of the creative fire. Prajāpati cried. His tears fell on Manyu, and Manyu became Rudra of a hundred heads, a thousand eyes, and a hundred quivers, his bow strung and his arrow fitted to the string (*ŚB*.9.1.1.6). God Wrath who stayed with Prajāpati is the creative fury of Prajāpati. God Manyu was fecundated by the hot tears of the Lord of Generation, and he became hundred-headed, thousand-eyed Rudra—like unto Puruṣa, the efficient cause of the universe—but he also had a hundred quivers. They belonged to Rudra as the fierce archer Śarva, now brought to life by the tears of the Lord of Generation, which inseminated his own fury. In this way, too, Rudra was generated by Prajāpati; he became the son of the Lord of Generation. But it was Rudra-Agni who made this cosmic manifestation of his come about. The fire genealogy of cosmic, hundred-quivered Rudra begins with Agni-Rudra, who prepared the seed for the Father, in whom sexual passion was still burning when the fire of Rudra's arrow turned it into wrath. Wrath was kindled in Prajāpati by Rudra. Prajāpati's hot tears fell on Manyu, and Manyu was born as Rudra's true self. He was Rudra. The gods were afraid of him.

Rudra, whether born as cosmic giant from the golden bowl of Prajāpati, from the gold in the Creator, or from Manyu (Wrath), remains an archer as he was in the primordial scene. As Puruṣa, Cosmic Man, his hunting ground is the entire world. Woman has no part in either the birth from Manyu or in that of the Lord as Ekavrātya, and only participates at a double remove in the birth from the golden bowl. The sons of Prajāpati shed their seed by merely seeing their lovely sister Dawn, the daughter of Prajāpati. From that seed in a golden bowl held by Prajāpati, Rudra is born.

The gods who were afraid of Rudra-Manyu were advised by Prajāpati to offer food to him in order to appease him. They offered to him the four hundred twenty-five offerings of the *Śatarudriya* sacrifice,[5] and appeased him with the enormous offering and grandiose litany (*ŚB*.9.1.1.7). The birth of Rudra / Manyu (*ŚB*.9.1.1.6) is a sacrificially cosmic event that parallels the birth of the ravenously hungry cosmic archer of the *Kauṣītaki Brāhmaṇa* (*KB*.6.1-2). Sacrifices are the food by which gods live. Man provides the food; by sacrificing, he consecrates himself. When Rudra / Manyu, the newborn child of Prajāpati, longed for food, he stood hungry and aflame on the fire altar that had now been completed. Agni had become Rudra. The gods made him immortal (*ŚB*.9.1.1.1).

The gods were not immortal from the beginning. They became immortal by drinking Soma, the elixir of immortality. They were dependent on man, on Soma, and on the sacrifice.

Rudra wanted to be immortal as were the other gods. But he also wanted to be born. His birth was presaged in the primordial dawn. He was born as Wrath, he was born as Puruṣa, Cosmic Man, he was born as the Lord, Ekavrātya, he was born as a child, the son of Prajāpati.

From the beginning, Rudra the Wild God was unlike the other gods. He wanted to be on one level with them ritually. His status as god had to be confirmed sacrificially. Beyond this, his metaphysical reality needed cosmic reification. He had to be born into the world for the cosmos to be his body.

c. *The Memory of the Initial Evil*

The Brāhmaṇa of a Hundred Paths tells of Prajāpati, who was alone in the beginning. "He desired, 'May I exist, may I reproduce myself!' "[6] He did *tapas*; he practiced austerities (*ŚB*.6.1.3.1). His son would not be a child of uncontrolled passion, such as had seized the Father in the beginning of things, according to the *raudra brahman*. On the contrary, Prajāpati practiced *tapas*, a technique of concentrating the heat of the body, the vital energy, in ardent meditation, so that its full intensity becomes available for any extraordinary endeavor. It is a tech-

[5] *Śatapatha Brāhmaṇa (ŚB)*, tr. J. Eggeling, 1963, part IV, p. 150.
[6] *Ibid.*, part III, p. 157.

nique of asceticism or yoga like that of the ascent or retention of semen (*ūrdhvaretas*); but unlike the discipline of *ūrdhvaretas*, the practice of *tapas* is not directed toward emancipation only, but also seeks fulfillment of other aims, particularly and only seemingly paradoxically procreation. Prajāpati as the householder, with Uṣas (Dawn) as his wife, held a sacrificial session for a year. The Lord of Generation shed seed in Uṣas. In a year, a boy (Kumāra) was born; he cried (*ŚB*.6.1.3.7-8).

A human, homely atmosphere has spread over the primal scene, that violent rape of Dawn, the Father's daughter. Instead, Prajāpati is here the master of the house. He and Dawn are a couple established in their home, the world. In due course, their child is born. No one interferes with its begetting. The traumatic, portentous incident at the critical moment of the intercourse with Dawn seems forgotten. But the infant cries as soon as he is born. This does not seem surprising in the humanized setting of the story of the birth of a god. However, it worries the boy's father, the Lord of Generation. The mother apparently takes no interest in her child. The god, a newborn child, cries and demands to be named (*ŚB*.6.1.3.9).

Newborn in his shape as Cosmic Archer, he voices the identical demand. In either shape he persists in demanding name after name, eight names in all. Only then is he satisfied. The newborn god is equally clamorous in either of his shapes and he is satisfied when he receives his eighth name. The infant stops crying, and the Cosmic Archer who had aimed at his father releases his hold of Prajāpati when he has received his last name (*KB*.6.2-9). However, the insistence of the newborn god is prompted by an entirely different reason in each of his two shapes.

As Puruṣa or Cosmic Man, the god is born at a sacrificial session and out of a golden bowl held by Prajāpati. Arisen, the overpowering figure grasps the father and demands to be given a name, saying, "for without a name assigned, I shall not eat food here" (*KB*.6.2) in this world.[7] Bhava, Existence, was the first name given to him by his father (*KB*.6.2).

With unforeseen suddenness, the theophany of the Cosmic Archer rising from a golden bowl of an arrow's flight's proportions, aims at Prajāpati, although in a forethought Prajāpati had collected the

[7] *Kauṣītaki Brāhmaṇa (KB)*, tr. A. B. Keith, 1920, p. 377.

sperm of fire and wind, of sun and moon, his sons whom he had just then created. Prajāpati of the *Śatapatha Brāhmaṇa*, however, was alone in the beginning. There was nothing else. He created the earth and the seasons. Desire overcame him to be, to know himself, to procreate and see the living proof of his existence. Subsequently, a boy was born to him and to Uṣas, the Dawn. The child cried; indeed, he wept. Concerned, Prajāpati asked the child the reason for his crying. The boy replied that he cried because he was not freed from evil, for no name had been given him. "Give me a name." The newborn god knew why he cried and demanded to be named. He knew what evil he wanted to be freed from. Many names had to be summoned to free him from the primordial evil when Dawn fled from its scene. The powers that were in him from the beginning had to be evoked at his birth and confirmed by their names. Being called by their names, they guarded him with his own power. Their presence in him accounted for his demand for name after name. The child remembered his past. It lived in his memory. By his memory the newborn god established his identity. Unlike his birth as Cosmic Archer, he bore no visible cognizance.

In both his shapes, as Cosmic Archer and as infant, the newborn god, son of Prajāpati, remembers the past. As Cosmic Archer, his shape proclaims it a hundredfold. In each of these shapes he demands his names eight times, eight names. His father, the Lord of Generation, then names the newborn god: "You are Rudra." "And because he gave him that name, Agni became such like . . . , for Rudra is Agni" (*ŚB*.6.1.3.10).[8] The *Śatapatha Brāhmaṇa* furthermore explains by popular etymology that Rudra is so called because he cried (*rud*; *ŚB*.6.1.3.10; cf. *TS*.1.5.1.1). The Wild God is now the crying, weeping god. But the newborn god is not satisfied; he knows himself to be mightier even than that name. He asks for one more name, and when that is given to him he wants yet another, and is not satisfied until he has received altogether eight names (*ŚB*.6.1.3.10-18). The enormity of the primordial evil is greater than the power inherent in any one of the eight names. Only in their eightfold totality are they commensurate with the primordial evil. Only after receiving all eight does the newborn god ask his father for no other name (*ŚB*.6.1.3.17; *VāP*.27.5-16).[9]

[8] *Śatapatha Brāhmaṇa (ŚB)*, tr. J. Eggeling, 1963, part III, p. 159.

[9] The order of the names given in the *Vāyu Purāṇa* is: Rudra, Bhava, Śiva, Paśūnāmpati, Īśa, Bhīma, Ugra, and Mahādeva.

When the Father gives his son his first name, his identity at once reveals itself. He is Rudra-Agni, the Wild God, the fire of creation. This is not the first time that the Lord of Generation gave name and status to the god as yet nameless—or whose name should not be uttered. Paśupati, Lord of Animals, was the name the Father had given, in fear, to the archer so that the hunter might spare him. But now Prajāpati gives a name, not to an unknown, threatening, archer but to his own child, knowing in his heart that the newborn god and the hunter are one in essence. Not satisfied with one name only, Rudra asks for more names. Name by name they are promptly given, one after the other as the child goes on asking for them: Śarva, Paśupati, Ugra, Aśani, Bhava, Mahādeva, and Īśāna, eight in all, including Rudra (*ŚB*.6.1.3.10-17).

Prajāpati was preoccupied with the primordial drama when the name Śarva, the thrower of the arrow, came to his lips; the name Paśupati came next. Formidable are these names. The next name, Ugra, the Ferocious, conveys their terror. It strikes like lightning (*aśani*), which is another name given to the child; lightning is the manifestation of fire in mid-air. These are names of dread and fire. Bhava, however, connotes Existence. Mahādeva is the Great God, and Īśāna the Lord or Ruler. "These are the eight names of Agni-Rudra. Kumāra (the boy) is the ninth" (*ŚB*.6.1.3.18; *KB*.6.2-9).[10] The "boy" (Kumāra) is the newborn god. The numbers eight and nine have secret significance. Assuming the eight names, the boy is the ninth, the new. He is never seen as a mere boy; he is seen in those forms that he has entered one by one (*ŚB*.6.1.3.19). "The great god of eight names" (*KB*.6.9) shows his fierce might in his name Ugra. Elsewhere, instead of Aśani "lightning," he is called Bhīma, the Frightful (*HGS*.2.8.6-7).

It was a Vrātya wandering about who, in his illumination, saw this entire world extended toward the four directions and pervaded by his god: Rudra in the center, Bhava, Śarva, Paśupati, and Ugra in the four directions, Mahādeva above and Īśāna in every direction. The eighth name of his god is the Sole Vrātya of the *Atharva Veda*, a transfiguration of the visionary Vrātya. All the eight names are invoked in the *Yajur Veda* (*VS*.39.8) and receive their offerings.[11]

[10] In the *Kauṣītaki Brāhmaṇa*, the order of the names given by Prajāpati is Bhava, Śarva, Paśupati, Ugra, Mahādeva, Rudra, Īśāna, Aśani (*KB*.6.2-9).

[11] The eight names given in *VS*.39.8 are Agni, Aśani, Paśupati, Bhava, Śarva, Īśāna, Manyu, and Mahādeva.

Only Rudra and Paśupati are mythic names. Bhava signifies existence itself, and he is the ruler and Lord, Īśāna (*RV*.2.33.9); he is the Great God, Mahādeva. In cosmic greatness the newborn god received his ancient names from his father Prajāpati. They were chosen by Prajāpati as they had been chosen before, from many others to whom homage is paid, in the *Śatarudriya*, the hymn of Rudra a hundredfold, though even in this laud not all the names are invoked under which the god had then been known. Thus he is called in the *Ṛg Veda* (*RV*.6.49.10) Father of the world or Father of living beings. Though this name was not, could not have been, among those that readily came to Prajāpati's mind, its meaning was in abeyance and waited to raise its head in the ongoing myth of the newborn god.

Uttering name after name, Prajāpati assigned to each a domain. The domain was neither territorial nor situated in any specific direction, as were the stations of the archers in the cosmic pyramid of the Sole Vrātya. The domains were qualitative and elemental, ingrained in the substance of the cosmos, its order, and man's consciousness of it. The newborn god did not stop crying until he had received his eighth name. He knew that he needed each name, together with the reality or domain that Prajāpati was going to give to him.

d. *The Investiture with the Cosmos*

The eight domains are those of the Vasus, the eight component powers of the Universe. These ancient gods dwell each in his sphere, and are one with it in name; from them develops the physical world. Their ogdoad is invoked in the *Ṛg Veda* (*RV*.2.31.1; 3.8.8; 6.62.8; 10.48.11; 10.125.1; 10.128.9). It consists of the pentad of the five elements. They are earth, the support of all creatures; fire that warms, illumines, and destroys them; water, purifying and fertilizing; air that breathes through the universe; and ether or space that pervades them all. To the pentad of existence constituted by the elements are added sun and moon, by whose light time is measured in hot glow and cold sheen. Together with the five elements, they form the heptad of existence. To this heptad are added the stars to form the ogdoad of the eight domains or realities of the manifest cosmos (cf. *ŚB*.11.6.3.6; *BṛUp*.3.9.3; *MBh*.1.60.17). Prajāpati assigns fire, water, plants, air, lightning, rain, moon, and sun to Rudra as his domains (*ŚB*.6.1.3.10-17), adumbrating, as does Ṛṣi Taṇḍi in his hymn in the *Mahābhārata* (*MBh*.13.16.35, 54), the eight concrete realities (*aṣṭamūrti*) with which

Prajāpati endowed his son. The *Purāṇas* name them clearly. They describe the newborn child as it sat crying—glowing red and deep blue (*nīla-lohita*) through both the sectors of the spectrum—on the lap of its father (*VāP*.27.3-5; *PP*.5.3.189-90). To this crying child his father—whom the *Purāṇas* know as Brahmā—assigns his eight domains.[12] They are those of the ogdoad of the Vasus: the pentad of the elements and the dyad of sun and moon (*VāP*.27.17-19). However, the eighth domain with which Prajāpati endows his son is not that of the far-away luminaries; their place within the body of the eight realities, the *aṣṭamūrti*, is ceded to man, the sacrificer or initiated *brāhmanaḥ* (*VāP*.27.19),[13] who is an embodiment of mind. "Mind is the form of the Sacrificer" (*ŚB*.12.8.2.4).[14] Mind embodied in man, among the domains of Rudra, takes the place of the stars among the Vasus. Mind first came into existence when life stirred in the dark void of the primeval flood (*RV*.10.129.4). In the eightfold cosmos of Rudra, his eighth domain, mind, is within man, the microcosm.

But not only man as mind, but also everyman is Rudra's domain (*LP*.2.13.20), for man the microcosm is homologous with the cosmos. Not only does the eye see with the light of the sun and the glow that is Rudra (*VāP*.27.40; *LP*.2.13.24-25), but each of the different faculties and functions of the living being represents one of the eight forms of the god. For instance, the vital energies (*prāṇa*) are the domain of Īśāna (*VāP*.27.43); Paśupati's domain is in the digestive fire (44). Rudra dwells in the functioning of the total psycho-physical body of man; as Mahādeva he lives in man's immortal being and he comes into existence anew, again and again.

The newborn god, having received his names and stations, makes no further demand on Prajāpati. He is freed from the evil whose memory had made him cry. The evil of that first morning of the primordial aeon is now allayed. Now Kumāra the "boy" starts out into his new world. He is the "ninth," "the New," in and as each of the eight realities of the cosmos and of man, the microcosm. Rudra had to be *born* to end the memory of the primordial evil. It persisted until, name by name and reality upon reality, the evil was eradicated from his memory. Now a new world under the dispensation of Rudra be-

[12] *Mārkaṇḍeya Purāṇa (MāP)*, tr. F. E. Pargiter, 1904, pp. 268-69 (= 52.3-9).

[13] The eighth domain in the *Vāyupurāṇa* is *dīkṣito brāhmaṇas* . . . (*VāP*. 27.19); H. Meinhard, "Beiträge zur Kenntnis des Sivaismus nach den Purāṇas," 1928, pp. 11, 12.

[14] *Śatapatha Brāhmaṇa (ŚB)*, tr. J. Eggeling, 1963, part V, p. 240.

gins. It is permeated by Rudra in each of its eight realities. This sacred ogdoad comprises the pentad of the elements and of the senses that perceive them and the dyad of the controlling agents, sun and moon, the measurers of time. These luminaries act at the same time as symbols of the hot and the cold and of currents caused by them. Mind or consciousness of the initiated completes the triad of the elements and luminaries, as also the ogdoad. The newborn god is all of them in one. The memory of the primordial evil is not allayed until the last name, Mahādeva, the Great God, is given to the child. The Great God entered into his domains as Aṣṭamūrti, God in the cosmos and in man (cf. *LP*.1.41.35-36; cf. *DStotra* 9).

The dialogue of Prajāpati with his demanding newborn son, dark blue and red in color, is a rite of expiation devised by the newborn god and performed by Prajāpati. It was Rudra's memory of the primordial evil that prompted the dialogue.

In the ongoing myth of Rudra/Śiva, events unfold across the aeons. Similarly, many hundreds of years may lie between different versions of one particular myth, or between the narrative and its related visual image. Among the most perfect works of Indian art are the images of Śiva dancing. The image of Śiva Naṭarāja, the king of the dance, cast in bronze or carved in stone is a visual embodiment of Śiva Aṣṭamūrti, or the eight realities.[15] In images of this and other modes of Śiva's dance, South Indian sculptures from the eighth century onward show the figure of the dancing god with his gyrating body standing on the prostrate shape of an infant with a snake in its hand.[16] The name of the prostrate shape is Apasmāra Puruṣa, and it is generally taken to be a demon and a symbol of ignorance.[17] However, its name says that the infant shape is that of "a being without memory." Its lusciously modeled flesh, neither plagued nor activated by memory, is pinned down by the foot of the dancing lord. The chubby babe Forgetfulness offers the greatest contrast to the newborn child of Prajāpati. That child cried for its name in order to be freed from evil that it remembered so well. Because the newborn god remembered the primordial evil, that memory kept the ancient evil in abeyance as the infant de-

[15] C. Sivaramamurti, *Naṭarāja in Art, Thought and Literature*, pp. 25, 31.

[16] K. R. Srinivasan, *Bronzes of South India*, 1963, figs. 54, 55, 93, 169, 169B: the serpent is said to have fallen from the arm of the Lord; C. Sivaramamurti, *South Indian Bronzes*, 1963, pls. 16, 22a, 24, 26, 27b, 28b; D. Barrett, *Early Cola Bronzes*, pls. 57, 58.

[17] J. N. Banerjea, *The Development of Hindu Iconography*, pp. 274-75, 472.

manded its names and received them from Prajāpati. The world of Rudra / Śiva began young and anew. But for the pained memory of the newborn god, no demands would have been made and no response elicited; the world of Śiva would not have come to be for Śiva Aṣṭamūrti to dance in the cosmos and in the heart of man.

The Wild God, guardian of the Uncreate and avenger of its violation, had to fail in preventing the violation so as to allow the seed to fall that he as Agni had prepared. The fire seed of creation deposited in the Father held the mystery of its origin and that of its descent. Rudra-Agni, the bearer of the seed, was to be born from that seed, metaphysically his own self and son, mythically the son of the Lord of Generation, Prajāpati. The newborn god wrested from Prajāpati his recognition and confirmation as ruler, Īśāna, and as Mahādeva, the Great God in his domain, the universe and man, in which he is embodied. And he is known as the eight-formed Lord who is identical with all the worlds (*LP*.2.13.29). The world is suffused with his presence, which is encountered wheresoever, in whomsoever. The *Śatarudriya*, the hundredfold laud of the Lord, knows where to find him; the *Liṅga Purāṇa*, dating from nearly two thousand years later, knows how to show that he has been found. Giving help to everyone and showing kindness to all is called the highest worship of the Lord of eight forms (*LP*.2.13.35-36).

2. The Birth from Brahmā

a. *Preparations for Rudra's Birth*

The world of Rudra has come to exist. It will run its course, and, in the end, it will be consumed by Rudra, who is Agni, Fire, the sole witness of the dissolution of this cosmos. His eight realities constitute the substance of the cosmos and of man, the microcosm. The two are homologous, and they also interact, for man represents and comprehends them. As such, he himself is the eighth reality, namely, mind (*manas*). Man, here, is the initiate, the mental exemplar in the universe of Aṣṭamūrti, the scheme of things to be. In the context of Śiva's myth, however, man has not yet been created in the flesh. To bring about man in his physical concrete existence as human being will be the task assigned to Rudra-Śiva by his father, the Lord of Generation, who is known in the *Purāṇas* as Brahmā, the Creator. He will create the aeon where the noumenal universe that is Rudra's body will come to life in all its parts, and its ingredients will combine in sentient creatures born to live and to die.

The Father who shed the seed, Prajāpati, and Brahmā, successively in the ongoing narrative of sacred tradition, play the role of the Creator. They are identical in essence, though mythically differentiated from the *Ṛg Veda* to the *Purāṇas*. They are assigned to different aeons.

Prajāpati, the Lord of Generation, felt alone. When a son was born to him, the relation of Rudra to the Father at the dawn of a former aeon was redeemed as soon as Prajāpati, at the newborn god's demand, invested the crying child with the constituents of the cosmos as they would exist in the universe and in man. Out of his own loneliness, before his son was born, Prajāpati gave to Rudra the double assurance of his existence in the universe and in man. In the world of Rudra man would not be alone. He would live with the cosmos, sharing the eightfold reality of Mahādeva, the Great God, Īśāna, the Lord. The cycle of the fire seed of creation had fulfilled itself in the birth of Mahādeva, the Great God, born of Prajāpati. When this aeon passes into the night of cosmic dissolution, another aeon will arise when Rudra will be born again from the Creator, whose name will now be Brahmā.

Man himself had not as yet come to exist, and after a long sleep Brahmā awoke in a new aeon (*kalpa*) (*LP*.1.41.37-38). The past aeon in which Rudra was born of Prajāpati saw the Great God indwelling in the cosmos, throughout existence, and in the consciousness of man. That aeon with its universe was ideational. It adumbrated the forecast; it provided the setting of a world where man would live and die. As yet man had not been born in the flesh. He existed only as the vehicle of mind. He was the consciousness in creation, himself as yet not created. Though this aeon had passed, its framework would emerge at the end of the cosmic night, and the world of Aṣṭamūrti would be filled with human beings destined to live and to die. But in between these two aeons night brooded over the waters of the cosmic flood in the darkness of dissolution. "This (universe) existed in the shape of Darkness, unperceived, destitute of distinctive marks, unattainable by reasoning, unknowable, wholly immersed, as it were, in deep sleep" (*M*.1.5).[18] Brahmā, the creator, meditated on the principles of things-

[18] *Mārkaṇḍeya Purāṇa (MāP)*, tr. F. Eden Pargiter, 1904, pp. 237-38 (= 49.3-10).

to-be evolving out of prematter (*prakṛti*) (cf. *VP*.1.5.3-4), and there appeared to him delusion covered with darkness (*tamas*) in which the real form of things remained unknown, in which next to darkness appeared illusion, great confusion, anger, and blindness (*ŚP*.7.1.12.1-2; cf. *VP*.1.5.3-6; *BhP*.3.12.2). Brahmā was not pleased with this creation of his (*BhP*.3.12.3). In his desire to create living beings who themselves would procreate, he exerted himself and created couples who could mate and produce offspring only once, at the end of life.[19] But this he deemed unsatisfactory, and he created a quantity of living creatures, so many that the three worlds were crowded, without room to breathe (*MBh*.12.284.13-14). It was a catastrophe. Again he practiced *tapas*. He exerted himself, and from his mind four or seven or more sons were born to him (*ŚP*.7.1.12.19-20; *VāP*.9.18-19; *MP*.3.5-8; *KūP*.1.10.12-13; *BhP*.3.12.3-4). However, they were disinterested in the course of the world; they had achieved mastery over their senses, they were free from desire, they were yogis and munis, who had silenced their roving minds. They did not produce progeny. Through yoga power they held their seminal energy upward, since Release was their ultimate aim (*BhP*.3.12.4-5; *ŚP*.7.1.12.20-21). Brahmā's purpose was not served by them (*MP*.4.26-27). He exerted himself once more, and once more his progeny were mind-born sages (*VāP*.9.67-69). Something was going counter to Brahmā's intention. First, the dark night of dissolution seemed to be clinging to his mind, the anguish of creation smothered its drive; Brahmā was critical and self-destructive. Brahmā, the creator of this new aeon, reacted to his frustration altogether differently from the Father, who, at the beginning of things, almost demented by physical frustration, lost his bearing. Aeons separate the Creator, the Father, from Brahmā. Having passed through the dark night of gestation prior to their birth, his mind-born sons, when born, failed Brahmā in his purpose to people the world. Being yogis of undeviating self-control, and born from his mind, they were embodied reactions to the primordial loss of control of the Father. They acted against the incontinence of the Father in that distant past that had slumbered uneasily in Brahmā's mind whence they were born. It is said that on finding them averse to the procreation of progeny, Brahmā became despondent and desperate about the creation of living beings. He exerted himself in most severe

[19] *Mānava Dharmaśāstra (M)*, tr. G. Bühler, 1969, p. 2.

austerities; his mind concentrated on the creation of mankind. Nothing happened. He waited in grief and his grief turned to anger. He cried in anger. Goblins and ghosts come out of his tears. Brahmā swore at himself when he saw the offspring of his tears (*KūP*.1.10.15-21; *ŚP*.7.1.12.19-24).

b. *Rudra Issues from the Head of Brahmā*

In utter distress, Brahmā breathed his last. And from his mouth Rudra came forth; the breath of life itself, glorious as a thousand suns and blazing like the doomsday fire (*KūP*.1.10.21-22; *LP*.1.41,42-43). Rudra then imparted the vital breaths to Brahmā, and brought him back to life (*ŚP*.7.1.12.31-32). According to another version, Rudra sprang from the forehead of Brahmā, darkened with rage (*BhP.* 3.12.6-10). The *Mahābhārata* lists the eleven mind-born sons of Rudra, here called Sthāṇu, with the six mind-born sons of Brahmā (*MBh*.1.60.1-4).

Rudra, the avenger, at the dawn of creation was born into creation from Brahmā's wrath, from the middle of his forehead, where the world of the senses and the intellect meet. Or he left the body of Brahmā by his mouth as his life breath, as the breath itself of life (*KūP*.1.10.22). Or "Brahmā created Rudra, born of his irate self. . . . From his wrath a being was born with the effulgence of the sun" (*VāP*.9.70,75; *KūP*.1.2.5-6; cf. *VrP*.2.48-49; cf. *BhP*.3.12.7). Radiant, glorious Rudra, the breath itself of life (cf. *BṛUp*.3.9.4), light of the sun and fire of doomsday, was born of Brahmā's anger. Anger had rankled in the Creator over the aeons from the beginning, when Rudra had aimed his arrow against the Father, against Prajāpati, the Lord of Generation. When the Creator in this present aeon sends into the world his mind-born sons, ascetics withdrawn from the world, he is no longer the Lord of Generation.

He also is no longer the Father, but is henceforth called Pitāmaha, the grandfather of the universe (*MBh*.1.1.30; *KūP*.1.2.5), and becomes Brahmā, the Creator, the theomorph of the *brahman*, the absolute, the undefinable plenum, the Uncreate. As such his mind-born sons are in direct descent from the Uncreate, Rudra being his last son. At the same time, however, Brahmā the Creator as well as Prajāpati are but successive forms of the Father, whose wrath or anger—the Father foamed like a bull when his intercourse was interrupted (cf. *RV*.10.61.8)—finally triggers in Brahmā the creation of Rudra.

Rudra, son of Brahmā, is born from Brahmā's wrath in this aeon, as he was born from that of Prajāpati before, when in the shape of Manyu he did not abandon the Lord of Generation. "Wrath (Manyu) was born instantly as a blue-red boy from between the brows of Prajāpati" (*BhP*.3.12.7).

Rudra is born from Brahmā's wrath, breath, and thought. He is born as the breath of life. When born from Prajāpati in a former aeon, he was a crying child or also Cosmic Man in his hunger, and he became the cosmos. Born from Brahmā, he is mind-born. The seed that he had prepared for the Father had become himself, the son of Prajāpati. Prajāpati freed his newborn child from evil; he also stilled his hunger, and the newborn god of eight names and stations became Aṣṭamūrti, the cosmos.

Now Rudra enters a new aeon, born not from the seed but from the mind of the Creator. He is born from the head of Brahmā—mind-born, as were the other ascetic sons of Brahmā. Or he issues from the mouth of Brahmā as the breath of life itself in its fire and radiance. According to one ancient myth, it was from the mouth of the Creator, Prajāpati, who alone existed in the beginning and considered how to reproduce himself, that Agni, Fire, was generated (*ŚB*.2.2.4.1). Rudra is Agni, Fire. As *prāṇa*, the life breath, he is the fire, the vitality of life itself. Rudra, the fire-seed of creation, son of Prajāpati, is Rudra, the breath of life, issued from Brahmā the creator.

But another myth relates how Rudra was born from a drop of Brahmā's blood. It oozed from Brahmā's forehead when he wiped away the sweat as he sacrificed into the fire caused by his self-glory. The drop of blood became Nīla-Lohita Rudra, the dark blue-red god (*SkP*.5.1.2.24-26). Carnal though not sexual, this birth of Rudra is also from the forehead of the Creator. The blood magic of *nīla-lohita* is reincarnated in this birth story.

The shock of Rudra's primordial shot stayed with the Creator. When Rudra released his arrow against the Father, he projected himself into this target. The avenger injected his wrath into his aim. The Father broke out in rage. All the gods abandoned Prajāpati when he had spent himself into creation. Only god Manyu (Wrath) stayed with him and became his son, Archer and Cosmic Man (Puruṣa) in one. When Brahmā, the Creator, labored in the agony of creation, anger seized him. The sons that in the end were born from his mind were all ascetics. Finally from his wrath Rudra, the Great Yogi, appeared, the breath itself of life. In the primordial scene Rudra the yogi had assumed the appearance of an archer. He was the guardian of hitherto unspent metacosmic integrity. Avenging the dissemination of its substance by the Creator, the full impact of the ascetic god hit Prajāpati. It occupied the mind of Brahmā, the Creator, and from it was born Rudra.

Leaving the head of Brahmā, Rudra entered the world as an ascetic or an androgyne (Ch. VIII) so as paradoxically to carry out Brahmā's desire for progeny, his desire for the creation of mankind.

VI

THE REFUSAL TO PROCREATE AND THE ENCOUNTERS WITH DEATH

1. Sthāṇu, the Pillar

As soon as he was born, Rudra cried violently, and Brahmā—as Prajāpati had done—gave him his names and stations (*KūP*.1.10.23-27; *BhP*.3.12.8-12). The investiture of the newborn god had become a rite. It had been first performed by Prajāpati (Ch. V.1.d). With its completion, all was within the great Lord, all that he had desired. Then he gave up all desire. Maheśvara, God of Gods, renounced the world. His mind fixed on the ultimate real, he drank deep of this supreme nectar, the uncreate and undecaying *brahman* (*KūP*.1.10.30-31). He was absorbed in contemplation when Brahmā ordered him to create progeny.

Brahmā, following his own unsuccessful attempts, insisted that Rudra create living creatures, that he bring mankind into being (*BhP*.3.12.14; cf. *VrP*.21.6) and beget children (*VāP*.10.43). Rudra responded to Brahmā's command in a manner conforming with his ascetic primordial nature. He followed the example of the earlier mind-born sons of Brahmā in that he would not procreate. Yet he also followed the example of Brahmā: he created from his own self mind-born sons, Rudras, equal to himself (*BhP*.3.12.15; *VāP*.10.44-45; *KūP*.1.10.32). He next discharged from his body lightning, thunder, and the meters (*MP*.4.29).[1] But this did not further Brahmā's pur-

[1] In this version of Brahmā's creation, Rudra appears as Śiva / Vāmadeva (cf. *MP*.4.27 ff.).

pose: the creation of mortals to populate the earth. Brahmā's plan was doubly contrary to Rudra's nature: *he* is the prototypal ascetic, and would not think of carnal progeny. He is also Śiva, the compassionate god, who wants to prevent the imperfections and suffering of the human condition. The world thus was at a standstill.

The mind-born sons of Rudra, the Rudras, are not all ascetics or sages, yet they acted as unlimited editions of possibilities and arabesques of Rudra's multiple nature. Not all were Nīla-Lohitas, dark and red. They were as multicolored as they were multiform (*VāP.* 10.44-54). Rudra's mental issue resembled but was unlike the innumerable thousands of Rudras of the *Śatarudriya* hymn (*VS.*16.54-66).

The Rudras of the *Śatarudriya* litany were reverberations of the presence of Rudra; the Rudras of the *Purāṇas* were his self-begotten sons, who were discharged from his mind by the Great Yogi before he stood in stillness.

The Rudras vibrate the universe and man with Rudra's breath. They leap into man's awareness out of his food, in the street, in the wood, at any place, and at any time, in the wealth and elation of the *Śatarudriya* hymn. They are turbulent and disturbing, invisible and full of energy (*LP.*1.70.312-13), free from attachment, riders on large bulls (*KūP.*1.10.33-34). Some are hunch-backed, some are dwarfs and crooked (*MP.*183.64). Or they are 840 million celestials called Sādhyas, three-eyed and without fear of getting old (*MP.*4.30). They are yogis, teachers, students. Some emit smoke and blaze; some have eight curved fangs, two tongues, and three eyes. Some have thousands of eyes, some are merciful and patient. They meditate, hold skulls, rush and leap everywhere between heaven and earth. Fully armed, they roam about and their mere glance may kill (*LP.*1.70.305-13). Yet, on the whole, their multitudes are more human, less elemental than those of the Rudras of the great litany; they are, though less spectacular, less irresistible and more compassionate, akin to those companions of Rudra whom Aśvatthāman saw in the uncertain light, blazing from the guardian of the camp of the Pāṇḍavas and whom Rudra looked upon as his legitimate sons (*MBh.*10.7.41-42). When Rudra-Śiva bade them work for the welfare of the world, they cried and ran about; the world is pervaded by them and they are devoted to all beings (*VāP.*9.77-81). Rudra's mind-born sons, unlike Brahmā's, did not all monotonously withdraw from the world. On the contrary, they activate the movement in creation. They are the breath (*prāṇa*) of life (*LP*.1.22.24; *ŚP*.7.1.12.25-30) in all beings, for Rudra is the origin of that breath (*MBh*.7.173.92-93). At Mahādeva's command, the Rudras are to be worshiped together with the other gods (*VāP*.10.58-61; *BP*.1.2.9.82-86). They are the indomitable, deathless stirrings and vibrations of creation, unformed, misformed, correct, and overstated until—worshiped with the other gods—they find their norm and form. Rudra discharged from his being these animating, vivifying powers and withdrew into his core of stillness.

When Brahmā saw the Rudras, he warned Rudra, "Do not create such people, exempt from death; create others who are bound by birth and death" (*KūP*.1.10.36; cf. *BP*.1.2.9.79-80). He should "create only such beings as would reap the fruit of their own karmas" (*MP*.4.31-32).[2] But Rudra remonstrated that he would not create offspring subject to death and old age. He firmly stated his position: "I am standing by. You create people" (*VāP*.10.56-57; *LP*.1.70.316). Thereafter Rudra did not procreate (*VāP*.10.63; *LP*.1.70.323). "Keeping the semen drawn up, Sthāṇu stood still until the great deluge. Because he said: 'Here I stand (*sthito'smi*),' he is known as Sthāṇu (one who stands)" (*VāP*.10.64; *BP*.1.2.9.89; cf. *MP*.4.32; cf. *KūP*.1.10.38; *LP*.1.70.323-24; cf. *SkP*.7.2.9.14; *ŚP*.7.1.14.14-21).[3] Rudra became Sthāṇu, a motionless pillar, a branchless stem. He stood in aeviternal illumination.

Sthāṇu (from the root *sthā*, "to stand"), "a post," is Rudra's concrete symbol. Its upward direction shows his inflexible stance across the universe (cf. *LP*.1.86.139), as well as suggesting the upward withdrawal of his semen. The visual concept of Sthāṇu, the pillar, is the paradoxical negation of the erect phallus, which the pillar shape suggests. This image is the monument in which the Lord of Yoga became Sthāṇu, or *liṅga*-formed. But for its implied meaning, this theophany is without any visual anthropomorphic trait. The whole of ascetic Rudra's being is within its pillar shape. If the pyramid of the Sole Vrātya was built mentally in a vision, a monument of the inner realization of that god, the verticality of Sthāṇu is a presentation of Rudra-Śiva, the yogi. This abstract pillar shape stands firm by the tension of the implied procreative force, its mastery, and negation.

The motionless pillar is Śiva, the ascetic, in whom the fire of life burns upward inwardly while he stands still. This is the mystery of

[2] *Matsya Purāṇa (MP)*, tr. "A Taluqdar of Oudh," 1916, part 1, p. 15.

[3] *Ibid*., p. 15n.

Sthāṇu (cf. *MBh*.17.173.92). He is motionless, like a log in which the potentiality of fire is latent (cf. *ŚUp*.1.13) and controlled. Sthāṇu is Śiva the yogi, an aeviternal, immovable presence, pillar of the world.

Rudra did not carry out Brahmā's command. He did not create mortals, whose sorry lot he foresaw. He stood still as a pillar, his organ of procreation itself motionless and pointing upward as a sign of the semen drawn upward, contained, consumed or transubstantiated within the body. The erect phallus of the yogi signifies the opposite of what this position conveys naturally, yet the erection is the basis for the conversion of its meaning.

"Since Rudra stands burning upward, and since he stands and exists as the origin of life, and since the *liṅga* is aeviternally erect, he is known as Sthāṇu" (*MBh*.7.173.92). The *Mahābhārata* sees Sthāṇu not in his immutability as master over sexual power but as the immutability of that power itself—and as the origin of life. Rudra does not procreate at Brahmā's behest, but stands still forever in the shape of the *liṅga* as Sthāṇu, the pillar. Sthāṇu in the simplicity of its shape is the monument of Rudra's paradoxical truth. Its dual significance comprises the irreducible nature of Rudra, the Fire, the origin of life, and Rudra, the Great Yogi, who, counter to nature, is master of the unspent life-giving power.

Before going into stasis, Rudra had created his mind-born sons, hosts of turbulent Rudras. Although unpredictable and frightening, the Rudras, these uncanny vital powers, are recognized; they are to be accepted and worshiped along with the other gods. They are the movement of breath itself (*prāṇa*), whose origin is Rudra. The creation and conversion of the Rudras is a prelude to and accompaniment of Rudra's stasis. In their restlessness they are Sthāṇu's alter ego. He discharged them from his mind and made them his sons.

The myth of Rudra-Śiva unfolds from aeon to aeon. Each new cosmos repeats and carries further the fundamental themes. When Rudra becomes Sthāṇu, his eight cosmic names are in abeyance. When Śiva-Aṣṭamūrti dances his cosmic dance, his bronze image as Naṭarāja, king of dancers, shows the gyration of his flexed limbs upheld by the stasis of the central axis of the flux of his movement. The immortal, invisible Rudras circulate in its rhythm.

The Rudras cried and ran about; they pervade this world and are devoted to it. But Brahmā rejected these immortal sons of Rudra because they could not fulfill his purpose (*BP*.1.2.9.70-80). They were not themselves, nor would they propagate,. mortals. Then Rudra withdrew into himself. He became Sthāṇu, motionless in aeviternal *samādhi*, ceaseless illumination, contained within himself, his seed withdrawn into himself (*BP*.1.2.9.88-89). In his pillar shape Rudra restores the unspent wholeness of the Uncreate. His seed and his breath are held. The fire seed of creation and the breath of life are held within his motionless shape. No mortals will ever be created by Rudra, but such things as knowledge, truth, asceticism, and illumination are in him, and he is in the gods, sages, and all beings; he is honored by all the gods (*BP*.1.2.9.89-92). The gods are "this side of creation" (*RV*.10.129.6). Rudra at the beginning of things acted as the guardian of the Uncreate, and became its pillar in the myth of creation.

As the bearer of the fire-seed of creation, from before the beginning of things, Rudra is his own counter player and the ultimate cause of his own birth. As Sthāṇu, standing withdrawn into the godhead, into himself, while Brahmā wants to create mortals, he resumes his ambivalence without which creation could not have begun, and without which death would become the end of everything.

When Rudra was told to create mortals instead of the mind-born Rudras, he decreed that these noble and mighty beings would roam about in his company (*ŚP*.7.1.14, 17-19; cf. *KūP*.1.10.38). Yet he stands in yogic trance until the dissolution of the universe. While he desists from creation and withdraws into himself, the Rudras play around the motionless Sthāṇu, who is the pillar of containment pervading the universe (cf. *LP*.1.70.320-24; *LP*.1.86.139). Having refused to engender mortals and having ceased to create immortals, the Great God says of himself: "I stand as the destroyer. Because I stand like a pillar, so I am *sthāṇu*" (*SkP*.7.2.9.13-14). His withdrawal from the world signals his destruction of the world. Sthāṇu, the pillar of containment, stands as a marker across the entire creation. On the unchartered road from before the beginning of time, when Rudra, the hunter, arose as the avenger of the Uncreate, Sthāṇu stands until the end of the aeon (*VāP*.10.64), when Śiva will destroy the cosmos, dancing it out of existence, the sole witness of its destruction (*KūP*.1.10.64-65).

Sthāṇu the ascetic rises into the empyrean between Rudra the avenger and Śiva the destroyer. His motionless shape has only one direction, upward. The self-contained shape holds within itself the power of life and of withdrawal from it. Within himself Sthāṇu restores the unspent integrity that was before the beginning of things. Standing *in* creation here and now, he is beyond creation. At the end of the aeon Śiva will destroy the cosmos, absorb it back into himself, into the undifferentiated darkness of cosmic night—a periodically renewed reflex of the Uncreate.

In declaring his nature to Brahmā, Śiva established his shape as Sthāṇu. Henceforward Sthāṇu becomes a name of Rudra-Śiva. In this name the Great God will act in his myth as the motionless pillar beyond time, and the cycles of time will move around him.

2. The Creation of Death and the Cycles of Time

Sthāṇu withdrew from procreation, frustrating Brahmā. But Brahmā persisted in his creative urge. Having produced his few mind-born sons and Sthāṇu, who had turned away from the task of procreation, Brahmā now produced people. In fact, he was overwhelmed by the profusion of creatures he created. They crowded the three worlds. Their number kept increasing, for they did not die (*MBh*.12.248.13-14). They were the very opposite of the innumerable and immortal Rudras, who were born deathless as the throbbing itself of life. The creatures of Brahmā, however, were sent into the world as a population that as yet had not met death. Bewildered and angered by the uncontrollable profusion of creatures he had brought about, Brahmā flared up and his wrath broke out of his body in a fiery fury. It set the universe ablaze, and all living beings were about to be annihilated, once and for all, in the holocaust. Then Sthāṇu, the Pillar, addressed Brahmā, asking him to show his grace by allowing the threefold universe, past, present, and future, to exist. Brahmā also had appointed Sthāṇu to preside over living beings, and now Sthāṇu asked the creator for a boon. Sthāṇu asked that living creatures might come back into the world for repeated births and repeated deaths. Then Brahmā drew his own fiery energy back within himself and permitted the fire to abate. Brahmā, in his infinite power, decreed that henceforth activity in the outer world (*pravṛtti*) would be followed by withdrawal (*nivṛtti*) in ever-renewed cycles (*MBh*.7, app. 1, no. 8, lines 69-116).

When Brahmā had withdrawn the fire of his fury into himself and let it subside, he granted Śiva's boon of repeated births and deaths. Then, from all the openings of his body, a maiden came out. She was dark and dressed in red (*MBh*.7, app. 1, no. 8, lines 118-19). Her stark colors, black and red (*kṛṣṇa* and *rakta*), resembled those of Rudra's body (*nīla-lohita*) (cf. *BhP*.3.12.7). Brahmā saluted her whom he had summoned in his anger to kill all creatures, fools and sages alike, namely, Death. The lotus-eyed young goddess in her sorrow began to weep as she implored Brahmā to release her from this cruel task that seemed to her to go against cosmic order (*dharma*). She asked for his permission to practice severe austerities. Then she fell silent. Brahmā acquiesced and let her go to practice the severest asceticism for millions and millions of years. Still she could not bring herself to obey Brahmā. The great god then granted her another wish that was in her heart. He reassured her of the righteousness of her assignment, that it was free from inequity. She would be with all creatures and act impartially, impeccably. But she did not agree. Finally Brahmā convinced her that her task was necessary and inevitable, as it conformed with the world order. Shed in compassion, her tears were to become terrible diseases, and people would succumb to them and die at their appointed time. She would send desire and anger together, when the time came for the end of living creatures. This relentless insistence of Brahmā made Death afraid that he would curse her and she agreed to destroy living creatures (*MBh*.7, app. 1, no. 8, lines 120-249). It was not in the power of young, compassionate, and ascetic goddess Death to prevent the pain of the dying and that of the living at their death; and she assumed the cruel task of destroying all their bodies when their time would come.

The death of the body is inevitable. Brahmā had to compel Death herself to accept this stern truth. Without it Brahmā could not have given the boon that Rudra had asked of him—the boon that living creatures may come back into the world for renewed births and repeated deaths. All human beings, at the time of death, go to the other world and then return (*MBh*.12.250.38).

Creation-destruction and then the pause before a new life begins on earth are ordained by Brahmā, but they are willed by Rudra-Śiva, the compassionate, who himself is beyond time, a motionless pillar (Sthāṇu). Śiva, throughout this myth of the introduction of recurrent deaths and renewed lives of man—and of the cosmos—acts as Sthāṇu. Sthāṇu or "pillar" signifies the timeless, motionless state of *samādhi* in which the Lord of Yoga dwells. Himself beyond time, Rudra the Lord in his compassion causes cyclical time to take its course, and alleviate the condition of mortals wherein past, present, and future will now sustain recurrent themes. The pause, the withdrawal from activity (*nivṛtti*) in its quiescence, is a reflex, in and beyond creation, of the Uncreate that is before and above all times and things.

The rupture of the Uncreate marked the beginning of the myth of Rudra. The Creator himself caused the break. Prajāpati let flow into creation some of the precious substance of the plenum, the Uncreate. Rudra, the threatening archer and guardian of the Uncreate, appeared just at the moment when the shedding of the seed could no longer be prevented. The Gandharva Kṛśānu, the archer and guardian of Soma, did no better. His arrow grazed the falcon who had stolen the Soma; it did not stop the bird from bringing the elixir of immortality to mortal man. The falcon lost a feather; it fell, a witness to the failure of Kṛśānu, the archer. The speed of the flight of the falcon, the surging passion and flow of the seed of Prajāpati, and the speed of the discharge of the arrow are embodiments of time that defied the intention of the archers. Time at the inception of Prajāpati's creation was the antagonist of Rudra, the avenger.

When Brahmā's progeny increased out of bounds and he could not regulate its growth, a holocaust seemed the only remedy. The creator in his anger was about to burn his deathless progeny. Its incalculable increase had already overwhelmed the three worlds. Rudra, moved by pity for the victims of Brahmā's unchecked productivity, directed the wrath of Brahmā away from the scheme of destruction, and Brahmā fulfilled the request of Rudra not to let the universe end in an irreparable cataclysm. Brahmā consented to let life go on in living beings to the appointed time, when it would be withdrawn from them; and, after a pause, they would return in other bodies until their time came to leave this world. This movement would go on till doomsday, when the entire universe would be destroyed and lie in dark quiescence until a new aeon would arise in the dawn of a new cosmos. Rudra, the ineffective guardian of the Uncreate, acted as the protector of creation. He unraveled the proliferating mass of Brahmā's helpless progeny by letting the creatures move along the river of time, with its waves surging and subsiding and the lives of the people flowing along through periods of activity and quiescence.

In the beginning, creation came about when Rudra as guardian of the absolute was defeated by time. At that very moment, however, time cooperated with Rudra-Agni, who had prepared the seed that then was flowing into creation. Now, when Brahmā was about to create—and destroy—mortals, different roles were assigned to the actors. The fire of destruction was subdued by Rudra, and time was given a saving dimension by Rudra. Not the flight but the flux of time would carry man through repeated deaths and renewed lives. It is this quality of time that Rudra gave to the world. To allow the renewal of life there must be death at the appointed time, the cyclical rhythm of Rudra's time.

The pathos of dying, however, seized the young goddess Death, who joined Brahmā and Rudra at the moment when the Creator fulfilled Rudra's wish and was about to give effect to it. The dark immaculate maiden was tormented by the pain she would be forced to inflict on mortals. It seemed to her against the order of the cosmos that she should have stepped out into the world from all the openings of Brahmā's sentient body to inflict the suffering of dying. Brahmā, however, was adamant about death's cosmic necessity. Rudra, Brahmā, and the young compassionate and blameless goddess finally cooperated in bringing death into the world. Rudra alloted to death its position in the order of cyclical time. Death would be the open gate through which the current of time would take its course. Brahmā had to be relentless in his insistence on the necessity of death—he knew what the world had been without it. Rudra brought the cyclical sequence of time into the cosmos as a remedy; Brahmā summoned Death from within himself to make the remedy effective, to keep intact the order of the cosmos. But the existence of death required the process of dying and the goddess knew its agony.

The time that Rudra brought into the world is a lived time, inwardly experienced. It came to be when Rudra was moved to pity by the imminence of total extinction. He arrested and distributed it so that it would alternate with life in recurrent rhythms. Rudra's time is a form of his compassion flowing through creation around Sthāṇu's immobile shape.

Among his diverse attempts to create human beings, Brahmā here succeeded with the help of his ascetic son Sthāṇu. Consistent in his stance while seemingly paradoxical in his actions—paradoxical himself already as a motionless pillar in action—Sthāṇu caused the Creator to introduce the renewal of life for his creatures who had been unable to die. Rudra, who had refused to create mortals and thereby bring into the world failure and suffering, had created immortals exempt from both. They were his mind-born sons, exuberant improvisations, arabesques and transmogrifications of the human condition, reflected in the mind of Rudra and agitating a world of freedom. Brahmā's progeny, on the other hand, trod the earth and exceeded the bounds of space and time. The earth was about to be overrun by their throng, and there was no limit to the continuation of such a predicament. The immortality of his crowd was a state of deprivation; mankind lacked death. Brahmā started a holocaust and Sthāṇu, the motionless, moved by pity, diverted the cataclysm. Contrary to his original intention, he cooperated with Brahmā in making bearable the human condition. He did this by offering the prospect of an aeviternal return in accordance with which each death would lead to another life.

Time had been the antagonist of Rudra, who was at the very beginning the hunter and avenger. But for this, the arrow of the hunter would have struck its target as soon as Rudra had noticed the Father's behavior. The union of Father and daughter would have been prevented and no seed would have been shed. In another sense, time cooperated with Agni-Rudra, who had prepared the seed—its purpose being to be shed—whereas time antagonized Rudra. Time interposed itself between the intention of the hunter and his target, and made the arrow hit the target at the most vulnerable moment so that some of the seed was spilled and fell down to the earth. Rudra, guardian of the Uncreate, partakes of its timelessness, but insofar as he played his part, time itself meted out his actions. Time carried his arrow at its own speed, as it did that of Kṛśānu. The guardians of the timeless Uncreate were overtaken by the delaying action of time.

The transition from the Uncreate into creation, from timelessness into time is a danger zone. The wound that Rudra inflicted causes havoc among the gods—from aeon to aeon.

But when Brahmā was about to consume in a holocaust the cosmos he had created, the moment had come for Rudra to confront time and to infuse it with his being.

Although time does not appear as a persona in the myth of the creation of death, its presence lurks in the urgency of the fire of total extinction born of Brahmā's wrath. Sthāṇu, the motionless pillar, moved, although quiescent, by pity for the creatures of Brahmā threatened with total extinction, begs him to grant them renewed life and the activity arising out of and alternating with death and quiescence. For them time will not end with death: they will return after a period of quiescence in a new birth. Time will carry them through repeated births and deaths to the end of the aeon. Rudra's time is a form of the Great God's pity for all creatures. That pity for man is the vehicle by which Sthāṇu diffuses his quiescence into the structure of time. Time will not prolong the lives of men; it will not defer their death. It will bring them back again into a new youth and a life resonant with their past. In time their life will be ready for death—and rebirth. Sthāṇu, out of the quiescence of his stance, prevailed on Brahmā. Death and rebirth thenceforth came to be interwoven in the pattern of time, due to Sthāṇu's compassion for creatures. The paradox of the motionless ascetic withdrawn from the world yet moved by pity for its creatures is resolved by a form of time that carries quiescence in its structure. Sthāṇu will stand by while the perennial renewal of its pattern will cease only at doomsday.

Sthāṇu in his concern for the life of creatures fulfills the hope expressed in the *Mahāmṛtyuñjaya mantra* of Rudra Tryambaka, whose power is over life and death (*RV*.7.59.12; *VS*.3.60; *ŚB*.2.6.2.14). Tryambaka liberates from death when he allows life not to be cut off by it. Sthāṇu gives death its place in the renewal of life, a transpersonal life carrying the here and now in indefinite repetition to quiescence and a new beginning, until the Great God absorbs in his dance of annihilation the uncounted rhythms he has released.

3. Rudra Plunges into the Waters and Castrates Himself

Charged by Brahmā to create living beings, Rudra created immortals of deathless vitality before he turned into a motionless pillar, self-contained in stillness. According to another tradition, however, the Great Yogi carried out Brahmā's command to create living beings by plunging into the water and then by castrating himself when asked to produce creatures (*MBh*.10.17.10-11, 21). Saying at first that he was unable to produce creatures, Rudra plunged into the water (*VrP*.21.6). He practiced *tapas*, austere in creative fervor, over a long time. Rudra, deeply immersed in the water, was absorbed in the task to which he had responded according to his yogic nature, believing that "one without fervent austerities is not able to create creatures" (*VrP*.21.7). Full of expectation, Brahmā waited all that time. Nothing happened, and Brahmā turned to another being whose name was Dakṣa

(*KūP*.1.15.1; *VrP*.21.9). Brahmā made Dakṣa the creator of all living beings. Seeing Rudra immersed in the waters, Dakṣa, his substitute, created living creatures. As soon as they were born, they ran toward him. They were hungry and wanted to devour him. Dakṣa turned to Brahmā to protect him and to assign food for the living creatures. Brahmā gave them herbs and plants, and gave the weaker creatures as food for the stronger. Then the living beings ate and multiplied by mating with their own kind and moved around the world. Brahmā was pleased (*MBh*.10.17.12-20). He had every reason to be pleased. According to the *Śatapatha Brāhmaṇa*, in the beginning Prajāpati, desiring offspring, sacrificed. He was Dakṣa (*ŚB*.2.4.4.1-2). Brahmā, the Purāṇic version of Prajāpati, in creating Dakṣa recreated himself.

At last Rudra rose from the waters and saw the living creation. At the sight he became angry, tore out his phallus and caused it to fall into the ground, since no purpose would be served by it (*MBh*.10.17.20-24). By his ardent exertion he had diffused his splendor into the waters, created the plants and healing herbs for all creatures. The plants would multiply like those whose food they were to be. Without them the living beings would have died. Cheerless and in rage, Rudra went to the foot of Mount Mūjavat to practice asceticism (*MBh*.10.17.25-26).

Rudra is Agni, Fire. He plunged into the waters where life was generated by his heat, by the fervor of his asceticism. The waters are Agni's resting place (*MBh*.13.84.24), his secret refuge when he—like Rudra—is charged at the sacrifice with an onerous task to perform (*RV*.10.51.1).[4] His flight from the sacrifice into the flowing waters is a withdrawal from action, a merging of himself in himself (cf. *MBh*.13.84.24). Agni hides in the waters, but at other times he is seen, a shaft of light from on high speeding to the shiny plane and resting there, the pillar of heaven (*RV*.4.13.5) glowing like the sun. It is the leg of the sun. With its one foot it steps out of the beyond. Thus its name is Aja Ekapād, the uncreate One-Foot (*RV*.2.31.6; 6.50.14; 10.65.13; cf. 1.67.3; 1.164.6; 8.41.10; 10.82.6). The light from on high plunges into the waters—as Rudra did—and shines forth, vibrating from the body of Rudra in solar and lunar rays (cf. *MBh*.7.173.66; cf. *LP*.2.12.7-23). Agni and Aja Ekapād merge the images of their light with that of Rudra. Rudra, who is the very self of

[4] *Ṛg Veda Saṃhitā (RV)*, tr. R.T.H. Griffith, 1973, p. 567.

yoga, is often described in terms of effulgent light (*MBh*.13.17.55, 65, 80). Light is the progenitive power (*TS*.7.1.1.1; *ŚB*.8.7.1.16).[5] Bathed by the water, Rudra, the young ascetic, kindles the waters with his creative fervor (*tapas*), and life stirs in them. Plants grow from the contact. The plants will be the food of living creatures moving about on earth.

When Rudra entered the waters, he was like that great wondrous presence (*yakṣa*) that strode in creative fervor on the crest of the sea (*AV*.10.7.38). That mighty presence was a *brahmacārin*, a consecrated celibate, as Rudra is, young and ardent. Absorbed in creative fervor, the *brahmacārin* stood in the sea, in the ocean. He shone on the earth (*AV*.11.5.26). He glowed with utmost inner exertion, the heat of creation.

Agni in the waters, Aja Ekapād, the uncreate One-Foot, and the young, chaste *brahmacārin* are likenesses of Rudra. In the particular situation of Rudra's taking refuge in the waters, they are identical with him. Agni and the uncreate One-Foot are cosmic figures. The world of man, however, lends the human figure to the *brahmacārin*, a student who fervently exerts himself in mastering, transmuting, and transcending the psycho-physical body. The *brahmacārin* is seen transfigured into a numinous presence, a *yakṣa*.

Rudra had sprung from the wrath of the Creator, from the fury of his frustration; he was meant to create mortals who would propagate. A mind-born son of Brahmā, he was like the others before him, who were sages by birth and had overcome the world as soon as they were born. Rudra, however, sprung from Brahmā's angry mind, was also bid by Brahmā to carry out a task in which Brahmā had failed. Though he was Brahmā's mind-born ascetic son, he accepted the paternal mandate and created life, though not through procreation. He plunged into the water, where the plants derived their nourishment from his presence. They pass it on to man. Rudra is "the food of the living beings everywhere" (*LP*.1.86.92).

Rudra tarried in the water, and once again time was against him, as it was when creation began and the Wild God let his arrow fly too late to prevent the emission of seed by the Father. Again, too late Rudra emerged from the water, only to see the population another had already created.

[5] Cf. M. Eliade, "Spirit, Light and Seed," 1971, p. 3.

In a rage, Rudra rid himself of his phallus, which sank into the ground. Rudra withdrew to the mountains to practice the most arduous *tapas*. Self-castration out of the rage of disappointment was the sequel to the wound Rudra had inflicted on the Father. Rudra had intended to prevent creation by sexual intercourse in which the Father was engaged, but he had not succeeded. Now, charged by Brahmā, his father, with the task of creating living beings who would propagate, Rudra compromised and created vegetation, the food of life. He did not people the world with living and moving creatures. Instead he rid himself in fury of his phallus that now had no purpose, whereas all the while that Rudra was in the water he, in his total being, was the life-giving cosmic phallic power of which the sun-pillar is the figure.

Rudra is that *brahmacārin*, the sun, the vital and vitalizing power in manifestation. The sun itself, however, is but a figure in front of the inexhaustible, unspent source in the beyond. It was the spending of this power that Rudra, the Wild God, avenged. He had acted as its guardian. Rudra, in agreeing to Brahmā's command to create living beings, seemed to evade the task by his plunge into the water, whereas he did cooperate, though he circumvented the implied mode of execution. Rudra is an ascetic according to human standards. But human standards do not apply to the god, who acts in accordance with them merely in order to approach the understanding of man. Rudra is the ascetic who guards the Uncreate and avenges the flowing of its substance into creation. With the primordial shot of his arrow he inserts his fury and his asceticism into the Creator who, as Brahmā, creates mind-born ascetic sons and, paradoxically, delegates the task of creating living beings to one of them, namely, Rudra. Brahmā, injected with Rudra's ascetic nature, assumes the role of his ascetic son, yet disregards the asceticism of Rudra, knowing that Rudra is Fire and had prepared the seed for the Father. Rudra submerged in the waters is the hidden light and fire by which the plants stir into life and become the sustenance of living beings.

Everything alive is dependent on food; it is Rudra, who caused it to be (cf. *LP*.1.86.92-95). Rudra is the fire and the food of life; he is absorbed by and in all creatures.

Emerging from the water and confronted with mankind whom he did not create, his anger flared up. He roared and flames shot forth; ghouls, ghosts, and others appeared (*VrP*.21.25-32). It was an anger of frustration, for creatures had come to exist and multiply while he had been absent preparing the food for them (*MBh*.10.17.20-25). Beneath this anger burned the fiercer rage of revulsion against sexual creation by which mankind had come to multiply. He wanted to do away with this mode of creation in which he had played no part, and rid himself of his procreative organ (*ŚP*, *DhS*.49.82).

Rudra, creative fire, mind-born son of Brahmā, turned away from sexual creation. He did so spectacularly, not calmly, as Brahmā's former mind-born sons had done. He had plunged into the water, then, emerging, severed his phallus out of anger and in revolt against sexual contact, by which mankind in his absence was made by Dakṣa to people the earth. His rage belonged to Rudra the Fire; his revulsion to Rudra the yogi. He left his phallus, which entered the earth (cf. *ŚP*, *DhS*.49.82-83).

As the Fire in the waters, Rudra warmed them to fertility. Vegetation would be their issue on which mankind would subsist, even though Rudra by plunging into the waters had refused to create those for whom this nourishment was intended.

Rudra in the waters evaded sexual procreation. He acted as the mind-born son of Brahmā, issued from the head of the creator as his very life breath. The Father, Prajāpati-Brahmā, had raised his procreative level from his animality at the time when he himself, in the shape of an antelope, had made Rudra the Lord of Animals, Paśupati. Rudra introduced his own yoga nature into the Lord of Generation when he let fly the arrow against the procreative act. Now, Rudra, from the high level of his birth, plunged into the waters. He carried out the command of Brahmā by his own creative, ascetic fervor. Plants resulted from it. As a yogi, Rudra turned away from carnal sex; as Agni, he diffused creative heat in the water until once again time was against him. He tarried a long while, during which Dakṣa brought mankind into being. Then, emerging from the waters, the fire of wrath leapt up in Rudra and he tore out his now useless phallus, having rejected its services when Brahmā had asked for them. The severed phallus fell to the ground—into the lap of the earth. On becoming Sthāṇu, the Great God had discharged into creation the Rudras from within his being. On emerging from the waters, he tore out his phallus. It fell down to the earth, as did the seed of Prajāpati.

Rudra the avenger had hurled the fire arrow of his rage against the Father at the climax of the latter's sexual activity. Rudra injected his own avenging rage into the Father, instilling into Prajāpati the blazing intensity of his own revulsion for the act by which the integrity of the absolute had been ruptured. This revulsion did its work in the Lord of Generation, so that he as Brahmā produced mind-born sons. Rudra, on the other hand, as Brahmā's mind-born son, was charged paradoxically with the task of creating carnal creatures. The other mind-born sons of Brahmā had been true ascetics, and Brahmā did not disturb their way of life. Rudra was more intimately linked with his father than with these single-minded, mind-born sages. Like them he was a yogi; but unlike him, the sages were not Agni the Fire. Rudra's plunge into the waters conformed with Rudra's nature as a yogi and Agni at the same time. As yogi, in the waters he had turned away from carnal creation, but the intensity of his *tapas* glowed in the waters, and life was engendered in them by his mere presence, perfected in calmness. The light that he radiated in the waters was as soft as moonlight. With his auspicious form that is half Soma and half fire, Rudra practiced chastity (*brahmacarya*) (*MBh*.7.173.95-97). Soma, the moon, is the lord of plants (*RV*.10.97.18, 19) that grow in his mild light as it shimmers in the luminosity of Rudra in the water. The rays of sun and moon are his hair. While Rudra remained immersed, time had taken its course on land. When he emerged from the waters his heat flared up in fury, for Brahmā had found another to carry out his task, and the earth teamed with couples and their children. Rudra castrated himself. His severed member fell to the ground.

Rudra, the archer, had aimed at the Father embracing his daughter. They parted when their intercourse was arrested. Rudra, the mind-born son of Brahmā, castrated himself. The coming into existence of mankind was threatened but not prevented by Rudra. His fierceness matched his naked asceticism. Essentially he was the Great Yogi aflame in ardor, adverse to procreation by which Dakṣa, his substitute, peopled this earth. And yet Rudra severed his member only when, after emerging from water, he saw living creatures who had come into existence while he abstained from creating them. No purpose would now have been served by his phallus. What purpose, other than as an instrument to be controlled, had it served for the mind-born yogi from the beginning? Different from the earlier sons of Brahmā, Rudra was not a world-renouncing sage only; he was Fire throughout, in his asceticism and in his rage. In the waters, the intensity of his asceticism was the life-giving fire. Emerging from the water, his rage was now spent against himself, the yogi, whom Brahmā had bypassed in the creation of living beings. It equaled his rage against the Father in sexual embrace, in the process of procreation.

By a fraction of time—which was then just about to begin its course—Rudra failed to prevent the violation of the Uncreate and the creation of living beings, when as a hunter he had attacked the Father. As Brahmā's mind-born son doing *tapas*, he stayed too long immersed in the waters, and the creator bypassed him and appointed a substitute for him who carried out Brahmā's bidding. Time once more seemed to be against Rudra, but time was also his ally, inasmuch as it made Brahmā transfer his mandate to a substitute. This should have been in accord with Rudra's detachment from procreation. Instead, he literally detached, on rising from the waters, his own procreative member. By this act he demonstrated his total detachment, and that he was not moved toward procreation.

The Great God severed his *liṅga* in fury. He severed it because it was the procreative organ. In this action Rudra who is Wrath and Fire prevailed over Rudra, the Lord of Yoga. The severed *liṅga* retained the ambivalence of his two natures. Severed, the *liṅga* fell into the earth, then rose in space, went to the *ākāśa*, where it stood as the endless fire pillar whose beginning and end neither Viṣṇu nor Brahmā could reach (*ŚP, DhS*.49.82-85).

4. The Meetings with Kāvya Uśanas

a. *Uśanas / Śukra, the Seed and Planet*

To the command of Brahmā to create mortals, Rudra, the Lord of Yoga, responded in two ways. In total introversion he turned into a motionless pillar. He became Sthāṇu. Or he plunged into the waters to practice asceticism, and he remained submerged for innumerable years. The glow of his ascetic energy irradiated the waters, and the plants began their life in them. Like the numinous being (*yakṣa*), the *brahmacārin* shining in a shaft of sunlight had entered their glistening plane.

In another myth, Rudra's asceticism in the waters has a different prelude as well as different consequences. Before he entered the waters and stayed absorbed in the most severe austerities for millions of years, Rudra had swallowed the great yogi Bhārgava (*MBh*.12.278.19-27).

All this took place in mythical time, whose duration not only exceeds the years of human reckoning and whose validity is unaffected by time, but also accommodates in its fullness the several myths like islands. Each of the islands observes the time that the course of its myth demands. Each island receives its light from Rudra and reflects it in its own way. The concern is not with when Rudra entered the water, but that he entered it in one situation or the other, either bid by Brahmā to create mortals or when provoked by Bhārgava.

Bhārgava, as the name implies, was descended from Bhṛgu, who was born of a spark from the flaming lake of the semen of Prajāpati (*AB*.3.34; also *MP*.195.7-8). Or, according to another Purāṇic tradition, Bhṛgu was one of the ten mind-born sons of Brahmā (*MP*.3.5-8; *BhP*.3.12.21-22). The proper name of this scion of Bhṛgu is Uśanas, and he is called Kāvya Uśanas on account of his omniscience. It was with Kāvya Uśanas that Indra, king of gods and creator of the cosmos of an earlier aeon, drank Soma, the drink of inspiration and elixir of life, the drink of immortality (*RV*.1.51.11).[6] Kāvya Uśanas also made for Indra the Vajra, his irresistible weapon (*RV*.1.121.12). In fact, by his own might, he made Indra's might (*RV*.1.51.10), for Uśanas gave Indra the great weapon (*RV*.5.34.2). Uśanas, the immensely powerful celestial ṛṣi, friend of Indra (*RV*.6.20.11), left the gods and became the priest of the demons (*MBh*.1.71.6).

Kāvya Uśanas, according to the *Mahābhārata*, was a great yogi, possessed of magic power (*siddhi*) (cf. *MBh*.12.278.16). By its exercise he entered Kubera, lord of the city Alakā in the Himālayas on Mount Kailāsa (*VāP*.47.1), chief of the yakṣas and rākṣasas, who are the genii and goblins, and the lord of treasures. The great ascetic Bhārgava / Kāvya Uśanas by means of yoga entered Kubera and deprived him of his wealth and liberty. Kubera went to the Great God and told him what had happened. Śiva, filled with rage, took up his lance. Uśanas, who had watched from a distance, by his magic placed himself on the tip of Śiva's weapon. Śiva bent it with his hand, and it assumed the shape of a bow, it became Pināka, Śiva's bow. Mahādeva, the Great God, took Uśanas in his hand and with care put Bhārgava into his open mouth, swallowed him, and entered the water. There Śiva stood motionless, absorbed in austerities for millions of years (*MBh*.12.278.7-22). Then he rose from the waters. Brahmā ap-

[6] *Ṛg Veda Saṃhitā (RV)*, tr. R.T.H. Griffith, 1973, p. 34 n. 11.

proached him and enquired about the progress of his austerities. Though Śiva replied that they had been properly observed, he saw that Uśanas, who was in his belly, had waxed in greatness on account of Śiva's own asceticism. Uśanas now began to wander about in Śiva's belly. He sang a hymn of praise to Śiva, for he wanted to get out, but Śiva had closed all the outlets from his body, except the semen passage, and he asked Uśanas to get out that way. Therefore Kāvya Uśanas became Śukra (*MBh*.12.278.23-32). Śukra means "shining," and also "semen." Śukra furthermore is the name of the planet Venus, which he became. Because he came out of the semen passage, he did not reach the center of the firmament (*MBh*.12.278.32). When Śiva saw him emerge from his penis shining with energy, he became angry and wanted to kill him. Umā prevented it, and Śiva let Śukra, the shining planet, go wherever he wanted. Śukra became Umā's son (*MBh*.12.278.33-36).

More is told elsewhere in the *Mahābhārata* and the *Purāṇas* about the relation of Śiva and Uśanas. The *Vāmana Purāṇa* does not favor Uśanas with the privilege of being swallowed by Śiva on this occasion. It describes how the long austerities of Rudra the yogi in the waters shook the universe. Brahmā and the gods, in order to stop the agitation of the cosmos, asked Rudra to terminate his austerities. Rudra rose from the water, but the earth continued to quake. Then Rudra wandered about and saw the ascetic Uśanas practicing austerities on the bank of a river. Rudra asked Uśanas the purpose of his austerities, and Uśanas replied that their purpose was to win from Śiva the spell (*vidyā*) Sañjīvanī that revives the dead. Rudra then gave Uśanas the spell (*VmP*.36.33-43).

Uśanas, the priest of the Asuras, desperately needed this spell because, in the battle between the gods and the demons, the latter were put to flight and their ranks were depleted (*MBh*.1.71.7). The *Matsya Purāṇa* adds that Śiva made Uśanas fulfill a vow in order to obtain the spell. Head down, Uśanas would have to inhale smoke from the sacrificial fire pit for a thousand years. Uśanas fulfilled the vow. Śiva gave him the spell and promised him that he would attain all his goals, but this was to be kept secret. Śiva also gave Uśanas the lordship over creatures and wealth, and made him invincible (*MP*.47.81-126).[7] Uśanas revived the slain Asuras by the spell for instantaneous revival,

[7] Cf. W. D. O'Flaherty, *Hindu Myths: A Sourcebook Translated from the Sanskrit*, 1975, pp. 292, 297 and pp. 337-38 for additional versions and discussions of the myth.

the Sañjīvanī Vidyā. They rose from death and were the same as before (*MBh*.1.71.7-9).

In the Uśanas myth, Rudra in the water is Sthāṇu, the immovable pillar. He is the ascetic absorbed in yoga, the Great God with his trident straight as the pillar. Sthāṇu, however, as occasion demands, actively intervenes in the course of things. He saved the living beings from total extinction and made Brahmā, the Creator, introduce the aeviternal return of life and death into the time structure of the cosmos.

In Śiva's encounter with Kāvya Uśanas, the great yogi and priest of the demons received from Śiva the spell that brings the dead back to life, even though Kāvya Uśanas had put to evil use his own magic power. He had deprived Kubera of his wealth and liberty, and to escape the onslaught of Rudra's weapon had placed himself on its tip. Rudra, the cosmic pillar, bent his lance and it became his bow, Pināka, of which the rainbow is one figure and the vault of the firmament another.

There the planet Śukra has his place. His is not the highest place on the firmament, and the myth explicitly states why Śukra, the planet, in his wanderings cannot reach the highest station (*MBh*.12.278.32). Though close to the sun, as morning star (Lucifer) and as evening star the planet Śukra is not seen in the cosmic North, in the center of the firmament where the sun-pillar—Sthāṇu—meets the sky. Sun and Venus / Śukra are the planetary figures whose positions in the sky illumine the relation of Śukra to Śiva. Among the planets, Śukra's position is lower than Śiva's; Śiva has the sun for his metaphor. Among stars, it is Sirius who represents Rudra. Each of these luminaries in its own light conveys the splendor of Rudra, shining from the sky.

The reason given for Śukra's not attaining the highest position in the sky is that he came out of Śiva's penis, out of the lower part of the body of the god. Similarly, Śukra had to fulfill his vow of smoke inhalation, holding his head down over a pit of fire. He had to learn humility. As priest of the demons, Kāvya Uśanas had fallen from the station that he had held as the power behind Indra, the creator of the cosmos and king of gods.

For a moment Kāvya Uśanas was seen by Rudra on the tip of his trident, but Rudra brought him low even before he let him find his way out of his semen passage.

Uśanas lost the high position among the gods that was his when Indra was the creator, though he retained great power by virtue of yoga. This he proved by entering Kubera, the guardian of Indra's treasure. While in him, Uśanas robbed Kubera of his wealth and will power. Kubera, whose capital, Alakā, is in the north where Śiva dwells on the mountain, sought Śiva's help. As Uśanas had entered Kubera, so Śiva, taking Uśanas into his hand, made him enter his body. There Uśanas dwelt for a long time and grew in might by the asceticism of Rudra. Uśanas had depleted Kubera, whom he had entered, and he grew as a result of Śiva's austerities while he was within the body of Rudra, by whom he had been swallowed.

The attitude of Rudra, Lord of Yogis, toward Uśanas, the great yogi, is ambiguous. Rudra had Uśanas in his power, yet he gave to Uśanas of his own power—only to feel murderous toward him when Śukra / Uśanas emerged shining with energy from Rudra's body.

Kāvya Uśanas, who was the power behind Indra, was overpowered by Rudra. Rudra, within the course of Indian theogony, has taken over many traits of Indra.[8] By swallowing Uśanas, Lord Śiva took into himself the power that was Uśanas's and Indra's. At the same time, the Lord of Yogis communicated his own magic power to Kāvya Uśanas in his belly, thereby increasing the power of his captive. When the latter came out of Rudra's body, the Great God let Śukra / Uśanas go wherever his wanderings as a planet would take him.

The exit of Śukra from the body of Śiva is told differently in the basic myth of Indian architecture (Ch. III.5). Uśanas, the priest of the Asuras (who had been defeated by the gods), sacrificed a goat. When the sweat of his anger fell on the sacrificial animal, it grew to cosmic size and drove the gods from heaven. In order to save them, Śiva let the fire from his third eye pursue Uśanas, who could find no refuge except in Śiva. By his yoga power Uśanas made himself small, entered Śiva's ear, and found refuge in the belly of the god, where he saw the whole universe resting in comfort. Śiva, pleased by the diplomacy of Uśanas, discharged him through his semen (*śukra*) passage and bestowed on him sovereignty as the planet Śukra. At the request of Śukra, the Lord also granted a boon to the defeated goat demon. This goat demon would be given a place of rest on earth, where the gods would reside on its extended shape, in the archetypal plan of every

[8] W. D. O'Flaherty, *Asceticism and Eroticism in the Mythology of Śiva*, 1973, pp. 83-89, discusses the qualities and characteristics that Indra has in common with Śiva, and that the latter inherited from the former.

temple (*ĪPad*.3.26.93-125). The gods were supported by the sacrificial meaning of the goat demon while they held in check its demonic power.

Śiva assigned this residence to the former goat demon and made him protector of the site (*vāstupa*). The prostrate shape of the goat demon, meted out to and occupied by the gods, who took their stations on him, underlies the structured order of the building. Śukra's defeated and pardoned demon lies at the base of sacred architecture here on earth.

Śukra himself, however, having become the seed and son of Śiva, was raised by him to the sky, shining brightly in the firmament as a planet, though this "Lucifer" cannot ever rise to the zenith, the cosmic North, the home of Śiva.

Śiva, by swallowing Uśanas, had taken to himself the ancient power of Indra. Yet, in return, Śiva increased by his asceticism the power of Uśanas, the great yogi, and placed him as planet in the firmament, and on earth Śiva placed the fallen goat demon for temples to rise above it.

More than that, the Lord of Yoga gave to Uśanas the spell for reviving the dead. Uśanas had proved himself worthy to receive it, for he had not only performed world-shaking austerities and kept his "smoke vow," head down, but, in a preceding aeon, he had been Kāvya Uśanas, who had served Soma, the elixir of immortality, to Indra. Now Rudra, who from the beginning had power over life and death, imparted to Uśanas the secret for reviving the dead. It was an application to a demonic purpose of his power over death.

From the beginning, Rudra had power over life and death. He spared the life of Prajāpati and became Paśupati. Although it rested with Rudra Tryambaka to cut short the life of mortals or to let them enjoy its full span, Sthāṇu, withdrawn into himself, projected his energy of withdrawal into a continuum where the activity of life would alternate with quiescence to the end of days. As Tryambaka, Rudra was the lord of time, of living creatures, of the present—in which to cherish past and future. As Sthāṇu, he introduced the aeviternal pattern of renewed life into the fabric of existence. To the priest of the demons, however, Rudra gave the spell for instant restitution of life cut short, a magic remedy against the death of the body and for the survival of the individual as an identical entity in the very same body.

Śiva let dwell on earth the prostrate shape of the goat demon arisen from Bhārgava's sacrifice. He gave to him, assigned to him, the basic position underlying the creative work of the architect. Moreover, he gave to the goat demon one of his own names, and called him Vāstupa.

Kāvya Uśanas, the antagonist and protégé of Rudra, was the power that had incited and driven Indra to the heroic feats by which this creator god established his cosmos. Kāvya Uśanas was a great yogi, who used his power to inspire the Creator himself; he provided weapons to the conqueror of the dragon Vṛtra. When, subsequently, Uśanas became the chief priest of the demons, his sacrificial power in the shape of a goat demon assumed a destructive transcosmic dimension. Śiva subdued the goat demon and gave it the basic position underlying the architecture of the temple in which all the gods have their place.

In Vedic ritual, Śukra's power had its symbol in the Śukra cup (*MS*.4.6.3). As such, "Śukra is the sun" (*TS*.6.4.10.2; *ŚB*.4.2.1.1). While Kāvya Uśanas was with the gods, his sun-power activated their king toward creation. Having left the gods, this mighty yogi, as priest of the demons, is Rudra's antagonist, whom the great god swallows as effortlessly as he bends his lance into the shape of a bow. Once Śiva has drawn Uśanas within himself, the Lord of Yoga, absorbed in austerities, allows his own asceticism to increase the power of his captive antagonist, just as he imparts to Kāvya Uśanas the Sañjīvanī Vidyā. The great god is bounteous to his antagonist, who previously had deprived Kubera, the brother of Śiva, of his strength and treasure.

b. *The Origin of the Knowledge of Reviving the Dead*

Tradition is not unanimous about the origin of the Sañjīvanī Vidyā. The *Mahābhārata* assigns to Uśanas ownership of the spell for reviving the dead (*MBh*.1.71.7-9). Śiva came to know through Nandin, his main attendant, that in the battle between the gods and the demons Uśanas restored the dead demons to life. He did this by means of his Sañjīvanī spell. Śiva ordered Nandin to bring Uśanas to him, and he swallowed the latter. The gods became victorious, since the fallen demons were not restored to life while Uśanas was in the belly of Śiva. When Śukra came out from Śiva's penis, Śiva made him his son (*VmP*.43.1-42). Śukra, in this version of the myth, himself possessed the power or spell for reviving the dead. The memory of the ancient life-giving sun power of Kāvya Uśanas / Śukra survives in this tradition.

Kāvya Uśanas, throughout his checkered career, retained his original character, though his pristine might declined into magic. He was the life-giving power and, as such, he came to play the role of Śukra or semen, the seed of life. The semen that was emitted by Śiva, however, was not his own seed; he allowed Kāvya Uśanas to appear as his seed, and when the latter came out shining, Rudra became angry (cf. *MBh*.12.278.33-36). Śukra, because of his past when he was the sun, was qualified to appear as Rudra's semen. Rudra did not shed his own seed, since this would have gone against his *brahmacarya*. Nevertheless, by granting permission to Uśanas—waxed in greatness by Śiva's yoga—to emerge by way of his semen passage and no other opening of his body, Rudra made the image of the pillar of containment appear as that of the shedder of seed.

Rudra's sojourn in the water had widely different consequences. When he had emerged with the intention of creating mortals and saw that this had been accomplished by Dakṣa, Rudra in fury castrated himself. When Rudra emerged with Kāvya Uśanas in his belly, seed was shed, and a star began to shine in the firmament as Śiva's son.

Ekavrātya, the Sole Vrātya, who is Rudra, took to himself a bow. It was Indra's (*AV*.15.1.6). With it he took from Indra all that the bow encompassed—the wide earth under the vault of the sky. He became its ruler: Īśāna, the Lord. When Uśanas, with deft wit, escaped being attacked by Rudra and settled himself on the tip of the lance of the Great God, he at once found himself on Rudra's bow, into which shape the latter had bent his weapon. Prognostically, Uśanas found his place on the arc of the firmament, a position he was to occupy when Rudra, after gently having put him into his mouth, let him wander in his body and leave his belly as Śukra, the planet. In between the swallowing and the emission, Uśanas had waxed in might. He was strong through his ancient Soma-Vajra power, which Rudra further increased by his asceticism. As Rudra had taken up the bow of Indra, so Uśanas held within himself the might of Indra. Rudra incorporated that ancient power—and discharged it to shine from the sky.

The encounters of Rudra with Kāvya Uśanas are multifaceted, ambivalent events. They do not lie within the main direction that extends from the beyond through the Father-Prajāpati-Brahmā to Śiva, but are linked to it where Rudra plunges into the water. Thence a road opens on which Kāvya Uśanas traveled, where he met Kubera, after a long journey from the world of Indra. When Uśanas found himself trapped in the body of Śiva, he grew in power through Rudra's austerities in the water. Brahmā was interested in the outcome of those austerities. He solicitously inquired about their success, and was reassured by Rudra (*MBh*.12.278.23-24). The power and glory of Indra had been incorporated in Rudra, and Śukra arose shining in that world. But the power of Uśanas had also increased through Rudra's yoga while Uśanas was in Rudra's belly (*MBh*.12.278.25-28).

The transfer of the kingdom of one god to another was conducted without bloodshed. It merely caused Rudra some passing anger. At his birth Rudra, the Great God, had been established in and as the cosmos by Prajāpati, his father, who gave him his names and domains. This was the beginning of Rudra's cosmos. His was not the first cosmos to come into existence. Indra, king of gods, had established an earlier aeon when he killed Vṛtra, the precosmic serpent, who at that time was the guardian of the Uncreate. Indra received his inspiration and energy for the fight with the dragon from Kāvya Uśanas, who gave him his weapon. Indra, moreover, had killed his father and made his mother a widow (*RV*.4.18.12) before he became king of gods. By incorporating within his body Kāvya Uśanas, Rudra incorporated the kingdom of Indra within his realm. The only casualty in this theomachy was Rudra's lance. Even so it did not break; it bent and vaulted over Rudra's world. The world of Indra and Kāvya Uśanas had heroes for gods. They fought armed with weapons and wit to release the waters of heaven and the sun, which Vṛtra kept imprisoned in the Uncreate. The task before Indra and Kāvya Uśanas was clear and, for all its difficulties, simple. Vṛtra, the guardian of the Uncreate, was the enemy. Indra fought Vṛtra in order to bring into existence the manifest cosmos. Indra killed his father right at the beginning. He then had no rival, and he had made a clean break with the past.

Before he was born into his world, Rudra was not a warrior. Though he was an archer, he was essentially a hunter and, like Vṛtra, a guardian of the Uncreate. He observed *brahmacarya*. He lashed out in fiery rage when he saw the Father shed his seed.

The story has here been told how, eventually, Rudra was born; how he assumed the state of being born as his manifest form, which subsumed his primordial appearance as a hunter. He became the cosmos and remained the archer, the guardian of the Uncreate and the avenger of its violation by the Father. After his birth from Brahmā, Rudra did not sever the bond with his father. It was elastic and tenacious. Rudra neither broke it nor did he annihilate the Father; though he killed him, he brought him back to life (*SkP*.3.1.40.16, 36-42). When the Father asked Rudra to create mortals, Rudra showed himself as Sthāṇu, withdrawn into himself by his asceticism. Or he plunged into the water and created the plants. Or, standing as Sthāṇu in the waters, by way of his asceticism he made Uśanas in his belly wax in power. Rudra had swallowed the ancient, heroic cosmos. Śukra was to rise as the morning star of Rudra's cosmos. It is the cosmos of the Great God who dwells in it, and, while he is its Lord, he remains the guardian of the Uncreate, whereas Vṛtra, killed once and for all by Indra, lies at the bottom of the waters, which flow over his dead body.

c. *Kāvya Uśanas and the Fallen Titans*

Mythologically, the figure of Kāvya Uśanas links the cosmos of Indra with that of Rudra. Cosmologically, it links the worlds of the gods and the Asuras, who became demons. The encounter between Rudra and Kāvya Uśanas took place late in the career of the ancient sage. Kāvya Uśanas drank Soma with Indra (*RV*.1.51.11). Indra needed Soma. As soon as he was born, he drank it in his father's house (*RV*.3.48.2). Gods such as Viṣṇu, the Maruts, or Trita Āptya treated Indra to this drink of immortality (*RV*.8.12.16). Originally Soma was in Vṛtra (*RV*.10.124.4-6).[9] There lay its source in the days before creation.

Before Indra created the cosmos, Vṛtra had withheld the waters and the light, the flowing light of the godhead. He also held captive the ancient gods, Agni, Soma, and Varuṇa. Indra asked Agni, Soma, and Varuṇa to emerge and leave Vṛtra's darkness: "The rule has changed. . . . The Asuras lost their power" (*RV*.10.124.1-5). The Asuras were the Titans, the ancient gods, before Indra's rule. Soma, Agni, and Varuṇa were Titans who went over to Indra and became gods.

Kāvya Uśanas / Śukra was the priest of these gods. In that capacity, Kāvya Uśanas "made Indra's might" (*RV*.1.51.10). The Asuras who left Vṛtra, joined Indra and became gods of his cosmos. The other

[9] Cf. A. Bergaigne, *La Religion védique*, 3:145-49; *Ṛg Veda Saṃhitā (RV)*, tr. K. F. Geldner, 1951, 3:354.

Titans stayed in darkness; they fell, when Vṛtra died, into the netherworld, where they retained their name of Asura. As denizens of the netherworld their position, however, was that of demons.

In the *Ṛg Veda*, Śukra was with the gods, and judging by his actions and importance he seemed to be Indra's elder, the guru of the younger god in his new world. In the *Brāhmaṇas*, however, Śukra was the priest of the demons (*JB*.1.125). Nonetheless, he went back from the demons to the gods: the gods won him over with wishing cows (*TmB*.7.5.20). When he was the guru of the gods he received great wealth from the Asuras (*BŚS*.18.47). Wealth attracted Kāvya Uśanas. He entered Kubera, the god of riches, and stole his wealth. This infuriated Śiva (*MBh*.12.278.7-13).

The riches of Kubera, the great weapons that Śukra possessed, and the wealth that he received from the Asuras were of a special kind. They were treasures akin to Soma, a wealth not to be hoarded, a magic, potent wealth to be used. This wealth constituted a body of knowledge of which the Sañjīvanī Vidyā, the science of resuscitation or the spell for reviving the dead, was part. Śukra was said to be the only one who had this power (*MBh*.1.71.7-9), though it was said much earlier, in the *Śatapatha Brāhmaṇa*, that the gods resuscitated those slain in battle by means of a sacrifice to the Fathers (*ŚB*.2.6.1.1). Apparently, the sacrifice to the Fathers was effective on that particular occasion, though one does not hear that the gods used it for this purpose at any other time; they would have been badly in need of the Sañjīvanī Vidyā during their perpetual war with the demons. Rudra did not impart this Vidyā to the gods; he reserved it for Uśanas.

Śukra employed the science of resuscitation only for the benefit of the demons. He brought back to life the demons who had fallen in battle, and he kept their ranks at an even strength (*VmP*.43.1-8). However, Śukra himself did not hesitate to leave the demons and go over to the gods when things were going badly for the demons. Śukra deserted them and joined the gods, who were powerful at that moment. The demons had to confine themselves to the netherworld. Soon, however, Śukra, feeling sorry for them, returned and assured them of his help. As only a few of them were left, he asked them not to continue the fight and to practice asceticism. Surprisingly, he said he would go to Śiva to acquire the spells for victory (*MP*.47.61-80; *PP*.5.13.204-17).

Śukra received the spell from Śiva (*VmP*.36.33-43). This happened when the demon kings Hiraṇyakaśipu (Gold Cloth) and Bali were ruling (cf. *MP*.47.34-39).

Later on, when Andhaka became the king of the demons, Śukra successfully applied his knowledge of revival to those fallen in battle. However, Nandin, Śiva's chief of gaṇas, informed Śiva of Śukra's Vidyā. Śiva ordered Nandin to seize Śukra; he did so, and presented him to Śiva. Thereupon Śiva threw Śukra into his mouth. Śukra wandered through Śiva's belly, where he roamed through the entire cosmos contained therein. Tiring of this experience, he clamored to be let out of the body of Śiva. The Great God complied, let Śukra out through the semen passage and declared him to be his son (cf. Ch. VI.4.a). Śukra returned to the army of the demons (*VmP*.43.1-44).

The movement of Śukra from the demons to the gods and back again was a continuation of his original descent from the Asuras as Titans and gods to the Asuras who had become demons. The first descent of Śukra made possible his freedom of movement between the two worlds, that of the gods and that of the demons, whose realms, after the fall of the Titans, had become separated and were as far apart as heaven and the netherworld. For this reason it was said that the wise Śukra became the guru of both the demons and the gods (*MBh*.1.60.40-42).

Śukra was originally the priest of the Titans, the Asuras. When Soma, Agni, and Varuṇa, these mighty Asuras, followed the change of rule, left Vṛtra, and followed Indra, the Ṛṣi Śukra went with these gods, who had been Asuras. When with the death of Vṛtra the Titans fell, Śukra again became their guru. For a short while he went back to the gods; he was a seer, and Siddha, a magician, wise and crafty, and he soon returned to the demons. Śukra exercised the power of resuscitation only for the sake of the demons. Like Soma, the elixir of immortality, the Sañjīvanī Vidyā was secret knowledge. Essentially it belonged to the Asuras.

Uśanas put into practice a power that before creation had rested in the unknowable mystery of life-to-be that filled the Uncreate. Rudra, in the beginning of things, meant to preserve its integrity. Śukra, the priest of the Asuras, however, put to work some of the power that had lain in the Uncreate. The Asuras, when fallen, benefitted by Śukra's power of resuscitation.

Surprisingly, Śukra did not practice this power at every occasion that called for it. When the ranks of the demons fighting against the gods were depleted, Śukra asked them to stop fighting. He went to Śiva and acquired the charms necessary for victory. Śiva made Śukra perform the smoke vow and granted him all the boons. Obviously Śukra, at that time, did not have the power to resuscitate the demons. He asked them to stop fighting. He expected to receive the spells from Śiva. While it was certain that Śukra would succeed in winning this boon from Śiva, the lord over life and death, it was equally clear that Śukra could no longer rely on his own power. The rule had changed once more since the time when some of the Titans had become gods and the others had become demons. Śiva had become Mahādeva, the Great God who had every power.

The encounters of Śiva with Kāvya Uśanas were of two kinds. From one of them Śukra emerged as Śiva's son and as a planet. In the other, he had, at Śiva's bidding, to perform the smoke vow before Śiva granted him the knowledge for reviving the dead.

Śukra having received it and used it to the detriment of the gods, Nandin, foremost of Śiva's gaṇas, represented to Śiva that the revivification of the dead demons was intolerable (*VmP*.43.10). Nandin resented Śukra's power—unaware that it was given to him by Śiva. Nandin spoke of it as if it had been Śukra's very own.

Indeed, Uśanas alone had the power of resuscitation (*MBh*.1.71.7-9). When this mighty magician and priest of the demons encountered Śiva, Śiva swallowed him. Together with his magic power, Uśanas was kept within Śiva practicing *tapas*, and Uśanas waxed in power through Śiva's austerities. A reciprocal increase of power resulted from Uśanas's stay in Śiva's body, and the Sañjīvanī Vidyā became Śiva's secret.

Its power was not integral to Śiva. He gave (back) to Uśanas the Sañjīvanī Vidyā; he even gave him the lordship over creatures and made him invincible, the glory of conquering all the gods would be Uśanas's (*MP*.47.123-126; 249.4-6). Thus Śiva, in the battle of the gods and the demons, helped the demons who, though fallen, had been Asuras, the powers before the cosmos was created by Indra.

5. The Swallowing of the World Poison

The gods did not do well in their fight with the demons, whose strength persisted undiminished due to the magic spell for resuscitating those who had fallen in battle that Kāvya Uśanas had received from Śiva. The worried gods asked Brahmā for his advice, and he counseled them to cooperate with, rather than fight, the demons. The gods thereupon suggested to the demons that together they should churn the ocean for *amṛta*, the elixir of immortality (*MP*.249.3-22). This proposal appealed to the demons, because by winning *amṛta* and drinking it they would save themselves from being killed in battle. This was preferable to being resuscitated by the Sañjīvanī Vidyā.

Accordingly, the demons and the gods churned the ocean. Their churning stick was the mountain Mandara. The cosmic serpent Ananta uprooted the mountain with all its trees and creepers. Indra fastened the tip of the mountain on the back of the king of tortoises. The serpent Vāsuki was the rope. As the gods and demons began the churn, the gods held Vāsuki by the tail, the demons clutched him by the head. Fire and smoke arose from his mouth and turned into clouds and lightning. Then a thunderous noise came from the whirlpool of the deep as the trees crashed from the revolving mountain. Fire broke out from their friction, killing the forest animals and those under water, while the resins of the trees and the juices of the plants exuded into the ocean and mixed with its waters. After churning for a long time, the gods and demons became tired. However, the god Viṣṇu-Nārāyaṇa gave them strength, and they stirred the ocean with renewed vigor (*MBh*.1.16.6-32; cf. *MP*.249.23-82).

Then wonderful things arose from the ocean: the moon and the sun, Śrī (the goddess Luck), the Kaustubha gem of Viṣṇu, and other treasures, one after another (*MBh*.1.16.33-36; *MP*.250.1-5).

The churning went on with great vehemence, as the gods and the demons were avid for ambrosia. A burning mass of poison, the terrible Kālakūṭa, came out of the ocean. It blazed with venomous fumes, which asphyxiated the triple world. Entranced, the hallowed Great Lord Mantramūrti, "Form-of-mantra," at the request of Brahmā and in order to protect everyone, swallowed the poison. He held it in his throat. The Kālakūṭa poison left a dark blue mark forever on Śiva's throat (*MP*.250.14-61). From that time he was called Nīlakaṇṭha, the Blue-throated (*MBh*.1.16.38N, insert 274, lines 5-7). When Brahmā saw the blue lotus-like throat of Śiva that looked as though a serpent, as though Takṣaka—the king of serpents—was licking it, he exclaimed: "O Śiva, you look beautiful with this throat" (*VāP*.54.91-92; cf. *MSt*.14). Although the dark Kālakūṭa poison burned like the doomsday fire (*VāP*.54.85-87), it did not harm Mantramūrti, the

Great Lord, who held it in his throat, where the center of purity (*viśuddha cakra*)[10] is situated, and whence the Word which is the body of the universe becomes manifest. The poison did not stain this subtle center in Śiva's body. It left a blue mark (cf. *SkP*.5.2.14.9) on the throat of the god, by which he is recognized as the liberator from death and destruction.

At another occasion he had drunk poison with a long-haired muni in ecstasy. The effect of the drink had carried Keśin in timeless transport across celestial fields, whereas Śiva absorbed within himself the Kālakūṭa poison. By drinking the Kālakūṭa poison, Rudra conquered its deadly power. As Mṛtyuñjaya, the conqueror of death (*SkP*. 1.1.10.68), he reabsorbed into himself its deadly darkness (*kāla*), the destruction of phenomenal existence. The gods said to Śiva, "we strove for *amṛta*, for immortality, but found death" (*SkP*.5.2.14.5); and they confessed that they had churned the ocean out of greed (*SkP*.5.2.14.6). In their distress they declared that they should be blamed. Their greed had turned into poison. When Śiva heard the confession of the gods, he was moved by compassion and drank the great, terrible dark poison (*SkP*.5.2.14.9).

The Kālakūṭa poison was a mass compacted of agony and greed. As it rose from the churn it broke out in flames; "by the anger of Rudra, by the fire of Kālakūṭa the universe was burned to ashes" (*SkP*.1.1.10.1, 3). The black mass of agony and greed flamed up as the anger of Rudra, threatening or consuming the universe. The Great Lord swallowed it all and took back into himself the fire of his anger as, on another occasion, moved by compassion, he had made Brahmā take back into himself his fiery energy by which the Creator had threatened to destroy all that he had created. Brahmā complied, and out of all the pores of his body came Death, the young, dark goddess. Śiva swallowed the flaming Kālakūṭa and held it in his throat, which it beautified with the color of the peacock (*SkP*.5.2.14.9).

Now the churning could continue. Further treasures came up and, at last, the gods and demons churned up *amṛta*. It rose in a white vessel held by Dhanvantari, the physician of the gods (*MBh*.1.16.37; *MP*.251.5-6). Dhanvantari here appears playing the role of the healer, which formerly belonged to Rudra (Ch. II.3). The hallowed

[10] The *viśuddha cakra* is the fifth in ascending order of the six centers of subtle energy within the human body. Meditating on it, the yogi realizes the secret meaning of the four Vedas (Cf. *ŚS*.5.90-91).

Mantramūrti saved the gods and the demons from death, so that Dhanvantari could come with the coveted ambrosia. It brought no happiness. Strife over the *amṛta*, cunning, and deception broke out between the gods and the demons. It all ended with a tumultuous battle. The gods won the *amṛta* and deposited this elixir of deathlessness with Viṣṇu for safekeeping (*MBh*.1.16.38-40; 1.17.1-30; *MP*.251.5-36).

Śiva saved the cosmos from destruction by swallowing the Kālakūṭa poison—also called Halāhala—compacted of poisonous greed and the agonies caused by it, and blazing with angry flames. Greed and pain formed the vicious poison that burst into choking fumes and flames; the latter are the anger of the Great Lord. The anger of Rudra was not directed in particular against the greedy gods; it was all-consuming, and, when the gods admitted their greed, the Great Lord was moved to compassion. The formation of the Kālakūṭa poison out of greed and suffering was due to a natural process that led to catastrophe. Through the intercession of Rudra it was avoided. Mantramūrti swallowed the whole of it and became Nīlakaṇṭha of sinister beauty, with his dark blue throat.

While the blessed Lord in trance, as Mantramūrti, swallowed the world poison and became Nīlakaṇṭha, he remained what he had been from the beginning. Manyu, "Wrath," is one of Rudra's names (*BhP*.3.12.12), and denotes that part of his being that consumes the cosmos. Out of compassion the Lord took the fire of the poison—the fire of wrath—back into himself. The Great Yogi held it in his throat.

After Śiva had drunk the flaming poison that had threatened to destroy everything living, Lord Nīlakaṇṭha went back to his cave in Mount Meru, the world mountain. The sages who had assembled there bowed to the Lord and lauded him who had swallowed Kālakūṭa and allayed the cosmic turmoil. But Nīla-Lohita, the blue-red god, smilingly disparaged his conquest of Kālakūṭa, since there was yet another and more terrible poison. Kālakūṭa was no poison at all when compared to mundane existence. This is the real poison, consisting of desire and attachment. This poison is overcome by detachment and withdrawal. These, more arduous than the swallowing of Kālakūṭa, liberate and set free (cf. *LP*.1.86.4-20). The greed of the gods and demons for immortality was but a special form of desire and attachment.

To Śiva, the Lord of Yoga, the conquest of death counted for less than the conquest of passion and delusion, and the Great God smiled in the knowledge that in the end his fire would burn the universe to ashes. Then, toward the end of the cosmic night of dissolution, his fire would rise as a pillar of flames.

In the churning of the ocean, Śiva acted for the sake of gods, men, and demons. Gods and demons cooperated, a rare occurrence brought about by the common purpose of the winning of ambrosia, the nectar of immortality (*R*.1.44.14-16). It was a joint endeavor, and had been going on for some time before the help of Śiva was invoked by Brahmā as the leader of all the gods (*MP*.250.27), or, according to another version, by Viṣṇu (*R*.1, app. 1, no. 8, lines 8-12).

The version of this myth (*MP*.249-251) already considered, and first narrated in the *Mahābhārata* (*MBh*.1.16-17), is not the only one. Another version, first recounted in the *Rāmāyaṇa*, relates that the poison arose first, and it was only after Lord Śiva swallowed the deadly stuff that the treasures arose from the ocean. The poison, moreover, did not come up from the waters directly: it was venom vomited by the serpent king Vāsuki after he let himself be used as the churning rope for a thousand years (*R*.1, app. 1, no. 8, lines 1-3). He had become weary and angered by the seemingly endless double pull of the gods, who held his tail, and the demons who pulled from the front. These positions had been assigned to them by Kṛṣṇa, the avatar of Viṣṇu. The demons, thinking they had been given preferential treatment, were, in fact, scorched by the flames issuing from the mouth of Vāsuki. On the advice of Viṣṇu, the gods and demons threw herbs and medicinal plants into the ocean to invigorate its waters so that they would yield *amṛta*. Viṣṇu saw to it that the gods and demons cooperated in their shared venture to acquire the elixir of immortality. However, while Viṣṇu promised an equal portion to each of the parties, he knowingly deceived the demons, from whom he withheld the precious draught (*VP*.1.9.82-109; *BhP*.8.9.1-13).

In the myth, as told in the *Viṣṇu Purāṇa*, the deceit of Viṣṇu pervades the ambience of the churning of the ocean. In it Viṣṇu literally carried great weight: the cosmic mountain, Mandara, used as a churning stick, rested on a tortoise, which was Viṣṇu himself in one of his animal avatars. Moreover, Viṣṇu was also enthroned on the summit of the mountain; he occupied the pivotal position (*VP*.1.9.88-90).

When Vāsuki struck his teeth on the rocks, he vomited the frightful Halāhala poison, which burned the entire world. The gods could not bear it and approached Viṣṇu. Viṣṇu invoked Śiva, the Great God. Because Śiva is the foremost of the gods, he must receive what was first produced by the churning of the ocean; he must accept the venom as the gift of the first fruit. The blessed Lord Śiva, moved by the distress of the gods and by the words of Viṣṇu, drank the Halāhala poison as though it were *amṛta*, and then departed (*R.*1, app. 1, no. 8, lines 1-16).

Viṣṇu, in the myth as told in the *Rāmāyaṇa*, acted in character with his multiple role as portrayed in the *Viṣṇu Purāṇa.* His invocation of Śiva bristled with irony. Lord Śiva, however, moved by the plight of the gods and by the truth that the words of Viṣṇu conveyed, ignoring their irony, drank the Halāhala poison—the venom of the serpent. Śiva took it into himself with the grace that is his as a dancer, as the Great Yogi, and as the compassionate Lord.

The churning of the ocean, *samudra-manthana*, a multilayered myth, is based on the diurnal annual cyclical movement of the sun. Its rising and setting was seen as due to a churning of heaven and earth. In the *Ṛg Veda*, the churning was the work of the Aśvins (*RV.*10.24.4). These celestials, who, like Rudra, were healers, agitated the cosmic tree in opposite directions in order to liberate Saptavadhri (*RV.*5.78.6), a personification of the celestial fire.[11]

The churning of the cosmic ocean had the mountain rather than the tree as its pivot, and the labor of the two Aśvins of an earlier time was performed by the gods and the demons; their churning rod was the cosmic serpent. They pulled it this way and that way. The position of Viṣṇu was pivotal; he was the fundament and crown of the churning stick. When the churning was about to lead to a catastrophe, Viṣṇu or Brahmā sought the help of Lord Śiva on behalf of the gods.

In the narrative of the *Viṣṇu Purāṇa*, where Viṣṇu was present in his shape of the tortoise and was also enthroned on the crest of Mount Mandara, no appeal was made to Śiva to save the world from destruction by the Kālakūṭa poison. In this version of the churning of the ocean, Śiva did not figure as the savior from the deadly Halāhala poison. The poison risen from the ocean was taken possession of by the Nāgas, the serpent gods (*VP.*1.9.97). Lord Śiva had no part in its disposal. He did not swallow the burning, deadly, black poison. Just before the appearance of the Kālakūṭa, he took to himself one of the

[11] Cf. A. Bergaigne, *La Religion védique*, 2:467.

treasures, the cool-rayed moon, as soon as it emerged from the waters (*VP*.1.9.97). Ever since, Lord Śiva has carried the crescent moon in his matted hair. Its delicate arc is said to be the sixteenth segment of the moon. Eternal and immovable, it governs and stands above the alternating succession of the white and black fortnights, a symbol of consciousness that contains the ideas of all that will be.[12]

This lovely ornament, the moon, with its cool rays, and holding in its cup Soma, the elixir of life, was all that Śiva took from the cosmic ocean in the myth as told in the *Viṣṇu Purāṇa*. There, no beautiful blue mark was left on the throat of the Great God. The poison was taken care of by the serpents, the Nāgas; their king Vāsuki had spat it into the ocean.

The world poison made its appearance in the Kṛta Yuga, the first and—not so—"Perfect Age." Later on, the blue-throated Lord was seen by people engaged in their daily pursuits. The herdsmen and the women saw him as they carried home water from pond or well. They saw the Great, formidable, God, the Savior, who had averted a premature destruction of the cosmos. They recognized him by the blue mark imprinted on his throat by the world poison.

Tradition is not unanimous as to whether the deadly venom appeared first when gods and demons had begun to churn the ocean for *amṛta*, or whether the serpent threw it up after having been pulled back and forth as a churning rope. Formed by greed and deceit, the world poison rose from the cosmic ocean in the first, the Perfect, age, threatened the destruction of the cosmos, and was consumed by Śiva, the destroyer of destruction, the Lord of Yoga, whose throat it beautified and whose body it did not harm. Or the poison Kālakūṭa stayed with the Nāgas, the serpents, the owners of treasure.

The name Kālakūṭa has two literal meanings: "black (*kāla*) mass (*kūṭa*)" and also "time (*kāla*) puzzle (*kūṭa*)." Both are simultaneously valid; the first hints at the dark secret of the other. Its darkness is that of death (cf. *SkP*.1.1.10.68). The gods saw clearly that, while they had been churning for immortality, they had also churned up death.

Śiva Nīlakaṇṭha, who swallowed the world poison in the first world age, the Kṛta Yuga, was but another form of Śiva Mahākāla, who will consume the time-world at the end of days. The gods spoke in human metaphors of emotion and conscience. In cosmic terms, however,

[12] Cf. G. Tucci, *The Theory and Practice of the Maṇḍala*, 1961, p. 12.

they had participated in and witnessed the commotion called Time, signaled in the first world age by the lights of heaven, by day and night. Time enveloped them like an all-consuming, deadly fire that had issued from the churning. Time, Kāla, was the world poison. Śiva, the Great Yogi, swallowed this venom unharmed. It marked his throat with sinister peacock beauty, dark blue, as if a serpent had kissed it.

VII

LIṄGA

1. The Falling of the *Liṅga* in the Deodar Forest

At the churning of the ocean, when the Kālakūṭa poison, dark and flaming, rose from the water and Śiva swallowed it, a mark of somber beauty was left on his throat. The moment of the rising of the poison from the waters was a portentous one; it marked the transition from potentiality to act. Formed in the waters, the poison coagulated under the violence of the avidity of the churning gods and demons; a glistening, viscous lump surged and, with its flames, engulfed heaven and earth. This was the anger itself of Rudra.

When Rudra emerged from the waters into which he had plunged in response to the command of Brahmā, his anger rose when he saw this command executed by another, by Dakṣa. In fury he tore off his phallus, drawing the extreme consequence of his asceticism (*MBh.* 10.17.10-23). Śiva practiced asceticism while under water; when he emerged he acted as the destroyer (cf. *MBh.*7.173.97-99), his hair "red as the rays of newborn sun, / like flame arising from the ripened heat / of his ascetic trance"[1] (*Subh.*4.26). The god cast his *liṅga* on earth, and the earth received it as she had received the semen of Prajāpati.

In the beginning, Rudra violated the procreative act of the Father. Now he did violence to his own procreative member, the target of the anger that Dakṣa had provoked. From this moment, Dakṣa became the antagonist of Rudra, who henceforth was confronted with two procreative figures against whose existence he played his consistent

[1] D.H.H. Ingalls, tr., *An Anthology of Sanskrit Court Poetry: Vidyākara's "Subhāṣitaratnakoṣa,"* 1965, p. 79.

roles. However, not Dakṣa but Rudra's own phallus was the immediate victim of the rage that inflamed his ascetic nature (*MBh*.10.17.20-24). At this extreme moment, Rudra no longer observed the vow of *brahmacarya*. He severed its instrument, and this was not the only time that the *liṅga* of the Great God, the Lord of Yoga, was severed. The *liṅga* was torn off another time and fell on the earth in the forest of Deodar trees. The body and the life of Śiva are only metaphors. Although anthropomorphic references bring the god nearer to human understanding, that likeness to man does not limit him by contingencies of body or time or the imperfections of the human condition.

Tradition is not unanimous on how and when the Lord came to the forest of Deodar trees. Deodar literally means "God wood." God Agni, the Fire, on becoming the priest of the gods, shook off his body. His bones became the Deodar tree (*BD*.7.75-78). A hidden fire burnt within and sustained the mighty evergreen trees in the forest where the *liṅga* of the Lord fell.

In this retreat, sages, with their families lived the life of recluses, observing the established rites. The peace of the hermitage was interrupted when a young stranger appeared on the scene, a naked yogi smeared with ashes, holding out his begging bowl for alms. Irresistibly fascinated, the wives and daughters of the ṛṣis rushed to bring him fruits and other food (*KūP*.2.37.1-13; *VmP*, *SM*.22.53-58; *ŚP*.4.12.9-11). He excited them so much that they were beside themselves. His attraction was such that he seemed extraordinarily handsome (*VmP*, *SM*.22.59-61; *LP*.1.29.10) or, on the contrary, he looked horrible with terrific, painted teeth (*BP*.1.2.27.11). "His penis and testicles were like red chalk, the tip ornamented with black and white chalk" (*BP*.1.2.27.12).[2] The Purāṇic descriptions suggest one who seemed to observe dreadful vows and practices. Yet, the wives and daughters of the sages were driven mad with passion. They took hold of his hands, embraced him and lost all self-control (*ŚP*.4.12.12-13). They had always been exemplary in their way of life, but now they knew no restraint. Their hair disheveled, shedding their ornaments and clothes (*KūP*.2.37.14-15), they could not tear themselves away from the intruder. Sometimes he laughed, sang, and danced beautifully; sometimes he roared repeatedly (*BP*.1.2.27.13); he was naked, his hair was

[2] W. D. O'Flaherty, *Hindu Myths: A Sourcebook Translated from the Sanskrit*, p. 142.

horripilating, his penis large (*MBh*.13, app. 1, no. 4, lines 66-67). In this manner he sported with the wives and the daughters of the sages.

The ṛṣis, bewildered, pained, and infuriated, asked the strange mendicant his name. He remained silent. Outraged and stupefied, the sages did not recognize him (*ŚP*,*JS*.42.13-15).

Some say that the sages pulled out his phallus (*VmP*, *SM*.22.68), others that they made it fall by their curse (*VmP*.6.65; *ŚP*.4.12.17; *ŚP*, *JS*.42.16), still others that they ordered him to castrate himself (*KūP*.2.37.38-41; cf. *SkP*.6.1.20). But it is also said that only he could do so (*BP*.1.2.27.30-33).

The sages had been stupefied and deluded for their own good by Śiva's power of illusion (*māyā*) (cf. *ŚP*.4.12.11). He put them to the test, and they did not recognize him. In one version of the story found in the *Vāmana Purāṇa*, his visit to the hermitage in the Deodar forest was an act of grace at Umā's request (*VmP*, *SM*.22.45-52). The sages were ascetics only because they observed established conventions. They failed when the Lord tested them with his outrageous ways and inner calm. But the women were fascinated; they were drawn to him, seeing him in beauty or in ugliness, both equally seductive. They came closer to him than the sages, though they too were deluded. They were aroused to erotic frenzy while he remained calm. He paid no heed to his effect on them (*VmP*, *SM*.22.53-68). He was a yogi, he had come begging in fulfillment of a vow; or he had been wandering about like one insane; his passion had burnt itself out in longing and grief for dead Satī, his wife, who had consumed her body in flames (*VmP*.6.26-29, 58-66). It was after this or another, even more profound, crisis that Śiva came to the forest of Deodar trees.

Images of Śiva cast in bronze or carved in stone show him as Bhikṣāṭana, the supreme mendicant. They celebrate the nakedness of the god. In them the Great God is shown not with the *ūrdhvaliṅga*, large, raised, and controlled by yoga, but, on the contrary, with the phallus small and pendant.[3]

It was Śiva's purpose to enlighten the false sages by allowing them to humiliate him. It was an act of grace on his part (*BP*.1.2.27.10; *ŚP*.4.12.11), but they were lost in anger (*VmP*, *SM*.22.67, 74). The Lord allowed himself to be assaulted and beaten by them. He ac-

[3] D. Barrett, *Early Cola Bronzes*, pls. 41, 53, 101.

cepted humiliation in the image that met the eye of the sages, as he had let himself be humiliated at the place of the sacrifice (Ch. III.2.b). He willed his *liṅga* to fall, and, unwittingly, the sages were his instruments when they made it fall. Or he tore it out himself, as he did when he had risen from the waters. There he severed it as an instrument of procreation. In his play in the Deodar forest, he severed it as an instrument of lust. The severance of the phallus was the purpose of his play. He played convincingly. Though he revealed his true nature when he danced, yet so great was his power to delude that the ṛṣis did not recognize him. Even though he appeared horribly fascinating, holding firebrands in his hands (*BP*.1.2.27.11-13), proclaiming himself as fire, these signals did not identify him. Though he aroused the women as the source of their desire, they were unable to see him as the killer of all desire (cf. *MBh*.13.17.51). They would touch but could not hold him who was free in frenzy and divine madness, the still core of the flame.

The *liṅga* of the Great God fell (*VmP*, *SM*.22.68). He threw it on the surface of the earth and vanished from the sight of the sages. All things, moving and unmoving, were destroyed (*VmP*, *SM*.22.69). The *liṅga* broke through the earth into the netherworld and went to the very sky (*VmP*.6.67; *ŚP*.4.12.20; *ŚP*,*JS*.42.17-18; *SkP*.6.1.21). The terrible, the marvelous *liṅga* of Śiva turned into the *liṅga* that pervades the *ākāśa*, and whose beginning and end Brahmā and Viṣṇu cannot reach (*ŚP*, *DhS*.49.82-85). Severed, it is the same great phallus that the *brahmacārin* of the *Atharva Veda* introduced into the earth (*AV*.11.5.12). Then its pillar shape was seen extending from heaven to earth. Now it is seen rising from below, from the netherworld to the sky. One way or the other, it is seen in its cosmic integrity.

Even though Śiva castrated himself by his own hand when he rose from the waters, or by his will through the agency or the curse of the sages, or once again by his own hand, Śiva is not a castrated god. The *liṅga* may be restored to his body (*SkP*.6.1.47-52; cf. *VmP*.6.84, 93) or Śiva may refuse to have it restored (cf. *SkP*.7.1.187.34-35), indifferent to the question of the completeness of the anthropomorphic metaphor of his body.

Yet by such a metaphor, by his naked body, he excited the forest dwellers. This was inevitable, for he was not an ordinary young ascetic but Śiva, and his dark skin glowed with his fire. He showed himself in his nakedness, undisguised and incarnate. The women of the sages pined to yield to him their carnal selves. The Lord, the Great Yogi, let this effect of his have its play, it was part of his unaccountable behavior, by which he shocked the righteous ṛṣis—the establishment—to whom the naked truth in the immediacy of self-revelation was strange and suspect.

This is how the Great God in the Deodar forest sported with the wives and daughters of the ṛṣis. Deluded by his *māyā*, they did not see that this great ascetic was free to play on lust as an instrument for purposes of his own. Calmly he accepted the consequences of the effect that he had created in the minds of the ṛṣis. He had provoked their false accusations and welcomed their assault, which precipitated the fall of the *liṅga* and fulfilled the purpose of the Great God. He vanished, and then the *liṅga* traversed the cosmos.

Bhikṣāṭana, the Supreme Beggar, ambiguously naked, phallic, and ascetic, startled the sages and their women, and they transgressed all bounds, swayed by frenzy and fury. Had they noticed his begging bowl? It was a skull stuck to his palm (*KūP*.2.31.64, 73).

Śiva, the Lord, the naked beggar in disguise, inscrutably seductive (*LP*.1.29.9-12), took them out of themselves and readied them for the climax, the severance of his phallus.

Images of Śiva in stone and bronze, other than those of Bhikṣāṭana, differentiate Śiva from other gods when they show his mighty *ūrdhvaliṇga*. But as a rule, images of Śiva, like those of other gods, are shown wearing rich jewelry and garments around the loins that deemphasize the presence of the *liṅga*. However, the *liṅga* is not meant to be absent, as is the case in images of the Buddha, on whose figure the organs of sex are said to have withdrawn.[4] Their absence is one of the signs of the *mahāpuruṣa*, the Buddha as supernal being. In other images, the *liṅga* is not erect, or its shape is concealed by garments and ornaments, but it is meant to be there.

Śiva as Bhikṣāṭana, Supreme Beggar, a form he had assumed when he visited the Deodar forest, is represented naked. The sky is his garment; yet he wears ornaments. A serpent is coiled around his hips.

[4] *Mahāpadāna Suttanta* in *Dīgha Nikāya (DN)*, ed. T. W. Rhys Davids and J. Estlin Carpenter, 1903, 2:17; *Lakkhaṇa Suttanta* in *Dīgha Nikāya (DN)*, tr, T. W. and C.A.F. Rhys Davids, 1921, 3:138; A. Wayman, "Contributions Regarding the Thirty-two Characteristics of the Great Person," 1957, 5:3 and 4, p. 253.

His *liṅga* is not raised—it conveys neither lust nor yogic control. Śiva as Bhikṣāṭana, in the tradition of the image makers, appears in divine spontaneity, aloof from the emotions that his *māyā* provoked in the ṛṣis and their women.

Śiva willed his phallus (*liṅga*) to fall. Now it was separated from his body. This cognizance (*liṅga*) of the Great Lord would be seen by the gods in flaming glory, and the sages would worship it on earth (*VmP*, *SM*.23.9-11), its shape of stone—or any other material—meted out in proportions of sacred geometry. It would rise through the millennia, as an abstract shape that implies the invisible presence of the Lord in the innermost sanctuary of a temple, the edifice surrounded on the outside by the many images in which Śiva is seen as the main actor in his cosmic play.

2. Transfiguration of the *Liṅga*: The Pillar of Flames

With Rudra's castration a cycle came to a close. It started at the beginning of time with Rudra, the hunter, who shot his arrow of fire right into the copulation of the Father and the daughter. Now Rudra, the cosmic ascetic, turned against himself and did violence to his own organ of sex. He severed it from his body, or the deluded sages in the Deodar forest were instrumental in its fall. The *liṅga* fell and proceeded to burn everything in its path. Wherever it went, it burned (*ŚP*, *JS*.42.16-17). It broke through the earth into the netherworld, and thence up to the sky (*ŚP*.4.12.17-20). Out of Rudra's mouth flames had come; they turned into demons, ghosts, and yogis (*VrP*.33.8). The demoniac, ghostly, and ascetic ambience of flames that Rudra exhaled into a burning universe was a prelude to the sovereign, awful grandeur of the cosmic fire *liṅga*. Flaming, soaring without beginning or end, its power loomed in the dark night of a world that had ended; the flaming *liṅga* pillar was its one and only light. After the fall of the *liṅga* to the ground, it rose in its own right, aflame in darkness, with consuming power, from the netherworld. It extended into heaven, whence the golden shaft of sunlight had descended into the cosmic waters of another aeon, impregnating them with the limpid sheen of Rudra's presence.

The descent of the impregnating light of heaven and the counter thrust of the ascending, flaming, phallic pillar are visionary complements. As soon as the *liṅga* had fallen, Rudra, the Lord of Yoga, left the scene and retreated into the solitude of Mount Mūjavat, where he practiced further austerities.

The fertilization of the waters by the light from beyond was an impregnation of matter with spirit. From it the plants were born, the staff of life, wherein Rudra's presence would feed mankind. The fallen phallus of Rudra, transfigured as cosmic phallic pillar flaming upward from the netherworld into heaven, was the counter player of the light from beyond. The pillar rose in the cosmic night in terrible splendor from immeasurable depths.

In the darkness of the flood, it was seen by Brahmā and Viṣṇu. In the total homogeneity of a dissolved universe, Viṣṇu and Brahmā were arguing over their relative supremacy when they were interrupted suddenly by the superluminous glow of a strange pillar of fire. Joined by Brahmā, Viṣṇu sped toward the indescribable flaming light, which grew before their eyes into infinity, rending heaven and earth. Overwhelmed and terrified by their unfathomable vision, the two gods sought the beginning and end of its burning immensity. Brahmā, flying upward with the wings of his bird shape—the wild gander—could not see its top, nor could Viṣṇu, diving down for a thousand years in his shape of a boar, see the bottom of that fire *liṅga* of him who is the light and destruction of the universe. Both of the bewildered gods returned exhausted to the level they had started from, and within the flaming *liṅga* they beheld Śiva in golden glory. He illumined the dark flood, and the two gods, Viṣṇu and Brahmā, bowed before him. Thunderous laughter, or the sound *AUM*, issued from the pillar, filled the sky, and Śiva dispelled their fear (*VāP*.55.13-57; cf. *LP*.1.17.32-59; cf. *KūP*.1.25.67-101).

Rudra's theophany in the *liṅga* took place in the interval between the destruction and reabsorption of one world age and the beginning of a new aeon. In the darkness of the flood, there were only two witnesses to the spectacle. They were Brahmā and Viṣṇu, each unable to fathom the greatness of the flaming pillar.

The epiphany of Rudra in the flaming *liṅga* was his self-revelation as Agni, the glowing, flaming pillar of fire connecting heaven and earth. That is how he arose on the altar of Aśvatthāman. When Agni comes through the sun-door from heaven to earth, he is the celestial light that glistens on the surface as he enters the waters.

Agni travels between heaven and earth, but when the god tires of his work as the messenger of the gods to men and of men to gods, he takes creative rest in the waters, as Rudra did before he arose and severed his phallus. Fallen to the ground, the *liṅga* sank into the earth. It cleft its way into the netherworld, and from this subterranean region of unprobed extent it shot upward, a flaming sign of Rudra's presence. It was the sign (*liṅga*) and at the same time the phallus (*liṅga*) of Rudra. It had no end and no beginning, but it had direction, flaming upward as does the earthly fire, pointing upward as does the *liṅga* of the ascetic, whose semen is consumed ascending by his *tapas* within his body. Transfigured, the detached creative limb, in its transcendent autonomy, revealed to the gods Rudra's presence within its flames. The gods bowed to the Great God, the mystery of whose *liṅga* they could not fathom.

In the flaming *liṅga* sign and abode, Śiva manifested himself to the gods. The *liṅga* appeared like a hundred fires of dissolution, with a thousand garlands of flame, void of decrease or increase, with no beginning, middle, or end (*ŚP*.2.1.7.48). Humbled and overawed by its mystery, the gods accepted its presence and bowed to it. Then Śiva's revelation to the gods by revealing himself through the *liṅga* of fire, which their minds first failed to grasp, had for its setting the cosmic night of dissolution, whence a new world would arise again. The *liṅga* of fire was its herald. It was the transfiguration of the severed phallus of Śiva. Having torn out the organ of procreation, and having let the instrument of lust fall to the ground, the Great God vanished from the scene. He revealed himself in glory within the transfigured *liṅga* to the gods who bowed to him (*ŚP, DhS*.10.12-16, 22-24). His ambience was fire, to which the *liṅga* had lent its pillar shape. The Great God himself was at its core. The two gods saw him. By divine sight they saw what no human eye can see and no words can define: the source of the light in the flames of the cosmic *liṅga*.

3. The Establishment of the *Liṅga* on Earth

Within the cosmic, flaming *liṅga*, Śiva was seen by the gods in the vast darkness of the night of dissolution. So that he could be realized within the *liṅga* here on earth, the *liṅga* fallen in the Deodar forest was taken up by an elephant in its *liṅga*-like trunk. Śiva himself had assumed for this purpose the shape of an elephant. The *liṅga* was transported by him from the Deodar forest, where neither the gods nor the sages could lift it, to a lake where grew a great banyan tree, the embodiment of Sthāṇu. There Brahmā established a stone *liṅga* on the primordial *liṅga*, which the elephant had set down and by which the stone became illumined. The lake where this and other miracles happened became the primordial *tīrtha* or place of pilgrimage. There liberation was attained by the sight of the *liṅga* and the touch of the banyan tree (*VmP*, *SM*.22.7-11, 37-38; 23.9-34; 24.17-25). Sthāṇu, rooted as a banyan tree in the middle of the lake of the primordial *tīrtha*, and the stone *liṅga*, reinforced the presence of Śiva here in this world. In the age-old symbols of omphalos stone and tree at the Sāṃnihatya lake, Śiva henceforth was accessible to man.

The banyan tree as Sthāṇu, the primordial *liṅga* in the waters as Śiva himself submerged in them, the omphalos stone as a replica of the primordial *liṅga*, are transparent in their several meanings, one sliding over the other. Across them shines the holiness of the *tīrtha* toward which the Śiva elephant had carried the felled *liṅga* in his trunk, which resembled a *liṅga*.

The mystery of the metamorphosis of the severed phallus of the god into a pillar of flames reverberated in the liberating sound *AUM* (cf. *LP*.1.17.49). It rang across the vastness of the cosmic night as Śiva revealed himself from within the *liṅga* to Brahmā and Viṣṇu.

The vision of the flaming *liṅga* seen by the gods and the legend of the establishment of the stone *liṅga* in the Sāṃnihatya lake introduced the worship of the *liṅga*.

The mystery of the stone *liṅga* set down by the Śiva-elephant in the Sāṃnihatya lake goes deeper than this legend: it was in the water of this lake that Rudra had been immersed in yogic trance. When he emerged, he tore out his *liṅga* in fury. He hurled it down into the lake and it stood there erect. Ever since, the *liṅga* has been known as Sthāṇu (*VmP*, *SM*.28.22-34). Like a magnet, the Sāṃnihatya *tīrtha* drew to itself the two myths of the fallen *liṅga*. Overlapping, they intensified the sanctity of the stone *liṅga* set up to be worshiped on earth.

It is also said that the gods overcame Śiva's reluctance to take back the severed *liṅga*. He agreed to carry it if gods and men would worship it. Thereupon the gods set up the *liṅga* and worshiped it (*SkP*.7.1.55-62). In one way or another, in one *tīrtha* or another, *liṅga* worship became established on earth.

4. The Meaning of the *Liṅga*

In the cosmic night of an earlier age, the Padma Kalpa or Lotus aeon, Śiva also had revealed himself to Brahmā and Viṣṇu. Viṣṇu was lying on the serpent "Endless," his couch in the vast flood full of darkness. A large lotus had grown from his navel, and he was playing with it when Brahmā happened to come by. The two gods, benumbed by Śiva's *māyā*, did not quite recognize each other, though Viṣṇu introduced himself, saying that the whole universe was his realm, while he noticed that Brahmā had the universe for his body. Brahmā then said that he too was the demiurge. Viṣṇu wondered and, with Brahmā's consent, entered through Brahmā's mouth and saw all the worlds contained within the belly of Brahmā. He roamed through them for a thousand years and, after coming out of the mouth of Brahmā, he invited Brahmā to enter his belly. Brahmā then found all the worlds within Viṣṇu's body. Viṣṇu had gone to sleep, however, and Brahmā could find no way out except through the lotus stalk in Viṣṇu's navel. Brahmā seated himself in the shining lotus flower (*LP*.1.20.1-32).

While Brahmā and Viṣṇu were arguing about their relative greatness and precedence, Śiva had appeared wading across the flood. Winds blew hot and cold and shook the lotus flower; they were Śiva's breath. As his agitated body rapidly splashed through the ocean, his fangs gleamed in his huge face, surrounded by his disheveled hair. He tossed masses of water to the invisible sky. He had ten arms and eyes going all around him. With his huge phallus erect, he roared terribly. Clad in pure golden raiments and wearing a girdle of *muñja* grass, he held a trident. Brahmā did not recognize him, but Viṣṇu knew he was the cause of the universe, the possessor of the seeds and their light. Viṣṇu beheld Lord Śiva by the splendor of his great yoga (*LP*.1.20.33-37, 59-62, 69-73).

Then Viṣṇu explained to Brahmā how Brahmā himself had sprung from Śiva through Viṣṇu, into whose womb Śiva had placed the shining seed (*LP*.1.20.78-82). Though this theogony, in praise of Śiva, seems to run counter to the mythic account of Śiva having sprung from Brahmā, it is valid in a context that sees Śiva as the timeless cause and origin from which the Creator himself has sprung. The apparent reversal of the relation of Brahmā and Śiva results from two different levels of speaking about Śiva. In one, the gods act as anthropomorphic symbols, in the other they are ontic realities. Śiva, as cause of causes and source of all creativity, is the cause of Brahmā's being. Śiva-Rudra reveals his causality by successively playing the roles of Agni, who prepared the seed for the father (Ch. I), and of the crying child on the lap of Brahmā (the Creator and his father) (Ch. V).

In the cosmic night of the Padma Kalpa, Śiva in ebullient abandon splashed the waters of the flood. He appeared on a lower level of realization than that of his manifestation from within the flaming *liṅga* pillar during the cosmic night of another Kalpa (*VāP*.55.13-57). He appeared, also, on a lower level of mythic significance, and with less depth of meaning than in the tale of his immersion in the calm waters in which he chose to plunge in response to Brahmā's command (*MBh*.10.17.10-26).

Yet the knowledge of the two stations in the waters is subjacent to the baroque epiphany of the Lord as the bearer of seed agitating the waters of the cosmic night of the lotus aeon. Śiva showed the paradox of his nature here: the wild potency of sex surging through his enormous body, distending his phallus. This potency sharpened his fangs and tossed his mane of hair, while he was clad in pure golden raiments and girt with an ascetic's belt. For he, "the possessor of seed," is the goal of ascetics (*LP*.1.20.72,73). As fire, Agni, he had prepared the seed for the Father (*RV*.1.71.5, 8). His fire glowed in the immense *liṅga* pillar that appeared in the cosmic night preceding the present kalpa. But, in this night preceding an earlier aeon, he was clad in gold, and illumined the flood as he irradiated the waters in whose depth he had practiced *tapas*. The roaring epiphany of his sex-charged shape, though clasped by an ascetic's girdle, was an anticlimax to his form of Sthāṇu, the ascetic, a motionless pillar. But its exuberant shape was the necessary complement whence his asceticism derived nourishment. Sex is the fuel of the fiery ardor of asceticism. It would burn itself out in arid waste if not sustained by the power of sex, which it consumes and transforms. Śiva shows these forms of his nature at will, they being at one within him. Thus, agitated, roaring, shining, the Lord was seen by the demiurges. He showed himself ten-armed and seeing with innumerable eyes. Whatever may be the number of his eyes, arms, or heads, he is the god who reveals and also severs his one and only phallus.

The stone *liṅga* of Śiva has been set up in the center of the innermost sanctuary of every Śiva temple over the last two thousand years. The *liṅga* has been worshiped as a vertical stone, "grown by itself" from the ground (*svāyambhuva* "self-existent"), and most sacred. Or it is a portable pebble smoothed into shape by the waves of a river. Or a shape made by the hand of man in clay, wood, stone, precious stones, or metal. A *liṅga* can be made of any material. It can be seen and worshiped anywhere: "even the circular luminous spot which the sun casts on a mirror, and which, for its resemblance to the shape of a lingam is called the phallic emblem of the solar rays" (*AP*.54.6).[5] A *liṅga* is tied to the body of the newborn child in a Vīraśaiva or Liṅgayat family, and every Liṅgayat wears throughout his life a *liṅga*, which is kept in a silver receptacle hung from around the neck; this "liṅga represents the wearer's soul, which is not different from the divinity, Śiva."[6] Less ostensibly, the *liṅga* is fixed in the heart of yogis (*KūP*.2.11.94, 98), and in South India a *liṅga* is set up above the place of burial of a *sannyāsin*.[7]

Liṅga-like shapes of clay have been found in Mohenjo-daro and Harappa.[8] They would date as far back as the seal discussed earlier, with the figure of a god whose phallus is shown pointing upward, in tune with the yoga posture (*āsana*) of the body.

As A. Bharati has pointed out, the ithyphallic shape, as part of a figure represented in a yoga posture (*āsana*), would be inconsistent if interpreted as in "priapic" condition. The ithyphallic representation of the erect shape connotes the very opposite in this context. It stands for "seminal retention," and it represents Śiva as "he stands for complete control of the senses, and for supreme carnal renunciation."[9] The yogi does not deny sex, rather he transforms sexual urge and directs it away from procreation and pleasure toward intuited wisdom, toward freedom and bliss. The ascetic god, whose seed is raised up, whose *liṅga* is raised up (*MBh*.13.17.45), is one with, though he stands at the other pole from, the god who is the bearer of seeds. The one creates the world of pleasure and pain, the other liberates from it. Their polarity is not that of eros and thanatos, of love and death, but of desire (*kāma*) and liberation (*mokṣa*). Between these two poles Śiva stretches the path of yoga, of which he is the lord. On this diameter

[5] *Agni Purāṇa (AP)*, tr. M. N. Dutt, 1903-1904, p. 194.

[6] W. McCormack, "On Lingayat Culture," in A. K. Ramanujan, tr., *Speaking of Śiva*, 1973, p. 179.

[7] J. Marshall, *Mohenjo-Daro and the Indus Civilization*, 1:58-61, pls. 13, 14.

[8] M. S. Vats, *Excavations at Harappa*, 1974, 1:56.

[9] A. Bharati, *The Tantric Tradition*, p. 296.

of his boundless ambience the god operates at every point. There, in one of his modes, he is Time (*Kāla*), and, being Time, who consumes life, he is Death (*Kāla*). Once a part of his role was delegated to a goddess who resembled him (*MBh*.7, app. 1, no. 8, lines 113-31). But the god who shows himself as Time-and-Death would not be Śiva if he did not rule over Time-and-Death and overcome both. A legend tells of Śiva breaking out of the *liṅga* in which he had been immanent. The Lord saved from death young Mārkaṇḍeya, his devotee, who was doomed to die at the age of sixteen. When Death approached the lad, who was worshiping the *liṅga*, Śiva appeared and warded off its threatening figure. Śiva blessed Mārkaṇḍeya to be always sixteen years old, an immortal youth (cf. *ŚP*.7.1.30.48).[10] And when the sage Śveta, whom Death had bound, called out Rudra's name, Death asked him, "Where is your Rudra? . . . Is he in the *liṅga*?" Śiva appeared and Death freed Śveta (*LP*.1.30.15-21).

Is Śiva in the *liṅga* the source of life that gives eternal youth? He saved from death and had the power to bring the dead back to life. In one version of his myth, Bhārgava installed and worshiped a *liṅga* in order to obtain the spell for the resuscitation of the dead. He exerted himself in terrible austerities, and finally Śiva came out of the *liṅga*. Bhārgava / Śukra praised him as Śiva the god of eight forms and the fire and the giver of calm at every step. Śiva gave to Bhārgava the *mṛtasañjīvanī mantra*, by which the dead are brought back to life (*ŚP*.2.5.50.1-18, 23, 27, 41-43). The *mṛtyuñjaya mantra* coalesced with the Sañjīvanī spell. Similarly, it was by the *liṅga* form (*liṅgarūpa*) that Śiva resuscitated the gods and demons killed by the Kālakūṭa poison. By his mercy, they arose as though from a deep sleep (*SkP*.1.1.10.51-55). Does the *liṅga* contain the god who is the source and secret of life? Śiva revealed himself to the gods in the flaming *liṅga* pillar.

The *liṅga* is the object of the greatest sanctity, more sacred than any anthropomorphic image. It is set up in the innermost sanctuary of every Śiva temple. The earliest sculptures that are definitely identifiable as *Śiva-liṅgas* are from Guḍimallam in South India[11] and from Mathurā,[12] and show a pillar shape; the rounded top is demarcated and clearly represents the glans, so that the shaft represents not only

[10] T. A. Gopinatha Rao, *Elements of Hindu Iconography*, vol. 2, part 1, pp. 156-58.

[11] *Ibid.*, p. 65, pls. II and III.

[12] N. P. Joshi, *Catalogue of the Brahmanical Sculptures in the State Museum, Lucknow*, 1972, part I, figs. 24-27.

a pillar but also a phallus. Moreover, Śiva stands in front of the *liṅga*, his back contiguous with its ascending shape; the phallus of the anthropomorph is shown pendant in the Guḍimallam sculpture, and as *ūrdhvaliṅga* in the Mathurā figure.[13] Subsequently, the rounded tops of the pillars were given different curvatures, representing different conic sections, with the shaft subdivided into three sections according to geometrical propositions. The total shape of the *liṅga* rises as a stark, geometrically proportioned volume.

The form of and the verbal references to the *liṅga* are charged with complex meaning. "Brahmā has for his cognizance (*aṅka*) the lotus. For Viṣṇu it is the discus; and Indra has for his cognizance the thunderbolt. But the creatures of this world do not have any of the signs that distinguish these gods. On the other hand, all creatures have a *liṅga* (penis) or a *bhaga* (womb). Hence all creatures of this world must be thought of as belonging to Śiva and to his consort" (*MBh*.13.14, note 102, insert 113, lines 1-2). The consort of Śiva has not as yet been considered. She is essential, though not in the primordial morning of Rudra's attack of the Father in the ongoing myth of Śiva. Indeed, it is said in the *Kena Upaniṣad* that "Umā, the daughter of Himavat, who being always in the company of the all-knowing Lord (Mahādeva) had the power of knowing *brahman*,"[14] which is here supreme knowledge, and that she explained the marvelous appearance of *brahman* as a *yakṣa* to Indra (*KUp*.3.1-2; 3.12; 4.1).[15]

The *liṅga* of Śiva has three significations. They are *liṅga* as sign; *liṅga* as phallus, and *liṅga* as cosmic substance (*prakṛti* or *pradhāna*), which is the subtle body (*liṅga śarīra*) of Śiva, who is the absolute real-

[13] A. K. Coomaraswamy, *History of Indian and Indonesian Art*, 1965, fig. 80. Since the first appearance of Coomaraswamy's work in 1927, this figure, identified by Coomaraswamy as a Bodhisattva, has been reidentified as a figure of Śiva.

[14] *Kena Upaniṣad (KUp)*, tr. Śriśa Chandra Vidyārnava, 1974, p. 112. This is Śaṅkara's commentary on *KUp*.3.12.

[15] S. Bhattacharji, *The Indian Theogony*, 1970, p. 158, discusses the names of the consort of Rudra as they appear in the pre-epic texts. Excepting Umā-Haimavatī, hardly anything but their names is known. The names of Rodasī and the Pṛśni cow have to be added, and their significance in relation to Rudra and the Maruts has yet to be clarified. Rudra's "paternity" of the Maruts, the mother being Pṛśni (*RV*.2.34.2; 5.52.16; 5.60.5; 6.66.3), is of a special kind, for the Pṛśni cow is also a bull (cf. A. Bergaigne, *La Religion védique*, 2:397-98). *Ṛg Veda Saṃhitā (RV)*, tr. K. F. Geldner, 1951, 2:168 on *RV*.6.66.3 suggests Rudra as the male half of the androgynous cow-bull, and that this would anticipate Śiva, the androgyne. The progenitive cow-bull, Pṛśni, however, corresponds to the progenitive bull-cow Tvaṣṭṛ-Savitṛ-Viśvarūpa (*RV*.3.38.4,8), rather than to Agni, the self-perpetuating bull-cow.

ity, "the imperishable Puruṣa" (*LP*.1.20.70). The original meaning of the word *liṅga* is "sign," a mark that proves the existence of a thing. Thus, the *Śvetāśvatara Upaniṣad*, where this word is used for the first time in the sacred tradition, says that Śiva, the supreme lord, has no *liṅga* or mark (*ŚUp*.6.9), meaning that he is transcendent, beyond any characteristic. As a distinguishing mark, *liṅga* also means a characteristic and, specifically, the sign of gender or sex.[16] *Liṅga*, "sign," not only signifies the existence of perceptible things, but also denotes the imperceptible essence of a thing even before the thing in its concrete shape has come to exist. Thus the form of fire, which exists in the kindling stick in a latent form, may not be seen, yet its *liṅga* is not destroyed but may be seized again by another kindling stick (*ŚUp*.1.13). Fire in its latent condition, unkindled, the potential of fire, its imperceptible essence, is the *liṅga* of fire, in contrast with and indispensable to its visible form (*rūpa*). The imperceptible essence of a thing, in its potentiality, is the *liṅga* of the thing. The insight of the *Śvetāśvatara Upaniṣad* conveyed through the word *liṅga* is formulated explicitly in the Sāṁkhya and Yoga schools or ways of looking at things (*darśana*), that is, by looking at their appearance and at ultimate reality. *Liṅga* here denotes the "subtle body" (*liṅga śarīra*) underlying and ontologically preceding anything perceptible. The perceptible state, in this context, is the gross body (*sthūla śarīra*), or concrete reality as it appears to the sense organs. In between the ultimate and concrete reality is *prakṛti*, also called *pradhāna*. Out of this imperceptible cosmic substance all things have come, and to it they will return.

As already discussed (Ch. IV.2), *prakṛti* consists of three *guṇas* or "strands." They are *sattva*, *rajas*, and *tamas*, and function as tendencies through which the principles and powers of cosmic substance cohere. The principles are: *mahat*, "cosmic intelligence or revelation"; *ahaṁkāra*, "individuation"; and *manas*, "mind." From these evolve the powers (*indriya*) of cognition that enable hearing, feeling, seeing, tasting, and smelling and their corresponding subtle elements (*tanmātra*) to exist. From these supersensible *tanmātras* the sense particulars (*mahābhūta*) come into being. They are ether or space, air, fire, water, and earth. They are the vehicles of the *tanmātras*, and constitute the gross body of concrete, perceptible, and particularized reality. The subtle body (*liṅga śarīra*) is the subtle prototype of the gross body. It

[16] Cf. M. Mayrhofer, *Concise Etymological Sanskrit Dictionary*, *s.v.*, and V. S. Apte, *The Practical Sanskrit-English Dictionary*, *s.v.*

is the imperceptible stuff of energy by which all phenomena are projected into concrete reality, like fire from its latency. The subtle body, itself changeless, accompanies the life-of-the-individual (*jīva*) through the cycles of births and deaths, and is finally reabsorbed into the principles and powers of which it is composed.

The two demiurges saw Śiva in one of the intervals between two aeons in the cosmic night of dissolution of the Lotus aeon. They saw the bearer of seed (*bījin*), irradiating the dark cosmic flood with the light of his yoga, with the light of his seed (*LP*.1.20.69-70). His huge phallus had risen beneath the pure golden raiment cinctured by a girdle of *muñja* grass.

The anthropomorphic shape functions as the "gross body" of the god. It is a superabundant evocation of fierce potency on a cosmic scale, and while it appears crassly phallic, it is much more than that. Greater in ambience than the vast body of the god is the light around him. It vibrates in waves of yoga, it emanates from the seed of Śiva, under the golden cloth held to the body by the ascetic's girdle. By the huge shape, by the many arms, by such quantitative excesses in size and number, the superhuman quality of the divine vision is rendered in visual terms of fascinating horror. The bearer of the seed rages with the vehemence of sex.

While the two demiurges, in turn, measured the extent of their domain, the cosmos, the Great God shattered their desire for precedence by his self-revelation as the power that inseminates, with his light, all creation-to-be. He is the power of creativity. His seed is the light. The superhuman phallus carries and emits the light. In his tempestuous appearance in the cosmic night of dissolution, he illumines the flood, wading across its waters as he strides on them, a *brahmacārin* in the daylight of a Vedic hymn (cf. *AV*.11.5.26). The girdle of *muñja* grass shows him to be a brahmin, an ascetic, even while his body is fiercely phallic. The vision of Śiva in the *pralaya*, in the dissolution of the cosmos, preceding the Lotus aeon, is an image of the night. In daylight, that of a cosmic day, Rudra-Śiva is Sthāṇu, the pillar, his entire self withdrawn, a motionless monument of containment. In yet another mode of his being, Rudra cut off his *liṅga*. It fell, sank into the earth, to arise in the cosmic night of another kalpa. Within this *liṅga* Śiva revealed himself.

The foregoing myths of Śiva, the bearer of the phallus or *liṅga*, the bearer of the seed, the motionless pillar (*sthāṇu*), and the flaming *liṅga* pillar, play around Śiva, the changeless, ancient Puruṣa, the cause of the universe (*LP*.1.20.70).

In the first myth, the anthropomorphic image harnesses a multiplicity of limbs to a body of superhuman proportions, capable of expressing more than human states and power. In such anthropomorphic shapes, the god addresses himself to the devotee and lifts him into his being. In the second myth, the sudden and complete transition from the god thought of, though not explicitly evoked, in the shape of man to that of an inert pillar has the immediacy of a miracle. The pillar shape remains its constant reminder. It is a symbol of self-containment in every section of its ascending volume. It rises upward, like the phallus of the yogi who draws his seed upward. *Sthāṇu*, the pillar, is a symbol in its own volumetric shape. Moreover, it carries the connotation of *ūrdhvaliṅga*, the *liṅga* or sign that rises upward as the seed is withdrawn upwards (*ūrdhvaretas*) (cf. *MBh*.13.17.45). This symbol abrogates any other meaning. The God has entered it totally. In the third myth, the pillar rises before the gods. It has no precedent, though it has a past. Mysteriously, it flames upward, and from within it the god is manifest. *Sthāṇu*, the inert post, is a conversion of god into pillar. The flaming *liṅga*-pillar, in which the god appears, is the sheath of a theophany.

The pillar form of Śiva, as such, is a manifestation of the god *modus geometrico*. In this respect it is akin to Ekavrātya, the transmundane, pyramidal four-sided *maṇḍala*. This pyramid, however, is a monument to an enthusiastic Vrātya's transformation into Rudra. In that pyramid Rudra had his station in the center of its ascending shape (*AV*.15.5.5), just as Śiva is manifest in the *liṅga* (*MBh*.13.17.74). Śiva is present in the *liṅga* as pillar. The pillar is his symbolic equivalent. Śiva turned into a pillar and became Sthāṇu. This is one way of realizing his presence in the *liṅga*. It presupposes an awareness of the sacred in the pillar, whether wooden post or stone. The pillar shape is assimilated to that of the *liṅga*, the erect phallus. Or Śiva is present in the *liṅga*, the phallus. The phallus is his symbol. It contains the seed. As the seed cannot be seen while in the phallus, so Śiva is invisibly present in the *liṅga*. The *liṅga* is not the Great God: it is the shape in which he dwells invisible. The Great God is known within his *liṅga* form (*MBh*.7.172.86-90). The *liṅga*, or phallus, is the form in and through which Śiva operates. While it is full with life yet to be, in that very state it is restrained; the seed is held drawn up. Siva, "whose seed is drawn up, whose *liṅga* is raised" (*MBh*.13.17.45), is a *brahmacārin* (*MBh*.13.17.72). He always observes the vow of chastity (*brahmacarya*). The sages, gods, gandharvas, and apsarases always worship his *liṅga* standing upright (*MBh*.7.173.84).

The *liṅga* is the phallus of Śiva. Śiva is in the phallus. God resides in whatever is part of god. The erect *liṅga* is full of seed. Śiva is the carrier of the seed. At will, he may release or restrain it. As Lord of Yoga he restrains its movement, absorbs the seed in his total being. As the *Mahābhārata* expresses it, he is the yogi; he holds the great (cosmic) seed; he is one with *tapas*, fire and fervent self-control; he is one with the golden seed (*MBh*.13.17.39). He effects and is the transition from transitive action to an intransitive state. He is God, and he is the seed of the universe (*MP*.47.130). The seed is golden with the radiance of light, the radiance of the sun—the inseminator.[17] He is the god of four faces; he is seen in the great *liṅga*, the beautiful beloved *liṅga*; he is lord of the *liṅga*, lord of the seed, and the maker of the seed (*MBh*.13.17.74-75). In this paean to the *liṅga* he, who from the beginning of things had prepared the seed, is known as its lord, whose domain is the *liṅga*—the cosmic substance of things to be, the "subtle body" (*liṅga śarīra*) of all that lives.[18]

Śiva's *liṅga* has many levels. They are worded in metaphor and synecdoche, and supported by symbols. Moreover, while these interpenetrate, they retain their primary significance in mystical coherence. The meaning of the Śiva *liṅga* is in the phallus, it is in the pillar, motionless or flaming, concrete or imagined, just as the *liṅga* can be shaped in clay, wood, or stone. Its substance, also, can be space itself. As such, the *ākāśa liṅga* is set up in the temple of Chidambaram. The walls of the sanctuary enclose the presence of Śiva in the symbol of *ākāśa*, the first element of manifestation that spreads in all directions and makes space possible. *Ākāśa* penetrates the other four elements and all that is manifest. The meaning of the Śiva *liṅga* is in each of its forms, whether verbal or visual. Even more than in any one of these shapes, it is between them, a diapason that vibrates with Śiva's presence, while he is beyond sound, word, and form. It is this that their upright shapes proclaim. It is perhaps appropriate that Umā, in the

[17] M. Eliade, "Spirit, Light, and Seed," pp. 3-4. Eliade discusses here the relationship of these three elements in several religions.

[18] Cf. Nīlakaṇṭha's commentary on *MBh*.13.17.77-78, ed. K. S. Gurjar, *Mahābhārata with Nīlakaṇṭha's Commentary*, 1888-1890.

Kena Upaniṣad, recognized the numinous being, the *yakṣa*, whose identity had baffled the other gods; she knew the *yakṣa* as the Lord, whose ultimate reality (*brahman*) had eluded the other gods.

On another occasion, a being (*yakṣa*) had been seen as he stood in the flood, high up in the cosmic ocean (*AV*.10.7.38). Glowing with *tapas*, this young ascetic carried the shining *brahman*. This cosmic ascetic (*brahmacārin*) carried supreme reality (*brahman*), while he stood in the waters (*AV*.11.5.24-26), like the flame *liṅga* that appeared in the flood of the cosmic night. When the demiurges (Viṣṇu and Brahmā) bowed to it, the sound *AUM* rang loudly from the flame *liṅga* (*LP*.1.17.49).

AUM, the indestructible syllable, is all that exists. The past, the present, the future are included in the one syllable *AUM*, and what is beyond the threefold time is also in the syllable *AUM* (*MāUp*.1.1). The gods saw the flame pillar and heard the sound that came from it. In these signs the ultimate reality that is Śiva was manifested to them at the time of total dissolution (*pralaya*), before a new cosmos was to consolidate and emerge in the morning of a renewed world.

The flame *liṅga* and the indestructible syllable are the signs by which the presence of transcendental Śiva is directly communicated to the demiurges. As such, Śiva is without any sign (*liṅga*). The Great God, "though devoid of *liṅga*" (*liṅgavarjita*), is "stationed in the *liṅga*" (*LP*.1.19.5).

The play on the word *liṅga* serves as a commentary on the connotations of *liṅga*. Śiva, who, as ultimate reality itself, is without any *liṅga* or characterizing mark (there is a faint undertone of Śiva self-castrated and devoid of his *liṅga*), is stationed in the *liṅga*. What is the relation of the *liṅga* to Śiva, who is *a-liṅga*? The *Liṅga Purāṇa* answers: "*Pradhāna* is *liṅga*; Śiva is the *liṅgin*" (*LP*.1.17.5). *Pradhāna* or *prakṛti*, the cosmic substance, is the *liṅga*. The *liṅgin* is the Lord in his transcendency (Parameśvara) (*LP*.1.17.5). *Liṅga* is the "subtle body"; Śiva, the *liṅgin*, has this subtle body. It is neither visible nor tangible: it consists of the conceptualized potentialities of *prakṛti* at work, and is the ontological foreshadowing of the manifest world. The *Liṅga Purāṇa* clearly says: "The *a-liṅga* (the noncharacterized) is the root of the *liṅga* (the characterized). The Unmanifest (*avyakta*) [*prakṛti*] is the characterized (*liṅga*); Śiva is the noncharacterized (*a-liṅga*), and the characterized (*liṅga*) is understood as related to Śiva" (*LP*.1.3.1; cf. also *KūP*.2.10.1). While these semantic and metaphysical relations of *a-liṅga* and *liṅga* clarify the meaning underlying the phallic pillar, its form, as it is set up for worship in the innermost sanctuary of a temple of Śiva, is not accounted for by them. Yet this link between meaning and symbol is in the word *liṅga* itself, denoting as it does the sign of sex. This meaning is undeniably given form in the earliest *liṅgas* carved in stone. The significance of *liṅga* as the "subtle body" of Śiva, however, was paramount in the sacred tradition, though the phallic meaning remained strong. This is clearly worded in the *Śiva Purāṇa* in a statement concerning Śiva as either *niṣkala* or *sakala* (1.5.8-11). The term *niṣkala* in its ambiguity clarifies the relation of the pillar, a visual and symbolic form, to the conceptual term *liṅga* in its metaphysical, as well as phallic, significance. *Niṣkala* literally means impartite, without parts and, thus, without definable parts, without and beyond definition. In this latter sense its meaning comprises both the subtle body (*liṅga śarīra, prakṛti*), and also the unmanifest absolute (*a-liṅga*). Moreover, the term *niṣkala* in Hindu iconography means aniconic in contrast to *sakala*, that is, possessed of distinguishable parts.[19] The anthropomorphic image of the deity is termed *sakala*, whereas the aniconic shape is *niṣkala* (*ŚP*.1.5.8-11). Thus, the *Śiva Purāṇa* helps to clarify the complex relation of pillar, phallus, and subtle body in the *liṅga*, the "aniconic" symbol of the Supreme Lord. Further, the *Śiva Purāṇa* explains the apparition of Śiva, the supreme lord, Parameśvara, in the flaming pillar to Brahmā and Viṣṇu: "He showed his own form (*rūpa*) by the form (*rūpa*) of a *niṣkala* [or aniconic] pillar." Thus, for the welfare of the world, Śiva showed his own *liṅga*, undifferentiated from the pillar because of the character of his own *liṅga* (*ŚP*.1.5.28-29).

From that time on, the *Śiva Purāṇa* continues, the *niṣkala liṅga* and the *sakala* icon were assigned to Śiva alone (*ŚP*.1.5.30). The iconic form of other gods bestows enjoyment, but the iconic and aniconic forms of Śiva grant enjoyment and release (*ŚP*.1.5.31). The same text explains that Śiva is *niṣkala*, for he is supreme reality (*brahman*) itself (*ŚP*.1.5.10). Hence, the *niṣkala liṅga* is used in his worship in the innermost sanctuary only. Yet he also has a form in image; his *sakala* icons are of many kinds. In the worship of all other gods, the iconic (*sakala*) form is used (*ŚP*.1.5.11-13, 20-24). Literally, *sakala* and *niṣkala* mean, respectively, "with parts" and "without parts." These words, as

[19] T. A. Gopinatha Rao, *Elements of Hindu Iconography*, vol. 2, part 2, pp. 361-62, discusses the meaning of these terms according to the *Vātulaśuddhāgama*.

applied to the form of concrete objects used in worship, may be rendered as "iconic" and "aniconic." Applied to ultimate reality, and to the cosmic substance, *sakala* and *niṣkala* may be rendered as "with" or "without" perceptible form, respectively. Śiva showed his *niṣkala liṅga*, his unmanifest imperceptible body of potentiality, his cosmic substance, by means of an aniconic pillar. Yet this pillar also evokes his phallus. As an aniconic shape, the pillar signifies a purely conceptual reality, the invisible cosmic substance that, as his "subtle body," belongs to Śiva, the ultimate reality. Visually, however, the aniconic shape of the cylindrical pillar with a rounded top resembles that of the phallus.

The *liṅga* pillar stands upright; it flames upward. Śiva, the ascetic, had severed his phallus. He did not want to procreate, to create human beings. The phallus, which the sages saw as an instrument of lust, was severed. The *liṅga* fell to the ground. It penetrated the earth. Aflame and beyond measure, it appeared in the waters of the cosmic night, like hundreds of doomsday fires with thousands of flames (cf. *LP*.1.17.34). *Liṅga* is said to be derived from "*layana* / *laya*," "dissolution," because everything is absorbed into it (*LP*.1.19.16).[20] Aflame, its light is the focus of all creative-procreative potentialities. The *liṅga* is also the locus of their yogic redirection as powers of reintegration, or of dissolution. The powers of creation, liberation, and annihilation dwell in the *liṅga*.

The body of God, though it is conceived as resembling the body of man, is not like it. Its substance is *prakṛti*, not matter. Yet the figures of myth show themselves in anthropomorphic or theriomorphic allusions or semblance without which, paradoxically, they could not act, be recognized, or communicate their meaning. Man, in his physical body, is but a halting place, a condensation that *prakṛti* deposits on earth, before this body is dissolved and annihilated. Yet the likeness of the physical body of man and its parts is lent to the images of the gods. Through them the gods communicate their being. The *liṅga* pillar, in which the shape of *liṅga* (phallus) and pillar are integrated, is thus, to some degree, both an iconic and aniconic symbol of Śiva's presence. The phallic component slumbers at the bottom of the realization of the *liṅga*. While it lends its shape to the abstract stereometry

[20] A similar statement is made in the *Suprabhedāgama*, quoted *ibid.*, vol. 2, part 2, p. 364 and n. 1.

of the *liṅga* as cult object, the *liṅga* is of the nature of transcendent bliss, and of the nature of knowledge, and it abides in the heart of yogis (*KūP*.2.11.94).

The *Ṛg Veda* (*RV*.7.21.5; 10.99.3) disparagingly spoke of those who made the penis (*śiśna*) their god. Those people were kept away from the Vedic sacrifice. Moreover, Indra slew them. Whoever they were, the object of their worship survives to this day in the form of the *liṅga*. No other god but Śiva is worshiped in the *liṅga* pillar. The other gods are worshiped in their icons. Besides the innumerable *liṅgas*, iconic images of Śiva abound, though no iconic image of Śiva occupies the center of the innermost sanctuary of a Śiva temple. In an apparent contradiction, the two forms (iconic and aniconic), are combined to illustrate the story of Viṣṇu and Brahmā bewildered by the flaming pillar of Śiva. In the middle of the flame pillar, Śiva reveals himself to the gods, as he reveals himself to his devotee. Carved within the *liṅga* pillar in a mandorla-like opening, the figure of Śiva stands straight as a post.[21] This visual paradox has intuitive clarity. The small icon of the unfathomable god is the cognizance by which god and man are able to recognize the presence of Śiva himself within the inscrutable *liṅga* (see however the juxtaposition of *liṅga* and image, p. 166).

Śaiva sacred tradition assigns different levels in the hierarchy of manifestation to the flame *liṅga* that appeared to the gods in the cosmic night and to the *liṅga* set up for worship. The *Vātulaśuddhāgama*[22] specifies the principles (*tattva*) and powers (*śakti*) in direct ontological descent from Śiva, the ultimate reality, down to the *liṅga* set up for worship. Śiva, the ultimate reality, is beyond form, limitless, and unknowable by any mode of proof. At the end of the destruction of an aeon, however, Śiva wills his transcendental power (*Parā Śakti*) to evolve from him, which is but a thousandth part of himself. From a thousandth part of this transcendental power emerges *Ādi Śakti*, "the primordial power"; similarly and in succession, the three powers of *Icchā Śakti*, "willing"; *Jñāna Śakti*, "knowing"; and *Kriyā Śakti*, "acting" evolve.[23] From a tenth part of *Parā Śakti*, "the transcendental power," comes the quiddity or principle of Sadāśiva, the eternal Śiva: "it exists everywhere as a subtle divine light, bright as the lightning and pervades the space in the universe."[24] From a tenth part of *Ādi*

[21] *Ibid.*, vol. 2, part 2, pp. 105-107, 110, and pl. XIV.

[22] Cf. *ibid.*, vol. 2, part 2, pp. 361 ff.

[23] *Ibid.*, vol. 2, part 2, pp. 361-62.

[24] *Ibid.*, vol. 2, part 2, pp. 363-64.

Śakti, the primordial power, the quiddity Īśāna-Śiva evolves. It exists as a pillar of the most intense luminosity, like that of a hundred thousand suns, and is called the celestial pillar (*divya liṅga*). As everything originates from this pillar, it is also called the root-pillar (*mūla stambha*). In the end everything also returns to it. The two highest ontological levels, here called Sadāśiva and Īśāna Śiva, in the descent from Śiva, the ultimate, totally transcendent reality, are without form (*niṣkala*).[25]

The quiddity of the third level, proceeding from the power of willing, also exists as a celestial *liṅga*. It has the brightness of fire with flames of fire flaring around it. This quiddity is no longer without form. It is more concrete (*mūrta*), and is considered as *sakala*. On the fourth level, or in the fourth stage, the celestial pillar is crystal clear and immense. The fifth and last quiddity exists as the *liṅga* set up on its plinth in the innermost sanctuary of the temple.[26]

Myth and doctrine, though cognate, apply the same terms with some latitude. The fire pillar, though celestial (*divya*)—as are its ontologically preceding celestial pillars—is, however, no longer considered to be "without form." The fire pillar is conceived as endowed with form, because it had been seen, if only by the gods. The *Vātulaśuddhāgama*, moreover, describes a figure of Śiva. This text beholds Śiva on the crystal-clear pillar of the next or fourth ontological phase or level as four-faced, twelve-eyed, and twelve-armed.[27] The icon of Śiva in the fire *liṅga* of the *Purāṇas* thus rightly occupies the aniconic *liṅga*. *Purāṇa* and *Āgama* differ with regard to the limits they define for the realm of form (*sakala*). The *Āgama* tradition sees the world of myth as situated within the world of form and beholds its images as concrete (*mūrta*). In the last stage, that of physical reality, inhere all the ontological principles and powers, for each level contains within itself the powers and principles that in turn preceded it. This inherent ontological hierarchy sanctifies the physical shape of the *liṅga* in its concrete reality.

Starting from below the absolute, transcendent Śiva, who cannot be conceived in any likeness whatsoever, the evolving Śiva principles are couched in terms of light. They correspond to his subtle body (*liṅga śarīra*). All-pervasive, with the imminence of lightning, it exists. It then condenses into a pillar, shining with the light of a hundred thou-

[25] *Ibid.*, vol. 2, part 2, p. 364.

[26] *Ibid.*, vol. 2, part 2, pp. 364-66.

[27] *Ibid.*, vol. 2, part 2, p. 365.

sand suns. This concentrate of effulgence is the celestial *liṅga*, the root-pillar (*mūla stambha*), whence everything originates and in which everything is dissolved. The primordial root-pillar, as yet imperceptible (*niṣkala*) to gods and man, prefigures the flaming *liṅga* pillar, which is *sakala*. The gods saw it. With it the fulguration, sunblast, and fire miracles in the ideation of the creative process subside in the crystal clarity and *sakala* immensity of the last of the three "celestial *liṅgas*" (*divya liṅga*) in which they prefigure the *sakala liṅga* in manifestation, in its material body, the *sthūla śarīra* set up for worship, or "self existent." The terminology of the *Āgamas* distinguishes the levels of the subtle body itself as *niṣkala* in the two higher levels and as *sakala* in the three successively lower planes, whereas the *Purāṇas* consider as *niṣkala* the entire subtle body. The conception of the pillar (*stambha*) traverses all the planes except the highest, which is entirely pervaded by the sharp, clear intensity of the light that is Śiva. On the next lower plane the pillar of light is realized ontologically as the celestial pillar. The celestial pillar, by which Īśāna-Śiva is known to exist in the invisible empyrean, has its architectural symbol in the *ākāśa* or space *liṅga*.[28] This *ākāśa liṅga* does not consist of space. On the contrary, it is a solid shape and functions as the finial of the tower (*śikhara*) on Śiva temples (*AP*.102.4); it can be found on such temples in Orissa and Andhra Pradesh of the seventh to tenth centuries. It rises high in space directly above the *liṅga* on the ground in the innermost sanctuary, the womb chamber (*garbha-gṛha*) of the temple.

Returning to the *Vātulaśuddhāgama*, on each of the next two ontological levels, the abstract pillar shape of fire or of crystal is associated with an iconic image of Śiva—the two planes being considered as *sakala*. In this context, the clear-cut definition of the *Śiva Purāṇa* speaks of Śiva manifesting his own form (*svarūpa*) through the form of a *niṣkala stambha*, an amalgam of pillar, phallus, and subtle body (*ŚP*. 1.5.28-29).

The combination of the conceptual form, as in the *Vātulaśuddhāgama*, of the *liṅga* and iconic figure stems from the purpose that these different visions and visualizations serve. They are symbols that support and evoke the presence of Śiva, the ultimate reality, the unmanifest, invisible, and unknowable source of creation. The purpose is fulfilled by the stereometric *liṅga* and the icon. They belong to the realm of form (*rūpa*), the realm of art in the age of the *Puraṇas*.

[28] M. A. Dhaky, "The 'Ākāśaliṅga' Finial," 1974, p. 307.

In the great rock-cut cave temple of Śiva in Elephanta, the *liṅga*, a cylinder rounded off on top, rises in stark purity within the small innermost sanctuary in the same spacious hall where, in supreme grandeur, the partly iconic shape of Sadāśiva (Pls. 1, 2, 4), integrating within its structure the verticality of the *liṅga*, presents in subtlest nuances of form the innermost essence of Śiva. Myth, ontology, and art, interrelated creative modes of the realization of Śiva, incorporate heterogeneous traditions and convert them into complex, startlingly coherent immediacy.

The *liṅga* in the abstract stereometry of its evocative phallic shape is an ontological symbol. It holds the unmanifest and invisible source of creativity. The image of Sadāśiva in Elephanta (Pl. 4), created from within this source, gives form to it. As the gods of the *raudra brahman* of the *Ṛg Veda* carved Rudra-Vāstoṣpati out of a *mantra*, so did the sculptor of Sadāśiva in Elephanta invest this image of Śiva, in visible terms, with the mystery of the *liṅga*. Śiva tore out his *liṅga* and separated from himself the organ of procreation and the instrument of lust. The *liṅga* touched ground, entered the earth, and flamed on a cosmic scale, consuming its substantiality in fire, yet retaining its shape, a transmundane sign glowing from the netherworld to the sky whence, incandescent, it soared to further horizons imperceptible to the eye. The transubstantiation of the severed *liṅga* into fire, thence into light, is a cosmic analogy to the transmutation of the yogi who experiences in himself the reabsorption of the elements of which his body is constituted until he obtains a body made of fire (cf. *ŚUp*.2.12; cf. *ŚS*.1.69-78). The flaming *liṅga* was seen by the gods; the *liṅga* of light was within and beyond the flames, beyond and through which they could not see. The epiphany of Śiva from within the flames enlightened them.

The pillars of flame and light, described in the *Vātulaśuddhāgama*, are precipitations of yogic realizations. The concrete *liṅga*, which is worshiped here on earth, is the result of the same sequence—in reverse—by which the yogi transmutes his body, implying in its materiality (be it clay, stone, or gold) the transcendental, indescribable source at its core.

The motionless pillar of the *liṅga* rises from the ground in which it is embedded, so that it stands firmly established.

According to another version, however, the severed *liṅga*, fallen to the ground, did not come to rest, but moved about, burning everything, until it found the *yoni* or lap of the goddess (*ŚP*.4.12.18-19, 32, 48). But the combined symbol of *liṅga* and *yoni* presupposes the existence of the Great Goddess, whose entry into the myth of Śiva—mythically an exit from Śiva's body—is an alternative response of the Great God to Brahmā's command that he create mortals. He did not create mortals. He is the unknowable source itself of life. The invisible presence of the source is ontologically implied in the concrete shape of the symbol *liṅga*. This symbol has the shape of a pillar; it resembles a phallus and calls to mind the motionless figure of Sthāṇu.

A South Indian legend about a local *liṅga* at Kāñcipuram tells of Śiva having destroyed, in the course of one night, everything that existed in creation. He danced and proceeded toward the creation of a new universe. He appeared as a "*liṅga* of light." Having entered the *liṅga*, Śiva created all that he had destroyed—nature, stars, gods, man, animals, plants, and so on. After worshiping this *liṅga*, Brahmā obtained the power of creation.[29]

The apparent paradox of Brahmā, the Creator, obtaining the power of creation from the Śiva *liṅga* has its mythical past in Rudra having prepared the seed for the Father. In the legend from Kāñcipuram, Śiva, having danced a dance of creation, enters the *liṅga* of light in which he appears. Image enters into symbol. They interpenetrate on the hallowed ground of the *liṅga*.

5. The *Liṅga* and the Face of Śiva

The concretization of the supernal light in the material shape, the *liṅga*, rises as phallic pillar, a symbol complete in the simplicity of its stereometric appearance. Some *liṅgas*, however, carry the head of Śiva, either one head alone, or a head in each of the four directions and a fifth head, invisible as a rule, but of the highest significance, as its name and position denote. The heads project from the curved plane of the pillar, and are modeled from the ears forward. They are integrally part of the *liṅga*, which they enlarge and whose content they make explicit. They are expositions of the meaning of the *liṅga* in manifestation, that is of its ontological reality and concrete existence. Among the *mukhaliṅgas*, or *liṅgas* combined with the face

[29] P. Dessigane, P. Z. Pattabiramin, and J. Filliozat, *Les Légendes çivaites de Kāñcipuram*, 1964, p. 29.

(*mukha*) of Śiva, the four-faced *liṅgas* predominate. The fifth, invisible, head is implied in the overall conception. This type of *liṅga* is the visual equivalent of the five *mantras* or *brahmans*. Inasmuch as a *mantra* is a thought form, particularly one in which deity is felt to be present, each of the faces of the *liṅga* corresponds to one of the five *mantras*, and represents a particular manifestation of Śiva. The faces are anthropomorphic and are executed in a concrete material. They are images (*mūrti*) corresponding to *mantras*. Face-*liṅgas* with one or five faces, as the *liṅga* from Bhīṭā shows, are known from the second century B.C.[30] The five-fold *mantra* is first known from the *Taittirīya Āraṇyaka* (*TĀ*.10.43-47), which is assigned to the third century B.C., if not earlier. This complex of thought-forms, embodied in representational shapes, appears as if precipitated into the form of the *Pañcamukha liṅga*, in which the "abstract" *liṅga* pillar coalesces with the anthropomorphic faces (cf. Sāyaṇa on *TĀ*.10.43-47).

The combination of pillar and head is known in India in several different contexts, the abstract vertical shape ending with or surmounted by the head. To this day, wooden pillars are set up that terminate with a human head. Several varieties of this configuration representing a god or deified hero exist in Bihar, in eastern India. They show the two component parts, pillar and head, demarcated from each other or coalesced, shoulders and arms of the globular head merging in low relief with the cylindrical post.[31] In this latter mode, the fifth head of the stone Bhīṭā *liṅga* rises from the central post, to which the four other heads of Śiva adhere in low relief. The Bhīṭā *liṅga* is exceptional in its coalesced shape of post and figurative components. Moreover, the fifth head, on top, is fully carved in the round and very conspicuous. As a rule, however, it is present in name only, the plain dome shape terminating the *liṅga*. There, the fifth head is to be thought of, symbol of an invisible, metaphysical reality.

While the Bhīṭā *liṅga* incorporates the presence of Śiva in the coalescence of pillar and human shape, another *liṅga*, of about the same time, in Guḍimallam, South India, boldly shows the entire anthropomorphic figure of Rudra-Agni standing in front of the towering and explicitly phallic *liṅga*.[32] Both these visualizations combine abstract

[30] B. N. Sharma, *Iconography of Sadāśiva*, 1976, pl. 1; T. A. Gopinatha Rao, *Elements of Hindu Iconography*, vol. 2, part 2, pp. 63-65 and pl. I.

[31] W. G. Archer, *The Vertical Man*, 1947, pls. 33-36, 42-43.

[32] T. A. Gopinatha Rao, *Elements of Hindu Iconography*, vol. 2, part 1, pls. II and III.

stereometric and anthropomorphic shapes, the phallic association being vested in that of the pillar.

A different combination of vertical and upright head is described in an early Buddhist text. The *Mahākapi Jātaka* relates that the skull of the Buddha, encrusted with gold, was to be set up on the point of a lance.[33] Though the implications of this memorial have no direct bearing on a *mukhaliṅga*, it shows a combination of a vertical object, a staff—though not a pillar—with the "human" head. The skull of the Buddha, inlaid with gold, the imperishable substance, would indicate that the relic and emblem of death had been made a symbol of immortality.

The vertical is the direction of the sacred; it is a symbol of ascent, pointing to heaven and transcendent regions. A vertical megalith, considered to be the seat of the spirit of a dead person and, for this reason, a focus of power, protects the living and ensures the fertility of the fields and women. The megalith acts as an instrument of fecundation in Dravidian and Munda, and also in Bhil, Gond, and other tribal traditions.[34] Within Śaivism, special sacredness accrues to the *svāyambhuva liṅgas*. These *liṅgas*, according to the *Kāmikāgama*, have come into existence by themselves, as their name implies—and are believed to have existed since time immemorial.[35] They are believed not to have been made by the hand of man. Their natural, spontaneous, apparently inexplicable origin invests the *svāyambhuva*, or self-existent, stone *liṅgas* with extraordinary sanctity. Inasmuch as the sanctity inheres in the natural hardness and durability of stone, the man-made *liṅgas* partake of it. The enduring quality of stone invests every stone *liṅga* as if the primordial substance (*prakṛti*) were ingrained in it. In its wide ambience of associated constituents, the shape of the *liṅga* may include urns and vessels made of clay, exhibiting on their walls a likeness of a human face. All these forms and traditions were available for or concurred with the conception of the *mukhaliṅga*, a precipitate of *mantra* into visible, tangible form, a solidification of sacred sound.

The combination of *liṅga* and head, the latter clinging to its pillar shape, reinforces the verticalism of the sacred object and emphasizes its meaning. The vertical *liṅga* (*ūrdhvaliṅga*), pointing upward, con-

[33] *Jātaka*, ed. and tr. E. B. Cowell, 1973, 3:227 (book VII, no. 407).

[34] M. Eliade, *Traité d'histoire des religions*, 1953, p. 192.

[35] T. A. Gopinatha Rao, *Elements of Hindu Iconography*, vol. 2, part 1, pp. 80-82.

veys not only the retention of the seed once "stirred" but its upward conduction, "through the spinal cord to the brain,"[36] retaining its integrity as creative substance, while being transformed and absorbed mentally as *bodhicitta*, the "thought of Awakening."[37] This tantric realization is seen in the *mukhaliṅga* or "face-*liṅga*," the two overlapping components forming a visual unity, an artistically potent symbol of the ascent and transmutation of sexual into mental power, a channeling of the procreative into creative faculty. As if to confirm this ancient knowledge, villagers in Girnar, a village about eleven miles from Nasik in Maharashtra, told a Peace Corps volunteer that in the winter they put woolen scarves around their head in order to keep warm their semen that is stored there.[38] The belief of village people of the present, tantric realization and practice, and the form of the *mukhaliṅga*, though on different levels of awareness, form part of the same tradition. The *mukhaliṅga* of one or five faces, of which the fifth as a rule is invisible, represents an inner realization by symbolic configuration.

At the same time, the *liṅga*, set up for worship, whatever its material, is the reification and concrete symbol of the light beyond perception, a light that took shape so that the eyes of the gods could see it wreathed in flames. The symbolical penetration of supernal light and its transformation in the concrete material shape of the *liṅga* is a process cognate with ontological thought. Once the vision of descending, condensing light strikes the terrestrial base and assumes concrete extension, its volume is situated in space. While the vertical direction of the pillar remains essential, it is ensconced in matter and takes on volumetric extensiveness. Though the upper part of the *liṅga* is circular, its lowest part is square; it is oriented in the four directions. This lowest part is sunk into the ground or into the pedestal of the *liṅga*. The square section is basic to the *liṅga*, although it is not visible. As the main part of the volumetric shape, the cylindrical shaft with the four heads incorporates the theme of the four directions. The heads face them in the most explicit iconography, which hinges on the embodied equation of *mantra* and deity, of sacred sound and vision.

Four is the sacred number of manifestation and orientation. Five,

[36] W. D. O'Flaherty, *Asceticism and Eroticism in the Mythology of Śiva*, pp. 261-62.

[37] M. Eliade, *Yoga: Immortality and Freedom*, p. 251; cf. A. Bharati, *The Tantric Tradition*, pp. 177-78.

[38] Reported in 1974 by Marilyn Hirsh to the writer.

the quintessential number, is not only that of the center but, by vertical extension, of a significance above, and symbolically beyond, the realm of the four directions on the terrestrial horizontal plane. Technically, the *liṅga* being a stereometric solid, the fifth head is assigned to the top, as in the Bhīṭā *liṅga*. This, however, is an exceptional instance. The *pañcamukha liṅga*, of which the texts speak, in its sculptural form shows the four heads encircling the shaft. The top of the *liṅga* is without a head, for the fifth head of the five-faced, or *pañcamukha liṅga* is a symbol of Śiva in transcendency, invisibly present in the pentad. Thus the color of the fifth head is said to be that of crystal.

Five is the sacred number of Śiva. Each of the five "letters" or syllables of the mantra of Śiva, *namaḥ śivāya*, has its equivalents on many levels of realization, while together the five syllables say "Obeisance to Śiva," signifying the assent and total commitment to Śiva by his devotee. In more expanded thought-forms amounting to verbally articulate incantations of Śiva, the *pañcabrahmans* invoke, one by one, five different forms of Śiva. They are Sadyojāta, Vāmadeva, Aghora, Tatpuruṣa, and Īśāna. They are represented by the five faces of Śiva, which have their correspondents in the five elements, in the five senses, in the five organs of perception, and the five organs of action[39] (see chart). "One should know all things of the phenomenal world as of a fivefold character, for the reason that the eternal verity of Śiva is of the character of the fivefold Brahman" (*PBUp*.31).[40] Śiva, in manifestation, is perceived in the five senses and in the five elements. He dwells in each, as he is in the five organs of actions, from those of sex to those of speech (*LP*.2.14.1-31).

The eight realities of Śiva, as Aṣṭamūrti, constitute the cosmos. The five *mantras*, the *pañcabrahmans*, of which the five-faced *liṅga* is the concrete shape, hold the total reality of Śiva, transcendent and immanent. It is realized within man, the microcosm, himself image and also part of the cosmos. The four visible faces of the *liṅga* are directed toward the world in which man lives, and in which each of the faces of god has its own countenance.

Sadyojāta is "born all at once." His is possibly the one and only face looking out from an *ekamukha liṅga* (a *liṅga* with one face only). It confronts the devotee as existence itself, for Sadyojāta, whose *mantra* is

[39] H. Meinhard, *Beiträge zur Kenntnis des Śivaismus nach den Purāṇas*, p. 17.

[40] *Pañcabrahma Upaniṣad (PBUp)*, tr. T.R.S. Ayyangar and ed. G. S. Murti, 1953, p. 112.

Śiva as the Five *Mantras* (*Pañcabrahmans*)

Mantras	*Transcendental* *Principles*	*Powers* (Śakti)	*Ontological/ Cosmogonic Principles*	*Sense powers* (indriya) *of the organs of* *Cognition*	*Action*	*Elements* *subtle* (tanmātra)	*gross* (mahābhūta)	*Directions*	*Colors*	***Deities***
Īśāna	*Śiva Tattva*	*Cit* (*Parā*)	*Kṣetrajña* (*Puruṣa*)	Hearing (ear)	Speech	Sound	Ether (space)	Upward	Crystal	Sadāśiva
Tatpuruṣa	*Śakti Tattva*	*Ānanda* (*Ādi*)	*Prakṛti*	Feeling (skin)	Grasping (hands)	Touch	Wind (air)	East	Yellow	Mahādeva
Aghora	*Sadāśiva*	*Jñāna*	*Buddhi* (*Mahat*)	Seeing (eye)	Moving (feet)	Form	Fire	South	Black	Bhairava
Vāmadeva	*Īśvara*	*Icchā*	*Ahaṁkāra*	Tasting (tongue)	Excretion	Taste	Water	North	Red	Umā
Sadyojāta	*Sadvidyā*	*Kriyā*	*Manas*	Smelling (nose)	Procreation	Smell	Earth	West	White	Nandin

Sources: *LP*.2.14.1-31; 2.21.9-11; columns 2 and 3 according to Śāradātilaka 1.15-24 and Vātulaśuddhāgama, in T.A.G. Rao 2.2.361-66; and column 11 according to *VDhP*.3.48.1-8.

the first of the pentad, is invoked in it as Bhava, existence. The face of Existence appears a miracle of sudden eruption into this world of the senses from the side of the pillar-shaped body of the *liṅga*. According to the *Liṅga Purāṇa*, his appellation is a secret word of power (*brahman*), for Sadyojāta, who is Śiva, the Unborn, the source of birth, is not beyond existence in this world (*LP*.1.23.5-6; 16.9-10). The face of Sadyojāta as shown on *pañcamukha liṅgas* resembles that of Tatpuruṣa, who is Mahādeva, the Great God.[41] Aghora, a euphemism for Ghora, the Frightful, is Rudra at his fiercest; he is Śarva, according to the *mantra*. Ghora is terrible and black, resembles Death, and is Time. But he who knows Śiva and that it is he who has assumed this terrifying form, has no terror and is full of peace (*LP*.1.23.18-22). Vāmadeva is the name of the face of god on the left (*vāma*). *Vāma*, moreover, means "lovely." The fivefold *mantra*, bodied forth from the *liṅga*, compacts and coordinates the hierarchy of manifestation, from the sense powers and subtle elements to the sense-particulars. Each of the five faces of the *liṅga* has its equivalent on two ontological levels, that of the "subtle elements" (*tanmātra*) and of the gross elements (*mahābhūta*). Besides these categories, the five faces of the *liṅga* are also the symbols of the metaphysical levels, from *manas* (cosmic mind) upward to *ahaṁkāra*, the individuating principle, to *mahat* and finally to *prakṛti* and *puruṣa*, cosmic substance and spirit. Through these transcendent categories, Śiva, the ultimate reality, becomes the efficient and material cause of all that exists. *Śiva-tattva* (the ultimate reality) has its symbol in the usually invisible face of the Lord, Īśāna, who is "the knower of the field" (*kṣetrajña*); his presence vibrates in his *mantra*. Tatpuruṣa is the symbol of *prakṛti*; Aghora is the symbol of *mahat* (*buddhi*) or cosmic intellect; Vāmadeva, the symbol of *ahaṁkāra*, and Sadyojāta the symbol of *manas* (mind) (*LP*.2.14.6-10). While the five faces are equivalent images of the world of the senses, they are at the same time symbols of the transcendental categories, so that Sadyojāta, "born all at once" as the symbol of mind has, in the world of the senses, the power of sex and the element earth as equivalent references (*LP*.2.14.20, 25). Each has its particular color. In this way the five-faced *liṅga* is the comprehensive symbol of the five-times-fivefold reality, Śiva, in whom are all the twenty-five *tattvas* or ontological

[41] K. Kumar, "A Dhyāna-Yoga Maheśamūrti and Some Reflections on the Iconography of the Maheśamūrti Images," 1975, p. 107 and pls. V and VI.

principles, from the unfathomable beyond to concrete existence (*LP*.2.14.31-33).

Sadyojāta, "born all at once," symbol of mind (*manas*)—who was generated first, is the first of the five *mantras*, and is existence itself—appears to occupy, in the symbolism of the *pañcamukha liṅga*, the position of the initiated, who represents *manas*, the eighth reality of Aṣṭamūrti Śiva.

The five *mantra* faces of the *liṅga* are those of Śiva. As faces of god they have their own names and iconography, and are shown not infrequently as busts with arms that carry their particular emblems. Sadyojāta is equated with Nandin, the foremost attendant and doorkeeper of Śiva. Vāmadeva, the "lovely" face of the left, is Umā, the Great Goddess, as consort of Śiva. Aghora is Bhairava, the horrible, frightening form of the Great God. Tatpuruṣa is Mahādeva, the Great God. Īśāna, whose face is generally not shown, indicates the presence of Śiva, the eternal Sadāśiva, in whom is evoked Śiva in utter transcendency (*VDhP*.3.48.1-8).[42] Once Umā asked Śiva why he had four visible faces. Śiva explained that the eastern face conveyed the supernatural and the perennial practice of asceticism, the western face expressed the sustenance of the universe, and the northern face showed meditation of the *Veda*, the sum total of all knowledge. The northern and western faces were auspicious, whereas the southern face meant the destruction of progeny (*MBh*.13, app. 1, no. 15, lines 278-81, 301-305).

The categories of the *Liṅga Purāṇa* are those of the Sāṁkhya system. Its ontology, in the *Viṣṇudharmottara Purāṇa*, is represented as a theophany. Differences in coordination occur in the *Purāṇas*, however; in the *Agni Purāṇa*, for instance, white is associated with Tatpuruṣa and yellow with Sadyojāta (*AP*.304.25).

While the *Purāṇas*, in explaining the meaning of the five faces of the *liṅga*, adhere to the Sāṁkhya system, a late Śaiva *Upaniṣad*, the *Pañcabrahma Upaniṣad*, and Śaiva philosophy account for the meaning of the *mantras* themselves, which are figured on the five-faced *liṅga*. Accordingly, Īśāna, Tatpuruṣa, Aghora, Vāmadeva, and Sadyojāta, the five *mantras*, the *pañcabrahmans*, are sound-forms that constitute Śiva in transcendency.[43] They are represented by the anthropo-

[42] *Viṣṇudharmottara Purāṇa (VDhP)*, cf. tr. S. Kramrisch, Part III, 1928, p. 71.

[43] *Pañcabrahma Upaniṣad (PBUp)*, tr. T.R.S. Ayyangar and ed. G. S. Murti, pp. 110, 111.

morphic symbols of the five faces of the *liṅga*. These also represent the five aspects of the power or *śakti* of Paramaśiva. Paramaśiva, or the Supreme Śiva, in utmost transcendency, is pure creativity, pure changeless consciousness, the godhead in which all things inhere. Paramaśiva, boundless plenum of pure consciousness, by its inherent power represents itself as *Śiva Tattva*, consciousness, together with *Śakti Tattva*, the power of consciousness to act. *Śiva Tattva*, and *Śakti Tattva*, the Śiva principle and the Śakti principle, are unproduced, eternal. They coexist monadically. Their polarization inheres in the *Sadāśiva Tattva*, the first evolute of consciousness, wherein "I—this" (*aham-idam*), or consciousness and its subject, arise in close embrace. Thence *Īśvara Tattva* evolves, the principle wherein consciousness gazes at itself as the object. In the next evolute, the *Sadvidyā Tattva*, consciousness, looks first at *aham*, "I," and then at *idam*, "this." In this third stage of the increasing distance of "I" and "this," all things are created. They are prefigured in the universal consciousness before its transcendental unity displays itself as duality by the power of *māyā*. The ontological hierarchy of the five transcendental principles of Śiva, Śakti, Sadāśiva, Īśvara, and Sadvidyā, which are "pure principles" or *Śuddha Tattvas*, has its point of reference in Paramaśiva, that is in pure, changeless consciousness, in pure creativity, or, only seemingly paradoxically, in the Uncreate.

The transcendental aspects of *śakti* or power associated with the five pure principles (*tattva*) are, respectively: *cit* or *parāśakti*, the power of transcendental consciousness; *ānanda*, bliss, the primordial or *ādi śakti*; and the transcendental powers of knowing, willing, and acting (*jñāna śakti, icchā śakti, krīyā śakti*).

The immutable pure principles and their powers, by an ongoing increase of the distance of *aham-idam*, give rise to duality, to discrimination, because of the finitizing or defining power of consciousness. This power or *śakti* is *māyā*, the power that brings about the prefiguration of mind and matter. *Māyā*, delusion, according to Kashmiri Śaivism, is an eternal power dormant in consciousness, which disrupts the transcendental unity of the pure principles and effects the impure duality of the manifest world. By the activity of *māyā* the pure principles and powers are transmitted to and transmuted in the realm of pure-impure (*śuddha-aśuddha*) principles, a metaphysical limbo between the transcendental and the phenomenal in which *aham* and *idam* are distinct as *Puruṣa* (cosmic creator) and *Prakṛti* (cosmic substance). Hence, the cosmos evolves in its subtle and gross aspects, from cosmic intelligence (*mahat*), the individuating principle (*ahaṁkāra*), and cosmic mind (*manas*), to the sense powers (*indriya*) and subtle elements (*tanmātra*), and down to Earth. The realm of the "impure principles" (*aśuddha tattva*) of Śaiva ontology is identical with that of the ontology of the Sāṁkhya philosophy, while being permeated by the presence of Paramaśiva, the ultimate point of reference of every *tattva* and each particular of knowledge, action, and concrete reality.

In the ontological theophany of Śiva, the body of god consisting of *mantra* (*mantra-mūrti*) is represented by the five-faced *liṅga*. The symbol of the presence of god on each and all levels of realization and reality is vested within the audible / inaudible sound of *mantra* over and above the luminance of the *liṅga* pillar.

The *Pañcabrahma Upaniṣad*, a text possibly prior to the *Viṣṇudharmottara Purāṇa*, assigns control of all *śaktis* to Tatpuruṣa (*PBUp.* 15), whereas *jñāna*, *icchā*, and *kriyā śakti* are specifically associated with Vāmadeva, Aghora, and Sadyojāta, respectively (*PBUp*.12, 8, 6). Besides, Tatpuruṣa is associated with the north (commentary on *PBUp.* 15); Vāmadeva, Aghora, and Sadyojāta with the south, west, and east, respectively (commentary on *PBUp*.10, 7, 5). The *Vātulaśuddhāgama*, on the other hand, gives precedence to *icchā śakti* instead of *jñāna śakti*.[44] Doctrinal differences, as well as possible errors in transmission, may account for changes in attribution, but they do not alter the main structure of Śaiva ontology. The doctrines were at their peak in the latter part of the first millennium of the present era; they coincided with the living tradition of the myths and imagery of the *Purāṇas*, adhering to Sāṁkhya doctrine, while the *pañcabrahman mantras* themselves were embodied in the *Taittirīya Āraṇyaka* (10.43-47) in about the third century B.C.

The *Pañcabrahma Upaniṣad* says: "With the knowing of the fivefold Brahmans, consisting of Sadyojāta and others, as the preliminary step, one should know that all this phenomenal world is the Parabrahman, Śiva, of the character of the fivefold Brahmans, nay he should know whatever is seen or heard of or falls within or lies beyond the range of his inner and outer senses, as Śiva of the character of the fivefold Brahmans alone" (*PBUp*.26).[45] The *Upaniṣad* continues: "In

[44] Cf. T. A. Gopinatha Rao, *Elements of Hindu Iconography*, vol. 2, part 2, pp. 361-63.

[45] *Pañcabrahma Upaniṣad (PBUp)*, tr. T.R.S. Ayyangar and ed. G. S. Murti, p. 111.

the Brahmapura (the body that is the city of the Brahman, wherein is the abode of the Brahman of the Microcosm), wherein is the abode of the form of a white lotus (the heart), known as the Dahara, . . . in the middle of it is the ether known as Daharākāśa. That ether is Śiva, the infinite existence, nondual consciousness and unsurpassed bliss. . . . This Śiva is the witness established in the hearts of all beings . . . and manifests himself to the seeker, in accord with the strength of vision and degree of spiritual development attained by the seeker. Hence this Śiva is known as the heart of all beings and the liberator from the bonds of worldly existence" (*PBUp*.40-41 and commentary).[46]

Reverting from the metaphysical and ontological meaning of the *pañcamukha liṅga* to the myth of the *liṅga* of the Great God: the *liṅga* was seen torn out and fallen on the earth, just as the seed of the Creator had fallen in the beginning of things. Fire consumed the lake of the seed of Prajāpati. The severed *liṅga* of Śiva entered the earth, vanished, and rose as a pillar of flame that only gods could see. Rudra was born; he arose from the seed of Prajāpati, and he sprang from the head of Brahmā. He was born anew from aeon to aeon. The myth of his creation, in successive aeons, holds the mystery of his birth, implied in the symbol of sex and in that of the head. Rudra is seed-born, mind-born, breath-born, though Uncreate. He is the Great Yogi, whose *ūrdhvaliṅga* is a sign of self-containment. He becomes Sthāṇu, the post, when Brahmā asks him, his own mindborn son, to create mortals. Rudra infused his own asceticism into his father Brahmā, who created him from his head, unlike Prajāpati, who had engendered him from his seed. Head and sex lie close together in the myth of Rudra and in the concrete shape of the *mukhaliṅga*, which is made of stone or any other substance.

The heads, one invisible, the others manifest, are united with the *liṅga* of Śiva in their proper places. Invested with their form and meaning, the *liṅga* is the concrete shape permeated by the vibrations of the light and of the *mantras* of Śiva. With its five faces, the *liṅga* projects its meaning beyond the perimeter of its abstract phallic shape into an ambience where *mantra* and image coincide. Śiva Mantramūrti is at the same time Sadyojāta-Nandin, "just born" in the mind of his devotee, and, facing in the opposite direction, he is Tatpuruṣa-

[46] *Ibid.*, p. 114.

Mahādeva, "suchness" and the Great God. The faces of Nandin and Mahādeva resemble each other.[47]

Along the other axis, and facing in opposite directions, the dreadful countenance of Aghora-Bhairava is the antithesis of the loveliness of Vāmadeva-Umā.[48] Aghora-Bhairava is Rudra, the Wild God at his fiercest. Vāmadeva, "the god of the left," is the Great Goddess, she is Umā, part of Śiva and his consort. Her face, suffused with tenderness, is to the left of that of Mahādeva. Although the *mantra* of Vāmadeva does not explicitly invoke the goddess, the face of Umā, to the left of the Great God, surges from the *liṅga*, swelled by the invisible presence of *Prakṛti* (Plates 4, 6, 10).

6. *Liṅga*, *Mantra*, Time, and Eternity

Transcendental reality and ontological becoming, together with phenomenal existence, have their symbol in the *liṅga*. With reference to the latter, and inasmuch as the four visible faces of the *liṅga* are oriented in the four directions, the movement of the sun, that is of time, is built into the conception of the four-faced *liṅga*. The number four is symbolically that of the four directions. It was transferred from the four cardinal points, together with their respective faces, to an allegory of time, as seen in each of the four yugas or world ages—the Kṛta, Tretā, Dvāpara, and Kali Yugas. These ages follow one upon the other in each aeon (kalpa). The *Vāyu Purāṇa* relates that the gods were worried when the yugas came into being, for they were controlled by Kāla, the dread god of four faces, who is Time. In their fear of Kāla, the gods resorted to Mahādeva, the Great God. For a thousand years they propitiated him (*VāP*.32.6-10), for only Mahādeva the Great God would know the four-faced Kāla. The Great God addressed himself to Kāla and calmed him. God Kāla then felt free to introduce each of his four faces to the Lord. He identified each with one of the four world ages, beginning with the white face, which was that of the Kṛta Yuga, the Perfect Age. He then introduced the red face as that of the Tretā Yuga, and the tawny yellow face as that of the Dvāpara Age. He introduced last the terrible black face with

[47] K. Kumar, "A Dhyāna-Yoga Maheśamūrti," pp. 107, 109, and pls. V-VIII.
[48] *Ibid*.

threatening red eyes (*VāP*.32.11-19). It showed that this last age, the Kali Yuga, the present age, could know no happiness, for Kāla in that age would grab everyone (*VāP*.32.19-20). When god Kāla, who is time and death, had introduced each of his four faces, Lord Śiva, who all the while had known their identity, declared that in the fourth face or age he himself was to be worshiped; in fact, he inhered in each of them (*VāP*.32.21-22). All four faces were those of Maheśvara, the Great Lord, who makes time roll on, and who has five faces, the fifth face being placed above the others.

God Kāla, however, has no fifth face; he carries only four faces of Lord Śiva, for time does not exist in transcendency, which the fifth face of Śiva symbolizes. Below it, under the sun, in the revolving world of time, each world age has its own clear and strong color. Yet it is particularly in the darkness of the present yuga that Kāla, who is time and death, resembles Lord Śiva.

In the beginning, when the Perfect Age emerged at the first dawn, time was the antagonist of Śiva. Though as yet it did not show its face and was not personified, it acted against Rudra. It did not permit him to prevent the rupture of the Uncreate. Subsequently, when Rudra had agreed to, but tarried in carrying out, Brahmā's command, time again ran its course, seemingly counter to Rudra's purpose. Dakṣa had superseded Rudra. Though time (Kāla) thus far had not shown its face but had made its actions felt, it now revealed four faces. They were Śiva's masks and mouthpieces.

Each of the faces has its own significance, but the four faces of god Kāla speak with more than one tongue. Although the white face of Kāla had four tongues, their number subsequently dwindled (*VāP*.32.14-19). In the last, the present, age, the horrendous black face with its one black tongue says that Kāla, time, death, and Rudra are one. While in this yuga, the Kali Yuga, there is no happiness (*VāP*.32.20), there also is no fear for him who recognizes in the dark face of Kāla the face of the Great Lord (*VāP*.32.23-25).

The allegory of the four-faced god Time is analogous to, and closely fits the conception of, the four-faced *liṅga*. As Śiva dwells in both, the two shapes coalesce; the faces of Kāla are masks of Śiva. The four faces of the *liṅga*, inasmuch as they face the four directions, greet the sun at the four significant stages of its annual cycle. They are oriented in time. Whereas the ontological symbolism of the *liṅga* includes the element space, conceptually it does not provide for the dimension of time that abides in Śiva.

In the Kṛta, the Perfect Age, the great Ṛṣi Taṇḍi praised Lord Śiva as the passage of time in the year, the yuga, and so on (*MBh.*13.16.46). Through the encounter of the Great God with and his self-recognition in Kāla, the *liṅga*, the ontological symbol of Śiva, became vested with the dimension of time. The *liṅga* now encompassed the sense powers and the elements together with time, the condition for their existence. In the world of concrete reality they cannot function if time be taken from them. Their relation would dissolve, they would disintegrate. While death appears to be the alternative of the temporal condition in this world, death is built into the structure of time. Death says that she is powerless and acts under the authority of Time. All modes of behavior are directed by time (*MBh.*13.1.58-60). Kāla operates in all creatures. The universe is suffused with time; all acts and all attitudes, all modes of behavior are conditioned by Kāla.

Thus we see that Death, the beautiful young goddess, carried out the dictate of Kāla. She did not act on her own account but was directed by Kāla, whose dark presence loomed over the aftermath of Brahmā's extinguished conflagration of the cosmos that he had created. At this moment, Rudra as Sthāṇu imparted his yoga power of withdrawal to Time. He inserted the pause of quiescence into its speeding course and assuaged the immutable fact of dying by making the Creator accept the aeviternal rhythm of cyclical time, thus allowing for periods of withdrawal and rest between those of activity. Sthāṇu, the motionless pillar, held in himself the timeless, indivisible eternity of the absolute that is realized by yogis in *samādhi*. Absolute, undivided Time is a quality of the realization of the absolute. The Great God, the Lord of Yoga, as Sthāṇu, is an embodiment of the paradox of absolute Time. As such his image is that of the god Mahākāla, "great" or transcendental Time, in contradistinction to Kāla, relative time, the condition for the existence of the universe.

Relative time showed itself first, just before the primordial sunrise. Its flight, which was that of Rudra's arrow, caused the Father to withdraw from the embrace of his daughter. His seed, the seed of creation, fell to the earth.

In his primordial action, Rudra caused time to become manifest. Though Rudra was its cause, time acted against the purpose of

Rudra; but in that respect it followed the pattern that Rudra himself had established. He did this by first preparing the seed and then obstructing the consequence of his action. There was no unilinear path leading into creation.

Rudra, Lord of Yoga, held within himself motionless, indivisible, absolute Time, his inner equivalent of the Uncreate. He became the cause of relative time, the condition for the existence of the universe. Like time, Rudra, the Wild Archer, brings death. The great, mythical Ṛṣi Taṇḍi—who sang his hymn to Rudra in the first, the Perfect, Age, the Kṛta Yuga—knew the Great God not only as the passing of time in the year (*MBh.*13.16.46) but also as Death, as Time, and the ultimate cause of time, and he knew him as eternity (*MBh.*13.16.51). The vision of Ṛṣi Taṇḍi in the Kṛta Yuga foresaw and comprised Kāla and Mahādeva as they would appear in the Kali Yuga.

The Wild God of the *Ṛg Veda*, in the dawn of the world, did not reveal his face. His bow and arrows sufficed to establish the identity of him who had the power to cut short the span of life of man and beast. Rudra Tryambaka acted in the way in which the features of Kāla-Aghora's face are cast.[49]

At the dawn of creation, the Wild Archer aimed his arrow at the procreative act. The arrow would have prevented the inception of life had not time intervened and allowed the seed of the Creator to fall. Time then was against Rudra; it cooperated with the purpose of the Creator by providing the field for Rudra's action. Time played an ambiguous part, as did Rudra himself. The Wild Hunter, having prepared the seed for the Father, obstructed the consequence. Creation came about, borne by tensions of ambiguity. Rudra, the Lord of Yoga, resolved them within his unqualified quiescence. When he himself came to be born from the mind or breath of Brahmā, the Creator, he chose the shape of Sthāṇu, the pillar, as his own. This was in response to Brahmā's having charged him with the creation of mortals. Or he chose an alternative response and plunged into the waters. Plants came to life in the water as his light irradiated them. He dwelled in the waters for a long time; for him, in his trance, time did not exist. Time, however, mattered to Brahmā, the Creator, who assigned to another, to Dakṣa, the work of populating the wide earth. When at

[49] Cf. *ibid.*, pl. VII and p. 107.

last Rudra rose from the water and saw all the people whom he had not created, he raged.

Time once again had been Rudra's antagonist, or an ambiguous helpmate. At the moment of primeval dawn, time had been part of the scene in which Rudra sent forth his arrow. The scene was set on the border of the timeless Uncreate of which Rudra acted as guardian. Since then, Rudra had come to be born from Prajāpati, the Lord of Generation; Prajāpati gave his son his names, as well as his domains. They comprised the total manifest cosmos together with sun and moon, the measurers of time. Rudra henceforth comprised the entire manifest world in his cosmic body. While he stayed under water, time was drowned in his yogic absorption, but he kept Brahmā waiting, and made him transfer to Dakṣa the responsibility of creating mortals. Although Rudra raged when he rose from the waters for having been bypassed by the Creator, he owed this not altogether unwelcome, and probably not unforeseen, treatment to his cosmic as well as yogic power over time; past, present, and future lay within him while he practiced *tapas* in the waters.

In his shape as Sthāṇu, Rudra's alternative response to Brahmā's order to create mortals, time was kept in abeyance by Rudra's resolve to stay motionless until the end of the world.

When Brahmā, however, distressed by the miscarriage of one of his experiments in creating mortals, had been about to consume his creation in a holocaust, Rudra, the pillar, moved by pity, came to its rescue. He implored Brahmā to allow the triple universe—the future, the past, and the present—to exist (*MBh*.7, app. 1, no. 8, lines 69-98). In his great concern for creatures, Rudra asked for even more than that. He begged of Brahmā that all creatures, having lived their lives, would go to rest and come back to a new period of activity. Out of his timeless being Rudra introduced into the dimension of relative time a rhythm of movement and pause, an aeviternal return of life and of cosmic cycles.

Pity moved Sthāṇu, the pillar. Out of his concern for life, he who had turned away from the creation of mortals made the creator extend their life beyond the life span of their mortal bodies, so that when life withdrew from one body it would, after a period of rest, return to new activity in another. Rudra, the Great Yogi, who had laid time to rest within himself, projected from within himself a pause into the course of time. The Great Lord, moved by pity, had taken unto himself his primeval antagonist, time, had laid it to rest, and had imparted to its flight a new quality, a cyclical rhythm of pause and return.

In their fear of Kāla, who is time, the gods had resorted to Mahādeva, for none but the Great Lord would know him. Śiva recognized himself in the four faces of Kāla—the yugas—and made time roll on.

In yet another vision, carrying, paradoxically, the movement of time even beyond the four faces of Kāla, the five faces or *mantras* of Śiva are beheld manifesting in time, one after the other, in the vastness of succeeding cycles—not of yugas or world ages but of aeons (kalpa); one kalpa equals one day of Brahmā, or 1,000 times the 432,000,000 years of four yugas (*LP*.1.4.4; 1.4.24-36). In this context, the twenty-ninth aeon (kalpa) was singled out for the manifestation of Sadyojāta (*VāP*.22.9-14; *LP*.1.11.2-5; 1.23.1-6). This particular aeon, the twenty-ninth, may have been chosen for one particular reason. When twenty-eight aeons have passed, a vast revolution of world ages has been completed; this revolution is analogous to the briefer movement of the moon across its twenty-eight mansions; or it is analogous to the duration of a *manvantara*, which comprises four yugas repeated seven times. After such a vast period of ages, the time comes for the total manifestation of Śiva as the *Pañcabrahmans*, his five *mantras*, beginning with Sadyojāta.[50]

When Śiva was born to Prajāpati, he appeared as Nīla-Lohita, a boy, blue and red. This child, comprising the colors of the spectrum, suddenly sat on the lap of Prajāpati (*VāP*.27.3-5). Now, as Brahmā desired a son from aeon to aeon, he meditated, and a youth appeared to him in one aeon after the other, each time of a different color. Sadyojāta was the first to appear to Brahmā: the child was pure white (*LP*.1.11.1-8; 1.23.1-3; *VāP*.22.8-14). The other *mantra* manifestations appeared successively, in red (*LP*.1.12.1-3; *VāP*.22.21-25), in yellow (*VāP*.23.1-10; *LP*.1.13.1-3), or black (*LP*.1.14.3-4; *VāP*.23.22-29), or in the color of crystal (cf. *LP*.1.16.4-5; cf. *VāP*.23.36-40). Īśāna, the ruler, whose face of crystal color in principle and as a rule is invisible

[50] According to the *Liṅga Purāṇa*, Sadyojāta is manifest in the twenty-ninth kalpa (*LP*.1.11.2-5), Vāmadeva is manifest in the thirtieth kalpa (*LP*.1.12.1-5), Tatpuruṣa in the thirty-first kalpa (*LP*.1.13.1), Aghora in the thirty-second kalpa (*LP*.1.14.1-6), and *LP*.1.16.1-6 treats of the kalpa of Īśāna.

and above—that is "beyond"—the other faces on the *liṅga*, is here coordinated with the other youths, just as the *Īśāna mantra* is coordinated as the fifth *mantra* with the other four. In conjunction with each of these five blessed youths appeared disciples of the same respective colors, who showed by their actions the way to reunion in Lord Śiva (*LP*.1.11.6-11; 1.12.6-13; 1.13.16-21; 1.14.7-13; 1.16.36-39; *VāP*. 22.8-35; 23.1-40, 58-61). The impact of Śiva's birth is manifestation from Prajāpati-Brahmā resounded through the aeons in the five *mantra*-youths and their disciples. They carried into the sequence of aeons the presence of him who is Sadāśiva, the eternal, who is supreme, eternal bliss, who projects all beings into existence and withdraws them again into himself, the origin of the worlds, and who is called Time, the destroyer (cf. Hymn of Taṇḍi, *MBh*.13.16.51).

The projection of embodied *mantras* into aeonic sequence reduces their significance, eternal verities becoming temporal truths. Whereas it is in the nature of sound, the conveyance of *mantras*, to be located in time, the five *mantras* were also known to constitute Śiva's body, which though imaged anthropomorphically was known to be a "body of pure energy" (*śakti śarīra*) having no substance (*prakṛti*).[51] The five *mantras* constitute its head, face, heart, sex, and feet (*SDS* p. 82).[52] Sound is one of the subtle elements (*tanmātra*) within the impure principles (*aśuddha tattva*) of manifestation, and inheres in *ākāśa*, that is, ether or space. Sound is but a conveyance for *mantra*. *Mantra*, however, is more recondite than sound. Its origin lies in the realm of the pure principles. There are five kinds of sound in relation to *mantra*. The ultimate principle of sound is *parā vāc*. *Parā vāc* or transcendental sound belongs to *Śiva tattva*, the first Principle of Deity manifesting. In ontological hierarchy, *Śakti tattva* is the abode of *paśyantī vāc* or "seeing sound," whereas *Sadāśiva tattva*, the abode of *madhyamā vāc*, is the midpoint between the first stage of manifestation of sound and sound as substance (*vaikharī vāc*). *Madhyamā vāc* is differentiated though not articulate, like words one utters to oneself without using the vocal cords; *vaikharī vāc* is sound as vibration. It is of two kinds, subtle or inaudible sound—belonging to *Īśvara tattva*—operating on a

[51] *Sarvadarśanasaṃgraha (SDS)*, tr. E. B. Cowell and A. E. Gough, 1908, p. 117 and n. 3.

[52] Cf. V. A. Devasenapathi, *Śaiva Siddhānta*, 1966, pp. 46-47, which varies in the physical regions assigned to Vāmadeva and Sadyojāta.

much higher or lower frequency than is audible to the physical ear; and gross *vaikharī vāc*. Gross *vaikharī vāc* belongs to *Sadvidyā tattva*. The element *ākāśa* is the vehicle of gross *vaikharī vāc*.[53]

The hierarchy of sound has its origin in the pure principles; in its lowest state it manifests as audible sound and reaches the ear of man. Thus Īśāna, represented by the quintessential, invisible face of Śiva, "adorned with the sound *AUM*" (*PBUp*.19), controls all the sounds. Śiva, whose body is *mantra* (cf. *PBUp*.6), by this very body links his devotee to himself, audibly, inaudibly, simultaneously in the world of the senses and the empyrean.

[53] S. S. Suryanarayana Sastri, "The Philosophy of Śaivism," pp. 388-93.

VIII

THE ANDROGYNE GOD

1. Prolegomena to the Creation of the Great Goddess

Brahmā raged against himself when he, the Creator, had failed in his several attempts to create mortals who would produce offspring by carnal intercourse and die at their appointed time. The people he had created increased beyond measure, for death as yet had not come into being to keep their throng in check. The overpopulation filled the three worlds (*MBh*.12.248.13-14). Or the pairs of human beings that Brahmā carefully grouped according to their emotional, moral, and intellectual endowment, as he created them in descending order from his mouth and chest to his thighs and feet, though they hastened to sexual intercourse, failed to produce children, except once—and then only at the close of life.[1] This did not meet the population density required in mythical time. Looking back at such self-defeating experiments, Brahmā wondered, "how can real knowledge dawn on one who is engaged in activities of creation?" (*ŚP*.2.1.15.13).[2] Brahmā dwelled in his mind on the state of abiding in ultimate reality beyond creation, the Uncreate, that had been ruptured at the beginning of things by the intercourse of the Father with his daughter, and resorted to purely mental creation. His mental issue, however, consisted of sons who were ascetic sages, lost to the world, altogether disinterested in procreation or sex (*BhP*.3.12.3-5). Then Rudra sprang forth as his mental son from his furrowed brow (*BhP*.3.12.6-10), or from his mouth, which was breathing with the exertions of *tapas* and also

[1] *Mārkaṇḍeya Purāṇa (MāP)*, tr. F. E. Pargiter, 1904, pp. 237-38 (= 49.3-11).
[2] *Śiva Purāṇa (ŚP)*, tr. "A Board of Scholars" and ed. J. L. Shastri, 1973, 1:245.

with rage (*ŚP*.7.1.12.26; *LP*.1.41.42-43). Brahmā delegated to Rudra the task of creating mortals.

Brahmā, in the anger of frustration, remembered, we might presume, that it had been Rudra who prepared the seed for the Father and, also, that he had let his arrow fly against him, when the Father was shedding that seed into creation. He, Brahmā, we may also presume, remembered that Prajāpati had made Rudra Lord of Animals, Paśupati, for sparing his life. He knew that Rudra had the power to extend or to withhold life.

Rudra responded in more than one way to the command of Brahmā. He refused to cooperate with Brahmā and left the creation of fallible, vulnerable mortals to Brahmā. Rudra withdrew into himself; he became Sthāṇu and, in the sparse, motionless shape of the pillar of self-containment, he then and for all time upheld what he had guarded before creation had become an issue: the inviolate integrity of a state beyond words, to which as Lord of Yogis he now showed the way. This was, however, not the only response the Great Lord gave to the Creator. As Rudra had been born from his father in more than one way, so the Great God reacted to the command of Brahmā in more than one way. Brahmā, on his part, also approached his immense son in more than one way.

In one version of the castration myth, Brahmā created Gaurī, of shining beauty, to be the wife of Rudra; Rudra was pleased. But when Brahmā asked him to beget progeny, the great, mighty Rudra plunged into the water. The Lord immersed himself in the water, thinking that a man without inner incandescence, without *tapas*, cannot create progeny. While Rudra went on with his ascetic austerities, Brahmā took back into himself that daughter of his (*VrP*.21.2-8). Though Rudra had been pleased by Gaurī, he chose *tapas*, the exercise of the inner light and fire, and not the woman, not the goddess, as the means to create progeny. He stayed submerged for a long while and, risen from the waters, paradoxically, he castrated himself. Drastically, he severed his procreative limb from his vast body and set his *liṅga* free. It assumed cosmic dimension and metaphysical significance proportionate to the decision of Rudra. Brahmā, not having foreseen this act of his son, found it exceeded his understanding. He also could not believe the fire miracle of the flaming pillar until Śiva revealed himself within the *liṅga* to the Creator. When Brahmā could not fathom the *liṅga's* transcending greatness, he went so far as to resort to a lie. This lie was to cost him his fifth head (Ch. IX.2). But before he lost it, he worshiped Rudra, who had revealed himself to the gods in the transcosmic fire *liṅga*, while on earth the *liṅga* of stone or some other material will be worshiped by mortals.

It mattered to Rudra that gods and man worship the *liṅga*. He foresaw that the *liṅga* would be installed on earth and worshiped (*VmP*, *SM*.23.9-11). On the other hand, he at first refused to take his phallus back (*SkP*.7.1.187.34), but finally he returned it to his body (*SkP*.6.1.62). The anthropomorphic metaphor of the body of the Lord slides over the other metaphor of his body, whose extent is the universe. When the *liṅga* had been severed from the body, it appeared in the limitless darkness of a cosmic night before a new cosmos was to arise. In its fiery light it held all the potentialities of becoming, that constitute the existence of the cosmos and of man, the microcosm. Śiva is Aṣṭamūrti, his body the manifest universe. The *liṅga* is his ontological symbol. Anthropomorphic and cosmic metaphors combine and hint at the mystery of Śiva and the *liṅga*.

In his Sthāṇu shape, Rudra established self-containment as an intrinsic form of being. The one-pointed shape of the pillar is the paradigm that the god implanted in the vertical body of man. In his self-castration, however, the Lord of Yogis separated from his vast body the manifest cosmos, the creative principles and powers by which the cosmos comes to exist. The *liṅga* is their symbol. The Great Lord, from his transcendental being, set forth his cosmic presence, perceptible in his eightfold reality as Aṣṭamūrti; it is knowable ontologically and worshiped as *liṅga*. By turning into a motionless pillar, by becoming Sthāṇu, where he is described as having his seed drawn up (*LP*.1.70.323; *ŚP*.7.1.14.21), and, again, by severing his *liṅga*, Rudra each time answered in his way the command of Brahmā to create. Neither response satisfied Brahmā. Undaunted by the self-revelation of Rudra—in lieu of procreation—that his command had effected, Brahmā gave this last mind-born son of his a third and last chance to carry out his bidding to create mortals.

2. The Divided God

The setting was the same as before. Rudra issued from the head of Brahmā, from his prolonged anger, which arose when the mind-born sons of the Creator showed no interest in sex and procreation. None knows how Rudra looked when he issued from the forehead or the mouth of Brahmā, either to become Sthāṇu or to sever his *liṅga* from his body. Obviously he appeared as a male. Charging Rudra with his task to create mortals, Brahmā received in response a self-declaration by his son of his own being. Sthāṇu was the total form of the Great God as Lord of Yoga, withdrawn in *samādhi*. In this motionless state he had restored within himself the integrality of the Uncreate. By his second response, the severance of the *liṅga* and its transfiguration, the Lord Śiva revealed the ontology of his being as the cosmos in its relation to the Uncreate. Both these symbolic shapes came into being by the will of the Lord.

The third response to the Creator was given by Lord Śiva, the lord of yogis (cf. *SP*.24.55-65; 25.5-29), as soon as he sprang from Brahmā's mouth. His vast figure was like fire, terrible to behold (*KūP*.1.11.2-3; cf. *VāP*.9.75; *LP*.1.70.325); it was half male and half female (*VāP*.9.75; *LP*.1.70.325; *VP*.1.7.12-13; *LP*.1.41.7-9; *LP*.1.5.28; *ŚP*.2.1.15.55-56; *KūP*.1.11.3). Brahmā asked the Lord to divide himself, and then Brahmā disappeared out of fear (*KūP*.1.11.3).

Lord Śiva appeared from Brahmā's forehead, his fierce, immense body a glowing mass, half man, half woman (*LP*.1.41.7-9). This form presaged the human race in its two constituents, the male and the female, the right and left halves of the body of Lord Śiva. His androgynous body had been conceived in Brahmā's mind. When it emerged from Brahmā's head, it was terrifying to behold, glowing like the sun, hot because of Brahmā's anger and because it was the shape of Rudra, who is Fire.

Rudra is Agni. Agni, the Fire, had for his highest symbol "the bull who is also a cow" (*RV*.10.5.7; cf. *RV*.1.141.2; 4.3.10). This image of Fire loomed at the last frontier that the mind of the Vedic seers, in quest of the ultimate, could reach (*RV*.10.5.6). There, it would seem, it burned itself into the mind of the Creator. The theriomorphic image of totality in its bovine shape of power was a seal and sentinel beyond which thought, vision, and word could not penetrate. Beyond this image of totality lay the Uncreate. The bull-cow was also, in the most ancient aeon, the image of Viśvarūpa, the primordial Creator (*RV*.3.38.4, 5, 7; 3.56.3).[3]

[3] The bull-cow Agni (Ch. I.4), unlike the progenitive bull-cow Viśvarūpa, is self-perpetuating, Agni being his own son (*tanūnapāt*), (cf. A. A. Macdonell, *Vedic Mythology*, pp. 99-100 and Ch. VII n. 15).

The bull-cow, the theriomorphic image of Agni, stored in the mind of the Creator desiring to create mortals, assumed anthropomorphic shape; Rudra, who is Agni, issued from Brahmā's head as Ardhanārīśvara, a figure half man, half woman. When the image of Ardhanārīśvara "the Lord whose half is woman" formed itself in the brooding mind of the Creator, the memory of sexual intercourse as a means of creating mortal creatures came back to him with renewed force. Having the Supreme Lord in view, Brahmā exerted himself in austerities, in order to create mortals who would multiply (*LP*.1.41.7-9). The dependence of the Creator on Rudra's help in bringing about creation was rooted in the traumatic experience of the Father Prajāpati, the Lord of Generation, whose progenitive act Rudra, a fierce hunter, had threatened by his sudden appearance. For sparing him, however, Prajāpati made Rudra Paśupati, Lord of Animals. Now it was Brahmā, in his plight of creating mortals, who sought the assistance of Rudra; he knew that this wild, ascetic god had the power to withhold death and thus give life.

In order to allay the misery of Brahmā, and to multiply his subjects, Rudra became the son of Brahmā (*ŚP*.7.1.14.3-4). Rudra was born an androgyne, the right half male, the left female, but the male and female halves had no procreative association. In their contiguous closeness there was no room for desire. When Brahmā saw his androgynous son, he asked him to divide himself, whereupon Rudra split his undivided male-female self into a male and a female entity. He continued the process and split the male entity into eleven Rudras (*VāP*.9.75-77; *ŚP*.7.1.12.27), this time condensing their indefinite number. Before he became Sthāṇu, he had discharged them from himself in an unlimited edition of his own being (Ch. VI.1). The number eleven had the sanction of a previous aeon, when the eleven Rudras were part of the three times eleven or thirty-three gods (*RV*.1.139.11; 3.6.9; 8.35.3). This number comprised the Vedic gods, including the group of the eight Vasus, who subsequently entered the domain of Rudra, and also the group of twelve gods, the Ādityas, which included all the suns that ever shone (cf. *ŚB*.11.6.3.5; *AB*.2.18). The Rudras carried the breaths (*prāṇas*) of the one Rudra, the *Ātman*, the inmost self, into all there is (cf. *BṛUp*.3.9.4). They were concerned with all beings and permeated the three worlds (*VāP*.9.80-81; cf. *ŚP*.7.1.12.29-30). The Rudras were the vital energies, the vital breaths (*prāṇa*) in all that lived (cf. *ŚP*.7.1.12.30; *ChUp*.3.16.3).

Though Brahmā had pondered over creation by sexual intercourse, the Creator could not people the earth with human beings, since women had not yet emerged from Śiva (*ŚP*.7.1.15.2). Brahmā, in his austerities, had contemplated the Lord as Ardhanārīśvara, the form of the Great God in which he is perpetually together with the woman in him, the Great Goddess, who is his *śakti*, his power. Brahmā knew that without Śiva's power, progeny would not be born, and with love in his heart, thinking about Lord Śiva united with the great Śakti called Śivā, he practiced *tapas* (*ŚP*.3.3.2-6). Pleased by the austerities of Brahmā, the Lord whose half is a woman granted the Creator the fulfillment of his wish. Having divided himself and set up his male domain elevenfold (*ŚP*.7.1.12.27), he created the Goddess from the other half of his body. Śakti manifested from the body of Śiva. She had all the divine qualities of the Great God. Though she pervaded everything, she appeared like a wonderfully embodied woman, bewildering the entire world with her *māyā*, her magic illusion, for in reality she is unborn, though apparently born of Śiva (*ŚP*.7.1.16.6-11).

The Great Goddess, the highly illustrious one, sharing half the body of the Lord, on having been separated by him, became Satī, "The Real" (*LP*.1.70.326-27). This was the image of herself in which Śiva was to know her as his wife in the universe. In his image as Ardhanārīśvara, the Lord manifested the signs of both sexes as the cause of creation. All creatures bear these signs (cf. *MBh*.13.14, note 102, insert 113, lines 1-8). For the sake of the welfare of the world, the Great Goddess became Satī among mortals (cf. *LP*.1.70.327-28; *KūP*.1.11.57).[4] All the women in the three worlds are born from her alone. She is everything in the feminine gender, and Rudra is everything masculine (*LP*.1.5.29-30). Now, however, since the Goddess proved to be the more fascinating by being barely discernible to the sight of the gods, it is said that Śiva requested her, for the sake of creation, to divide herself in halves, one white, the other black (*LP*.1.70.328).

This polarity was an anticipatory epitome of all the goddesses that were to spring from it. They were to guide and agitate a posterity that Brahmā yearned to establish with the help of Śiva. The names of the goddesses are infinite. The entire universe was pervaded by them. Black and white, working weal and woe, of multifarious shapes and

[4] The gods figure and act here as mortals whose shape Satī assumed.

propensities, they were known as so many shapes of *prajñā* or gnosis, and also of *śrī* or luck (*LP*.1.70.333-344).

Śiva hypostasized; he separated from himself the Goddess so that Brahmā, wishing to increase mankind through sexual intercourse, could address himself to her. Brahmā bowed to Śivā. He told the Goddess in a hyperbole of deference that he, Brahmā, had been created by her consort, the lord of gods, and ordered by him to create progeny. Mentally, Brahmā had created the gods and others, but they did not multiply. They had to be created again and again. But now Brahmā wanted creation to originate by means of copulation. The female sex, however, had not as yet issued from Śivā, and Brahmā—according to the *Śiva Purāṇa*—lacked the power to create women (*ŚP*.3.3.2-6; 7.1.16.1-6, 15-18).

All *śaktis*, all female powers, spring from the Great Goddess. Hence Brahmā asked Śivā to give him the power to create women (*ŚP*.3.3.7-20). Brahmā then asked the Great Goddess for yet another boon. He, the Creator, implored her, the mother of the universe, to be born as the daughter of Dakṣa, his son. The supreme goddess, Śivā, the *śakti* of Śiva, consented and granted Brahmā his request. From the middle of her brow she created a *śakti* equal in glory to herself. Lord Śiva, the ocean of mercy, then smilingly asked Śakti to fulfill the desire of Brahmā, and she became Satī, the daughter of Dakṣa (*ŚP*.3.3.21-27). Then the Great Goddess, the goddess Śivā, reentered the body of Śiva, and Lord Śiva vanished (*ŚP*.3.3.28). From that time, womankind was created in the world, procreation became sexual, the enjoyment of pleasure in woman was established, and Brahmā was happy (*ŚP*.3.3.29; 7.1.16.25; *SP*.25.5-29).

Satī is the Great Goddess. As Satī she acted the part she had to play in the myth of Śiva; she issued from and represented the Great Goddess, who had returned into Śiva. The Great Goddess, as idea, would be eternally within Śiva, while as image she would be Satī, whom Śiva would love as his wife. Before that could happen, she had to become the daughter of Dakṣa. She had to be born, and though she was an image of the Great Goddess, she was but an aspect of her whole unfathomable being.

Before the Great Goddess consented to be born in her role as the daughter of Dakṣa, she had allowed *śaktis* to become apparent everywhere (*ŚP*.7.1.16.19-22). But none of these *śaktis* or powers would hold the attention of Śiva, and none had to be born as anyone's daughter. They remained intangible powers to be reckoned with, indefinitely large in number, like that of the Rudras prior to their being represented by their Vedic number symbol of eleven.

The Great Goddess, by order of Brahmā, had to be born as the daughter of Dakṣa so as to become the wife of Śiva. By the order of Brahmā, Satī was given to Rudra by Dakṣa (*SkP*.7.2.9.11). This son of Brahmā was born from his mind or, according to other—in this connection more relevant because phallically suggestive—accounts, from his thumb (*MP*.3.9; *VP*.4.1.6; cf. *SkP*.7.1.19.57).[5] It was Dakṣa who filled the earth with mortals, his own progeny, while Rudra tarried, immersed in the waters (Ch. VI.3). Dakṣa, son of Brahmā, played a role intermediate between Brahmā, the Creator, and Śiva, his mind-born, ascetic son. According to the *Harivaṃśa*, Dakṣa, in a subsequent aeon born of Māriṣā and the ten Pracetasas, produced moving and stationary creatures by his mind, then created women and married them to other beings, whence arose creation by intercourse (*H*.2.45-49). Dakṣa was a progenitor, a Prajāpati, a Lord of Generation, a title of the Father in Vedic days.[6] Subsequently, however, this role was shared by a number of patriarchs, all mind-born sons of Brahmā.

Satī was to act out her own destiny and follow her own will. She had issued from the Great Goddess, and had become the daughter of the patriarch Dakṣa. The Great Goddess, having been separated from Śiva and having brought Satī into existence, reentered the body of Śiva. Śiva was the cause, by two removes, of the creation of women, of intercourse and sensual fulfillment. The Great Goddess is their proximate origin. Only insofar as she herself had manifested from Śiva is the Great God their source. Moreover, the Great Goddess on her own did not create Satī. The cooperation of Dakṣa was needed, who at the command of Brahmā let the *śakti* of the Great Goddess become his daughter Satī.

The detachment of Rudra, the Great Yogi, was so great that in one version of the myth, in the *Skānda Purāṇa*, Rudra subsequently accepted as his wedded wife Satī, whom Dakṣa, at the command of Brahmā, had given to him. But when Brahmā told Rudra to procreate, Rudra refused. Creation was the duty of Brahmā, whereas he himself was the destroyer. He stood firm as a post and showed himself

[5] *Mārkaṇḍeya Purāṇa (MāP)*, tr. F. E. Pargiter, 1904, p. 551 (= 101.9-10).

[6] The *Harivaṃśa* even notes this interchange of identity at one point by referring to Dakṣa as Dakṣa Prajāpati (*H*.2.42 and 45; cf. *MP*.3.9).

as Sthāṇu (*SkP*.7.2.9.7-17; *VrP*.21.2-8; Ch. VI, supra). As a bridegroom, he took the form of Sthāṇu. The Great Yogi had directed inward the outward drive of sexual power. He had withdrawn it into himself, where he, the Fire of life, burned perpetually upward. When born from Brahmā as Ardhanārīśvara, however, the Lord shone forth a flaming seal of undivided wholeness, male and female in one. Obeying the command of the Creator, he divided himself. His separated female half became the Great Goddess. In her own right, she let issue from her the *śakti* who was to become Satī, her image. Although woman and sexual pleasure had emanated from the Great Goddess, Rudra neither procreated children with Satī nor created mortals.

He mentally created the Rudras exactly like himself, free from fear, old age, and death, when Brahmā wanted him to create mortals (*ŚP*.7.1.14.14-17). Though it is said that Śiva, when thinking of Satī, created the innumerable Rudras, they were still mentally created by him (*VāP*.10.43-54; *LP*.1.70.303-304; 1.6.11). Even though Satī dwelled in his mind, his mentation did not bring about her maternity. Nowhere does Satī figure as the mother of the Rudras.[7]

Ardhanārīśvara, born from Brahmā's forehead, was commanded by Brahmā. Thence the Great Goddess stepped forth and was born as Satī, the prefiguration of woman and bride-to-be of Śiva, the Lord of Yoga.

Seen in the cycle of revolving aeons, Ardhanārīśvara will be born at the beginning of a new creation in the same way as in the past. In a vision recorded in the *Liṅga Purāṇa*, the androgynous god blazing forth from Brahmā's forehead burned Brahmā, who thus had no chance to command Ardhanārīśvara to divide himself. Then, by the path of yoga, Ardhanārīśvara enjoyed his own half, the Supreme Goddess. He created Viṣṇu and Brahmā in her (*LP*.1.41.9-12). In another version, Viṣṇu created Brahmā, who in turn created Rudra. In another aeon (kalpa), Rudra created Brahmā. Then, in another aeon, Viṣṇu created Brahmā, then Brahmā created Viṣṇu, and then Lord Śiva created Brahmā. Brahmā, seeing the misery in the world, left off

[7] The Rudras issued or were discharged from Rudra. Another Vedic group of gods, the Maruts, were sons of Rudra (*RV*.2.33.1). The Pṛśni cow and Rudra were their father and mother (*RV*.5.52.16). Rudra put the germ into Pṛśni (*RV*.6.66.3). However, the Pṛśni cow was androgynous (cf. A. Bergaigne, *La Religion védique*, 2:397-98); her milk flowed from the udder of the bull Pṛśni (*RV*.4.3.10). Rudra's participation in this cow-bull and in the birth of the Maruts from Pṛśni await clarification; cf. Ch. VII n. 15.

the activity of creation. Motionless like a rock, he remained in *samādhi* for ten thousand years (*LP*.1.41.15-20).

In the middle of the lotus in his heart he installed Lord Śiva (*LP*.1.41.20-22). Then the Lord pierced through Brahmā's forehead. The original color of Lord Śiva was dark (*nīla*) but he became red (*lohita*) from inner contact with fire; hence he is like Kāla—who is Time and Death. He was named Nīla-Lohita (*LP*.1.41.25-27).

In a dizzying, reciprocal, transaeonic theogony, Brahmā, initially burnt up by the androgyne god, returned in cycles. He returned less frequently as the creator of Śiva and Viṣṇu than as one created by these gods. Śiva Ardhanārīśvara, the yogi, enjoying by the path of yoga his own undivided, twofold being, set in motion the cycles of a reciprocal theogony. In its vortex, the tensions of the father-son relation of Brahmā and Śiva were set at nought. No room was left for them in the heart of Brahmā.

As Brahmā inhaled, the lotus within the cavity of his heart faced downward. As he held his breath, the lotus, facing upward, expanded its petals, and Brahmā installed the Great Lord Śiva in the infinitesimally small space within his heart (*LP*.1.41.20-22). Another aeon was about to begin.

In the vision of the *Liṅga Purāṇa*, the androgyne god was Parameśvara Śiva, one with Parameśvarī origin and pivot of Śiva or Rudra in manifestation. In the latter aspect, Śiva, the Destroyer, was coordinated with Brahmā, the Creator, and Viṣṇu, the Preserver, each a demiurge, subordinate to Parameśvara Śiva. Each in turn was vested with the full power of deity in manifestation. The reciprocal, concatenated filiation of the three gods was a paradox unfolding through the aeons, that is in time, whereas the supreme, timeless paradox was that of Ardhanārīśvara, the androgyne yogi enjoying by the path of yoga the other half of his being, the Supreme Goddess.

Brahmā installed Īśvara, the Lord, within the lotus of his heart, and once again Śiva was to be born from Brahmā's forehead, but this was aeons away from Śiva's burning of Brahmā. Now Śiva took the form of Aṣṭamūrti as he stood before Brahmā. By the grace of Aṣṭamūrti, Brahmā took up again the work of creation and, having created the world, he slept for a thousand world ages (yuga). When he awoke he desired to create living beings. Thus he performed austerities, but nothing happened. His sorrow at his failure turned into anger. Consumed by fury he breathed his last, and Rudra issued from his mouth, the breath of life (*prāṇa*) itself, and became Ardhanārīśvara (*LP*.1.41.35-43). Brahmā's life was restored by Ardhanārīśvara (*LP*.1.41. 48-49). A new cycle began in which Brahmā willed to engender mortals and Ardhanārīśvara let the Great Goddess step out of his own being and send her power to be born in the shape of woman.

3. The Genealogy of Desire

To Brahmā, the Creator, creating Rudra from his forehead or his mouth had been an act of anger and despair. It did not have the desired result, for, as yet, through the creation of Ardhanārīśvara and the Great Goddess, only the possibility of sexual enjoyment and sensual fulfillment had been created. Brahmā therefore continued the work of creation, and in the end succeeded in creating mortals. This task Rudra had shunned, inasmuch as he had thought Brahmā properly should perform it. The birth of Rudra from Brahmā's head was but an interlude in the course of creation. Having asked androgynous Rudra to separate himself into male and female, and having witnessed the division of the male half into the eleven Rudras, Brahmā created Manu Svāyambhuva out of, and like, himself. At the same time he created Śatarūpā, the immaculate. Manu Svāyambhuva married her.[8] From that time, living beings began to multiply rapidly (*VP*.1.7.14-21). Brahmā's first mind-born sons, ascetics disinterested in procreation, had been found ineffective for his purpose. Brahmā at last took recourse to himself, and not only literally reproduced himself as Manu Svāyambhuva but also created at the same time Śatarūpā "of a hundred forms," the female half of himself. Manu and Śatarūpā became the paradigmatic progenitive couple. By becoming his son—while yet remaining himself—Brahmā gained some distance from himself; he stepped out of himself toward the creaturely world.

When Brahmā commanded Rudra to divide himself, he spoke from within his own being. As the creator of the universe, Brahmā disposed of and fully activated all the powers of creation, but not necessarily all at the same time. Thus, his desire to create mortals who would multiply through sexual intercourse had remained unfulfilled for a long time. The shape of Ardhanārīśvara, his mind-born son, a totality half male and half female, seemed to Brahmā to have the making of a pro-

[8] *Mārkaṇḍeya Purāṇa* (*MāP*), tr. F. D. Pargiter, 1904, pp. 247-48 (= 50.7-15).

genitive couple. Rudra, however, having separated his two halves, bifurcated his male-female potency throughout the cosmos. He divided the male half into eleven Rudras. He requested the Great Goddess, whom he had separated from his body, to divide herself in two, whereupon an untold number of goddesses came forth. Brahmā then asked the Great Goddess to allow the race of women to emerge from her. Without the archetypal image of woman before him, Brahmā felt himself unable to create women. Although the Great Goddess created a *śakti* from within herself and fulfilled the request of Brahmā to permit Śakti to be born as Satī, the daughter of Dakṣa, the expectation of Brahmā remained unfulfilled. The Great Goddess returned into Śiva, and Satī, who was to become the wife of Śiva (cf. *SkP*.7.2.9.11-12), never gave birth from her womb to a child engendered by Śiva. Even as the Great God had refused to create mortals, so, fittingly, the gods who became his sons were not born in the usual way of mortals. This should not have been expected of any god, and least of all of those who were the sons of Śiva, even though they were not his mind-born sons.

Brahmā saw at last that he could not depend on Śiva's help in engendering mortals. The task with which Brahmā had charged him gave the Great God an opportunity only to manifest his otherness from Brahmā. Thus Brahmā, thrown back on himself, reproduced himself and fulfilled the role he had meant to assign to Rudra. Without further delegating the work of creation to any of his sons, and having gained distance from his various experiments in creation, some nearly disastrous (Ch. VI.3) and others unsatisfactory, Brahmā finally followed his true and ancient nature as Creator. He created Manu, the paradigm and progenitor of man. Mankind, seen from the world contained in the myth of Śiva, could have been established only after Ardhanārīśvara had let the Goddess step out from his being, and Satī, the celestial idea of woman, was born.

Brahmā, the Creator, was preceded by Prajāpati, the Lord of Generation. The themes of the myth of Prajāpati / Brahmā and those of the myth of Rudra / Śiva interact in counterpoint. While the myth of Śiva carries the leading melody, that of Brahmā, the Creator, contributes its ancient themes, which are basic to the myth of Śiva Ardhanārīśvara. Śiva was ordered by Brahmā to complete and carry out Brahmā's work of creation. Twice Śiva had complied according to his own nature, and the result had not served Brahmā's purpose. The third time, as Ardhanārīśvara, Śiva conformed with the Creator. The Lord of Yoga took up, in a new key, the work of Brahmā / Prajāpati, the Creator, the Lord of Generation.

The myth of the creation of man by Prajāpati is told in the *Śatapatha Brāhmaṇa* (*ŚB*.6.1.1.8 to 6.1.2.11; cf. *TmB*.7.6.1-6). "Prajāpati, having created these worlds, was firmly established on the earth" (*ŚB*. 6.1.2.11).[9] Rudra in this creation myth did not disturb the formation of the cosmos of Prajāpati. While Rudra played no part in this myth of the sovereignty of Prajāpati, the mode of operation of Prajāpati, as Creator, brought into focus the figure of Ardhanārīśvara.

The *Brāhmaṇa of a Hundred Paths* relates how Prajāpati desired to reproduce himself. To this end he practiced austerities and created the *Vedas* (*ŚB*.6.1.1.8). Again he practiced austerities and created the waters out of Vāc, who is Speech, for *vāc* belonged to him (*ŚB*.6.1.1.9). Prajāpati desired to be reproduced from the waters, and he entered them with the *Vedas* (*ŚB*.6.1.1.10). An egg arose. From the egg the *Vedas* were first created (*ŚB*.6.1.1.10). In ascetic effort, practicing *tapas*, Prajāpati conceived the *Vedas*, sum of all knowledge, and he created the waters, the realm of fertility, out of Speech. Speech was his, articulating the Revelation. The transformation of the intuited knowledge, of the conception, into the spoken word of the *Vedas* came about in the waters. From the egg formed in the waters the *Veda* arose, conceived by the Creator and made into Word through *vāc*. Th embryo in that egg was fire and the shell of the egg was earth (*ŚB*.6.1.1.8-11).

Again Prajāpati desired to multiply, and he, as fire, united with the earth (*ŚB*.6.1.2.1). The embryo was the wind and the eggshell the air (*ŚB*.6.1.2.2). As Vāyu, Wind, Prajāpati cohabited with air; from the egg that formed itself, the sun was created; the eggshell was the sky (*ŚB*.6.1.2.3). And again Prajāpati desired to multiply, to reproduce himself. As the sun he united with the sky. From the egg that then arose the moon was created; the eggshell became the four quarters of the world (*ŚB*.6.1.2.4).

Having created earth, air, sky, and the four regions, Prajāpati desired to create creatures that would be his in these worlds (*ŚB*.6.1.2.5). Through his mind he united with Speech, and became pregnant (*ŚB*.6.1.2.6). Four times he consorted with Vāc (Speech); the eight Vasus, the eleven Rudras, and the twelve Ādityas, the sun gods, were

[9] *Śatapatha Brāhmaṇa* (*ŚB*), tr. J. Eggeling, 1963, part III, p. 150.

thus created, and the Viśvedevas, the "all-gods." Prajāpati placed these groups of beings on earth, in the air, in the sky, and in the four directions, respectively (*ŚB*.6.1.2.6-9). Then Prajāpati created everything that exists (*ŚB*.6.1.2.11).

Prajāpati, the lord of progeny, conceived the *Vedas*, the sum of all knowledge. This was his first creative act; he also created the waters out of Speech, for Speech belonged to him. Speech, Vāc, was a woman; her gender made her female; she was Prajāpati's speech. Prajāpati immersed himself in its fluency, and the *Vedas* arose from an egg that had formed itself by his contact with the waters of creation. The embryo inside the egg was fire.

Prajāpati's desire to reproduce himself continued from one copulation to the next. In each an egg was formed and an embryo within it. Prajāpati took the shape of each successive embryo: he was fire, the embryo in the shell of the earth, in one "generation," and in the next he was fire, the consort of the earth, renewing himself in each generation, like the mother who becomes the wife of the son, who becomes her lover (cf. *AB*.7.13; cf. *BṛUp*.6.4.2).

Prajāpati's creation *per generationem* was an ongoing renewal / reversal, a concatenation, whose resilient links transmitted the past to the future and held in each loop the memory and promise of an eternal now.

Having created the cosmos on the firm foundation of the *Vedas* (*ŚB*.6.1.1.8), the Creator desired to create creatures. By his Mind he united with Speech and became pregnant. By the union of the creative intellect and articulate speech, the cosmos came to exist and all who have their place in it, gods and mortals. From the upper vital functions (*prāṇa*) Prajāpati produced the gods, and from the lower vital functions, the mortals (*ŚB*.6.1.2.11).

"The creative power is always a unity of conjoint principles."[10] Manas (Mind) and Vāc (Speech) were a creative, procreative couple, but it was Prajāpati, the Lord of Generation, who became pregnant.

Sexual images abound in the world of Prajāpati. Prajāpati, who was Mind, conceived. Thus he became pregnant. The Indian image makers of later millennia show Brahmā as pot-bellied, a pregnant male, rendering visually the identity in god of creation and procreation. Though pregnant, Prajāpati was not an androgyne. The images of

[10] A. K. Coomaraswamy, "The Vedic Doctrine of Silence," in *Coomaraswamy*, 1977, 2:206 n. 15.

Brahmā, there being no images of Prajāpati, do not show a combination of male and female features, but reveal the uniquely female condition of pregnancy in the distended abdomen of a powerful and altogether male figure. Manas and Vāc were so closely one in the Creator that he carried her condition in his shape. "He [Prajāpati] laid the power of reproduction into his own self " (*ŚB*.11.1.6.7). In the image of Brahmā, the figure of Prajāpati survived the actuality of the Lord of Generation, whom the *Vedas* and *Brāhmaṇas* celebrate.[11]

Brahmā, of whom the *Manu Smṛti* and the *Purāṇas* speak, unlike Prajāpati in *his* creation of man, was not the ultimate cause. He was the efficient and material cause, first in the line of descent from the Self-Existent, or Svayambhū. An autarchic genealogy led from the inconceivable, indiscernible Svayambhū to Manu, the paradigm of man. This was so according to an essentially male genealogy, in which the female was intermingled with, separated from, and united with the male. Brahmā in his Purāṇic nascent universe—and unlike his sculptural representations—was neither a pregnant male nor an androgyne. Having split himself, Brahmā became a male and a female. Before that, no such distinction could be seen in Brahmā. In contrast to Śiva, no androgynous images of Brahmā exist. The androgyne was a modality of Agni, Fire, who was the bull-cow; of Viśvarūpa, though functioning differently, the primordial, manifesting Creator of a long past aeon; and of Śiva, the "Lord whose half is woman."

The creation of Brahmā had its beginning in the mind of the utterly indefinable Self-existent. His seed was deposited in the waters and became a golden egg. It floated in the waters. Brahmā was born in the golden egg (*M*.1.8-9). The *Manu Smṛti*, in its *Purāṇa*-like account of the universe of Brahmā, tells of the substantiation of the metaphysical Self-existent as it extended, station by station, down to Manu. It emerged from the total darkness that was before the beginning. This total darkness was already a reification of the altogether indescribable Uncreate.

In the total darkness in which the universe lay immersed, as if in deep sleep, was the Self-existent, Svayambhū, who is inconceivable, indiscernible, and eternal, and who contains all created beings. He

[11] For images of Brahmā, see Sir Leigh Ashton, ed., *The Art of India and Pakistan*, 1949, pl. 32, fig. 217, gilt bronze image from Mirpur Khas, Sindh, c. 500 A.D. (now in the Karachi Museum, Pakistan); and P. Pal, *Bronzes of Kashmir*, 1975, pl. 3, p. 55, bronze image of the 7th century.

desired to produce creatures of many kinds from his own inconceivable body. First, with a thought, he created the waters and placed his seed in them. That seed became a golden egg, brilliant like the sun. In that egg he himself was born a male, as Brahmā, the progenitor of the whole world. He dwelled in that egg for one whole year. Then, by his thought, he divided it into two halves. Out of the halves he formed heaven and earth. Dividing his own body, Brahmā became a male and a female. Through the female he produced Virāj, who is the plan or prefiguration of the cosmos. The male, Virāj, having performed austerities, produced Manu Svāyambhuva, the progenitor of the whole world (*M*.1.1-34).

The unknowable, unfathomable Self-existent reproduced himself (*M*.1.7-9; *VP*.1.7.16). For this purpose he as Brahmā split in two the golden egg formed from the seed of Svayambhū, the Self-existent. Out of the two halves of the egg he formed this world of heaven and earth. Just as he divided the egg and it became heaven and earth, so Brahmā divided his own body and it became a male and a female. Prior to his self-division, Brahmā was not an androgyne. It was on division only that Brahmā, the male, became differentiated as male and female, as the egg on division became the two separate and complementary entities of heaven and earth. It was not unusual for the cosmic egg to be split in this manner. God Indra, albeit from the outside, had performed the feat of separating heaven and earth in the aeon under his dispensation (*RV*.5.31.6; 6.44.24; 10.44.8).

Brahmā, the Creator, was not androgynous, although following the mode of Ardhanārīśvara, not only Brahmā but also Viṣṇu were indeed beheld as androgyne, each viewed as creator of the universe and, as such, identical with one another (*H*, app. 37, lines 40-47). Prajāpati also had not been androgynous, although he became pregnant when he entered by his Mind (Manas) into union with Speech (Vāc) and created gods and mortals (*ŚB*.6.1.2.6ff). The pregnant Creator, a potent maternal male (cf. *Vedagarbha*; *BhP*.3.12.1), was a reservoir of conjoint creativity, male in appearance and female in the state of gestation and the power of reproduction that he laid into his own self. His figure was without a clear line of division between two adjacent halves, one male, the other female.

Svayambhū, the Self-existent, created the waters and placed his seed in their lap. When it grew into an egg, the foetus within the egg was Brahmā, in whom the unfathomable Svayambhū had acquired substantiality. In the course of one year—time hitherto had not yet existed (cf. *ŚB*.11.1.6.1-2)—Brahmā split the egg from within. Heaven and earth lay in it in close embrace. Brahmā also divided his body. One half became male, the other female. Only after division did the male and the female become distinct. Indistinguishable they had lain in Brahmā's body. When the female was created he engendered in her Virāj, a male (*M*.1.32). Virāj, who practiced austerities and created the world, is himself Manu Svāyambhuva, the scion of Svayambhū, the Self-existent (*M*.1.33; *KūP*.1.8.6-9). It is from Manu that all mankind has descended (*MBh*.1.70.11). Manu Svāyambhuva, the paradigm and progenitor of man, was the lineal descendent of Svayambhū. Following the fission of Brahmā, the union of the male and the female thus created the male Virāj, by which Manu came into being. In this coessential lineage of self-descent, Brahmā, the male, as efficient and material cause, separated the female out of himself.

The creation by Brahmā, recounted in the *Manu Smṛti*, proceeded from the mind and seed of the Self-existent. The mind of Svayambhū activated the golden, germinal substance that swelled into the egg shape in which Svayambhū became substantiated or "born" as Brahmā. Brahmā became the form of Svayambhū, or his incarnation. As such he carried the thought of Svayambhū into action. After a year of gestation he split the egg (cf. *ŚB*.11.1.6.2), as also his own body. The halves of each became definite entities; those of his own body became male and female. From their union Virāj, the plan of the cosmos, came into existence. Manu, the progenitor of man, was Virāj. Manu descended in direct line from the mind (*manas*) of the Self-existent.

The creation of Brahmā proceeded without hindrance from the metaphysical plane into existence. Brahmā was only a halting point in the substantiation of the intent of Svayambhū. When Brahmā, in other myths, played the role of the Creator, his mind seemed still to be in the grip of the darkness before the beginning of things. He was caught in the turmoil and agony of gestation, and his creation miscarried. Was he, the Creator, aware or apprehensive of another's presence, as the Father had been when he embraced his daughter at the beginning of things? Rudra stepped out of his forehead when Brahmā's creation faltered.

The vision of the approach of the hunter, the Wild God, is told within Revelation (*śruti*), the *Veda*, whereas the creation of Brahmā from Svayambhū downward is not recorded in the *Veda*. It is stored in memory (*smṛti*), of which the *Manu Smṛti* is a record. Brahmā's experiments with creation are told in the epics and the *Purāṇas*. The main currents, with their eddies, of the myths of Brahmā and of Rudra flow on, from the one to the other, and intermingle.

Although the creation myth of Svāyambhuva Manu is not told prior to the *Manu Smṛti*, where apparently it is a later, Purāṇic addition,[12] it is inserted here as background for the Vedic myth of Rudra. Manu, the father of man (*RV*.2.33.13) and initiator of the sacrifice (*RV*.10.63.7), is known in the *Ṛg Veda* as son of Vivasvat, the Sun (*RV*.8.52.1).[13] Manu in the *Ṛg Veda* is not descended from the Self-existent, Svayambhū. Though the ultimate ancestor of man on earth is not named in the *Ṛg Veda*, his conception is prefigured in the creation hymn that sings of Ābhu, the life principle (*RV*.10.129.3).[14] Svayambhū and Ābhu are closely related.

In an often retold and contracted version of the myth of Brahmā's creation, the genealogy of Manu is shortened. The male and the female produced by Brahmā's division were Manu, one in essence with Brahmā, and Śatarūpā (*VP*.1.7.16-18; cf. *AP*.17.7-10). From their union sprang two sons and two daughters (*KūP*.1.8.9-11). Prasūti, "the birth-giving," one of the two daughters of Manu and Śatarūpā, was given in marriage to Dakṣa, one of Brahmā's mind-born sons (*KūP*.1.8.11). Dakṣa had many daughters; one of them was Satī, the Great Goddess herself incarnate (*KūP*.1.8.16-17). After Dakṣa, son of Brahmā, was reborn as the son of the Ten Pracetasas and Māriṣā, procreation came about by sexual intercourse. Before that time it had resulted from mental conception, sight, or touch (*LP*.1.63.2; cf. *KūP*.1.15.1-2).

The universe of Brahmā, in which Manu Svāyambhuva was perfect or paradigmatic man, unfolded placidly. Svayambhū, the Self-existent, desired to produce creatures. Although he was unknowable and inconceivable, the mere fact that he desired to produce creatures placed him at one remove from the Uncreate, of which nothing what-

[12] Cf. J. Muir, *Original Sanskrit Texts*, 1976, 4:30, where Muir relates *M*.1.5-13 to earlier texts (*RV*.10.129 and *SB*) "with an intermixture of more modern doctrines."

[13] A. A. Macdonell, *Vedic Mythology*, p. 139.

[14] Cf. H. Grassmann, *Wörterbuch zum Rigveda*, 1964, *s.v.*, where he interprets Ābhu as "leer"; A. A. Macdonell, tr., *Hymns from the Rigveda*, also interprets the term as "void," p. 19. *Ṛg Veda Saṃhitā (RV)*, tr. K. F. Geldner, 1951, 3:360, however, translates Ābhu as "*das Lebenskräftige*."

soever could be predicated. Svayambhū, being a personification, necessarily and paradoxically brought the fathomless Uncreate within the range of human empathy. The Self-existent desired and created through thinking, as well as by placing his seed in the waters that his thought had created. Without friction or interruption, as though by an organic process, Svayambhū extended and substantiated himself as Brahmā in the cosmic egg.

Logically and cosmologically, by taking the liberty of presenting a sequence of myths in the reverse order of their appearance in their respective texts, the *Ṛg Veda* and the *Manu Smṛti*, the descent of Brahmā from Svayambhū would have preceded the appearance of the Wild God on the cosmic stage. Incipiently, as described in the *Ṛg Veda*, Ābhu, the arch-potential, the will-to-live, the first stage of manifesting Mind, hot with creative fervor (*tapas*), floated in the flood, and desire (*kāma*) overcame it as the first seed of mind (*RV*.10.129.1-4). Desire (*kāma*) was the first seed of the mind of the Creator.

Svayambhū, the Self-existent, and his substantiation as Brahmā, were not conceived in Vedic time. Svayambhū, the Self-existent, and Ābhu of the *Ṛg Veda* (*RV*.10.129.3), the life potential, each denote a starting point, a prime locus of creation. But, whereas Ābhu is the life germ nascent in the dark flood of emptiness of a cosmos as yet uncreated, Svayambhū is Self-existent as if Uncreate that is beyond form and image, beyond darkness, flood, or emptiness. Yet Svayambhū, indefinable as is the Uncreate itself, paradoxically, by being its personification, thinks and desires. Thus, utter transcendency touches upon the as yet uncreated, which will become created.

Svayambhū was "born" as Brahmā, who, by splitting himself, created heaven and earth and man and woman. Svayambhū, Brahmā, and Svāyambhuva Manu—of immutable essence and increasingly compact substance—were stages from creative desire in the Self-existent to creation. The seed, the golden egg, was its substance. Śatarūpā, the woman of a hundred shapes, cosubstantial with Brahmā, cooperated with him.

Brahmā, after dividing himself, carried into the world not only the unfathomable reality of Svayambhū, to which Manu became the heir, but also the desire that had swelled the seed of Svayambhū in the waters. It was at one with the first seed of the mind of the Creator (*RV*.10.129.3).

The genealogy of desire was traced first in the creation hymn of the

Ṛg Veda (*RV*.10.129) and in the *Śatapatha Brāhmaṇa* (*ŚB*.10.5.3.1, 3; 11.1.6.1). According to the hymn, there was in the beginning neither nonexistence nor existence, neither death nor life. Ensconced in an impenetrable flood of dark emptiness there was mind only; in inner incandescence (*tapas*), mind became, was "born" as Ābhu, the life potential. It was overcome by desire (*kāma*) and "that one" (*tad ekam*) was the first seed of mind (*manas*) (*RV*.10.129.1-4).[15] From this seed sprouted the entire creation.

Svayambhū, the Self-existent, and Ābhu, the essential existent, the life potential, were close in meaning. While Ābhu, the life potential, was created by the fervor (*tapas*) of mind, Svayambhū created by his mind. In the *Ṛg Veda* hymn, desire (*kāma*) overcame the life potential and became the seed of mind. *Kāma*, in the lineage of Svayambhū, arose from the seed of Svayambhū when Brahmā, who was Svayambhū now born of his own substance, split the golden egg (cf. *ŚB*.11.1.6.2) and himself.

Mind effected its own concretization through *tapas*, its indwelling fervor, and desire overcame the life potential, Ābhu, that had formed itself in the inner incandescence of mind, in the dark waters of the flood of the void.

Ābhu, the life germ, praised in the *Ṛg Veda* hymn, was personified as Svayambhū in the *Manu Smṛti*, comprising in his germinal person both mind and desire. Growing in substance, Svayambhū became the cosmic egg as well as Brahmā, the Creator. Brahmā (like Prajāpati; *ŚB*.11.1.6.2) dwelled in his egg, the cosmic substance, for one year. The year of growth was one cycle of time. Time grew organically in the substance of the cosmic egg. Before that it was nonexistent. *Kāma*, the desire in Svayambhū, was prior to, and also within, Brahmā.

Tradition is not unanimous about the manner in which Manu came to be. Although the direct line of his descent remained unchallenged, it lost its unruffled smoothness when attention focused on Brahmā, the Creator. Brahmā's unsuccessful attempts at creating mortals also cast their shadow on the events that led to the birth of Manu. Thus, the *Matsya Purāṇa* relates that Brahmā, dissatisfied with his creative work, invoked goddess Gāyatrī, who is Śatarūpā in the form of sacred speech (*MP*.3.30-32; cf. *BhP*.3.12.28-33); she is the most hallowed

[15] W. N. Brown, "Theories of Creation in the Rig Veda," pp. 33-34.

mantra of the *Ṛg Veda*, the mother of all, giving inspiration and illumination (*RV*.3.62.10). She appeared from Brahmā's half. Brahmā first mistook her for his daughter (cf. Ch. I.1); seeing her exquisite beauty, he was overcome by desire, while she, worshiping the Creator reverentially, circumambulated him. Brahmā, struck by desire, could not take his eyes off her loveliness, but ashamed in front of his mind-born sons to turn his head and follow Gāyatrī as she walked around him, he sprouted four heads, one in each direction. Gāyatrī, to escape the lustful stare of Brahmā, went to heaven with Brahmā's mind-born sons, and Brahmā sprouted a fifth head on top of the four, looking upward toward her ascension. After that, Brahmā lost the creative power that he had acquired by his austerities (*MP*.3.32-40).

Nonetheless, Brahmā, transfixed by the arrows of desire, in the end married Gāyatrī. For a hundred years he enjoyed her company inside a lotus. After a long time Manu was born to them (*MP*.3.41-44). Manu, in this myth, was engendered by Brahmā; he did not gain his status as Brahmā's separated half. Moreover, as Brahmā and Manu were identical in essence, it was Brahmā who married Śatarūpā, and Manu became their son.

This intermezzo in the creation of Manu, enlivened by Brahmā's acquisition of his five heads, was brought about by the upsurge of desire in Brahmā for Gāyatrī / Sarasvatī / Śatarūpā. Brahmā was ashamed of having yielded to desire in front of his mind-born sons. He cursed desire (*kāma*), and Kāma, the god, stood before him (*MP*.4.11).

As Brahmā was cursing Kāma, Rudra came to his mind. The curse turned into a double curse, of Kāma as the aggressor and Rudra as his future, potential victim. "The object with which you made me the target of your arrows will ere long lead you to be reduced to ashes by Śiva, when you similarly behave with Him" (*MP*.4.12)[16] was Brahmā's curse. Brahmā was upset by the vehemence of Kāma's attack and, while he cursed him to be reduced to ashes, he thought of Rudra, the fire, as the means of destroying both Kāma and Rudra himself—the ascetic, the Great Yogi, whom Brahmā meant to see in an even greater predicament than his own. Brahmā solicited Rudra's help in destroying Kāma and at the same time cursed Rudra to be victimized by

[16] *Matsya Purāṇa (MP)*, tr. "A Taluqdar of Oudh," 1916," part I, p. 13.

Kāma. Impulsively, Brahmā had cursed Kāma. But the involvement of Rudra in this curse was provoked by Brahmā's deep-seated resentment of Rudra. Its cause lay as far back as the beginning of things.

Kāma released his arrows against Brahmā. They inflamed Brahmā with lust. Kāma was an archer like Rudra. Brahmā, the Creator, was his target. Aeons ago, at the beginning of things, Rudra had let his arrow fly against the Father / Prajāpati. The arrows of Kāma and of Rudra flew in opposite directions. Rudra's arrow was sent against the Creator, against the inception of life on earth. The arrow of Kāma incited Brahmā with passion and toward procreation. Between these two attacks on the Creator—the one the beginning of the myth of Rudra and the other of god Kāma—Rudra had come to be born from Brahmā. Whereas Rudra, in the course of his ongoing myth, became the son of Brahmā, Kāma (desire) brought about, and from the beginning of things was part of, Brahmā. Kāma was ingrained in Brahmā, as it was in Ābhu, the life potential.

Kāma was the urge in the creative mind toward manifestation, condensation, and substance. The arrows of Kāma—of which the *Purāṇas* speak—were directed hitherward. God Kāma with his arrows, the arrows of desire, intensified from the outside the urge that had been shaping Brahmā even before Brahmā had come to be. Kāma, the god, made Brahmā flare up in passion when Brahmā had seen Gāyatrī, who had sprung from half of his body, and whom he first mistook for his daughter.

The arrows of Kāma flew toward this world; they would wound but not kill, they would incite passion. Rudra released but one arrow, aiming back and away from creation, at a target that had arisen on the horizon. *Kāma*, desire, in the creation hymn of the *Ṛg Veda*, was the urge into substance, into life embodied in form. Brahmā had been sustained for one year within the cosmic egg before he split the egg into which the seed had grown. The egg was as much a symbol of Brahmā's world as the *liṅga* was the symbol of Śiva's world.

In the myth of Rudra, the seed had been made ready for the Father by Rudra. Rudra, the Fire, the spark of life out of the source in the beyond, the Uncreate, was its guardian and avenger. The arrow of Rudra flew against the Father—against the act of procreation—for the sake of the integrity of the Uncreate. When the arrows of Kāma hit the Creator, their sting incited the passion of Brahmā for his daughter. Brahmā and Kāma were cosubstantial. However, although

Brahmā—he disliked to admit it—played the role of the Father vis-à-vis his daughter, and also that of the father of Rudra, Rudra of the *Ṛg Veda* had not entered the scene of his own myth as son of the Father / Prajāpati. Rudra, the Fire, was to become the son of Prajāpati / Brahmā; Kāma, desire, was ingrained in Brahmā. Before Kāma, the god, appeared on the stage of the *Purāṇas*, *kāma* had been in Brahmā; they were one in origin from Svayambhū.

As desire (*kāma*) overcame Ābhu, so Kāma, Desire, overcame Brahmā: god Kāma shot his arrows at Brahmā. They excited Brahmā as he gazed at his daughter Sāvitrī, or Gāyatrī. Brahmā sprouted five heads in order better to see Sāvitrī as she walked around him worshipfully and soared upward, escaping from his lustful gaze (*MP*.3.35-40).

The scene between Brahmā and Sāvitrī was a reenactment of the primordial scene augmented by the presence and reactions of the sages, the mind-born sons of Brahmā, and punctuated by the then-acquired five heads of Brahmā. Rudra, the protagonist in the primordial scene, though he did not act in its restaged version, was present in Brahmā's curse of Kāma. The latter had taken Rudra's place as the assailant of the Creator. Hence Kāma, "born from Brahmā's heart" (*MP*.3.10), was to direct his arrows from the universe of Brahmā toward Rudra, the Great Yogi.

According to another version of the myth, Kāma was born from the mind (*manas*) of Brahmā. This occurred when Brahmā had created by his mind beautiful Sandhyā, the Twilight. (She had been Dawn, daughter of the Father, primordially.) Brahmā, aroused by her beauty, created Kāma (*ŚP*.2.2.2.18-23, 35-36). A late version of the myth in the *Skānda Purāṇa*, relates that Kāma was born of Brahmā after his mind-born sons, and, like them, refused to carry out the command of Brahmā to procreate. In this version, Kāma, in his attitude toward the command of Brahmā, acted like Śiva, the ascetic son of Brahmā, though he soon gave up this stance. His flower-arrows would not let him maintain it. They were destined to fly off to arouse desire and make it blossom (*SkP*.5.2.13.2-20). They were not, as a rule, directed fatally to pierce to the root. Kāma—like Rudra, the avenger—was an archer. Kāma and Rudra aimed with different purposes at the same target, the Creator himself, whose mind-born sons they were.

The genealogy of Kāma had been contained within the universe of

Brahmā. In the myth of Rudra, the figures of the Father, Prajāpati, and Brahmā successively acted out their essential identity. Kāma entered the universe of Rudra after Ardhanārīśvara let the Great Goddess send forth her *śakti*, her power. Then Rudra became the target of Kāma. Desire entered the world of Rudra. The Great Goddess had prepared the way.

4. The Birth of Satī

According to a version of Brahmā's myth—a version in the thrall of Śiva—it was at the prompting of Śiva, present within Brahmā, that the Creator divided himself in two, male and female (*ŚP*.2.1.16.10-11). It is generally held, however, that Brahmā, following his own nature and precedent, had commanded Śiva to divide himself (*VāP*.9.75-76). The exchange of roles gave to Śiva precedence over and assigned to him immanence in Brahmā, whose son he was. Such fluctuations and inversions moved around a fixed center outside time, though time was just about to begin. The center lay between Rudra, the androgyne, and Brahmā, who split the cosmic egg as he split his body. Agni, the bull-cow, had been Rudra's theriomorphic image. In anthropomorphic likeness the Great God was Ardhanārīśvara, the Lord whose half is woman. In the visual image created by art, the figure of Śiva as Ardhanārīśvara balances wide-flung curves of the left, female half of his body with the firm verticals of the right and male half.[17] The image of Ardhanārīśvara comprises their diversity, being an indivisible whole of two related but different and complementary halves. Brahmā, on the other hand, is never depicted as androgynous. His portly male shape carries a big belly. All the world, in the multitude of its shapes, rests within his pregnancy. The image of the male, potbellied Brahmā stays through Indian art as that of the parent, whose issue, however, is born from his seed or from his mind.

Śiva, the Lord whose half is woman, is an image of wholeness in which equivalent parts show their distinction, right and left. Straight and static on the one side, of flexed posture and flowing lines on the other, the two halves combine in the image of Ardhanārīśvara in as many varieties of assimilation or contrast as will make whole the image of the Lord. He shows himself half-male, half-female, comprising

[17] The figure of Ardhanārīśvara in Elephanta (pls. 3, 11, 12) overemphasizes Śiva's left half, giving the image a poignancy unrivaled by images of the goddess herself.

both natures. They exist in god. In the image of Ardhanārīśvara they are marked in the difference that their shapes affirm, and that their axis in common upholds and denies. Along the vertical axis of the figure of Ardhanārīśvara, cast in bronze or carved in stone, the male and female characteristics are iconographically distinct and visually complementary. By assuming the mind-made shape of Ardhanārīśvara, Lord Śiva, paradoxically revealed himself totally in anthropomorphic terms. In neither of his two other births from Brahmā's head had he gone so far as to incorporate comprehensively a human likeness in his shape. Before he became Sthāṇu he discharged from himself the innumerable wild Rudras, and withdrew into his immutable stillness as the pillar of self-containment, of tensionless, solidified intensity, faceless and without body. In his second response he tore out his *liṅga* in a blaze of fury and set it free. The shape of his severed organ of sex became one with the pillar and was accepted by gods and man as the cosmic symbol of the Lord.

Sexual terms and situations are basic to and abound in the myth of Śiva. Their elementary power, supported by a living tradition and its symbols, seizes the devotee and allows him to rise to the level he is capable of reaching in approaching Śiva. The *liṅga*, the comprehensive symbol of Śiva in his myth, had to be severed from his body. When Brahmā asked Śiva Ardhanārīśvara to divide himself, Śiva had already done so, though not in his half-man, half-woman shape. Divided, or severed from the body of the Lord, the *liṅga* is the total symbol of being and becoming, and signifies Śiva, who is before and beyond either.

Sthāṇu and *liṅga* are each Śiva in his wholeness, the one psychologically, the other ontologically. Sthāṇu is the symbol of the destroyer, who, as the Great Yogi, abolished all demands and commands that would fetter the freedom of his integral state. Being the Lord of Yoga, Śiva became Sthāṇu. Being the Wild God, Rudra tore off his *liṅga*. It arose as a flaming pillar, the word *liṅga* hermeneutically signifying the destroyer, as Sthāṇu defined himself (Ch. VI.1). In neither of his two responses to Brahmā did Śiva fulfill the demand of Brahmā; he did not create mortals. He did not engender progeny in any womb other than that of *prakṛti*, and from it, the original *māyā*, the entire universe is born (cf. *KūP*.2.8.3).

Ardhanārīśvara—half man, half woman—issued from the mouth of Brahmā, when Brahmā, infuriated that all his ascetic exertions did not have the desired result, gave up his life. From the tears he had shed in his anger, ghosts and goblins sprang up (*LP*.1.41.40-43). They were adorned with *svastikas*. Brahmā cursed his austerities that had brought about these destructive creatures. As he expired, the vital energies, the breaths of life, left his body. Rudra restored to Brahmā his vital breath, and Brahmā, hearing Rudra address him as though in a dream, saw standing before him Rudra Ardhanārīśvara with eight cosmic bodies and elevenfold (*LP*.1.41.40-55).

The Lord whose half is woman both divided himself and remained as Rudra. The female half became the Great Goddess, Umā (*LP*.1.41.44, 55). While each of his former halves, now god and goddess, continued to divide themselves, they carried out literally the earlier order of Brahmā (*VāP*.9.75-76; cf. *LP*.1.70.314-15). They did this as though unaware of its implied purpose. They neither created nor did they procreate mortals. True, the eleven Rudras carried the breath of Rudra into all that lived. Specifically, the Great Goddess, on being commanded by Śiva, divided herself into the polarities of her nature, such as black and white, Prajñā and Śrī, wisdom and wealth. From these polarities all the goddesses originated, thousands of them; all life was in their thrall (*LP*.1.70.328-344; *VāP*.9.82-87).

The proliferation of female power by Śiva's will, and in execution of Brahmā's order, continued, but did not meet Brahmā's need. Brahmā finally appealed to the Great Goddess. He did not bypass Śiva. On the contrary, he bowed to Śiva's will, giving up at last his futile efforts at procreating mankind. He prostrated himself before Śiva Ardhanārīśvara, without whose power progeny would not be born. Brahmā addressed himself to Śiva Ardhanārīśvara as though the bipartite sexual unity of the Great God prefigured progenitive couples. Thereupon, Śiva, in his majesty and mercy, detached his female half from his body. Brahmā introduced himself to Śivā, whose shape was that of the Great Goddess, the Śakti of Lord Śiva. Brahmā told her that he had been created by Śiva, her consort, the lord of gods (*ŚP*.3.3.2-10, 13-15). Such a deferential reversal of the relationship of Brahmā and Śiva would seem hyperbolic flattery, instead of a graceful abdication by Brahmā, as Pitāmaha, the grandfather, from his role as Creator. That role he now passed on to Śiva. Brahmā, the Creator, the Father who had been the target of Rudra, the archer, at the beginning of things, and who became the father of Rudra / Śiva, the Great God, now made over to the Lord the role of the Creator.

Rudra's asceticism, which, at the beginning, he had injected into the Father, had worked insidiously in the Creator. His mind-born sons were ascetics adverse to the ways of the world. Rudra-Śiva himself, by a coincidence of cause and effect, became the mind-born son of Brahmā. Brahmā could not go further in spiritualizing his procreative role. In fact, the spiritualization of his procreative role was a reawakening in Brahmā of the primordial mode of creation when Mind only became the seed of creation. But this lay far back in the genesis of the cosmos. The Creator, however, in his role of the Father or Prajāpati, Lord of Generation, had been engaged in sexual intercourse when he was struck by Rudra. Brahmā raised the procreative activity to his head, whence Rudra was born. This was Rudra's second place of birth. In his first birth he had arisen from the seed of Prajāpati, the lord of progeny.

Brahmā, having come near the end of his mental resources, appealed to Śiva, his son—half man, half woman. From this form of his son, Brahmā anticipated a fruition of his own asceticism. The inner heat generated by his fervid exertions, his *tapas*, would promote the fulfillment of his wish. This hope was founded in the seemingly paradoxical effect of asceticism upon sexual and procreative power. He relied on the harnessing, concentrating, heightening of his powers by *tapas*. They would achieve the desired result. Lord Śiva, the Great Yogi, was delighted with Brahmā's asceticism, and fulfilled his wish by indirection. Ardhanārīśvara detached the Great Goddess from his body; he created her by separating the female half from his body (*SP*.25.4-9) so that Brahmā could address himself directly to her. She gave Brahmā the power to create women. She agreed to be born as the daughter of Dakṣa, the mind-born son of Brahmā. For this purpose the Great Goddess Śivā created a Śakti equal in splendor to herself, who issued from between the brows of the Great Goddess. When Śiva saw Śakti, the Great God smiled and played his part in the celestial game. He admonished this Śakti, a projection of the Great Goddess and equal to her in glory, to fulfill the desire of Brahmā and become the daughter of Dakṣa. The Great Goddess, having given to Brahmā the power to create women, reentered the body of Śiva. Ever since, womankind has been created in the world, and creation became sexual (*ŚP*.3.3.20-29; *SP*.25.10-28).

Even before Brahmā told Śivā that he was created by her consort, Śiva had addressed Brahmā as his dear son (*ŚP*.3.3.11). He did this in a happy frame of mind, and Brahmā confirmed their relationship in his appeal to Śiva. Not on every occasion when the question of paternity was to arise between Brahmā and Śiva was inversion or exchange of fatherhood and sonship accepted as gracefully. The essential dialogue here, however, was not between Śiva and Brahmā but between the Great Goddess and Brahmā; it was Śivā who helped Brahmā to overcome the hitherto all-male creative situation. Śiva here seemed to act only as an intermediary between Brahmā and the Great Goddess, who, her mission fulfilled, reentered the body of Lord Śiva. It was a return into the wholeness of Lord Śiva, whence she had sprung. Thus Śiva, after all, if indirectly, played the leading part in the creation of the idea of woman. It was now left to Brahmā to find a partner for her and to set in motion procreation by sexual intercourse. Brahmā's immediate concern, however, was not to find a mate for the Śakti, who was as brilliant as the Great Goddess and had sprung from her brow. Instead, he secured a father for her, namely, Dakṣa, his son. Although Dakṣa was to have many daughters, there was none to compare with the Śakti, who was alike to the Great Goddess and whose name was to be Satī, the Real.

Śiva, into whom the Great Goddess returned, who was the ocean of mercy and her origin, stood by almost like Sthāṇu during the dialogue of Brahmā, the Creator, with the Great Goddess. Ardhanārīśvara knew that those who would be born of women, owing to the exertions of Brahmā, would not see the light of day as the children of Śiva. Though the Lord whose half is woman encompassed both sexes, and though the Great Goddess, after her detachment from the Great God and her meeting with Brahmā, rejoined Śiva Ardhanārīśvara, no mortals issued from that unity. Śakti, on the other hand, who had sprung from and was alike to the Great Goddess, having become the daughter of Dakṣa, was destined for Śiva. Aeon after aeon the Great Goddess was to be born to become the bride of Śiva. As Satī she became the daughter of Dakṣa; in a later aeon she was born as Pārvatī, daughter of Parvata Rāja, the Mountain Lord. The union of Śiva and Satī was childless, although it is said that Śiva begat four sons in Dākṣāyāṇī: they were Hari, Kṛṣṇa, Nara, and Nārāyaṇa (*VmP*.6.1-2). These four names designate Viṣṇu and some of his avatars. The sonship of all the gods or of Viṣṇu, in particular, was to show the supremacy of Satī, the bride-to-be of Śiva, as the Great Goddess and "mother of the world" (*ŚP*.3.3.21). Related to such theogonies is the vivid paradox and mythical anomaly of Ardhanārīśvara, who "by the path of yoga enjoyed the female half of himself. . . . In her he created Viṣṇu and Brahmā" (*LP*.1.41.10-12). Indeed, Śiva meditated on Satī when *he* created the Rudras (*VāP*.10.43-54; *LP*.1.70.303-304). But when Brahmā told Rudra, the lord of Satī, to perform creation, Rudra said he would not perform creation, he would become Sthāṇu, and left for Kailāsa with Satī (cf. *SkP*.7.2.9.5-17; cf. Ch. X.A.1).

Human beings were not the progeny of Śiva and Pārvatī, nor was any immortal born from the sexual union of Śiva and the daughter of the Mountain Lord. Each of these statements allows for a partial exception, one being the birth of Kārttikeya from Pārvatī after she drank the water of the golden lake of seed (*MP*.158.34-49; 159.1-3), the other being the human incarnation of Śiva as King Candraśekhara.[18]

Śiva did not create mortals. He stood by as the Great Goddess, his Śakti, who stemmed from him, gave Brahmā the power to create women. She gave to him of herself, of her own power (*śakti*) when a Śakti issued from her forehead. Brahmā gave her to Dakṣa, his son, the progenitor, to be his daughter. In this way the power (*śakti*) of Śiva, on being detached from Ardhanārīśvara, was transferred to the progeny of Brahmā—to Dakṣa, the progenitor. Satī, at Brahmā's behest, was born as the daughter of Dakṣa. Brahmā took the leading part in establishing Satī in his family or universe. Having discharged in anger fiercely glowing Ardhanārīśvara from his forehead, however, and having asked him to separate himself, Brahmā performed a similar operation on himself, converting his substance into Manu and Śatarūpā. They begat children by sexual intercourse.

Brahmā's many experiments with and modes of creation led in the end to his dividing himself into a progenitive couple: Manu and Śatarūpā. They had four children: two sons and two daughters. One of the daughters, Prasūti, the "birth giving," Brahmā bestowed on Dakṣa, the effective instrument of manifestation, his mind-born son, who proved his competence by producing twenty-four daughters with Prasūti (*VP*.1.7.16-19, 22). Those who from the age of the *Brāhmaṇas* had charged Prajāpati with incest and had not been silenced by the age of the *Purāṇas* were comforted when they understood that

[18] One version of the story is succinctly translated in W. D. O'Flaherty, *Asceticism and Eroticism in the Mythology of Śiva*, pp. 206-207. The full story is told in *Kālikā Purāṇa (KP)*, chapters 46-52.

Brahmā embodied the four *Vedas* and that Śatarūpā, of a hundred forms, in her form as Sāvitrī and Gāyatrī was the essence itself of the *Vedas* (cf. *MP*.4.7-10). This redeeming relationship did not help Brahmā recover from the passion he had felt as Prajāpati—and as the Father of mankind—for his daughter Uṣas, the Dawn. Desire overcame him when he saw Śatarūpā in one or the other of her forms.

Creation by self-division had been Brahmā's proper mode of operation from the time he had split the cosmic egg, in which he was born and where he had dwelled for a year. The seed of Svayambhū, the Self-existent, had grown into the cosmic egg. Desire had made Svayambhū, who contained all the creatures, shed seed so as to produce creatures of many kinds from his body. Desire was in Svayambhū when he reproduced himself and became Brahmā.

The universe of Brahmā, born from the golden egg, carried Kāma in its substance, since Svayambhū, the Self-existent, deposited his seed in the water, until the stage at which Manu, the paradigm of man, was created. For this purpose Kāma had assumed divine shape. The Great Goddess, Śivā, in her own right, had created a goddess like herself. When that goddess became the daughter of Dakṣa, the son of Brahmā, the world opened up for women, intercourse, and the pleasure of sex. They were awaiting Manu when he married Śatarūpā, his cosubstantial consort.

From the left side of Śiva and by indirection, the fire of the fierce god was transmitted by the Great Goddess to Satī. She needed to be born to Dakṣa, son of Brahmā, to become real, to exist. Without Satī's birth into the universe of Brahmā, the flower arrows of Kāma would have wilted and fallen to the ground.

When the curtain rose at the beginning of things, only three figures could be discerned in the crepuscule of a nascent cosmos: the Father, together with his daughter, and the Wild Hunter aiming his arrow at the interlocked pair. Now the curtain rises for the second time, and the same gods, some with new names and playing several roles, continue the play. Brahmā has taken over the part of the Father and lord of progeny, Prajāpati. The Wild Hunter appears in several changes of costume. He had already shown himself as the formidable androgyne, radiant, fierce, and vast (*VP*.1.7.12-14), difficult to look at and extremely terrible as Ardhanārīśvara (*KūP*.1.11.3). He detached from himself his Śakti, the Great Goddess, who held the stage for only a short while to reappear later as Dakṣa's daughter, given to him by

Brahmā. Three male figures sprang from Brahmā: two mind-born ones, the protagonist Rudra-Śiva and Dakṣa; and Kāma, ingrained in Brahmā and said to have sprung from the heart of Brahmā. These and Satī, daughter of Dakṣa, carry on the divine play, the *līlā* of Śiva, the Great Lord. But for the presence of another, invisible actor, it would never have started. He was an antagonist of Rudra, and one whose delaying action interfered with the intent of the Wild God, the avenger. He made his presence felt subsequently when Rudra tarried under water and Dakṣa performed the task assigned to Rudra by the Creator. Though the invisible actor was not named in either of these relevant scenes, he was most intimately connected with Rudra. He appeared to be antagonistic to Rudra, the avenger, the Lord of Yoga, by interfering with his intent, yet he furthered the course of the play that had Rudra for its principle actor. A third time his presence loomed large, when Sthāṇu prevented Brahmā from burning up his universe. At that time Sthāṇu communicated his own being to the silent, invisible player. Yet another time Rudra recognized himself in this actor, who at that meeting had assumed a definite shape and revealed his name as Kāla, "Time" (Ch. VII.6). If Kāma (Desire) is cosubstantial with Brahmā (the Creator), Kāla (Time) is one with Rudra in creation and beyond. There Rudra's name is Mahākāla (Ch. IX.5).

5. Creation of Woman, Sex, and Sensual Fulfillment

In the ongoing myth of Śiva, the predicament of Brahmā had been that he could not create mortals by means of sexual intercourse (*ŚP*.3.3.4). This insurmountable difficulty went back to the traumatic experience of the Father when his intercourse with the daughter had been disturbed by the Wild Hunter. The memory of that early morning, aeons ago, had not left the Creator, although he had, on several occasions, produced creatures who mated and multiplied. It is not explicitly stated in what manner the people whom Brahmā had created multiplied uncontrollably. The Creator, at that time, found no other remedy to stop the unforeseen disastrous increase of living beings than by a total conflagration of his universe (*MBh*.12.248.13-17). Although much had happened since that early morning at the beginning, the Creator, the Lord of Generation, remembered his assailant. Though the Lord of Generation at that time, in the far away past, had immediately bestowed on his attacker lordship over animals for sparing his life, the incident had not been closed. In a much later aeon, when the Creator was referred to as Brahmā and was desperately straining to produce creatures through sexual intercourse, he remembered the shock he had experienced, when he himself for the first time in creation was engaged in that act. His assailant, Rudra, the Wild God, came to his mind—and was born from his mind. He, who, in the past, had attacked and nearly killed the Creator and disrupted his sexual union, would now be the one to enable him to create by sexual union. Rudra had the power over life and death, the power to avert death and bring about the inception of life. Twice, when Brahmā had summoned his mind-born son, he disappointed his father. Though Rudra was the Lord who comprised the entire cosmos, he was primordially the Lord of Yoga. Not that he only sat absorbed in meditation; he showed his asceticism in his actions, from the time when he had appeared as a Wild Hunter to the moment when Brahmā summoned him and he appeared from the head of the Creator and became Sthāṇu, or plunged into the water and cut off his *liṅga*. When Brahmā summoned Rudra for the third time, the Great God had taken androgynous shape in the mind of the Creator. In this shape, too, Rudra manifested once again as Lord of Yoga. Ardhanārīśvara, the Lord whose half is woman, immense and fiercely blazing, issued from the head of the Creator. He had assumed this heraldic device to proclaim the unity of his bipartite appearance. The unity was a symbol of his completeness, two halves upheld by him, the Pillar, the axis of the ambivalent shape. He had let the male and female shape coalesce in a design whose figures had been those of bull and cow when he stood as Agni, the Fire of creation, on its border with the Uncreate. Brahmā, however, intent on sexual procreation, commanded Ardhanārīśvara to divide himself. Śiva carried out Brahmā's command, and before the eyes of Brahmā, the Great God and the Great Goddess stood face to face. At once Śivā, the Great Goddess, after granting Brahmā the boon he desired, was back again within Śiva Ardhanārīśvara. In the short moment of her separateness from the Lord, she, like Brahmā himself, let issue from her own forehead another celestial, a *śakti*, who was to be born as Satī, the daughter of Dakṣa. Satī, the Real, incarnate as goddess, was to be the woman in the life of Śiva. Emanating from the Great Goddess, she was sent into the world of the gods to participate in the mystic play in which Śiva and Śivā are "the sanctifiers of living beings in the entire universe; the couple whose bodies are devoid of birth and death and who have taken the bodies of an excellent man and a youthful maiden" (*ŚP*.7.1.15.35).[19] In the complexities of the divine play into which the Great God entered, he assumed a shape, resembling that of man, in company with Śivā, the goddess.

Brahmā had felt himself unable to produce creatures through sexual intercourse, since womankind had not emerged from Śiva (*ŚP*.7.1.15.2). Rudra had discharged from himself the Rudras, whose features prognostically included and whimsically portrayed a wide range of human types and their activities. But none of them was feminine. A male universe was taken for granted. Brahmā himself had created couples, and Dakṣa his son was to populate heaven and earth, but in these efforts of the progenitors woman played no part in her own right. She functioned as a copulative adjunct. This was true even though the Lord of Generation, Prajāpati, having given Nīla-Lohita (the blue and red god) his names, had, according to Purāṇic tradition, provided each of them with a wife duly named (*VP*.1.8.2-9; *BhP*.3.12.10-14). This had been in an earlier aeon, and the wives were goddesses and abstractions. Prajāpati at that time rewarded the insistence of his demanding son by giving all he had asked and even more, in order to establish him fully in the cosmos. At that time Prajāpati did all he could for his son. Now, however, it was Brahmā who needed help, troubled as he was by his repeated failure. Something, Brahmā felt, was lacking, and he knew himself incapable of its creation. Śiva had failed him when Brahmā had charged him with the creation of mortals. Brahmā had to accept his refusal to procreate, but now a vision hitherto not conjured by the Creator arose in his mind, and once more he let the Lord be born from his forehead. He had the shape of Ardhanārīśvara. Beholding this immense form, one half of which was as much like as it was unlike the other, Brahmā asked Ardhanārīśvara to divide himself. Then Śiva, the Great God, divided himself, and his left half, the Great Goddess, stood before Brahmā. She had been in Śiva and now, on her own, assumed the role of the Creator. She let issue from her forehead her power (*śakti*) into the cosmos. To become real (*sat*), Śakti had to be born from Dakṣa, the progenitor. The Great Goddess, having sent forth her *śakti*, reentered Śiva. The Śakti went into the world of the gods, where she was born from Dakṣa as Satī.

[19] *Śiva Purāṇa (ŚP)*, tr. "A Board of Scholars" and ed. J. L. Shastri, 1973, p. 1,825.

Woman was first in god. So that woman should come to be, Lord Śiva, the Great God, placed the woman in him—she was half of himself—outside himself. Then he saw the Great Goddess. Seen separately, she was the Great Goddess. She emanated her own power into the cosmos to be born by Dakṣa, the progenitor. She became real (*sat*), she became Satī, for she had been born, had been given substantiality. Her progenitor Dakṣa passed it on to her from Brahmā, the egg-born, his father.

In this way woman, immanent in the Lord, emanated from Ardhanārīśvara and showed herself as the Great Goddess. Standing in transcendency she released her own power to be born in the line of Brahmā, the Creator. From this side of her ancestry Satī was endowed with substantiality, for Brahmā, the Pitāmaha, the grandfather, had been born of and spent a year in the cosmic egg. Along with substantiality, desire was ingrained in her paternal lineage. Desire had come to Brahmā himself from Svayambhū; it was the first seed of Mind. Lord Śiva Ardhanārīśvara created woman, the Great Goddess, who, thus empowered, sent out her own power to be embodied as Satī, the Real, when viewed from transcendency, and as the idea of woman, when viewed from the world of mortals, who thenceforward would be born from the sexual union of a man and a woman.

In his form of Ardhanārīśvara, Rudra completed the work of the Creator (*ŚP*.3.3.1). In none of his other forms had he manifested the goddess within him. He had discharged the Rudras into creation, and the universe reverberated with the rhythms of life, but the goddess he had retained within him when he became Sthāṇu. His total asceticism required the female element to be implicated in his self-absorbed ardor. Then, as Ardhanārīśvara, the Lord whose half is woman, he divided himself and faced the Great Goddess. Her presence was all power. She was transcendental power (*Parā Śakti*), she who would discharge her power in innumerable śaktis, potent goddesses, who would dispense it to all who were destined to exist on earth, their home. They would fill it in increasing number, born from the sexual embrace of man and woman, children of sensual delight. The immense fire-shape of Ardhanārīśvara scintillated in innumerable colors of union when the Great Goddess reentered the Lord and Satī was being born from Dakṣa, the son of Brahmā. Brahmā, having reproduced himself as his son Manu, the progenitor of mankind, cohabited with her of a hundred forms, Śatarūpā, his daughter. She was totally of Brahmā's substance, and Prasūti, her daughter, who was procreation in person, continued the line of Brahmā. Satī, born into the lineage of Dakṣa, brought to it the power that had descended to her from the Great Goddess, the left half of the immense, frightening fire in the shape of Ardhanārīśvara.

This is how Śiva completed the work of Brahmā, the Creator. He was called—and Brahmā called him—to complete this work, for it was he who had begun it. He, the Fire in creation, had prepared the seed for the Father, the inseminator, the Lord of Generation, Prajāpati; and he caused the seed to fall on the earth when he surprised, frightened, or killed Prajāpati in sexual embrace.

Prajāpati was not only the inseminator, he himself prefigured the universe: he was its golden germ, Hiraṇyagarbha (*RV*.10.121.1; *TS*.5.5.1.2; *ŚB*.11.1.6.2-7), the golden egg from which was born Brahmā. Ontologically, the hierarchy of Brahmā began with Svayambhū, but historically, in post-Vedic tradition, Brahmā came to take the place of Prajāpati. Svayambhū, the Self-existent, was the ultimate origin of Brahmā, a substantiation of mind whereas the seed of the Father was prepared by Fire, the spark of life.

In the universe of the Self-existent, Manu and Śatarūpā, male and female, were the separate manifestations of Brahmā, "split up through the desire of creating; and these are declared as the parents of the creation that sprang into existence" (*KS*.2.7).[20] Creation proceeded in the cosmos and continued as procreation when Brahmā reproduced himself as Manu Svāyambhuva. Manu is the final progenitor of mankind, himself the embodiment of the Self-existent. His lineage was flawless, and all was well in the world of Brahmā of the golden egg, a world of organic metaphysics.

Prajāpati, the inseminator, however, acknowledged Rudra as born from his seed. The newborn god had not forgotten the primal scene, and he made his father free him from the memory. Shedding his seed, the immortal substance, the Father had violated the integrity of the Uncreate. Rudra, the Fire, having prepared the seed for the Father, had incited the Father, who became the target of the arrow of the Wild God. When Rudra was born from the seed of the Father, the Creator, the double memory of that morning was allayed for Rudra. The memory, however, stayed with Brahmā, the Creator. Similarly,

[20] *Kumārasaṃbhava (KS)*, ed. & tr. M. R. Kale, 1967, translation p. 7.

Manyu, "Wrath" had stayed with Prajāpati (Ch. V.1.b). It impeded his creative activity. The sexual act at the beginning of things, by which he had violated the Uncreate and during which he himself was wounded by the Wild God, became the stumbling block in his task of creating mankind. The arrow of Rudra, as it struck the Father, had injected into him the asceticism of the Great Yogi together with the fury of the Wild Hunter. Brahmā resorted to mental creation, and his mind-born sons were ascetics averse to sexual procreation. At that phase Brahmā, the Creator, conceived by his mind Rudra, who had been born from the seed of Prajāpati, the Lord of Generation. When Brahmā called Rudra to his mind, the Great God issued from the head of Brahmā and proved himself to be the Great Yogi that he had been from the beginning. He who had been the guardian of the Uncreate and avenger of its violation showed its integrity within his own being and became Sthāṇu. A second time, when Brahmā thought of Rudra and let him be born from his mind, the Lord of Yoga resorted to the waters and remained immersed in them. This was an ambiguous response. He clarified it on emerging from the water. He tore off his organ of sex. He did it in anger, perhaps as a gesture of expiation for having originally struck the Father while he was engaged in the sexual act. Rudra set free his *liṅga*.

The third time Brahmā called upon Rudra, the Great God, the Lord of Yogis, he manifested from the head of Brahmā as the Lord whose half is woman. To Brahmā this manifestation in its fiery glow appeared to hold the promise of becoming a couple that would unite sexually. Brahmā's mind was set on sexual procreation as the condition for mortals to people the earth.

Once, aeons ago, when nothing else existed but Puruṣa, and creation had not yet begun, supernal man let himself become two. From that arose husband and wife. He united with her. From that union mankind was born (*BṛUp*.1.4.3). Puruṣa divided himself because he was alone; nothing existed besides himself. He was afraid, but had no reason to be afraid, since there was none to fear (*BṛUp*.1.4.2). Yet, being alone, he also had no delight, and for this reason desired a second (*BṛUp*.1.4.3). Ardhanārīśvara had no desire. He was not alone. He was all in one, male and female, a single unity. At Brahmā's command the Lord Śiva, whose half is woman, divided himself and let his Power, his Śakti, be seen by him and by Brahmā. She was the Great Goddess, a woman in shape, all fire. Woman is fire; the delights of sex are its sparks (cf. *BṛUp*.6.2.13). The Great Goddess, the transcendental Śakti, sent forth her power to be born as Satī, real in the world of Brahmā.

Rudra, who is Agni, Fire, sent forth one-half of his glowing self, which had the shape of woman. The Great Goddess had already reentered the Lord when her fire power had burned its way into the lap of Satī, who was to become the bride of Śiva. Rudra, in the form of Ardhanārīśvara, divided his body of fire. The Great Goddess stood before him, glowing, and then reentered his shape. The Lord had separated her from himself to send her glowing ardor, shaped like her, like a woman, into the world of the gods, which was ready to receive her. Brahmā granted this boon to the Great Goddess, who became the daughter of his mind-born or thumb-born son Dakṣa. In his own substance, and following upon the self-division of Ardhanārīśvara, Brahmā reproduced himself as Manu and Śatarūpā.[21] The progeny from the union of Manu and Śatarūpā were not carnal humanity (*VP*.1.7.16-35). Their progeny represented the qualities, propensities, aspirations, predicaments, and activities that were prognostications of the human condition (*VP*.1.7.20-35; *VāP*.10.16-28).[22] These Rudra had been loath to create. Even so, they were the issue of Brahmā's or Manu's intercourse with Śatarūpā, and intercourse would not have come to be had not the Great Goddess sent her Śakti to be born as the reality of woman, that is as the idea or archetype of woman, comprising all her faculties, including her sex and sexuality. That the Great Goddess sent out her power in the likeness of herself into the sexual act and its joy was due to Ardhanārīśvara's self-division. Then only could Manu—or Brahmā—and Śatarūpā beget the human race as it came forth, adumbrated by all its qualifications.

Ardhanārīśvara sent out of himself his fire power, his *śakti*, and let it be born as the idea of woman, sex, and sensuality. Śiva did not create mankind. Mankind was eventually born in the line of Brahmā. From that line Satī had received just enough substantiality to make her real as the idea of woman, while also being essentially the Great Goddess.

Sthāṇu, the post, withdrawn into himself, let his fire burn perpetually upward, consuming and destroying all but itself. The Great Yogi is one in nature with the Lord whose half is woman. At will, be it even

[21] *Mārkaṇḍeya Purāṇa (MāP)*, tr. F. E. Pargiter, 1904, p. 248 (= 50.9-15).

[22] *Ibid.*, pp. 248-49 (= 50.15-25).

at the command of Brahmā, Lord Śiva directs his fire to create or to destroy, to create while destroying, or even to destroy while creating the objects that change their names and shapes while the fire keeps burning.

In his form of Ardhanārīśvara, Rudra completed the work of the Creator. The Wild God, as Agni, had begun it. In the shape of an archer he had interrupted the first sexual embrace in which the Father shed the substance of the Uncreate. It was a rape; Dawn, his daughter and partner, fled. In his form of Ardhanārīśvara, Rudra let the Great Goddess out of himself to transmit her power to Satī, who was at once like the Great Goddess and like woman-to-be. She would bring to every sexual embrace the fire of the goddess who stems from Śiva, the Lord. Brahmā experienced bliss as creation became sexual (*ŚP*.3.3.27-29).

The sexualization of Śiva's world was channeled from the Great God through his Supreme Śakti, who was one with him as Ardhanārīśvara, to her Power or Śakti. She was born as Satī, the daughter of Dakṣa. The emblematic unity of Ardhanārīśvara was split and diffused in a heterosexual world, which the Great Goddess had brought about at the request of Brahmā. Just as Śiva had severed his *liṅga* and set it free in the cosmos, the Lord whose half is woman let the Great Goddess step out of his body and create the female sex. Śiva took the *liṅga* back to his body, and the Great Goddess reentered the Lord. Each of these separations was of abiding consequence; they refer back to the unity whence they have sprung. The Great Goddess played her own part as Satī and, in another aeon, as Umā or Pārvatī, the daughter of the Mountain and consort of Śiva. The togetherness, meetings, and separations of the Great God and the Great Goddess, as Śiva and Satī or Śiva and Pārvatī, play on all the strings of sensibility, passion, and understanding that resound in human beings. Embodied among the other gods, the transcendental Śakti took upon herself her tragic role as Satī, and the Great God mourned her death. Śiva and Satī, Śiva and Pārvatī, for the sake of mortals, were to play their roles among the gods as if they were human. In this way Śiva and Brahmā came to terms. Brahmā had wanted his recalcitrant son to create mortals, and Śiva carried out this command by creating the possibilities and patterns of human life prefigured in the world of the gods.

The Supreme Śakti, the Great Goddess, her mission fulfilled, entered Ardhanārīśvara. The visual image of the androgyne, though timeless, answered to both stages in the myth of Ardhanārīśvara. In this manifestation, Lord Śiva was born androgyne. When the transcendental Śakti returned into his body, he was once more the androgyne Lord, which he had not ceased to be. The eternal image, having discharged its meaning into the action of the myth, resorbed it. The timeless, changeless image was a seal that comprised, in its paradoxical unity, the simultaneous and equivalent existence of opposite entities.

A reflection of this image, transposed into temporal sequence, may be seen in a legend transmitted in varying accounts from the *Rāmāyaṇa* (7.78-81) to a late *Purāṇa* version (*BDP*.1.53.50-55). In the legend as told in the *Rāmāyaṇa*, the state of androgyny is phased in successive stages of one month's duration. Here is told the tale of King Ila, son of Kardama Prajāpati, a powerful and just ruler (*R*.7.78.3-7). It takes place at a time when, after the death of Satī, Śiva had married Pārvatī.

Once, while hunting in a forest and having killed hundreds of thousands of wild animals, King Ila entered a grove, the pleasance of Śiva. On that occasion the Lord, in order to please the goddess, who was then his wife Umā, the daughter of the Mountain (Pārvatī), had assumed the shape of a woman (*R*.7.78.8-12), and, accordingly, all male creatures in the forest were changed into females: there were no male animals to be seen anywhere in the forest (*R*.7.78.12-13). On entering the forest Ila and his retinue all became women (*R*.7.78.14-15). The grove had been enchanted. Ila felt sorry for himself, but he was filled with fear when he realized that all the femininity had been caused by the Lord of Umā (*R*.7.78.16). King Ila then entered into the presence of Śiva. The Great Lord spoke smilingly and let Ila ask for any boon of his choice, except manhood (*R*.7.78.17-19). King Ila refrained from asking Śiva for any boon and addressed himself to Pārvatī. With the consent of Rudra, Devī gave Ila a boon, half of it on her behalf, the other on that of Śiva. The boon was that Ila would live half of his life as a woman and the other half as a man. Ila was pleased. He suggested to the goddess that he live as a very beautiful woman for one month and as a man for the next month (*R*.7.78.20-26). The goddess agreed but added that while male, Ila would not remember his female form, and while female he would not remember his male form (*R*.7.78.27-28).

In the first month Ilā, the most beautiful woman in the three worlds, wandering in the forest, came to a pond. There she saw Budha (the planet Mercury), shining like the moon, himself the son of the moon, practicing austerities in the water. Ilā marveled at the sight (*R*.7.79.5-11). Budha, on seeing the girl, more beautiful than any celestial being, thought her fit to become his wife. He came out of the water and, on hearing that she was her own mistress and had no husband, proposed that she with her friends dwell on the mountain with him (*R*.7.79.12-24). Budha made love to Ilā in the month of Mādhu (March-April) (*R*.7.80.6-8). When the month was over, Ilā, becoming Ila, awoke one morning and saw Budha doing *tapas* in the pond, his arms raised to the sky. King Ila was persuaded by Budha to remain in the forest. In the ninth month Ilā gave birth to the son of Budha and turned the child over to its father (*R*.7.80.9-25). When Ilā had once more become a man, Budha undertook to remedy Ila's state, and hence a horse sacrifice to Śiva was undertaken. Śiva was pleased, and granted Ila his manhood (*R*.7.81.4-19). King Ila founded the city of Pratiṣṭhāna (*R*.7.81.21), and his son Purūravas succeeded him (*R*.7.81.22-23). According to the *Mahābhārata*, Ila is remembered as both mother and father of Purūravas (*MBh*.1.70.16). This mode of parentage would have been more appropriate in Brahmā's world than in Śiva's.

The effect on Śiva of his creation of the goddess from within himself was so powerful that the Great God himself, as told in the *Rāmāyaṇa* story of Ila, assumed the shape of a woman in order to please the goddess (*R*.7.78.11-12) by being like her. The grove that surrounded Śiva and Umā responded: its trees and the animals also became female. The mighty King Ila, entering the grove, succumbed to the spell and became a woman, Ilā. Śiva, having already as Ardhanārīśvara hypostasized the woman in himself, now to please the goddess took the shape of woman and caused all life in the enchanted grove to become female. King Ila, shocked at the transformation and realizing that Śiva had brought it about, was allowed by Śiva to ask for any boon—except that of manhood. Ilā, dumbfounded, did not respond to the Great God held in the thrall of the feminine. She turned to the goddess, who, in her equanimity and with the consent of Śiva, gave the boon, half on her own account, half on that of Śiva. The boon given to Ilā was a divided life. During one half she would be a woman, during the other a man. Ilā expressed her gratitude, while asking for a modification of the boon. The modification involved the question of timing the gift, so that she might change her sex every month. Umā granted the request on condition that no memory would connect the two sexes of Ila / Ilā. Ila / Ilā was thus the first androgyne in the world of time, leading a split life that ran its course on a level below that of the timeless validity of the transcendental image of the Supreme Lord whose half is woman.

In between the transcendental plane, whence the image of the Supreme Lord whose half is woman shines forth, and the creaturely world, lies the region of the gods, where Śiva together with Pārvatī had taken residence on Mount Kailāsa. Umā, beseeched by Ilā and with due reference to Śiva, favored her with a decision that meticulously did justice to the equality of the male and the female factors on the side of the givers and the recipients of the boon. It was conceded, however, with one particular clause, involving the lack of memory of Ila as Ilā and of Ilā as Ila. The unity of the male and female in Ardhanārīśvara was withheld from Ilā as well as from Ila. Like beads of two different colors, the male and the female condition were strung without interval and without consciousness of one another. They were strung on the thread of the life of Ilā, who was not to know that she was and would be again King Ila. At the end, Ilā having fulfilled her female role in giving birth to Purūravas, and having once more become Ila, Lord Śiva granted lifelong manhood to King Ila. The desire for manhood prevailed over the satisfaction that Ilā experienced in the months when she enjoyed extreme beauty and motherhood.

In other versions of the legend of Ila / Ilā, it was Pārvatī who not only gave the boon to Ilā but also caused the spell to be cast over the sacred grove. Once, when the seven sages had come to the sacred grove to see Śiva, they found the god and Pārvatī making love. The goddess, getting up naked and ashamed, said to Śiva that anyone in the future who would cross the boundary of the grove and enter the hermitage would become a woman (*VāP*.85.25). Or again it was Śiva, who, for the satisfaction of Pārvatī, cast a spell over the grove, promising her the transformation of any future intruder (*DBhP*.1.12.16-23; *BhP*.9.1.23-33; cf. *MP*.11.45-46).

Regardless of whether it was Pārvatī herself or Śiva who cast the spell over the sacred grove, the goddess was its cause. She had entered first, in an earlier aeon, the life of Śiva as Satī. Born in the present aeon as Pārvatī, the goddess in the exercise of her sexual role used her spell-binding power when her love-making with Śiva was interrupted. Śiva, the Lord whose half is woman on the transcendental plane, was, on the level of the gods, the husband of the goddess Pārvatī, who herself or through her lord asserted herself. The spell to which Ila succumbed was an application, on the level of the gods, of the power that the Great Goddess had discharged from herself. Caught and offended by the sages in the exercise of her sexual role, she remonstrated by turning, on her own account or by the will of Śiva, male into female. Thus, the state of transcendental unity, which she had left, was adjusted to the dimension of time. She carried her spell even further and deprived Ila / Ilā of memory, identity, or wholeness. The legend of Ila / Ilā is a sequel in reverse to the manifestation of Śiva, the Great God, as androgyne.

The discontinuity in the form of Ila / Ilā changing sex terminated when Ila regained his manhood permanently. This he did by means of a horse sacrifice to Śiva, and Śiva was pleased (*R*.7.81.14-15). The legend of Ila's changes of sex, accompanied by a loss of memory, has a happy end, inasmuch as his masculinity was restored forever. Though the goddess directly or indirectly had caused the change from male to female, in the end it was Śiva who restored Ila's manhood. King Ila was a mortal, his changing sex was but a refraction in the mirror of time of Ardhanārīśvara's timeless being.

Another king, similarly, though in the distant past, had also been destined to change his sex, a retribution by the god Indra, whom the king had annoyed. King Bhaṅgāśvana, however, changed into a woman, did not suffer a loss of memory, and was able to assess her life as woman and her life as man. Consequently, she implored Indra to allow her to remain a woman, for the affection of women is greater than that of men, and the pleasure that women enjoy during intercourse is always much greater than that of men. Indra fulfilled her wish (*MBh*.13.12.2-9, 29-49).

The Lord whose half is woman, having singled out that half from himself, made it possible for the Great Goddess to send her power into the world. This power was substantiated and realized among the gods in the shape of Satī, and it made itself felt henceforward in the female sex and in the joy of intercourse. These could not have come about had not Śiva "exposed" the goddess from his body. She stood in front of him; she was addressed by Brahmā before she returned into Śiva. Brahmā appealed to her power; and having made it come true, or realized it, she returned into the Lord. By sexualizing the world, Śiva enabled mortals, whom he did not himself create but whose birth, after much reluctance, he now had made possible, to delight in sex. By sending the Great Goddess out of himself, duality came into the world.

Ila / Ilā, the mortal, a king and thus in a privileged position, was given little choice when the female sex had already been imposed on him by Śiva. Śiva meant to deprive him of his manhood for having disturbed the love-making of the god and having annoyed the goddess, in particular. She, however, made Śiva agree to her suggestion of a compromise by which King Ila would have the benefit of alternating periods of masculinity and femininity. This was a questionable boon, as the goddess deprived him of the memory of his life in one state when he was in the other (*R*.7.78.20-28). It was left to a star, Budha, the planet Mercury, to initiate the horse sacrifice to Śiva, by means of which King Ila remained a man for the rest of his life. Whereas it is not reported if King Ila was allowed to recollect his past and link in his person the double experience, another king, Bhaṅgāśvana, another plaything in the hands of a god, successively experienced the joys and sufferings of the life of a woman and that of a man. Given the freedom of choice out of his comprehensive sexual experience, he decided to be a woman (*MBh*.13.12.29-49).

Ardhanārīśvara, whose image prefigured in one body the possibility of sexual awareness of both sexes, completed the creation of Brahmā. Though he did not create mortals, he made it possible for them to come into existence by issuing the half of him that is the Great Goddess into the world. Her sex came into existence with the birth of Satī, who was destined by Brahmā to become the true bride of Śiva. This goddess consumed her body in the fire of her yoga. In a later aeon, the sexual union of Śiva and Pārvatī was beyond compare; on one occasion Śiva made love to her for a thousand years (*ŚP*.2.4.1.27-28). The love-making of Śiva and Pārvatī was as hot as fire, for Rudra is Fire, and there was no end to their love play, for the Great Yogi retained the semen in his body. The love-making of the Great God, even considering that he was the Lord of Yoga, was different from any other, human or divine. "The great god, Maheśvara, never delights with a wife distinct from his own self. . . . The joy within him is called the goddess. Śivā is not outside him" (*KūP*.2.31.20-21).

Rudra, the Fire, had prepared the seed for the Father. Ardhanārīśvara sent out of himself the woman in him, his creative power, his *śakti*, into the universe of Brahmā. She was born, became "real." Satī was the idea of woman realized on the level of the gods. From that time the consciousness and exercise of sex came into the world. By its power, gods, demons, sages, the ancestors (*pitṛ*), and kings were created (*M*.1.34-37), the hierarchy of the human condition, whose progenitors were Manu and Dakṣa (*VP*.1.7.16-22). Sending his power, the Goddess, into the world, Śiva completed the creation of Brahmā. From that time sexuality came into the world, as did mortal men and women (cf. *SP*.25.5-28).

In his primordial manifestation, Rudra, the archer, interrupted the sexual act of the Father. Seed was shed. The substance of the Uncreate fell on the earth. This was at the beginning of the myth of Rudra, as told in the *Ṛg Veda*. From Prajāpati, the Lord of Generation, according to the *Brāhmaṇas*, Rudra arose. He was born into the cosmos and he, the son of Brahmā, became the cosmos, Aṣṭamūrti. The elements, time, space, and man—the initiate—were his domain. In the fivefold universe of the *Pañcabrahmans* sex played no part in heaven or on earth; although in transcendency, Puruṣa was distinguished from Prakṛti. The *liṅga* implied these two categories (Ch. VII.4). Śiva permitted to step out from within himself the Great Goddess, who is an image of Prakṛti in the form she had within Ardhanārīśvara. By the power of the Great Goddess, Satī came to be born as a daughter of Dakṣa, the progenitor.

Rudra, the archer, was the avenger of the rupture of the Uncreate. Its integral substance had flowed into creation. Rudra, the mind-born son of Brahmā, his seed drawn up within Sthāṇu, became the pillar of self-containment, a form as abstract in shape as it was anthropomorphic by allusion. This shape of Rudra the yogi, the ascetic, was a symbol of the state of transcendental wholeness as it had been before anything came to be. Yogic austerities were the means of attaining that state. As lord of yogis (*SP*.24.64-66), Śiva became Ardhanārīśvara (*SP*.25.5-9). His shape as androgyne had the vertical of the pillar for its axis. Sthāṇu and Ardhanārīśvara were cognate forms of Śiva, born from Brahmā, consistent in the opposed meanings that coexist within Lord Śiva. Rudra had so deeply injected his asceticism into Brahmā that the Creator had become impotent as procreator of the human race. It was for Śiva to remedy this incapacity. At Brahmā's request, Ardhanārīśvara gave half of his glowing self out into the world, which became sensitized with sexuality and peopled by mortals, susceptible to the arrows of Kāma. It was Kāma who, bewildering men and women with his five flower-arrows, carried on the eternal creation (*ŚP*.2.2.2.37).

6. *Yoni* AND *Liṅga*

Kāma, desire, had arisen in the heat (*tapas*) of the nascent cosmos of *Tad Ekam* "That One," the arch-potential, Ābhu (*RV*.10.129.2). Full-fledged, god Kāma manifested in front of Brahmā when Brahmā desired Gāyatrī. Kāma let fly his arrows in all directions. Brahmā was the nearest victim, and Rudra, the lord of yogis, was the ultimate target. Prior to the attack of Kāma, Śiva did not ever yield to desire. He glowed with heat and fire, radiant as Nīla-Lohita. His eyes were sun, moon, and fire itself (*KūP*.2.5.9), shining and flaming. Downward from the thighs he was blazing fire; the upper half of his body was like the moon. With that auspicious moon quality he practiced asceticism, while his terrible blazing form below burned everything, devouring flesh, blood, and marrow (*MBh*.7.173.95-98). Thus, with the lower half of his self he was the destroyer, but there also burned the fire of sex.

In the Deodar forest, the Lord had played with it. He held his naked *liṅga* in his hand; the sight inflamed the women of the sages (*ŚP*.4.12.10-13). If he himself was aloof, his mere presence spelled seduction. It roused the sages to action. The *liṅga*, the organ of lust, had to fall. The Lord, the Supreme Beggar, in a situation of escalating passion and fury, let his *liṅga* be torn off by the ṛṣis, or by himself. He had been playing an ambiguous game. It was terminated by the cataclysmic fall of the *liṅga*, whether the sages cursed the *liṅga* to fall (*ŚP*.4.12.17-18), or whether it was Śiva's will to let it fall (*BP*.1.2.27.32-33). When it fell, it burned everything before it like fire. It did not stop anywhere, went into hell and heaven, and agitated all creatures on earth (*ŚP*.4.12.19-21). It is said that the sages, who had not recognized the god, went to Brahmā to ask his help against the devastating power of the *liṅga* set free, of sex let loose (*ŚP*.4.12.22). Brahmā, knowing that no good would come to the three worlds as long as the *liṅga* could not be made to stand still, advised the desperate sages to propitiate Devī, to beseech the Great Goddess to take the form of the *yoni*, the womb. There the *liṅga* would come to rest (*ŚP*.4.12.28-32). Then the sages and the gods worshiped Śiva. He assured them of happiness when his *liṅga* would be held in a *yoni*, but no woman except Pārvatī would be able to hold the *liṅga* of Śiva. Held by her, the *liṅga* would at once become still (*ŚP*.4.12.43-46). Hence, Pārvatī in the form of the *yoni* would be the pedestal in which the *liṅga* would be installed.

At the end of its journey, the raging, severed *liṅga* of the lord stood still, in yogic control, in Pārvatī's *yoni*. The goddess, reduced to the female sex organ in its form as architectural symbol and cult object, was conceived as the counterpart of and supplement to the severed *liṅga*. Together they were installed on earth, their place of worship. The cult object of the *liṅga* combined with a *yoni* shows the cylindrical shape of the former rising from a pedestal with a spout-like elongation. The latter fulfills a practical purpose: it allows the water, poured in worship over the "burning hot" stone *liṅga*, to flow off its base. The pedestal, serving a utilitarian purpose, came to signify the *yoni*. The *ūrdhvaliṅga* rises from this base as Agni, the flame of fire, rose from the sacrificial altar, its *yoni* (*RV*.1.140.1; 3.5.7; 10.91.4). The *liṅga* does not enter the *yoni*.

The *liṅga* in the *yoni* is a paradoxical visual symbol. In ancient times, the *ūrdhvaliṅga* of the Lord, set up for worship, rose from the ground or a plinth, and no *yoni* was part of the sacred symbol. The mythical account of the entry of the *liṅga* into the *yoni* related in the *Śiva Purāṇa* reduced the cosmic dimension of the *liṅga* to its basic function as penis. The reduction in meaning as conveyed by the myth, however, was in line with the naturalism of the shape of the earliest *liṅgas* set up for worship. Between the explicitly phallic shape of the earliest *liṅgas* and the later, abstract pillar shape of the *liṅga* lay the symbolic saturation of this vertical sign with ontological meaning. Between the abstract pillar shape by itself and its setting in the *yoni* lay a return to the primary phallic meaning. If the early "naturalistic" shape was shown turgid with life-giving power in which inhered all the possibilities of generation and modalities of existence, the *liṅga* in the *yoni* focuses on the sexual situation of coitus, introducing into it, however, the paradox of the *ūrdhvaliṅga* as a sign of *ūrdhvaretas* (Ch. I.3). The latter connotes the retention, ascent, and transformation of the seed within the body of the lord of yogis. The abstract, geometrical shape, however, of the *ūrdhvaliṅga*, the repository of the ontology of existence, placed on the *yoni* as its pedestal, rises out of the *yoni*, the womb; it does not enter it. The "*liṅga* in the *yoni*" emerges from the *yoni*; it does not penetrate it. This paradox in the coital proximity of the sexual symbols is consonant with and amplifies that of the *liṅga* itself.

Śiva as Sthāṇu, the pillar, and Śiva in the millennial embrace of Pārvatī are seemingly antithetic images, in each of which, however—though different in emphasis—the Great God reveals his yogic and phallic being. It was during the endless love-making of the Lord with the goddess that the sage Bhṛgu called on Śiva. The sage wanted to find out if Śiva truly was the greatest god. Śiva, however, did not receive the sage, because he was in union with the goddess. Offended, Bhṛgu cursed Śiva that he would have the shape of *yoni*-and-*liṅga* (*PP*.6.282.19-31).

Here Śiva, cursed by Bhṛgu, took the shape of *yoni*-and-*liṅga*. The *liṅga-yoni* symbol was not the only form of Śiva resulting from a curse by a sage. When the *liṅga* fell in the Deodar forest, the future worship of the *liṅga* also resulted from a curse. In that myth, "in some versions, Śiva is said to be cursed to be worshipped as the *liṅga*, while in others he himself curses the sages to worship him as the *liṅga*."[23] The excess of sexual power emanating from the Great God was hard for the sages to endure. The object of their aversion was cursed, or they were cursed by Śiva to worship the *liṅga*.

In ancient times, the phallus worshipers were kept away from the sacrifice (*RV*.7.21.5), and god Indra made short shrift of them. They were slain by him (*RV*.10.99.3). The sages, who, in their own way, adhered to the tradition of the sacrifice, were cursed by Śiva to become *liṅga* worshipers, while they themselves cursed Śiva to be worshiped in the *liṅga*. It was an uneasy transition for the sages, from sacrificial offerings to *liṅga* worship. In the ongoing myth of Śiva, moreover, *liṅga* and *yoni* not only retained their value as mere symbols but became actors.

According to the *Bṛhaddharma Purāṇa*, Śiva, absorbed in yogic trance, was apprehended by the goddess. She failed to arouse him from his meditation, but he could not help noticing her presence, as she had taken the shape of a foul-smelling corpse. Śiva returned to his trance. The Great Yogi then assumed the shape of the *liṅga*, and the goddess took the shape of the *yoni*. She placed the *liṅga* within her

[23] W. D. O'Flaherty, *Asceticism and Eroticism in the Mythology of Śiva*, p. 180.

and plunged into the water to create progeny (*BDP*.1.31.16-36), carrying out what Śiva had postponed and avoided when he had plunged into the water (Ch. VI.3). The combined symbol shape of *liṅga* and *yoni* in this late, Tantric myth was separated into its constituent parts, which were personified as god and goddess until they resumed their original position in nature during coitus. The active part was played by the goddess. In the above parable, her anthropomorphic, symbolic shape was that of a putrid corpse.

The goddess, in anthropomorphic form and not in the shape of the *yoni*, became part of the *liṅga* in the homology of the *Viṣṇudharmottara Purāṇa* (*VDhP*.3.48.4-8).[24] There, the five *mantras* or thought forms of Śiva embodied in the *liṅga* with its five faces were homologized with five different aspects of the Lord. The *Vāmadeva mantra*, represented by the face of Vāmadeva, was equated with that of Umā or Pārvatī, the Great Goddess. The face of Vāmadeva, the lovely (*vāma*) god, was that of woman, adorable in her absorption in *samādhi*, fulfilled like the open lotus flower in her hand (Pl. 10). Vāmadeva evoked woman and sex. A chant, based on intercourse, is called the *Vāmadevya sāman* or chanted meditation on Vāmadeva (*ChUp*.2.13.1-2). The chant is structured, or progresses, like the ritual of love. It begins with the invitation or invocation of the deity, proceeds to the request, which is the preliminary laud, on to the lying down with the woman, which is the hymn of glory, and on to the parting, which is the concluding hymn.[25] The structure of the Vedic ritual is at one with the progress of the lovers in the *Vāmadevya* chant of the *Chāndogya Upaniṣad*, just as the goddess and Śiva Mantramūrti coincide in the Vāmadeva face of the image carved in Elephanta and described in the *Viṣṇudharmottara Purāṇa*.

The goddess was sent out from within Ardhanārīśvara, and she reentered his body. Between these two movements, Satī, her likeness, came to exist, the image of femininity. She was Prakṛti given anthropomorphic shape, and her ways, though they prefigured those of the human condition, were transposed to the world of the gods. She was to be the bride of Śiva, who was her origin. Their union would be a reunion, with the *liṅga* in the *yoni* as its sign.

[24] *Viṣṇudharmottara (VDhP)*, cf. tr. S. Kramrisch, 1928, part III, p. 71.

[25] A. Daniélou, *Hindu Polytheism*, p. 224. The translator of this text (S. Chandra Vasu)

By a further reduction of the *liṅga* to its natural function, it is said that the universe was created from the seed emitted from the *liṅga* of Śiva during the sexual act, and the gods worshiped that *liṅga*.[26]

The obvious phallic basis of the sign of the Great God was never forgotten in any of the myths or forms of the Śiva *liṅga*, but no myth, it would seem, tells the story of how the universe was created from the seed that poured out of the *liṅga* of Śiva. It was the seed of Prajāpati that fulfilled that function when it flowed down so copiously that it formed a lake (Ch. III.1). Reversal of the roles of Prajāpati-Brahmā and Śiva was part of the relationship of these gods as father and son. Their relation was considered reversible from the age of the *Brāhmaṇas*: it was the twofold relation of Prajāpati and Agni, of Agni and Prajāpati, as father and son (*ŚB*.6.1.2.27). The two gods embodied the Creator as substance of life and as spark of life, both the cause of life, material and efficient cause, in the conjoint work of creation. The interaction of the two gods was fundamental to the myth of Rudra-Śiva.[27] Whereas the reversible relationship as father and son cost Brahmā his fifth head, the Śiva-*liṅga*, almost ironically, by an appropriation of Prajāpati's mode of operation, was represented as sexual creator. Invested with this meaning, the *liṅga* stood diametrically opposite to the avenger of the primal, procreative act of the Father, for whom Rudra had prepared the seed. Rudra, the yogi and bearer of the seed, restrained the seed within himself, or he let it flow at will; by indirection only, one or the other god or sage was to arise from it. For this purpose Rudra had to be born from the seed of Prajāpati, the Lord of Generation, who endowed his son with the cosmos; and Rudra had to be born as Ardhanārīśvara from the torment and fury of Brahmā's, the Creator's, mind. In creation, Rudra, of innumerable names and shapes, has but one sign of his totality, the *ūrdhvaliṅga*, unmistakable in its shape, ambiguous in its meaning. Ardhanārīśvara was born fierce and ambivalent in order to complete the work of Brahmā's creation. In Ardhanārīśvara, who embraced both the sexes

---

presents a long note on the interpretation of the chant as a "description of the union of the human soul with the Divine Beloved," p. 131.

[26] Cf. *ibid*., p. 228.

[27] The opposition and identity of Prajāpati-Brahmā and Agni-Rudra and also, most cogently, their complementarity have been demonstrated at length by W. D. O'Flaherty, *Ascetisicm and Eroticism in the Mythology of Śiva*, pp. 111-40.

and was beyond them, was the intimate and ultimate origin of the communion of the male and female principles, a paradoxical prognosis of sensual fulfilment. Desire had no part in the world of Ardhanārīśvara.

Kāma, Desire, the god of love, had not as yet intruded into the myth of Śiva. His attack on the lord of yogis was still to come. Still, it is said that because Śiva remembered Kāma, the eternal *liṅga* of Śiva rose on earth (*SkP*.7.1.200.9-30). Kāma, it seems, lived in the perfect and prognostic memory of Śiva, the Great Yogi, just as the primordial scene had been stored in the memory of the newborn Nīla-Lohita (Ch. V.3). The overtones of desire, however, sounded first in the world of Brahmā, when Kāma strung his bow and made Brahmā his victim.

Prognostic memory as well as a reversal of time are effective in the relation of other events in which Ardhanārīśvara and the *liṅga* are connected in the continuity of their myth. Thus, the *Liṅga Purāṇa* says that the goddess is the mother of the universe. Her name is Bhagā (womb). She is the altar of the god who has the form of the *liṅga*. The *liṅga* is the Lord. Together they created the universe. Śiva in the form of the *liṅga* is the light that abides above the darkness (*LP*.1.99.6-7). God and goddess, *liṅga* and *yoni*, are the cocreators of the universe. In this view, Śiva's invisible presence does not inhere in the *liṅga*, which is Prakṛti (Ch. VII.4). Prakṛti here is the goddess as the dark womb and altar, from which rises the divine splendor. Bhagā is the sacrificial ground and the *liṅga* is Agni, the flame of fire. Having transferred *prakṛti* from the *liṅga* to the *yoni*, the *Liṅga Purāṇa* continues to say that from the union of *liṅga* and *yoni* [*vedi*] came Ardhanārīśvara. First, he created Brahmā, his son, the four-faced Lord. Śiva granted cosmic knowledge to Brahmā, and Brahmā asked Śiva to divide himself. From the left side of his body he created the Goddess as his wife (*LP*.1.99.8-12). The reversed roles of Brahmā and Śiva as father and son are interwoven with the *liṅga-yoni* ensemble. This pregnant formula, according to the above context, required Śiva to become Ardhanārīśvara. Teleologically, the *liṅga-yoni* symbol prevailed over the image of Ardhanārīśvara, and Śiva prevailed over Brahmā as Brahmā became the son of Śiva. In another account from the same text, the Lord became the son of Brahmā. He then became male and female Ardhanārīśvara and, as the Lord, burned Brahmā. Thereafter, for the purpose of the increase of the world, Ardhanārīśvara, by the path of yoga, enjoyed the female half of himself. In her he created Viṣṇu and Brahmā (*LP*.1.41.9-12). Thus Brahmā was egg-born, lotus-born, and born also from the body of the Lord (*LP*.1.41.13).

In this version, Ardhanārīśvara as the son of Brahmā divided himself into a male and a female. He enjoyed her who had been half of himself. This relation, though by way of yoga, was counter to the archetypal image of Ardhanārīśvara with its axial male-female division of the body, precluding any sexual position of union. Nonetheless, Ardhanārīśvara not only turned—by the path of yoga—into a progenitive couple but became the father of Viṣṇu and of Brahmā. Before that, Ardhanārīśvara Śiva burned Brahmā, whose son he was, so that Brahmā could be born again from Śiva. This was Brahmā's third mode of birth; his other births were in the waters, where the cosmic egg floated, his original place of birth, and in the cosmic lotus flower, the ancient birthplace of the goddess Lakṣmī, the lotus-born (Padmajā). The death and birth of Brahmā were due to the greatness of Śiva, while the triple birth of Brahmā was a synopsis of the several living traditions about the birth of the Creator. Moreover, not only Brahmā but also Viṣṇu became Śiva's son.

In creation, on the level of the gods, a world full of anthropomorphic metaphor, the gods of the *Purāṇas* were prone to demonstrate their superiority among each other. Śiva manifesting out of the flame *liṅga* humbled Brahmā and Viṣṇu in their aspects as demiurges. The relation, however, of Brahmā and Śiva, which is that of father and son, is complex, intimate, and reciprocal. Related to the reversibility of origin is the flexibility of overlapping situations and conceptual levels. Time and space, as mythical dimensions, allow not only the same objects or symbols but also the same actions to be grouped in several ways. Thus, when, according to one account, Ardhanārīśvara had divided himself, Dakṣa took the female half, gave her to Rudra, and asked him to perform creation. Rudra refused and asked Brahmā to create and let him destroy. "I will become Sthāṇu." Then Śiva with Satī went to Kailāsa (*SkP*.7.2.9.5-17). Śiva, who as Ardhanārīśvara was to complete Brahmā's creation, had recourse to his ascetic nature and resumed his position as Śiva-Sthāṇu; then Śiva went to Kailāsa with Satī, taking for granted and as part of himself his resolve to be Sthāṇu, withdrawn into himself, the destroyer of all fetters. Śiva in his togetherness with Satī, Śiva as Sthāṇu, and Śiva as

Ardhanārīśvara are aspects of the many-sided Great God. Each has its myth; while it is intoned, its resonance touches other facets of the myth, and their vibrations meet. Because the various aspects are ingrained in the body of Śiva, they are simultaneously present and made visible at will. The Lord Śiva, on his own accord, shows forth one or another side of his nature (cf. *MS*.2.9.7), each having a myth of its own. They lie ready within his total being. If one aspect is activated, one or the other aspect may also be summoned. While one myth of Śiva is being told, its episodes, spaced on several threads, are knotted in various patterns. Their themes, lying ready, are taken up and placed, fittingly or tendentiously, into the current of the story. Such myths, in their complexity, yield a kaleidoscopic theophany, rather than a narrative along the arrow of time: Ardhanārīśvara, from within his own manifestation, let step out the goddess. She, in turn, at Brahmā's command sent her Śakti into the world of Dakṣa, where her power entered Vīriṇī, the wife of Dakṣa (*ŚP*.2.2.14.12-14), and the Great Goddess was born as his daughter Satī. By being born, Satī acquired the body of her own reality. It was the idea of woman represented by the female sex. The *yoni* was its seat and symbol. Henceforward, the female element and the consciousness of sex dwelled in Śiva's sacred grove. The Great Yogi, having destroyed all fetters and become Sthāṇu, went with Satī to Kailāsa (*SkP*.7.2.9.5-17).

In the dual symbol of *yoni* and *liṅga*, *prakṛti* appears extrapolated from the comprehensive *liṅga* symbol and transposed into the *yoni*. In the *Īśvara Gītā*, the song of the Lord, of the *Kūrma Purāṇa*, the Lord (Īśvara) says, "Mahat Brahman [that is, Prakṛti] is my womb; I cast the seed [of creation] in that and it is called the original *Māyā* of which the entire universe is born" (*KūP*.2.8.3).[28] Succinctly stated, the triple world arises from the union of *liṅga* and *yoni* (cf. *MBh*.13.14, note 102, lines 7-8; cf. *ŚS*.1.92). *Māyā* is the womb of the Lord impregnated by his seed (cf. *KūP*.2.8.2-3). *Prakṛti*, prematter, though transcendent, is not ultimate reality. Impregnated by the seed of the Lord, *prakṛti* becomes *māyā*, holding his presence and covering it. The veil of *māyā* is the magic paradox that hides and also reveals the Lord. The Lord said: "All creatures are made of me. Deluded by my *Māyā* they do not see me, their father" (*KūP*.2.8.6). The Lord and his *māyā* are the father and mother of all creatures. The wise men who know the Great

[28] *Kūrma Purāṇa (KūP)*, ed. A. S. Gupta and tr. A. Bhattacharya (part I) and S. Mukherji, V. K. Varma, and G. S. Rai (part II), 1972, p. 323.

God as the father who casts the seed are never bewildered (*KūP*.2.8.7-8).

The knowledge of ultimate reality and of contingent reality, in which the former dwells, has the *liṅga* in the *yoni* as its visual equivalent. Yet, the *ūrdvaliṅga*, facing upward, rises from the *yoni*, away from it, in the opposite direction. It stands for Śiva, the ascetic, who is always seen along with the goddess (*KūP*.2.31.47). The apparent paradoxes support one another. The composite shape of *yoni* and *liṅga* is an epistemological symbol set up for worship. To the eye of knowledge, focused on the symbol, the presence of Śiva is revealed. The Lord lifts the veil of *māyā*, that he, the cosmic dancer, holds in his raised hand (Pls. 22-24).

IX

BHAIRAVA

1. One, Four, Five Heads of the Creator

Rudra had prepared the seed for the Father; Rudra shot the Father while he, the Lord of Generation, Prajāpati, was spending his seed into creation. Creation is a destructive activity. It violates the integrity of the indefinable absolute, making manifest and disseminating its contents.

Rudra, the avenger of the primordial act of the Father, was born in another aeon from the seed of Prajāpati. To assuage the memory of the primordial scene that troubled his newborn son, Prajāpati invested Rudra with the cosmos.

In yet another aeon, Rudra was born from the head of Brahmā. The Father, Prajāpati, and Brahmā are successive names of the Creator, *per generationem*. Rudra, who had prepared the seed for the Father, carried within himself the fire seed of life. Born as a mental son of Brahmā and being Consciousness itself, the Great God and Lord of Yoga acted out fully his role as avenger. He severed his *liṅga* from his body. He cut off the head of Brahmā.

When Prajāpati and his daughter consorted as antelopes, Prajāpati was pierced by the arrow of Rudra; he bounded to the sky and became the constellation Mṛga, the antelope (*AB*.3.33; cf. *ŚB*.1.7.4.1-3); or Prajāpati, pierced by the arrow, abandoned his body, and became the constellation Mṛgaśiras (*ŚB*.2.1.2.9). Mṛgaśiras, the antelope's head, is the head of Prajāpati (*ŚB*.2.1.2.8), though this constellation may also represent the abandoned body of Prajāpati (*ŚB*.2.1.2.9). In the sky among the stars, Prajāpati became established as Mṛgaśiras, the head of the antelope, for the body of Prajāpati, struck by the arrow, fell to the ground (*SkP*.3.1.40.12). As Prajāpati, pierced, abandoned his body (*ŚB*.2.1.2.9), a great light arose from it, went to the sky, and became the star Mṛgaśiras (*SkP*.3.1.40.13). Mahādeva, that ocean and treasury of compassion (*SkP*.3.1.40.26, 35), who had severed the head of the Creator of the world (*SkP*.3.1.40.30), revived Prajāpati-Brahmā and placed four heads on his body. They were those of Nandin, the leader of Śiva's host, and of others of his gaṇas. Having lost his one head and received four, four-headed Brahmā praised Śiva. Henceforward, according to this version of the myth, Brahmā had four heads (*SkP*.3.1.40.39-49). The head of the antelope had become a separate reality. To this day it looks down from the sky. Brahmā, however, acquired his four heads in more than one way.

The four heads of Brahmā faced the four directions. The four directions constitute the extent of the manifest world; the four orients refer to the movement of the sun. They indicate the cosmos under the rule of time. Four being the comprehensive number of the total manifestation, is also the number of revelation—completely made Word in the four *Vedas*. Brahmā, the Creator, was fittingly given four heads. It did not matter on whose shoulders each had formerly sat; their number was all that mattered, for it showed the comprehensiveness of Brahmā's being.

Even so, this number of heads proved to be insufficient when Brahmā had to cope with the appearance of a lovely girl, dark, slender, and with beautiful eyes (cf. *VmP*, *SM*.28.4-5, 20). She appeared from one half of his body (Ch. VIII.3) as he invoked Sāvitrī, the most sacred *mantra*, the essence of the *Vedas*, whose other name is Gāyatrī (*MP*.3.30-32). Sāvitrī manifested in response to Brahmā's dissatisfaction with his creation of mind-born sons and as he was conceiving a new plan for the creation of living beings. She was one of Śatarūpā's hundred forms (*MP*.3.31). Brahmā first thought she was his daughter, and he desired her. He could not take his eyes off Sāvitrī, and did not want to turn his head. Instead, by his own will he grew four heads in the four directions in order to see her while she walked around him. Śatarūpā, embarrassed, moved heavenward (*MP*.3.32-40; cf. Ch. VIII.3).

The self-acquired four heads of Brahmā resulted from his lusting after his daughter. In them he set forth into the world in the four directions his hitherto undivided self. The heads had sprouted from his desire for something no longer within himself. It was Gāyatrī, the goddess who had appeared from his own half. True to the ancient pattern, she was his daughter. Being his daughter she carried within her the knowledge of her celestial origin.

Her ascension provoked the appearance of one more, the fifth, the quintessential head on top of the four. Brahmā covered it with his long, matted hair. Its abundance showed his virile power; its uncared-for tangled look gave him the appearance of a yogi. Nevertheless, due to his desire for congress with his daughter, Brahmā lost all the power accumulated by his austerities (*tapas*) that he needed for the creation of the universe (*MP*.3.39-40).[1]

Brahmā's desire for his daughter was aroused by her beauty, but it was caused by Kāma, who was born just then as Brahmā's mental son (*ŚP*.2.2.2.23, 35-36). Kāma was born to madden and delude people, and for this purpose Brahmā gave him magic arrows. Kāma immediately tested them and pierced Brahmā. They had the desired effect. Seen in this amorous state by his other mind-born sons, the ascetics, Brahmā was ashamed (*MP*.4.11). He became angry with Kāma and cursed him. The curse of the Creator meant death to Kāma, and implicated Śiva in this fatality. Brahmā cursed Kāma that he would be reduced to ashes when he made Śiva his target. Kāma cried out in anguish that Brahmā had created him to captivate the minds and arouse love in whomever his arrows hit, and that he had carried out Brahmā's instruction. Then Brahmā promised him that he would become incarnate again. Kāma, sad on account of the curse but relieved by its modification, departed (*MP*.4.11-21).

Brahmā in his curse of Kāma meant to avenge his own passion on Śiva, exposing him to the same predicament that had befallen his own person. Primordially, when Prajāpati had become a victim of Rudra's

[1] A forerunner of five-headed Brahmā is King Soma as/or Prajāpati having five mouths or heads. According to *KBUp*.2.9, one should worship the moon with the words "You are King Soma, the far seeing, *pañcamukho'si prajāpatir*," that is, the "five-faced Prajāpati" or the "five-mouthed Lord of Generation." The five mouths of King Soma are the Brahmin, the King, the Hawk and the Fire. With these mouths he eats the kings, the people, the birds, the regions, and with the fifth mouth he eats all the beings. In *KBUp*.2.10, 11, however, Prajāpati, the Lord of Generation, and not King Soma is spoken of. King Soma as Lord of Generation shades over into Prajāpati, the Lord of Generation, the five heads a forecast of Brahmā's five heads.

arrow, he made Rudra Lord of Animals, and Paśupati, the lord of creatures, spared the life of Prajāpati. Now, however, Brahmā had been victimized, not by Rudra but by Kāma, desire, which had seized the Creator at the very beginning of creation. Though Brahmā cursed Kāma, the Creator revenged himself on Rudra / Śiva. Like Brahmā, Śiva would become a victim of Kāma and his victory would be the death of Kāma and his resurrection.

Exhausted by his curse of Kāma and by his own shame, Brahmā abandoned his body. His daughter, seeing her father dead, killed herself, but both were revived by Viṣṇu. Viṣṇu then gave her in marriage to Kāma and named her Rati, the goddess Lust (*BVP*.4.35.38-73, 101). Śatarūpā, of a hundred forms, Brahmā's daughter, when she died in loyalty to her father, was called Sandhyā, Twilight (*ŚP*.2.2.5.7-10; 2.2.7.1-5). Long ago, when creation began, she had been Uṣas, the first Dawn of a nascent cosmos. At that time Prajāpati was pierced by the arrow of Rudra. Now he was a victim of Kāma's arrow and he left his body in shame. According to the *Brahmavaivarta Purāṇa*, Sandhyā killed herself and became the goddess Lust, Rati, the wife of Kāma (*BVP*.4.35.71-73, 101). But this was not her only fate. Her other fate was to become Arundhatī, the embodiment of conjugal chastity (*ŚP*.2.2.5.8). Just as a god or goddess may be born more than once, each may have more than one fate and live it out in more than one shape.

The number of Brahmā's heads and the manner in which they came to be convey metaphysical and lesser problems. Together with the inherent significance of the numbers one, four, and five, the existence or acquisition of the respective number of heads and the loss of one of them—be it the first and only one or the fifth and last—form an intricate pattern. The light thrown on it by several versions of the myth moves around a central sensitive knot in which the identities of Śiva and Brahmā are tied up. The pattern of the threads, seen in this uncertain light, appears positive from one angle, negative from another, but out of seeming contradictions the heads sit or fall in the appointed place.

Thus, it was Śiva who gave Brahmā his four heads in compensation for the one he had caused to be severed. Or Brahmā himself sprouted all his five heads. Prajāpati had been felled by Rudra-Śiva, because he had emitted into creation some of the substance of the Uncreate. It fell into creation as its seed. Prajāpati, the Lord of Generation, was lustful and incontinent. Rudra avenged the violation of the wholeness of the Uncreate. The incontinence of the progenitive act of Prajāpati was his target. The head that had allowed it was severed and transferred up to the sky, to the stars. Śiva, the Great God, full of compassion, compensated the severance of the one and only head of the Head of the World by placing four heads on Brahmā's shoulders. In renewed wholeness, Brahmā's eyes now beheld the whole world and he carried the sum of all knowledge, the fourfold *Veda*, within him and held it in his hand in the shape of a book, as his images show. Thus Brahmā, the Creator, got four heads. He got them by the grace of Śiva.

Others, however, know that Brahmā the lotus-born (*BhP*.3.8.16), Brahmā the egg-born (*PP*.5.14.88; *MP*.2.35-36), had four heads from the beginning (*BhP*.3.8.16). The myth of Brahmā, the Creator, belongs to an aeon long after the one head of Prajāpati, the Lord of Generation, had found its place in the sky. On the other hand, Brahmā got himself his five heads. One by one, they appeared on his neck for the same reason for which Prajāpati's one and only head had been severed from his body. The intercourse of Prajāpati with his daughter and the desire of Brahmā for his daughter are symbols through which was acted out the primordial violation of the Uncreate by the Creator.

Uṣas, first Dawn of the world, having been the partner in the traumatic, primeval scene, marked the transition into creation. Though in union with the Father, she had not been the target of Rudra's arrow. As Sandhyā, Twilight, a kind glance from Śiva's eye freed her from all shortcomings and, delighted with her asceticism, Śiva told Sandhyā that she had become pure (*ŚP*.2.2.3.59; 2.2.6.30-40).

Sandhyā was reborn from the sweat of Dakṣa as Rati, Lust, his daughter (*ŚP*.2.2.3.51-59); or she entered the sacrificial fire, where, at the end of the sacrifice, sage Medhātithi found her as his daughter in the sacrificial pit (*ŚP*.2.2.7.1-5, 14). Uṣas, cosmic Dawn, in mythical transformation, descended to being Sandhyā, the twilight of each ritual day and, after her voluntary death, was reborn as lust or as conjugal fidelity, the one considered to be the opposite of the other.

Brahmā did not retain his fifth head for long. It had arisen above the four heads as Brahmā sought not to lose sight of his daughter in her flight from this earth. The fifth head looked heavenward. It differed from the other four heads by its position, above their level.

In this respect, the fifth head of Brahmā resembled Īśāna, the head of Śiva. Śiva, being Mantramūrti, necessarily had five heads. His *mantra*, *Namaḥ Śivāya*, is of five syllables; his fivefold evocation in the *Taittirīya Āraṇyaka* and its form as the *liṅga* of five faces showed the pentad to be Śiva's comprehensive numerical symbol. Of the five faces of Śiva, that of Īśāna, the Lord, towered above the others; it represented a higher plane in the total reality of the god.

Brahmā had four heads and the fifth was supernumerary, excessive, the outgrowth of Brahmā's surpassing desire for his daughter, who took flight heavenward. Uṣas had run away from the Father, *post factum*, to the south, the region of perdition. It is also said that Brahmā grabbed his daughter in order to cohabit with her. Before she vanished she told Brahmā that five faces were not becoming to him; four faces, full of *Veda*, would be proper (*BhvP*.3.4.13.1-5).

With his five heads, Brahmā numerically rivaled Śiva, whose fivefold being was conveyed from ancient times by his five *mantras*. The exalted position of the fifth head of Śiva had a pejorative counterpart in Brahmā's fifth head. Position and number of the heads of the two gods were deceptively similar, but Brahmā's fifth head negated all that Śiva's fifth head meant. The elevated position of Brahmā's fifth head singled it out for an assault by Śiva. It was a reenactment of Rudra's primeval onslaught on the Father. The target, however, was not in the region of sex. It had moved up to the head. The attack did not come from a Wild Hunter, his name unuttered because of fear. The attack came from Śiva, born from Brahmā's head. Brahmā as father of mind-born sons seems to have had not more than one head, the birth-giving head.

Brahmā, it would appear, enjoyed the manner in which he had acquired his five heads, that is, by looking at the beauty of his daughter while she reverentially circumambulated him, for, on another occasion, he created the celestial maiden Tilottamā, of unrivaled beauty. As her name implies, she was made of the minutest particles of jewels. Tilottamā walked around the assembly of the gods. When she came near Śiva and was at his side, another face of Śiva appeared. When she was behind him another face of the god appeared, and as she walked on, a fourth face. Śiva manifested his sovereignty of the universe with the face looking toward the east. With the face turned to the north he sported with the Great Goddess. With the face toward the west he showed himself as the ordainer of the happiness of creatures, and with the southern face he showed himself as their destroyer (*MBh*.13.128.1-6). He revealed himself to Tilottamā, the lovely temptress, as the Five *Brahmans*, though she could not see his fifth, invisible face.

The archetype of all the many heads, eyes, and limbs of the Great God is Supernal Man, the Puruṣa, in whose likeness Rudra was born. The numbers, a hundred or a thousand, hint at the innumerable, whereas any number smaller than ten is not a cypher but a symbol, the number four standing primarily for the directions of space, the number five, in this context, being the quintessential number of the center raised above the four other heads. In Brahmā's case, the fifth, supererogatory head was evil; in the episode of Tilottamā, Brahmā created a situation similar to that in which he had found himself when Sāvitrī appeared before him. In the assembly of the gods, Brahmā seemed to mean to ensnare Śiva in a situation parallel to the one that had produced his own fifth head, but Śiva put out only four heads. Brahmā thought of humbling Śiva by inducing him toward the production of several, but he had not exceeded four visible heads, whereas Brahmā had achieved five heads in his amorous pursuit. Brahmā retaliated for having been in a position where he compulsively copied the pentad of Śiva's head by bringing about a similar situation; but Śiva did not produce more than four heads—the number, as Sāvitrī, his daughter, had said, that was becoming to Brahmā.

Brahmā's fifth head, an outgrowth of uncontrolled desire, seen against the fifth, invisible head of Śiva, that of Īśāna, dwelling in transcendency, amounted to a sacrilege.

According to another point of view, the five heads were given to Brahmā long ago by Śiva as a special sign (*ŚP*.1.8.7), in a rite, as it were, of initiation to invest Brahmā with the power to create. Śiva with five faces spoke the five syllables—*Namaḥ Śivāya*—with his five mouths to Brahmā. Brahmā grasped them with his five faces or mouths (*LP*.1.85.13-14).

In a complete reversal of positions, the five heads of Śiva are said to have appeared during an argument between Śiva and Brahmā. Śiva stared at Brahmā's fifth face when five-faced Brahmā emerged from the cosmic ocean. After an angry exchange between the two gods, the five faces of Śiva manifested (*VmP*.2.23-34; cf. Ch. IX n. 1).

The reciprocal relation of Śiva's and Brahmā's five heads is even more involved, but also resolved in other myths. When Brahmā was unable to create and asked Śiva to be his son, Śiva said he would cut off Brahmā's head. Śiva was born from Brahmā's head, from the mouth breath, or forehead of Brahmā. Brahmā, having created five-headed Śiva, became overweening; his fifth head generated heated energy, it shone brighter than the sun, it outshone the splendor of the gods and incapacitated them. Śiva cut off the fifth head and kept it in his hand to prevent it from burning the earth and drying up the ocean (*BrP*.113.1-18; cf. *SkP*.5.1.2.7-26; cf. *PP*.5.14.92-115).[2] The severed head of Brahmā, held in Śiva's hand, was to cling to it. The head became a skull and served Śiva as his begging bowl (cf. Ch. IX.2). Or Brahmaśiras, the head of Brahmā, retained its formidable energy and became the Pāśupata weapon, which Śiva gave to Arjuna, the Pāṇḍava hero and son of Indra (*MBh*.3.41.7-8, 13).[3]

Arjuna had subjected himself to ascetic austerities when, to obtain a sight of Śiva, he went into the Himālayan wilderness (*MBh*.3.39.10-12). There the Pāṇḍava hero encountered a wild hunter, a Kirāta, of powerful build. At that moment a boar was about to attack Arjuna. Though the boar was struck down simultaneously by the arrows of Arjuna and of the Kirāta, Arjuna and the Kirāta began to fight as to who had first aimed at the boar. The Kirāta proved to be invulnerable and got hold of Arjuna's bow Gāṇḍiva (*MBh*.3.40.1-25, 39).

Pleased with Arjuna's courage in battle, Śiva revealed himself to Arjuna. Arjuna prostrated himself before Śiva, the Wild Hunter. Smilingly, Śiva, holding Arjuna's hands, pardoned him (*MBh*.3.40.52-61). Śiva granted his request for the Brahmaśiras weapon. Thus, Śiva gave to Arjuna the Pāśupata weapon, which can be hurled by the mind, by the eye, by words, and by the bow (*MBh*.3.41.13-16). The Kirāta also returned the Gāṇḍiva bow to Arjuna (*MBh*.3.41.25). Brahmaśiras, "the head of Brahmā" had become a most powerful weapon, the Pāśupata weapon, which was no other than the Pāśupata

[2] Cf. W. D. O'Flaherty, *The Origins of Evil in Hindu Mythology*, 1976, p. 284.

[3] The Brahmaśiras weapon destroys all the three worlds at the end of a yuga. Cf. M. Biardeau, "Études de mythologie hindoue, IV," 1976, p. 124.

Vrata (cf. *AUp*.67), the vow by which alone *kaivalya*, liberation from the fetters of existence, can be obtained (commentary on *AUp*.67).

Rudra / Śiva, the Wild Hunter from the beginning of things, whom Prajāpati, the Lord of Generation, had made Paśupati, Lord of Animals, lord of creatures, took the shape of a Kirāta. As a Kirāta, a tribal huntsman without caste, he imparted to Arjuna, the warrior, the infallible weapon of the Pāśupata vow by his gift of the Brahmaśiras, the magical power inherent in Brahmā's severed head.

Śiva, the Wild Hunter, the Kirāta, had a following of women, thousands of Kirāta women (*MBh*.3.40.17). In another shape, that of Bhikṣāṭana, the Supreme Beggar, Śiva had enlightened the sages in their forest hermitage. There, the women of the ṛṣis followed him, entranced by the mysterious beggar.

The bacchantic women who followed Bhikṣāṭana / Bhairava and the Kirāta amazons were groups of enthusiasts, ecstatics, and jungle dwellers who recognized Lord Śiva; they were drawn to him, followed and praised him, even though their men, the sages in the Deodar forest, were averse to him.

In another hermitage, the wife of sage Atri, for example, unwilling to live in subjection to her husband, left him and sought the protection of Lord Śiva, subjecting herself to great austerities (*MBh*.13.14.65-66). Yet another woman, the mother of Upamanyu, blessed with the knowledge of Śiva, lived as an ascetic in the wilderness. Once her son asked her to cook some dish with milk, for he had tasted milk on his visit to another hermitage. She had none to cook, for, living in the woods, roots and fruits were her only food, and asceticism together with the recitation of sacred *mantras* were the daily practices of the recluses. Having no sweet milk to give to her son, the mother of Ṛṣi Upamanyu told him about Śiva, the giver of everything (*MBh*.13.14.75-84). The mother of Upamanyu praised Mahādeva, the Great God who is incomprehensible to ordinary, unenlightened man, though he resides in the hearts of all creatures. Many are the forms of his grace (*MBh*.13, app. 1, no. 4, lines 11-18).

The laud of Mahādeva by the mother of Upamanyu was imbued with the knowledge and fervor of the *Śatarudriya* hymn. She added to the "hundred" forms of Rudra, hailed in that paean, those of the Kirāta and the Śabara, representatives of the wild tribes of the jungle; she added the shapes of tortoise, fish, conch, and snake; the demonic and ghoulish form of Preta, Piśāca, Rākṣasa; of lizard, leopard, crow, and peacock, of many other beasts, birds, and of every man. She saw the Great God girt with snakes; his earrings, girdle, and sacred thread made of snakes. She saw him wearing an elephant skin but also perfectly naked, fair complexioned, dark complexioned, pale, ruddy, white with ashes smeared all over his body, and the crescent moon shining from his forehead. She saw him dance and wander over cremation grounds, and she saw him sport with the daughters and wives of the ṛṣis. She heard him sing and play on many instruments; she heard him laugh, cry, and make others cry, or he appeared to her like a madman. She knew him as the very breath of life, its principle (*jīva*); she knew him as the conscious mind and its transcendence, yoga itself, Maheśvara, the Great Lord, the destroyer of all creatures and on whom all creatures rest (*MBh*.13, app. 1, no. 4, lines 27-77).

The mother of Upamanyu, unable to give her son the milk that nourished other ṛṣis living closer to village and pasture than her retreat in the mountain forest, saw the Wild God as a Kirāta. As a Kirāta, a wild hunter, the Great God gave to Arjuna his missile, the Brahmaśiras, the "Head of Brahmā," that is, the Pāśupata weapon or Pāśupata vow. It was a powerful weapon. Its magic worked in many ways, for it could be aimed by the mind, by the eye, by words, and by the bow. But before the Brahmaśiras weapon, the head of Brahmā, could become effective, Śiva had to sever the head of Brahmā, his fifth head. In the myth of the Kirāta, Arjuna received the Brahmaśiras weapon from the hand of Śiva. In the myth of Bhairava, the head of Brahmā clung to the hand of Śiva. It became a skull (*kapāla*), the begging bowl of Śiva as Bhikṣāṭana.

2. The Severed Head: The Cause of Its Fall

The fifth head of Brahmā had to fall, for more than one reason. The *Skānda Purāṇa* remembers the one fundamental, primordial cause. It says that formerly, in the very beginning of the Kṛta Yuga, the golden age, Brahmā was enamored of his youthful daughter and was about to cohabit with her. Seeing this, Śiva cut off with a sword the fifth head of Brahmā (*SkP*.2.3.2.3-4; cf. 3.1.40.5-16). The primal scene, at the beginning of days, is staged here in the costume of a later age, when the figure of the Father Prajāpati had acquired the features of Brahmā, including the fifth head, the physiognomical projection skyward of his lust that had gone to his head. Rudra, in this setting, did not direct his arrow toward the sex of Prajāpati. Instead, he wielded a sword by which he cut off the obnoxious head.[4] But for the change in costume and iconography, the primordial scene has remained intact.

According to other accounts, the site of the decapitation of Brahmā was not the stark vastness of a nascent world but the sublime peak of Mount Meru, the cosmic mountain (*KūP*.2.31.3). There, the great sages asked Brahmā which god was the imperishable, supreme reality. Deluded by Śiva's *māyā*, Brahmā declared himself as the supreme reality (*KūP*.2.31.4-6). Viṣṇu made the same claim for himself (*KūP*.2.31.8-10). The *Vedas* declared Śiva to be the ultimate reality in whom all beings reside, the highest reality that the yogis know, the Great Lord who makes the wheel of existence revolve, Śaṅkara, the bringer of peace, Mahādeva, the Great God, Puruṣa, the primal being, Rudra (*KūP*.2.31.13-16). Hearing these words, Brahmā in his delusion laughed and asked: "How is it that the Supreme Spirit, the Brahman, free of all attachment, lustily sports with his wife and the very haughty Pramathas, the churn-spirits?" (*KūP*.2.31.17-18; cf. *ŚP*.3.8.31-32; *SkP*.3.1.24.16).

Brahmā, in this contest of supremacy, assumed an aggressive stance against Śiva, who was not present in the assembly of the gods and sages on the peak of Mount Meru. It was under the spell of the *māyā* of Lord Śiva that the two demiurges acted as they did. Brahmā inveighed against Śiva for the same reason that—in the opinion of some of the gods—Rudra had attacked Prajāpati in the primordial scene. The intercourse of Prajāpati and his daughter, however, had been a signal only that the wholeness of the absolute was being ruptured by the flow of its substance into creation. Subsequently, the meaning of the symbol sank into, and was submerged in, its sexual impact. It rose to Brahmā's uneasy and deluded mind when he attacked Śiva, the Great Yogi, apparently in the thrall of lust and thus disqualified from being supreme reality, free from all attachment.

The final word in the assembly of gods and sages was spoken by a formless one that had taken on a form, the sound *AUM*, the primordial sound, the *praṇava*, the source of all *mantras* (*KūP*.2.31.19). *Praṇava* said, "Never does the Great Lord Rudra-Śiva take delight in any wife who would be separate from his own self. The glorious Lord is

[4] W. D. O'Flaherty, *The Origins of Evil in Hindu Mythology*, p. 284, on the removal of the "in auspicious first head."

self-luminous, eternal. His delight in himself is called Devī, the goddess. Śivā is not outside Śiva" (*KūP*.2.31.20-21; cf. *ŚP*.3.8.34-35; cf. *SkP*.3.1.24.18-19). He is that ascetic who, by his very nature, is "always in close union with the goddess" (*KūP*.2.31.47).[5]

Prajāpati had cohabited with his daughter. She was his self-begotten duality. Śiva held within him the goddess, his state of bliss. In this way he was one with her, in self-contained fulfillment of deity. Its incandescence dissolved their lineaments. The alternative of the Lord and the goddess within him had manifested as Ardhanārīśvara, the right and left, male and female in equal parts within the Lord.

Praṇava, pure sound, ethereal vibration in which the cosmos chants itself, if it reached Brahmā's ear, failed to convey its message to him, deluded as he was by Śiva's inscrutable *māyā* (*KūP*.2.31.22). At this impasse a celestial light irradiated the firmament, a shining orb (*KūP*.2.31.23-24; *SkP*.3.1.24.28-30), or a mass of flames from heaven to earth (*ŚP*.3.8.37), or was it Puruṣa, carrying a trident? The crescent moon was his head ornament, a third eye shone in his forehead, and he was wreathed in serpents (*ŚP*.3.8.37-41). Brahmā's fifth head looked up and burned with rage, and he saw Nīla-Lohita (*KūP*.2.31.26). The fifth head of Brahmā burned with anger (*ŚP*.3.8.39). Having created this fifth head, Brahmā spoke to the Supreme Lord: "O Great God, I know you. In the past you sprang from my forehead. You were my son named Rudra. Come to me. I will protect you" (*KūP*.2.31.28; *ŚP*.3.8.42-43; *SkP*.3.1.24.31-34; cf. *MP*.183.84-86). As Maheśvara, the Lord, heard these arrogant words, he sent forth Kālabhairava (*KūP*.2.31.29; *SkP*.3.1.24.35) of dread appearance, Kālarāja, the lord of time of whom even time is afraid.

There are no words for the fearfulness of Bhairava, for his terror. Bhairava is the complete form of Śiva. Fools, deluded by Śiva's *māyā*, do not know him (*ŚP*.3.8.2). Bhairava, the Kālapuruṣa, Time who controls time, who controls everything (*KūP*.2.31.29, 45), cut off that head with the nail of his left thumb (*VrP*.97.6-7), or with the tips of the nails of the fingers of his left hand (*ŚP*.3.8.52), or simply cut it off after a great battle (*KūP*.2.31.30).

The severed head became attached to Rudra's hand (*VrP*.97.7). Its skull did not leave the palm of Bhairava's left hand.

Bhairava is Śiva at his most fearful. He is Śiva entire, whether spo-

[5] *Kūrma Purāṇa (KūP)*, ed. A. S. Gupta and tr. A. Bhattacharya (part I) and S. Mukherji, V. K. Varma and G. S. Rai (part II), 1972, p. 456.

ken of as emanated from Śiva, or, seen on the highest level of Śiva, as Mahādeva Kālabhairava, the Great God Kālabhairava. It was the same left hand that severed the head and to which clung the skull of Brahmā. According to the *Kūrma Purāṇa*, Śiva acted out his being, facing himself in multiple unity. Mahādeva, the Great God, enjoined Nīla-Lohita, who stood in front of him, to carry the skull as his begging bowl, and collect alms for the expiation of the sin that he had committed. The Great Lord said to Kālāgni, who is Time, the devouring Fire, and who became Bhairava, "Roam constantly begging alms." Mahādeva Kālabhairava of dark countenance and beauty then wandered through the world (*KūP*.2.31.61-73). Much as he wanted to be freed from it, the skull remained in his hand while he expiated his sin (*ŚP*.3.8.61-62).

The unnamed god whose arrow struck the Father in his organ of sex and Śiva-Bhairava, who cut off Brahmā's fifth head, are one in essence.

Brahmā's fifth head taunted Lord Śiva manifesting in glory; it belittled the Great God for having been born as Brahmā's son and offered paternal protection to Mahādeva. Śiva, however, had anticipated the animadversion of Brahmā. At the time when Brahmā had desired Śiva to be born as his son so that Brahmā could create living beings, Śiva had assured Brahmā that he would cut off the overbearing fifth head of Brahmā (*SkP*.5.1.2.20-21).

The fifth head of Brahmā was that of a horse (*BhvP*.1.22.13-16). The horse's head is known to crown Viṣṇu: he is called Hayamukha, "horse-faced one" (*MBh*. 1.20, note 10, 299, line 2), but a similar form, Hayagrīva, is the name of a demon killed by Viṣṇu (*MBh*.5.128.49). The ambiguity of the horse's head stems from the sun, vivifying and also scorching, of which the horse is a symbol. Thus, also, the horse's head holds and gives away secret knowledge (*RV*.1.116.12; 1.117.22; 1.119.9).[6] The fifth head of Brahmā recited indiscretely, though prognostically, the *Ātharvaṇa mantra*, " 'O Kapālin,' 'Skull-bearer,' O Rudra, . . . protect the world . . ." as Rudra, just born, sat on the shoulder of his father (*VrP*.97.3-5).

The fifth head of Brahmā, self-acquired by his lust or arrogance, had to fall because of its foreknowledge and indiscretion in having in-

[6] A. A. Macdonell, *Vedic Mythology*, p. 141, on the cut-off head and the horse's head; cf. S. Kramrisch, "The Mahāvīra Vessel and the Plant Pūtika," 1975, pp. 224-26.

voked and provoked the newborn god as Kapālin, a title he was to earn once he had cut off Brahmā's head, and the head had turned into a skull clinging to his hand as he went begging with this bowl that had held Brahmā's most compelling drive and ambition. Hearing the words of the *mantra*, "O Skull-bearer, O Rudra . . . ," from Brahmā's mouth, Rudra Nīla-Lohita, Bhairava, cut off the fifth head of Brahmā with the nail of his left thumb (*VrP*.97.5-7).

Misgivings based on their father-son relationship prompted Brahmā's fifth head to a fatal indiscretion. If the fifth head gave away its foreknowledge in order to infuriate Śiva, it did do worse when, according to another version of the myth, it lied. This took place on the battlefield when Brahmā and Viṣṇu fought, not with words but with their weapons, so as to prove by the victor's sovereignty, his ultimate reality. Śiva, seeing that the flaming weapons of the fighting demiurges were about to burn the world, appeared on the battlefield as a huge column of fire. The gods, wondering what this blazing pillar was, attempted to fathom its extent, as they had done when the flaming pillar arose from the flood of a cosmic night. They failed to reach either bottom or top, but Brahmā, on his return from on high, where he had flown in the shape of a wild gander, lied to Viṣṇu that he had seen the top of the pillar. What he had seen was a Ketakī flower that had floated down from high above when Śiva's head had shaken with laughter on seeing the fight of Brahmā and Viṣṇu. But when Viṣṇu bowed to Brahmā, believing that Brahmā had seen the top of the flaming pillar, Śiva manifested to punish Brahmā (*ŚP*.1.7.4-29). He created Bhairava from the middle of his forehead to chastise Brahmā (*ŚP*.1.8.1). In this myth, Mahādeva, the Great God, bid Bhairava to worship Brahmā with his sharp, quick sword. Bhairava caught hold of the hair of Brahmā's fifth head, which was arrogant and had lied; he raised his sword to strike (*ŚP*.1.8.3-4), and cut off Brahmā's fifth head (*ŚP*.3.8.52). The radical punishment of Brahmā on ethical grounds, because the Creator had lied, though it was meted out in a cosmic setting, obfuscated the metaphysical significance of Śiva's parricide of Brahmā, the Creator. To strengthen the argument on ethical grounds, not only did Brahmā himself lie, but he also made the Ketakī flower give false evidence by saying that it was the witness to the truth of Brahmā's assertion that he had seen the top of the *liṅga* (*ŚP*.1.7.24-25). In another version of the myth, Brahmā resolved to say that he had seen the end. He sprouted a fifth head in the form of a she-ass, to speak the lie that his other four faces could not (*BrP*.135.1-21).

The lie of Brahmā was a more ethically justifiable reason for his beheading than was the self-glory of the fifth head that, according to yet another version, made it outshine the radiance of all the other gods. For this overweaning brightness of the fifth head, Rudra, according to the *Padma Purāṇa*, cut off the head with the nail of his left thumb (*PP*.5.14.112-13). The *Skānda Purāṇa* amplifies this account. The fifth head of Brahmā, elated with pride, produced such fiery heat (*tejas*) that it destroyed the fire of gods and demons. They sought refuge with Śiva who, on their behalf, went to Brahmā. Brahmā—now overwhelmed by darkness—did not recognize Śiva, who laughed aloud. Brahmā, stupefied by Śiva's laughter and confused by his *tejas*, lost his head to the nail of Śiva's left thumb. Brahmā was so confused by the hot intensity (*tejas*) of Rudra that he did not know that his head had stuck to Rudra's hand. Stuck with the skull, Śiva danced (*SkP*.5.1.2.33-69).

So shattering was the truth of Śiva beheading the Creator that it had to be embellished, and was told on levels easier of access than that of the primordial scene. In one such story the two essential motifs, the desire of the Creator for his daughter and the severing of his head by Śiva, are linked causally. Sarasvatī was furious when Brahmā made amorous insinuations, and she cursed the mouth that had spoken inappropriately. In the future, Brahmā's fifth head would always speak objectionably and bray like a donkey. Then, one day, Śiva and Pārvatī came to see Brahmā. While the four heads of Brahmā welcomed Śiva worshipfully, the fifth mouth made some disagreeable sound. Śiva, annoyed with the evil fifth head, cut it off. It remained stuck to his hand during his wanderings all over the earth, though Śiva could have burned it (*ŚP*,*JS*.49.65-80).

The skull of the fifth, quintessential head of Brahmā, in which his lust and pride had reached their peak, had to fall. Śiva felled the head of Brahmā with the same inevitability that had directed the arrow of Rudra against the Father, Prajāpati. Brahmā's verbal provocation by overstating his paternal status, the rasping sound of his voice, and the telling of a lie at a crucial moment were but expressions of irritation that stemmed from a deep-seated cause.

The head of Brahmā had to fall. It was severed by Śiva, who for this purpose sent forth from himself Bhairava, his own other form (*ŚP*.3.8.60). Bhairava is the total, complete Śiva (*ŚP*.3.8.2). The nail of his left thumb sufficed for nipping off Brahmā's head (*ŚP*.3.8.52; *SkP*.5.1.2.65; *MP*.183.86). Bhairava looked so fierce that even Kāla, who is Time and Death, was afraid of him; hence he is Kālabhairava. Bhairava also was Kālarāja, lord of time and death. Terror emanated from Bhairava (*ŚP*.3.8.46-47). Tormented by fear, those who beheld him saw in him the source of their own fear. In the fulness of their fear they saw the embodiment of fear. Thus, his name describes the effect that he created in the frightened eyes of the beholder, dilated by fear, as those of the god were dilated by devastating fury. The word Bhairava is derived from *bhīru*, which means timid, fearful, in the sense of feeling fear.[7] Bhairava is an appellation by inversion, placing effect into cause. While the name of Rudra, unspeakable in its horror, was not to be pronounced, Bhairava's name did not denote the identity of the god, but intensified his frightfulness by communicating the effect of his frightfulness.

Bhairava in particular is Śiva, as Śarva was Rudra. The fierce hunter had changed his shape and mode of attack. He allowed no distance between himself and his victim. Their contact was close, one sharp touch by the hand of the god was final, neither time nor space intervened.

Śiva become Kapālin. The skull of Brahmā stuck to Bhairava's hand. The sin of brahminicide did not leave him. Like any murderer of a brahmin, Śiva / Bhairava had to expiate this greatest of all sins, though he was God. By making himself a sinner he became "the divine archetype of the Kāpālika ascetic."[8] The Kāpālika "symbolizes the perfected yogin precisely because on a mundane level he is the most debased of ascetics."[9] It was not for the first time that Rudra / Śiva abased himself (Ch. III.2.b).

3. Time, Death, and Timelessness: Kāla and Mahākāla

Time was deeply entrenched in the myth of Śiva. In the primordial scene, as an invisible actor, time had played a decisive and ambiguous role. It placed itself between the intent of Rudra and the actuality of

[7] H. von Stietencron, "Bhairava," 1969, p. 863 and n. 1.

[8] D. N. Lorenzen, *Kāpālikas and Kālāmukhas: Two Lost Śaivite Sects*, 1972, p. 20.

[9] *Ibid*., p. 70.

his shot. The actor was not only invisible but also had no name. We call him Time. Had Rudra's arrow hit its target as soon as the Wild Archer saw the mating couple, no seed would have been spilled, and no substance would have flowed from the Uncreate into creation. By intervening at the moment of Rudra's intent to halt the couple, at the moment when Rudra acted out his role as the guardian of the absolute and avenger of its infringement, Time entered the scene. Time had come into existence with the first movement of Rudra. Even before that, in the spontaneity of his being, Rudra was the carrier of the seed for the Father, in the limbo between the Uncreate and the creation of life. While Time obstructed the intent of Rudra and frustrated the immediate purpose of the attack on the Father by the Wild God, he was only seemingly Rudra's antagonist. His intervention was directed against Rudra, the avenger, and, at the same instant, undertaken *for* Rudra, the bearer of the seed.

Time reenacted the simultaneity of its twofold role on another occasion. Time intervened between Rudra's plunge into the water and his emergence from yogic absorption when under water. While Rudra had tarried, apparently to ready himself for the work of creation / procreation, Dakṣa was at hand and accomplished the task for the Creator with which Rudra had originally been charged. In both scenes, the one at the dawn of creation, the other on the banks of and in the water of Rudra's immersion, Time, the invisible, acted with Rudra, while giving the appearance of defeating Rudra's immediate purpose.

In creation, Rudra, the Wild God, the fierce archer, threatened the life of man. His arrows brought death; they cut off man from life, as a gourd is cut off from its stalk (*RV*.7.59.12), before it can ripen, before its time. The duration of life (*āyus*), the lived dimension of time, was in Rudra's hand. Time, the actor, invisibly present at the beginning of creation, insinuated itself into the life that Rudra had helped to bring about, so that it should ripen in the fullness of time, but Rudra had the power over life and time. He could shorten their span. The Wild God ruled over lived time (*āyus*).

Once, Rudra met Kāla, god Time (Ch. VII.6), and recognized himself in him, looking out from his eyes, although Time had only four faces and lacked the fifth face of Śiva that is beyond time. But for this difference, god Kāla and Śiva could be mistaken for one another. The fifth face of Śiva, the Lord, Īśāna, is beyond time. Thus, Śiva is Time,

Kāla, and he is beyond Time, Mahākāla. Inasmuch as he is Time, he has coalesced with time, his original antagonist, who from the beginning was within his ambience.

Time had invisibly entered the myth of Rudra at the beginning and presented his credentials to the archer. They were the present, past, and future set by him along his arrow, the arrow of unilineal time. In creation Rudra directed his own arrow toward living creatures. If not averted, it would cut short the duration of the life of animate beings. Their lifetime would be shortened; Kāla, Time, would stop their last breath and the beating of their heart.

God Kāla is Time, the Ender (*antaka*). He is Death to the living being and it is he who also ends the cosmos. He is the Destroyer of existence; he is the inalienable counterpart of life. He is Rudra, the Great God whose form as Kāla carries the fact of death. The misery of dying was entrusted to the dark and beautiful young goddess Death (Ch. VI.2). She had come out from all the pores of Brahmā, the Creator, who was intent on making a holocaust of his unmanageably proliferating, deathless creation. With tears in her eyes, she implored the Creator to let her desist from her appointed task. But this he would not grant to her. For all her tears and most severe austerities over millions of years, the young goddess had to acquiesce. She accepted the immutable fact of death. She accepted herself when cyclical time had come to be at the intervention of Śiva as Sthāṇu (*MBh*.12.248-50).

Kāla, the Ender, is a form of Śarva, the archer. From without he approaches the beings and terminates their vital energies (*prāṇa*). But, inasmuch as Rudra is himself the vital breath (*prāṇa*), even as he had been the carrier of the vital seed, it is he who from within, as much as from without, constitutes the life span, the lived time of mortals. Within the living organism time moves rhythmically. Breathing, pulsating, alternating like day and night, the vital breath is the microcosmic homology to cosmic time. The dance of Śiva begins within the inner rhythm of living beings and thence embraces the cosmos. Its stage is set in many places, in the heart of man, in the heights where Śiva is at home in Himālayan groves, in temples, or wherever a site is favorable, and also at the end of the world, before it is swallowed in the abyss of the cosmic flood.

Unilineal time, the time of the arrow and the archer, and the vibrant, palpitating rhythm within living beings are both Rudra's time, as the *Vedas* know it and the *Brāhmaṇas*. Rudra, however, the Wild Archer, is also the lord of yogis and he is Sthāṇu, who discharged from his being the tumultuous Rudras (Ch. VI.1). In the silence of his mind and body, time stood still. But when Brahmā, the Creator, was at a loss in his work of creating living beings, for their life went on and on because there was no stop to it (death as yet had not been created and the lifetime of his creatures stretched endlessly), Sthāṇu, compassionate and merciful, appeared on the scene of Brahmā's intended holocaust. He summoned triple time—past, present, and future—and requested Brahmā to instill into its flux the quiescence of his own being. Thus, periods of ongoing activity would alternate with periods of withdrawal, the business of living would subside and out of its pause life would begin again. In aeviternal rhythms the current of time would be channeled in the cosmos, reflecting not only the pulsation of life within the microcosm, but with it also the possibility of realization, in *samādhi*, of timelessness. Projected outward into the flux of time, *prāṇa* (the inner movement of life within the living being), and the state of withdrawal (holding the promise of at-one-ment within its stilled mind and body), these two (the vital breath and yogic stasis) would coalesce in a new order of time, carrying the assurance of an aeviternal return.

Straight, arrow-like time and the time of aeviternal return are Śiva's modalities of time within creation. By Sthāṇu's intervention Brahmā gave effect to the latter.

Before the arrival of Sthāṇu on the scene of the holocaust, Brahmā had lost his hold on time, for which, as Prajāpati, he had been the paradigm. The myth and rites of Prajāpati in his relation to time were recorded in the *Śatapatha Brāhmaṇa*. The human being as the sacrificer was implicated in the renewal of time by building up the fire altar, the terrestrial homology of the cycle of the year and of Prajāpati. By his participation in the piling up of the fire altar, by rites of architecture, the sacrificer recreated the body of Prajāpati, who had fallen down in sheer exhaustion after having spent himself into creation. By architectural rites, man participated in the reconstruction of Prajāpati and, at the same time, effected his own regeneration.

Prajāpati created all living creatures, whereas Brahmā, injected with Rudra's asceticism, produced only mental progeny. "Having created all existing things, he [Prajāpati] felt like one emptied out, and was afraid of death" (*ŚB*.10.4.2.2; 3.9.1.1; *TB*.1.2.6.1).[10] Creating, Prajāpati had dispersed himself into the manifold universe. The breath of life left him, and the gods abandoned him; he asked Agni, the Fire, to restore him (*ŚB*.6.1.2.12-13). Hence the gods built up Prajāpati and gave him the shape of the fire altar (*ŚB*.6.1.2.14-18). Brick by brick they built him up in the fullness of a year, the time in which nature renews and spends itself. The building of the altar was a paradigmatic rite in which Prajāpati was recomposed symbolically by the piling up of a structure. As the gods had done first, so man, the sacrificer, was to build up the fire altar as the counterpart of Prajāpati (cf. *ŚB*.11.1.8.3). By doing this sacred work, the sacrificer consecrated himself magically, for he meted out the proportions of the altar according to his own measure.[11] The fire altar thus became a work of identification, a homology by sacred, architectural rites, of man and the Creator. Reassembling the fallen, exhausted, dispersed Prajāpati by sacred knowledge and sacred work, the sacrificer restored the Creator to pristine totality, to last as long as time lasts in its cycles, of which the year is the unit. Prajāpati, who was weakened, is the year (*ŚB*.6.1.2.18, 19) and "the Year . . . is the same as Death, for he [Prajāpati, the year] . . . , by means of day and night, destroys the life of mortal beings" (*ŚB*.10.4.3.1).[12] Day and night are taken here not in their cyclical renewal but in their succession along the arrow of time.

Prajāpati, the Lord of Generation, is the year. Exhausted from creation, he was afraid of death, which he carried in himself in the succession of days and nights. Time and death were immanent in the work of the Creator, and in him inasmuch as he identified himself with his creation. Prajāpati was afraid of death, which he carried within him and into creation, for without death the year would have no form; not dying, it would have no end, no time to die in. Time pervaded the work of the Creator and himself at work. It held sway over him.

The visual figure of Prajāpati, the year, was a volumetric shape, an altar built of bricks and replete with the symbolic significance of each single brick. The year with its seasons and, with it, death, as the *Brāhmaṇa of a Hundred Paths* explicitly states, was built into its structure. It

[10] *Śatapatha Brāhmaṇa (ŚB)*, tr. J. Eggeling, 1963, part IV, p. 350.

[11] *Ibid.*, Introduction, pp. xv-xvii; S. Kramrisch, *The Hindu Temple*, pp. 68-70.

[12] *Śatapatha Brāhmaṇa (ŚB)*, tr. J. Eggeling, 1963, part IV, p. 356.

was not the movement of time but the sections of the year, the unit of recurrent time, that were symbolically laid out, their sequence in time conveyed by the spatial order according to which the brick symbols were laid down. The "time" of Prajāpati, or Prajāpati as Time, allowed itself to be laid out spatially in a work of architecture. The time of Śiva flowed into the movement of the limbs of Śiva, the lord of the dance. Works of sculpture and architecture demonstrate each in its own form the time of which they are the symbols. The building of the Vedic altar, by the accompanying words of the sacred rite of architecture, is self-explanatory. Symbolically, time, the time of the seasons, was built into the altar. The form of the altar comprised time, conceived as it were in terms of space.

Prajāpati, who sacrifices himself into creation and is ritually restored by sacrificial man, the builder of the altar, is a self-contained symbol of the renewal of life. The building of the altar is the means by which man, like the Creator himself, is restored to wholeness (cf. *ŚB*.11.1.8.4-6). Prajāpati's collapse is made good by his restoration. The symbol of his restoration, the altar, is piled, brick by brick; their layers make up its shape as the seasons make up the body of the year.

The other myth of Prajāpati was not enacted ritually by man on earth; it was seen in the sky by the gods. Prajāpati, the antelope, became the victim of Rudra. Pierced by his arrow, the wounded antelope fled to the sky and became a star. Some say that the star is the head of the antelope (Mṛgaśīrṣa) (*ŚB*.2.1.2.8), and that Prajāpati, pierced by Rudra's arrow or by the gods, abandoned his body, "for the body is a mere relic (or dwelling, vāstu)" (*ŚB*.2.1.2.9).[13] Even so, it was Prajāpati's body, the body of the sacrifice. It is also said that Prajāpati assumed the form of the sacrifice and that he gave himself up to be sacrificed (*ŚB*.11.1.8.2-3). Prajāpati the antelope, the sacrificed animal, and Prajāpati the year, the sacrificial altar, are here equivalent. The myths of Rudra "sacrificing" Prajāpati and of Prajāpati's self-sacrifice were drawn together.

The year, Prajāpati, was renewed each spring, at the vernal equinox, when a star was seen to rise before the sun. The star "supported" or heralded the rising sun and vanished when the sun had risen. With this spectacle in the sky began a new sacrificial year, a new cycle of life. The priest, watching the sky, uttered the *vaṣaṭ* call over the auspicious

[13] *Ibid.*, part I, p. 285.

star and began to perform the rites of the new year sacrifice when the star was no longer visible, and until the sun had come to the spot where the star was last seen.[14] For generations, the star that heralded the rising of the sun at the spring equinox was Orion; the beginning of the year was announced by the same star. Then over generations, the priest watching the sky observed that it was no longer Orion that rose before the sunrise of the spring equinox. The sun had moved away and rose in another star, Aldebaran. The beginning of the sacrificial year had moved from Orion to Aldebaran; Prajāpati had moved toward Rohiṇī. The precession of the equinoxes, watched over more than a millennium (from ca. 4500 to ca. 3400 B.C.),[15] was telescoped mythically in the image of Prajāpati moving toward Rohiṇī. Rudra (Sirius), seeing that Prajāpati had moved to Rohiṇī, aimed at him.

Astronomical time, that is, the movement of the stars, illuminates the mythical movement of Rudra's appearance on the primordial scene. Mythically, Rudra appeared on the scene of the primordial morning out of nowhere and no time, right out of the Uncreate. His arrow, however, sped along time that carried it from intent to target. Having entered the scene, Rudra brought with him time. Its length was that of the flight of his arrow.

Prajāpati as the embodiment of the annual cycle of vegetative life played his part in the dawn of that first morning. Astronomically, it began a new era, that of Rohiṇī. Mythically, however, that morning signified the beginning of time as such and the dawn of creation. Ritually, Prajāpati was built up as the altar. Its layers were the seasons. Sections of time were homologized with spatial extent. Noetically, the conception of time preceded its symbols. In the language of myth, Time would be the father of Prajāpati.

Thus, the *Atharva Veda* speaks of Time as the father of Prajāpati (*AV*.19.53.8). Father Time is in the highest heaven (*AV*.19.53.3), beyond the cosmos, beyond Prajāpati. He has engendered the past and the future (*AV*.19.53.5). His is the eternal present, a time beyond time, duration without beginning or end: timeless transcendency in the Uncreate. Time is the source of immortality and all beings (*AV*.19.53.2). Time transcended Prajāpati and became his son, living with his creatures as their past and future (cf. *AV*.19.53.4). In the

[14] B. G. Tilak, *The Orion*, pp. 26, 33, 125.

[15] See Ch. II n. 26.

Atharva Veda account, transcendent Time spontaneously flowed into creation. Neither violence nor sin accompanied its descent. The beatific epiphany of transcendental time in the temporality of the created world included Prajāpati.

Although Śiva played no part in the hymns of Time of the *Atharva Veda* (*AV*.19.53, 54), the *Śvetāśvatara Upaniṣad* knows Śiva as beyond time. "Higher and other than time . . . is he from whom the world revolves" (*ŚUp*.6.6). "He is the beginning, the impulse of the causes . . . beyond time, and without separate parts" (*ŚUp*.6.5). "Into him . . . in the beginning and at the end the universe is gathered" (*ŚUp*.4.1). "He is the maker of time" (*kālakāra*) (*ŚUp*.6.2, 16).

Time in manifestation, when the first sun was rising over a world of temporality, was Rudra's invisible, cooperating antagonist. Their interaction was set in motion from a source in the beyond. The *Atharva Veda* calls this originator Kāla in the highest heaven. The *Śvetāśvatara Upaniṣad* calls him Śiva.

Śiva is Time beyond time, Time undivided in its plenitude, as it was before and is beyond creation. Transcendental Time, as the fullness of eternity, pervades the Uncreate. Time in the Uncreate is the hidden source of the causes that unite the Uncreate with creation. At this junction, Rudra discharged his arrow. The motionless time of eternity, which permeates the Uncreate, set forth into creation as temporality. The Wild God together with his cooperating antagonist were its figures. The cause itself that set them forth bears their own names. It is called Kāla in the highest heaven or Śiva as Kālakāra, "the maker of time." The theophany of Śiva as Time has taken into itself Kāla in the highest heaven. From him the world revolves, in him is the origin of the revolving time world; he spins the universe, and draws its rotating axis back into timelessness.

Śiva, however, as transcendental Time as such, is called Mahākāla (*MBh*.12, app. 1, no. 28, line 249), time in its vastness; whereas within creation he is all movement in time, for this is how Time manifests. Śiva is the cosmic dancer, Rudra the hunter, whose arrow flies in time. As Rudra let the arrow fly and the sun was already rising over the primal scene, paradoxically undisturbed motionless Time took what is his—namely, time—put it between the intent of the maker of time and his target—and the seed of the Father flowed down on the earth.

The irruption of transcendental Time into creation, its transmutation into the temporality of this world, made itself felt as a searing, invisible combustion that consumed continuously the universe. Kāla, Time, came down in an uninterrupted current, imperceptibly assailing all beings, unnoticeably from instant to instant changing each creature, drawing it into obscurity, touching every part of man and the universe (*MBh*.12.217.18-59). The descent of transcendent Time into the world of temporality was an invisible, continuous combustion of existence, darkly insidious and silent. "In the conversation of people time moves along in imperceptible form" (*ŚP*.5.26.10).

Mythically, Time, the cooperating antagonist of Śiva, coalesced with Śiva. Cosmogonically, transcendent Time descended into the world, extending while consuming its substance from within, in an imperceptible process. From this ailing world as his background in manifestation, Śiva withdrew and became Sthāṇu, the post, in whom time stood still.

It was Sthāṇu who made Brahmā desist from the holocaust Brahmā had intended. At that time the Great Yogi, acknowledging the inexorable movement of time, which he transcends (*ŚUp*.6.5), and of which he himself is the cause (*ŚUp*.6.2), in the stillness of his stance appealed to Brahmā. Śiva as Sthāṇu, the pillar, the Great Yogi, had in himself that timeless state that he has as Kāla in the highest heaven. Brahmā inserted into the inexorable onrush of time the quiescence that was in Sthāṇu. Thenceforward time flowed rhythmically through the activity of life to the quietude of its cessation and on to a new life. The aeviternal return is a form of Śiva's yogic stasis projected into the ceaseless movement of time, a paradoxical entry of transcendental Time or timelessness in which the Great Yogi dwells, into the relentless passage of time. Cyclical time of alternating activity and withdrawal is a modality, created by Brahmā, of Śiva's, Sthāṇu's, being. This form of the "eternal return," brought about by Brahmā cooperating with Śiva, is related to Prajāpati, the year's recurrent time. Its cycle revolves in the life of nature; the other, the time of the "eternal return," flows through the hearts of the believer.

At another cosmic moment, at the churning of the ocean, Śiva took into himself the world poison that is time. He swallowed the poison that had risen from the ocean, or which Vāsuki, the king of serpents of the netherworld, had thrown up. Its flames and fumes would have asphyxiated gods and demons alike. Or it was not Vāsuki but Ananta, the Endless, the cosmic serpent, from whose mouth Kālakūṭa, the poison called time, had issued (cf. *KūP*.1.42.26-28).

Sthāṇu inserted his timeless being into time, giving it the rhythm of all who were to breathe in life and cease in death and start again in an ever-renewed systole and diastole. The aeviternal return is a form of time due to Śiva's compassion for living beings.

All the same, time proceeds relentlessly, composed of minute parts that are less than an instant (*kṣaṇa*), composed of days, months, and years; every fraction of Kāla is a form of Śiva (*MBh*.13.17.138; *ŚP*.7.1.7.6). Kāla is forever at work, changing at every moment the living bodies that he consumes. The inexorable power of Kāla cannot be fought because Kāla creates the beings and destroys them; everything is in Kāla's power, but Kāla is in no one else's power. He controls all this. Hence Kāla has been described as *prāṇa*, the vital breath (*KūP*.2.3.16-17). Imperceptibly, Kāla's identity slides over that of Rudra, the life breath in all beings, and Lord Śiva recognizes himself behind Kāla's mask (Ch. VII.6).

Śiva is "the maker of time" (*ŚUp*.6.2, 16). By *acting* as he did from the beginning, he created time, his cooperating antagonist. They appeared simultaneously on the scene of the world. Rudra the Fire, Agni, is also Kālāgni (Kāla-Agni), the Fire that destroys the world, the fire that is time. Time pervades the manifest universe, the world of *māyā*. In the song of the Lord, the *Īśvara Gītā*, Rudra says of himself that being the master of and one with *māyā*, he becomes united with Kāla, creates the universe, and also destroys it (*KūP*.2.3.22-23). Kāla, impelled by Rudra, creates the universe and gives it momentum. Rudra gives the impetus to Kāla just as he prepared the seed for the Father. Rudra is the prime mover, Kāla is the dark, world-destroying form of Lord Śiva, Śambhu, who is benevolent (*KūP*.1.42.29).

Rudra destroys the world by assuming the form of Kāla (*KūP*.1.42.28-29). Being but a form, an aspect issued from the Lord, Kāla is said to be born of Śaṅkara, the bringer of peace (*KūP*.1.42.29), as much as Kālāgni, the destroyer, who reduces everything to ashes, becomes Maheśvara, the Great Lord (*KūP*.2.44.2-3).

Kāla, whether as Rudra or born of Rudra (*MBh*.13.16.51), and breathing with him in all beings, retains his own aeviternal identity. He is Time, the Destroyer, Death, in every breath in creation. The gods were afraid of him. "All the gods, frightened by Kāla, saw the Great Lord who is Hara, the ravisher, and, calmed by him, became peaceful" (*KūP*.1.24.40). In their fear, the gods were drawn to Hara / Śiva, as fearful an aspect of the Great God as is Kāla. Hara took away their fear and restored peace to them. Kāla, Time, is but a nuance of Hara, the Destroyer. Kāla knows no peace. Kāla is perpetual movement, has and gives no rest, races along from beginning to end, without respite, merciless, offering no refuge. Śiva Kālāgni, the consuming fire of time, Śiva Śaṅkara, the bringer of peace "into whom at the beginning and at the end all the universe is gathered" (*ŚUp*.4.1), is the origin of the world and its destroyer (*MBh*.13.145.38-39; 13.14.182-85), so that it can arise anew.

The Time by which the worlds come to an end is different from the time that measures life (cf. *SSi*.1.10). Time that measures life is lived time; its desired duration for the human being is a hundred years. Rudra has the power to cut short its span. Inasmuch as Kāla is Rudra, Rudra is Death, or a form of death (*MBh*. 13.14.184). He consumes life by burning it up as Agni (*MBh*.13.14.184); he is Death (*Mṛtyu*) and the god of death (Yama); he is Kāla (Time) (*MBh*.13.16.51). Time is the universal destroyer (*MBh*.13.17.31-32). He burns the universe that he has created (*MBh*.13.14.129, 161). His form is time (*MBh*.13.17.104). He is past, present, and future (*ŚP*.7.1.7.4), and he is aeviternal time, form of the ceaseless succession of birth and death. Everything arises from Kāla and perishes through Kāla (*ŚP*.7.1.7.1). Kāla is relentless, unilineal time, Death, the Ender, unassuaged by the palliative of the aeviternal return into which Rudra let flow his yogic absorption, unamenable to elixirs (*ŚP*.7.1.7.14). Time is the universal fatality. "The whole universe caught in its mouth whirls like a wheel through the activities of creation and annihilation" (*ŚP*.7.1.7.2).[16] While Śiva recognizes himself as Time, opening that dangerous mouth; he recognizes himself in his own image spread over the firmament as Kālarūpin, the shape of time, the Zodiac (*VmP*.5.28-30; cf. *MBh*.13.17.104). Within Śiva's being, Śiva Kālarūpin is the antithesis of Śiva, the Lord of Yoga. As the Supreme Yogi, Śiva is the imaged symbol not of time but of eternity, the unfathomable dimension of the Uncreate realized, paradoxically, within embodied beings who are yogis (*ŚP*.5.26.12). Kāla, the inherent calamity of existence, is a form of Śiva, is under the control of Śiva, but Śiva is not subject to its control (*ŚP*.7.1.7.9-10).

Rudra *in* manifestation coalesced with his antagonist at the beginning of creation, and Rudra as Kālāgni-Rudra, the Fire that is Time, absorbs the world into his own self at the time of destruction (*AUp*.55

[16] *Śiva Purāṇa (ŚP)*, tr. "A Board of Scholars" and ed. J. L. Shastri, 1963, p. 1799.

and commentary). Thus, when the creation is to be dissolved, Rudra assumes the forms of Kāla, the all-consuming fire (*MBh*.13.14.184-85), and burns down the universe (*AP*.368.7-11). He burns it down and dances wildly (*SP*.33.28-29). The consuming fire of time is the Destroyer. Kāla devours existence in the dark abyss of his wide jaws.

The power of burning, devouring Kāla cooperates with *tamas*, "darkness," the tendency of disintegration. They are at one within Rudra, who draws the world into nonexistence. *Tamas*, a quality inherent in creation, has no mythical figure, as Kāla does. *Tamas*, the tendency of disintegration, like Kāla, all-consuming time, is active from the beginning. "Whatever destroys any existing thing, moveable or stationary"[17] is the Destroyer, Rudra (*VP*.1.22.39). Rudra to whom *tamas* belongs enters the night of destruction into which creation has been drawn. There, Kāla, of dark complexion (*LP*.1.95.41), as Kālāgni Rudra absorbs the world into himself (*AUp*.55 and commentary). Rudra remains even after all is gone at the end of the kalpa (*MBh*.13.14.185), even as he existed before creation and before time (*AUp*.2 and commentary). Then, however, there was no darkness and "when there is no darkness, then there is no day or night, nor being, nor nonbeing," only Śiva alone. "That is the Imperishable," "the adorable light of the Impeller, and the ancient wisdom proceeded from that" (*ŚUp*.4.18).[18]

Śiva's ambience comprises and exceeds the world of time. The Great Yogi, the destroyer of all fetters, is also the destroyer of time. Kāla's realm is the world, the entire manifestation. While he races through it unchecked, he leaves behind him the motionless bodies across which he has sped. Kāla means death to the body, to individual existence. Śiva, the Great God in transcendency, made and impelled Kāla, made him, in manifestation, share his entire domain, to unfold his innumerable illusions, while he from whom this world revolves is beyond and other than time (cf. *ŚUp*.6.6). Timelessness is an attribute that "undefines" the Uncreate. Rudra, the guardian of the Uncreate and avenger of its violation, in his form of Sthāṇu is the yogi in whom the Uncreate is restored in its integrity. *Mokṣa*, release from the fetters of contingency, is the recreated Uncreate, recreated by yoga, of which Rudra is the lord. The discipline of yoga is a mode of the creative

[17] *Viṣṇu Purāṇa (VP)*, tr. H. H. Wilson, 1961, p. 127.

[18] *Śvetāśvatara Upaniṣad (ŚUp)*, tr. R. E. Hume, 1951, p. 403.

power. "Yoga is called *māyā* (creative power) by the wise, and Mahādeva, the Great God, is called yogi and Lord of Yoga" (*KūP*.2.4.30).

Yoga is a fervent discipline or asceticism by which the human practitioner releases the power to dissolve his bondage to the world (cf. *ŚP*.5.26.12). By the same yoga, Mahādeva, the Great Lord of Yoga, creates this world in all its contingency and relativity in which ultimate reality is shrouded by his *māyā*. In his ultimate reality, Śiva does not unfold the veil of *māyā*. Being beyond action, he does not reveal the creative power by which he sets the world in motion. Setting it into motion, he is Kāla, whom he impels (*KūP*.2.4.28-29) aeviternally. This impulsion out of eternity, an act of supreme bliss, is Śiva's, the yogi's, eternal dance (*KūP*.2.4.33).

Impelled by the supreme joy of creative power, god Kāla is given his mandate, and by his own sport, aeon after aeon, he consumes the whole universe; and having consumed it, Kāla becomes Mahākāla (*SkP*.4.1.7.91). Kāla, the dark mode of Śiva, moves as an antiphony of Śiva's dance; the fire of creation becomes recognizable in the fire of destruction as it flares up again and again, until its extinction, when Kāla, Time, consumes itself and becomes Mahākāla, absolute Time or timelessness.

Kāla is the dark mode of Śiva. Kāla means "time," "death," and "black." It is equivalent to *tamas*, the dark tendency of disintegration, of which Śiva is the lord. As Kāla he swallows everything with the quality of darkness (*KūP*.1.10.82). Compacting the images and narrative of myth with Sāṁkhya philosophy, the *Kūrma Purāṇa* evokes the progress of Kālāgni, the Fire of Time, which burns everything to ashes. He burns the whole universe along with gods, demons, and men. Taking on a terrifying appearance and entering the sun's orb, he burns the entire world. After the conflagration of the gods, the Goddess stands alone, the sole witness; with a garland of the skulls of the gods as His ornament, He fills heaven. He has a thousand eyes, a thousand shapes, a thousand hands, a thousand feet, a thousand rays, huge arms, fangs in his dreadful face, eyes blazing, holding a trident, wearing animal skin, abiding in divine yoga, having drunk supreme, abundant, nectarine bliss, the Supreme Lord dances the Tāṇḍava dance. The highly blessed goddess, having drunk the nectar of the dance of her consort, through yoga enters the body of the trident-bearing god (*KūP*.2.44.2-12).

Leaving the ecstasy of the Tāṇḍava dance at his pleasure, the Lord sees the burning universe. Then the earth with all her properties dissolves into water. Fire devours the water; fire is dissolved in wind, wind in space, space in the sense organs; the gods are dissolved in one of the three modes of bondage constituting *ahaṁkāra* (the individuating principle); *ahaṁkāra* is dissolved in *mahat* (cosmic intellect), and *mahat* is dissolved in *brahman*. After dissolving the elements and the principles in this manner, the Great Lord separates *prakṛti* (cosmic substance) from *puruṣa* (spirit). Their dissolution does not come about by itself. It is willed by the Great Lord. *Prakṛti* nonmanifest is the equilibrium of the *guṇas*. *Prakṛti*, the womb of the world, is without consciousness. *Puruṣa*, Consciousness itself, the twenty-fifth principle (*tattva*), stands at the apex, apart, the Only One. The sages call him the witness. Thus, according to sacred tradition, does the perpetual power of the Great Lord Rudra burn everything, from *prakṛti* to atoms (*KūP*.2.44.13-24).

Kālāgni, the Fire of Time, operates within creation and devours it. Timelessness as it was before creation, before the beginning in which inheres the end, has its figure in god Mahākāla, Time as measureless immensity. Mahākāla is the ultimate paradox of time.

While Kāla and Kālāgni are degrees of Rudra in manifestation, at its end and beyond manifestation, Kāla alone has a witness and victim in every living being. Releasing his clutch on life as Kālāgni, in a consuming blaze of self-ignition, his metamorphosis is the metaphysical fulfillment of time as Mahākāla, eternity. The mythical figure of Mahākāla is Bhairava. The hierarchy of Time within Lord Śiva is acted out in the myth of Bhairava. The myth shows the overcoming of temporality that has its image in Kāla, the god who is Time and Death, gorging himself on the bodies of the living. As such, Kāla is committed to an act of continuous destruction, aeon after aeon. Then the Lord Kālāgni Rudra, the highest lord, the seed of the universe, the fire of annihilation "whose form is time and who has no form" (*KūP*.1.28.48), reduces everything to ashes and merges the self in his own Self (*KūP*.2.44.2-3).

4. Śiva's Dance for Ṛṣi Maṅkaṇaka

Śiva showed himself to each of his devotees in a shape that met the need of the worshiper. Once, in Saptasārasvata, a place of pilgrimage, Maṅkaṇaka, a ṛṣi, worshiped Śiva by muttering the five-syllabled *man-*

tra: Namaḥ Śivāya. Ṛṣi Maṅkaṇaka was aglow with fervid asceticism. In the transport of his joy that Rudra had come, he danced. Rudra asked him for what purpose he had danced. Although Maṅkaṇaka saw the Lord Rudra, he did not reply; he danced again and again. When the Lord, the holy one, saw Maṅkaṇaka wrapped up in self-gratifying pleasure and conceit, Rudra, to destroy the vanity of the ṛṣi, tore open his own body. Ashes came out of it, the proof of asceticism. Then Rudra, the destroyer of the moving universe, assumed a form of supreme majesty: he danced, thousand-headed, thousand-eyed, thousand-footed, his face dreadful with fangs, flame garlanded, terrifying (*KūP*.2.34.44-53). Then the Lord God resumed his former shape, embraced his devotee, and as a boon revealed himself to Maṅkaṇaka as Kāla and the maker of Kāla, the actuator who impels all (*KūP*.2.34.56-63).

The excitable Ṛṣi Maṅkaṇaka was one in name and legend with a seer who marked by his hermitage and history a particular *tīrtha* in Kurukṣetra (*MBh*.3.81.1, 97). The holy land of Kurukṣetra, to the south of the river Sarasvatī, abounded in lakes and sacred places of pilgrimage (*tīrtha*) (*MBh*.3.81.175-78). At the Gate of Kurukṣetra is the *tīrtha* of a famous *yakṣinī* (*MBh*.3.81.19-20); three other *yakṣas* guard the other gates: Macakruka, Tarantuka, and Arantuka (*MBh*.3.81.7, 13, 42; cf.178). Together, these four marked a sacred square. The sacred geography of India was laid out in squares, guarded at the four points by *yakṣas*, potent presences who sustained the wealth in the soil and the nourishment in the plants. The *yakṣas* had female counterparts, the *yakṣiṇīs*. Their weighty, colossal images, carved in stone, abounded in northern and mid-India. They were more ancient than the *Mahābhārata* and some are still in existence, though the *yakṣas* ceded their worship to other gods who superseded them.[19] One *tīrtha* belonging to the Great Goddess is known as Śākambharī; here the Goddess subsisted for a thousand celestial years on plants alone.[20] She attracted many ṛṣis, rich in asceticism. Because she entertained them with plants (*śāka*), she became known by the name Śākambharī (*MBh*.3.82.11-13). Did Ṛṣi Maṅkaṇaka, a *siddha* or sage possessed of magic powers, subsist on plants and feel their juice pulsate through his body, strengthening and elating him (*MBh*.

[19] Cf. V. S. Agrawala, *Matsya Purāṇa—A Study*, 1963, pp. 280-81.

[20] For Śākaṃbharī as an aspect of Devī, see J. N. Banerjea, *Development of Hindu Iconography*, p. 400.

3.81.97-98)? Did he, like Trita fallen into a well (*RV*.1.105.17; 10.8.7), on seeing a creeper hanging down into it, will mentally the juice of the plant to be the juice of Soma, the elixir of immortality (*MBh*.9.35.25-33)?

The *Mahābhārata* gives a different account of the meeting of Śiva and Ṛṣi Maṅkaṇaka. Once, when Maṅkaṇaka accidentally cut his finger with a blade of kuśa grass and plant juice flowed from his wound, his joy was boundless and he danced. Overwhelmed by the powerful skill of his dance, all the creatures and plants began to dance. The gods, however, went to Mahādeva requesting him to stop the dancing ṛṣi. It was then that the Great God appeared before the ṛṣi and asked the reason for the overwhelming joy that made him dance (*MBh*.3.81.97-103). The ṛṣi gave the miracle of the plant juice flowing from his wound as the reason for his joy and dancing. Śiva struck his thumb with one of his fingers and ashes as white as snow flowed from his wound. The ṛṣi fell at the feet of Lord Śiva and worshiped him as the creator and ordainer of the universe and to whom all return at the end of the yuga (*MBh*.3.81.104-109). In the legend, twice told in the *Mahābhārata* (cf. *MBh*.9.37.34-48), Śiva showed Maṅkaṇaka the snow-white heap of ashes that flowed from his body. Śiva, in these early versions of the legend, did not dance. He did not display his dance of Time and Death against Maṅkaṇaka's self-absorbed joyous transport. Śiva revealed himself in the stillness of ashes falling from the wound of his body, from a higher incandescence than that of vital exuberance or emotional transport.

The *siddha* / *ṛṣi* Maṅkaṇaka had absorbed into himself the nourishing juices of the plants of this earth or the Soma juice itself, and the juices retained their purity within the body of the *siddha*. When Maṅkaṇaka saw the plant juice flowing from his body, he felt freed from the bondage of blood. The flow of ashes, however, from the body of the Great God showed a higher degree of rarefication than the ṛṣi had achieved by the transformation of his blood into plant juice. Śiva had absorbed the world into his own self at the time of dissolution (*AUp*.55 and commentary). He showed himself as Kāla and the actuator of Kāla, the fire that burns to ashes the world and all its sins (cf. *KūP*.2.34.62). "What is Agni is ashes; what is air, is ashes; . . . what is all this (phenomenal world) is ashes; what are the mind and such as these, the eyes, are ashes alone; the *Avyakta* from which all these originate, is also ashes,"[21] runs the *Pāśupata Vrata*, the *mantra* of the lord of creatures (*AUp*.67). The elements or sense objects, the senses, mind, and its fabric are burned up, one in the other, in the ultimate conflagration that has its symbol in ashes and its Kālāgni-Rudra image in the dance of Śiva when Maṅkaṇaka trembled and bowed his head before the Lord (cf. *KūP*.2.34.55). He enlightened the sage, allowing him to see beyond the elation of the senses and the mind, when Śiva, the Fire, will dance the cosmos out of existence and nothing will remain but Śiva alone (cf. *SP*.33.28-39).

5. The Breakthrough from Time to Eternity

When the gods first observed with amazement that the equinoctial sun had moved from one star to another and that along with it the beginning of the year had moved from Orion, they had witnessed on the ecliptic the precession of the equinoxes, the greatest movement of time in the cosmos. Rudra, the Wild Hunter, aimed at Prajāpati, the year. Did he mean to arrest or undo the movement of time, as he had meant to prevent the flow of life out of the Uncreate? Prajāpati's mythical image was the antelope, whereas, ritually, the year was his form. Projected to the stars, the two modes of reference coalesced. The constellation Orion was beheld as the figure of Prajāpati, the antelope. As such, Prajāpati had his position fixed in the sky, whereas Prajāpati, the year, had his visual symbol on earth, in the architecture of the Vedic altar. It was, however, so it would seem, the movement of the vernal equinoctial point, which marked the beginning of the year, that is, Prajāpati, from Orion toward Aldebaran (Rohiṇī) that gave its meaning to the star myth.

Rudra was its protagonist, Time his unnamed, cooperating antagonist. Time began in consonant ambiguity with Rudra. The ambiguity of Kāla was to become the certainty of Death. Rudra as Śarva, the fierce archer, saw to it and Rudra as Mṛtyuñjaya freed from it. The world of Rudra, the Wild God, had this coherence. He established its pattern in the dawn of the world, when he became Paśupati, the Lord of Animals.

Rudra is Agni the Fire. Fire is a hunter. Time is a fire that burns its way through life; Kālāgni, the fire that is time, burns up life, ends it.

[21] *Atharvaśira Upaniṣad (AUp)*, tr. T.R.S. Ayyangar and ed. G. S. Murti, 1953, p. 49.

Kāla, Time, is Death. In its cosmic dimension he is Kālāgni, the doomsday fire consuming the entire creation.

Acting as the Wild Hunter, Rudra set time in motion and time took its course. It seemingly ran counter to Rudra's immediate intent, though it provided the dimension in which to manifest his actions. Rudra and Kāla were a syzygy whose momentum Rudra provided. As Kālāgni, at the end of the yugas, the fire that is Death consumes everything, including time. "Praise be to Kāla of dark complexion; praise to the destroyer of Kāla" (*LP*.1.95.41). Śiva, in ultimate fulfillment of his nature, the Fire engulfing the darkness (*tamas*) of time, ends time itself. Śiva, the prime mover, as Kālakāla (*SP*.23.24), Time beyond time, full of the highest bliss, dances at the end of the world (*SP*.23.42). Encircled by flames he dances the world out of existence. All its forms dissolve in the vehemence of his dance, and their essence is reabsorbed in the universal consciousness, in Śiva. During *pralaya*, the state of dissolution, manifestation lies dormant until its slumbering potentialities shine forth in the dawn of a new creation. There, they germinate out of eternity into time.

Time, the antagonist and alter ego of Śiva, has the manifest world as his field of action. In the shape of *āyus*, the length of life or lived, experienced time, he stood as "fulcrum in the nest of the Highest" (*RV*.10.5.6).[22] This image was one of the signs marking the frontier of human understanding and of absolute transcendency. The "nest of the Highest," in which life is hatched, was located, like the bull-cow, the image of Agni, on the razor-sharp yet insubstantial line that forbids entry into ultimate reality. In itself without dimension, it is out of bounds to human understanding, for whose sake the signs were set up on the border.

With his first shot Rudra signaled that creation, the time-world of movement and action, had begun. Paradoxically, his arrow was directed away from the nascent world of beings. Rudra had aimed in the other direction whence the seed was about to leave its source. Thence, he derived his own momentum when, as Śarva, he let his arrows fly into creation. Rudra started his work as a hunter, an archer, and he fulfilled it as a dancer. His first witness and victim had been the Father. At the end he remains himself the only witness of the time-world consumed by his flames.

[22] Cf. A. Bergaigne, *La Religion védique*, 2:107.

As the cosmic dancer, Śiva's work was completed, though not terminated. At the end of each aeon, the Great God dances the cosmos out of existence. Creation / destruction, an aeviternal process, takes place in temporality, the time world of Rudra-Śiva.

It was of his own making and as son of Brahmā, the Creator, that he let himself be born into it. Brahmā wanted his son to complete the work of creation, whereupon Rudra became Sthāṇu, motionless, detached, withdrawn, drawing within himself the life that Prajāpati had meant him to bring into the world. As Sthāṇu, the post, Rudra showed himself the counterpart of the tree of life, unconsumed fuel to his fire, potent in seemingly arid starkness, as were the white ashes that he let flow from his body for Ṛṣi Maṅkaṇaka to see.

Sthāṇu stood by, leaving Brahmā's work unachieved, making himself the sign of a reality that though without definition was capable of being realized. As sign of cessation, Sthāṇu, the post, stood for the arrest of time, a state beyond death. The symbol shape of Śiva Sthāṇu, the branchless stem, stands opposite to the image of dancing Śiva, his many arms, his flowing hair filling the cosmos with the rhythms of his being. Sthāṇu standing by the moving universe is a symbol of the timeless state attainable in *samādhi*. Śiva, the Lord of Yoga, dwells in timeless eternity, while Śiva, the dancer, performs his aeviternal dance at the end of each aeon across which Kāla speeds.

Out of the timelessness of his stasis, Sthāṇu communicated his being to Time. The presence of Sthāṇu, when Brahmā had willed to terminate in a holocaust his flawed creation, made the Creator adjust the straight line of time running from past to future to alternating phases of movement and rest. Sthāṇu, in ascetic withdrawal from the world, motionless and beyond time, represents eternity realized from within. The post is a symbol of the restitution in creation of timelessness that was and is in the Uncreate. The shape of the post points upward. It supports nothing but the empyrean, and signifies its realized presence in the world of time, in the heart of man. Moved by pity, Śiva Sthāṇu made Brahmā impart the pause of quiescence—a reflex of eternity—to the stream of time whence life and action would resurge once more.

Rudra, the Wild God, had set time into motion—past, present, and future, a fiery, consuming current. Sthāṇu, the Great Yogi, through Brahmā's agency communicated the quiescence of timelessness in which he dwelled to the rushing stream of time. Even so, the waves of time rolled on, through periods of activity and withdrawal until a final conflagration and dissolution (*pralaya*).

Pralaya is the cosmic homology of absolute, transcendental Time, "Kāla in the highest heaven" or Mahākāla, before the descent of time into the world. At the end of the time-world, Kālāgni Rudra, the fire that is time and annihilation, becomes Mahākāla. As the last flame of Kālāgni flares up, it expires in Mahākāla. In that instant, Kālāgni becomes and is Bhairava, in a leap from the dissolution of the cosmos into the metaphysical realm. The dissolution of the cosmos takes place in what had been manifestation. Its annihilation is but an image of transcendency, a homology of the Uncreate. In the leap from the annihilation of the cosmos to the metaphysical realm or transcendency, Kālāgni becomes Bhairava. His explicit name is Kālabhairava (cf. *KūP*.2.31.71, 30). Because even Kāla fears him, he is called Kālabhairava (*ŚP*.3.8.47), or Kālarāja, the Lord of Kāla (*ŚP*.3.8.46). Bhairava is a form of Śiva (*ŚP*.3.8.60); more than that, Bhairava is Śiva's integral form. It was Bhairava or Śiva as Bhairava who snipped off Brahmā's overweening head (*KūP*.2.31.30; *SkP*.3.1.24.39; 4.1.31.41, 48).

The mythical identity of Bhairava corresponds with the explicit epistemological definition given to Bhairava in Śaiva thought,[23] from the ninth to the fourteenth century, in Kashmir and in South India. In the words of H. von Stietencron, "Bhairava [in Śaiva philosophy, especially in Kashmiri Śaivism] is a designation for the undifferentiated universal consciousness . . . ,"[24] comprising the entire cosmos as an unqualified and undivided whole. It is a state of supreme plenitude of the absolute and the realization of this plenitude on the level of mental experience. "The state of absolute unity is at the same time the ultimate source of all creation." It is the first of "three fundamental planes" of experience or realization. The third and last plane "is that of resorption, of dissolution of the world in deity." "Employing a cosmic image, this is the instant when the god takes back into himself, i.e. swallows up, the play of the universe that he produced."[25]

Brahmā's assumed fifth head was severed by Bhairava. Libidinous from the start, overbearing and evil-tongued, it had appeared competing with Śiva's fifth head in transcendency, provoking Śiva and its own fate.

[23] H. von Stietencron, "Bhairava," pp. 868-69.
[24] *Ibid.*, p. 869.
[25] *Ibid.*, in reference to Abhinavagupta's *Tantrāloka*, III.268-85.

Bhairava's shape was a syndrome of terror. The gods who put together the most terrible shapes in order to compose an adequate form of Paśupati's frightfulness (Ch. I.2) exhausted their resources in giving plausibility to the appearance of the Wild God on his entry into the first act of the drama of creation. This conglomerate of horror, the guise of Rudra contrived by the gods, became threadbare in the course of more than a thousand years, and allowed the naked terror of the god to assume anthropomorphic features. No image of any other aspect of Śiva comprises as many contrasting iconographic types as that of Bhairava, such as the frenzied, sinewy skeleton figure of Atiriktāṅga Bhairava[26] or the staring, bloated, pot-bellied shape of Bhairava that the *Viṣṇudharmottara Purāṇa* (*VDh.P*.3.59.1-5) describes.[27] Bhairava, having swallowed up and consumed Time, had taken into himself the agonies of all time, the death pang of creatures, the hollow horrors of life. Fed by them, he needed nothing more than the nail of his left thumb to cut off Brahmā's head.

The Father was wounded in his genitals by the Wild God who avenged the loss of integrity of the absolute that the Lord of Generation had caused. Rudra carried out a paradoxical task, for the fullness of the Uncreate is not ever depleted. It flowed into creation that came to recognize Rudra, the Lord, in his many shapes. In his ultimate, integral shape, the Great God reenacted the primordial scene: he assaulted the Creator, and the head of Brahmā fell.

Śiva, son of Brahmā, was born from the head of the Creator, from his breath, from his mind. Brahmā, sarcastically, in order to humble

[26] Powerful images of Atiriktāṅga Bhairava are in the Rāmeśvara Cave (Cave 21) in Ellora, of the sixth century. (See T. A. Gopinatha Rao, *Elements of Hindu Iconography*, vol. 2, part 1, pl. 43); on the Vaital Deul, Bhuvaneśvar, Orissa, see M. E. Adiceam, "Les images de Śiva dans l'Inde du Sud, IV. Kaṇkāla Mūrti," 1965, p. 36, fig. 13.

[27] This type is represented by images of the Pāla and Sena school of eastern India (cf. R. D. Banerjee, *The Eastern Indian School of Medieval Sculpture*, 1933, pl. LV(c). Of special significance are also the iconographic type of Vaṭuka Bhairava, riding on a dog (T. A. Gopinatha Rao, *Elements of Hindu Iconography*, vol. 2, part 1, p. 178) and the South Indian images of Śiva standing in front of a large dog (M. Adiceam, "Les Images de Śiva dans l'Inde du Sud, II. Bhairava," 1965, pp. 23-44, figs. 1-4, 7, 8) in lieu of Nandin, who conveys Śiva. The Śatarudriya renders special homage to the dogs (*TS*.4.5.4), and Vāstoṣpati/Sirius is the dog star. The howling, large-mouthed dogs (AV.11.2.30) belong to Rudra, the hunter and dweller in cremation grounds, as well. A small bronze sculpture of about the fourteenth century from Nepal, P. Pal, *Nepal, Where the Gods Are Young*, 1975, pp. 94, 128, pl. 64 shows a shrine surrounded by a cremation ground. In the center of the shrine a dog is seated, his mouth open. The dog in the center of the shrine is Bhairava.

the Great God, reminded Śiva of his place of origin. Bhairava cut off the fifth mocking head, in its most exposed, most vulnerable position. With one, barely perceptible gesture, Bhairava deleted in that head the consciousness of Rudra's birth into the cosmos. Kālāgni Rudra, the destroyer of creation (*SkP*.7.1.9.1, 5), cut back the arrogant head, together with the memory it had held. Cutting off the head of the Creator, Kāla Bhairava relieved Brahmā of the evil that had been stored in his head.

The head of Brahmā fell and he died (*SkP*.3.1.24.39). The head stuck to the hand of Bhairava. Once more Rudra had acted as a parricide. His guilt was not lessened when Īśvara, the Lord Śiva, brought Brahmā back to life (*SkP*.3.1.24.40). Or Śiva consoled Brahmā: though Śiva had cut one of Brahmā's heads, Brahmā had four heads left that would never perish. Śiva admonished Brahmā not to worry over a predestined incident (*VmP*, *SM*.28.4-5, 19-20).

Time entered the cosmic scene when the Father cohabited with the daughter and Rudra set his arrow flying. Rudra set time into motion, allowing time to unfold. In a fiery stream it would burn itself into all living things, and consume them in the darkness of Kāla, god Time who is Death (*ŚP*.7.1.7.14) to the living, who is Kālāgni, the Fire of doomsday, the conflagration of the cosmos. Everything will be annihilated through Kāla, as everything has originated from Kāla (cf. *ŚP*.7.1.7.1), Rudra's cooperating antagonist whom Rudra himself had set into motion, intent on preserving the integrity of the absolute, while its substance was already beginning to flow into creation.

Everything is Kālāgni's fuel until Rudra's unfettered being breaks through the flames. The breakthrough from time into timelessness is the *mysterium tremendum* of Śiva Bhairava. It is the restitution of timelessness as it was before the beginning, the timelessness of the Uncreate. Bhairava is the integral Rudra at the instant of the breakthrough from time (Kāla) into the timeless immensity (Mahākāla) of the Uncreate.

At this instant, Bhairava, with the nail of his thumb, snipped off the fifth head of the Head of the Universe. The head fell straight into his hand, stuck to his left palm, and would never leave it (*VmP*.2.36-37). Mahādeva made Bhairava, his "other form" and integral self, take upon him the Kāpālika vow that he would go begging all over the world with his skull-bowl, collecting alms until the skull would fall from his hand. Bhairava had to undertake this vow, the *Kāpālika*

Vrata (*ŚP*.3.8.60-62; *VrP*.97.9-10; cf. *KūP*.2.31.64-65; 67-68; *SkP*. 4.1.31.5.1-53; cf. *VmP*.2.38-43), in expiation of his sin for having cut off the fifth head of the Head of the World, the head of the Creator, his father. Worse than a parricide, Bhairava had cut off the head of Brahmā, who was a brahmin, and brahminicide was known from ancient days as the most heinous of all crimes (cf. *ŚB*.13.3.5.3).

The head of Brahmā stuck to Bhairava's palm. When god Indra twisted off the head of demon Namuci, it did not let him go, rolled after him, and accused him (*RV*.5.30.7; 6.20.6; *TB*.1.7.1.6-7). Brahmā's severed head clung fast to Bhairava's palm. Its accusation took the shape of a dreadful fury, called *brahmahatyā*, the sin of brahminicide.

Sthāṇu and Bhairava are symbol and image of Śiva as transcendental reality with reference to creation. Sthāṇu is the symbol standing by creation; Bhairava takes off from the created world. Both are figures of return from the world of time to the Uncreate, the latter with reference to cosmic, the former with reference to microcosmic or yogic realization.

6. The Wanderings of Bhairava as the Supreme Beggar

Mahādeva Kālabhairava roamed over the three worlds with the skull in his hand. He came to the Deodar forest (*KūP*.2.31.73-78). The sages who dwelled in the forest did not recognize the naked mendicant holding out his bowl. They were immersed in practicing austerities and tending the sacrificial fires. They conformed with sanctioned conventions. They had lost the way to release from bondage (*KūP*.2.37.2-4).

They were shocked and provoked by the naked mendicant who had entered their establishment. Bhairava appeared in his form of Bhikṣāṭana, the Supreme Beggar. As Kāpālika / Kapālin, "bearer of the skull bowl," Śiva had been known in the *Mahābhārata* (*MBh*. 13.17.100); there too he was known as Mahākāla (*MBh*. 12, app. 1, no. 28, line 249).

Bhairava-Bhikṣāṭana, young, stark naked, with no distinguishing attribute except his begging bowl and a garland of forest flowers, attracted the women and infuriated the ṛṣis. The Supreme Beggar, looking and behaving unlike anyone they had ever seen, put the ṛṣis to the test. He outraged their sense of propriety and excited their jealousy. They were less concerned about the interruption of their austerities and the loss of power that they had gained by these arduous exertions and that had accrued to them by the faithfulness of their wives.[28]

The subsequent castration of the Lord, along with the fall of the *liṅga* of the Supreme Beggar in the Deodar forest on Mount Himavan and its transfiguration, was as momentous an event as was the fall of Brahmā's head, witnessed by the *Vedas*, on the peak of Mount Meru. Śiva-Bhairava felled the head of Brahmā, the seat of consciousness of the Creator. Bhairava ended the mythical time that had begun when the Father embraced the daughter and Rudra shot his arrow. By cutting off the head of Brahmā, Rudra, who was Kāla, became Mahākāla, the paradox of time in transcendency or the realization of eternity. The empty skull of Brahmā stuck to the hand of Bhairava. As the begging bowl of the Supreme Mendicant it needed to be filled.

The breakthrough of Kāla, or time experienced, into the realization of metaphysical time or timelessness marked the beginning of Bhairava's pilgrimage in the triple world. He was naked, had no other garment than the sky. He held out his empty begging bowl; readily the entranced women in the Deodar forest put in their alms. When he was castrated, his *liṅga* did not fall as easily as had Brahmā's head. But when it did fall, it was transfigured as a fiery pillar without beginning or end, and traversed the cosmos.

In a former aeon, when Rudra emerged from the water, he tore out his *liṅga* in a rage. The *liṅga* was of no use to him, as he was unwilling to procreate mortals, and someone else, Dakṣa, had fulfilled this command of Brahmā. This was not Rudra's, the Wild God's, the Great Yogi's, task. In the Deodar forest, the strangely seductive mendicant yogi let his *liṅga* fall. The sages cursed the organ of lust of the Supreme Beggar, the terrible god Bhairava. Had they not been outraged by his startling, unseeming ways, and had they looked at his begging bowl, they would have seen death staring at them from the skull that it was. Maybe the strange yogi was insane; he howled, danced, and smiled in bliss and terror. He offended all conventions, for he had broken through all limitations. He had overcome death, he was beyond time, but at the same time he was a murderer. He had murdered his father, the Creator, a brahmin. The head of Brahmā

[28] W. D. O'Flaherty, *Asceticism and Eroticism in the Mythology of Śiva*, pp. 178-79.

stuck to him, the skull did not leave his palm; *brahmahatyā*, his sin, followed him. The forest dwellers did not know that the young intruder into their settled ways of life was expiating his crime, was carrying out the Kāpālika vow. As he went through the forest an antelope would raise its head, would rise on its hind legs toward the hand of the Great God. Off and on he would hold out to it some young leaves. This is how Indian sculptors and painters remembered and imaged Bhikṣāṭana, the Supreme Beggar.[29] With tenderness they gave shape to the animal (*mṛga*). At the beginning of things, it was the Father (Prajāpati) who had taken the shape of an antelope.

Rudra let his *liṅga* fall because the sages were hostile to it (*KūP*.2.37.39-40), to the organ of lust in its naked display. Where the forest dwellers had seen seduction at play they had taken part in the mystery of Rudra-Bhairava. Having severed the head of Brahmā, he had risen above himself as Time and Death. It was a breakthrough from his manifestation in the created world into the Uncreate. In the Deodar forest, Rudra let fall, like a ripe fruit, the severed *liṅga* from his body. As the *liṅga* touched the ground, frightening portents announced its transfiguration.

Bhairava and the *liṅga* are each the integral Śiva, the one abiding beyond time in the timelessness of the Uncreate, the other traversing the cosmos. Though the forest dwellers had not recognized the Lord in his naked shape of Bhairava, they took part in the falling of the phallus and witnessed its transfiguration. They worshiped the Lord in the *liṅga*, and found peace. When the *liṅga* fell, Śiva vanished (*VmP*, *SM*.22.67-68; *KūP*.2.37.41).

Kālabhairava, Śaṅkara, the bringer of peace, continued his pilgrimage; the women followed him. They sang and danced in front of the black-faced lord, Kālabhairava. Śaṅkara then came to the abode of Viṣṇu (*KūP*.2.31.77-79).

In the Deodar forest, Kāla Bhairava did not show the blackness of his countenance, though some could see the terrific teeth in the strange beggar's face (*BP*.1.2.27.11). Lord Śiva in the Deodar forest did not look the same to all who saw him, nor were his movements interpreted by them in the same way. He had come to the Deodar forest on his pilgrimage of expiation, true to his Kāpālika vow. He had

[29] Cf. D. Barrett, *Early Cola Bronzes*, pls. 41 and 42; C. Sivaramamurti, *South Indian Painting*, 1968, figs. 78, 79; C. Sivaramamurti, *The Art of India*, 1977, p. 349, fig. 304.

come to impart the knowledge of withdrawal and peace (*nivṛtti*; *KūP*.2.37.5). He showed himself in his nakedness; as he went along, he baffled, enraged, tested, and enlightened the sages when he allowed himself to be maimed. This was part of his pilgrimage, and he continued his progress.

To the forest dwellers who had not recognized the god, he appeared gold-complexioned, most handsome (*KūP*.2.37.6-7), or ugly and deformed (*LP*.1.29.9). They also saw him having come by himself, or they beheld him accompanied by a beautiful woman, who was Viṣṇu in disguise (*KūP*.2.37.9). The sons of the sages desired her (*KūP*.2.37.15), but this, though it brought further confusion, did not change the course of events. The *liṅga* of Śiva fell and Śiva vanished (*KūP*.2.37.39-41). After terrible portents, the sages realized through Anusūyā, Atri's wife, that Śiva had been there, and they sought advice from Brahmā (*KūP*.2.37.42-45). On Brahmā's instruction, the worship of the Śiva *liṅga* became established on earth (*KūP*.2.37.87-88). When the Lord appeared once more in the Deodar forest, accompanied by Pārvatī, the sages recognized and praised him, though he was smeared with ashes, his eyes were reddened, and he held a firebrand (*KūP*.2.37.99-105).

The appearance of Śiva with Pārvatī in the Deodar forest, while it echoed, also climaxed the appearance of Śiva with entrancing Mohinī, Delusion, a form of Viṣṇu. The sages asked Śiva how they should worship him, and the Lord told them to observe the Pāśupata vow (*KūP*.2.37.126-40). Then Śiva and Pārvatī vanished, having assured the sages they would come to them if the sages meditated on them (*KūP*.2.37.149). As the sages meditated, Pārvatī and then Śiva alone were seen by them in glory (*KūP*.2.37.153-57). The sages, having taken the Pāśupata vow (cf. *AUp*.67), realized Śiva as the only and eternal reality. All else was delusion. He had appeared with the firebrand that inflamed in them the fire of knowledge of the ultimate reality (cf. *KūP*.2.37.100). This fire burns everything to ashes. Fire itself and the sense objects—the senses too—and the mind turn into ashes.

This time the sages had seen the Lord smeared with ashes when he entered the Deodar forest. The very appearance of the Lord imbued them with the Pāśupata doctrine. Before that, from his very entry into the Deodar forest, the sages had witnessed the Supreme Beggar carrying out the Kāpālika vow. The worship of the *liṅga* as well as the

Kāpālika and Pāśupata mode of realizing Śiva were established in the archetypal forest of Deodar trees, the vital center of the realization of the fire of god in which everything is burned to ashes, while the magic play (*līlā*) of the Lord retains its validity.

The Deodar forest was twice hallowed by the visit of the Supreme Beggar. By his first coming the worship of the *liṅga* became established. It was in his second visit that the Pāśupata vow was established among the sages. Śiva himself had made it lead to release (*vimukti*) (*KūP*.2.37.140-43).

The introduction of the Goddess, amplifying the effect of Śiva's *māyā* on the forest dwellers, lent more than an operatic grandeur to the Lord's play. The presence of the Goddess added overtones to the passing of Śiva, the Supreme God, the naked beggar, through the Deodar forest. In a final vision granted to the sages (*KūP*.2.37.153-62), the Goddess, Śiva's *śakti* or power, appeared in the sky, in a garland of flames (*KūP*.2.37.154) preceding the manifestation of the lord of *māyā*, Śiva himself, with whom she is one (*KūP*.2.37.161).

The scene in the Deodar forest allowed for ambiguities and perplexities not only in the reactions of the sages, their wives, daughters, and sons but also in the minds of the myth makers. Some understood the visit of the strange mendicant as a rite of passage enacted by Śiva Bhairava. Others saw Lord Śiva entering the forest distraught after the death of Satī (*VmP*.6.58; *SkP*.7.3.39.5-12). They knew that she had consumed herself by means of yoga in flames of grief, because Śiva, the Great God, her husband, had been excluded, on the ground that he was a Kapālin, by Dakṣa, her father, from the sacrifice he was performing (cf. *VmP*.4.1-16). Śiva, the Kapālin, the carrier of the skull bowl, is Śiva Bhairava, the ultimate cause of the death of Satī. The forest of Deodar trees was witness to the maddening grief of Śiva, as it had been the scene of his frenzy when he had cut off the head of Brahmā.

In another myth, Śiva comes to the Deodar forest full of desire. Śiva, not satisfied by making love to Pārvatī, went naked and full of desire to the Deodar forest, there to make love with the wives of the sages (*ŚP*, *DhS*.10.78-80).

At all times, Śiva showed himself to his *bhakta* or devotee in the shape and to the extent in which his worshiper was ready to see him. The Lord's play in the Deodar forest thus attracted to itself situations and modes of Śiva's being that were peripheral to the plot of the play.

Similarly, but with an opposite effect, diverse forms of Śiva would enter, if by their name only, a narrative without any obvious connection of that name to the actuality of the story. When Maṅkaṇaka, for example, bowed down before Śiva, he bowed down before Girīśa, the Lord of the Mountain; Hara, the Ravisher; Tripurasūdana, the Destroyer of the Three Cities of the Asuras (*KūP*.2.34.58). None of these epithets had any direct bearing on the legend of Maṅkaṇaka, yet they evoked the presence of Lord Śiva in the vastness and power that Maṅkaṇaka came to realize. Episodes were condensed into epithets denoting permanent aspects of deity. They referred to actions that happened once as significant events in which the permanent being of deity shone forth. Thus, these incidents became part of, defined, and accentuated the image of the god.

The Deodar forest drew Śiva to itself in the most intense moments of his manifestation, while roaming over the country frenzied with guilt, in the agony of mourning, and, as some say, maddened by sex. Within the sacred geography of India, the Deodar forest on its Himālayan slope was Śiva's place of passage, whereas he never left Vārāṇasī once Brahmā's skull had fallen from his hand.

The play in the Deodar forest, in drawing to itself various events from the myth of Śiva, had but little concern with their sequence. Śiva had entered the Deodar forest as a Kapālin, the bearer of Brahmā's skull, while expiating the sin of brahminicide. As a Kapālin, Śiva Bhairava, following his decapitation of Brahmā, had come to the Deodar forest. There, Śiva became castrated.

In the Dakṣa / Satī myth, however, Śiva entered the Deodar forest after the death of Satī, which she inflicted on herself in consequence of Śiva's exclusion from the sacrifice because he was a Kapālin.

In the context of Pārvatī's estrangement, Śiva entered the Deodar forest after his dissatisfaction with Pārvatī, his wife whom he had married after Satī had died. Whatever were the reasons seen in Śiva's visit to the Deodar forest, and whether the visit was interrupted and renewed (*LP*.1.29.7-24, 36-42; 1.31.20-37; *KūP*.2.37.2-163), it was one and the same visit differently accounted for and variously celebrated. What happened in the Deodar forest happened once and for all. The *liṅga* of the god fell and was transfigured. The different preludes and circumstances of Śiva's advent led to the same climax, and its aftermath was revealed in the mystery play in the Deodar forest.

Śaṅkara, the Bringer of Peace, left the Deodar forest with his begging bowl and, on his wanderings through the three worlds, where he visited the countries of gods and demons, came to the abode of Viṣṇu (*KūP*.2.31.73-79). All the while Brahmahatyā, the ghoulish figure of brahminicide personified, followed Bhairava. Nīla-Lohita, as soon as he had asked Bhairava to observe the vow of expiation, had sent this fury, a figure of his guilt, to accompany Bhairava. She would not leave Bhairava until they came to Vārāṇasī. She was gruesome to look at (*KūP*.2.31.68-70).

Viṣvaksena, the gatekeeper of Viṣṇu's residence and himself born from a portion of Viṣṇu, not knowing the purpose of the visit, nor recognizing the Supreme Lord, Parameśvara, checked Bhairava, who held the *kapāla* and a trident in his hand (*KūP*.2.31.79-82). Bhairava sent forth a terrible attendant, who fought with Viṣvaksena, and the Great God, Mahādeva, pierced Viṣvaksena with his trident. Carrying aloft on his trident the dead body of Viṣṇu's doorkeeper, Śiva entered Viṣṇu's residence and faced the god who maintains the universe (*KūP*.2.31.83-88). On seeing Śiva holding out his bowl, the blessed Lord Viṣṇu asked Śiva, the lord of the universe, why he went a-begging (*ŚP*.3.9.23). Then Viṣṇu opened a vein in his forehead. A stream of blood gushed forth into the skull; for a thousand years it kept on flowing (*KūP*.2.31.89-91). Even so, the skull bowl was not filled completely by Viṣṇu's offering (*KūP*.2.31.91; *MP*.183.90), nor could Viṣṇu persuade Brahmahatyā to leave the trident bearer (KūP. 2.31.94-95). Viṣṇu repeated the advice given by Śiva Nīla-Lohita to Śiva Bhairava: Bhairava should proceed to Vārāṇasī, the holy city, where Brahmā's skull and the sin would fall from Bhairava (*KūP*.2.31.96).

Śiva Bhairava left the house of Viṣṇu; he went away intending to visit all the sites and shrines of deep mystery. Praising the Lord, the Pramathas, the "churn spirits," as always, accompanied the Great Ascetic Śiva Bhairava, as he danced on his way holding the trident with Viṣvaksena's body transfixed on it. Anxious to see the dance of the Lord, Viṣṇu rushed after him. Mahādeva, the Great God, infinite yoga itself, on seeing Viṣṇu, danced again and again. Accompanied by Viṣṇu, Brahmahatyā, and his host of churn spirits, with his splendid bull Dharma as his vehicle, Bhairava approached Vārāṇasī. As the lord of gods entered the holy city, the miserable Brahmahatyā with a shriek went to hell. In Vārāṇasī, Śaṅkara placed the skull in front of his hosts, the gaṇas, and returned Viṣvaksena, his life restored, to Viṣṇu (*KūP*.2.31.96-104).

Bhairava, embodiment of the breakthrough into the Uncreate—Bhairava, the symbol of the shattering of contingency—having left the forest accompanied by the frenzied women (*KūP*.2.31.77-78), in the course of his pilgrimage came to the house of Viṣṇu, the sustainer. Viṣvaksena, the doorkeeper, who did not recognize Mahādeva and obstructed his entry into Viṣṇu's abode, for his lack of perceptiveness and for his dutiful obstruction found himself pierced on Śiva's trident. Bhairava, balancing the corpse of Viṣvaksena on his long-stemmed weapon, and holding out his left hand with the skull bowl, entered the building. Having learned Śiva's reason for begging alms, Viṣṇu, the sustainer of the universe, made his blood spurt from his forehead into the skull bowl, without being able to fill it.

Bhairava had to move on and continue his pilgrimage. Dancing in holy madness, he proceeded in the direction of Vārāṇasī. Viṣṇu could not resist rushing after the dancing god. There was no end to the dance of Śiva, himself absorbed in endless yoga (*KūP*.2.31.100), until the Great God, Śaṅkara, the bringer of peace, reached Vārāṇasī. The skull of the Creator, the blood of the sustainer of the universe, and the corpse of Viṣvaksena swayed in the hands of dancing Rudra, the Destroyer of all fetters, the liberator.

In Vārāṇasī, as Parameśvara Śiva had decreed, the sin of *brahmahatyā* left Bhairava. Ever since, whoever comes to Vārāṇasī with devotion is freed from sin, even that of brahminicide. The holy center where the skull of Brahmā fell to the ground became known as Kapālamocana, "liberating from the skull." It was on the eighth day of the month of Mārgaśiras, the "Head of the Antelope," that Śiva appeared in the shape of Bhairava (*ŚP*.3.9.54-56, 59-60, 63).

The coming down to earth of Bhairava, the death of Death, to the holy city of Vārāṇasī, the city of liberation, is told in the *Purāṇas* with slight variations. Viṣṇu, even before putting his question to Bhairava, had recognized Mahādeva, for he asked the Great God the reason for playing this role, and on hearing the reason he conceded to Bhairava, "you play as you please" (*SkP*.4.1.31.86). He saw through the play Mahādeva had staged for the sake of the sages and gods; he knew that he, the Supreme Spirit, took his forms at will, that it was the Lord's playfulness to appear before him as he did. Śiva's sight alone liberated (*SkP*.4.1.31.99-101).

Śiva danced as the skull fell from his hand (cf. *SkP*.5.1.2.69). Whether, as in one version, Śiva danced on his way to the holy city as he had danced, in a different mode, in the Deodar forest, or whether he danced out of joy in Vārāṇasī at the fall of the skull from his hand, it is said that Śiva manifested as Bhairava on the eighth day of the dark half of Mārgaśiras, the month called after the constellation Mṛgaśiras, the head of Prajāpati.

Vārāṇasī is not the only sacred site where Bhairava was freed from the skull of Brahmā, the *kapāla*; but no other final station of Bhairava's pilgrimage was equal in sacredness to Vārāṇasī, nor had as mighty a myth. The legend of the sanctuary of Kapāleśvara, the lord of the skull tells of a sacrifice in heaven held by Brahmā and Gāyatrī. A fierce, naked, abject-looking man came, skull bowl in hand, and said, "give me food." The participants in the sacrifice wanted to drive away the sinful, naked Kapālin, bearing a skull, unfit for sacrificial rites. The awful-looking beggar said that on hearing of Brahmā's sacrifice, he had come from afar. He was hungry. Why did they revile him? The brahmins insisted that he leave quickly, for their sacrificial hall was not a place for one emaciated by hunger. When the intruder heard this, he threw the skull on the floor. The brahmins asked him to throw it out. As the beggar did not stir, the brahmins asked someone to remove the skull with a stick. This was done—and immediately another skull appeared on the spot. When that skull was thrown out, yet another cropped up, and so it went on for a hundred thousand years. Hosts of skulls appeared and polluted the sacrifice. Finally, Brahmā asked the intruder why he spoiled the sacrifice. Śiva then said to Brahmā: "you know that not the same offerings are made to me as to the other gods. I get a special portion." Brahmā assured Śiva that in the future no sacrifice would be complete without taking Śiva into account. There would always be a special chant for him. He would stand near the gate, skull in hand, and would be known as Kapāleśvara, lord of the skull. Śiva then destroyed all the skulls (cf. *SkP*.6.1.182.1-41).

In this skull fantasy, replacing the one skull that clung to Śiva's hand by a series of self-renewing skulls, Bhikṣāṭana, the Supreme Mendicant, appeared as a hungry, naked beggar; some, however, say he was dressed in tattered rags, dirty and dusty (*SkP*.7.1.103.3). The humiliated and subsequently accepted intruder was Rudra, the stranger who appeared darkly clad at the Vedic sacrifice (Ch. III.2) before Brahmā had been heard of in Indian myth.

Brahmā, it is told elsewhere, had provoked his decapitation when Rudra, his newborn son, sat on his shoulder and the fifth head of Brahmā prognostically chanted the *Ātharvaṇa mantra*. "O Kapālin, O Rudra, . . . protect the world. . . ." Subsequently, Rudra cut off his father's head (*VrP*.97.3-7). He became a Kapālin and observed the Kāpālika vow (*VrP*.97.10-11), enjoined for murderers of brahmins (*M*.11.73).[30] The fulfillment of the vow took him to Vārāṇasī (*KūP*.2.31.96, 101). On his wanderings over the earth, Rudra divided the head of Brahmā, keeping one piece of the skull in hand and putting the other pieces in his own hair, made himself a sacred thread out of its hair, and made the beads of his rosary and garlands out of the "big" bone (*VrP*.97.11-14). A skull grins from the parting of the hair of an uncannily lovely Bhikṣāṭana bronze image of the eleventh century.[31]

In this version, not only did Śiva carry the head of Brahmā resting in his hand and hair, but he was seen wearing a garland of heads, thousands of heads, thousands of them Brahmā heads (cf. *SkP*.7.1.9.5, 6), and he loved the place where corpses are burned (*KSS*.2.8-15). On such recreation grounds, also, Śiva danced. To him who had overcome death, its shapes—the skulls and bones—were but ornaments swaying with his dancing body.

The macabre exuberance of Śiva's death ornaments was but a sequel to Śiva's orgiastic entry into Viṣṇu's house. With Brahmā's, the Creator's, skull stuck to one hand, Bhairava speared Viṣvaksena, the dutiful if not perceptive gatekeeper. Flaunting the corpse of Viṣvaksena on his trident, the Wild God stepped across the threshold and faced god Viṣṇu, the Preserver of the universe. Lord Viṣṇu, despite the intrusion of Śiva into his house and the presence of the corpse of his gatekeeper held aloft on Śiva's trident, offered his own blood into the *kapāla* in Śiva's hand. He let it spurt from his forehead (*KūP*.2.31.89-90), or from his right hand, which he held out to his guest (*PP*.5.14.14-15) so that his blood might fill the empty skull bowl.

[30] H. von Stietencron, "Bhairava," p. 867 and n. 13.

[31] D. Barrett, *Early Cola Bronzes*, pl. 53.

It has never yet been filled. Śiva's fire eye again and again consumed what was offered into the skull that stuck to his palm.[32] Śiva himself once said of the *kapāla* that this world, resembling a skull, rested in his hand (*KSS*.2.15).[33]

Śiva, the Destroyer, having forcibly entered the house of Viṣṇu, the Preserver, was given a guest offering such as only the Sustainer of the World could offer him. Viṣṇu gave Bhairava his own life blood and, in ecstasy, he followed Bhairava, who danced his way to Vārāṇasī. God Viṣṇu himself, like the women of the sages in the forest who had followed the naked mendicant, left his home to be near the dancing beggar. God Viṣṇu, as Śiva was departing, joined the wild, ghastly cortege of the skull-bearer wielding his trident with the corpse of Viṣṇu's gatekeeper impaled on it. The dead body of him who was to have guarded the house of Viṣṇu decorated Śiva's trident and swayed in the joyous dance of the Lord. The horrible Brahmahatyā followed the God all the while on the way to Vārāṇasī.

Carrying the skull of Brahmā and the corpse of Viṣvaksena, Bhairava danced, a moving figure of Consciousness that had transcended, while in its fullness it comprised all conditions in which God manifests to the eye of mortals. Having severed the head of the Creator and killed the guardian of the house of the Sustainer of creation, Bhairava had cut through all fetters. Horrendous, abject, naked, or in rags that emphasized his nakedness, self-contradictory and consistent with his unspeakable being, with an entrancing smile on his lips he bared his fangs. The images of the Lord show him young and in glory as Bhikṣāṭanamūrti, the Supreme Beggar. They show him as Kaṅkālamūrti, carrying the impaled body of Viṣvaksena; or emaciated and deathlike in his image as Bhairava; or stern, bloated, his matted hair surrounded by flames, fiercely ponderous, and black as Kāla and Mahākāla. No contradictions were adequate and no single iconographic likeness sufficed to render the total, tremendous mystery of Bhairava. The furthest outreach of contradictory qualities was gathered in the intensity of the myth, and split in the variety of images in bronze and stone. They adumbrate the breakthrough from time into eternity, from Kāla to Mahākāla, from creation back into the Uncreate.

The head of Brahmā was cut off by Śiva Bhairava. The gatekeeper

[32] Cf. W. Jahn, "Die Legende vom Devadāruvana," 1915, p. 532.

[33] *Kathāsaritsāgara (KSS)*, tr. C. H. Tawney and ed. N. M. Penzer, 1:10.

at the threshold of Viṣṇu's house was pierced to death by the trident of Śiva Bhairava. He entered the house of Viṣṇu, the Preserver of the World, and left, at Viṣṇu's advice, for Vārāṇasī. Unable to resist, Viṣṇu left his house to follow the dancing god on the way to Vārāṇasī, where sin, guilt, and the skull of Brahmā fell from Śiva. The skull broke into a thousand pieces (*MP*.183.99-100); with a shriek Brahmahatyā sank into the netherworld. When the frenzy of the ecstatic pilgrimage of Bhairava on earth came to its end, the god was then and there released from all fetters of his own making (cf. *VmP*.3.42-44). After he had taken his bath in a wonderful pond, full of lotuses, the pond became known as Kapālamocana, "releasing of the skull" (*VmP*.3.47-51).

Having been freed from the cut-off head of Brahmā, Śiva returned into transcendency whence the Wild Hunter from out of nowhere had appeared in the primordial scene.

At Kapālamocana, Śiva was freed from his sin of having cut off the head of Brahmā. The site forever remains the most holy abode of Lord Śiva on earth. It was called Avimukta, the region never forsaken by the Great God (*MP*.181.13-15; 183.99; 184.25-28). In his terrible shape, motionless and stable like a pillar, Lord Śiva stays there until the dissolution of the world (*MP*.182.3-4). His abode is invisible to ordinary man, in space (*antarikṣa*) above the cremation ground; only yogis, *brahmacārins*, and those who know the *Veda* can see it (*MP*. 182.5-8). Those who go to Avimukta obtain not only freedom from sin but also freedom from the cycle of births and deaths; they obtain final release and union with Śiva (*MP*.182.11-27). The Great God resides in Avimukta with all his attendants. Some have faces like infuriated lions and wolves, others are hunchbacked, some are dwarfs, others are contorted; armed giants guard the sacred grove of Avimukta (*MP*.183.63-67).

The motley crowd of the freakish retinue of Śiva is part of his ambience. Indefinitely variable in its monstrosity, wit, and vitality, it includes the misshapen as possibilities within his orbit. Rudra refused to create mortals because they were imperfect. The retinue of Śiva, *bhūtas, gaṇas, pramathas, pāriṣadas, kumbhāṇḍas, rākṣasas*, and *piśācas*—different types of spirits, sprites, ghosts, and ghouls—do not belong to the pitiable class of mortals; they are part of Rudra's being, tremors, resonances of his nature, byproducts of tensions that sustain his contradictory wholeness. They are scintillations of the Rudras, smithereens of the terrifying glory of Rudra-Śiva himself.

His abode was the burning ground, which was "covered with hair and bones, full of skulls and heads, thick with vultures and jackals, covered with a hundred funeral pyres, an unclean place covered with flesh, a mire of marrow and blood, scattered piles of flesh, resounding with the cries of jackals" (*MBh*.13.128.13-15). Indeed, in his wanderings all over the earth, the Great God had always been in search of a hallowed spot. "There is nothing purer than a cremation ground," Śiva declared (*MBh*.13.128.16). The hosts of ghostly beings that are his companions loved to dwell there, and Śiva did not like to stay anywhere without them (*MBh*.13.128.18).

Revulsion as a means of detachment had its form in the imagery of the cremation ground. It dwelt not on the cessation of life and the purgation of the mortal body through the consuming fire, but on the byproducts of physical disintegration. Though gruesome, they were less terrifying than disgusting.

Revulsion in its last degree of sublimation reaches up to holiness. As part of the divine play of the Great God, it hovers above the cremation ground, shedding its odor in the ethereal purity of the *antarikṣa*.

The burning ground offers its extreme situation after the end of the life of the body, full of debris in which the ghouls delight, the ghouls whose company Śiva never liked to be without. The residence of Śiva, above the burning ground in Avimukta, is never without Śiva, as the word Avimukta implies. The forest of Deodar trees, on the other hand, was but a place of passage for Śiva on his wanderings. It was the place of the critical moment, after Śiva had decapitated his father the Creator, or after he lost his wife Satī by her self-immolation. The Deodar forest was the place of the highest pitch of the god's passion. He danced, laughed, acted like a madman, and was inwardly calm when his *liṅga* fell.

In his divine play, Rudra-Śiva, the Wild God, assumed many guises or shapes, but he did not wear a mask. As Bhairava, his fearful countenance revealed his fangs and revoked the smile that came to the lips of the Great God every so often when he addressed himself to the gods. His laughter resounded from the measureless flaming *liṅga* that traversed a cosmic night.

The macabre setting of the burning ground was the locale of the detachment of Lord Śiva. The smile and laughter of the god, which he released on so many occasions, were similarly expressions of his aloofness from whatever situation he summoned. They conveyed the surpassing joy that set his play going—in heaven, on earth, and in the nether world. It was staged from Śiva's abode in the space of the cremation ground, "for who could live, who could breathe, if there were not this bliss in the space?" (*TUp*.2.7).[34]

[34] J. M. van Boetzelaer, tr., *Sureśvara's Taittirīyopaniṣadbhāṣyavārtikam*, p. 128.

X

THE FAMILY OF ŚIVA

A. THE LINEAGE OF DAKṢA, THE PROGENITOR

1. Life and Death of Satī

a. *The Spring of Love*

The Perfect Age, the Kṛta Yuga, had passed. It was perfect inasmuch as it contained the abiding themes on which the myth of Mahādeva, the Great God, was built. They were to sustain and determine the ongoing structure of his presence. The Kṛta Yuga, however, was less than perfect if it were to be assessed in human terms. It began with the fall, the fall of the seed of the Creator, the fall from the Uncreate into creation.

At the beginning of the next, even less perfect age, the Tretā Yuga, the sixty daughters of Dakṣa were born (*ŚP*.2.2.6.55; 14.4),[1] of whom Satī was the first (*VāP*.30.40-41). It is also said that Satī / Śivā was the middle or the last-born (*ŚP*.2.2.14.9). The latter alternatives have little to commend themselves, for the race of women had not been created prior to Satī's incarnation. But myth has its own inconsistencies or differing versions. The general view that Satī should be born from Dakṣa and one of his wives runs counter to another statement made in the *Harivaṃśa* that after creating all moving and unmoving creatures, both bipeds and quadrupeds, by his mind, Dakṣa then created women, whom he gave to various gods; hence arose reproduction through couples (*H*.2.46-49). Dakṣa's first birth was in the distant past, at the beginning of things, when he was born from Aditi, and

[1] The number of Dakṣa's daughters is said to have been twenty-four (*VP*.1.7.22) or sixty (*VP*.1.15.103) or fifty (*VP*.1.15.77-78).

Aditi was born from Dakṣa (*RV*.10.72.4). The birth of Dakṣa from Aditi is on the same level as Agni, the bull-cow, that is, at the furthest reach of metaphor (cf. *RV*.10.5.7, Ch. I.4). Dakṣa had traveled far through the aeons, from his birth from Aditi, to his becoming Brahmā's son,[2] and father of Satī.

Twenty-seven of his daughters he gave to the moon in marriage (*ŚP*.2.2.6.56). They were the Nakṣatras, the twenty-seven lunar mansions. Satī, however, was to become the bride of Śiva (*VāP*.30.41). With that purpose, the Great Goddess out of her own will assumed human shape and was born from Vīriṇī, Dakṣa's wife (*ŚP*.2.2.14.12-14, 24).

Brahmā had prayed to the Great Goddess to fascinate Śiva, for he did not think that Śiva, the yogi, detached from the world, would on his own account take to himself a goddess as his wife. If he, the cause of the universe, remained detached, creation would not come about. The Great Goddess would have to enthrall the great ascetic to fulfill Brahmā's plan (*ŚP*.2.2.11.18-28). The cosmic goddess appeared as Yoganidrā, "slumbering wakefulness" (*ŚP*.2.2.11.6). She glistened like collyrium (*ŚP*.2.2.11.7) as she assured Brahmā of her endeavor to delude Śiva so that he would take a bride (*ŚP*.2.2.11.45-46). Dakṣa, having performed austerities for three thousand years with great devotion to Śiva, saw the dark, primordial goddess before him. She was the Great Goddess in her cosmic form; as the power of the Great Goddess, she had emanated from her. She appeared to Dakṣa in her dark cosmic form sparkling with Ardhanārīśvara's fire. Its superluminous radiance scintillated out of her darkness. In this form she was Kālikā, the Dark, the primordial, cosmic goddess. Dakṣa, in a prognostic vision of her iconic shape, conceived of her seated on a lion; she held a blue lotus and a sword in two of her four hands. At Brahmā's bidding, Dakṣa worshiped her who had not as yet been embodied in corporeal shape. He prayed to her that she be born as his daughter, to fascinate and enthrall Śiva. She alone had this power. Kālikā granted the boon that Dakṣa asked of her. As Śiva had been born as Brahmā's son, so Śivā would be born as Dakṣa's daughter. By this divine play of hers, the Great Goddess would fulfill the purpose of the entire world. The Great Goddess in her cosmic form agreed to be Śiva's beloved in every incarnation (*ŚP*.2.2.12.6-29).

[2] J. Dowson, *A Classical Dictionary of Hindu Mythology and Religion*, 1928, p. 76.

Brahmā had a willing Great Goddess to cooperate with him in his plot of enticing Śiva, the great ascetic, to take a wife. Since she had left the form of Ardhanārīśvara and had chosen to be born as Dakṣa's daughter, assuming human appearance and becoming Śiva's bride was her way of returning to Śiva. Darkly glittering, the Great Goddess had already left bipartite wholeness for the world of duality, the realm of Kālikā, the cosmic power of the Great Goddess. Willing to be born as Dakṣa's daughter and to fascinate Śiva, Kālikā listened to Dakṣa's prayer. Dakṣa knew that no other woman would be competent to enthrall Śiva. Toward this tremendous task the goddess Kālikā—whose other names are Caṇḍikā, the Fierce, and Durgā, the Difficult to Reach (*ŚP*.2.2.11.3, 6)—was ready to become Dakṣa's daughter, but first she made one condition: if ever in future Dakṣa should show her less respect, she would cast off her body and withdraw into her inmost self, or take up another shape (*ŚP*.2.2.12.33-34).

Dakṣa named his daughter Umā (*ŚP*.2.2.14.49), a name rich in possible meanings. It could have alluded to the night-splendor of her beauty, or it could have singled her out as the "Mother of the Universe," by which appellation Dakṣa paid homage to Satī (*ŚP*.2.2.14.27-28). As the Mother of the Universe she would have been in line with Umu, the Sumerian "Mother"[3] and with Ommo, the name of the Goddess, the consort of Śiva, inscribed on a coin of Huviṣka, the Kuṣāṇa king.[4] The Goddess appears in the *Taittirīya Āraṇyaka* (*TĀ*.10.12 and Sāyaṇa on same). Under the name Umā she explains to Indra the identity of the Supreme Brahman, which had eluded the other gods (*KUp*.3.12 and 4.1).

Brahmā's plan to see the Great Goddess, Kālikā, the Mother of the Universe, take birth as Dakṣa's daughter for the purpose of entrancing Śiva was only part of a total design for diverting Śiva, the Lord of Yoga, from his true nature—asceticism—and making him subservient to the Creator's purpose, the creation of mortals. Satī's task in the seduction of Śiva was part of a twofold plan devised by Brahmā. Satī knew that only by asceticism could she draw the great ascetic toward herself. While Brahmā had no need to intensify her asceticism, he exerted himself in rendering Śiva susceptible to her incomparable beauty. Brahmā's design for the temptation of Śiva was complex and deep-rooted. It had more than one cause.

[3] M. Mayrhofer, *Concise Etymological Sanskrit Dictionary, s.v.* Umā.

[4] J. Rosenfield, *The Dynastic Arts of the Kushans*, p. 94.

Brahmā still smarted from the loss of his head. It had been preceded by the loss of his mind when he, full of lust, had stared at his daughter Sandhyā (also called Sāvitrī, Ch. IX.1). His infatuation on that occasion had spread to his sons, including Dakṣa. Brahmā and his sons were helpless, for they were hit by the arrows of a wonderfully handsome being who appeared as Brahmā's creation, just as Brahmā stared at Sandhyā. That wonderful being, born with a bow and five flower arrows, was Kāma. He started his work even while Brahmā assigned to him his task: to fascinate men and women and carry on the aeviternal work of procreation. Even the gods Brahmā, Viṣṇu, and Śiva would be in his power (*ŚP*.2.2.2.22-39). Hit by Kāma's arrows, Brahmā was seen in this state by Śiva, who saw everything from high in the air. Śiva laughed and mocked Brahmā (*ŚP*.2.2.3.36-45). Shamed and angry, Brahmā cursed Kāma, who had brought about his ludicrous plight, and included in his curse Śiva, who had ridiculed him: Kāma was cursed to be burned by the fire of Śiva's eye after doing the same thing to him (*ŚP*.2.2.3.61-64).

Brahmā shed drops of sweat. From them the *pitṛs*, "the Fathers" were born. They had for their mother Sandhyā, after whom Brahmā had lusted (*ŚP*.2.2.3.48, 58-59). Dakṣa, in a similar though lesser plight, had also perspired and from his sweat Rati, the goddess Lust, was born (*ŚP*.2.2.3.51-53). She was to become the wife of Kāma (*ŚP*.2.2.4.4-6). Brahmā particularly resented having been seen by Śiva in a scene analogous to the primordial one in which Rudra, the Wild Hunter, far from being an amused spectator, had aggressively taken a vitally fateful part. Now, however, it was Kāma's arrow, not Śiva's, that hit Brahmā. Brahmā cursed Kāma, but he also meant to confront the two archers, Kāma and Śiva. Brahmā wanted Śiva to succumb to Desire, whereas Kāma would be burned to ashes by the fire shooting from Śiva's eye (*MP*.4.12; *ŚP*.2.2.3.64). Brahmā's curse was directed as much against Śiva as it was against Kāma; the double target, moreover, revealed also Brahmā's duplicity in regard to Śiva. He wanted Śiva to be struck by the arrow of Desire in order to avenge Rudra's primordial attack on Prajāpati engaged in intercourse. Interlocked with Brahmā's vengefulness was his wish to turn Śiva away from his asceticism and to inflame him by the same erotic passion that had led to Brahmā's disgrace. The motives of Brahmā, far from pure, reinforced one another. His vindictiveness against Śiva sharpened the curse against Kāma, made it all the more effective, because Brahmā wanted to avenge himself on Kāma and he wanted Śiva to succumb to Kāma for the sake of creation, which Brahmā alone was unable to accomplish. Brahmā's revenge was directed primarily against Śiva, who had wanted to prevent creation, having primordially assaulted Prajāpati and interrupted him in the act of procreation, and who had mocked Brahmā in his erotic excitement.

On hearing Brahmā's curse, Kāma shuddered with fear. He cried out in dismay, entreating Brahmā to save him from the effect of the curse. Kāma was not to blame for having aimed at Brahmā: he had only carried out Brahmā's command not to spare anyone, not even Brahmā. Moved, Brahmā modified his curse, though he maintained that Śiva's glance would reduce Kāma to ashes and he would become bodiless. But this curse would end; Kāma's body would be restored when Śiva took a wife (*ŚP*.2.2.3.68-76). Then Brahmā would be happy (*ŚP*.2.2.8.15).

Brahmā's plot approached Śiva in two stages. Satī was to attract Śiva by her asceticism and captivate him by her loveliness. Then Kāma was to wound and inflame Śiva. Seeking release from Brahmā's curse, Kāma helped Brahmā in his strategy. He left Brahmā's presence in sorrow for having been cursed, but glad that the curse had been modified and that his body would be restored to him (*MP*.4.21; *ŚP*.2.2.3.78).

When the Great Goddess had descended into Vīriṇī's womb, though she was conceived like any child, Dakṣa, her father, recognized his daughter as the Great Goddess and worshiped her. From her early childhood, when playing with other children, she drew pictures of Śiva, her songs were about Śiva, her mind was directed toward Śiva, and when Brahmā came on a visit and told her to marry Śiva, she was not surprised. Worshiping Śiva day by day, Satī grew up subjecting herself to increasingly arduous austerities with Śiva as her goal. Her desire for him grew daily, and she meditated on Śiva with concentrated devotion (*ŚP*.2.2.14.13-27, 55-57; 15.1-28). Her austerities strengthened her desire.

Meanwhile the gods and sages went to Kailāsa where they praised Śiva, the Lord of Yoga, who is neither god nor demon, neither man nor beast, neither male, female, nor eunuch. What remains after all negations—*that* is Śiva (*ŚP*.2.2.15.33, 61-62). Brahmā urged Śiva to take a wife, as all the other gods had done. Śiva replied that it would be improper for him to marry because he was detached from the world and always practiced yoga. What use had he for a loving wife? Further, he was always dirty and inauspicious, completely absorbed in the realization of the absolute; marriage was a bondage and did not interest him (*ŚP*.2.2.16.26-27, 31-34). But, for the sake of his devotees, he would marry. The woman would have to be of a very special kind, beautiful and practicing yoga. "She must be a Yoginī when I practice Yoga and a loving woman when I indulge in love" (*ŚP*.2.2.16.36-39).[5] When Śiva would be absorbed in his imperishable nature, in utter transcendency, wretched be anyone who would disturb him. There was another condition on which Śiva insisted: should she ever doubt his words, he would abandon her (*ŚP*.2.2.16.40-44).

Brahmā then spoke to Śiva of Satī, practicing austerities in order to win Śiva as her husband. Śiva in his mercy should grant her the desired boon and should marry her lovingly. Smiling, Lord Śiva agreed (*ŚP*.2.2.16.46-51, 57).

Satī was devoted to Śiva. She practiced yoga, not in order to gain release but to ready herself for Śiva and at the same time draw him to herself. She did not know that Śiva, the Lord of Yoga, persuaded by Brahmā, had resolved to make her his wife for the sake of his devotees and creation. Śiva let the yoga power of Satī, the magic of her concentrated will, and his own compassion for his devotees do their work.

Satī was absorbed in meditation when Śiva became visible to her: handsome, radiant, five-faced and three-eyed, four-armed, the crescent moon on his forehead, his throat blue. The celestial Gaṅgā adorned his head (*ŚP*.2.2.17.3-5). Continuing her meditation, she bent her head in worship. Śiva wanted to give her the fruit of her austerities, and he wanted to hear her voice. He asked her to choose whatever boon she desired. She could not speak, shy with love for Śiva; and when at last she asked for the boon, she could not complete the sentence. As she prayed that Śiva, the giver of boons, the bridegroom of her desire, would fulfill her desire—Śiva completed her thought and asked her to be his wife. Silent, in dark, glowing beauty she stood before his crystal clarity. When she found words, she joyously requested the Lord of the universe to take her with due marital rites in the presence of her parents, and Śiva consented (*ŚP*.2.2.17.7-23).

[5] *Śiva Purāṇa (ŚP)*, tr. "A Board of Scholars" and ed. J. L. Shastri, 1973, p. 345.

Love had entered their hearts. Śiva responded to Satī erotically, a form of love that hitherto his anthropomorphic shape had not experienced, while in his symbol shape, the *liṅga*, the erotic fire flamed upward all the while. He was thought of as acting in the shape of man. Love of more than one kind dwelled in Śiva—the benign, as his name implies, though even Vedic Rudra, the Wild God, was invoked for his benevolence (*RV*.1.114.3; 1.122.1; 2.33.14; 5.41.2; 5.51.13), his exceeding benevolence (cf. *TS*.4.5.1.1), and for healing (*TS*.4.5.1.1). Out of love for his devotees, he saved from death Śveta and Mārkaṇḍeya. Out of love for his devotees, Śiva projected his *māyā* and acted as the protagonist in the play that touched the hearts of the people and showed them the Great Yogi assuming the part of the lover.

Out of compassion, for the sake of the gods and his devotees, the Great God showed himself to the Goddess in his supernatural shape. He agreed to take in marriage, according to custom established among mortals, the Goddess embodied in human shape.

Henceforth Śiva and Satī will appear to act like mortals; in this manner, the play (*līlā*) of the Great God will be understood by mortals. While playing his divine play and entering into its mood, the Great God, who conjures up this play, remains aloof in his transcendental reality. It shimmers through his *māyā*, the magic veil of his presence.

Satī returned to her parents' house and Śiva went to his Himālayan hermitage, his meditation disturbed by his longing for Satī. Still, Kāma was given no chance to attack Śiva. Excited like any mortal in love, Śiva had abandoned his meditation on the Supreme Self, which he was, and thought of Satī.

Śiva had readily accepted Brahmā's plan, but he had made certain conditions. His stipulation that his future wife should be a yoginī, if he was ever to marry, was in tune with his own nature. His stipulation that she should be a loving woman when he indulged in love was not in character with Śiva the ascetic. But the ascetic god meant to act in conformity with Brahmā's plan. Thinking further about his future wife, he anticipated the possibility of her interfering with his utter absorption in himself, with his transcendency. In that case he would curse her. The prospect of marriage, to which Śiva had readily agreed, did not really appeal to Lord Śiva. He even thought of the possibility of leaving Satī should she not fully believe in him. In short, Śiva did not unconditionally accept Brahmā's plan. But he had begun to be stirred by Satī. Also, he thought of marrying her for the sake of his devotees. He felt disturbed.

Satī, on the other hand, wholly devoted to Śiva, had neither questions nor premonitions. It had been withheld from her that Dakṣa had been compelled by Brahmā to give his daughter in marriage to Śiva.

Brahmā made Dakṣa agree to an early wedding of Śiva and Satī (*ŚP*.2.2.17.30-36, 68-69). Then, the preparations for the wedding completed, Śiva started in the month of Caitra from his hermitage on Kailāsa. Brahmā, Viṣṇu, and all the gods and sages accompanied Śiva to Dakṣa's house. The hides of elephant, tiger, and serpents, the crescent moon, and the ascetic's matted hair, by Śiva's will, became his wedding ornaments (*ŚP*.2.2.18.20-24). Dakṣa welcomed Śiva worshipfully and announced the marriage agreement to his guests (*ŚP*.2.2.18.30). Brahmā was chosen to perform the marriage rites (*ŚP*.2.2.18.31). When the stars were in auspicious conjunction with the planets, Dakṣa happily gave his own daughter Satī to Śiva (*ŚP*.2.2.18.33). Viṣṇu praised Śiva as the Father and Satī as the Mother of the World. He praised them for having entered the world for their own pleasure, for the safety of the good and the suppression of evil. Thus, standing close to the Lord who shone with the collyrium-dark luster of the goddess, Viṣṇu counseled Śiva to kill any man who would lust after Satī. Śiva laughed but promised to act accordingly. Viṣṇu then left the wedding, and Brahmā performed the sacrificial rites (*ŚP*.2.2.19.3-10).

The descent of the power (*śakti*) of the Great Goddess into the cosmos, as Kālikā, the Mother of the Universe, and her resolve to act as a mortal on becoming Satī, a real woman, were fraught with apprehension and forebodings. Kālikā, the Mother of the Universe, granting to Dakṣa the boon of becoming his daughter, uttered a solemn warning: she would cast off her body were Dakṣa in the future, after becoming her father, less respectful toward her than when he asked her the boon of becoming his daughter (*ŚP*.2.2.12.34). Even as the Cosmic Goddess Kālikā was uncertain about Dakṣa's future relation to Satī, so also was Śiva uncertain about the steadiness of Satī's feelings toward himself. Were she ever to show disbelief in his word, he would abandon her (*ŚP*.2.2.16.44). To these prognostic fears of Śiva and Kālikā, Viṣṇu added a further apprehension through his advice: should any man lust after Satī, Śiva should kill him (*ŚP*.2.2.19.7).

The time had now come in the marriage ritual for the bridal pair to walk around the sacred fire, which Brahmā as the chief priest was tending. He saw Satī's bare feet protrude below her garment, and was smitten with lust. He stared at her. Anxious to see her face covered by her veil, he put wet branches on the fire to make it smoke, and as Śiva covered his eyes smarting from the smoke, Brahmā lifted Satī's veil and looked at her face again and again with growing excitement. He covered up the four drops of semen that he let fall to the ground. Śiva, though blinded by smoke, saw it all and raised his trident to kill Brahmā, but Viṣṇu, who had anticipated the episode, intervened, pleading that he, Brahmā, and Śiva were but manifestations of Śiva in transcendency, from whom they and all else had emanated. Śiva, knowing this to be the truth, desisted from killing Brahmā (*ŚP*.2.2.19.17-76).

Brahmā's incontinence at the wedding of Śiva and Satī was a grotesque replica of the Father / Prajāpati's primordial transgression. This archetypal exploit already had one replica, in the myth of Brahmā lusting after Sandhyā. There, it cost him his head. Here it was a shameful incident that Śiva could afford to overlook, as a peccadillo of the Creator deluded by Śiva's *māyā*. Śiva was in a generous and playful mood. He urged Brahmā not to be afraid, and requested him to touch his own, Brahmā's, head with his hand. Brahmā obeyed and obtained the form of Śiva's vehicle, the bull. Brahmā, having thus become Śiva's vehicle, was told he would be born as a man with a bull's head and would roam over the earth. Any man who, lusting after another man's wife, would hear Brahmā's story would be free from that sin, whereas Brahmā would be laughed at. To be held in ridicule by people was to be Brahmā's abasement. At the same time, as many a man was sure to find himself in this position, Brahmā's sin would gradually decrease, and he would become pure (*ŚP*.2.2.20.7-20).

Ribald, absurd, and amusing, this vignette added to the wedding of Śiva and Satī was part of the play of the Lord to assure his devotees of his mercy and humor. The four drops of semen shed by Brahmā, however, did not bring about any progeny; on the contrary, they swelled and became the four great clouds—Saṃvartaka, Āvarta, Puṣkara, and Droṇa—that bring about the dissolution of the universe (*ŚP*.2.2.20.21-24), when Śiva will dance the cosmos out of existence. Brahmā's untimely propensity turned into a harbinger of destruction.

Brahmā concluded the wedding rite. Śiva and Satī mounted his vehicle, the bull, and followed by his gaṇas, rode to Kailāsa. Dakṣa accompanied Śiva half way, happy with Śiva's love (ŚP.2.2.20.47-51). It was, according to the *Śiva Purāṇa*, under the rule of Svāyambhuva Manu that the marriage of Śiva and Satī took place (ŚP.2.2.20.58). When Śiva reached his home, the snow-clad mountains, the Himālaya, the gods and sages took leave of him (ŚP.2.2.20.53-55). Śiva discharged his gaṇas, Nandin, and all others from his mountain cave. He was alone with Satī, played with her, caressed and teased her; they sported in verdant groves and dark caves. Then, climbing Himālayan ridges, Śiva remembered Kāma of his own accord (ŚP.2.2.21.8-28). When Kāma arrived, Spring spread his splendors: trees blossomed and the waters were full of lotus flowers (ŚP.2.2.21.29-30). Entranced by Satī, Śiva made love with her; it was as though she entered his body (ŚP.2.2.21.42). Holding her in close embrace or, full of fun, wreathing flower garlands around her, as well as conversing with her, he gave her knowledge of the Self, of the principle of life, and of the Supreme Spirit (ŚP.2.2.21.43-44). In this way Mahādeva, the Great God, the naked yogi, revealed himself to her. Enthralled by her, Śiva sported with Satī, the Great Goddess, day after day for twenty-five years according to the reckoning of the gods (ŚP.2.2.21.47). Śiva, the protagonist of his divine play, abandoned himself to his new role to the point where it appeared to him as his own reality.

Satī knew that her austerities had been performed to win the Lord of Yoga as her husband. His love would not be like that of any god or mortal. She won him in the only way he could be won, by yoga, and now he loved her in a way that only the Lord of Yoga could achieve. He held his semen within his body, and while his fervor never decreased, the Great Yogi remained collected within himself. Moreover, Śiva had set forth the condition that his beautiful bride must be a yoginī when he practiced yoga and a loving woman when he was intent on love (ŚP.2.2.16.39). But he indulged in love as a yogi, with his seed drawn up, experiencing erotic pleasure while restraining his body, his consciousness calm. He was always engaged in yoga (ŚP.2.2.16.30). It was the basic modality of his being and metaphor of his transcendence. The Lord of Yoga, however, was unapproachable for Satī while in *samādhi*.

b. *Satī's Frailty*

Following the long spring of their love, the summer season came with days of scorching sunshine and hot winds. Śiva and Satī took shelter in the shade of trees, for Śiva had no house of his own: he had always been a homeless wanderer. But when the rainy season came, the trees gave no protection from lightning and the pouring clouds, and Śiva had no money to build a house; all he had was the tiger skin that he wore and the snakes that were his sacred thread, his armlets, bracelets, earring, and girdle around his hips. He laughed away Satī's faintheartedness, and took her up on a cloud where no rain could fall. Hence, Śiva became known as Jīmūtaketu, "having a cloud as his banner" (*VmP*.1.11-30). Or he led her high up to the top of the Himālayas, where even the clouds do not reach. There Śiva lived with Satī for ten thousand years of the gods (*ŚP*.2.2.22.1-65). Occasionally he visited Mount Meru, where the gods were, or he went to different places on earth. Still, he found happiness only with Satī (*ŚP*.2.2.22.66-68).

After sporting with Śiva until satisfied, the bride of Śiva became very indifferent. She told Śiva that her mind had turned away from the delights of love, blessed though she was to have become Śiva's wife (*ŚP*.2.2.23.1-7). She knew that the Lord had married her out of love for his devotees (*ŚP*.2.2.23.6). She knew that Mahādeva out of love for his devotees let his *māyā*, his power of illusion, stage the divine play that would draw his devotees to him by bringing him and Satī near to them. It was a sublime play in which god and goddess showed themselves swept by emotion and joined in passion while calm in their immutable selves. "All this is Śiva's play. The mighty one produces many plays; he is independent and changeless. Satī also is like this" (*ŚP*.2.2.24.16), though in principle rather than in action.

Satī wanted to know the secret of devotion for the sake of which Śiva created and acted out his plays. Śiva explained that there was no difference between devotion and perfect knowledge (*ŚP*.2.2.23.16). He meant that there was no difference in the object attained by them. The Great God was concerned that his devotees attain both release from the world and happiness in it (cf. *ŚP*.2.2.23.15-17). Prognostically, he had the Kali Yuga in mind, the present age in which his devotees live, and during which the knowledge of ultimate reality and detachment have grown old and lost their attraction (*ŚP*.2.2.23.39). No other path brings happiness as does devotion (*ŚP*.2.2.23.38). Resigned and aware of the disposition of man in the Kali Yuga, Śiva explained to Satī the virtue of devotion when perfect knowledge—the consciousness that "I am *brahman*"—was hard to obtain in this world, and that few men knew that Śiva was *brahman* (*ŚP*.2.2.23.13,14).

Śiva's explanation had satisfied Satī as it applied particularly to the

Kali Yuga, especially in need of the grace of Lord Śiva (*ŚP*.2.2.23.37-38). Thus Satī and Śiva, who are the embodiment of the Supreme *Brahman* and who give happiness to the three worlds, sported in the Himālayas and elsewhere (*ŚP*.2.2.23.55-56). All the same, things did not go well with Satī. She did not always follow the meaning of Śiva's divine play, and at times was deluded by his *māyā*. Once Śiva, having ascended his bull with Satī, roamed over the earth. They came to the Daṇḍaka forest and saw Rāma searching for his abducted wife (*ŚP*.2.2.24.21-23). Rāma was an avatar of Viṣṇu. In the past, Śiva had at one time crowned Lord Viṣṇu as the lord of the universe (*ŚP*.2.2.25.21). Having bestowed this lordship on Viṣṇu, Śiva bowed to Rāma, an incarnation of Viṣṇu, the lord of the universe (*ŚP*.2.2.24.27). Satī did not know of Viṣṇu's coronation by Śiva, and when she saw Śiva bow before Rāma, who was wailing for the abducted Sītā and roaming in the forest, she was puzzled (*ŚP*.2.2.24.29). Even though Śiva told her that Rāma was an avatar of Viṣṇu, Satī still doubted the divinity of Rāma (*ŚP*.2.2.24.39-41). Śiva then playfully urged the doubting Satī to test the divinity of Rāma (*ŚP*.2.2.24.43).

Satī staged a play of her own. She assumed the shape of Sītā, the abducted wife of Rāma. If Rāma indeed was an incarnation of Viṣṇu, he would see through her disguise. Disguised as Sītā, she went to Rāma, who on seeing her laughed and said, "Śivā!" Satī was alarmed and ashamed for not having believed Śiva and having doubted Rāma (*ŚP*.2.2.24.45-51). She repented, and grief-stricken she returned to Śiva (*ŚP*.2.2.25.41-46).

Śiva knew everything and recalled with distress the vow he had made in the presence of Viṣṇu that if she should ever doubt his word, he would abandon her. Were he now to retain his love for Satī, his vow would be broken (*ŚP*.2.2.25.48-50; 16.44). It was then that Śiva mentally abandoned Satī. He did not tell her the contents of the vow, and, to console the distressed goddess, he narrated many tales to her on their way back to Kailāsa. There Śiva, the yogi, entered *samādhi*, meditating on his transcendent, real, Self (*ŚP*.2.2.25.51-60).

When Śiva finished his meditation, Satī, agitated in her heart, went to him. Śiva tried to entertain and cheer her, telling stories of interest to her. She obtained happiness, as before, and Śiva did not forsake his vow (*ŚP*.2.2.25.63-66). But it would be wrong to speak of Śiva as having become estranged and separated from Satī. The two are not separate. While they play as they like, Satī and Śiva are united like a word and its meaning; but should they so wish, their separation can be imagined (ŚP.2.2.25.67-69). When the Great Goddess had stepped out of Ardhanārīśvara and sent her power into the cosmos to be born as Satī, Dakṣa's daughter, the Great Goddess returned into Ardhanārīśvara and Satī became the wife of Śiva. The Goddess became real as a woman born of the wife of Dakṣa; Satī was destined to become the bride of Śiva by the will of Brahmā. By her own will the dark, beautiful Satī practiced austerities. Her beauty and steadfast yoga attracted Śiva, the ascetic, and he asked the shy but determined Satī to be his wife. Suffused with love, Satī, the daughter of the ritualist Dakṣa, asked Śiva, the Lord of Yoga and of the universe, to take her according to the marital rites in the presence of her father (ŚP.2.2.17.22). This mattered to her greatly, for she had inherited from her father a sense of strict observance of rites. Little did she know that some time later she would be forsaken mentally by Śiva, who could not continue to love her the same way as before (ŚP.2.2.25.50-51), and that she was to blame.

At the wedding, Śiva wore a bridegroom's dress and ornaments: the elephant and tiger skins, and the serpents transformed at his will (ŚP.2.2.18.23). But when he went to live with Satī in the Himālayan solitudes, he returned to his usual attire. Although Satī had subjected herself to fasts and other austerities in the worship of Śiva, she had been accustomed to the style of life in her father's house, and became fainthearted living with Śiva through the heat of a summer where the shade of trees was the only refuge from the scorching rays of the sun. She feared the coming of the monsoon, the torrential rain, and Śiva took her up on a cloud; in voicing her fears of the coming monsoon, she revealed that she had not trusted Śiva to protect her.

Out of her own free will Satī had assumed human form (ŚP.2.2.15.8, 27); by her own power of illusion (*māyā*) she became and acted like a human (ŚP.2.2.14.40); she was petulant and weak in faith. When the long spring of their love had been drawing to an end, Śiva visited different places on earth; even so he found real happiness only when he was with Satī (ŚP.2.2.22.65-68). She, however, sated with love, let her mind dwell not on attachment, though her attachment had been to the Lord himself who is beyond attachment, but on detachment from the world and worldly bondage (ŚP.2.2.23.1-9). It was then that Śiva spoke to her of devotion (ŚP.2.2.23.12-17).

It so happened that some time after, when wandering over the earth in the company of Satī, the time of testing came. They encountered Rāma exiled and in distress in a southern forest. When Śiva bowed before the grief-stricken figure, Satī was astonished that the lord of the world should bow to any one, particularly such a distraught person, and when Śiva told her the reason, she was unconvinced and doubted him. She meant to find out for herself the reason for Śiva's deference to Rāma, and went to test Rāma, disguising herself as Rāma's wife. Instantly, she was recognized by Rāma. Shamefaced and pained, she returned to Śiva, for whom her test of Rāma was a test of herself, of her faith and belief in Śiva. Then Śiva mentally forsook Satī.

Such was the divine play of the Great God in which Satī acted her part as the mortal that she, the Great Goddess, had willed to become. All the same, the descent of the Great Goddess into human likeness, into the world, left intact her image as the Great Goddess who had stepped out of Ardhanārīśvara and, in a trice, had returned into him. The triple figures of Satī, of Kālikā, the cosmic goddess, and of the Great Goddess are overlapping transparencies on the luminous ground of Śiva Ardhanārīśvara.

The incarnation of the Great Goddess as Satī was her way back to Śiva through the failings and suffering of the human condition that she had chosen. When the first spring of their love was over and she had been with Śiva both as yoginī and loving woman, the young goddess became dissatisfied. Her mind needed answers that would clarify her longing for ultimate knowledge, her need for devotion, and the relation of both these essential strivings. She had assumed the role of a human being, and was born to a life of ease and elegance in Dakṣa's house. Though she had prepared herself for Śiva's ascetic ways and responded to them as being of his very nature, when exposed to the—not self-imposed—duress of living at the mercy of the elements, she turned petulant and was oblivious of Śiva's power. She began to doubt not only his actions but also his word, and by her lack of faith she lost the Great God. She had her own will; out of love for this stubborn child, he reluctantly let her have it, and she sought her own death out of love of Śiva as much as in anger for his humiliation by Dakṣa. She sacrificed herself in flames of anger, before the celebration of Dakṣa's sacrifice had begun. She regained her divinity and oneness with Śiva in the fire that consumed her body, while Śiva, moved by passion and compassion, could not overcome her loss.

c. *Renewed Humiliation of Śiva*

Śiva and Satī returned to the Himālayas. They lived on Mount Mandara whence, on occasion, they visited hallowed sites. Thus they attended a sacrifice held by the patriarchs and sages at Prayāga, at the confluence of the sacred rivers Gaṅgā and Yamunā. Śiva and Satī were already present when Dakṣa, the lord of patriarchs, arrived. Śiva did not rise and bow to Dakṣa as did the others assembled there. This insult infuriated Dakṣa. In his anger he accused Śiva of being like an outcast without religion and nobility, and cursed him to lose his share in the offerings (*BhP*.4.2.4-18). The curse only confirmed the status quo and gave it permanence (cf. Ch. III.2.b).

Dakṣa's curse was prompted by the insult to his pride. Actually, however, Śiva went against the very grain of Dakṣa (*VāP*.30.45-49), and Dakṣa's pent-up anger broke out in words of fury. Various *Purāṇas* show, by giving different reasons, or by stating that there was no reason (*BVP*.4.38.5), Dakṣa's deep-seated, congenital hatred of Śiva, who had let fly his arrow against Prajāpati / Brahmā, the father of Dakṣa. Dakṣa saw Śiva as shamelessly dwelling in cremation grounds, mad and vile, as well as absorbed in endless love making with Satī, the daughter he had given as a wife to Śiva. He had done it reluctantly, at Brahmā's command (*BhP*.4.2.4-16; *ŚP*.2.2.26.10-16). Dakṣa cursed Śiva to lose his share of the sacrifice (*BhP*.4.2.17-18; *ŚP*.2.2.26.18).

In his curse at the sacrifice in Prayāga, Dakṣa brought up to date and gave actuality to a situation that was not new to Śiva. He had been excluded from the sacrifice (*TS*.2.6.8.3; *GB*.2.1.2; *TmB*.7.9.16), and was treated as an outcast by the gods. They gathered and ate together, but they did not eat with Śiva. They contrived that no share of the offerings was to be assigned to Rudra in all sacrifices (*MBh*.10.18.2-4; 12.274.25-26; *VāP*.30.112-13; cf. *KūP*.1.14.8). At the sacrifice in Prayāga, Śiva's curse by Dakṣa was returned by Nandin, Śiva's chief of gaṇas and foremost devotee. He cursed Dakṣa to become a gross sensualist, worldly and vulgar. He would also be goat-faced (*BhP*.4.2.20-26; *ŚP*.2.2.26.30-39). This too was a dreadful curse, exposing pejoratively Dakṣa's nature, for this arch-patriarch with his bountiful progeny was the paradigm of the competent sacrificer and ritualist. The goat, if the least of the five kinds of sacrificial animals—man, horse, bull, ram, and goat—according to ancient tradition

(*ŚB*.10.2.1.1), remained the most common sacrificial victim. Besides, the goat was considered a lecherous animal. Dakṣa, as the account of the great sacrifice celebrated by him will show, indeed left it goat-headed (Ch. X.A.2.a). Iconographically, his goat head is Dakṣa's cognizance.

Hearing Nandin's curse, Śiva laughed and soothed his foremost devotee by making him understand that in truth Śiva had not been cursed, could not be cursed, being himself the sacrifice and the sacrificial rite as well as attached to and beyond the sacrifice (*ŚP*.2.2.26.43-47). Delighted, Śiva, accompanied by his gaṇas, left the assembly. Dakṣa, full of fury and ill will against Śiva, went to his home (*ŚP*.2.2.26.51-52).

When Śiva spoke of himself as being sacrifice and sacrificer in one, he referred to a time when he in the shape of Varuṇa performed a universal sacrifice. He, the foremost of the gods, so the *Mahābhārata* relates, assumed the shape of Varuṇa (*MBh*.13.85.1-2), the Overlord of the Universe (*RV*.2.28.6; 5.85.1; 7.82.2; 8.42.1).[6] All the gods, sages, *Vedas*, the *Upaniṣads*, the syllable *AUM*, Past, Present, and Future came to that sacrifice. The Great Lord offered himself as an oblation into himself. Then all the goddesses came to the sacrifice of Śiva / Varuṇa. When Brahmā, who acted as the main priest, saw the beautiful celestial women, he shed some seed on the earth. God Pūṣan gathered the seed and cast it as an oblation into the fire. From that seed offered into the fire all the sages arose, beginning with Bhṛgu, Aṅgiras, and Kavi, also the Rudras, Vasus, and Ādityas, the divisions of time, the stars, and planets (*MBh*.13.85.3-24). Though all of them were already present at the sacrifice, the myth relates how they came into being at this very sacrifice, accounting for the result by its cause, while reversing their sequence.

Mahādeva said, "This sacrifice is mine. I am the sacrificer. The first three offspring are mine" (*MBh*.13.85.25-26). Then Agni made a similar claim (*MBh*.13.85.27). Brahmā, however, declared as his own all that had come out of the sacrifice, for it was his seed that was poured into the fire whence everything had arisen (*MBh*.13.85.28-29). In the end all the gods praised Brahmā from whom the entire creation had sprung (*MBh*.13.85.30). On their pleading, Bhṛgu, the first-born of the sages, although born of Brahmā became Rudra's own child

[6] Cf. A. A. Macdonell, *Vedic Mythology*, p. 23.

(*MBh*.13.85.32). Aṅgiras became Agni's adopted son, and Kavi became Brahmā's son (*MBh*.13.85.33). The offspring of these three sages was to people the earth (*MBh*.13.85.35).

Rudra's role in the sacrifice was as the original impetus that brought it about and as the sacrificial act itself. Brahmā contributed his substance.

In this complex creation myth, which deviates from, though it is related to, the Rudra-Prajāpati creation myth (Ch. III.1), Rudra / Varuṇa as the Overlord of the Universe offered himself into creation. He claimed the outcome of the sacrifice as his own, just as he, in his horrendous shape of Paśupati, had claimed all that had remained after the lake of Prajāpati's seed had gone up in flames.

Rudra, lord of the sacrifice, in the shape of Varuṇa, the Overlord of the Universe, offered in his sacrifice his total self, like Puruṣa (*RV*.10.90). Brahmā, however, contributed the seed and substance to the sacrifice and made Rudra, the Lord of Yoga, the nominal and adoptive father of creation. Rudra in the *Ṛg Veda* was invoked, though once only, as "Father of the World" (*RV*.6.49.10) and its Lord (*RV*.2.33.9). Dakṣa, vituperating Rudra, had been unaware or oblivious of the position of Rudra, who was the sacrificer and the sacrifice.

When the rainy season had passed, Dakṣa himself, foremost of the patriarchs, the Prajāpatis, began the celebration of a great sacrifice (*VmP*.2.7) at Gaṅgādvāra in the foothills of the Himālayas (*VāP*.30.94). Dakṣa invited everyone, all his relatives, all the great gods, and the other celestials. He did not invite Rudra, his son-in-law, the husband of Satī, whom he had cursed at the sacrifice in Prayāga. This time his displeasure and disgust with Rudra was pinpointed on Rudra being a Kapālin, the bearer of the skull of Brahmā (*KP*.16.30-31; 17.7-12; 61.4-5; *VmP*.2.8-17; 4.1; cf. *KūP*.1.14.11; *ŚP*.2.2.27.22). Dakṣa's mind was full of Rudra, who had shown himself for what he was, Darkness (*tamas*) embodied, and he reviled Rudra for being naked, smeared all over with ashes of burnt corpses, wearing garlands of severed heads, and the bones of the dead as his ornaments. The hides of tiger and elephant dangled from his shoulders, his hair was disheveled as he roamed over cremation grounds like a madman, sometimes laughing, sometimes crying, a drunkard, riding a bull surrounded by ghastly hosts of ghouls, ghosts, and goblins, altogether impure (*PP*.5.5.42-50; *ŚP*.2.2.27.43-44; *BhP*.4.2.14-16). Having cut off the head of the Creator, Rudra had become macabre, gruesome, filthy, and demented in the eyes of Dakṣa, which was exactly how Rudra wanted to be seen, steeped in the horror of his own act, when he fulfilled his vow of expiation. Tormented, he had gone on his way to Release.

One day, Satī, who did not know of the great sacrifice that her father was about to hold at Gaṅgādvāra, saw the Moon with Rohiṇī going to Dakṣa's residence (*ŚP*.2.2.28.3). She told Vijayā, her lady-in-waiting, to ask the Moon where they were going (*ŚP*.2.2.28.5). When Vijayā brought back the news that it was to Dakṣa's sacrifice, Satī impetuously entered Śiva's council chamber and entreated him to come with her to her father's sacrificial hall. Śiva lovingly restrained her; did she not know, as Dakṣa did, that Śiva was his particular enemy? (*ŚP*.2.2.28.6-24). Śiva tried to dissuade Satī from a journey to her father's house, and firmly stated that he, not having been invited, was not going to Dakṣa's sacrifice (*ŚP*.2.2.28.25-30). He was not invited because he was Kapālin, he carried the skull of Brahmā, Dakṣa's father; Satī, being Kapālin's wife, was not invited, though she was Dakṣa's daughter. Little did Satī know that her father had given her in marriage to Śiva only because Brahmā had made him do so (*ŚP*.2.2.27.22-23, 42). Accepting Śiva's refusal to accompany her to Dakṣa's sacrifice, she won his permission to proceed to her father's house, for she was pained and anxious to know what was going on in the mind of Dakṣa and the assembled gods (*ŚP*.2.2.28.32-36). She went to Dakṣa's sacrifice in royal splendor, riding Śiva's richly ornamented bull and followed by sixty thousand of Śiva's attendants (*ŚP*.2.2.28.37-40). When they reached the gate of the sacrificial enclosure, Satī dismounted from Nandin (chief of the gaṇas, and Śiva's foremost attendant, who had the shape of a bull and the qualities of a noble devotee). She went alone inside the place of sacrifice and saw the portions laid out that had been allotted to all the gods. But nothing had been set apart for Śiva. She became intolerably angry (*ŚP*.2.2.29.1-7). Dakṣa wanted to know why she had come at all (*ŚP*.2.2.29.30). Forgetting the vow the goddess Kālikā had made him take before she became his daughter, that Satī would cast off her body should he treat her with disrespect, Dakṣa told Satī to her face that Śiva, king of ghosts, goblins, and spirits, of lowly origin, improperly and indecently dressed, had been accepted by him as his son-in-law because Brahmā induced him to this folly. But, as she had come all the way to the sacrifice, she could have her share (*ŚP*.2.2.29.31-34). Satī replied that she would cast off her body, abandon this contemptible body sprung from Dakṣa and gain happiness (*ŚP*.2.2.29.60-61). She added that Dakṣa himself, during the course of his sacrifice, would be killed by her lord, Mahādeva. He would be reborn as the son of the ten Pracetasas, not as a brahmin but as a kṣatriya (*MP*.13.13-15). Then the obscuration of Dakṣa's mind due to his anger left him and he saw Satī as the Mother of the Universe and prayed to her not to forsake him. He understood her resolve, but he was desperate. Fearing he had lost her, he wondered where he would ever find her again (*MP*.13.16-23). Satī consoled him by saying that "she was to be found at every time, in every region, in every being. There was nothing in the universe in which she was not to be found" (*MP*.13.24).[7]

She fell silent and became calm. Seated on the ground, she meditated on Śiva. She controlled her breath. Her inner, yogic fire consumed her body. Its ashes remained on the ground (*ŚP*.2.2.30.2-8; cf. *KūP*.1.13.59).

d. *The Agony of Śiva and Yakṣa Pāñcālika*

When Śiva heard of Satī's death, he tore out a bunch of his matted hair and threw it angrily at the top of the mountain. From his breath a hundred fevers were born (*ŚP*.2.2.32.20, 24).

Śiva went to Dakṣa's house and, after destroying the sacrifice, agreed to revive Dakṣa and the others, but Dakṣa would carry the head of a goat on his shoulders (*BhP*.4.7.2-3); or he cursed Dakṣa to be born in a kṣatriya family and to procreate a son in his own daughter (*KūP*.1.13.62). Creation by means of sexual intercourse would begin with the appearance of Dakṣa as the son of the Pracetasas (*LP*.1.63.2). Śiva gave vent to his rage by curses appropriate for Dakṣa, son of Brahmā / Prajāpati: Dakṣa would perform incest, a travesty of the primordial symbol of the violation of the Uncreate by Prajāpati. When Śiva came to the spot where Satī had consumed herself in the flames of her anger, Śiva smeared his body with her ashes. In agony and demented, he roamed over the country (*BVP*.4.43.27; 4.38.12-13). Or, according to another, tantric tradition, Satī's body that he had loved was still where she had shed it. Śiva, raving in fren-

[7] *Matsya Purāṇa (MP)*, tr. "A Taluqdar of Oudh," 1916, p. 41.

zied pain, embraced the dead body, his hot tears burnt the earth. The gods asked Śanaiścara, the planet Saturn, to hold the tears of Śiva, but Saturn was unable to contain them (*KP*.18.1-27). Śiva raised Satī's lifeless body and, placing it on his shoulders, balanced it on his head. He danced exceedingly, his arms flailing the regions. The stars were scattered by the swish of his hair. Death, love, and despair syncopated the escalating speed of his Tāṇḍava dance; the earth shook while Śiva went on dancing in frenzy, his eyes whirling. The gods wanted to calm him, and Viṣṇu thought of a device to end the orgiastic dance. As Śiva danced on and on, the body of Satī became lighter and lighter, and he saw that limbs and parts had fallen from it. Viṣṇu's disc had cut it part by part whenever Śiva's feet touched the earth. Śiva now had lost even the body of Satī, but then he saw her *yoni*, which had dropped in Kāmarūpa and had sunk into the netherworld. Shaken, Śiva changed into a mountain and in the shape of a rock *liṅga* upheld the *yoni*. Wherever a part of Satī had fallen there rose a *liṅga* (cf. *BDP*.1.40.13-54; cf. *DBhP*.7.30.44-50; cf. *KP*.18.36-54). Viṣṇu saved the earth from being shaken and destroyed by Śiva's impassioned dance, and Śiva became calm, though his sorrow did not leave him.

He had mentally forsaken Satī when she lived with him. She found him in the fire of her self-immolation. He clung to her charred, dead body, losing even that carnal residue of her existence, and turned into a rock to find permanent union with her in their symbol shape of *liṅga* and *yoni*. But this perennial symbol of his being, in the tantric context of this version of the myth, was a manifestation of a different kind from the one he assumed in his divine play, a manifestation of feeling and acting as a human being while also being a god. In this form he mourned Satī, wandering about distraught as if in search of her. Then Kāma espied Śiva. Kāma's five arrows may or may not have grazed Śiva in that Himālayan spring when Satī had lived with him, but now the arrow called "Maddening" smote Śiva and he went mad (*VmP*.6.26-27). Distraught, he roamed through the forests and fell into a river. The water was scorched by Śiva's heat and turned black. Thenceforward the water of the river Yamunā remained black (*VmP*.6.28-31), but Śiva wandered on in glades, along river beds, not knowing where he was, singing, wailing, weeping, brooding on Satī, dreaming of her. In his dreams he would implore her to return to him. When he awakened from his dream with a moan, Kāma smote him again (*VmP*.6.32-43). Smitten by the arrows "Insanity" (*unmāda*) and "Torment" (*santāpana*) Śiva noticed Yakṣa Pāñcālika, the son of Kubera, and transferred to Pāñcālika his insanity, torment, and yawning (*vijṛmbhaṇa*), for he knew Pāñcālika to be capable of bearing these afflictions (*VmP*.6.44-49). Pāñcālika took them over and Śiva bestowed a boon on Pāñcālika that "whoever will see you at any time in the month of Caitra, touch or worship you with devotion, be he an old man, a child, a young man, or a woman, shall go mad. O Yakṣa, they shall sing, dance, sport and play on their instruments with zeal."[8] Even as they speak mirthfully in front of Pāñcālika, they will have magic powers (*VmP*.6.50-53). It was in the spring, in the month of Caitra, that the magic of Yakṣa Pāñcālika had begun to work. Śiva's abysmal, crazed dance of mourning as he carried Satī's dead body had been changed, as if by a magic touch of the *yakṣa*; Śiva's madness had been converted into the lighthearted happiness of people dancing and singing and feeling the presence of Śiva, though they come in contact with a mere *yakṣa* only. In this way they would, unknown to themselves, celebrate the wedding anniversary of Lord Śiva. Satī, the bride of god, was present in them, as she was after her death in all beings (cf. *MP*.13.24).

When Śiva had sported with Satī in the spring of their love, the Great God was her gentle guide, initiating her into an understanding of herself, revealing to her the principle of life, and communicating to his beloved the presence of ultimate reality. In a vision, while meditating on him, she had seen him in divine radiance; at their wedding, she saw him as she beheld him in her vision, wearing all the shining ornaments of a bridegroom. Śiva had changed his frightening attire of the hunter and the yogi into dazzling splendor. She was not to know his fearsome shape, though Dakṣa had cursed it in her presence at the sacrifice in Prayāga. Her god and husband was her gentle, playful guide. He expected her to be strong in her faith, and when she doubted his word he abandoned her mentally and diverted her mind by telling her pleasant stories. She had failed in her devotion to him, although she had listened to Śiva's discourse on devotion (*bhakti*), the easy, pleasant path for those in the Kali Yuga. But this age had not come as yet, and Satī did not apply to herself Śiva's remarks. Her mind was shrouded in darkness, as was her body, like that of the Cosmic Goddess, whose incarnation she was. Down to the moment

[8] *Vāmana Purāṇa (VmP)*, ed. A. S. Gupta and tr. S. M. Mukhopadhyaya, A. Bhattacharya, N. C. Nath, and V. K. Verma, 1968, p. 30.

when she doubted Śiva—and realizing that Śiva had told her the truth, had returned to him—he had loved her so dearly that she seemed to enter his body, to be within him as she had been in Ardhanārīśvara. Mentally, Śiva abandoned her, only to love her the more when finally he lost her who sacrificed herself, albeit in anger, for the sake of her love for him. The young daughter of Dakṣa consecrated herself by her sacrifice, and Śiva, in pained frenzy, madly longed for her bodily nearness. Awake and asleep he dreamed of her, pleaded with her who was "constantly heard, seen, felt, admired, and embraced" (cf. *VmP*.6.38).[9] She was the true love of the Yogi who did not let his semen flow. Śiva's marriage with Satī had served Brahmā's purpose as little as did Śiva when he became Sthāṇu or plunged into the water.

Śiva transferred his woes to Yakṣa Pāñcālika, who would infect in the spring, in the month of Caitra, with contagious gaiety, dance, and music whomever might touch him.

Śiva unburdened his agonies on Yakṣa Pāñcālika. Obligingly, the *yakṣa* accepted them. By the alchemy of his *yakṣa* nature and the glance, touch, or devotion of a human being in the spring, in the month of Caitra, the woes of Śiva would turn into mirth, dance, and music. The pain and passion of the Great God, filtered through the *yakṣa*'s being, when touched by anyone, would turn into joy and creativity. The spring madness communicated by Yakṣa Pāñcālika, and rooted in the agony and passion of the Great God, informed a local celebration in the Pāñcāla country with intimations of deity. Śiva then bade Pāñcālika to journey through all the countries, bringing his spring miracle to everyone. Śiva then turned his steps toward the south, but there too Kāma pursued him and Śiva fled into the forest of Deodar trees (*VmP*.6.56-58; Ch. IX.6).

2. The Sacrifice of Dakṣa

a. *Destruction of the Sacrifice*

In the first shock of the news of Satī's death Śiva had torn out a fistful of hair. When he dashed it against the top of a mountain a terrific explosion was heard. The cluster of matted hair split into two halves. Vīrabhadra rose from one half of that cluster of hair (*ŚP*.2.2.32, 20-

[9] *Ibid.*, p. 28.

22). From the other half arose the dreadful Mahākālī (*ŚP*.2.2.25). This awful goddess was the female counterpart of Vīrabhadra. Elsewhere, however, it is said Vīrabhadra was created from Śiva's brow (*MBh*.12.274.36-38), while Bhadrakālī was born from the anger of the Great Goddess, just as Vīrabhadra was born from Rudra's anger (*MBh*.12, app. 1, no. 28, lines 118-19). Vīrabhadra, born from Śiva's potent hair, or from his mouth (*VāP*.30.122), was, like Puruṣa of the *Ṛg Veda*, of great strength and splendor, with a huge body, a great being (*VāP*.30.128-29). Like Puruṣa, the supernal male, he had a thousand heads, eyes, feet (*VāP*.30.123), but also terrible tusks projecting from his mouth (*VāP*.30.126) and numberless weapons (*VāP*.30.123-24). He had the size of any of the world mountains, was ablaze all over, and dripped with blood. The crescent moon shone on his head. He was girt with snakes, wore tiger and lion skins and a garland of flowers on his head. He was anointed with unguents and adorned with jewels. He rolled his eyes in rage. Sometimes he danced, sometimes he spoke sweetly or meditated intently. In short, he was a monstrous demon whose deceptive exterior disguised his true nature full of wisdom, detachment, sovereignty, asceticism, truth, patience, fortitude, lordship, and self-knowledge (*VāP*.30.125-36). He greatly resembled Śiva, whose emanation and emissary he was; or Śiva himself, according to an earlier account, destroyed the sacrifice (*MBh*. 12.274.31).

Vīrabhadra was charged by Śiva to destroy the sacrifice of Dakṣa, to burn Dakṣa, his wives and kinsmen, and to fell the gods Viṣṇu, Brahmā, and Indra (*ŚP*.2.2.32.47-58). Mahākālī, the active power of destruction, was accompanied by the nine Durgās (*ŚP*.2.2.33.11-12), whereas Vīrabhadra was followed by all the attendants of Rudra, who in hundreds of thousands had each assumed the shape of Rudra (*ŚP*.2.2.33.5). Over and above these, others joined the retinue of Vīrabhadra. There were thirty million dogs, born like Vīrabhadra himself of Śiva's hair (*ŚP*.2.2.33.36), the powerful issue of the one who as the Hound of Heaven scintillated from the *Ṛg Veda* sky (Ch. II.4). Śiva had remained faithful to his canine form. The dog stayed with him, his stately companion in his aspect of Bhairava, to which the South Indian image makers, in the beginning of the second millennium of our era, gave visible reality in art.

Vīrabhadra and his host set out in chariots drawn by ten thousand lions. Among his bodyguard were lions, tigers, crocodiles, fish, and elephants (*ŚP*.2.2.33.7-8). Sixty-four groups of angry yoginīs (divine sorceresses, demonesses, and fairies) and Ḍākinīs and Śākinīs, along with Bhūtas (ghosts), the *Pramathas* (churn spirits), the *Guhyakas* (guardians of hidden treasures), the *Bhairavas*, *Kṣetrapālas* (land guardians), and other types of spirits and fiends accompanied Vīrabhadra (*ŚP*.2.2.33.13-15).

Evil omens appeared: Dakṣa's left eye, arm, and thigh throbbed, stars shone billiantly in daylight, and thousands of vultures hovered over Dakṣa's head. Dakṣa and others vomited blood, pieces of flesh, and bones. Then darkness set in; it was shot across by a peculiar blaze. The gods fell senseless to the ground. There they lay like dead serpents, or they bounced up again like balls; they rolled and dashed against each other like tortoises. All the gods, even Viṣṇu, had their powers blunted (*ŚP*.2.2.34.2-20). After a great battle, the gods and others were put to flight and went to their respective worlds (*ŚP*.2.2.36.16-18). They came to understand that the whole catastrophe was brought about by Satī (*ŚP*.2.2.37.42).

The gods having left, all who depended on sacrifices were defeated. On seeing the destruction of the sacrifice, the sacrifice itself was frightened and, taking the shape of an antelope, it fled. Vīrabhadra seized the sacrifice in the form of an antelope fleeing up to the sky and beheaded it (*ŚP*. 2.2.37.44-46). This done, Vīrabhadra kicked the patriarchs and sages on their heads (*ŚP*.2.2.37.48). Caṇḍa, the Fierce, pulled out the teeth of Pūṣan, because—according to the *Śiva Purāṇa*—Pūṣan had shown his teeth when he laughed while Śiva was cursed by Dakṣa (*ŚP*.2.2.37.54). Nandin tore out the eyes of Bhaga, who had winked, approvingly, at Dakṣa uttering his curse (*ŚP*. 2.2.37.55). Vīrabhadra, in person, with the tip of his fingers cut off the nose of Sarasvatī, the consort of Brahmā (*ŚP*.2.2.37.49). Dakṣa, who was hiding behind the altar, was dragged out by Vīrabhadra, who tore off the head of Dakṣa—as Śiva had severed Brahmā's head—and threw it into the sacrificial fire pit, a last sacrificial offering (*ŚP*.2.2.37.58-61). When the entire sacrificial site with all that was left on it was burnt, Vīrabhadra's laugh rang across the three worlds. Flowers from the celestial gardens were wafted over Vīrabhadra by a cool, fragrant breeze as he, having accomplished his task, went to Kailāsa, to Lord Śiva (*ŚP*.2.2.37.63-67).

In other versions of the destruction of Dakṣa's sacrifice Śiva himself was the destroyer. In the evening, after the destruction, Śiva danced (*NŚ*.4.234).

A cycle had come to a close. Dakṣa's head was cut off by Vīrabhadra / Śiva in retribution for Dakṣa's not having invited Śiva to his sacrifice on account of Śiva being a Kapālin, having cut off the fifth head of Brahmā, Dakṣa's father. Dakṣa, carrying out Brahmā's will, had reluctantly become Śiva's father-in-law. He had to pay with his own head for having slighted Śiva, just as Brahmā had. Dakṣa's beheading was not only an aftermath but also a kind of replay in the chain of these beheadings.

After the destruction of Dakṣa's sacrifice, the defeated and mutilated gods went to Brahmā, and related their defeat. Brahmā was pained on account of Dakṣa, his son, whom he wanted to see restored to life and his sacrifice continued. Brahmā and the gods resolved to go to Kailāsa and ask Śiva's forgiveness (*ŚP*.2.2.40.3-6, 20-22). They found the Lord under the shady branches of his *vaṭa* (fig) tree where he went to practice yoga (*ŚP*.2.2.40.35-37). The gods eulogized the Lord as an ocean of mercy, Aṣṭamūrti, the primordial lord, and they asked him to revive both the uncompleted sacrifice of Prajāpati Dakṣa and Dakṣa himself, and to restore the organs and limbs of the mutilated gods. The gods promised that Śiva would be allotted his share in the sacrifice (*ŚP*.2.2.41.44-51). Śiva, acknowledging his delusion of the gods by his inscrutable *māyā* (*ŚP*.2.2.42.4), stated clearly that the destruction of Dakṣa's sacrifice was not *his* work, for if one hates another, it will recoil on him (*ŚP*.2.2.42.5). Lord Śiva then decreed that god Bhaga should again see by the eye of the sun, but Pūṣan would remain toothless (*ŚP*.2.2.42.7-8). Then Śiva, accompanied by the gods and sages, proceeded to the site of the sacrifice, where he saw the destruction that Vīrabhadra had wrought (*ŚP*.2.2.42.13-15). At Śiva's command, Vīrabhadra quickly threw Dakṣa's headless body in front of Śiva, and the gods put the head of a goat, the sacrificial animal, on the body of Dakṣa. Śiva glanced at the head joined to the body, and Dakṣa, regaining life, awoke as if from a deep sleep. Dakṣa was about to praise Lord Śiva but was overcome with emotion and love for Satī, his dead daughter. When he calmed down, he who formerly had hated Śiva now praised him (*ŚP*.2.2.42.21-32). Dakṣa completed the sacrifice and gave Śiva his full share in the sacrifice (*ŚP*.2.2.43.25-26).

Though Dakṣa's sacrifice was part of Śiva's divine play, it was the culmination of Rudra's aeviternal struggle for recognition by those gods who had been critical of him from the beginning. As described in the *Śiva Purāṇa*, the pageantry of Dakṣa's sacrifice served a moral. Earlier versions were free from this. Moreover, paradoxically, the plot of Dakṣa's sacrifice (*MBh*.12.274.23-26) had its precedent in which Dakṣa did not figure at all. There, it was the gods who excluded Rudra from the sacrifice (cf. *MBh*.10.18.2-4). Rudra's exclusion from the sacrifice, whether by the gods or by Dakṣa, and his winning his share by destroying the sacrifice, became the recurring themes in common to all versions of the myths (cf. *TS*.2.6.8.3; *ŚB*.1.7.4.1-17). This main theme, however, was the consequence, and served as a cloak to cover a fundamental situation: the assault by Rudra of the Father, Prajāpati. Rudra's arrow had pierced Prajāpati, the Creator / Progenitor, the god, the antelope. This was the primeval myth. Acted out ritually, Rudra pierced Prajāpati, the sacrifice.

Wounded Prajāpati, the antelope, the embodiment of the sacrifice, who had cohabited with his daughter in the shape of a female antelope, sprang up to heaven and, blazing in beauty, became the constellation Mṛga, the Antelope. Rudra, the hunter who followed the antelope across the sky, became the star Mṛgavyādha, the Hunter of the Antelope (*AB*.3.33; cf. *MS*.4.2.12; cf. *ŚB*.2.1.2.9; cf. *VāP*.30.157; cf. *MBh*.10.18.13-14; cf. *VmP*.5.26-27; cf. *LP*.1.100.34-35; cf. *ŚP*.2.2.37.45-46). The gods themselves had urged Rudra to pierce Prajāpati (*ŚB*.1.7.4.3, 4).

"When the anger of the gods subsided, they cured Prajāpati and cut out that dart of this (Rudra); for Prajāpati, doubtless, is this sacrifice" (*ŚB*.1.7.4.4).[10] The gods were anxious to save this small part of the sacrifice, this morsel of the Creator's body pierced by the arrow of Rudra. It should not get lost, should not be wasted. Small as it was, it should be the first part of the offering (*prāśitra*) (*GB*.2.1.2). The gods had it taken to Bhaga to eat. Bhaga looked at it. It burned his eyes and he became blind. They had it taken to Pūṣan, who tasted it and lost his teeth. It was not yet appeased. It was then taken to Bṛhaspati, the lord of the creative Word. He took it to Savitṛ, the "Impeller" (of the sun). He "impelled" it, and it did not harm him. It was appeased (*ŚB*.1.7.4.5-8; *GB*.2.1.2; cf. *TS*.2.6.8.3-6; cf. *KB*.6.13). Some *Purāṇas*, speaking about the gods injured by Rudra at the sacrifice, add to the

[10] *Śatapatha Brāhmaṇa (ŚB)*, tr. J. Eggeling, 1963, part I, p. 210.

ubiquitous figures of Bhaga and Pūṣan that of Kratu (the Sacrifice). Bhaga and Pūṣan lost their eyes and teeth, respectively, whereas Rudra cut off the testicles of Kratu. Kratu fell to the ground, his organ of procreation having been pierced (*VrP*.33.10-11; cf. *SkP*.4.2.89.43-44).

Although, in this account, Kratu is coordinated with the other gods at the sacrifice, the memory of the Vedic context knows that Rudra wounded the generative organ of Prajāpati, Kratu, the sacrifice. The small bit that the gods had cut out of Prajāpati was magically potent: it was that part of the Lord of Generation that had felt the entry of the arrow of Rudra and was in immediate contact with its searing thrust. It held the power of Rudra's arrow even when cut out of Prajāpati. That danger-laden morsel had to be offered right back to the source, to the lord of the creative Word, to Savitṛ, the Impeller of the sun, the vivifying power that illumines the cosmos and the mind.

The gods excluded Rudra from the sacrifice. They well knew for what reason. But then in a hysteron proteron, it is implied that Rudra pierced the sacrifice because the gods excluded him from the sacrifice (*TS*.2.6.8.3). Because they assigned no share to him, Rudra went after them and pierced the sacrifice. This inversion was a "translation" of the tremendous primordial mystery from mythical event into ritual performance. Because Rudra's arrow had struck Prajāpati, the Lord of Generation, the gods excluded Rudra from the sacrifice in the hope that the sacrifice would be effective for them. Then, Rudra pierced the sacrifice.

Mythically, Rudra pierced Prajāpati, the Lord of Generation, only once. This mythical feat was enacted ritually by Rudra piercing the sacrifice. It was now the task of the gods to propitiate Rudra by ritual means so that the sacrifice should be well offered and benefit them.

Whatever the first part of the offering may have been physically, symbolically it was the morsel of the Creator's body pierced by the arrow of Rudra. Its power was devastating. It deprived the gods of vision and creative potency. The teeth of Pūṣan symbolized the latter.[11] It was Pūṣan who cast Brahmā's seed into the sacrificial fire (Ch. X.A.1.c). Only Savitṛ himself, the Impeller of solar power, of light, sight, and creativeness, could appease the rabid morsel.

[11] S. Kramrisch, "Pūṣan," 1961, p. 120, referring to *BhP* 6.6.41, "Pūṣan became childless."

The primordial myth told in the *Ṛg Veda* and its ritual reenactment as described in the *Yajur Veda* and the *Brāhmaṇas* are substantially identical. The bridge from the aeviternal meaning of the myth to its sacrificial symbol connects different levels, one of intuited vision, the other of ritual practice. In consequence of the mythical assault against Prajāpati by Rudra, the seed of the Creator fell on the earth, which is the place of sacrifice, whatever be the location of any particular celebration. Mythically, the gods cut out of the body of Prajāpati the arrow stuck in the wound. As soon as it was seen, the perfervid might of this "fore-offering" assaulted the gods. Finally, they were able to allay its fierceness by offering it to Savitṛ, the Impeller. Ritual practice had for its model a myth, the myth of the dangerous, wounded spot of Prajāpati's body. Because it had been potent, endangered, and wounded, it became dangerous: the danger-causing arrow had stuck in it. The star myth of Prajāpati, the antelope, and the hunter in the sky had its ritual equivalent in the myth of the wounded flesh of Prajāpati and Rudra's arrow, which had inflicted the wound.

In Dakṣa's sacrifice, Vīrabhadra / Rudra pursued the antelope to the sky and beheaded the antelope, the sacrifice. Caṇḍa, the Violent, a subform of Rudra, knocked out the teeth of Pūṣan, and Nandin plucked out the eyes of Bhaga; Vīrabhadra cut off the nose of Sarasvatī and crushed Bhṛgu, whose moustache was torn out by Maṇibhadra (*ŚP*.2.2.37.45-55). The emanations and acolytes of Śiva impersonated the angry morsel charged with Rudra power, which the gods had cut out of the wounded, killed, or sacrificed Prajāpati.

The primordial sacrifice in which the Father / Prajāpati was the victim, the paradigmatic ritual sacrifice celebrated by the gods, and the sacrifice of Prajāpati Dakṣa succeeded and substituted for one another in the ongoing myth of Rudra.

According to the *Mahābhārata*, the sacrifice, following the primordial sacrificial pattern, was offered by the gods after the Kṛta Yuga had passed. Rudra was excluded from the sacrifice because the gods did not know him truly. Though he looked like a *brahmacārin*, clad in an antelope skin, he also carried a bow; he was Mahādeva, the Great God, whom the other gods had not recognized and to whom they had assigned no share. Enraged, Rudra went to the sacrifice and, while the earth trembled and the stars wandered in irregular courses, his arrow pierced the heart of the embodied sacrifice; in the shape of an antelope it fled to heaven. After the sacrifice had fled along with Agni, the sacrificial fire, the gods lost their creative powers. Rudra deprived Bhaga of his eyes and Pūṣan of his teeth. Laughing aloud, he paralyzed the other gods. They sought his protection. Gratified, Rudra threw his burning wrath into the ocean. There it dwelled, drinking the water of the ocean incessantly (*MBh*.10.18.1-21). Appeased, Rudra restored the mutilated gods. They assigned to Mahādeva all the oblations as his share (*MBh*.10.18.22-24). The Great God here appeared cruel and kind in one, that is, in his pristine nature.

Rudra / Mahādeva in this amplified version played the part of the baneful *prāśitra*, which in turn had contained his destructive power. In other words, Rudra destroyed the sacrifice from which the gods had excluded him. Having destroyed it, he made it whole again and won his share in the sacrifice. No wonder the gods did not know Rudra truly; it was difficult to know him, the Great God who was and looked like an ascetic and acted like a demon. They could not make sense of him, let alone make a *mantra* or poem, as the gods of the *Ṛg Veda* had done when they saw the Wild God, the formidable archer.

Fighting for his place in the sacrifice, Rudra gained a precarious admission to the world of the gods. He had to be born from Prajāpati, the Father; he had to receive from his mouth the names by which he was invested with the cosmos and became Mahādeva, the Great God. By his birth and the receiving of his names he was freed from evil. Even so, he remained outside the pale of the other gods, who celebrated sacrifices and received their share in them. Whereas the Father, Prajāpati, the Creator, had become Rudra's victim and made Rudra his son, Rudra did not gain recognition from the sacrificing gods. To gain admission to the sacrifice and the world of the gods Rudra, paradoxically, had to reenact his primordial feat. His shot now was aimed at the sacrifice. The sacrifice took the shape of an antelope, the same shape in which Prajāpati had become the target of the Wild Hunter. Prajāpati attacked by Rudra made him Paśupati, Lord of Animals.

Dakṣa appeared first in the myth of Rudra and the sacrifice in two other versions in the *Mahābhārata*. In both these versions Pārvatī and not Satī was the wife of Rudra (*MBh*.12.274.7 and 12, app. 1, no. 28, line 69). Satī does not appear in the *Mahābhārata*. Vīrabhadra, on the other hand, has his origin recorded in the *Mahābhārata*, obliquely in one instance (*MBh*.12.274.36-40) and directly in the other (*MBh*.12, app. 1, no. 28, lines 70-80). According to the first account, due to

Śiva's hot rage for not having been invited to the sacrifice, a drop of sweat fell on the earth from the forehead of Śiva, who was pursuing the fleeing antelope, the sacrifice, to the sky. From the blazing fire that shot up on the spot a dreadful being arose, covered with hair all over its black skin. It had bloodshot eyes and was dressed in the color of blood. That being devoured the antelope, the embodiment of the sacrifice. It then attacked the gods at Dakṣa's sacrifice. At the request of Brahmā, this fearful creature was made to wander over the earth and was named Fever, the dreadful energy of Mahādeva. Śiva distributed it in the earth as bitumen of the mountains, as a throat disease of horses, as a bilious attack in everyone, as hiccups of parrots, and in many other pains in which it was to enter tigers, men, and Vṛtra, the cosmic serpent (*MBh.* 12.274.23-56). Because fever is the dreadful energy of Śiva, none but Śiva can remove it. Thus Śiva is shown in his form of Jvarahareśvara, the lord who removes fever, dancing three-legged like an off-balance Naṭarāja, one arm thrown across his body pointing to the raised leg that gives grace and dances away the fever.[12] Elsewhere, however, it is said that the drop of sweat that fell from Śiva's forehead, on falling to the earth, became Vīrabhadra (*MP*.72.11-13). Or Vīrabhadra emanated from the mouth of Rudra (*MBh.*12, app. 1, no. 28, lines 70-71), and confined his destructive activity to the sacrifice of Dakṣa. Born from the contact of Śiva's hair and the rock, Vīrabhadra's birth also fulfilled different conventions established in Śiva's myth.

After Vīrabhadra destroyed the sacrifice, Śiva himself arose from the sacrificial pit and Dakṣa adored him in a hymn celebrating the one thousand and eight names of the Lord (*MBh.*12, app. 1, no. 28, lines 140-55). The emergence of Śiva, effulgent in glory and smiling, from the sacrificial pit in the narrative of the *Mahābhārata* took the place of Śiva's becoming Paśupati in the account of the *Maitrāyaṇī Saṃhitā* (4.2.12) and the *Brāhmaṇas* (cf. *AB*.3.33) and in the narrative of the *Purāṇas*.

b. *The Lord of Animals and the Pāśupata Vow*

Primordially, Rudra was made Paśupati, Lord of Animals, by Prajāpati for sparing his life; he earned this title anew in the course of his

[12] P. Z. Pattabiramin, "Notes d'iconographie dravidienne: III. Jvarahareśvara ou Jvaradeva," 1959, pp. 20-24, pl. 69.

ongoing myth. It acquired a new actuality. After Śiva had defeated the gods in Dakṣa's sacrifice, they were helpless. Their divine, creative powers had been taken from them. Deprived of their faculties of knowledge, they were reduced to the condition of animals. Because the gods had not given him his share of the sacrifice, Śiva had taken away their creative powers. Then the gods in their plight praised Śiva, as he decreed that they all were animals (*paśu*) and Śiva, their lord (*pati*), would release them. Śiva became the Lord of Animals, Paśupati. He gave back to Pūṣan his teeth, to Bhaga his eyes, and to each god his creative power and understanding (*VrP*.21.78-82; 33.25-28; cf. *MBh*.10.18.22-23). The gods recognized Śiva as the primordial and eternal lord of redeeming knowledge, the Lord of Animals, Paśupati.

Rudra reduced the gods to the state of animals. He made them animals in order to save them. He became the redeemer of those who had become his creatures (*paśu*). In the primordial scene, the Father / Prajāpati *was* the animal whose life Rudra saved. At the site of Dakṣa's destroyed sacrifice, the gods had to be humbled by Rudra; they had to become animals before Rudra could save them. The anguish of the creatures made possible their salvation. Paśupati, Lord of Animals, was the Lord and Savior of those who had been gods and who, fallen from their divinity by their pride as participants in Dakṣa's sacrifice, had become animals (*paśu*).

Rudra, the hunter of the antelope (*mṛga*), is the Lord of Animals, Paśupati. *Paśu*, as a rule, is taken to designate the tame, domestic animals or cattle such as belonged to Rudra in the sacrifice of the Aṅgirases. He made them over to Nābhānediṣṭha (Ch. III.2). Rudra as Śarva was a slayer of man and cattle. Because he was a slayer of cattle, the gods who had divided the sacrificial animals among themselves reluctantly gave Rudra a portion of the sacrifice (*TmB*.7.9.16-18). The animals (*paśu*), however, that Rudra claimed as his own from the ashes of the burned-out lake of Prajāpati's sperm included different kinds of antelopes, buffalo, camel, ass, tame and wild animals (*AB*.3.34). Similarly, animals that live in the air, in forest, and village are collectively called *paśu* (*RV*.10.90.8).[13] Man too is included among the *paśu* (*RV*.3.62.14).

The Pāśupata doctrine, one of five schools of religious doctrines mentioned in the *Mahābhārata* (*MBh*.12.337.59, 62), relates the animal

[13] Cf. *Ṛg Veda Saṃhitā (RV)*, tr. K. F. Geldner, 1951, 3:288.

(*paśu*), that is, the creature, the human being, or "soul" (*ātman*), to the Lord (*pati*) who breaks the snare (*pāśa*) that binds the unredeemed human being to worldly existence and its objects (*LP.*1.80.1). "Salvation in Pāśupata doctrine is the state called End of Sorrow (duḥkhānta)."[14] ". . . it is achieved only by the grace of God. Preliminary to this final liberation, however, is Yoga, . . . 'the union of the *ātman* and Īśvara.' The soul does not become absorbed or dissolved in Īśvara . . . but remains inseparably tied to God in the state . . . called *Rudrasāyujya*" (cf. *PS.*5.33).[15]

Although the Pāśupata doctrine may appear to be grafted onto the myth of Dakṣa's sacrifice, the two are intrinsically connected. They stem from the primordial scene and preserve its metaphysical ontology in terms of myth and religion. At the time of the *Purāṇas*, the Pāśupata doctrine had long been established.[16] Śiva himself had announced that by the power of his yogic illusion he would appear as a *brahmacārin* who, having entered a corpse on the cremation ground, would be known as Lakulin. This would come about at the holy site of Kāyāvatāra, the "Descent into a Corpse," the present-day Karvan, near Baroda. There, also, four ascetic sons would be born to Śiva (*LP.*1.24.127-32; *VāP.*23.219-24). The prophecy of Śiva referred to himself as Lakulīśa, the founder of the Pāśupata order, who most probably lived in the first half of the second century A.D.[17] The four sons—or disciples—represent the four sects following the Pāśupata doctrine.

In the first age of the gods, Prajāpati had given to Rudra the lordship over animals. Rudra became Paśupati. When this perfect age, the Kṛta Yuga, had passed,[18] Śiva gave the Pāśupata religion to Dakṣa, the son of Brahmā, Brahmā having taken over from Prajāpati the role of creator. A cycle had come to a close between Prajāpati, the Lord of Generation, and Prajāpati Dakṣa, the patriarch.

After the destruction of the sacrifice, Śiva manifested in glory, aris-

[14] D. N. Lorenzen, *The Kāpālikas and Kālāmukhas: Two Lost Śaivite Sects*, 1972, p. 191.

[15] *Ibid.*, p. 191.

[16] *Ibid.*, pp. 179-80, 182.

[17] *Ibid.*, pp. 180-81.

[18] The chronology according to yugas adopted here and elsewhere for the sake of a coherent narrative, though post-Ṛg Vedic, goes back to the beginning of the first millennium B.C.

ing from the sacrificial pit, and granted Dakṣa the boon of the restoration of the sacrifice. Dakṣa praised Śiva by uttering his thousand and eight names (*MBh*.12, app. 1, no. 28, lines 140-55). Carried away by their power and his own emotion, he concluded the hymn by stating the reason for not having invited Śiva to the sacrifice. Since Rudra was the creator, master, and indwelling spirit of all creatures—since Rudra was adored in all sacrifices—therefore Dakṣa had not invited him to his sacrifice (lines 381-84). Or perhaps Dakṣa failed to invite Śiva because he was stupefied by Śiva's power of delusion (lines 385-86). Śiva in his grace did not doubt the sincerity, and overlooked the discrepancies in Dakṣa's statement, that is, his sweeping eulogy of Śiva's universal acceptance at the sacrifice as the reason for his not inviting Śiva, while at the same time admitting that his delusion was the cause for not having invited Śiva. Dakṣa was no longer aware that he had stigmatized Rudra as a Kapālin, that he had even refused to know of Rudra's existence, when at the beginning of the sacrifice he had said that he knew many Rudras, he knew the eleven Rudras, but did not know Maheśvara (*BrP*.39.30-33; *MBh*.12, app. 1, no. 28, lines 40-41; *VāP*.30.105). Śiva granted Dakṣa salvation (*sāyujya*). Śiva made Dakṣa a leader of his host, the gaṇas (*LP*.1.100.49). Dakṣa would therefore dwell close to Paśupati on Mount Kailāsa when Śiva resided in his city called Bhogya, the Enjoyable (cf. *LP*.1.80.2).

c. *The City Called Bhogya*

Śiva lived in different styles in the Himālayan altitudes. He had no house, no shelter for himself and for Satī, his bride. He was an ascetic and at the same time newly married; he could be both, for he was the Wild God sporting in the forest, or taking his ease on a cloud. Nevertheless, for granting a sight of himself to the gods who had been *paśus*, Paśupati resided in his palace in Bhogya (*LP*.1.80.1-3). This city was built in eleven concentric and superimposed rings around the peak called Kailāsa. Viśvakarman, the architect of the gods, had built the palaces, mansions, and ramparts within the walls of the cities and their gate structures. The palace of Śiva was in the highest, the eleventh, city, which was perfectly round, right on the peak of Kailāsa (*LP*.1.80.9-23).

The city was full of beautiful women of the Rudras, gaṇas, and *siddhas*; there were thousands of Rudrakanyās, the Rudra virgins adept at conversation and music, both vocal and instrumental. Their eyes were roving, for the girls were slightly drunk. Many dancers lived in the city of Śiva, with Gandharvas and Apsarases, *yakṣas* and serpents. All were splendidly dressed in different fashions and jewelry, and all the people in Śiva's city were fond of pleasure and love (*LP*.1.80.30-40). The elegant and luxurious costumes of the people in Bhogya apparently had much to hide, for as is stated in one text, gods, sages, and people are born without clothes, but because they do not control their sense organs, they cover them with clothes (*BP*.1.2.27.118-19).

Dakṣa who had been cursed to be a sensualist, was now rewarded with a sight of the peak of delight in Śiva's city of Bhogya. Having lost his head in the destruction of his sacrifice, Dakṣa had been made whole again by the gods, who had put a goat's head on Dakṣa's shoulders, and Śiva's glance gave Dakṣa new life. In this restored identity Dakṣa won liberation on seeing Paśupati in his city of delights, where Śiva resided on appropriate occasions, away from what is called the world of shame, delusion, and fear that he had created (*BP*.1.2.27.117), a world of *paśus*, although he had refused Brahmā's command to create such a world (Ch. VI.1, 3).

The atmosphere of the city of Bhogya, heavy with the scent of flowers and women, though it lacked the fresh air of the mountain groves where Śiva used to sport with Satī, was free from the macabre fumes that rose toward Śiva's residence in Avimukta. There, high up in *ākāśa*, Śiva dwelt liberated from having been Kapālin, the bearer of Brahmā's skull. In Bhogya, Śiva, the Lord of Yoga, resided as *bhogī*. Yoga and *bhoga* (sensual enjoyment) seem diametrically opposed in human experience. Śiva, however, the Lord of Yoga, considered himself a yogi having supreme gnosis and a *bhogī* in full control of his senses (*ŚP*.2.2.10.25). Śiva imparted the Pāśupata Vrata, the Pāśupata vow and faith, to the assembled gods who had come to Bhogya for this purpose (*LP*.1.80.1-2, 54-56). The Pāśupata vow is a sacrament of fire and ashes. When the doomsday fire breaks out of Śiva's third eye, all creation is destroyed. Similarly, everything creaturely is destroyed in those who take upon themselves the Pāśupata vow. It rests on the knowledge that existence is a relation of consumer and consumed. Fire is the consumer and Soma, the essence of life, is the stuff consumed. Ashes are the very potency of Śiva. Whatever has become ashes has become sacred. By daubing the body with ashes, and having controlled anger and the senses, all sins are destroyed and there will be no more rebirth (cf. *BP*.1.2.27.86-88, 106-24).[19]

Śiva had danced for Ṛṣi Maṅkaṇaka the dance of Time. The earth had been shaken by the ṛṣi's jubilant dance when he had discovered that plant sap instead of blood flowed through his veins; Śiva put a stop to the sage's exuberance by dancing himself before Ṛṣi Maṅkaṇaka. The elation was halted when he saw the lightness of Śiva's dance, light as ashes. Śiva cut one of his own fingers and white ashes dusted the ground (*VmP*, *SM*.17.7-15). White and weightless, they showed to the sap-inspired ṛṣi a freedom from turbulence that the miraculous change in his own body, from blood to plant sap, had failed to achieve. But when Śiva anointed his body with ashes, they were those of Satī, who had consumed her body in the yoga fire of her love and anger. Now that she no longer existed in the body, her ashes cooled the agony Śiva suffered by being separated from her.[20]

Ashes are a potent and ambivalent dust of cooled embers, the product of fire and matter that have ceased to be. Having gone through fire, they not only are purified matter but themselves purify. Symbolically they are the essence, the spirit of matter, set free. They not only purify but are said to protect from evil the house of childbirth, in particular (*BP*.1.2.27.114). Even so, from ashes the fields are made fertile. Those who were covered with ashes, in control of their senses, calm, and came to Śiva attained Release (*BP*.1.2.27.115).[21] For those who had undertaken the Pāśupata vow the delights Bhogya had to offer were immaterial; they were able to enjoy without attachment whatever the city had to offer. According to Śiva's teachings, the sins of his devotees are destroyed after they bathe in ashes and meditate on Lord Śiva (*BP*.1.2.27.121-22), and tripling their effort and having thrice bathed in ashes they become Gaṇapatis or lords of Śiva's host (*BP*.1.2.27.122-23), like Dakṣa. Those who would meditate and go northward obtain immortality (*BP*.1.2.27.124); those who turn south to the cremation grounds, understanding the eight qualities of Śiva, become immortal (*BP*.1.2.27.124-26). Embodied as Lakulīśa in Kāyāvatāra, Śiva taught the Pāśupata doctrine on earth.

[19] Cf. W. D. O'Flaherty, *Asceticism and Eroticism in the Mythology of Śiva*, pp. 246-47.

[20] *Ibid.*, p. 245, where the erotic and creative significance of ashes is stressed. Here it is subsumed to their soothing effect on Śiva's agony.

[21] "There is nothing higher than the *Pāśupata vrata*" (*BP*.1.2.27.116).

d. *The Antelope*

In the myth of Śiva, the goat as sacrificial as well as demonic and lecherous animal was associated with Dakṣa. Its significance is less pervasive than that of the antelope.

From Vedic time, the antelope, a denizen of untamed nature, was the animal figure of Prajāpati in the spontaneity of his intercourse with his daughter. Rudra shot Prajāpati the antelope. Prajāpati—in a way even in this myth—sacrificed himself into creation, spent himself while creating. In the myth of the *Śatapatha Brāhmaṇa* (Ch. IX.3), Prajāpati, exhausted from creation, collapsed and fell apart (*ŚB*.6.1.2.12). Conceptualized as the year, Prajāpati of the *Śatapatha Brāhmaṇa* spent himself into creation (*ŚB*.6.1.2.18). He filled with his content the year, the unit of cyclical time. He was built up by the gods in the shape of the Vedic altar (*ŚB*.6.1.2.13-22). The human sacrificer imitated their example and by complex architectural rites built up the sacrifice in the shape of the altar. [22] Prajāpati was the sacrifice and the year (*ŚB*.11.1.1.1); and Prajāpati was the altar (*ŚB*.10.1.3.5). In the *Mahābhārata* and the *Purāṇas*, however, the sacrifice, threatened with destruction by Rudra / Vīrabhadra, fled to the sky in the shape of an antelope (*VmP*.5.26-27; *MBh*.12.274.34-35). It took its flight in the same figure in which Prajāpati had been shot at by Rudra.

Vedic Prajāpati, the antelope, frightened to death by Rudra, the Wild Hunter, made him Paśupati, Lord of Animals, for sparing Prajāpati's life. In Dakṣa's sacrifice as told in the *Mahābhārata*, however, the antelope, the "personified" sacrifice, was struck by Rudra's arrow right in the heart (*MBh*.10.18.13; cf. *LP*.1.100.34-35; cf. *ŚP*.2.2.37.45-46), and leapt up and fled to heaven, pursued forever by the Hunter of the Antelope. Mṛgavyādha, the hunter of the antelope, up in the sky is the star name of Rudra, the Lord of Animals, Paśupati.

Prajāpati Dakṣa, patriarch and sacrificer, his own head having been thrown into the sacrificial fire as a last offering, was given the head of a goat when his sacrifice was restored and completed by Śiva. When represented in art, the identity of Dakṣa is immediately recognizable by his head of a goat, though Agni on one occasion assumed the face

[22] *Śatapatha Brāhmaṇa (ŚB)*, tr. J. Eggeling, 1963, part III, p. 150 n. 3, where Eggeling notes that the restoring of Prajāpati is "symbolically identified with the building up of the fire-altar."

of a goat to amuse his child Kārttikeya (*MBh*.3.215.23). This was in character for the myth in which Agni lusted after the *kṛttikās*, the wives of the ṛṣis, who became the "mothers" of Kārttikeya.

The goat was the last and least of the five animals offered in Vedic sacrifices (cf. *ŚB*.10.2.1.1). The sacrificer redeemed himself by the animal that he offered (*ŚB*.11.7.1.3). Most anciently, the five kinds of sacrificial victims were man, horse, bull, ram, and goat (*ŚB*.10.2.1.1). Subsequently the goat alone remained the sacrificial animal (*ŚB*.6.2.1.5, 39; 6.2.2.1-6) that functioned as a proxy for the human sacrificer, for his animal nature that he sacrificed. By sacrificing it he consecrated himself.

The black antelope skin, on the other hand, symbolized the sacrifice itself (*ŚB*.6.4.1.6; 12.8.3.3; 14.1.2.2). The *brahmacārin* was clothed in a black antelope skin (*AV*.11.5.6). The rite of consecration was performed on a black antelope skin (*ŚB*.1.1.4.3; 3.2.1.1). During the year of initiation, the sacrificer wore a circular gold plate suspended on a triple cord of hemp from his neck down to his navel. The golden disc had twenty-one knobs comprising symbolically the totality of space and time. This golden disc was the sun, the twenty-one knobs its rays. Wearing the golden disc, man was transfigured from his human existence into his divine essence, for only then was he able to bear the fire of the sun, its seminal vital energy (*ŚB*.6.7.1.1-8). The golden disc was "sewn up in a black antelope's skin; for the black antelope skin is the sacrifice" (*ŚB*.6.7.1.6).[23] Between the body of the sacrificer and the solar energy of the golden disc lay the antelope skin as the means of protection and transfiguration.

The sacrificer was anointed on the black antelope skin (*ŚB*.9.3.4.10). Antelope and goat, in their symbolic significance, are clearly differentiated. Rudra's upper garment was a black antelope skin (*BP*.1.2.27.99). At a sacrifice, when Brahmā invested Rudra with the sword that he had created for him, Rudra showed himself wearing a black antelope skin studded with stars of gold (*MBh*.12.160.44-47). He wore it as Mṛgavyādha / Sirius, the Hunter of the Antelope.

"On a he-goat's skin should be anointed one desirous of prosperity, on a black antelope skin one desirous of spiritual lustre" (*ŚB*.9.3.4.14).[24] The goat skin was magically instrumental in securing worldly goods, whereas the black antelope skin was ritually effective

[23] *Ibid.*, part III, p. 266.

[24] *Ibid.*, part IV, p. 227.

in satisfying the longings of the mind and spirit for illumination. Should anyone desire both these fulfillments, he should be anointed on both skins (*ŚB*.9.3.4.14). The imparting of the Pāśupata vow in Bhogya, the city of Śiva, was not less accommodating.

The consecrating magic of the black antelope skin was vested in the black antelope, Rudra's victim. "Once upon a time the sacrifice escaped the gods, and having become a black antelope roamed about. The gods having thereupon found it, and stripped it of its skin" (*ŚB*.1.1.4.1).[25] The black antelope was homologized with the sacrifice. The land where the black antelope roamed was the land suitable for sacrifice, from the eastern to the western ocean, from Himālaya to Vindhya. What lay beyond it was the land of barbarians (*M*.2.21-23). Even so it was the skin of the black antelope (*kṛṣṇājina*) that sanctified and was homologized with the *brahman* (*KB*.4.11). The gods flayed the animal; Rudra had shot it.

Ironically though, by unerring logic, Rudra, who was excluded from the sacrifice, was the cause of the sacrificial, sanctifying magic emanating from the flayed skin of the black antelope, his victim.

Ritually, the black antelope was the sacrifice. Mythically and ritually, Prajāpati was the sacrifice. "With the sacrifice the gods sacrificed to the sacrifice" (*RV*.10.90.16; *VS*.31.16; *ŚB*.10.2.2.2).[26] The antelope was Prajāpati and, from the beginning, Rudra's animal victim.

The antelope became part of the iconography of Śiva. In bronze and stone images of many aspects of Śiva, the antelope remains closely associated with the Great Lord. He holds it in his hand; he displays it as an attribute as he displays his other attributes—the battle axe, trident, flame, drum, and skull—as insignia of his being. Playfully, the antelope—small in scale, for it is but an attribute—is shown leaping, supported by the fingers of the god's hand raised shoulder high, leaping toward the god or away from him, its head turned toward Śiva or in the opposite direction. The antelope is part of the image of Śiva in his manifestation as Candraśekhara, the lord crowned with the crescent moon. In this aspect the figure of Śiva stands straight like the cosmic pillar, like the *liṅga*, and this aspect is further emphasized in the image of Śiva Ekapāda or "One Foot," whose body

[25] *Ibid*., part I, p. 23.

[26] Cf. *Ṛg Veda Saṃhitā (RV)*, tr. K. F. Geldner, 1951, 3:289. Geldner notes that the sacrificial animal and the deity to whom the animal is sacrificed are one person.

is supported by a coalesced leg terminating in one foot.[27] The antelope is similarly balanced on the hand of Śiva in a flexed stance as Tripurāntaka,[28] the destroyer of the triple city of the demons; or it is shown on his hand as Viṣāpaharaṇa, Śiva having swallowed the world poison;[29] on his hand as Vīṇādhara-Dakṣiṇāmūrti, the Lord as the origin of music and all the arts;[30] or on the hand of Śiva Vṛṣabhavāhana[31] leaning on his conveyance, the bull. The antelope is on Śiva's hand when he is represented together with the Goddess, his bride, as Kalyāṇa Sundara;[32] when he stands his arm embracing the Great Goddess as Umāsahita;[33] or enthroned with her as Somāskanda, with the child Skanda/Kārttikeya between them.[34] Even the Great Goddess, shown by herself as Maheśvarī, upholds the cognizance of the antelope, as does the Great God himself.[35] In the image of Paśupati, however, though it is similar to that of Candraśekhara,[36] the figure of the antelope is substituted by a *kapāla*, the skull of Brahmā (*ŚRa*.2.22.114-16), demonstrating the parallel meaning of the hunter Rudra and the antelope / Prajāpati on the one hand, and that of Bhairava and Brahmā on the other. In contrast to this wealth of images, the standardized iconography of the image of Paśupati, but for its name, does not exhibit any feature that would visibly make it an image of the Lord of Animals.

From the Vedic myth of Paśupati to its epic and Purāṇic transpositions—the latter supported by a living faith, the Pāśupata religion—and by innumerable images of Śiva in many aspects, the antelope accompanies Śiva. Prajāpati, the antelope of the *Maitrāyaṇī Saṃhitā* (4.2.12), and the antelope, the embodied sacrifice, each Śiva's victim, are upheld playfully by one of Śiva's hands. The animal was integrated into the iconography and composition of the figure of Śiva itself; it was drawn into and became part of diverse manifestations of the Great God with the inscrutable smile.

Held in the upper left of Śiva's four hands and shown by iconographic convention balanced on or leaping from two fingers, the antelope was incorporated into the ambience of Śiva, as were his other

[27] S. Kramrisch, "Śiva the Archer," 1973, p. 142, fig. 133.

[28] C. Sivaramamurti, *South Indian Bronzes*, pl. 34.

[29] *Ibid*., pl. 30a.

[30] *Ibid*., pl. 31a.

[31] *Ibid*. pl. 20a.

[32] *Ibid*., pl. 21a.

[33] Cf. *ibid*., pl. 37b.

[34] *Ibid*., pl. 36a.

[35] *Ibid*., pl. 48a.

[36] *Ibid*., pl. 45a.

attributes: the weapons, the musical instruments, other objects, and the skull of Brahmā. The latter, related mythically to the Prajāpati-antelope, was confined to images of Śiva Paśupati and Bhairava, whereas the antelope graced many aspects of Śiva that did not directly refer to Śiva as the Hunter of the Antelope.

Instead of being carried by the hand of Śiva, the antelope is shown in much larger size by the side of Śiva as Bhikṣāṭana, the Supreme Beggar, and also as Kaṅkālamūrti, the "skeleton (-bearing) image," the latter carrying not only the skull of Brahmā but also the corpse of Viṣvaksena. Standing beside the god and raising itself on its hind legs is an antelope, its head looking toward Śiva's pendant hand, apparently holding out to the antelope some leaves. The god holding out his hand to the animal accentuates the meaning of this iconographical conception. To the left of Bhikṣāṭana, balancing the figure of the antelope on his right, a gaṇa carries on his head a large bowl, a receptacle for all the offerings presented to the Supreme Beggar, which he keeps in store for his devotees.[37] In his grace, the Lord holds out his hand to the antelope.

The antelope, the animal symbol of Prajāpati, the Lord of Generation, the Creator, implies also the creature, the animal or *paśu*, the human soul (*jīva*). The sage Jābālin, when asked to explain who the *paśus* were, answered, "The Jīvas are said to be the Paśus. Paśupati is so called because of his being the controller of the Paśus" (*JUp*.12-13).[38] In the work of the artists, the sculptors and painters, the figure of the antelope looks up to the image of Bhikṣāṭana holding out his hand to the animal. In all the other images, the figure of the *paśu*, the animal, the human soul, is in Śiva's hand.

B. THE LINEAGE OF PARVATA, THE MOUNTAIN

1. Lord Mountain and His Daughters

Dakṣa, the son of Brahmā, performed his great sacrifice in the age of Manu Cākṣuṣa (*VāP*.30.37-38). In a subsequent Manvantara when Manu Vaivasvata ruled, Dakṣa was reborn as a kṣatriya, the son of the

[37] D. Barrett, *Early Cola Bronzes*, pls. 41, 42; C. Sivaramamurti, *The Art of India*, fig. 79, p. 127, from the Bṛhadīśvara Temple in Tanjavur; C. Sivaramamurti, *South Indian Paintings*, fig. 79, p. 127, from Chidambaram, seventeenth century.

[38] *Jābāli Upaniṣad (JUp)*, tr. T.R.S. Ayyangar and ed. G. S. Murti, 1953, p. 89.

Ten Pracetasas (*MBh*.12, app. 1, no. 28, lines 1-2; *KūP*.1.13.53-62). Śiva had cursed Dakṣa by this rebirth on learning of his treatment of Satī and her consequent death (*KūP*.1.13.61-63).

Śiva's passionate grief for Satī was assuaged in the age of Manu Vaivasvata by the birth of Pārvatī, the daughter of Parvata, "the Mountain," and his wife Menā, "the Woman." Brahmā had planned that the Great Goddess who had been born as Satī would be reborn as Pārvatī, the daughter of the Mountain (*MP*.154.52, 60-61). In the meanwhile, the gods had fallen on evil days. They had been unable to hold their own against a formidable demon called Tāraka, "Star." Tāraka had practiced austerities as enormous as was his might. There lay the source of his power. He had approached Brahmā, who granted to the ascetic demon the boon that he asked for. "If a son born of Śiva becomes the commander-in-chief of an army and discharges weapons against me, let my death occur then" (*MP*.154.47-54; *ŚP*.2.3.15.41, 16.26).[39]

Before Pārvatī was to be born, Brahmā prayed to Rātri, the goddess Night, who had emanated from him first. She alone was able to accomplish the great work Brahmā had planned (*MP*.154.55-58). Brahmā praised the goddess Night, saying, "you are like lust itself to the sensuous, you are the play of those who are playful, the delusion of the mind, and you are Kālarātri, the Night of Demons, and the destroyer of all that exists" (*MP*.154. 78-84). Rātri was asked to aid the gods through the birth of Pārvatī (*MP*.154.70-74). Rātri went to the Mountain King's palace. As Rātri entered Menā's fragrant, luxurious bedroom, night set in. Parvata and Menā had gone to bed. As Menā began to feel sleepy, the goddess Rātri entered her mouth. Slowly the goddess Night found her way into Menā's womb and colored the embryo black. She remained in Menā's womb till the time of delivery (*MP*.154.90-95).

Pārvatī was born at midnight when the constellation Mṛgaśiras was in conjunction with the moon. The Goddess assumed her own form (*ŚP*.2.3.6.32-33). Seeing the lovely faced one born of her own will, Parvata was perplexed and terrified by her radiance, and asked the Great Goddess, "Who are you? I do not know you, my child" (*KūP*.1.11.56-61). The Goddess showed herself to the Mountain in her divine form of calmly fierce majesty and infinite wonder

[39] *Śiva Purāṇa (SP)*, tr. "A Board of Scholars" and ed. J. L. Shastri, 1973, p. 531.

(*KūP*.1.1.66-68). Parvata praised her with a thousand names (*KūP*.1.1.211). She showed the gentle, gracious form of glory, and the Mountain knew that she was the embodiment of the Self of all, she was Prakṛti, Śivā, the highest bliss. She was the goddess Maheśvarī, half of Śiva's body, called Śivā. She was all-pervading, endless, without division, but the seat of all distinctions. She was the highest *śakti* or power of Maheśvara, the Great Lord. Relying on her, the Great God created and destroyed the world. She was the best of creation in every category. With her alone, Śiva attained his own bliss (*KūP*.1.1.213-236). Maheśvarī was the Śakti (the embodied power) of the Lord, but it was he who possessed *śakti* (power). The yogis who contemplate the real truth see their complete oneness. Those who seek liberation find refuge in Pārvatī, the highest goddess, the self of all beings belonging to the self of Śiva. Parvata would abide by his daughter's wish and give the goddess in marriage to the Lord of Gods, to Śiva (*KūP*.1.11.316), who has no beginning and is unborn (*KūP*.1.11.302).

Parvata felt there was neither god nor demon in the world equal to him, since the Mother of the World had been born to him as his daughter (*KūP*.1.11.252), and he rejoiced as he looked at the child shining in dark splendor. Parvata, the Lord Mountain, named his daughter Kālī, the Black (*ŚP*.2.3.7.11).

Satī's mother, the daughter of sage Vīraṇa, was called Asiknī, Night (*ŚP*.2.2.29.4). Satī and Pārvatī were both darkly beautiful, like blue lotus flowers. But it was Rātri, the goddess Night, who entered the womb of Menā and painted the embryo black. Menā herself was a mind-born daughter of the Forefathers (*pitṛ*) (*VāP*.30.27-31). She was to become the mother of two, or as others say three daughters. According to the *Rāmāyaṇa*, Menā was the mother of two daughters, Gaṅgā, the elder, and Umā (Pārvatī), the younger (*R*.1.34.13-14). The *Vāmana Purāṇa* knows three daughters of Menā or Parvata: Rāgiṇī, the Red, who was all red and dressed in red; Kuṭilā, the Curvaceous, with curly dark hair and wearing a white garland and white dress; and Kālī, the Black, also called Pārvatī, who was the youngest (*VmP*.25.1-4). The two elder girls practiced austerities, for each wanted to become the mother of Śiva's son; they were seen by the gods, and each girl was taken to the heaven of Brahmā. Brahmā found the austerities of neither adequate to make her fit to give birth to a son of Śiva. The girls became angry and lost their tempers, particularly Kuṭilā. Thereupon Brahmā cursed them; Rāgiṇī, born of the Mountain, became

Sandhyā, the red evening twilight, conjoined with the body of the Pleiades (Kṛttikās). Kuṭilā, however, by the curse of Brahmā was burnt and subsequently turned into water. In that form she would be able to bear Śiva's seed, though not to the end; as a fast-flowing river she inundated the heaven of Brahmā (*VmP*.25.5-20). When Menā saw that her two elder daughters, the red and the white, were lost to her, she prevented her black daughter Kālī from practicing austerities, exclaiming: "U mā—do not (practice austerities)" (*VmP*.25.21).

The family of Pārvatī, in which the Great Goddess was incarnated as the daughter of Parvata, consisted of Menā, the Woman; her father Parvata, the Mountain; and her curvaceous sister Kuṭilā, who in the heaven of Brahmā turned into the overflowing celestial waters and became Gaṅgā (the Ganges), the name by which she is called in the *Rāmāyaṇa*. The other sister, Rāgiṇī—whose redness completed the triple color scheme of the three *guṇas*—became absorbed in the constellation of the Kṛttikās, the Pleiades.

Parvata the Mountain was as old as the rocks and the *Ṛg Veda*. There he was invoked together with the Waters, the Rivers, and Heaven and Earth, and with Indra, Savitṛ, and other gods (*RV*.6.49.14; 7.34.23).[40] Beyond this, the Mountain formed an essential part in the cosmogony that has god Indra for its hero. In that myth, the Mountain was a figure that stood for the intangibly high ambience that enclosed the world, closed it off from spaces of shimmering light toward which its slopes were rising. The Mountain enclosed the world and closed off the infinite regions of light in the beyond above its impenetrable extent (cf. *RV*.2.23.18; 5.56.4; 5.60.3), the region of the sun before it ever shone on earth. When Indra cleft the Mountain, the light of heaven flowed down to earth (cf. *RV*.1.32.1-4; 6.30.3-5; 10.89.7).[41] Parvata, the Mountain, keeping the light of heaven imprisoned, had been its guardian. In this respect Parvata, though inactive, was akin to Rudra, the archer, and to Kṛśānu, who by their actions intended to keep in its integrity the state *ante principium*, before creation. In the myth of Indra—which pervades the *Ṛg Veda*—the Uncreate was a pleroma of light closed off by the Mountain, and Indra brought it to the world. The pleroma of the Uncreate held the elixir and essence of Life: Soma, the elixir of life, and semen, the seed of life. Vṛtra, the serpent, had lain coiled around the cosmic

[40] Cf. A. A. Macdonell, *Vedic Mythology*, p. 154.

[41] Cf. H. Lüders, *Varuṇa*, 1951, 1:174.

mountain. Vṛtra was killed by Indra and fell to the bottom, into the abyss, when Indra shattered the mountain and released the streams to flow to the sea and freed the sun to shine in this world. But Indra's first act of creation was not yet complete, for the sun became engulfed in darkness in the cave at rock bottom, whence it had to be liberated and let out (*RV*.1.62.3, 5; 3.39.5; 6.17.5; 10.138.2) to rise in the spring of the world. Parvata was the rock bottom in the depths as well as the dome on high, the firmament, the sky, that had kept imprisoned the light and waters of life.

In the creation myth of Indra, the figures of the Mountain and of Vṛtra, the serpent coiled around it, correspond to those of Rudra and Kṛśānu, the archers. The Mountain was cleft, dead Vṛtra fell to its bottom, becoming Ahi Budhnya, the Serpent of the Deep. The shining rivers of light and life flowed down from heaven to the earth, and their waters filled the ocean. The sun, having shown its face on high, had yet to be liberated from the cave deep in the mountain, where it had been kept imprisoned by demons. Now Dawn could come forth and the sun could rise and set going the world of time. Like Vṛtra, the serpent, Rudra and Kṛśānu, too, failed to keep in its integrity the state *ante principium*, before creation. Their arrows could not arrest the flowing to earth of Soma, the elixir of life, and the semen that Prajāpati shed into creation. They had been in the Uncreate, described as a region of ineffable light that Parvata and Vṛtra had held unspent.

The precosmic power of the Mountain had to yield the streams of flowing light of which the celestial Gaṅgā, who was also called Kuṭilā, became the mythical image. Her sister Rāgiṇī, the "red," Dawn or Twilight, had been her fellow prisoner. Her figure, of indistinct contour in this myth, became merged with the Pleiades, the Kṛttikās, stars fixed in the firmament—the Mountain—becoming visible at the waning of the red evening twilight. Though liberated from the rock or Mountain, neither of these two daughters of Parvata was deemed adequate in her austerities to qualify as the future, potential mother of Śiva's son, although in the mythical universe of Śiva, Gaṅgā as well as the Kṛttikās (Rāgiṇī) cooperated in the birth of Śiva's son.

The bond that was to be forged between Śiva and Pārvatī links the Mountain, a figure of the precosmic state as imaged in the myth of Indra, with the cosmic presence of Śiva. The third and youngest daughter of Lord Parvata was Pārvatī, the bride-to-be of Śiva.

Within creation itself and in later Indian myth, the Mountain was seen rising from the center of the world into the regions where the gods are at home. Mount Meru, the cosmic mountain, carried the hierarchy of beings. Under the name of one of its peaks as cosmic axis, Mandara, the mountain functioned in the Churning of the Ocean.

The Mountain in the cosmos of Indian myth was the center of that cosmos; on its heights in heaven dwelled the great gods, in cities, palaces, and caves, enlivened by the presence of lesser celestials who moved about at will or rested on its slopes. Śiva dwelled in Kailāsa and also favored Mount Mandara. These mythic sites on high, envisioned from the earth, were assigned to the north, to the Himālayan altitudes. Cosmically and symbolically, the north signified the region of the pole star. Mythically, the Himālayan region was its proxy on earth. The king of these mountains was Parvata. Parvatarāja brought to his anthropomorphic representation his precosmic past. From him issued Gaṅgā the celestial river, whose other name is Kuṭilā, who flooded the heaven of Brahmā. Thence she flowed on earth, vivifying and bringing into this world her significance from before creation; when Parvata was forced open and had to let the flowing light from beyond into the world of man from the uncharted regions of transcendency, the inviolate and inexhaustible plenum, Parvata's eldest daughter, Sandhyā, the twilight or Dawn—the Father's Daughter—merged with the Kṛttikās. It is natural that a daughter of the Mountain should merge with the Pleiades, for in creation the Mountain had its cosmic figure as the night sky, where the light from beyond was seen shining forth in the shape of stars.

Gaṅgā, the elder daughter of Parvata, the Mountain, the stony dome of ancient heaven where in the world of later myth she flooded the heaven of Brahmā, was to occupy the highest position on Śiva's body. For a long while he held her captive in his hair on her precipitous descent from heaven. Had Śiva not supported her on his mighty head she would have crashed down to earth, shattered it, and flown into the netherworld. He sheltered her in the matted skeins of his hair, and let her flow on to fulfill her mission, flowing in heaven, on earth, and the netherworld, thrice herself, Tripathagā, moving on her path. She is called Mandākinī in heaven, Vegavatī or Gaṅgā on earth, Bhogavatī in the netherworld (*PP*.6.267.46-47).

She came from the apex of heaven to the moon, and flooded the heaven of Brahmā (*BhP*.5.17.1,4; *VP*.2.2.32).[42] She came down from heaven into the netherworld in order to redeem the sixty thousand ruthless sons of King Sagara (*R*.1.43.1-4; cf. *LP*.1.66.15-20).

The sixty thousand sons of Sagara were born to him by one of his two queens; the other queen had only one son (*R*.1.37.1-17). After some time Sagara decided to undertake a horse sacrifice (*R*.1.37.23-24; *MBh*.3.105.9). The rite required that the consecrated horse be set free to roam at will. The land over which it wandered would form part of the king's realm. At the end of the year the horse was sacrificed and the king became a Cakravartin, or sovereign of the entire domain. As the rite progressed, God Indra, for his own ends, abducted the horse and took it into the earth (*ŚP*.5.38.50). In vain did the sixty thousand sons who had accompanied the horse search for it. They went everywhere on earth, and then descended into the netherworld. After a long time they found the horse near the hermitage of sage Kapila (*MBh*.3.105.10-25). Ignoring the sage, the sons of Sagara quickly seized the horse (*MBh*.3.106.1). Angered, the sage opened his eyes, the fire of his *tejas* shot forth and burned to ashes the sixty thousand sons of King Sagara (*MBh*.3.106.2-3). They were found by Aṃśumat, the grandson of Sagara. He beseeched Ṛṣi Kapila to grant that those whom his anger had destroyed would ascend to heaven. The sage promised that they would attain heaven when Gaṅgā was brought from heaven to purify their ashes with her waters (*MBh*.3.106.20-27). This was beyond the power of the descendents of King Sagara until Bhagīratha, the grandson of Aṃśumat, by his asceticism and devotion to Śiva, moved the Great God to agree to sustain Gaṅgā, the daughter of the Mountain, during her descent to prevent the earth being split by the impact of her fall (*MBh*.3.108.1-6). Śiva caught the turbulent Gaṅgā like a garland of pearls on his forehead (*MBh*.3.108.9). She who had thought by raging whirlpools to press Śiva down into the netherworld could not find an outlet from the meshes of his hair, and floated on them like a flower. She at last reached the earth. Her waters flooded the ashes of the sons of Sagara. At last, the ancestors of Bhagīratha were redeemed. Gaṅgā flowed into the seas and her waters filled the ocean (*MBh*.3.108.12-17).[43]

[42] *Mārkaṇḍeya Purāṇa (MāP)*, tr. F. E. Pargiter, 1904, p. 280 (= 56.1-3). Seen from a Vaiṣṇava angle, the divine river Ganges issued from the foot of Viṣṇu / Nārāyaṇa.

[43] This story is found in several texts: *R*.1.37-43; *BhP*.9.8.8-31; 9.9.1-12; *ŚP*.5.38.48-57; 5.39.1-8.

Impetuous Gaṅgā, "who was as beautiful as the rays of the moon,"[44] not having been found capable by Brahmā to bear the seed of Śiva, insisted she was capable, that she would make the head of Śiva bow down by her austerities. Brahmā cursed her to become all water, and she inundated Brahmā's heaven (*VmP*.25.6-14). Though she wanted to bear Śiva's son, she resented her initial humiliation and wanted to show herself superior to Śiva, who had the power to support her on his head and imprison her in his hair. She was violent in her turbulence. She would crush Śiva so that pieces of his bones, like small bits of conch shells, would be mixed with her water and Nandin would have to search for them.[45] She was intensely desirous of Śiva, determined to hold him within her aqueous body, having broken him up all together. But he caught and entrapped her in his hair. There, he carried her on his head like an ornament, or let her glide like a mermaid along the waves of his hair when he danced. "As beautiful as the rays of the moon," she found herself close to the crescent moon that graced Śiva's brow. Its thin sickle showed it to be waning, for the gods had drunk its Soma nectar, leaving but this last part for the *pitṛs*, the Manes, to drink.[46] Gaṅgā, released from Śiva's hair, found her way to the sons of Sagara, dead and burned to ashes. She purified them by her water, and they ascended to heaven. Death associations decorate Śiva's head.

Gaṅgā's purpose in descending into the netherworld had been achieved. She purified the dead and they ascended to heaven. This mission the sacred river Ganges fulfills to this day.[47] Gaṅgā went through all the levels of the cosmos and of inner experience. She wanted to bear Śiva's son, but she also wanted to crush Śiva. Fierce and proud, this river goddess fulfilled her mission when first she flooded with her waves the ashes of the Sagara sons. From that time on her work never ceased. The water of the sacred river Ganges

[44] *Vāmana Purāṇa (VmP)*, ed. A. S. Gupta and tr. S. M. Mukhopadhyaya, A. Bhattacharya, N. C. Nath, and V. K. Verma, 1968, p. 244.

[45] Nīlakaṇṭha Dīkṣita, *Gaṅgāvataraṇa* 5.7, quoted by C. Sivaramamurti, *Gaṅgā*, 1976, p. 9.

[46] In the *Matsya Purāṇa* the waning of the moon is described according to how much is drunk and when, by the gods, the manes, and the sages (*MP*.126.61-72). The fifteenth portion of the moon in the dark half of the month is drunk by the fathers or manes (*MP*.126.72).

[47] Cf. H. von Stietencron, *Gaṅgā und Yamunā; zur symbolischen Bedeutung der Flussgöttinnen an Indisthen Tempeln*, 1972, pp. 50-57.

brings release to the dying who seek it, and she brings joy to the living. The Ganges is called "giver of release" (*mokṣadā*) and "giver of joy" (*bhogadā*). But she did not bring much joy to Pārvatī, who looked upon her as a rival.[48] Gaṅgā had never been in Śiva. She came to Śiva from on high; he caught her on his head and kept her in his hair. She floated with his locks spreading through the cosmos when he danced in ecstasy. Her foam caressed his hair, her hands reached out to the crescent moon on whose nectar the Manes feed. Pārvatī frowned at her (*MD*.50). Gaṅgā took no notice of Pārvatī's jealousy, which preoccupied the minds of poets and artists. She had a mission and temporarily had become Śiva's captive. She loved him destructively, but could not harm him. Her desire to become the mother of Śiva's son was fulfilled by indirection, while Pārvatī did not bear the seed of Śiva.

Pārvatī, the youngest daughter of the Mountain and of the "Woman" or Menā—whose name is shared by Apsarases, seductive nymphs arisen from the spray of the cosmic ocean at its churning—from before her birth was destined for the surpassing task, beyond her control, which her sisters could not fulfill by themselves: to become the mother of Śiva's son. For this purpose the goddess Night, her starry eyes closed, had entered Menā's womb and infused night's darkness into the embryo. She enveloped the embryo until birth. The goddess Night painted in Menā's womb the embryo with her darkness (*tamas*) (*MP*.154.61-70).

In this manner Brahmā prepared the birth of Pārvatī so that the Lord might fulfill the purpose of Brahmā. The Great Goddess cooperated with Brahmā and entered her second incarnation as the daughter of the Mountain. She fixed herself in the mind of Lord Mountain when he made love with Menā, and Menā conceived (*ŚP*.2.3.6.5-6). Brahmā's long-frustrated desire for the creation of mortal progeny through Śiva was now superseded by a new urgency. Only a supergod born of Śiva would be able to destroy the demon Tāraka.

Pārvatī was a full incarnation of the Great Goddess (*ŚP*.2.3.4.25). Previously, the Great Goddess had been incarnated in Satī, to win the love of Śiva. Now she decided to be born as the daughter of the Mountain and Menā (*ŚP*.2.3.6.2). She had taken this form in answer

[48] Cf. *Mudrārākṣasa* 1.1., quoted by C. Sivaramamurti, *Gaṅgā*, p. 23.

to the prayer of the gods that she again become the wife of Śiva (*ŚP*.2.3.4.18). The Great Goddess, the eternal Prakṛti (*ŚP*.2.3.5.26), remembered herself as Satī, who had cast off her body in anger at her father Dakṣa's disrespect for Śiva (*ŚP*.2.3.4.31). Before her yoga fire engulfed her, however, Satī had told Dakṣa that she could be found at any time, any place, in every being; there was nothing in the universe in which she could not be found (*MP*.13.24). Yet Śiva could not find her or peace anywhere. He made a garland of her bones. Like one who was not a god he wailed aloud; like a lover he spoke in a manner disordered by the pain of separation (*ŚP*.2.3.4.37-39). Although the Supreme Lord by his power of illusion had taken upon himself madness and pain, yet he is really unaltered, undistressed, and unconquered. Through any change in form whatever he is untainted by *māyā*; what use has he for love and delusion? (*ŚP*.2.3.4.40-41).

2. Śiva and Pārvatī

a. *The Goddess Night*

In the meanwhile, the demon Tāraka oppressed the gods, laid waste the celestial world, and invaded the sky-high mountain. No one, no god, had been able to subdue Tāraka, for he was a great ascetic and by his asceticism he had won the boon from Brahmā: Tāraka would be defeated by an infant seven days old; but his slayer was not yet born. The slayer of Tāraka was to be born as Śiva's son (*MP*.154.33-38, 47-49).

In due course the Great Goddess as Pārvatī was born from Menā; she cried like any newborn child. Although the little girl soon played with balls and dolls, the knowledge of her previous birth came to her (*SP*.2.3.7.1, 22, 24).

Pārvatī had privileges of birth similar to those of Satī. In addition, she had all the knowledge of the world of the gods (who acted like human beings), which Satī had not acquired in her short life. The lineage of her family, however, was different from that of Satī's. Dakṣa was a son of Brahmā, the Creator, whereas Parvata's original state lay far back, before the rule of the gods began and before the Asuras, the Titans, had become demons. One feature that these two incarnations of the Great Goddess had in common was the darkness that showed in their complexion, which they largely owed to the goddess Night, whose name Satī's mother had borne and who, in person, had entered Menā's womb. On her father's side, Pārvatī was heir to the hardness of the mountain.

The goddess Night, who had enveloped with her darkness Pārvatī while yet unborn, was to play a vital role in Pārvatī's relation with Śiva. According to Brahmā's plan, Pārvatī would practice austerities in order to be united with Śiva, and when united with him in marriage, the conjoint energies would be formidable. Even so, the destruction of the demon Tāraka seemed improbable. The conjoint *tapas* of Śiva and Pārvatī had to be made even stronger. With the help of Rātri, the goddess Night, their *tapas* would increase to a pitch of intensity at which their love making would create a son able to destroy Tāraka. To this purpose the goddess Night was to interrupt the love making of Śiva and Pārvatī by a quarrel between them. Śiva would chide Pārvatī in jest on account of her dark color. Pārvatī would be annoyed and leave Śiva to perform austerities in order to rid herself of her darkness. Śiva, too, would practice *tapas*. After this interruption, heightening their energies, the son born of their union would destroy the demon Tāraka (*MP*.154.58-70).

Brahmā instructed the goddess Night to work on the increase of sexual power of Śiva and Pārvatī by two means: *tapas* and quarrel. Their amorous enjoyment interrupted, their frustrated desire would demand even more compellingly to be satisfied. The quarrel itself, having heightened their emotional tension, would itself require further *tapas* to be allayed.[49] Then, with increased energy, their desire would bring together god and goddess in a union without compare from which their son, the victor over Tāraka, would be born. In the plan of Brahmā, the asceticism of the gods was meant to be subservient to their role as the future parents of the son who would save the world.

In order to make Śiva engender a supergod, Brahmā had to do more than merely command Śiva, as he had done hitherto when he wanted Śiva, the Great Yogi, to create mortals. Now, however, Brahmā's concern was the survival and creativity of the gods. Both were threatened by the demon Tāraka. A new god was needed, more powerful than Tāraka, more powerful than any god. He did not as

[49] Cf. W. D. O'Flaherty, *Asceticism and Eroticism in the Mythology of Śiva*, pp. 55-56, 152.

yet exist and could be born only from the union of Śiva and Pārvatī. Brahmā's purpose had changed: Śiva should not procreate mortals but a supergod to defeat an invincible demon.

b. *The Burning of Kāma*

In making his plan, Brahmā took part in the *līlā* of Śiva, in which the gods seem to behave like mortals. He took into account that *tapas* or asceticism can be practiced to more than one purpose. Pārvatī and Śiva practiced austerities (*tapas*). The austerities of Śiva, the Lord of Yoga, led him, in *samādhi*, to the reality of his utter transcendency. The austerities, however, that Pārvatī would practice were not to lead to *samādhi*, the abnegation of all outwardly directed activity and power. The strenuous discipline of will, though it was part of asceticism, was not the whole of yoga and stopped short of its end. For Pārvatī, austerities were the means for harnessing escalating power to her one purpose, winning Śiva as her husband. By *tapas* anything could be won—beauty, fame, and wealth in the world of man (cf. *VmP*.25.58) and in the world of the gods—and Pārvatī was certain that "desired objects are obtained by asceticism and there is nothing impossible for an ascetic" (*MP*.154.290).[50] She would even consume her body by austerities, for she had no doubt that by practicing *tapas* she would fascinate Śiva and draw him to her. She would win the love of the Great Yogi and become his wife (*MP*.154.289-92).

Pārvatī grew up in her parents' home and conquered the whole world by her beauty and intelligence. Ṛṣi Nārada read her palm and saw that one who was without father or mother, a naked yogi free from desire, would be her husband (*ŚP*.2.3.8.11; cf. *MP*.154.176-184), a description obviously referring to Śiva (*ŚP*. 2.3.8.13). None but Kāma, the god of love, could bring about their union (*MP*.154.207). Kāma, who could bring down gods, sages, demons, and others by the side glances of a beautiful woman (*ŚP*.2.3.17.20), should bring about the impossible and make Śiva his victim. At that moment, Indra thought of Kāma, who immediately with Rati, the goddess Lust, his wife, appeared before Indra. Charged by Indra with his nearly impossible mission, Kāma, accompanied by Rati and by Vasanta

[50] *Matsya Purāṇa (MP)*, tr. "A Taluqdar of Oudh," 1916, part II, p. 94.

(Spring), went to the hermitage of Śiva in order to disturb and interfere with his unshakeable asceticism (*MP*.154.208-20; *ŚP*.2.3.17.1-2, 28-43).

Kāma, the god of love, entered a verdant grove on the mountain peak, where he found Śiva seated in deep meditation in the hero posture on the coils of Vāsuki, the king of the serpents of the netherworld, holding the serpent's tail. Śiva's long, matted hair reached the ground, where a skull and a water vessel had been placed. Terrible serpents, coiled and with their hoods raised, adorned his hair, around his ears, and encircled his body like ornaments. A lion skin hung from his shoulders. His eyes were half closed in a face of indescribable beauty (*MP*.154.227-34).

The serpents of Śiva, conspicuous at all times around his body, were assembled more copiously and significantly than ever when Kāma was about to attack Śiva. In full excitement, their hoods raised, they coiled around his ears. They were breathing fire. Śiva held in his hand the tail of Vāsuki, on whose coils he was seated, in full mastery of the king of serpents of the netherworld, who served as his seat. The serpent, a multivalent symbol, poisonous and menacing, implying death and sex, protected Śiva's aloofness. He held the tail of the serpent king in his hand and used as ornaments the rest of the serpent brood. They encircled Śiva and guarded him, as their ancestor Vṛtra had lain coiled around the cosmos before creation, and as a serpent spreads its hood above the *liṅga* in uncounted representations of the present day.

Kāma went right into Śiva through his ears, and Śiva's *samādhi* vanished. But Śiva exercised his yoga power and was again in *samādhi*, while Kāma, affected by Śiva's yoga power, left Śiva's body, stationed himself outside, and discharged his flower arrow at Śiva's heart. A great flame of fire blazed from the third eye of the infuriated Śiva and burned Kāma to ashes (*MP*.154.235-50; cf. *MBh*.12.183.10. 3-5). The flame of fire in the shape of a mare entered the ocean and began to consume the water (*ŚP*.2.3.20.21; cf. *MBh*.7.173.75 and insert 1464 under n. 75). Rati, in distress, smeared Kāma's ashes all over her body. She wanted to kill herself. While Śiva consoled her by saying that Kāma would be born again (*MP*.154.259-74), he also rejoiced that Kāma had been reduced to ashes, for desire (*kāma*) leads to hell, from lust is born anger, from anger is born delusion, and because of delusion asceticism is destroyed (*ŚP*.2.3.24.27).

c. *Seduction of Śiva and His Marriage*

Śiva remained in his mountain retreat for many years, practicing austerities. When he came to the city Oṣadhiprastha, situated within the kingdom of Parvata, the latter, on hearing of Śiva's arrival, went to render homage to Śiva (*ŚP*.2.3.11.10). The Mountain King took with him his lovely daughter, exquisitely dressed. On their way through the forest they met the disconsolate Rati, who told her story. Parvata shuddered, whereas Rati's lament made Pārvatī see clearly that death was preferable to a life of pain and frustration. These, however, could be overcome by practicing austerities, and she resolved to obtain Śiva by her asceticism (*MP*.154.275-92).

Śiva was absorbed in meditation when Parvata-Rāja arrived, offering flowers, fruits, and his daughter to serve the Lord. Śiva saw Pārvatī in her great beauty. Regaining control over his nascent passion and closing his eyes, he meditated on himself, the ultimate reality (*ŚP*.2.3.12.1-12). Parvata, though doubtful, requested Śiva's permission to come daily and serve the Lord. Śiva broke his meditation. Opening his eyes he asked Parvata not to bring his daughter with him. What use was a woman to him, an ascetic, a yogi? (*ŚP*.2.3.12.13-30). Pārvatī, undaunted, addressed the Great Yogi: "Śiva, you practice arduous austerity because you have the energy to do so. That energy is Prakṛti, the cause of all action. How can the Great Lord of the *liṅga* exist without Prakṛti?" Śiva was delighted by Pārvatī's words and replied, "I destroy Prakṛti by great austerities; in my ultimate reality I am without Prakṛti." Śiva's words made Pārvatī smile inwardly, and she said, "Everything, at all times, is held together by Prakṛti. What you hear, what you eat, what you see, and what you are are all the activity of Prakṛti. O Lord, if you are greater than Prakṛti, why do you practice austerities here on this mountain?" Pārvatī, not wanting to argue with the Lord of ascetics and stating emphatically, "I am Prakṛti and you are Puruṣa," added that it was only through Prakṛti that Śiva had qualities and form. Without her Śiva was without attributes and unable to perform any activity. If he were really superior to Prakṛti, he need not fear being near her (*ŚP*.2.3.13.1-21). Moreover, her nearness would only stimulate and strengthen his yogic power of aloofness.

Śiva as well as Pārvatī was adept in the art of yoga. In their meeting they showed the effect of its solitary practice. Their nearness, moreover, and her beauty were welcome obstacles that increased their *tapas* and also their *tejas*. It was the intention of Brahmā to make Śiva desire Pārvatī, and to see to it that Pārvatī should make her future husband become the father of their son. This would have been an obvious demand had Śiva been any man or god. To induce, however, the Lord of Yoga to behave like natural man was tantamount to making him abandon what he essentially was.

Pārvatī's words voiced the Sāṁkhya viewpoint, whereas Śiva upheld the Vedānta point of view (*ŚP*.2.3.13.22). While Śiva and Pārvatī were engrossed in their universe of discourse, Brahmā assured the besieged gods that Tāraka would be destroyed. Brahmā himself, having given Tāraka the boon of a qualified invulnerability, could not destroy him. Śiva's cooperation was essential. If there were a son born of Śiva, he alone could kill Tāraka. Brahmā was certain that Śiva would marry Pārvatī; the gods would then have to ensure the descent of Śiva's semen into Pārvatī. Pārvatī alone is capable of making Śiva, who controls his semen upward, let his semen flow downward. No other woman would be capable of this. There was no time to be lost now for the gods to make Śiva desire Pārvatī as his wife (*ŚP*.2.3.16.20-35).

The battle between Śiva, the ascetic, and Kāma, fought in a sudden spring in the Himālayan mountains, continued within Śiva himself, whom Kāma had entered for a moment only. There, within the Great Yogi, the pendulum between self-control and desire kept swinging, the tremors of the one, the pull of the other, impeding, reinforcing, reciprocally acting on each other. They left unmoved the transcendental reality of Śiva.

Kāma had entered the world of Śiva from the universe of Brahmā. Kāma had been the first effective power in the chain of creation. Rudra, the ascetic, the Wild Hunter, though obstructing the act of creation / procreation which is one in the Father, in his capacity of or identity with Agni had prepared the seed for the Father. Though antagonistic to the uncontrolled outpouring or spontaneous generosity of the Creator, Rudra had prompted it. Rudra and the Father represented first principles. Only tenuously were they conceived anthropomorphically. Their actions were mythical symbols that adumbrated and clarified the relation of the absolute, or Uncreate, to the creation. The Wild God who *was* from the beginning had to be "born" in order to take possession of the cosmos. His cosmos became the scene of "the divine play of the Great God which protects the world" (*ŚP*.2.3.4.36).

Assuming for the sake of his devotee the role of god in the semblance of man,[51] the bearer of the seed and the yogi were one and the same, acting in a conceptually consistent, though logically conflicting, manner. A primary task of the yogi is the subduing of lust. Without desire, however, no conquest of desire can be undertaken. It is the stuff that yoga consumes. Hence its power. Śiva is both the Lord of Yoga and the destroyer of Kāma (*MBh*.13.17.51). Śiva the yogi presupposes Śiva as Kāma, the latter controlled by while sustaining the former. "Throughout the Purāṇas, the meaning of the conquest of Kāma by Śiva is undercut by qualifying episodes and even complete reversals: Śiva burns Kāma but is nevertheless sexually aroused; Śiva burns Kāma only to revive him in a more powerful form; . . . and, the final Hindu complication, Śiva *is* Kāma."[52] The dialogue between Śiva and Pārvatī was provoked by Kāma, the emissary of Indra. He was sent from the universe of Brahmā to set going Śiva's play. Kāma was doubly present in the play that had the seduction of Śiva by Pārvatī for its theme: once within Śiva himself, whom he entered if only for a moment through his ears, and again when he attacked Śiva from outside (*MP*.154.235-45). In fact, once burnt to ashes and bodiless, Kāma became omnipresent, existing "in the minds of all embodied creatures."[53]

The discourse of Śiva and Pārvatī, on the other hand, allowed the minds of those embodied creatures, who are Śiva's devotees, to participate in the divine play as if the Great Gods were human. Śiva staged his play out of concern for his devotees (cf. *ŚP*.2.3.25.64), making them see in a vivid drama the coherent roles of the male and female protagonists who in reality are Puruṣa and Prakṛti (cf. *LP*.2.11.3-4). Pārvatī herself told it to Śiva, who at that moment was not in a mood to listen (*ŚP*.2.3.13.17-20).

[51] Śiva explained to the Great Goddess that perfect knowledge, that is, consciousness that "I am *brahman*," was hard to find in the three worlds (*ŚP*.2.2.23.13-14). There was, however, no difference, between devotion and knowledge (*ŚP*.2.2.23.16). This concession allows for the statement made by Brahmā: "Everything is a sport of Śiva. The Lord indulges in many divine sports. He is independent and undecaying" (*ŚP*.2.2.24.16); *Śiva Purāṇa* (*ŚP*), tr. "A Board of Scholars" and ed. J. L. Shastri, 1973, 1:385. The divine sports are his plays (*līlā*) which he stages and performs in anthropomorphic semblance for the sake of his devotee. Through his *līlā* the Lord comes near to his devotee who is precluded from the consciousness, "I am *brahman*."

[52] W. D. O'Flaherty, *Asceticism and Eroticism in the Mythology of Śiva*, p. 145.

[53] *Ibid*., pp. 162-63 and *KSS*.20.70.

Pārvatī knew her own mind. Her determination was as firm as the Mountain, her father. Besides, she had the seductiveness of "Woman," her mother, who shared her name Menā with Apsarases. The beautiful princess Pārvatī became a yoginī in order to win by her austerities Śiva as her husband, so that their son would be born as the slayer of the hitherto invincible demon Tāraka. Pārvatī was free from the failings of Satī, who had shown herself vacillating as well as obstinate, when against Śiva's counsel she went uninvited to Dakṣa's sacrifice. Satī was also faint of heart; she had doubted Śiva's ability to shelter her from passing clouds. Worse than that, she doubted Śiva's word in the episode with Rāma. Nothing could make Pārvatī swerve from her path of asceticism. Her mind was set, with Śiva in her heart. By her asceticism she would move Śiva more surely than by her beauty or intelligence. Her austerities would lead Śiva away from his asceticism; he would marry her and beget a son on her. She was firm in her paradoxical purpose. In vain did Menā attempt to dissuade her daughter from leaving the palace and going into the wilderness to subject herself to ascetic rigors. Fasting, Pārvatī stood in the summer near blazing fires; during winter she remained in icy water, meditating on Śiva (*ŚP*.2.3.22.17-27, 40-42). The universe and the gods were scorched by her austerities. Viṣṇu and the gods went to Śiva, imploring him to marry Pārvatī and free the gods from the misery that Tāraka caused them. Lord Śiva should accept Pārvatī's hand in marriage (*ŚP*. 2.3.24.13-16). Śiva, rising from his trance, answered: "If the goddess Pārvatī, the most beautiful lady, were to be accepted by me, she will be able to resuscitate Kāma on account of the marriage. Then all the gods, sages and ascetics will become lusty and incompetent in the great path of Yoga" (*ŚP*.2.3.24.18-19).[54] Still, though Śiva considered marriage a great fetter, he decided to marry Pārvatī for the sake of begetting a son (*ŚP*.2.3.24.60, 75). He had drunk poison for the sake of the gods, and would not disappoint them now (*ŚP*.2.3.24.70). Śiva played his role of prospective bridegroom to perfection rather than leave room for doubt about his love for Pārvatī. He himself was in the thrall of his *māyā*, and took refuge in his assurance of serving his devotees and furthering the welfare of the gods.

He was swayed by Pārvatī, drawn to her as an ascetic and excited by her as a woman. Śiva decided to test Pārvatī's resolution (*ŚP*.

[54] *Śiva Purāṇa (ŚP)*, tr. "A Board of Scholars" and ed. J. L. Shastri, 1973, p. 566.

2.3.25.16), the intensity of her asceticism, the clarity of her mind, the purity of her devotion, and her knowledge of himself.

The fire of her asceticism had made all living beings shudder, so Indra sent the seven ṛṣis to Pārvatī. The seven sages told her that if she was attempting to have Lord Śiva as her husband, she meant to obtain the unattainable: the passionless ascetic whose fire had consumed Kāma. The sages tried to dissuade her from her resolve to win by extreme asceticism Śiva as her husband. They wanted to discourage her by describing the Great Yogi as "naked, ferocious, Dweller of the cremation grounds, the carrier of skulls, a hermit, statue-like in action, a beggar, mad, fond of collecting ugly and terrible things, and inauspiciousness incarnate. . . . He is the wearer of a necklace of gory heads, adorning Himself with terribly hissing snakes, . . . moving about with his ferocious attendants."[55] Did she think of gratifying sexual desires or getting any happiness with Śiva in this and the other world? Pārvatī replied that they did not know the Great God (*MP*.154.310-46). The disparagement by the ṛṣis only strengthened her resolve.

Happy with the result of their test, the seven sages went to Śiva. Taking his seat on an antelope skin, Śiva was pleased to hear of the successful visit of the sages with Pārvatī. Straight away the seven sages called on the Mountain King and Menā, for, Pārvatī having stood the test, Lord Śiva had asked for the hand of their daughter. The Mountain King should now give his daughter in marriage to Śiva in order to save the world. Parvata was overcome by emotion; Menā, however, was less certain about the wisdom of giving her daughter in marriage to Śiva, whose only qualification, if it were one, was his asceticism (*MP*.154.379-80, 389-91, 406-16).

Their mission fulfilled, the sages went to their home (*ŚP*.2.3.25.72-73), and Śiva longed to meet Pārvatī again. Again he wanted to test her. Approaching her, he took the appearance of an old ascetic and expressed his astonishment of seeing so beautiful a girl engaged in austerities in a forest. Light seemed to emanate from him. Pārvatī told him about her seemingly hopeless quest. In spite of her austerities she had not attained what she desired, and she was just about to enter the fire when the old brahmin arrived. She could not wait, and threw herself into the fire, which instantly became like sandal paste. Impressed

[55] *Matsya Purāṇa (MP)*, tr. "A Taluqdar of Oudh," 1916, part II, p. 95.

and smiling, the old brahmin wanted to hear the whole story (*ŚP*.2.3.26.1-30). Pārvatī told him that she had sought to attain Śiva by mind, by speech, and by action; she knew her object was very difficult to attain. The old brahmin advised Pārvatī to dismiss Śiva from her mind. He knew him, the naked, ash-smeared, serpent-wreathed ascetic, the skull-bearer who married Satī, who killed herself. Pārvatī should not throw herself away on Śiva, a homeless loner, whose birth was unknown and who was surrounded by ghosts and ghouls. He was completely unsuitable for her (*ŚP*.2.3.27.1-38). Pārvatī agreed with the old brahmin's words. They were true; they described some of Śiva's forms that he adopted in his divine play (*ŚP*.2.3.28.1-3). Did the old brahmin mean to denigrate Śiva? Exasperated, Pārvatī was about to leave when the old brahmin assumed the beautiful shape of the Lord Śiva in which Pārvatī had meditated on him; he clasped his beloved (*ŚP*.2.3.28.36-42). She addressed him, the lord of gods, as her husband, for she knew her father would accept him (*ŚP*.2.3.29.7-11). Then Śiva, laughing lovingly, praised Pārvatī as the great power of illusion, the primordial nature (*ŚP*.2.3.29.20), and she declared herself as his devotee, his wife always in every birth (*ŚP*.2.3.29.32). At the same time Pārvatī appreciated Śiva's different sports, while he remained intent upon himself, the Ultimate Reality (*ŚP*.2.3.29.34). Śiva allowed himself to be seduced into marriage by Pārvatī's beauty, her mind, her asceticism, but more than these by her infallible understanding of himself in the macabre horror in which he clad his transcendence. The tests were Śiva's key to their wedding chamber.

She returned to her parents, who received her with joy. Parvata celebrated the return of his daughter by the distribution of gifts and the recitation of hymns. Then he went to the river Ganges for a bath (*ŚP*.2.3.30.5, 23, 25).

Meanwhile, Śiva had assumed the appearance of a dancer. He was dressed in red, and carried a horn in his left hand and a drum in his right. He danced with great expertise and sang very charming songs. He blew the horn and played on the drum. It was an exquisite performance. People came crowding into the palace. They all were enraptured and became ecstatic. Pārvatī swooned from a vision of Śiva, his three eyes shining, his body smeared with ashes, wearing a serpent as his sacred thread and a garland of bones, and carrying his trident and all the other symbols. It was the unfathomable, ascetic god whom she desired. Śiva granted her the boon to be her husband. Then the vision vanished, while the dancing beggar continued his performance. Menā, delighted by his enchanting dance, offered him jewels in golden bowls. The dancer refused them. Instead, he asked for Pārvatī and started to dance and sing again. Menā was surprised and angry. In the meantime, Parvata returned from the Ganges and heard what had happened. Everyone wanted to drive out the dancer, but none could touch him who was like a great fire, shining and brilliant. Then the dancer showed his power to Parvata: he stood before Parvata in the shape of Viṣṇu and changed into Brahmā; he turned into the radiance of Śiva and Pārvatī. Then Parvata saw these shapes become a mass of splendor, undefinable in its formless expanse. And once more the mendicant begged for Pārvatī as alms. He accepted nothing else, and vanished. Himavat and Menā realized that it was Śiva who had been there and had now gone home (*ŚP*.2.3.30.26-53). Though he had chosen the shape of a beggar, Śiva danced before Menā a dance of enchantment. It swayed Pārvatī. Swooning, she saw the Great God who had come to her in his frightening beauty to ask her to be his bride. The vision vanished, but indeed the dancing beggar asked for Pārvatī's hand. When Parvata and all the others wanted to drive out the dancing beggar, he stood before Parvata as Viṣṇu, changed into Brahmā, changed into Śiva with Pārvatī herself, and then dissolved into sheer radiance. Śiva's wizardry touched those on different levels of readiness for him, delighting Menā by the beggar's dance, while Pārvatī swooned on recognizing Śiva in his macabre, ascetic shape. He enlightened Parvata by showing himself in his threefold divinity, his triple aspect of nameless light.

In order to win Parvata's consent to the marriage, but to have that consent given with reservations,[56] the gods requested Śiva to visit Parvata and to make disparaging remarks about himself (*ŚP*.2.3.31.9-11, 29). Once more Śiva appeared in disguise. Looking like a Vaiṣṇava brahmin, a matchmaker, Śiva went to the Lord of Mountains. None but Pārvatī recognized the god in his disguise. The matchmaker told her parents that he had heard of the possibility of Parvata giving his daughter to Śiva in marriage. He warned Parvata, saying that Śiva has no support, no connections; is a beggar, ill-shaped, without qualities;

[56] If the lord of the mountain were to give his daughter to Śiva with reservations in his heart about the marriage, he would not gain the fruit of his act immediately, and hence as a receptacle of many jewels would remain longer on the earth to the satisfaction of the gods (*ŚP*.2.3.31.2-5).

dwells in cremation grounds, looks like a snake catcher; is a yogi, naked, smeared with ashes, his matted hair unkempt; he is without pedigree, has a bad character, is ill-tempered; nobody knows his age, and he lacks good judgment. The brahmin stopped, and Śiva, calm, the player in various divine sports, went to his own home (*ŚP*.2.3.31.31-53).

Menā was disconsolate. She went into her "boudoir," took off her necklace and lay on the floor sobbing (*ŚP*.2.3.32.7). In the meanwhile Śiva, longing for Pārvatī, summoned the seven sages and sent them to Lord Mountain (*ŚP*.2.3.32.8-9, 34-36). The sages told the Mountain that Śiva was the father of the universe and Pārvatī its mother. Hence, Pārvatī should be given to Śiva, the Supreme Spirit (*ŚP*.2.3.33.1). The seven ṛṣis spoke the truth. Śiva and Pārvatī are the figures of Puruṣa and Prakṛti, the eternal principles of creation. "Śivā is the wife of Śiva in every birth" (*ŚP*.2.3.33.46). When the seven sages left, the Mountain sent out a letter of betrothal to Śiva, and the wedding invitations. All the mountains and rivers came to the wedding (*ŚP*.2.3.37.4-5, 9, 41-42). The gods sent Ṛṣi Nārada ahead. He arrived at the thousand-pillared palace of the Mountain King. It had been built by Viśvakarman, the creator *per artem*. Great was Nārada's surprise when he saw his own image made by Viśvakarman. Nārada was somewhat mystified, but, on entering the marriage hall, he was bewildered. Had Śiva, seated on his bull and surrounded by his gaṇas arrived already for the wedding? Had the gods, led by Viṣṇu, also arrived, and the sages and the other celestials? Nārada could not believe that he had been duped by the magic of Viśvakarman, who had made these true likenesses of celestial realities (*ŚP*.2.3.41.1-12). By the illusion that the portraits in his palace caused, the Mountain King subtly and gracefully had taken his revenge on Indra, who long ago had clipped the wings of the mountains and deprived them of their ability to fly (*ŚP*.2.3.41.23-29; *MS*.1.10.13). Now the Mountain King showed Indra and the gods that wings were, so to say, superfluous. The gods were present in effigy; they had come to the Mountain even before they had started out in the marriage procession of Śiva. The Mountain King, aided by Viśvakarman, had taken his creative revenge on Indra, who had deprived the mountains of their power to fly.

Śiva, having received Parvata's letter and accepted its contents, invited all the gods to Kailāsa before he started on his wedding procession (*ŚP*.2.3.39.5, 21-22). The seven mothers undertook the rite of the decoration of Śiva for his wedding. His usual attire became his wedding ornaments. The moon became the bridegroom's crown, his third eye became the beautiful *tilaka* on the forehead. The serpents around his ears became earrings studded with jewels, and the serpents on other parts of his body changed into the ornaments of the respective parts; all were studded with gems. The ashes became sandal paste and other unguents; the elephant hide became beautiful cloth (*ŚP*.2.3.39.36-41). The elephant hide in particular lent itself to becoming a suitable garment for this occasion. It had belonged to an elephant demon whom Śiva had slain (*ŚP*.2.5.57.1). Gajāsura, the demon, was a voluptuary, and since he had not controlled his senses, he became evil (*ŚP*.2.5.57.25-26). Śiva pierced him with his trident (*ŚP*.2.5.57.49). Pierced, he asked for a boon, which Śiva granted. Śiva should wear the hide of the demon, purified by the fire of his trident. Scorched by the flames of asceticism, the hide did not burn (*ŚP*.2.5.57.58-61). Dressed for his wedding, Śiva had a beautiful appearance extremely difficult to attain (*ŚP*.2.3.39.42). Starting out for the palace of Lord Mountain, "Śiva appeared to be completely overpowered by Kāma like an ordinary man" (*ŚP*.2.3.41.51).[57]

The marriage procession of Śiva was nearing the palace of the Mountain King. Menā was anxious to see the bridegroom. She stood on the terrace, and Śiva took delight in seeing her watching the procession, for he meant to delude her. The procession was arranged in groups. At the head came the handsome Gandharvas, richly dressed, riding in their vehicles with flags and banners. Groups of heavenly nymphs accompanied them. When Menā saw Maṇigrīva, the lord of *yakṣas*, she took him to be Śiva. She was told that he was only an attendant of Śiva, and when the next god surrounded by his retinue came within her sight, twice as splendid as Maṇigrīva, she was similarly mistaken. Thirteen times more Menā was taken in by the escalating splendor of each following god with his retinue. Her happiness and pride increased, became almost unbearable, until Nārada announced the arrival of Śiva. He was preceded and surrounded by his gaṇas of wondrous shapes; and by *bhūtas* and *pretas*, elementals and ghosts who dispelled the proud anticipation of Menā. Some had the form of wind murmuring through the banners. Their innumerable host showed, as was their wont, all the deformities one could think

[57] *Śiva Purāṇa (ŚP)*, tr. "A Board of Schoalrs" and ed. J. L. Shastri, 1973, p. 647.

of. When Menā saw Śiva in their midst, she trembled. Seated on his bull, he had five faces, three eyes, ashes smeared all over his body; the crescent moon in his matted hair, ten hands with the skull in one of them; he wore the hides of a tiger and an elephant and held his bow in one hand, his trident in another. He had an odd number of eyes, and was misshapen and untidy (*ŚP*.2.3.43.1-61).

Alarmed, trembling, and burdened with grief, Menā fell to the ground (*ŚP*.2.3.43.62-63). When she awakened from her swoon she bewailed her fate and that of Pārvatī. The reward of her daughter's austerities was painful to look at (*ŚP*.2.3.44.1-5); Menā wanted to cut off her head and run away (*ŚP*.2.3.44.22). The words of the sages failed to console her (*ŚP*.2.3.44.37-38). The Mountain King explained to her that Śiva had many names and many forms. Did she not recollect an earlier deception (as the dancing beggar) (*ŚP*.2.3.44.42-45)? Menā did not listen. She threatened to give up her life if the Mountain decided to give their daughter to Śiva (*ŚP*.2.3.44.50). Pārvatī told her disconsolate mother that she had wooed Śiva by mind, word, and action, and her mother could do as she liked. Menā, gnashing her teeth, seized Pārvatī and beat her. She threatened to poison her or throw her in a well (*ŚP*.2.3.44.60-62, 65). Menā ceased ranting when at last she was made to understand that Śiva had many forms, both hideous and handsome, but she agreed to give her daughter to him only if he took on a lovely appearance (*ŚP*.2.3.44.90-101). Śiva showed himself in his divine, compassionate beauty (*ŚP*.2.3.45.3-4).

Parvata and Menā started the marriage rites (*ŚP*.2.3.48.1-2). Śiva had to declare his lineage (*ŚP*.2.3.48.7). He was silent. Nārada, knowing the reason, with his mind fixed on Śiva began to play on the *vīṇā*. The Mountain asked Nārada to stop playing at this important moment (*ŚP*.2.3.48.8-11). Nārada stopped playing and told the Mountain that even Viṣṇu, Brahmā, and the other gods did not know Śiva's lineage or family (*ŚP*.2.3.48.16). Śiva was the formless Supreme *Brahman*; he was without attributes. According to his own wish he had qualities, a body, and many names. Even a wise man does not know him (*ŚP*.2.3.48.18, 19, 21). The Mountain listened with delight, and Nārada continued: *Nāda*, the primordial sound, is the lineage of Śiva, and Śiva is identical with *Nāda* (*ŚP*.2.3.48.25-28). It was for this reason, Nārada said, that he played on his lute when Parvata asked to be told Śiva's lineage (*ŚP*.2.3.48.30). This explanation of the mystery of Śiva satisfied the Mountain (*ŚP*.2.3.48.31), for *Nāda*, primordial sound, is the basic momentum or "substance" from which the world is made. It is the prototype of sound, and the condition necessary for creation to take place. *Ākāśa*, ether or space, the first element of manifestation, has sound for its quality (*ŚS*.1.70, 73; cf. *ŚS*.5.26, 29).

Now the Mountain King and the guests at the wedding knew that the lord of the three worlds was seen by them face to face (*ŚP*.2.3.48.34). Parvata gave his daughter Pārvatī in marriage to Śiva (*ŚP*.2.3.48.37). During the wedding rites, as the bridal pair were circumambulating the sacred fire, Brahmā, the main priest, kept staring at Pārvatī's feet (*ŚP*.2.3.49.3-5). The same weakness had overcome him at Satī's wedding. This time the spilled drops of semen did not turn into threatening clouds of doom; instead, thousands of sages arose from them, the Vālakhilyas (*ŚP*.2.3.49.7, 34-35). They greeted Brahmā, their father, and went to the mountain Gandhamādana (*ŚP*.2.3.49.36-38). Śiva, angered at first at Brahmā's incontinence, assured him that he had nothing to fear (*ŚP*.2.3.49.9, 46-47). Śiva was benignly contemptuous rather than murderous, as he had been at the same occurrence during Satī's wedding, when he had said that having killed the Creator he himself would create all living things, or he would create another Creator (*ŚP*.2.2.19.58-60). He had come to terms with the mechanism of Brahmā's sexuality, which was lacking in the emotional, erotic overtones that Kāma's arrows had released in Śiva's heart.

After the wedding, the time had come for Rati to bring Śiva the ashes of Kāma. Śiva glanced at them with compassion, and Kāma, as beautiful as before and wielding bow and arrows, emerged from the ashes (*ŚP*.2.3.51.1-15). Śiva with Pārvatī returned to his mountain home.

d. *The Sons of Pārvatī and of Śiva*

i. Gaṇeśa; the Sapling of the *Aśoka* Tree; Vīraka

In the groves and forest solitudes of Mount Mandara, the Great Yogi and the Great Goddess strolled and frolicked. They were young and carefree. As time went on, Pārvatī felt a longing for a son. Once, after having bathed, she rubbed scented oil and powder on her body. It mixed with the scruff of her skin and she shaped the matter into a human figure with an elephant's head. Then, out of fun, she threw the little figure into the Ganges, where it grew to such an extent that it became as large as the world. Pārvatī called him to her as her son. Gaṅgā, too, addressed him as her son. The gods worshiped him; he was called Vināyaka (*MP*.154.500-505), and Brahmā and Rudra made him the head of the gaṇas (*Yāj*.1.270). Thus was the birth of Gaṇeśa from Pārvatī. Though the birth of Gaṇeśa is told in different ways because of the difference in kalpas (*ŚP*.2.4.13.5), Gaṇeśa was born as Pārvatī's son; Śiva was his father only inasmuch as Pārvatī's longing for a son had arisen in her as Śiva's wife. It was by her own effort that Gaṇeśa was born from her body, albeit from its scruff. Some of Pārvatī's resentment that Śiva had not fathered the child could have gone into the substance from which she shaped Gaṇeśa.

Creating Gaṇeśa, however, did not altogether satisfy Pārvatī. Her longing for a son continued. This time she gratified her longing by planting a sapling of an *aśoka* tree, and she tended the young tree with great care. The gods rebuked her. They expected her to give birth to a son, but she disappointed them by her reply that one tree was worth ten sons (*MP*.154.506-12). Thus, for the time being, she assuaged her desire for a son.

After this incident, Śiva gently led her into his palace to play dice with her. Suddenly a tumultuous noise was heard, and Śiva explained to Pārvatī that the lords of gaṇas were amusing themselves. The gaṇas had been humans who had won Śiva's favor by austerities, fasts, celibacy, and pilgrimages. They were powerful and dear to Śiva; he could not live without them (*MP*.154.514-29). Their favored city was Bhogya, but they also chose other sacred cities, gardens, abandoned houses, bodies of demons, infants, mad men, and the cremation ground for their residence. They were addicted to music and dancing, and some were naked, while others looked like deer or birds (*MP*.154.530-41). They were like the Rudras of the *Śatarudriya* hymn (cf. Ch. IV.1).

Pārvatī was especially attracted to one gaṇa, clad in antelope skin and wearing a girdle of muñja grass and a garland of stone heads, who was beating his arms with slabs of stone. He was held in great esteem by the other gaṇas, Śiva told her, for his wonderful qualities. His name was Vīraka or Vīrabhadra. Pārvatī said she wished she could have a son like him. When would she be blessed with such a son? Śiva said he, Vīraka, would be her son and would call her "mother" (*MP*.154.542-47).

Vīraka / Vīrabhadra, in an earlier Manvantara, had come into existence when Śiva, in despair over Satī's death, dashed a bunch of his hair against a rock. Vīrabhadra acted as Śiva's alter ego and emissary, and destroyed Dakṣa's sacrifice (*ŚP*.2.2.32.20-22, 47-58; 2.2.37.44-46). In the Vaivasvata Manvantara, Vīraka, though still a child, had become a leader of Śiva's gaṇas. He resembled Śiva inasmuch as he wore a garland of human heads. They were, however, of stone. Vīraka playfully also slapped his arms with slabs of stone. This distinguished him from other gaṇas and attracted Pārvatī, the daughter of the Mountain or the Rock. Vīraka seemed predestined to become her son, to continue the line of her own father, the Mountain or Rock. Vīrabhadra was closely linked with Śiva, to whom he owed his existence, whether he appeared at the instant when Śiva struck the rock with a bunch of his hair, or whether, as the embodiment of Śiva's wrath, he emanated from Śiva's mouth for the destruction of Dakṣa's sacrifice (*VāP*.30.122; *MB*.12, app. 1, no. 28, lines 70-71). When Dakṣa Prajāpati at a different time held his sacrifice and did not invite Śiva, Pārvatī objected to Śiva and became miserable over his exclusion. Understanding what was in Pārvatī's heart, Śiva with his terrifying attendants destroyed the sacrifice himself (*MBh*.12.274.18-35). Pārvatī, however, was not Dakṣa's daughter and did not immolate herself in flames of love and anger when Śiva was excluded from the sacrifice.

Gaṇeśa was Pārvatī's son born from her own desire and the perfumed scruff of her body (*MP*.154.500-505); or he is said to have been born, as the result of Pārvatī's desire, from her dress and Śiva's kiss (*BDP*.1.60.7-32); or he was given to her as the result of a boon requested of Kṛṣṇa by Pārvatī after she had praised and then beheld the Great God (*BVP*.3.8.1, 8-9). Vīraka, on the other hand, was Śiva's creation, and Pārvatī played no part in his coming into existence. Vīraka became her son by inner affinity and Śiva's consent. Pārvatī seemed pleased, though in her inmost being she was dissatisfied.

ii. Birth of Kārttikeya

Ardhanārīśvara let the goddess step out from his total being. The Great Goddess discharged her power as Śakti, the Cosmic Goddess, who was born as Dakṣa's daughter Satī and reborn as Pārvatī, the daughter of the Mountain. The Great Goddess and the Cosmic Goddess are eternal presences. Satī and Pārvatī, her incarnations, were theophanies who for the sake of mankind acted out their destinies as if they were mortals, in the presence of the Great God whose partners they were in his divine play.

In whatever situation they met him face to face, they knew him in his ultimate reality, though they would doubt him, quarrel with him, or even denigrate him. In his love for them they felt the awful grandeur of the Lord as Time and Death, and his utter detachment as the Great Yogi. While they acted as if they were human, they were goddesses, essentially the Cosmic Goddess and ultimately the Great Goddess, his other half. He knew their tremors, for it was he who made them vibrate when playing on his lute, and he recollected them in his inscrutable smile.

In assuming his roles, Śiva had mankind—that is, his devotees—in view. The great performer and dancer remained wholly himself, though he varied his own role and created anew those of the principal players. Dakṣa and his daughter Satī were personages widely different from Parvata, his wife Menā, and their daughter Pārvatī. Each character acted out his own destiny. It rested on his mythical past, of which he was the living symbol. The significance of their actuality was embedded in it, or the outcome of situations whose remembrance imbued the play in which Pārvatī took the leading female part; Mahādeva remained the constant, principal figure, manifesting in whatever guise and mood his own ineffable, contradictory, and consistent, transcendent presence. Satī, the Real, had been the first coming to earth of the Cosmic Goddess. Satī maintained her divinity in her inborn determination to win, by the fervor of her self-imposed discipline, Śiva as her husband. She had been separated from him from before her birth, and was driven back to him in yogic effort and ecstasy. She found him only to lose him, inasmuch as she acted as a human—a young, inexperienced girl, weak in faith though strong in *tapas*. She lost Śiva through her lack of confidence in the word and power of the Lord, and sacrificed herself in flames of anger, hurt in her pride and love of Śiva.

As inborn as Satī's love of Śiva was Dakṣa's hatred of him. Satī carried in her being the Great Goddess who had separated from, and always is, in Śiva. Dakṣa, Brahmā's son, who had given his daughter to Śiva against his will because Brahmā had urged him (*BhP*.4.2.16; *SkP*.7.2.9.11), carried Brahmā's resentment of his decapitation by Śiva into hatred of Śiva, his son-in-law.

Satī's marriage to the Great God was without issue. It could not have been otherwise, for the love making of the Great Yogi was controlled, his seed was drawn up; his sexual power remained contained within his body, and its substance was transubstantiated into the self-realization of the god. Satī, herself a yoginī, knew and was with Śiva when he desired her. When he was in *samādhi*, she was in the presence of transcendence itself; she kept aloof. Śiva had warned her to stay away from his motionless body.

After the death of Satī, the Great Goddess was born as Pārvatī, the daughter of the Mountain and Menā. From her father, Pārvatī had inherited the firmness of the rock. This was not any rock, not even the rock of ages, but that all-embracing rock which, in the myth of Indra, had held within it the cosmos-to-be. This possessive Mountain had kept within itself the flowing light of the godhead. When the Mountain was shattered by Indra, the sun's rays and the flowing rivers were set free.

Pārvatī was not the only daughter of the Mountain. Her older sister was Kuṭilā / Gaṅgā, and the third sister was Twilight / Dawn, who merged with the Kṛttikās, the Pleiades. On her father's side, Pārvatī brought to her marriage with Śiva the power of a hoary cosmic myth. Her sister Gaṅgā was similarly endowed, and Śiva was to face the rivalry of the two sisters in relation to him. Menā, their mother, the "Woman," was earthbound, being the daughter of the Fathers, the *pitṛs*. She offered obstacles to Pārvatī's unconventional marriage. While she was enchanted by the mendicant Śiva's dance and music, she was appalled and became rabid when Śiva, in gruesome majesty, came to his wedding. Misjudging the total integrity of the Great God, she finally consented to give Pārvatī to Śiva of lovely shape.

Pārvatī before her marriage showed hardly any of the traits of her mother's character. Pārvatī's strength of mind, will, and emotion equaled Śiva's. She argued with him and held her own in metaphysical discourse. She won and held Śiva. Over and above everything, she had a mission to fulfill: to give birth to Śiva's son. For this purpose she had been painted black by the goddess Night while in her mother's womb. The goddess Night carried out a stratagem of Brahmā. Pārvatī's dark complexion had not disturbed Śiva before their marriage. Rather, her dark beauty enchanted him. After their marriage, one night as they were lying together, Śiva in his ashen white, unearthly sheen and the goddess embracing him, Śiva in jest compared her dark arms to a serpent encircling a tree. Pārvatī resented Śiva's words, spoken while the rays of the new moon were falling on her white garment. She looked like the night of the new moon (*MP*.155.1-2) that shed its *soma* beams from Śiva's locks on the goddess who herself is Soma, the elixir of immortality that suffuses Śiva who is fire (cf. *BP*.1.2.27.112; cf. *ŚP*.7.1.28.19). But neither her *soma* nature nor the moonlit peace around her assuaged Pārvatī. The Great God and the Goddess quarreled, and infuriated, Pārvatī left Śiva to practice austerities (*MP*.155.3-23). She remained surrounded by fire in the scorching sun of summer and stayed under water in the rainy season (*MP*.156.8-10). Brahmā having granted her wish to acquire a gold complexion so that she would be an ornament in the arms of her lord (*MP*.157.8-12), she returned to Śiva, who, after their quarrel, had been absorbed in austerities. Now they met and their love was stronger than before. In this respect, the goddess Night had completed her task. They made love immeasurably for a thousand years according to the reckoning of the gods (*ŚP*.2.4.1.24) as if it were a single night (*KS*.8.91). While the goddess Night had succeeded in heightening the erotic tension of the lovers, all that she effected was a change in the color of Pārvatī, who shed her black complexion, thus severing her connection with the goddess Night. Thereafter Pārvatī glowed in golden color, like Śiva's son-to-be, whom she was not to conceive.

As no son had been born to Pārvatī from Śiva, the distress of the gods was great. The very purpose of the marriage of Śiva and Pārvatī had remained unfulfilled, and the gods were helpless, for Tāraka's might was based on Brahmā's boon that none but Śiva's son would have the power to defeat and kill Tāraka. Brahmā had also anticipated that none but Pārvatī could seduce the Great Yogi to shed his seed in her. Kāma's death and resurrection seemed to have been in vain. The gods were in an unthought-of dilemma. Only the issue of Śiva and Pārvatī's conjoint power could defeat Tāraka, but being endowed with such power would he not be a threat to Indra himself, who had summoned Kāma to bring about the union of Śiva and Pārvatī? And who would dare to interrupt the seemingly endless love making of Śiva? The earth trembled under its weight (*ŚP*.2.4.1.44). But if a son were born to Śiva from Pārvatī, the entire universe would be burned by the issue of their combined energy. He would vanquish both the gods and the demons (*BVP*.3.1.26). The gods in their plight addressed themselves to Śiva himself (*R*.1.35.8-9). They asked Śiva for the favor that he would not beget a son in the goddess Umā. He should restrain his fiery energy. Śiva agreed and drew up his seed (cf. *R*.1.35.10-13). From that time, according to the *Mahābhārata*, he became known as *ūrdhvaretas* (*MBh*.13.83.41-47), one more instance of a hysteron proteron or inverted causality, for the Great Yogi had controlled his seed all the while.

All the same, the gods had had to interrupt this unending congress that left the world uncared for by Śiva, and from which no child was born (*R*.1.35.6-7). Moreover, the gods found themselves in a quandary. According to the *Śiva Purāṇa*, their distress at being besieged by Tāraka prevailed when they decided to approach Śiva in the arms of Pārvatī in the bedroom of his palace (*ŚP*.2.4.1.61-63). But whether they were more frightened by the danger to themselves of the power of Śiva's son should he be born (*BVP*.3.1.26), or by the threat to their existence posed by the demon Tāraka, for whose conquest it was incumbent that Śiva's son should be born (*MBh*.13.84.1-2; *MP*.154.47-55), the outcome was the same. Śiva rose from his love making, the seemingly interminable intensity of which in itself had been a threat to the world. Only Śiva, the Lord of Yoga, in the fury of his love making, could have held the semen within him (*ŚP*.2.4.2.1).

It was Agni the Fire who, on behalf of the gods, in the shape of a bird—a gander, dove, or parrot according to different accounts—had unobservedly entered the bedroom and disturbed the couple in their embrace (*VmP*.28.38-43). Śiva got up and went to meet the gods who had been waiting outside, and after hearing their request, let his semen fall on the ground, where Agni in the form of a dove swallowed it (*ŚP*.2.4.2.1-11).

As Śiva took a long time to return, Pārvatī came out, and when she saw the gods and heard what had happened, she cursed the gods (*ŚP*.2.4.2.11-17). Since they had hindered her in her desire for a son, they should have no offspring of their own (*R*.1.35.20-21; cf. *MBh*.13.83.48-49). Pārvatī indicated that Śiva had desired to procreate (*MBh*.13.83.49). This was what she must have wishfully been thinking.

The curse of Pārvatī, entailing the childlessness of all gods and goddesses, was but a continuation of Śiva's refusal to procreate. She transferred to the world of the gods Śiva's resolution not to create mortal progeny. Pārvatī, thinking in terms of mortal women, considered childlessness to be a curse. This was contrary to a view held even by

Brahmā himself about the descent of man. When Brahmā first created human couples, they hastened to sexual intercourse and had no children except at the end of life, when they produced pairs of children. They lived in heaven, without iniquity and strife. Thereafter, they fell from heaven and became passionate; the women conceived frequently, and in the course of time people became possessive and avaricious. Discord grew among them.[58] Pārvatī, the Great Goddess, felt like a woman. Childlessness was her greatest sorrow; it made her suffer even more acutely than the interruption of her congress with Śiva and the falling of his seed on the earth (cf. *BVP*.3.2.23-24). According to one version of the myth found in the *Vāmana Purāṇa*, Pārvatī, having pronounced her curse, went to take a bath. While rubbing her skin with scented ointments she made Gaṇeśa out of the scruff of her skin (*VmP*.28.56-66). At whatever phase of her married life Pārvatī created Gaṇeśa, it was an act of self-assertion against the disappointment of her failure to have a son by Śiva.

The seed of Śiva, which he discharged on the earth, leapt into a blaze of fire—or into the mouth of the Firebird. From this seed eventually Śiva's son was born. He was to have more than one mother. As Śiva's son he was called Kumāra, "the young boy," eternally celibate; he was Śiva's sheer essence. The name Kumāra had been waiting for him by predestination: it was Rudra's ninth name given by his father Prajāpati (Ch. V.1.a; *ŚB*.6.1.3.18), and it heralded the new god, the glowing energy (*tejas*) itself of Śiva, the one who is born from "that radiant seed surpassing the sun" (*MD*.43).[59] Pārvatī was not the mother of Kumāra. Her yoga power of seduction had failed to make Śiva fecundate her, and had been instrumental only in arousing the Lord of Yoga. He controlled the emission of his seed until it spurt into Fire.

Agni was exempt from Pārvatī's curse, as he was not present when she pronounced it (*MBh*.13.84.8). Agni carried Śiva's seed within him until, commanded by Brahmā, he threw it into the Gaṅgā, who carried it until she too could bear it no longer. She deposited the embryo on a mountain, where the Kṛttikās nursed it and adopted the child as their son. Hence his name Kārttikeya (*MBh*.9.43.6-16; 13.84.8-13). The child had six faces, as it had the six Pleiades as its "mothers" (*MBh*.9.43.12). The seed of Śiva had been carried by Agni and Gaṅgā,

[58] *Mārkaṇḍeya Purāṇa (MāP)*, tr. F. E. Pargiter, 1904, pp. 237-40 (= 49.1-36).

[59] L. Nathan, tr., *The Transport of Love: The Meghadūta of Kālidāsa*, 1976, p. 45.

and the Kṛttikās nursed the child. All three daughters of the Mountain were thus instrumental in the nativity of Śiva's son: Pārvatī had stirred Śiva but was deprived from receiving his seed; Gaṅgā had carried the embryo; and Rāgiṇī was merged with the Kṛttikās, who nursed the newborn child (*MBh*.9.43.12-13). Many more claimed to be his mothers (cf. *MBh*.3.213.1-2, 217.6-9), all by indirection, for by Pārvatī's curse all gods and goddesses were condemned to be childless.

Śiva's seed had been offered as an oblation into the mouth of Agni. Agni the Firebird was the altar for the offering. An altar in the form of a bird was Agni's ancient shape that received the Soma offering in Vedic times (*ŚB*.10.1.2.1). Śiva, having completed his role as his wife's yogic husband, offered his seed by sacrificing it not into the fire of her womb but into Fire itself. On another occasion, Śiva had offered his total self into the fire of his self-sacrifice. At that time, he assumed the shape of Varuṇa and offered his total self into creation; he offered his presence into all living beings. But, so that they should come into bodily existence, it was Brahmā who offered his seed (Ch. X.A.1.c). From the seed of Rudra, however, held within his body while consorting with Pārvatī for a thousand years and ejaculated into the Fire, his son came to be born through the aborted pregnancy of Gaṅgā, Pārvatī's sister who had received Śiva's seed from Agni (cf. *MBh*.9.43.6-9).

Śiva had gone to the end of the yogic path of the retention of the seed under extreme erotic and sexual provocation. Had he not been disturbed, he would have continued the great copulation beyond even a thousand years of the gods. Disturbed by the Firebird, he gave up being the Lord of Yoga and showed himself to the gods as sacrificer and sacrifice unto himself, for Agni is Rudra.

Pārvatī, having cursed all the deities to be childless like herself (*ŚP*.2.4.2.18), and having gone through an antithesis of the immaculate conception, made physical childlessness a condition common to all gods and goddesses. It was an empty revenge. Indeed, she was discontented (*ŚP*.2.4.2.22).

Śiva's sexual asceticism had several degrees. He was a yogi who had no use for a woman; he was a married yogi who did not consummate his marriage but indulged in love-play and copulation. Being inwardly detached, he could afford to take delight in this relation with Pārvatī. He was, however, no longer acting as a yogi when his seed fell and spurted into the fire. On other occasions he acted neither as yogi nor as sacrificer when he let fall his seed. It happened through lovely Mohinī (Delusion), and Śiva himself had asked for it. The occasion was the Churning of the Ocean; after Śiva had swallowed the world poison, the gods had won the elixir of immortality and the demons had stolen it from the gods. Viṣṇu came to the help of the gods. He took the shape of Mohinī—his form of seduction by which he also beguiled the sages in the Deodar forest—and by her charms won back the *amṛta* for the gods (*BhP*.8.8.41-46; 8.9.11-13). Thereupon Śiva, who was accompanied by Pārvatī, asked Viṣṇu to show once more his enticing shape. Viṣṇu again became Mohinī. Śiva seized her and his semen fell on the ground. It turned into gold and silver (*BhP*.8.12.1-3, 12-33). From the seed was born Śāstā / Aiyanār, the son of Śiva and Viṣṇu, and if Viṣṇu in this context is taken as a proxy for Pārvatī,[60] the situation would be akin to the birth of Śiva's son Kārttikeya. Iconographically, the image of Śiva known as Harihara shows Viṣṇu (Hari) on the left side, which is the place of the goddess in the image of Ardhanārīśvara.

Another time, Mohinī provoked the fall of Śiva's seed and Hanumān was born from it (*ŚP*.3.20.3-7). The seduction of Śiva by Viṣṇu / Mohinī as his female Power would amount to a progenitive self-seduction that the image of Ardhanārīśvara denies. In these myths, not only was Śiva struck by the arrows of Kāma but Kāma entered Śiva; he even was Śiva, while in the case of Mohinī (Delusion), Śiva was swayed by her.

The tremendous energy of Śiva, the Lord of Yoga, that went into his love making with Pārvatī prepared the birth of Skanda. In the subsequent shedding of the seed, Śiva no longer showed himself as yogi, but as Fire. As Fire, he had prepared the seed for the Father. As Fire, he offered his own seed into Fire whence his son, his glowing energy, was to be born.

The *Mahābhārata* was first to tell of the birth of Kārttikeya, who in this ancient myth was born from the seed of Agni, the celestial Fire (*MBh*.3.214.1-17). The identity of Agni and Rudra, explicitly reiterated in the *Mahābhārata* (*MBh*.3.218.27-30), pervades the myth of the birth of Kārttikeya, born of one fiery essence impersonated by Agni and Rudra. Agni carried Rudra's seed and shed it without physical

[60] M. Adiceam, *Contribution à l'étude d'Aiyanār-Śāstā*, 1967, p. 19.

contact into Gaṅgā. The goddess, unable to bear the glowing embryo, deposited it on a mountain (*MBh*.9.43.6-9; 13.84.8-12, 48-64). The infant glowed in golden splendor; everything around seemed transubstantiated into gold (*MBh*.13.84.68-70). In this way gold came to exist as the offspring of the god of blazing flames. Gold was the ingrained color of the son of Śiva. Pārvatī, who was not to be his mother, had acquired her golden color through her *tapas*. Though the goddess had shed her darkness, and Śiva and Pārvatī were reconciled after their quarrel, Pārvatī found other reasons to be discontented. She was jealous of Gaṅgā, with whom Agni / Rudra had consorted and who had carried the embryo in her womb (cf. *R*.1.36.7-31).

Agni in the *Mahābhārata* myth was Adbhuta Agni, the celestial Fire (*MBh*.3.213.1-2). He had come out of the disc of the sun and entered the sacrificial fire of the sacrifice of the celestial ṛṣis. There Agni saw the wives of the ṛṣis—the Kṛttikās or Pleiades (*MBh*.3.213.38-42). (In the Deodar forest their astral meaning was not obvious.) Agni fell in love with the wives of the ṛṣis (*MBh*.3.213.44). And here the myth of the birth of Kārttikeya begins.

One day when Indra saw the sun rising over the eastern mountain and the new moon gliding into the sun at the *raudra* moment of dread significance, he saw the gods and demons fighting on the eastern mountain. The morning twilight was spattered with red clouds. Agni, carrying the oblations of the ṛṣis, had entered the disc of the sun. As Indra saw the union of the sun and the moon, their fearful conjunction, and Agni entering the sun, Indra thought it wondrous. And he thought of Agni begetting a son who would be stronger than any other god and who would defeat the demons (*MBh*.3.213.26-36).

In other words, the vision of Indra took place when the sun was in the Kṛttikās. Agni, the celestial fire, having come to the sacrifice of the ṛṣis, saw their beautiful wives and decided to become the household fire in order to be near them (*MBh*.3.213.45-47). Their union, though veiled in complications, impersonations, and substitutions, resulted in the birth of their son Kārttikeya, so called after his foster mothers, the Kṛttikās. Thus, in the oldest allusion to the story, the leading figures are the celestial Agni and the Kṛttikās (*ŚB*.2.1.2.4-5). The latter were seen by Indra in a morning twilight spattered with red clouds. An anthropomorphic figure of this red dawn was Rāgiṇī, who merged with the Kṛttikās, the Pleiades (Ch. X.B.1). Agni, in his rapid flight between the household fire of the ṛṣis and the sun, was in the sun and the sun was in the Kṛttikās, or the celestial fire of the sun was in the Kṛttikās. At that moment the new moon was gliding into the sun. Though Indra saw all this, the moon did not figure any further among the complex events and transformations that preceded the birth of Kārttikeya. The Kṛttikās were his first "mothers." Pārvatī, her heart aching in her empty body, stood last in line as a potential mother of Kārttikeya. She was altogether absent from the earliest account of the prelude to the birth of Kārttikeya given in the *Mahābhārata*. Though Śiva also does not appear in this early version of the myth, his presence was prefigured by Agni. In the later Purāṇic versions of the myth, Agni played a role subsidiary to that of Śiva, and the Kṛttikās became foster mothers or nurses of Kārttikeya. Gaṅgā was given her share in carrying Śiva's seed, whereas the key role of Svāhā, who in the early version seduces Agni by impersonating the wives of the ṛṣis (*MBh*.3.213.50-52), was discontinued in the later version, which gave prominence to Pārvatī. The transfers and elaborations of the roles of the participants in the birth of Kārttikeya[61] have their starting point in the vision of Indra, which took place, though in mythical time, at an astronomically definable moment. The spring equinox when the sun was in the Pleiades, can be assigned to about 2300 B.C. The conjunction of the sun with the new moon further specifies the beginning of the month of the new year that started from the vernal equinox when the sun was in the Pleiades.[62]

The myth of Śiva as referred to the sun and the stars was seen in two of its most significant moments, at the spring equinox when the sun was in Aldebaran (Rohiṇī) and at the spring equinox when the sun was in the Pleiades. More remote than these two significant "moments" is the rising of the vernal equinoctial sun, heralded by Sirius / Vāstoṣpati, the Dog Star.

iii. The Blind Demon King

Once while Śiva was sporting with Pārvatī on Mount Mandara, she covered in jest with her golden, coral-like hands the three eyes of Śiva. Immediately the cosmos was steeped in blinding darkness. Her

[61] Cf. W. D. O'Flaherty, *Asceticism and Eroticism in the Mythology of Śiva*, pp. 94-98, which includes several variant forms of the myth of Agni and the sages and the birth of Kārttikeya.

[62] *Ibid*., p. 100, and B. Ya. Volchok, "Protoindiiskie paralleli k mifu o Skande," 1972, p. 307. See also Ch. II n. 26.

hands, resting on Śiva's forehead, perspired from the heat of the fire of Śiva's third eye; the rutting juice from her hands was heated by the fire in Śiva's forehead. A terrible creature was conceived. It was angry, black, with matted hair, and blind. It sang, cried, laughed, danced, and stuck out its tongue. Śiva told Pārvatī, "you did this by closing my eyes, O my beloved, why are you afraid of it?" Pārvatī, however, could not understand how and why such an ugly creature had come into existence. Śiva explained that the revolting and immensely powerful creature was born of his sweat, and that Pārvatī was the cause of the creation of that being. His name would be Andhaka, "Blind." Pārvatī would be responsible for his safety and well being: he was her own son (*ŚP*.2.5.42.15-26; *ŚP*, *DhS*.4.4-14).

At that time the demon king Hiraṇyākṣa or Gold Eye, who had remained childless and whose wife pined for a son, subjected himself to rigorous austerities in order to see Lord Śiva. Śiva, pleased by the self-control and self-abnegation of the demon king Gold Eye, granted him the boon of a son who would inherit the kingdom of the demons. Hiraṇyākṣa was granted a son by adoption. It was Andhaka whom Śiva gave to Gold Eye as his son (*ŚP*.2.5.42.28-40). Śiva, however, warned King Gold Eye: should Andhaka attempt vile deeds or covet the Mother of the Universe, Śiva himself would "purify" Andhaka's body. Nor could Andhaka obtain Pārvatī without defeating Śiva (*VmP*.37.6-16).

The demon king did not live long. He was killed by Viṣṇu, (*ŚP*.2.5.42.49) and Andhaka as his son became the new, immensely powerful king of the demons. The royal demon family resented Andhaka's kingship, for he was king by adoption only. Andhaka, though he appeased his paternal cousins, the sons of demon Hiraṇyakaśipu (Gold Cloth), he went to a forest where he underwent austerities more severe than any other god or demon could perform. Not only did he stand on one leg with his arms raised continuously, but every day he offered a piece of his flesh together with his blood into the sacred, blazing fire. When nothing but his bones were left and he was about to offer his bloodless skeleton to the fire, he was seen by the gods. They were frightened, as the power of these austerities threatened their existence, and Brahmā immediately offered Andhaka a boon: he could have whatever was very hard to get in the universe. Andhaka said that, being blind, he wanted divine vision and deathlessness. Neither gods—not even Viṣṇu and Śiva—nor demons, Gandharvas, *yakṣas*, serpents, or anyone should be able to kill him. Brahmā explained that there was no immunity from death for anyone born in any way. Andhaka modified the boon he desired and formulated it in terms that surprised Brahmā. Andhaka said, "who is the most excellent woman of all time, whether old, middle-aged, or young, shall be like a mother to me, even though she be unapproachable to all men in body, mind, and speech. Let me be destroyed if I desire her" (*ŚP*.2.5.44.1-16). Andhaka expressed the oedipal death wish that Śiva had foreseen because he had willed it.

Brahmā granted the boon. Then, at Andhaka's request, he restored flesh and blood to Andhaka's skeleton body. The demon king forthwith proceeded with his conquering army all over the earth. He lived the life of a demon king, full of pride and sex. He had every woman he wanted. He conquered the whole world, built a city on the Mandara Mountain, and gradually made people settle there. Once, his ministers saw a strange hermit in a mountain cave. The crescent moon adorned his head, he wore an elephant hide, serpents coiled around his body, and his necklace consisted of skulls. He held a trident, arrows, quiver, bow, and a rosary. Ashes were smeared over the splendor of his four-armed body. The ministers noticed a white bull nearby. They also saw a beautiful woman in the splendor of her youth and covered with jewelry. All this the ministers reported to Andhaka. He trembled with lustful anticipation and sent his emissaries back to the hermit with the order that the hermit should give his wife to Andhaka. The demon king's ministers taunted the hermit about the incongruity of his appearance, his absorption in performing austerities, and the presence of his ravishing woman companion. The hermit should surrender his weapons and carry on his austerities. Smilingly, Śiva revealed his identity to the ministers (*ŚP*.2.5.44.18-57).

Although some time had passed since the birth of Kārttikeya, Śiva now resolved to practice *tapas* (or the Pāśupata vow, as others say) in order to restore the energy and vitality he had lost in his endless love making with Pārvatī (*VmP*.34.2-3; *ŚP*.2.5.45.11-13). When urged to give Pārvatī to the demon king, Śiva said that the fiend could take whatever pleased him at the moment (*ŚP*.2.5.44.60). Andhaka had said that the daughter of the Mountain should be given to him, but she could do as she pleased. He had no power over her (*VmP*.40.45-49). Pārvatī remarked that Śiva and Andhaka were gamblers in a game of life, and whoever won would get her (*VmP*.40.51). Śiva stood quietly. Then, in order to carry out the great austerities by which Pārvatī would be free from sorrow, he left for the divine (Deodar) forest (*ŚP*.2.5.45.13).

The description of Pārvatī by Andhaka's ministers had inflamed the senses of the demon king. In vain did a son of Gold Cloth named Prahlāda who, though a demon, was a devotee of Viṣṇu, attempt to dissuade the blind demon king from his infatuation. He told Andhaka his past. Pārvatī, the Mother of the Universe, was the wife of Śiva, who was his father. They let their son be adopted by Gold Eye, the demon king. Śiva, at that time, had warned King Hiraṇyākṣa that if Andhaka should covet the Mother of the Universe, Śiva himself would "purify" Andhaka's body (*VmP*.37.3-11).

Prahlāda's words had no effect on blind Andhaka, blinded also by lust and arrogance. He rushed with his army to the Mountain cave where Pārvatī stayed during Śiva's absence, guarded by Vīraka, her son. Andhaka attacked Vīraka. Frightened, Pārvatī thought of Brahmā, Viṣṇu, Indra, and the other gods. They came, having assumed female appearance, as it would have not been seemly for the gods to enter the cave where the goddess resided (*ŚP*.2.5.45.16-27). Or, in another version of the myth, it was Pārvatī herself who took up a hundred forms in fear of the demon king (*VmP*.33.34). Pārvatī, blazing with fury, and standing among the hundred goddesses, set out herself with a vast army of divine women in whose velocity thousands of powerful currents were let loose, and Andhaka was repulsed (*VmP*.33.35-40). Śiva, having performed the Pāśupata vow, returned and embraced Pārvatī. She dismissed the many goddesses. Blind Andhaka, who had not been able to recognize Pārvatī, sent an emissary to Śiva challenging him as one who was not a true ascetic but only an enemy, and ordering him to surrender Pārvatī. Śiva invited Andhaka to fight with him (*ŚP*.2.5.45.42-51).

Although the army of the demons was kept intact by Śukra's science of resuscitation (*sañjīvanī vidyā*) (*VmP*.43.6-8), Nandin captured Śukra and brought him to Śiva, who swallowed him, ejaculated him through his penis, and made him his son (*VmP*.43.26-43; cf. Ch. VI.4.a). Śiva then produced Yawn and, infested by it, the demons opened wide their mouths and those gods whom they had swallowed came out; the army of the demons was defeated (*VmP*.43.63-68). Śiva danced, whirling his eighteen long arms; he meditated, worshiped the sun, and danced, joined by his gaṇas and the gods. Then he performed the twilight worship (*sandhyā*) and danced to the utmost of his desire. He was again ready to fight with Andhaka (*VmP*.43.69-74). The demon king, seeing his army defeated and Śiva invincible, had lost none of his lust for Pārvatī (*VmP*.43.75-78). He thought of a ruse that would subject Pārvatī to his desire. He would delude her by assuming the shape of Śiva, and enjoy her body. Andhaka ordered the demon Sunda to assume the shape of Nandin. Both he and Nandin appeared covered with wounds fresh from the recent battle (*VmP*.43.79-82). Pārvatī, seeing Śiva and Nandin wounded and coming to her apartment, made her maids bring dressings and ointments; tending Śiva's wounds, she failed to see the bull marks on his sides, knew that she had fallen victim to a deception, and ran away in fear (*VmP*.43.83-93). Andhaka, blind as he was with passion and by birth, pursued her but could not catch up with her, for she had vanished into a radiant, white *arka* flower. Andhaka resumed his own shape and returned to his army (*VmP*.43.94-97).

Pārvatī, taking refuge in an *arka* flower, took refuge in Śiva. Though the significance of the *arka* plant is not dwelt upon in the *Purāṇas*, it was ancient knowledge that the *arka* tree stood for Rudra. It had sprung from Rudra's resting place (*ŚB*.9.1.1.9), and was consubstantial with him. It sustained Rudra with its own life sap; it was the sacrificial food offered to Śiva ritually in the *Śatarudriya* sacrifice. When the God stood flaming on the altar longing for food, the gods gathered food for him. They offered wild sesamum to him by means of an *arka* leaf (*ŚB*.9.1.1.1-8). The leaf on which the food was offered and the food were looked upon as one. They were the offering for Agni / Rudra, to be consumed by him. They became one with him, and he revealed himself as "Agni, the *arka*" (*ŚB*.10.3.4.5).

While Pārvatī found refuge in the *arka* flower, the fiercest battle began to rage between the gods and the demons. Finally, only Śiva and Andhaka were left on the battlefield (*VmP*.44.19-22). Śiva pierced the heart of Andhaka with his trident (*VmP*.44.27). Andhaka was impaled on the trident that Śiva held aloft, high up in the air (*VmP*.44.39). The lower half of Andhaka's body was dried up by the rays of the sun, the upper half was drenched by the downpour of the clouds; his flesh withered (*ŚP*.2.5.46.38). Yet the demon Andhaka did not die. For a thousand years of the gods he remained impaled on Śiva Bhairava's trident, his body dried up by Śiva's eyes that are sun and fire (*VmP*.44.49). Having lost his demon kingdom and his demon nature

(*SkP*.6.229.26), the demon king became pure and free from sin by the fire of Śiva's (third) eye (*VmP*.44.50). On the stake held aloft by Śiva, Andhaka praised Śiva and cried out for protection, saying, "I am a sinner," and "I was born in sin." . . . "Do not be angry with me, O Lord of gods. You made me this way." . . . "Protect me. I have come to you for refuge" (*VmP*.44.51-66). Śiva, pleased with Andhaka, let him choose any boon he liked except Pārvatī (*VmP*.44.67-68). Andhaka replied that Pārvatī was his mother and Śiva his father, and chose the boon of becoming Śiva's devotee (*VmP*.44.69-71). Śiva, the ocean of compassion, made him a chieftain of his gaṇas named Bhṛṅgī (*VmP*.44.72; *ŚP*.2.5.46.39). He took Andhaka off the trident and, having passed his hands over Andhaka's body, made him whole again (*VmP*.44.73). Śiva, accompanied by Andhaka and Nandin, returned to his mountain home, where he saw the daughter of the Mountain in the white *arka* flower (*VmP*.44.84-85). She left the flower. Śiva embraced her and presented to her Andhaka, her son (*VmP*.44.86-89). He praised the Great Goddess, and she asked him to choose a boon. Bhṛṅgī said; "O Pārvatī, let my sins come to an end. O mother, let me be devoted to Śiva in eternity" (*VmP*.44.91-93). Thus, Śiva in his terrible form of Bhairava transformed the foremost demon into Bhṛṅgī due to his devotion.

Andhaka, hideous, black, and blind, owed his existence to a carefree, careless, playful, impulse of Pārvatī. She covered the three eyes of Śiva and darkness set in. Once already she had played a similar game. She covered Śiva's two eyes. As their light went out, Śiva opened a third eye that none had seen before. The fire of destruction shot out from the middle of his forehead, soared to heaven, and consumed the Himavat Mountain, Pārvatī's father. Śiva, however, out of compassion restored the Mountain and he forgave Pārvatī her lack of foresight (*MBh*.13.127.26-38). Pārvatī had failed to understand that the slightest obstruction caused to Śiva's body would have cosmic consequences. In this instance, Śiva restored the damage that had been done by his spontaneous, fiery outbreak, and he restored Pārvatī's confidence. It was a childish prank that could have destroyed the world. Instead, it released into the cosmos Śiva's power of destruction that was to clean the world from obsolescence and dross, and make possible a new beginning after the end of days. Moreover, it gave to Śiva his unique cognizance, the vertical third eye in the middle of his forehead. Artists first rendered this cognizance of Śiva by showing the third eye horizontally in the middle of the forehead. God Indra was also shown with the third eye, placed horizontally, in the middle of the forehead. Indra's third eye was but a singularization of the thousand eyes that had come to cover his entire body. These represented multiples of the physical organ, the eye (or also the vulva—but this latter significance has no bearing here), and like the eye their position was horizontal, whereas Śiva's third eye, in post-Kuṣāṇa sculptures, cut across the horizontal extent of the forehead and of the physical plane. Śiva's third eye was an outlet of the fire within himself, which he sent forth into the cosmos as the power of destruction / creation.

When Pārvatī covered with her coral-like hands the three eyes of Śiva, her hands were heated by the fire of Śiva's third eye. The perspiration from her hands and the heat from Śiva's forehead commingled, and from this Andhaka issued, blind, dark, hairy. The hideous creature showed himself to be Śiva's son. He danced, sang, laughed, and cried as Śiva did at times. He had the excessive intensity of Śiva's disposition. And he was furious. But it was Pārvatī who had caused him to come into existence by closing Śiva's eyes. By her frowardness, the light and fire within Śiva that keep the universe alive were occluded within Śiva. His forehead broke out in a sweat of frustration, anger, and nascent sexual excitement. Hideous Andhaka, more intimately than any other being, became the son of Śiva and Pārvatī, having been born from the direct touch and sweat of his parents. This scion of the two greatest divinities, in his ugly deformity, had no reason to be grateful to his parents, or to his mother in particular, who had provoked his coming into existence.

By demoniac coincidence, Gold Eye, the childless demon king, exerting himself in austerities in order to have a son, gave Śiva the opportunity of granting his wish by giving blind Andhaka to Gold Eye as his adopted son. Śiva knew why he gave Andhaka away to be adopted by the demon king. He knew Andhaka's vicious might, of which Andhaka's lusting after his mother was part. By making his son over to the demons, Śiva placed him where he belonged. It was the proper place from which Andhaka could exercise his power, and through which Śiva could lead into sin and later redeem his ill-begotten son.

The adoption by Gold Eye did not clear Andhaka's vision. Born blind, he became blind with passion and blind with arrogance. Though adoption had made Andhaka legitimately the son of Gold

Eye, Andhaka's cousins did not fully accept him and made him feel that his origin lay elsewhere than in the demon kingdom. Andhaka then subjected himself to self-immolating austerities, honing his body until only his skeleton was left. By this extreme yogic discipline he took revenge on himself for not being accepted as the scion of Gold Eye, and he took revenge on his original parents, particularly on Pārvatī, who had caused his plight. Born with the qualities of a demon, though himself of the highest divine descent, Andhaka was adopted by the king of demons, thus legally having the status of a demon, yet spurned by his demon family. Finding himself in this impossible situation, he meant to achieve the impossible. The gods were frightened for their own sake by his terrific penance, and Brahmā offered him the boon that indeed he could attain whatever was inaccessible. Andhaka being blind and of divine origin, wanted divine vision. He wanted to be exempt from death, but this Brahmā could not grant anyone. Then by his own impulse Andhaka formulated the boon he craved: the most excellent woman in the world should be like a mother to him, though she be unapproachable to any man. Should, however, Andhaka covet her, he should be destroyed. Unwittingly, he had repeated the warning Śiva gave when he made over Andhaka to Gold Eye for adoption.

Hideous, black, blind Andhaka acted out his destiny. Born through an act of indiscretion on the part of his mother, abandoned by both parents, and made over by Śiva to the demons, where by looks and disposition he belonged, legally confirmed in his new status but repudiated by his new family, Andhaka in anguish longed for a mother of supernal perfection, and desired her who was unapproachable. As king of the demons, Andhaka had any woman he wanted.

Nearly giving himself away in asking for his boon, he pulled himself together and added, to Brahmā's surprise, his wish to be destroyed should he covet his mother. His wish for destruction overwhelmed him. As powerful in his kingdom as he was desperate in his life, he longed for his divine mother who abandoned him after having caused his blindness and ugliness. He wanted divine vision. Brahmā granted Andhaka's wish *de profundis*. He also restored his body.

The blind demon king, having conquered the three worlds and enjoyed all they had to offer, stayed in his new city in the Himālayas and heard from his ministers about an uncanny hermit and a most beautiful woman who stayed near him. Their description of the woman aroused in him an insane desire for her. He refused to listen to his cousin Prahlāda, who informed Andhaka about his own past as it had settled down in and disturbed the recesses of his mind. Andhaka insisted on demanding the beautiful woman from the strange yogi, who was Śiva. Immersed in the observance of the Pāśupata vow, Śiva let Pārvatī decide for herself her response to the demon's demand. It was somewhat cynical, but Śiva trusted Pārvatī to stand on her own, which she did, for she had all the power of the Great Goddess, and it assisted her in the shape of all the women that the gods had become in order to defend her when Andhaka and his soldiers drew near her cave guarded by Vīraka. When Śiva returned, having fulfilled the Pāśupata vow, Andhaka in his blindness did not see him, nor could he in his blind lust discern Pārvatī amid the waves of divine femininity whose impact engulfed him. In the ensuing battle between Śiva and Andhaka, the army of the demons was defeated and Śiva exulted in a cosmic dance, sinking into meditation whenever he paused. This was the moment when Andhaka, realizing that his army was defeated and that Śiva was invincible in battle, decided to seize Pārvatī, disguising himself as Śiva wounded in the war. Pārvatī, finding the body of the demon king without certain marks she knew to be on Śiva's body, saw through Andhaka's deception, ran away, and escaped him. Blind and impassioned as he was, he could not reach her, nor could he see her. He resumed his own hideous shape and continued the fight with Śiva, who impaled him on his trident. Though pierced through the heart, Andhaka did not die. Impaled, he meditated on Śiva until his flesh withered away, and he praised the Lord until he was released from the great fear of his sin. Śiva forgave his son his base lust of Pārvatī (*ŚP*.2.5.49.4-20; *VmP*.44.72). At last he could worship Pārvatī and pray to the mother that he be eternally Śiva's devotee (*VmP*.44.90-93).

Andhaka, pierced in his heart, impaled on the trident of Śiva, and reduced to a skeleton was not the same Andhaka who by his tremendous demonic energy practiced austerities in order to obtain the boon from Brahmā that astounded even the Creator. Andhaka then had cut off all his flesh and drained away his blood until only a skeleton remained. The boon he desired was complex: divine vision; deathlessness; the most excellent woman, unapproachable to all men, as his mother; and destruction should he covet her.

Impaled on Śiva's trident, blind Andhaka in new austerities dried up until only his bones remained, but he did not die. He obtained divine vision—he saw Pārvatī as the Mother. Along with his flesh his infatuation had dried up, and he had lost a demon's kingdom.

Pārvatī, the cause of Andhaka's blindness, had confronted the sightless demon king in multiples, each a furious defensive shape of herself. He could not recognize her whom he coveted because he could not see her in that outburst of female power. He attempted to seize her by assuming Śiva's shape, but blind by birth and passion, he could not catch her when she ran away and fled into a white *arka* flower. For all this blindness of his—by birth, lust, and pride—Andhaka should have died. He was saved by Śiva's grace when impaled and withered; held aloft on Śiva's trident, he meditated and obtained divine wisdom. Śiva then took Andhaka to Pārvatī, his mother.

Andhaka, of divine origin, had been destined to lead a tortured life of demonic lust, power, passion, rejection, ascetic self-destruction, and longing for divine vision and the perfect woman, the Mother of the Universe who had abandoned him. Though he lived in darkness, divine vision and the Mother of the Universe were his by birth. Obsessed by demonic, unconsciously incestuous desire, he drove himself to his own defeat; his death was a purification by Śiva, who had willed his redemption and return to his origin.

Images of Śiva together with Pārvatī (Umā-Maheśvara) and also of other forms of Śiva include the skeletal figure of Bhṛṅgī. An etiological myth identifies this figure with a ṛṣi of that name,[63] unaware that Bhṛṅgī, who had been Andhaka, was part of the "holy family" of Śiva along with Gaṇeśa, Kārttikeya, and Nandin.

[63] Cf. T. A. Gopinatha Rao, *Elements of Hindu Iconography*, vol. 2, part 1, pp. 322-23; and W. D. O'Flaherty, *Asceticism and Eroticism in the Mythology of Śiva*, pp. 307-308.

XI

THE DEMONS

1. Demons of Sex

a. *Āḍi*

Though Andhaka looked and acted like a demon from the moment of his birth, he was of divine origin and was led back to the gods. The demon had appeared spontaneously in consequence of an unpremeditated, playful movement of Pārvatī's hands. On another occasion, it was Śiva who teased Pārvatī during their love making. She resented his calling her black and she left the house, only to have a demon enter in her absence. In those tension-charged, amorous moments, the slightest dissonance released forces beyond control. A playful gesture or word during the love making of the gods brought about one demon and attracted another.

Śiva had teasingly commented on Pārvatī's darkness one night as they were lying together, her arm like a dark serpent around his white sandal-treelike body. She also looked like the night of the new moon. As Śiva called her Kālī, "Black," Pārvatī withdrew from his embrace. Angered, she called Śiva more than black, Mahākāla, the great or transcendent darkness. Then Śiva told her she was as hard as rock, like the Mountain, her father, cold as snow, and crooked like the winding Himālayan footpaths. Pārvatī rejoined that Śiva, like ashes, knew no affection, that he lived in cremation grounds, shameless, naked, fond of disgusting things, and wearing skulls (*MP*.155.1-23). Pārvatī hurled reproaches at Śiva which before their marriage she had defended Śiva against, not only accepting but enthralled by the inscrutably abhorrent traits of the Great God.

Brahmā's dark scheme worked. Pārvatī took as a personal slight Śiva's description of their contrasting colors that set off their separate and combined beauty. She exaggerated a possibly implied ambiguity and hurled its pejorative meaning back at Śiva, overlooking in her irritation that serpents were dear to Śiva and served as his ornaments, and that he wore on his head the crescent moon whose rays rested on her white garment. Pārvatī was leaving the palace in order to win by renewed austerities a golden complexion so as to be loved more truly by her lord when Vīraka came running, imploring her not to leave. But she was firm in her resolve and spite; she instructed Vīraka to guard the gate and not to let any woman enter in her absence, for Śiva was covetous of women (*MP*.155.24-34).

Āḍi, a demon and son of Andhaka, learning that Pārvatī had left Śiva, thought the time had come for him to kill Śiva, who had ended the life and rule of his father, the demon king. Āḍi ignored, or did not want to know, the transfiguration of Andhaka speared on Śiva's trident. By his own austerities Āḍi had won a boon from Brahmā that he himself could not be killed if he did not change his shape. Anxious to revenge himself on Śiva, he entered the palace unseen by Vīraka, for he crawled in shaped like a serpent; once in the palace, the serpent assumed the shape of Pārvatī. Śiva at first was happily surprised on seeing her return, for his longing was great. But when Pārvatī said she had returned driven by love, Śiva realized that she had come back without fulfilling her purpose, and he knew the woman could not be Pārvatī. He also noticed on her body a clump of hair where Pārvatī's body had the mark of a lotus. Śiva, seeing through the hoax of the satanic demon, fixed a thunderbolt on his penis that rendered ineffective the strong sharp teeth that Āḍi had put into the vagina of his Pārvatī disguise. Śiva killed the demon Āḍi (*MP*.156.11-37). The real Pārvatī, engaged in austerities, heard from Vāyu, the Wind, of a woman dead in Śiva's palace and cursed rock-born Vīraka that his mother should turn into a stone, without heart, inanimate, and rugged, which Pārvatī craved to become (*MP*.156.37-39; 157.1-2).

Pārvatī completed her austerities, and her color became golden. Like a sheath the darkness had fallen from her, transforming itself into the goddess Night (*MP*.157.13-14). Pārvatī returned to Śiva's palace, revealed herself in her golden identity to Vīraka, her son, whose innocence she acknowledged by modifying her curse. Śiva quickly made love to Pārvatī and did not desist for a thousand years of the gods (*MP*.158.6-28; cf. *PP*.5.41.1-121).[1]

The sequence of events in Śiva's married life varies according to different traditions. Thus, Gaṇeśa is said to have been born before or after the birth of Kārttikeya. On the other hand, the Āḍi episode took place before the birth of Kārttikeya, and Andhaka was impaled by Śiva after the birth of Kārttikeya. Āḍi, however, is said to have been Andhaka's son, who meant to avenge his father's death on Śiva. Each of the several myths is valid in its own right. They are strung together like manifold beads on a chain, some of more recent make, some ancient. Their colors and shapes may be gathered in one sequence or another, and enhance the figure for whose sake they have been assembled.

After their marriage, Pārvatī did not see Śiva in the same light as that in which he had appeared to her before the wedding and in the long years of her ascetic life of readying herself for Śiva and drawing him to her. Living with Śiva, she became irritable when Śiva lovingly teased her; or grew insouciant when she playfully touched him. From that contact of her hand Andhaka was born and, when she left Śiva following their quarrel, Āḍi entered. Demons sprang from or entered into the erotic life of Śiva and Pārvatī. Andhaka, their son, was redeemed by his inner conversion while impaled on Śiva's trident. His son Āḍi found his death through another weapon, the thunderbolt of Śiva's penis. Śiva administered death to the demon by means of sex, a method the demon had meant to practice successfully on Śiva. Pārvatī had given Āḍi the opportunity to find his death through Śiva. Having meant to kill Śiva by deceitful seduction, he became the victim of Śiva. The weapon that Śiva used was his *liṅga* equipped with adamantine power. The lethal power of sex was provoked in Śiva by the demon's deceit and sexual fantasy. Kālī's black color had set afoot this far-reaching effect. The demon had crept into Śiva's apartment in the guise of a serpent; it was, however, Śiva who had likened Pārvatī embracing him to a serpent coiled around a tree. This remark, offensive to Pārvatī, brought magically to Śiva's apartment the serpent-shaped demon who meant to act as Pārvatī. In serpent shape the demon entered his death chamber where, disguised as Pārvatī, he made love

[1] The same story is told in greater detail in the *Skānda Purāṇa* 1.2.27.60-84; 1.2.28.1-14; 1.2.29.1-82.

with Śiva. Śiva did not see the serpent, he only saw the woman who looked like Pārvatī.

Āḍi's serpent shape appeared to serve his purpose; it was an appropriate disguise for entering the presence of Śiva, whose ambience the serpents form. They surrounded Śiva when Kāma attacked him. He mastered their power. They functioned as his amulets and ornaments, they guarded the Uncreate. They were the protection of Śiva, who is called the one who wears black serpents (*ŚP*.2.5.13.26). They also were his weapons, his bow and arrow. Kṛṣṇa and Arjuna saw these terrible snakes become Śiva's bow and arrow (*MBh*.7.57.72). Indeed, the Pināka, Śiva's bow which is like a thousand rainbows, was really a mighty snake (*MBh*.13.14.122). Protective ornaments or aggressive weapon, the serpent belongs to Rudra. It is strong with ancient Asura power. Kāvya Uśanas, acting as the priest of the demons whom Śiva attacked, tore out a lock of his hair and hurled it against Śiva. From that lock of hair sprang many serpents. They began to bite Śiva, and his throat turned blue (*MBh*.12.329.15). From Vṛtra, the serpent guardian of the Uncreate, whence also the demons received it, the serpent power had come to Śiva. In the shape of Kuṇḍalinī, according to the symbolic language of Tantra, the serpent power lies coiled around his *liṅga* in the lowermost *cakra* or center of realization of the body, which is associated with the element earth.[2] The chthonic abode of the serpents and the region of sex are tantric symbolic equivalents of the same center. In the sex myth of Śiva and the demon Āḍi, the serpent with sinister intent made its way to Śiva, but changed into the semblance of Pārvatī before reaching Śiva, who killed the demon who had changed his shape twice. The bite of the serpent issued from a lock of Uśanas turned into a mark that appears as an ornament on Śiva's throat. This mark is also said to be due to the world poison that arose during the Churning of the Ocean (Ch. VI.5). According to some, the serpent Vāsuki had spat the poison into the water.

b. *Pārvatī's Ballgame*

Śiva's *liṅga* was fatal to the demon by virtue of the thunderbolt power ostensibly added on to it, but in fact inherent in it. The adamantine

[2] Cf. P. H. Pott, *Yoga and Yantra: Their Interrelationship and Their Significance for Indian Archaeology*, 1946, pp. 8-9, 38, and table I; M. Eliade, *Yoga: Immortality and Freedom*, p. 245.

power of the *vajra* or thunderbolt was, moreover, of a double nature, inasmuch as *vajra* in tantric usage signified transcendentally the absolute, while also implying its other meaning of phallus.[3] The latter meaning is obvious in the scene described in the myth, while the other meaning, though not inherent in the narrative, hovers over the crassly sexual situation. It was Śiva's *liṅga* that annihilated the demon. The effectiveness of Śiva's *vajra liṅga* in the Āḍi myth looms at the opposite end of the *ūrdhvaliṅga* of the Great Yogi. Śiva's deadly power of sex was activated against a demon attempting in the shape of Pārvatī to cohabit with Śiva.

The demons once saw her playing ball. She enjoyed the game, and two lustful demons got excited as they watched her. Pārvatī hit both of them at the same instant with one ball; they fell to the ground like ripe fruits or like mountain peaks struck by a thunderbolt, and the ball changed into a *liṅga* (*ŚP*.2.5.59.16-27). The thunderbolt power of Śiva's *liṅga* directed against demons by Pārvatī's hand protected Pārvatī's chastity. The paradox of Śiva's death-bringing *vajra liṅga* was centered on Pārvatī, who was saved from being raped by the demons through Śiva's sexual power, which brought death to them.

The episode of Pārvatī's ball game, which fatefully attracted the two mighty demons Vidala and Utpala, whose names but for this incident would be unknown, was brought about indirectly by Śiva himself. These demons had harassed the gods; Brahmā thought of Śiva, and Śiva sent Nārada, the celestial sage, to the demons, singing the glory of Pārvatī's beauty. They responded by getting excited and resolved to abduct the goddess. The moment had come, so they thought, when one day, flying in the air, they saw Pārvatī playing ball (*ŚP*.2.5.59.2-17). Śiva played his own game, not far away from Pārvatī. He used her beauty as bait, and they both enjoyed the game.

c. *Jalandhara*

At another and more crucial phase of the perennial battle of the gods and demons, Śiva, indirectly through Nārada, the celestial sage whom he commissioned, made similar use of Pārvatī's beauty while she, on her own, went one step further and caused the death of Vṛndā, the flawless, devoted wife of Jalandhara, then the emperor of the demons and a "son" of Śiva. The tragic myth of Jalandhara begins with Śiva

[3] A. Bharaṭi, *The Tantric Tradition*, p. 175.

casting off into the ocean the fire of fury of his third eye. Indra and Bṛhaspati had gone to Kailāsa to see Lord Śiva. A naked yogi with matted hair and radiant face blocked the way. Indra, not recognizing Lord Śiva, who meant to test their knowledge, asked the yogi repeatedly who he was and received no reply. Enraged, Indra threatened Śiva with his thunderbolt, and Indra's arm was paralyzed (*ŚP*.2.5.13.4-18). Śiva mastered his rising fury; so that the fire of his third eye that was about to kill Indra should not hurt him, Śiva cast it into the ocean (*ŚP*.2.5.13.48-50). Instantly, the fire of Śiva, born of the eye in the forehead and cast into the salt ocean at the mouth of the Ganges, assumed the form of a boy. As the child cried terribly, Brahmā descended from heaven. Although the Ocean could not tell Brahmā anything about the origin of the child, Brahmā said that the boy Jalandhara would become the emperor of the demons. None except Śiva would be able to slay him, and he would return to the place of his origin (*ŚP*.2.5.14.4-28).

Śukra (Kāvya Uśanas) performed the rites of coronation, and soon Jalandhara grew into a handsome man and was married to Vṛndā, the daughter of the great demon Kālanemi. Jalandhara then ruled over the Asuras with the assistance of Śukra (*ŚP*.2.5.14.30-40).

Jalandhara ruled over the earth with justice and nobility, but he resented the churning of the Ocean, his "father," whose treasure, the *amṛta*, the gods had treacherously taken (*ŚP*.2.5.15.17-19). Hence, the gods were unhappy under Jalandhara's rule. Distressed, they sought Śiva's help. Śiva sent Ṛṣi Nārada to act on behalf of the gods who suffered under Jalandhara (*ŚP*.2.5.18.1-5). After consulting with the gods, the celestial sage Nārada went to see Jalandhara (*ŚP*.2.5.18.18-19). Nārada, on being asked whence he had come and what was the purpose of his visit, described to Jalandhara the residence of Śiva in its celestial beauty. Nārada had wondered if there were any other place to match Śiva's residence; in response Jalandhara showed off his wealth. Nārada commented that Jalandhara, who possessed the most beautiful of everything, lacked only the best jewel among women. Nārada then returned to his description of Śiva's residence. Śiva lived there as a naked yogi with Pārvatī, his wife of exquisite beauty. Her charm was such that she had even subjugated Śiva, the Great Yogi. Jalandhara, though he was surrounded by all the wealth in existence, could not boast of such beauty near him. Nārada exerted himself to make Jalandhara covet Pārvatī, and he succeeded in exciting the king of demons (*ŚP*.2.5.18.22-50). Infatuated, Jalandhara, who had conquered the world and ruled over the gods, sent his messenger, Rāhu, to Śiva. He demanded that Śiva give Pārvatī to Jalandhara. He was the ruler; it was for him to enjoy all excellent things. What use was the incomparable beauty of Pārvatī to the Great Yogi attended by ghosts, spirits, and demons? Her place should be with Jalandhara, who had seized and enjoyed the most precious possession of every god (*ŚP*.2.5.19.3-16). Rāhu placed Jalandhara's message before Śiva, the Great God, who appeared in regal splendor, celestial ornaments adorning his perfect body white with ashes. After listening to Rāhu's message, a terrifying creature burst out from between Śiva's eyebrows. Huge with the face of a lion, it got hold of Rāhu and started to devour him. Śiva restrained the hungry creature and made it devour its own body. When the creature was left only with its head, Śiva made it his gaṇa and doorkeeper Kīrttimukha (*ŚP*.2.5.19.18-48), the apotropaic face that guards the entrance of the house of god.

Jalandhara, angered by the failure of his emissary, mobilized the entire army of the demons against Śiva's gaṇas (*ŚP*.2.5.20.7-8). It was a hopeless battle for the gaṇas, because the demons by the magic power of resuscitation exercised by Śukra kept their ranks undiminished, until Śiva, in great fury, sent forth a sorceress from his mouth (*ŚP*.2.5.20.49-52). Her mouth was cavernous, her breasts crushed trees (*ŚP*.2.5.20.52); she had teeth and eyes in her womb. She went to the battleground and stuffed Śukra into her vagina, where she kept him for the time being (*ŚP*.2.5.20.55; *PP*.6.18.82-90). Śukra (the Seed), the wielder of the magic of resuscitation, was held captive in the womb of the witch, and the fight of the demons and Śiva's gaṇas remained undecided until Śiva himself, in his terrible form and laughing, went into the battle, riding on his bull (*ŚP*.2.5.22.1). Jalandhara saw that his powers of warfare were useless against Śiva, and took recourse to his magic power, conjuring up an illusion of Gandharvas and Apsarases, dancing and singing. They held Śiva's interest while Jalandhara, driven by lust and assuming the shape of Śiva, ten-armed, five-faced, and three-eyed, went toward Pārvatī. She came to meet him. Overwhelmed by her beauty, his seed fell and he was paralyzed. From this Pārvatī realized that he was a demon, that he did not have the stamina of a god, and she vanished. She told Viṣṇu about the incident, for it struck her that Jalandhara unwittingly had shown her the way to his own destruction. As Jalandhara had attempted to subject her to his lust, so Viṣṇu should violate the chastity of Vṛndā, the wife of Jalandhara. Viṣṇu thereupon went to Jalandhara's city to carry out his deception (*ŚP*.2.5.22.33-52). First, Viṣṇu made Vṛndā have bad dreams and see evil omens, even the death of Jalandhara killed by Śiva. None could restore Jalandhara to life once Śiva had killed him. Yet, an ascetic who was Viṣṇu in disguise achieved the impossible to the eyes of Vṛndā: he restored Jalandhara to life. Little did she know that it was Viṣṇu who now had assumed the appearance of Jalandhara. Vṛndā and Jalandhara embraced and made love. Only at the end did Vṛndā realize that she had made love with Viṣṇu. She cursed Viṣṇu and entered the fire. Having sacrificed herself, her sheer inner light (*tejas*) reached the world of Śiva and was absorbed into Pārvatī (*ŚP*.2.5.23.3-49).

Jalandhara, having been unable to deceive Pārvatī, returned to the battlefield. By that time the dancing and singing Gandharvas and Apsarases had vanished from Śiva's vision. Finding himself back on the battlefield, Śiva fought with Jalandhara. Once more Jalandhara exercised his *māyā* and made Śiva see Pārvatī, this time bound in her chariot and beaten by demons. Śiva became distressed, but as Jalandhara attacked him the delusion vanished (*ŚP*.2.5.24.2-14). Śiva decided to kill Jalandhara. Then, in great fury and for sport, Śiva with his big toe drew a wondrous terrible discus in the waters. Laughing, he challenged Jalandhara to lift the wheel created in the waters. Should he lift it up, he would be able to fight with Śiva. Jalandhara in reply boasted of his former exploits, among them his having seized Vaḍavā, the fire-mare—the submarine fire—and having closed her flaming mouth that devoured the water of the ocean. Śiva laughed and became enraged. He held in his hand Sudarśana, the discus he had drawn with his toe. He threw the discus, bright like a hundred thousand suns and the fire of dissolution, and he severed the head of Jalandhara (*ŚP*.2.5.24.25-47). The *tejas* departed from Jalandhara's body and merged into Śiva, just as the *tejas* from Vṛndā's body had merged into Pārvatī. The entire universe then resumed its normal course (*ŚP*.2.5.24.52, 58).

While Andhaka was more a son of Pārvatī than of Śiva, and became a demon only by adoption even though he looked and acted like a demon from birth, Jalandhara was born from Śiva's ire. Pārvatī had no share in the making of Jalandhara. He assumed his shape in the Ocean whose son he became: he was destined by Brahmā to become emperor of the demons. Jalandhara was fair-minded yet, being a demon, he was an enemy of the gods. The war between the gods and the demons that had Śiva and Jalandhara as protagonists was waged in two domains: that of arms, demanding power and skill, and that of sex and deception, with Pārvatī and Vṛndā as pawns. Śiva played an equivocal part. Jalandhara was his own issue, whom none could kill except Śiva himself. To this end Śiva sent Nārada to tempt Jalandhara with his description of Pārvatī's beauty; moreover, he made the steadfast, faithful demon king's slowly rising desire appear justified on account of Śiva's, the yogi's, unsuitability as Pārvatī's husband. Jalandhara's demand for Pārvatī, in the end, almost seemed reasonable for one who ruled over the gods and possessed everything excellent except Pārvatī. When Jalandhara succumbed to the temptation of Nārada's description of Pārvatī and sent Rāhu to Śiva to demand Pārvatī, Śiva received Rāhu with devouring fury. Śiva's indirect offer of Pārvatī to the demon king having miscarried, the war of the gods and demons continued. Śiva either knew from the beginning that Nārada's mission would be unsuccessful, or else he left it to Pārvatī to act on her own vis-à-vis Jalandhara, as he had done in the case of Andhaka, the demon king.

Śiva played a safe and cruel game in tempting Jalandhara, for Pārvatī and Śiva were inseparable, like a word and its meaning. To those who did not know this truth and thought of them as separate, Śiva's attitude toward Pārvatī could have seemed cynical and calculated.

Pārvatī, less subtle than Śiva and more demonical than Jalandhara, retaliated. She made Viṣṇu exercise his power of illusion on Vṛndā, the devoted wife of Jalandhara. Pārvatī made Viṣṇu make love with Vṛndā, revenging Jalandhara's aborted attempt on herself. But in contrast to Jalandhara's clumsy and revealing behavior, Viṣṇu in the course of his *māyā*, using psychological tactics, twice disguised himself. Posing as an ascetic, he knew how to win Vṛndā's confidence. The false ascetic conjured before her eyes the illusion of the maimed, dead body of her husband; he followed this up by himself assuming the shape of Jalandhara, whom in the meanwhile he had restored to life. He revived, rose, embraced, and kissed Vṛndā. Overwhelmed, Vṛndā yielded to him whom she believed to be Jalandhara, but who was Viṣṇu. Then, realizing his deception and what she had done, Vṛndā killed herself.

Pārvatī had taken her revenge on Jalandhara; she dealt a fateful blow to him by Vṛndā's death. Śiva then decided to kill the weakened Jalandhara in battle by means of the discus called Sudarśana. Śiva created this sharp wheel in the waters of the ocean by stirring them playfully with his big toe (*ŚP*.2.5.24.26, 46). The wheel, an ancient symbol of the turning of heaven around the cosmic axis (cf. *RV*.10.89.4), according to the Jalandhara myth was created in the cosmic waters, the domain where Jalandhara was born. Śiva challenged the demon king to lift the wheel created by Śiva in the waters. If he could perform this feat, he would be competent to fight with Śiva. As Jalandhara did not stir, Śiva laughed and became angry; he hurled the Sudarśana wheel, as bright as a hundred thousand suns, and severed the head of the emperor of the demons from his body (*ŚP*.2.5.24.28, 44-47).

The cosmic Sudarśana weapon in Śiva's hand, destructive of the world power of the demons, ended the life of Jalandhara, while it was Śiva's trident that had pierced the heart of Andhaka. The movement of heaven around the cosmic axis and the cosmic axis itself were the respective weapons signifying the annihilation of cosmic rule of the demons and establishment of that of the gods.

Jalandhara, unable to take up the Sudarśana but glorifying in his previous achievements, told Śiva that he had closed the mouth of the submarine fire (*ŚP*.2.5.24.38). Jalandhara the demon king had originated from the cast-off fire of Śiva's third eye. It had broken out to kill Indra, king of the gods (*ŚP*.2.5.13.49-50; 2.5.14.4), as it had killed Kāma. That fire of Śiva's anger, the fire that killed Kāma, became a mare (Vaḍavā) and was taken by Brahmā to the ocean to feed on its water (*ŚP*.2.3.20.14-19).

Both Jalandhara and Vaḍavā, the submarine fire-mare, originated from the fire of Śiva's third eye, and each became a demonic power in its own right. In their relation to Vṛndā and Jalandhara, the gods acted like demons, whereas Vṛndā, of unalloyed demonic extraction and nobility in her essence and energy (*tejas*), became one with Pārvatī. The fire of Śiva's third eye created demonic powers in the water, or it heated his forehead so that when Pārvatī laid her hands on Śiva's eyes and darkness engulfed the cosmos, from the fire of Śiva's forehead and the sweat from her hands Andhaka was born (*ŚP*.2.5.42.16-19; *ŚP*, *DhS*.4.6-7), who like Jalandhara, the "son of the Ocean," became king of the demons by adoption. While Andhaka, though of celestial descent, was diabolic from the start, Jalandhara had to be perverted by Nārada for the sake of the gods by Śiva's command. Śiva took back to himself the *tejas* of his son Jalandhara whom he had led astray. The *tejas* of Vṛndā, the blameless victim of Pārvatī, merged into the Great Goddess. Jalandhara and his passionate, trusting wife were lost to the world of the demons. Śiva and Pārvatī, having depraved, deceived, and deprived Jalandhara and Vṛndā of their lives, took the demons' energies (*tejas*) into themselves. The two noble demons were joined with the Great Gods. They had gone through their fated trials and, having played their parts in the game devised by the gods, Jalandhara was taken back by Śiva, and Vṛndā, the sorely tried demoness, joined the Great Goddess. Unlike fierce Andhaka, they acted out their destiny without attaining release while still embodied.

2. Śiva's Demon

Though the gods and the demons were perpetually at war, the gods, the Devas, the shining ones, had many traits in common with the demons, who frequently extended their rule beyond Pātāla, the netherworld, their home after the fall of the Titans, the Asuras. The Asuras, more ancient than the gods and nearer to the undefinable Uncreate, were beyond good and evil; potentially they held the germs of both, but it was only after their fall, when the shining Devas arose, that the Asuras, relegated to the netherworld, became demons. They were the "others" and therefore enemies, and thought of as evil by the gods who, for this reason, felt free to treat them with evil intent. The character of the gods and the demons did not coincide with the dichotomy of good and evil. The two pairs of opposites overlapped as much as they intersected in changing patterns. Śiva / Vīrabhadra raged with demoniac furor as he destroyed the sacrifice of Dakṣa. To destroy sacrifices to the gods was one of the main purposes of a demon, for in this way the gods were deprived of their food. Under a different kind of stress Śiva danced with demonic frenzy as he carried the dead body of Satī, whom he had loved exceedingly. The excessiveness of his grief—as well as of his elation—was an outburst in which Śiva's demon revealed himself. It was for the demon's sake, also, that Śiva would show his outwardly unprovoked smile or let his laugh be heard. The tension and bond between god and demon found its release in Śiva's smile and laugh. The demon was in the god from before the beginning. God Rudra was essentially an Asura (*RV*.5.42.11); his Asura nature never left him (*RV*.2.33.9).

The inscrutable smile of the god is spread over the countenance of innumerable images of Śiva. His laugh—or was it the sound *AUM*—rung over the waters of dissolution as the god manifested from within the cosmic *liṅga* (Ch. VII.2). Besides, the excess that was in Śiva manifested in the shape of the Rudras, gaṇas, and Pramathas, who were Śiva's entourage and kept his ambience astir with movement. Before becoming Sthāṇu, Śiva dismissed the turbulent Rudras from his being. Their demonic traits, however, subsisted in the grotesque physiognomies of innumerable gaṇas who formed Śiva's host, prognostications or caricatures of possibilities of the human condition. Busy in making themselves felt, the gaṇas were the comparatively infinitesimal quantities replete with the impulsion of his presence that swelled the host of the Great God. Some had attained the status of gaṇas and had become leaders of troops after having been defeated in other forms and having "died," as was the case with Dakṣa and Andhaka. The Pramathas or churn spirits, another component of Śiva's host, formed an elite of whirling impetuosity. Nothing could stagnate where the Pramathas appeared. The demonism and density of Śiva's entourage, which throbbed with the invisible and varied texture of feeling alive, was tinged with grotesque and lugubrious hues. Others, the *bhūtas*, *rākṣasas*, and *piśācas*, ghosts and fiends, belonged to more dangerous categories. Śiva preferred to stay with them in cremation grounds.

Śiva explained his liking for cemeteries to Umā when she asked him the reason for his dwelling in cremation grounds, which were full of hair, bones, and skulls, jackals and vultures, and the smoke rising from corpses, when he had so many beautiful residences. Maheśvara, the Great Lord, replied to the Goddess that in the past he had been looking a long time for a pure place to dwell in. He could not find one, was frustrated, and out of anger against procreation he created the terrible *piśācas*, flesh-eating ghouls and goblins, and the *rākṣasas*, intent on killing people. Out of compassion and to protect people and alleviate their fear, however, he kept these ghosts and fiends in cremation grounds. Since he did not want to live without the *bhūtas* and gaṇas, he chose to live in a cemetery. The brahmins worshiped him in daily sacrifices, whereas those who desired liberation took the terrible Rudra vow. Only heroes (*vīra*) could stay in such a place. It was not fit for seekers of long life or for the impure. None but Rudra could free people from fear. When the ghosts stayed with him, they caused no harm. It was for the well-being of the world that Rudra lived in cemeteries (*MBh*.13, app. 1, no. 15, lines 358-95).

The Rudras, gaṇas, and Pramathas, demonic contingents of vital energies that only Rudra can control, were complemented by dreadful hordes of ghosts and ghouls whom Rudra out of consideration for mankind kept with him in cemeteries. Even so, it was he who had created the Rudras. It was out of anger against procreation that he discharged them. It was due to the fiery fury shooting out of Śiva's third eye that Jalandhara, the demon king, was born and the submarine mare came to be. Rudra himself was born from Brahmā's anger. As Manyu, Anger, he was born from Prajāpati.

The cemetery had its place at the opposite end of procreation. When horror, disgust, and revulsion are overcome in the charnel ground, ashes remain. From them the animals were born at the burnt-out lake of Prajāpati's semen (Ch. III.1), and ashes make fertile the fields. Śiva has smeared them all over his body.

The anger of Śiva was a creative counterpart of his *samādhi*. From his anger demons came forth and joined the ranks of those who had fallen into the netherworld. The former were god-created demons, the others were demons descended from the Asuras. The latter's domicile was the netherworld, whereas the innumerable hosts of Śiva accompanied him in heaven, and the most macabre ones were kept in bounds on earth, in cemeteries, a guard of honor of the elect, the heroes (*vīra*) who had overcome their animal nature, who had nothing to fear because they had attained freedom from fear.

Implied in Śiva's answer to Pārvatī was his nature as Tryambaka, lord over life and death (*RV*.7.59.12), and Yogeśvara, Lord of Yoga, who had discharged his aversion to procreation in the shape of the Rudras. He was the lord over the life of creatures and the master of his own virility, which he controlled and kept unspent. He had turned away from procreation and dwelled in the cemeteries where he liked to stay. His "necrophilia" complemented his aversion to procreation, and he rationalized, for the sake of Pārvatī or for his devotee, his spontaneous predilection for cemeteries. The explanation that the dreadful ghosts concentrated there around him would not harm people who thus could live free from fear was only part of his entire statement—which meant that those who feared the awful ghosts were destined to remain outsiders. Only heroes could be near him in the cremation ground, heroes who had defied death and liberated themselves from passions and fear. These were the true devotees of Rudra in his form of dread.

The metaphor of the cemetery is on the same level of intensity of realization with the myths of Śiva dancing while he carried Satī's dead body, and with the death of Āḍi by monstrous sex. These extreme situations are symbols of Śiva's power that defies death. A fierce bliss of agonized compassion shaped the physiognomy of some of the images of Bhairava as represented in art. Śiva liked his ghostly entourage. It attracted to his presence those who had nothing to fear, who had mastered the onslaught of the multiple categories of threatening powers that were fatal to those who were less than heroes, and who could not control the frightening phantoms because they had not controlled themselves. Śiva, the yogi, in his compassion, kept them away from his macabre residence, his preferred dwelling in the world of mortals.

In a lighter vein, basing Śiva's liking of cemeteries on the god's own past and cosmic role, Kāṇabhūti, a *piśāca* or meat-eating ghoul in the *Kathāsaritsāgara*, relates Śiva's answer to Pārvatī's question. Śiva himself told it to the demon in the burning ground at Ujjain. Śiva said he was asked by Pārvatī as to where his delight in skulls and cremation grounds came from. Śiva then told her that having cut off the head of arrogant Brahmā, he felt remorse and undertook a difficult vow. Thus it came about that he carried a skull in his hand and loved the places where corpses are burned. "Moreover, this world, resembling a skull, rests in my hand; for the two skull-shaped halves of the egg before mentioned are called heaven and earth" (*KSS*.2.8-15).[4]

According to Śiva's answer to Pārvatī in the *Mahābhārata*, however, the cremation ground was a testing ground for the *vīra*, the hero, while Śiva, withholding the fear of death from the living who were unable to overcome it, was at home among death's figures, liked their variety, and kept them contained by his presence.

By another act of containment, by the power of yoga, Śiva, the Great God, more than any other god, was an Asura. The great gods of the *Ṛg Veda* still bore that title.[5] They possessed *māyā*, creativity, which filled the Uncreate. All things to be created, to be manifested,

[4] *Kathāsaritsāgara (KSS)*, tr. C. H. Tawney and ed. N. M. Penzer, 1968, 1:10.

[5] In *RV*.1.24.1, Varuṇa is invoked as the "wise *asura*," and in *RV*.1.174.1, Indra is called *asura*; Agni is called an *asura* in *RV*.5.15.1. Cf. A. A. Macdonell, *Vedic Mythology*, pp. 156-57, for a discussion of the meanings of the word *asura* in Vedic texts and various explanations for the development from *asura* "god" to *asura* "demon."

they held within this power in a state of potentiality before the sun had risen and revealed the flowing light of the godhead. This was their treasure. The Mountain and Vṛtra, the serpent that had lain coiled around it, guarded the treasure. It also had other guardians—the Gandharva Kṛśānu and Rudra.

The Great Asura Vṛtra tenaciously guarded the treasure, but he was defeated by Indra, who made him lose his hold. The serpent was killed by the young, new, conquering god, and the mountain was shattered. Then the treasure of the Asuras became manifest for all to see, under the light of the sun. It had been a hard battle and long fight as the demons, the *paṇis*, clung to their treasure, unwilling to open up the cave and have the treasure dispersed (*RV*.6.39.2; 10.108.1-11). They clung to it like misers to their gold.

Seen from the manifest world of which Indra became the creator, the vice of the Asuras was their unwillingness to part with their treasures: the sun, the light, the rivers. Indra killed the serpent Vṛtra who enclosed them, and shattered the mountain where they were held captive. For the same reason Indra threw away the three heads of the Titan Viśvarūpa, the son of Tvaṣṭṛ Viśvarūpa, after Trita Āptya had killed the avaricious Titan, who did not live up to the name Viśvarūpa, "All-Form," which he had inherited from his father, the shaper of all form among the Asuras (*RV*.10.8.7-9). The world of the Titans was a world of potentiality. It held all the powers and forms of creation, and withheld them from creation. In this sense the Asuras were considered demons by those among them who left and followed Indra.

The *paṇis* or misers explicitly represented this Asuric or demonic trait. After Vṛtra had been slain, they kept hidden in a cave deep down in the mountain their treasure, cows, and horses. Not only Indra (*RV*.6.39.2; 6.20.4) but also Agni (*RV*.7.9.2) or Agni and Soma (*RV*.1.93.4), who had left the Asuras, as well as the Aṅgirases (*RV*.1.83.4) had to free the treasure that the *paṇis* refused to share when the river Rasā was already flowing in the emerging cosmos.[6]

Cosmically, in the mythic world of Indra, the treasure of the Asuras was dispersed all over creation. Vitally and in the human metaphor of the creation myth that has Prajāpati and Rudra as protagonists, the seed of Prajāpati fell down onto the earth and life had its beginning.

[6] Cf. A. A. Macdonell, *Vedic Mythology*, pp. 157 and 63.

Soma, the elixir of immortality and of creative inspiration that had belonged to the Asuras and that was with them when they were *in* Vṛtra and encoiled by the serpent, had been brought down to man. Visibly, physically, the treasure of the Asuras was dispersed in the cosmos. Its metaphysical reality, whether concentrated as Soma in Indra's myth, or as semen in Rudra's myth, by the power of yoga was vested in Rudra / Śiva. Serpents guarded the Great God at any time, and particularly when god Kāma attacked him. The Great Yogi retained the treasure; he did not shed it into the lap of woman. The self-containment of the Lord of Yoga, formulated in terms of sex, had its illustration in the myth of Śiva and Pārvatī. From the outset, she knew the mystery of the treasure of the Asuras that Śiva carried and, in the course of the myth, she responded on more than one level to Śiva's demon. And we see "the dark neck of Śiva, which the God of Love has, so to speak, surrounded with nooses in the form of the alluring looks of Pārvatī reclining on his bosom . . ." (*KSS*.1.1)[7] when the goddess wants to know why Śiva delights in skulls and charnel grounds.

3. Cosmic Demons

a. *The Domicile in the Netherworld*

Śiva Aṣṭamūrti permeated the universe as soon as Prajāpati had invested the newborn god and given him his names (Ch. V.1). Receiving his names, the child became free from evil. It was the primordial evil inherent in the inception of life on earth that the divine child, given his names, overcame.

Evil, however, had more than one origin.[8] It sprang up when the Asuras were besieged by Indra, some of them going over to his rule. Indra and the gods who, like Viṣṇu, had been on his side, as well as the Asuras who left Vṛtra, became the victorious gods of a new cosmos, the Devas, the shining ones. The Asuras who had not joined Indra fell into the netherworld, whence they emerged again and again to extend their power over heaven and earth. Originally, the Asuras were precosmic powers. They were roused from potentiality to act by the assault of god Indra. Later Vedic theogony, however, only faintly remembering the precosmic precedence of the Asuras, was con-

[7] *Kathāsaritsāgara (KSS)*, tr. C. H. Tawney and ed. N. M. Penzer, 1968, 1:1.

[8] W. D. O'Flaherty, *The Origins of Evil in Hindu Mythology*, treats admirably and exhaustively of the problem in the light of theodicy.

cerned with the created world, having Prajāpati as the Creator of the cosmos, and assigned to him the creation of both the gods and the Asuras. "There were two classes of the descendants of Prajāpati, the gods and the Asuras; the younger ones were the gods, the elder ones were the Asuras" (*BṛUp*.1.3.1).[9] Conceding seniority to the Asuras, however, was not the only criterion by which the *Brāhmaṇas* distinguished between the two categories. The gods, as a rule, issued from the upper part of Prajāpati's body, the Asuras from the lower part[10] (*ŚB*.11.1.6.7-9; cf. *VP*.1.5.31-33).[11] The gods emerged as superior not only by the respective position of their origin, but also by their association with light and goodness, while the Asuras were seen together with darkness and evil (*ŚB*.11.1.6.7-9). The inscrutability of the precosmic Asuras, the Titans, in Brahmā's creation condensed into darkness. Fallen, the Asuras were assigned a lower position and an evil disposition. The Titans became demons. In the *Brāhmaṇas*, their origin from the lower portion of Prajāpati was tantamount to their fall. On account of the low position to which they now were "born," they were doomed to be evil. The gods and the demons, both born from Prajāpati, were vying with each other for supremacy (*ŚB*.1.2.5.1; *BṛUp*.1.3.1; *ChUp*.1.2.1). In spite of their lowly position, the demons defeated the gods, thought that the world belonged to them, and wanted to divide it. When the gods heard of it, they went to the Asuras with god Viṣṇu at their head and the desire of sharing the earth with the demons. The demons proposed to give to the gods as much land as Viṣṇu could lie upon. Viṣṇu was a dwarf, but he also represented the sacrifice, and the sacrifice was as large as the whole earth (*ŚB*.1.2.5.1-7).

Though the Asuras were generous in their offer to divide the earth between themselves and the gods, they had not meant to share it with them in equal parts; they meant to give them just as much as the dwarf-god, lying down, could cover. Little did the demons know that Viṣṇu was the sacrifice and thus as large as the earth. The gods had tricked the Asuras, who were left landless. The sly gods were worse than the demons.

[9] The texts vary, but in two sources the *asuras* are born first: cf. *Mārkaṇḍeya Purāṇa (MāP)*, tr. F. E. Pargiter, 1904, p. 233 (= 48.4-8); and *VP*.1.5.31-33.

[10] *Mārkaṇḍeya Purāṇa (MāP)*, tr. F. E. Pargiter, 1904, p. 233 (= 48.5-8).

[11] The *Viṣṇu Purāṇa* here and elsewhere uses the designations Brahmā and Prajāpati interchangeably.

Inasmuch as the demons were afflicted with evil on account of their low birth—equivalent to their fall—they were victims of circumstance, whereas the gods who tricked them abused their high station and were more evil than the demons. Or it is said that the demons regarded themselves as equal to the gods and vied with them (*MBh*.12.160.28-29). They made the initial mistake of considering themselves equal with the gods because both had been born of Prajāpati. They did not take into account that Prajāpati, the Creator, had himself smitten them with evil when he saw that he had created darkness, which he equated with evil. Evil had its origin in the Creator.

Thus the demons were righteous from the beginning, and the goddess Śrī, "Fortune" dwelled with them. She attached herself always to those who lived according to the *dharma* or norm of their own station. The demons were law-abiding, self-disciplined, generous, and compassionate; they lived gracefully, free from envy and greed. But in the course of time the demons began to yield to desire and anger. They became quarrelsome, self-indulgent, and took pleasure in entertainments where men dressed as women and women as men. The goddess Śrī, therefore, left the demons and went over to the gods (*MBh*.12.221.26-83). As the demons degenerated, their good fortune left them. Desire and greed, self-indulgence and anger, as time went on, destroyed their *dharma*. They changed, but not in their pride. They regarded themselves as equal to the gods, and to make up for what they had lost of their initial assets in the course of time, they strove against the gods (cf. *MBh*.12.160.28-30). Their deterioration kept pace with that of mankind in the course of the yugas (Ch. VII.6). They became evil and fought with the gods, whom they generally worsted, only to be defeated by the gods' guile and trickery. The demons recovered quickly, as they could rely on their knowledge of resuscitating the dead.

On the intellectual and ethical levels, the demons did not do better than in the emotional sphere. "The gods and the demons, born from Prajāpati, received their father's inheritance, namely speech: truth and untruth. They both spoke truth, and they both spoke untruth; they were alike" (*ŚB*.9.5.1.12). Then the gods left untruth and held to truth, and the Asuras did just the opposite. The truth that had been in the Asuras saw this change and went to the gods. The untruth that had been in the gods thereupon went to the demons. The result was that the gods, who spoke nothing but truth, became very poor and despised, whereas the demons who spoke untruth throve and were very prosperous; but in the end they came to nought (*ŚB*.9.5.1.13-17). Then the gods started performing sacrifices and spreading the truth. The demons went there to fetch what originally had been theirs. When the gods saw the demons, they stopped the sacrifice and did something else. The demons went away, but they came back again and interrupted the sacrificing gods at each step (*ŚB*.9.5.1.18 ff.) until the gods, by performing certain rites, besieged on the earth, in the air, and in the sky the three cities that the demons had built (see infra, XI.3.b; *ŚB*.3.4.4.3-4; cf. *ŚB*.10.2.5.2) after Tāraka had been defeated by Kārttikeya.

Up to that time, the demons, comprising the Daityas and the Dānavas, lived in Rasātala in the netherworld called Pātāla.[12] The Daityas were descended from Diti, the Dānavas from Dānu (cf. *MBh.* 1.58.30). Both these demonesses, at the time of the *Mahābhārata*, were looked upon as daughters of Dakṣa (*MBh*.1.59.11-12). Dānu, however, before the Titans fell, had been the mother of Vṛtra, the Asura, the cosmic serpent (*RV*.1.32.9). After their fall, the demons became city dwellers. Their cities were better than those of mortals, more splendid even than those of the gods. Their capital, Hiraṇyapura, the golden city, had been built by Viśvakarman, the architect of the gods, and created in his mind by Maya, the architect of the Asuras (*MBh*.5.98.1-2). Maya was the planner. The gods had no objection to letting their architect execute the work and build the capital city of the Asuras. It was a way of acknowledging their foes as superior to them. The city had beautiful facilities for luxurious recreation and sport (*MBh*.5.98.9-15).

Pātāla, the lowest region of the netherworld, is said to be so named because here fall all the forms of water (*MBh*.5.97.6). Daityas and Dānavas worshipfully frequented Pātāla, and many sinful Dānavas had made it their home (*MBh*.5.97.1, 11). The source of life was there. An egg of great beauty lay in its waters. It was there from the beginning of creation; none knew its origin. When the end of the world was to come, a mighty flame of fire would rise from it and con-

[12] Pātāla is the name of the netherworld. It has seven levels or regions, Rasātala being the fourth, and the lowermost region again being called Pātāla. Rasātala of the *Purāṇas* owes its name to Rasā, the "heavenly stream" (S. S. Bhave, *The Soma Hymns of the Ṛg Veda*, 1960, 2:81). For suggested identification of the river Rasā with the ecliptic, cf. S. Kramrisch, "The Indian Great Goddess," p. 241.

sume the three worlds (*MBh*.5.97.17-19). There also blazed the Asura fire, known as the fire-mare, Vaḍavā, the submarine fire, that feeds on water (*MBh*.5.97.3).[13] It had left Śiva as his wrath, though the origin of the submarine fire outside the Śaiva tradition was also differently accounted for as Asura fire. There also the (sun-) horse rose from the primal source (cf. *RV*.1.163.1).[14] There also the celestial elephant Airāvata took up the cool water and imparted it to the clouds, whence Indra shed it down on earth as rain (*MBh*.5.97.7). Aquatic monsters lived there who subsisted on the rays of the moon (*MBh*.5.97.8). Many kinds of creatures that died in the daytime, pierced by the rays of the sun, came back to life in Pātāla in the night, as the rays of the moon revived them with *amṛta* (*MBh*.5.97.9-10). It was there that the gods, after defeating the Asuras, drank the *amṛta* and deposited it (*MBh*.5.97.4).

The domicile of the Asuras after their fall, after Indra had killed Vṛtra, or after they were born from Prajāpati / Brahmā, was down below the level of the earth: the demons had entered the earth (*ŚB*.11.1.6.8). They went into the darkness, though not into hell. Hell was below the netherworld, a fathomless dark pit reserved for evil-doers, particularly of human birth (*RV*.2.29.6; 7.104.3, 11, 17; 9.73.9), and was called Naraka (*AV*. 12.4.36). It was furnished, according to the *Purāṇas*, with accoutrements of exquisite torture, in a hot hell, a cold hell—altogether seven of them, one above the other.[15] The entrance to hell was at the mare's head, Vaḍavāmukha, where the submarine fire, Vaḍavānala, issued from her mouth, in the Southern Ocean,[16] near the celestial south pole. The south, at all times, from the *Ṛg Veda* on, was known as the region of death. This was the cosmic south, below the earth. Pātāla, the netherworld, was above it. Hell was a place of punishment. Nāgas, guilty of the crime of brahminicide, had to go to hell and leave Pātāla,[17] the stratum of the netherworld deepest in position as well as significance.

[13] On the submarine fire, see W. D. O'Flaherty, "The Submarine Mare in the Mythology of Śiva," 1971, pp. 10, 11.

[14] In *RV*.1.163.1, the horse is the archetypal horse risen from the ocean or the primal source. This primal source whence the "sun horse" rises would be in a region that corresponds in later mythology to Pātāla.

[15] *Mārkaṇḍeya Purāṇa (MāP)*, tr. F. E. Pargiter, 1904, pp. 71-74 (= ch. 12).

[16] Cf. W. D. O'Flaherty, *The Origins of Evil in Hindu Mythology*, p. 346; and *Asceticism and Eroticism in the Mythology of Śiva*, pp. 289, 291.

[17] *Mārkaṇḍeya Purāṇa (MāP)*, tr. F. E. Pargiter, 1904, p. 661 (= 131.9).

Pātāla had become the deep region of mystery after god Indra's onslaught of the cosmic mountain. There the waters fell and cradled an egg that held creation and also destruction. It floated in the waters, which were laced with *amṛta* and lit up by the flaming mare's head. This subterranean, sublunar domain, sheltered from the scorching sun, lay below the domicile of the demons, who before the creation of the cosmos had been Titans.

The embryo of the waters and of the moving and unmoving (*RV*.1.70.2), and the horse that emerged from the waters (*RV*.1.163.1) were images *de profundis* of fire hidden in the deep. The horse that has its seat in the ocean is a manifestation of Agni (*VS*.17.87).

From their sumptuous domicile in the netherworld the fallen and subsequently more and more corrupted Asuras or demons made frequent forays. They emerged in order to disturb the sacrifices, so as to deprive the gods of sustenance, and their armies overran heaven and earth. Though the demons were always defeated, they rose again. They were irrepressible, and this was unavoidable in the world of dichotomy, where light is set against darkness, white against black, good against evil, and gods against demons. While sons of god, like Andhaka or Jalandhara, could become demons, none born as a demon became a god, whereas Kāvya Uśanas, who was a Titan, officiated at different phases of his long career as priest of the gods and priest of the demons. From their abode in the netherworld the demons, in their perpetual war with the gods, threatened heaven and earth, where they made themselves at home and ruled over conquered land from their newly built fortified cities. Andhaka's exploit was but one of their innumerable, if temporary conquests.

Their fortresses originally were built of stone. There were hundreds of them (*RV*.4.30.20), that gave them as much or as little security as the Mountain where the Titans had dwelled. They did not, however, build stone fortresses only. Their citadels were of iron (*RV*.2.20.8); they also had golden strongholds (*AV*.10.6.10), and Śuṣṇa, the demon, had a moving fortress (*RV*.8.1.28), though it is not stated what it was built of. They needed these strongholds, for they were sorely besieged by the gods, whom they also wanted to baffle by the splendor of their fortifications. In the course of time they altogether relied on metal fortifications on earth, in the air, and in the sky.

b. *The Destruction of the Triple City of the Demons*

"The Asuras had three citadels; the lowest was of iron, then there was one of silver, then one of gold. The gods could not conquer them; they sought to conquer them by siege. . . . They made ready an arrow, Agni as the point, Soma as the socket, Viṣṇu as the shaft. They said, 'Who shall shoot it?' . . . 'Rudra,' they said, 'Rudra is cruel, let him shoot it.' He said, 'Let me choose a boon; let me be overlord of animals.' Therefore is Rudra overlord of animals. Rudra let it go; it cleft the three citadels and drove the Asuras away from these worlds." (*TS*.6.2.3.1-2).[18] This was not the only time that Rudra became Lord of Animals, for this status had been conferred on him by Prajāpati, and the gods contrived his fearful shape (Ch. I.2). Rudra's request to the gods would seem unexpected, unless by his renewed shot he wanted to have his title confirmed. Or the myth of the three cities, taking no cognizance of the primordial myth, assigns to its own setting Rudra's becoming Paśupati (Ch. X.A,2.b).

Rudra let his arrow fly against the three citadels of the Asuras. The citadels were burned and the demons were driven from the earth, the air, and the sky. Or, it is said, the gods themselves discharged the arrow (*KB*.8.8). Again, when the Asuras made the worlds into their forts, the gods performed certain sacrificial rites of siege whereby the Asuras were defeated (ŚB.3.4.4.3-4). Or from the rite of siege was made an arrow with Agni, Fire, as its tip (*AB*.1.25). Agni then took possession of the citadels, his body occupied each one of them; encased in iron, silver, and gold, he chased away the threatening Asuras (cf. *VS*.5.8; *KāS*.24.10; *ŚB*.3.4.4.23-25). Thus, the forts of the demons, each now encasing Agni, were conquered by the gods, who had besieged them by having ritually set up the fire altar and accessory parts as their citadels, whence they besieged the demons and conquered their fortresses on earth, in the air, and the sky. Hence an amulet made of three bands—one of gold, one of silver, and one of iron—will protect the wearer from the demons or dangers that threaten him from the sky, the air, and on earth, and he will overcome whoever hates him (*AV*.5.28.9, 10). In the ritual myth, the demons made the three worlds into their forts; their forts were as large as these worlds themselves. The demons, at that time, did not build their forts *in* the

[18] *Taittirīya Saṃhitā (TS)*, tr. A. B. Keith, 1914, p. 504.

three worlds—as they were subsequently said to have done. They converted the triple world into fortresses of their own. The gods defended themselves from their own fortresses; these were the sacrificial buildings and the rites of siege (*upasad*).

Ritual and magical practice in their own effectiveness corresponded to the myth of Rudra, the archer, and the fire of his arrow. His primordial myth, valid at all times, was actualized, though the target was not Prajāpati, the Creator procreating, but a demonized universe. The myth of the burning of the three citadels of the Asuras was a reassessment of Prajāpati's primordial intercourse in the light of that morning of the world when it had become the target of Rudra's arrow. The shot rang through hundreds and thousands of years from the *Ṛg Veda* through the *Brāhmaṇas*, and, though it did not gather momentum, it was heard through the *Mahābhārata*, and its reverberations became louder and louder in the centuries of the *Purāṇas*, in the ongoing myth of Rudra.

After Tāraka was defeated by Kārttikeya, the son of Śiva, the three sons of Tāraka—the demons Tārakākṣa, Kamalākṣa, and Vidyunmālin, or Sun-Eye, Lotus-Eye, and Lightning-Wreathed, respectively—practiced austerities, and Brahmā granted a boon to these ascetics. They asked for immortality, but Brahmā never granted this boon because he was unable to give it. They then asked for another boon that would, so they hoped, be practically as efficacious. They wanted to live in three fortified cities, whence they would rove all over the world. After a thousand years they would come together, and their cities would be united into one. Only that god who could pierce the three cities with one arrow would be able to cause their destruction (*MBh*.8.24.4-12).

Indra had been unable to defeat the troublesome demons. The gods asked Rudra to slay them, and promised that the animals slain in every sacrifice would be his (*MBh*.7.173.52-55). The gods offered Rudra his share in the sacrifice. They accepted his condition, for they had no other chance of victory over the demons; even their own survival was threatened.

The three Asuras commissioned Maya, their master architect, to build the three cities—one each of gold, silver, and iron—in the sky, air, and on earth, respectively (*MBh*.8.24.13-16). From their cities, the three demon kings soon assailed the three worlds (*MBh*.8.24.19). The demons were full of energy, for Maya fulfilled the wish of everyone living in the three cities (*MBh*.8.24.22). Within their metal walls, the cities were equipped with every convenience and luxury, including parks and ponds. What is more, Hari, the son of Star-Eye and himself a great ascetic, won a boon from Brahmā. It was a pond of a special kind, for it brought back to life those slain in battle when their bodies were thrown into the reviving water (*MBh*.8.24.23-26). Or it was a well, full of *amṛta*, and with the same properties of restoration, which Maya created (*MP*.136.8-16).

The magic lake or well in the golden city, with its vivifying water, produced by the *tapas* of Hari and a boon from Brahmā, or by the *māyā* of Maya the Asura, was a replica of Gold-Eye's city, or derived from the waters in the netherworld wherein burned the perpetual flame of Vaḍavā's head, born of the fire of Rudra. The fire-mare lived in the waters, at the bottom of the netherworld, whither the waters had fallen from the Beyond, where they had been held captive, by the great Asura Vṛtra. These vivifying waters, guarded by the great Asura, on his defeat and death by Indra's hand had fallen into Pātāla, the netherworld, the substratum and source of the enjoyments that Rasātala, the domicile of the fallen demons, provided for them. The austerities of the demon Hari, and a boon of Brahmā, had created the lake in the golden city. Its miraculous water had fallen from the deathless Beyond, the Uncreate, the source of life, into the netherworld, flooding its fields with the power vested in it by its origin and now rendered available to the demons in their dispersion all over the world, once their dead bodies were immersed in the lake of the golden city. From the same source Kāvya Uśanas, priest of the Asuras, had received the secret of bringing the dead back to life. By the possession of the well or pond whose water revived the dead fallen in battle, the demons possessed a limited substitute for the freedom from death that Brahmā had been unable to grant them.

In spite, however, or because of their opulence and abundance, all did not go well with the demons. Though they had everything, they became overbearing and, insensate in their greed, they began to invade and ruin the towns and cities all over the world (*MBh*.8.24.28-30). Now the time had come for the gods to appeal to Śiva. They praised him who is unborn and is Lord of the Universe, robed in animal skins, the lord of all trees, of all kine, the lord of all sacrifices (*MBh*.8.24.36-51). Śiva agreed to slay the demons, and preparations for the attack on the three cities commenced (*MBh*.8.24.64-65).

Under the instructions of Viśvakarman, their architect, the gods began to build the chariot of Śiva (*MBh*.8.24.67). The mind was the ground on which the chariot stood; the earth was the body of the chariot; sun and moon were the chariot's wheels, the four *Vedas* the four steeds, and Brahmā was the charioteer (*MBh*.8.24.75, 68, 71, 103, 108). Śiva mounted his chariot (*MBh*.8.24.93). In ancient times, as Rudra, he had sat on the seat of his chariot, piercing with his weapon like a wild beast (*RV*.2.33.11). The chariot set out for Tripura, the triple city. As Śiva ascended the chariot, the horses fell to the ground on their knees, but Brahmā, seizing the reins, urged on the horses. With horses swift as the wind, they approached the three cities. Śiva strung the bow and, when the three cities became united, Śiva discharged the arrow and the triple city began to fall. Burning, the Asuras sank into the western ocean (*MBh*.8.24.110-21; cf. *MP*.138.39, 40).

The Tripura myth is told in the *Purāṇas* in many versions concerned with the deterioration and corruption of the demons, which justified Śiva's attack.[19] Tripura, the demon city, had become a site of religious dissent, heresies, and lawlessness. It had sunk from the world of myth into that of history, and was ripe for destruction when Śiva mounted his chariot.

i. The Bull, Viṣṇu, and Śiva

Viṣṇu had come to Śiva's aid and had raised his chariot when, contrary to all expectation, this glorious vehicle, the earth, replete with all the powers of the cosmos, had begun to sink (*MP*.136.54-59; *ŚP*.2.5.9.7-8; *LP*.1.72.28-31). Viṣṇu alone could raise the earth. Once before he had raised the earth when she had sunk. At that time she had sunk into the ocean, depressed by all the evil perpetrated on her. At that time Viṣṇu had taken the shape of a boar;[20] now, however, Viṣṇu took the appropriate shape of a bull, Śiva's bull who is Dharma (*VDhP*.3.48.18),[21] law and order in the cosmos and in the world of man. Viṣṇu, the bull, raised Śiva's chariot by his horns (*MP*.136.58-59).

Viṣṇu as a bull gave double support to Śiva. By his own will god Viṣṇu had come out of Śiva's arrow (cf. *LP*.1.72.24) to raise his chariot

[19] W. D. O'Flaherty, *The Origins of Evil in Hindu Mythology*, pp. 180-89.

[20] Cf. *ibid.*, pp. 222-23; and *MBh*.3, app. 1, no. 16, lines 70-122.

[21] The *Viṣṇudharmottarapurāṇa* (3.48.18) calls the bull Dharma, as both have four feet.

and, giving this support in the shape of a bull, Viṣṇu became Śiva's own trusted vehicle, which from ancient times had "conveyed" Śiva in both senses of the word. Śiva, "bull of bulls," who can be approached by yoga only had the bull as vehicle and cognizance of his power. But when the bull conveyed the Great Yogi who rides or dances on its back (Śiva images from eastern India of about the eleventh century A.D. show Śiva dancing on Nandin), the bull named Nandin, "joy," is Dharma itself, an image of controlled power.

Having raised Śiva's chariot, Viṣṇu the bull trampled over the demons and right into Tripura, where he destroyed the flower beds and drank up all the *amṛta* in the lake. Then he returned to Śiva (*MP*.136.63-65). Viṣṇu acted according to the *dharma* of his self-chosen station.

Another time, after the Churning of the Ocean, Śiva himself took the shape of a bull in order to set things right when they had gone out of control. As the *amṛta* emerged from the ocean, bewitching girls appeared from the drops of spray. They were Apsarases, nymphs (*ŚP*.3.22.20-22). The demons quickly took them to their lavish houses in the netherworld (*ŚP*.3.22.36-37). Viṣṇu, in pursuit of the vanquished demons, on seeing the young enchantresses made love with them and engendered many wanton sons who ravaged heaven and earth (*ŚP*.3.22.41-48). Śiva saw the havoc done by Viṣṇu's sons (*ŚP*.3.22.55). He entered the netherworld, bellowing terribly, for he had taken the shape of a bull. With his horns and hoofs he killed them and kicked Viṣṇu, who had invited all divine beings to take part in the orgy, back to his senses (*ŚP*.3.23.1-13). Having cursed them all, Śiva said that whoever except a self-contained sage or a demon born of Śiva enters that place will die immediately (*ŚP*.3.23.33). Śiva himself provided for both exceptions. He himself fulfilled the first condition, for his senses were controlled, and he had demons as his sons. A self-controlled sage would either take no notice at all of the enchantresses, or he would not be affected whether he took one or many of them; in fact, his *tapas* would increase in their tempting presence that could not erotically excite his emotion while he experienced sexual pleasure, whereas the demons would succumb to temptations (*ŚP*.2.3.18.44; *KS*.1.59).[22] When Viṣṇu had assumed the shape of Śiva's bull, he also assumed its nature and its mission to defeat unruly demon powers.

[22] Cf. W. D. O'Flaherty, *Asceticism and Eroticism in the Mythology of Śiva*, p. 260.

ii. The Child on Pārvatī's Lap

While the triple city began to burn, Pārvatī came to see the spectacle. She had then on her lap a child with five tufts of hair on his otherwise bald head. She asked the gods who that child was. Indra did not like it, and was about to strike the child with his thunderbolt. Smiling, the child paralyzed Indra's arm. Indra and the gods went to Brahmā and told him about the strange happening. Brahmā knew that the child was Śiva. Brahmā asked the Great God to be gracious to Indra. The gods then praised Śiva in a magnificent hymn (*MBh*.7.173.57-69; 13.145.28-41).

Pārvatī had come as a spectator, when the battle was won and the triple city of the Asuras was being consumed by flames. Suddenly, a child was on her lap. She did not know it, and she asked the gods who that child was. She was baffled by its appearance, Indra resented it, but Brahmā knew its identity. It bore Śiva's sacred number five on its head as a cognizance. It was Śiva, the cruel god, whom the gods on account of his cruelty had chosen to burn the three cities. But the child, smiling in its cruelty, became the gracious god and restored Indra's arm.

Pārvatī, the Great Goddess, the childless goddess, found Śiva—her child, as it were—on her lap. He was Mahādeva, the Great God, born from no mother and at the height of his power. He had conquered the demons in the manifest world, his realm, which they had invaded. In the hour of his triumph, Pārvatī found the Great God anew. He had come to the lap that he had left barren, and she felt his presence, cradling the infant as if he were her son.

In another context, Śiva, in the form of an infant crying in the cremation ground full of ghosts, drew the Great Goddess toward him. She had assumed the dark horrendous shape of Kālī, and had just defeated the demon Dāruka. She was still full of fury, which Śiva was eager to imbibe. Deluded by Śiva's *māyā* and not recognizing him, the goddess bent down and took up the crying infant, kissed it, and suckled it. He drank the fury of the dire goddess along with her milk. Śiva then assumed his Aṣṭamūrti form; he showed himself as the entire universe, in which her excessive fury had been allayed. At dusk, the lord of gods, in order to propitiate the goddess, danced the Tāṇḍava dance. His host of ghosts and the leaders of goblins accompanied the dance. The Great Goddess drank in the ambrosial flavor of the dance, and danced herself in the midst of the ghosts, along with the yoginīs (*LP*.1.106.14-26).

Before Tripura, Śiva gave himself to the goddess as her child, though leaving her unaware whence it had come and who it was. She received the Lord, a formidable gift, her child. Or he let himself be found by her, let her, the dread goddess, feel motherly so that he could absorb within himself her anger. Leaving behind the deceptive *māyā* shape of the infant, the lord of gods, the Prime Mover of all, showed himself as the cosmos. Refreshed by the goddess's maternal milk of fury, he danced the Tāṇḍava at dusk in the cremation ground, and the goddess joined the dance of the lord of destruction-creation in the burning grounds.

Śiva danced and caused others to dance. The holy family danced. It was before Tripura that Kārttikeya danced. A late Purāṇic myth times Pārvatī's appearance before Tripura differently from the *Mahābhārata*. She had been with Śiva when he decided to destroy the triple city of the demons. Playfully, she diverted his attention to Kārttikeya, their son, beautifully groomed by his mothers, the Kṛttikās and Svāhā (the last-named, though his primary mother, has not been accounted for in the present context). Śiva feasted his eyes on him. Forgetting the harassed gods and the demons, he embraced his son and asked him to dance. The leading gaṇas danced along with him and, at the command of Śiva, the entire three worlds danced. The gods were puzzled, then excited, and finally dejected, until Nandin, riding on his white bull, admonished the gods to build Śiva's chariot, as the triple city was as good as destroyed (*LP*.1.71.117-63). Śiva let himself express his joy through his son, to the delight of Pārvatī. Even so, the gods began to build the stupendous war chariot for Śiva, who ascended the glorious though somewhat overweight vehicle.

iii. Tripura in the Microcosm

The ancient myth of the burning of the three cities was envisioned in the *Mahābhārata* (*MBh*.8.24) as enacted in the cosmos by the gods and the demons. The latter had invaded and usurped the triple world. The same myth, however, was also thought of as having the body of man for its scene. The actors were the same, even though they had different names: the Asuras entered the bodies of men. Then pride, which destroys man's *dharma*, arose. From pride arose anger, then shameful behavior, then delusion. People did as they pleased. Then the gods appealed to Śiva. With a single arrow they felled three demons, together with their habitations. The chief of the demons, called Bhīma, who struck the gods with terror, was slain by Śiva. When this chief of the demons was slain people regained their former nature (*MBh*.12.283.8-17).

The moralized version with the human being, the microcosm, for its playground was implicit in the cosmic myth. As told in the *Mahābhārata*, the world calmed down and became normal after the defeat of the Asuras. The microcosmic version relates that the chief of the demons was slain by Śiva himself; the other demons were felled by one arrow of the gods.

The destruction of their three cities and the expulsion of the demons from the cosmos was Śiva's victory. He was persuaded, according to the *Mahābhārata*, by the promise that animals slain in every sacrifice would be his (*MBh*.7.173.55; 13.145.26), whereas in the earliest account of his victory over the Asuras, in the *Taittirīya Saṃhitā*, he had asked to be made Lord of Animals (*TS*.6.2.3.1-2). The moralized version contained the implication that the demons who entered the bodies of men were the passions and failings that make man their habitat, their Tripura. The leaders of these demons were Pride, Anger, Shameful Behavior, and Delusion; their habitat was "natural" man, the *paśu*, the unregenerate human being.

The moralized version, equating the three mighty demons plus a leader with the powerful passions, would be appropriate for the time when the truth that originally was in the Asuras had left them and had gone to the gods, and the untruth that was originally in the gods had left *them* and had gone to the Asuras. The demons, however, who flocked from the netherworld to settle in the three cities (*MP*.131.4-5) in the sky, in the air, and on earth, lived virtuously. They lived in the pursuit of the three aims of life: in *dharma*, in accordance with their own station, and in the legitimate enjoyment of wealth and pleasure (*artha* and *kāma*) (*MP*.131.10), for they got all they wanted through Maya's *māyā* (*MP*.131.6), the magic, creative power of their great architect, who had built the three cities.

iv. The Drama in the Sky

Maya was a great ascetic, and through Brahmā's boon he built the three cities, each impregnable by itself. By his *māyā* the great architect built another civilization, that of the demons (*MP*.129.23-25; 130.1-

11). Its standards and achievements were analogous to those of the gods and men. The demons passed their life as happily as the gods in heaven (*MP*.131.11). Maya also built a temple of Śiva, for the demons worshiped Śiva (*MP*.131.13). Maya had built and completed the three cities when the moon was in conjunction with the asterism Puṣya (*MP*.129.31; 130.11-12; 132.15-16). It would also be at the time of the conjunction of the asterism Puṣya with the moon that the three cities would rise and meet the firmament (*MP*.139.3-5). Whoever would attack these three cities at the time of their conjunction could destroy them by one arrow only (*MP*.129.31-33). Who else but Lord Śiva could destroy these three cities? (*MP*.129.36; *ŚP*.2.5.1.51-52; *SP*.35.30-34).

Puṣya is one of the twenty-seven lunar mansions, a constellation conspicuous neither for its size nor its brilliance. The name Puṣya does not figure in the early myth of Rudra, when this star was known as Tiṣya (Ch. II.4). At that time, its mythical association with Rudra appears to have been established, although Rudra's star form was the Hunter of the Antelope, the star Mṛgavyādha or Sirius. Yet, as it was said explicitly that Tiṣya was Rudra (*TS*.2.2.10.1-2), it has now to be shown what might have led to the transfer of Rudra's association with Sirius to the Nakṣatra or lunar station called Tiṣya and subsequently Puṣya.

Sirius, the brilliant star, may be seen shooting rays like arrows, whereas Tiṣya is a star conspicuous neither by size nor brightness. The *Ṛg Veda* (*RV*.10.64.8) invoked "Agni, Kṛśānu, Tiṣya, the archers, Rudra, the true Rudra among Rudras" to come to the sacrifice. Whether the archers invoked here were Tiṣya and Rudra, the true Rudra among Rudras, or Kṛśānu and Tiṣya who is Rudra, is left open to interpretation. The *Taittirīya Saṃhitā*, however, left no doubt about the identity of Tiṣya and Rudra.

What would have been the reason or one of the reasons of making Tiṣya the star of Rudra? A favorable time for performing the bull sacrifice (*śūlagava*) to Rudra was after the full moon of Tiṣya / Puṣya (*GGS*.3.10.18; *ŚŚS*.4.17.1-3 and commentary; cf. *TS*.2.2.10.1).[23] This sacrificial date was Rudra's, apparently even before he was admitted by the other gods to their sacrifices.

The name Puṣya as that of the sixth lunar mansion occurs already

[23] Cf. A. Weber, tr., *Die Vedischen Nachrichten von den naxatra (Mondstationen)*, 1860, pp. 324, 337.

in the *Atharva Veda*.[24] It was synonymous with Tiṣya, and, in the end, the name Tiṣya was replaced altogether by Puṣya as that of the sixth house of the moon.[25]

The three cities of the Asuras were situated on the earth, in the air, and in the sky (*MP*.129.33-34). They had to come together, be aligned, and form one city. Then only could they be pierced by Rudra's arrow. The cities rose from the earth and the air, and met the city in the sky; they formed the "Three-fort" city, Tripura. Rudra pierced it with one arrow and, burning, it fell into the western ocean. When he had discharged his arrow, Lord Śiva the Great God wept on account of Maya, who would perish (*MP*.140.44-49). Śiva saved Maya and his palace from under the sea (*MP*.140.50-52, 75). The palace was then seen where Dhruva, the Pole Star is, but Maya moved to another region where he felt safe (*MP*.140.80).

The cities of the Asuras had been the enemy's bastions in the triple world. They had fortification walls of shiny metal. When they came together in the sky they were dazzling.

To begin with, in the *Brāhmaṇas*, the strongholds of the Asuras were the three worlds. Having conquered them, the demons occupied them and made these, their worlds, into forts. Rudra sent his fire arrow, or the gods did it by the power of their rites, and the three forts—the universe—were filled with fire. It was a world conquest, a universal conflagration that wiped out the demons from earth, air, and sky, and left them untouched in their domicile, the netherworld. This was the late Vedic conception of the three strongholds of the Asuras.

Subsequently, in the *Mahābhārata*, the three strongholds of the demons were said to have been built as fortified cities *in* the three worlds and thence, from these cities, the demons would roam all over the worlds. These three cities were the work of the demon mastermind, Maya. They revolved, each on its level; they were part of a revolving universe. The *Matsya Purāṇa* specifies that each city occupied a square of one hundred *yojanas* (*MP*.129.31), that is, eight hundred or nine hundred miles. The square plan was basic in Indian architecture,[26]

[24] Cf. M. Mayrhofer, *Concise Etymological Sanskrit Dictionary, s.v.*

[25] Cf. A. Weber, tr., *Die Vedischen Nachrichten von den naxatra (Mondstationen)*, p. 324; *TS*.2.2.10.1; *ŚŚS*.4.17.1-3 and commentary.

[26] S. Kramrisch, *The Hindu Temple*, pp. 41-53.

and its size mythical. Whereas the *Mahābhārata* describes the cities as rotating, the *Matsya Purāṇa* says the cities would go anywhere where they willed (*MP*.130.15). Extent and mobility of the three strongholds changed. Originally conterminous with the extent—and subsequently also with the motion—of the manifest world, they were assigned a shape and size of their own and, according to the *Matsya Purāṇa*, also a motion of their own, as they would go anywhere they willed. Originally, the arrow that pierced the three strongholds set the whole world afire. Subsequently, the three strongholds were no longer conterminous with the extent of the three levels of the cosmos on which they were built; and lastly, they were given movements of their own.

The Tripura myth changed in the course of time from the conception of the triple universe usurped by the demons to that of three strongholds of large, though limited, extent, built on its levels and moving with them; and, finally, the movement of the cities was according to will; the strongholds were envisioned as shiny units, having their own movements. They would have to come together in the sky so that they could be pierced by one arrow.

Originally the Tripura myth had a cosmo-symbolical dimension. Rudra regained for the gods a universe from which they had been ousted. His mythical arrow was equivalent in efficacy with the *upasad* rites performed by the gods with Agni as their agent. In the course of time, this coming together of the strongholds in one universal conflagration, in which Agni lay in triple armor encased in iron, silver, and gold, yielded to a vision no longer of mythic, universal significance but of temporal, astronomical urgency. Although no explicit data were given in the *Purāṇas* other than the time of the *Puṣya yoga* for the three cities to come together, or be aligned in such a way that Rudra could pierce them with one arrow, and other than that these three strongholds had their own movements, still the three strongholds, it would appear, were seen as three planets that at a certain *Puṣya yoga* were close together and in one line with the position of Rudra, the archer. Their triple conjunction had to be in one straight line with Sirius.

The triple conjunction of planets could have been seen in the vicinity of Orion at more than one date. No further specification, however, being given in the *Purāṇas*, the particular date of the cyclically recurrent phenomenon of three planets in conjunction near Orion and aligned with Sirius cannot immediately be ascertained.[27] At the time of its observation, mythical thinking recognized Rudra, the archer, his arrow directed toward his target, Tripura. The triple city had arisen in the region of the sky near Orion, the antelope, and was in one line with Sirius, whence Rudra, the Hunter of the Antelope, was seen to have let fly his first arrow, aimed at the Father, Prajāpati. Between this primeval initiating deed and the destruction of Tripura extends the ageless myth of Rudra. Though the destruction of Tripura was enacted in mythical time, cosmic phenomena were adduced as witnesses. The change in the scenario of the Tripura myth was linked, it appears, with a particular, observed astronomical configuration.

Rudra, who became Kāla, Time, was the main actor in his primordial myth when Prajāpati moved toward Rohiṇī and made love to her. Prajāpati the year had transferred its beginning from its accustomed station in Orion toward Aldebaran.

The beginning of the year, the renewal of life, had been considered fixed with the sun's rising in one and the same star. When this observed *and* believed-in phenomenon was observed not to be an aeviternal reality, but had changed so that the vernal equinoctial sun no longer rose in Orion, but had left that position, had gone toward Aldebaran, the shock of this observation—though it must have been made over a very long time—had its mythical image in Prajāpati's unpardonable movement toward Rohiṇī (Aldebaran). The precession of the equinoxes that was known in its fulness and named by the Greek astronomer Hipparchus in 127 B.C. only, but which must have been observed in India over a very long time—even before and when the spring equinox moved from Orion toward Aldebaran—became the cosmic, astronomically verified "moment," synchronized with the Father's approach to his daughter.

Another moment, ominous and in this instance predictive, was witnessed by Indra in his vision of a battle of gods and demons as the sun was rising in the Kṛttikās and the new moon was gliding into the sun, a moment predicting the birth of Kārttikeya heralded by the sun rising in the Kṛttikās, the Pleiades;[28] the rising of the vernal equinoctial

[27] M. Raja Rao, "The Astronomical Background of Vedic Rudra and Purāṇic Śiva," 1952, pp. 167-68, using the planetary tables of the Indian ephemeris by Swami Kannu Pillai, suggests either 2270 B.C. or 503 B.C. as possible dates.

[28] B. Ya. Volchok, "Protoindiiskie paralleli k mifu o Skande," pp. 305-12.

sun of an earlier aeon, in Aldebaran; and in a most distant past in Sirius—these significant moments in the myth of Rudra (and Indra) were linked with the visible cosmos, the stage on which the gods were clothed with their imagined shapes and trappings. The stars signaled the events of their myths, they were the cosmic code that myth deciphered and translated in its own language.

The time when the sun at the vernal equinox no longer rose in Orion but moved to Aldebaran was after 4500 B.C. More than a millennium later, the sun rose at the vernal equinox in Rohiṇī / Aldebaran and, more than another millennium after that, about 2200 B.C.,[29] the sun at the vernal equinox rose in the Kṛttikās, the Pleiades (Ch. IX.3).

The fourth myth of Rudra / Śiva linked with a definite movement in the sky was that of the burning of the triple city of the Asuras by Rudra. In its last phase, it seems to have referred to a special conjunction of the moon and a star (Puṣya) that coincided with a particular configuration of certain planets and the star Sirius.

If from the *Matsya Purāṇa* onward an astronomical date was assigned to the burning of Tripura, elsewhere a *terminus post quem* is given by laying the corruption of the virtuous demons to the activities of a heretic teacher, who was the creation of Viṣṇu. This teacher converted the demons to Buddhism with the sole purpose of diverting them from their worship of Śiva (*ŚP*.2.5.3.45-2.5.6.28; cf. *LP*.1.71.73-96; *SP*.34.24-71). The teacher of Buddhism as a creation of Viṣṇu would have been no other than the Buddha avatar of Viṣṇu. The Buddha avatar of Viṣṇu was established in Hinduism about a millennium after Gautama Buddha himself, that is, around the sixth century A.D.[30] It may have been introduced earlier.

The introduction into the narrative of the myth of a historically datable occurrence such as the teaching of Buddhism—a heretic religion put into the mouth of the Buddha avatar of Viṣṇu, which depraved the virtuous demons—is secondary in importance to the inclusion, in the texture of the myth, of the luminaries, the signals of time. In the Vedic age, the occurrences in the sky were of paramount importance

[29] J. Deppert, *Rudras Geburt*, p. 189, gives a precise date, about 210 B.C. see Ch. II n.26.

[30] Cf. R. C. Hazra, *Studies in the Purāṇic Records on Hindu Rites and Customs*, 1975, pp. 41-42, 103.

for the timing of the sacrifices. Astronomy was a science ancillary to the *Veda*. The life of the gods depended on the sacrifices, their sustenance.

Rudra, as soon as he entered his myth, was confronted by time, without which no action is possible. He let his arrow fly in mythical time—which lies before and is valid for all time—at the dawn of a sunrise that saw the paradigmatic event in which Rudra revealed his being. Time then was his antagonist, for that great Asura Rudra / Agni had just stepped out of the Uncreate, making ready the seed for the Father.

Rudra, in his ongoing myth, became Time itself, Kāla, and his myth, at significant points, was linked with momentous movements observed in the sky. God Indra was struck by a particular sunrise of ominous portent, in the Kṛttikās, the Pleiades, which heralded the birth of Kārttikeya, whom the Pleiades were to nurse.

The age of the linking of the myth of Rudra / Paśupati, on the one hand, and of the myth of the vision of Indra heralding the birth of Kārttikeya, on the other, with astronomical events observed by the unaided eye of god or man, his priest, can be ascertained astronomically, whereas the latest versions of the burning of Tripura would be from an age cognizant of Buddha's word, enounced by the Buddha avatar of Viṣṇu, datable historically.

v. Śiva's Animals

The demons were worshipers of Śiva. They were true devotees. Whether they were good or evil did not matter, for even though they would commit sin, they would be absolved from it and were protected by worshiping Śiva (*ŚP*.2.5.3.5-7; *LP*.1.71.67-71). The situation was complicated, for the demons were the enemies of the gods, and therefore had to be destroyed whether they were good or bad. But whatever they were mattered little, because although they were the enemies of the gods, they were worshipers of Śiva, and the loyalty of the god to his devotees was intense. A means had to be found to make it possible for Śiva, in whom the gods saw their only savior, and who had committed himself to saving them, to destroy the demons of Tripura.

Viṣṇu once again came to Śiva's aid. By his *māyā* Viṣṇu succeeded in obstructing the worship of Śiva, and he won the demons away from Śiva. Viṣṇu, however, was not a free agent. It was by Śiva's command that Viṣṇu deluded the demons (*ŚP*.2.5.3.45-50). The divine means of leading the demons away from the worship of Śiva were more devious than the corruption that they effected. The corruption consisted in leading the demons away from the worship of Śiva, and in leading their wives, separately deluded by Ṛṣi Nārada, to promiscuity (*ŚP*. 2.5.4.1-19; 2.5.55-61; *LP*. 1.71.92). The entire Tripura became converted and demoralized; Viṣṇu was satisfied, and Śiva felt free to attack Tripura (*ŚP*.2.5.6.2-3, 34-35; *LP*.1.71.94-95, 117-19). The heresy of the demons as motivation to induce Śiva to destroy the demons—though he had his scruples—was a theme introduced in the later *Purāṇas*. Tripura lost its mythical dimension and became a center of religious polemics and politics. Oppressed by their weight, Viṣṇu—in his bull shape—slipped. When Śiva got into his chariot made of the entire earth with all its riches and values, the *Veda*-horses fell headlong down to earth, and Viṣṇu, "the supporter of the earth," taking the shape of a bull, only for a moment succeeded in raising the chariot; in the next moment he fell to the ground on his knees. At the instance of Śiva, Brahmā as the charioteer finally succeeded in steadying the chariot and, with his mind as swift as the wind, drove on to the triple city (*LP*.1.72.29-33). Just then the three strongholds were seen in the sky (*ŚP*.2.5.9.12). It was then that Śiva asked the gods to give him lordship over the animals (*ŚP*.2.5.9.13). This was the crucial point in the victory of the gods over the demons. At this moment Śiva asked the gods to give him the lordship over animals (*TS*.6.2.3.1-2; *ŚP*.2.5.9.13; *LP*.1.72.34), or the gods promised him that animals slain in every sacrifice would be his (*MBh*.7.173.55). Prajāpati, at the beginning, on the first morning of Rudra's myth, had offered the cruel, Wild God the lordship over animals if Rudra desisted from killing him. Before the fall of Tripura, Śiva demanded the lordship over animals before he would kill the demons and free the gods from fear. Prajāpati, for the latter reason, had made Rudra Lord of Animals, Paśupati, in return for Rudra's grace.

Rudra had put forth his claim to the animals at the burnt-out lake of Prajāpati's seed, for its embers and ashes had turned into animals and he had relinquished his claim. He gave to Nābhānediṣṭha, nearest to him of Vedic seers, the cattle due to Rudra himself at the sacrifice of the Aṅgirases. Again and again Rudra, Lord of Animals, asserted his claim to the animals. The animals sacrificed at every sacrifice were to be his. The Vedic sacrificial animals were goat, sheep, horse, bull, and finally man, for whom the other animals substituted as sacrificial victims. All creatures were the animals of Lord Śiva, and he made the gods his animals not only at Tripura but also at Dakṣa's sacrifice, from which he had been excluded. It was an act of retribution by the Wild God. He destroyed the sacrifice, maimed the gods, deprived them of their creativity and senses. They had come to know the destructive power of Rudra by indirection, when they themselves, in their anxiousness to preserve it, took the first part of the offering, the *prāśitra*, to one god after the other; it injured and maimed each one when he tasted it. The first part of the offering was charged with Rudra's power. As his arrow, it had pierced Prajāpati. That pierced part was the fore-offering, the *prāśitra*, that wreaked havoc among the Vedic gods. Later, when they graced Dakṣa's sacrifice with their presence, Śiva / Vīrabhadra made felt his unwanted presence. The act of depriving them of their creativity was a substitute for the wound inflicted by Rudra's arrow on Prajāpati.

At the sacrifice of Dakṣa, Śiva deprived the gods of their creative powers, reduced them to the state of animals, that very state in which Prajāpati the antelope could not help shedding his seed. Rudra avenged the animality of Prajāpati, the Creator procreating.

"How did the gods, including Brahmā, become animals?" ask the sages in the *Liṅga Purāṇa*. "How did Paśupati, the Great Lord, come to burn the three cities of the demons?" (*LP*.1.71.1-2). These questions were asked at the beginning of the chapters on the destruction of Tripura in the *Liṅga Purāṇa*. They follow the chapter on the process of creation (*LP*.1.70). The burning of the triple city of the demons was not the end of creation. A cleansed, regenerate world began with its fall. The demons had been corrupted. Śiva was ready to destroy the corrupted demons, but not before the gods had declared themselves to be animals. The gods were reluctant to accept this status, disinclined to admit that they were animals, unregenerate creatures, *paśus*. Śiva assured them that on recognizing him as their lord, they were freed from the fetters (*pāśa*) that bound them to the objects of their desire. To corrupt the demons so as to justify burning them was an act of exoneration of Śiva, for the demons, though the enemies of the gods, were his devotees. The gods, on the other hand, for whose sake Śiva was about to destroy Tripura, like human beings and all who are created, lived in their natural, congenital state, which they took for granted. Śiva made them *see* themselves as animals, and having thus *made* them into animals (*paśu*), he alone could free them and become their Lord, Paśupati Śiva, the lord of all sentient beings. They observed the Pāśupata *vrata*, and all the gods became the Lord's creatures. Śiva untied the snares (*pāśa*) of each *paśu*, of each individual (*ŚP*.2.5.9.13-24). In the meanwhile, when Śiva had decided to destroy Tripura, Pārvatī drew Śiva's attention to Kārttikeya, and Śiva asked him to dance. All the leading gaṇas danced with him, the entire universe danced at the moment (*LP*.1.71.119-31) of Śiva's resolve to destroy Tripura. As he stood in his chariot, Śiva glanced at the three cities. They were instantly reduced to ashes. The gods said that even though the cities had been burned by his mere glance, Śiva ought to discharge the arrow for their benefit. Then Śiva, laughing, discharged his arrow (*LP*.1.72.110-14; *SP*.35.42, 43).

Why indeed should Śiva, who could destroy the whole universe with his mind, have mounted his chariot accompanied by all his gaṇas to burn Tripura? It was just for the sake of his play (*līlā*). What other benefit had he to derive from this elaborate spectacle? (*LP*.1.72.95-97; *SP*.35.30-32).

From the entry of Fire into the iron, silver, and gold strongholds of the Asuras to the allegoric extravaganza of the *Purāṇas*, Śiva's fire-arrow loomed large. By its power Rudra became Paśupati, the Lord of Animals; they were his to be slain, left unscathed, protected, or released. The first animal in Rudra's power was the Creator himself; finally, all creatures became Rudra's animals. He liberated them from their animal nature, he removed their fetters; he was their savior. The recognition and designation of Rudra as Mahādeva, "the Great God," occurred, according to the *Mahābhārata*, when the gods decided to build his chariot on which he was to conquer Tripura (*MBh*.8.24.63).

From the beginning, the Wild Archer, the Hunter, had been made Lord of Animals by Prajāpati. Yet Rudra had not been accepted by the other gods until they had to recognize him as Mahādeva, to whom they gave half of all their energies (*MBh*.8.24.62), so that armed with bow and arrow he ascended his chariot. He had been slighted, humbled, excluded from the sacrifice. In the beginning the Creator himself, whether actually or potentially, had been his sacrificial animal, the victim of the first of Rudra's arrows sent forth in creation against the creaturely act of procreation, the shedding of the seed, the substance from out of the pleroma of the Uncreate.

XII

THE PRESENCE OF ŚIVA

1. Conspectus

"O Wealth, my treasure, honey, red flame of heavenly hosts that excels all lustre, embodied One, my kin, my flesh, heart within my flesh, image within my heart, my all-bestowing tree, my eye, pupil of my eye, image seen in that pupil, save me from the disease of the powerful *karma*,"[1] Saint Appar of the seventh century sang to Śiva. Flaming, glowing, palpably near, and in him, embodied in his own flesh, in his heart and eye, the saint saw the image of the Savior.

The Wild God, a hunter, his arrow afire, had been seen before life had come to be. Right into its nascent future he released his arrow—its searing thrust went deep. Its sharp, burning point fixed the beginning of life on earth in the world of Rudra. Had it not been for the terror of this entry of the god into his world, Appar could not have felt the god throbbing in his flesh, could not have seen the red flame of heavenly hosts carry the image that he held in his heart and that was reflected in his eye.

Rudra's world starts with the flight of his arrow precisely aimed at the Father, the Creator in the act of procreation. He shed seed and some of it fell on the earth. His seed held all life to be; it was a potent substance made ready by Agni / Rudra and never shed before. It was in the Father before it was stirred by the sight of his daughter, consubstantial with and hypostasized by him just then. Her separation from him provoked Prajāpati, the Lord of Generation, to seek union with her; spontaneously, the Creator seized her, united with her as

[1] M. Dhavamony, *Love of God, According to Śaiva Siddhānta*, 1971, p. 151.

creatures do. He acted as, and had the shape of, an animal, an antelope. While the seed of the Creator fell, the gods made of it a *brahman* and gave it the shape of Vāstoṣpati. It fell into creation. Before that the mysterious substance of the seed had been contained within the Uncreate, a state beyond and before creation. Inviolate in its integrity of total potentiality, the Uncreate was a pleroma, beyond existence, metaphysical, transcendent, beyond the reach of words, prior to and beyond action in which myth has its beginning. The Uncreate had its guardians, who knew this unconditioned, ultimate secret.

Prajāpati, the Lord of Generation, was about to release it when he became Rudra's target. Only an act of violence could prevent the violation of the Uncreate. Ablaze, Rudra discharged his arrow. He was Fire who had prepared the seed, heating it beyond Prajāpati's endurance, and the Lord of Generation let it flow down to earth.

Rudra / Agni, bivalent in his double attack on the Father, made sure of his prey, whom he had excited, incited, and caught in the act. Rudra was a fiery hunter, the fire *of* creation and *in* creation to be. Flaming, he had taken his stand at the boundary of the Uncreate beyond which no mind could reach. Thence he discharged his arrow. It flew at the first dawn of the inception of life, hit its target and nearly missed its aim. The arrow, sent flying as the Father embraced the daughter, struck as he cohabited with her, and some seed fell down on the earth.

Rudra, the guardian of the Uncreate, the Fire and cause of creation; the fierce Archer, by his first action brought about time. Without it no action can take place, nor can a place be reached without it. The arrow, a fraction of time too late, failed to separate the mating pair before seed was shed. The substance of the Uncreate flowed into creation.

Having incited it, Rudra interrupted Prajāpati's intercourse. Rudra, the Fire, caused and stimulated a result that the Wild God meant to prevent. As Agni he stood on the boundary of the Uncreate; his flame lashed hitherwards and heated the Father's seed. As Rudra he aimed at the procreating Father this side of the boundary. Prajāpati faced hitherwards, Rudra faced the Uncreate, whose guardian and exponent he was and whose integrity Time prevented him from preserving. He struck the creator / progenitor, and the arrow stuck in his genitals. He "killed" the Father only to revive him, or he spared his life.

Rudra, guardian of the Uncreate and avenger of its loss of integrity, was the antagonist of the creator / procreator who acted as animal (*paśu*) according to the spontaneous compulsion of its nature. Rudra spared the life of Prajāpati on the condition that the Lord of Generation make Rudra Lord of Animals. The Creator himself thus became Rudra's charge, as did every animal, every sentient being that would be created, man or god, and other animals, wild and tame. By the flight of his arrow, the Wild God, guardian of the Uncreate, became the murderer of the Father and the protector of all creatures, including the Creator. Inasmuch as he was Fire, Rudra had flared up at the limit of mind's grasp, at the frontier of the Uncreate; inasmuch as he was the Wild Hunter, he killed the Father; and inasmuch as he was God, he spared his victim's life and was acknowledged as Paśupati, the Lord of Animals, who protects the creature. The guardian of the Uncreate, the ultimate, unconditioned Reality, was fierce as Fire, a Wild Hunter incensed by the copulation of the Father and aiming to prevent the Father's emission of seed, prognostic of his own birth and the beginning of life on earth.

Though he did not succeed in this, his arrow stuck in the wound he had inflicted. The searing thrust of his arrow remained in the flesh of the Creator. The gods preserved the wounded part. It was not larger than a barley corn, and wreaked havoc from sacrifice to sacrifice through Rudra's myth until that morsel was appeased.

Rudra had acted in two directions, the one hitherwards into creation when he prepared the seed for the Father, the other backwards and away from this world. They lay on the same endless line that cuts across the boundary between the intelligible and the transcendental realms where Agni was stationed. Life came to earth in Prajāpati's seed that Rudra had made ready. Its potency was of the Uncreate, and was immeasurable like the Uncreate itself. Paradoxically, the measureless plenum of the Uncreate remained measureless as it had been and *is*—when realized in *samādhi* by the yogi. Withdrawn from action, Rudra the Wild Hunter is the Lord of Yoga, one with his Self, the measureless, inviolable homology of the Uncreate.

The myth of Rudra begins with the primordial action of the God. Implied in it is its ground, the Uncreate, the consciousness of which prompted Rudra's action. Rudra is Consciousness and his actions are its forms. The Uncreate is the abiding content. Each of his movements touches on it.

He assumed the appearance of a man of lowly station, a hunter in his primordial myth, uncanny and not gladly seen, though he was God. This the people felt, though they gave him as offerings only the remnants of their own food, or even things not fit to be eaten. They also celebrated sacrifices exclusively his own, but these had to take place outside the village. He was an outcast among gods; they did not want to see him at their own sacrifices, but the herdsmen saw him and the women on their way to get water from the pond. Those who were of low station and made their living in a demanding, hazardous, or devious way knew him, for he threatened or protected them. He had that power; their life was in his hands. They were afraid of him, and where he did not harm them they worshiped him in his power and grace. Perhaps they had no words to contain his awful greatness. The words were given to a seer who in divine vision witnessed the primordial scene and sang of it in the *raudra brahman* (*RV*.10.61.1), the "song of the seed" (*AB*.6.27).

In the primordial scene, Rudra not only showed his frightening power but also his control and, with it, his grace. He refrained from killing the Father, or if he did kill him he brought him back to life. Also, on more than one occasion, he refrained from taking the cattle that belonged to him (Ch. III.2.a). His way was the mastery over life, not only of the gods or the animals but also his own, for he was an ascetic who controlled his power, and he was the god who let flow from it his grace. Fierceness was his nature and the reason why the other gods, though unwilling to accept him as their equal, recognized him as their lord, the Lord of Animals, Paśupati. His fierce fire as a hunter was directed outward; as an ascetic he held it within and it illumined his being. He stood apart and was an outsider to the other Vedic gods. He could be recognized by his weird, mad looks. He seemed poor and uncared-for, neglectful of his appearance; the gods despised him, but he intentionally courted dishonor, he rejoiced in contempt and disregard, for "he who is despised lies happy, freed of all attachment" (*PS*.3.3 and commentary; cf. *PS*.3.7-9).[2] The fierce, self-humiliated Lord was a yogi, and inasmuch as he was Fire, he burned within himself by the heat of his asceticism the pride of self-abasement. He provoked contempt as a test of his detachment. It was confirmed by his willed exposure to contempt, by which he proved

[2] D.H.H. Ingalls, "Cynics and Pāśupatas, The Seeking of Dishonor," p. 286; cf. D. N. Lorenzen, *The Kāpālikas and Kālāmukhas*, p. 187.

himself to be above contempt. Similarly, on other occasions, he let himself be sexually tempted in order to prove, and persist in, his *brahmacarya*. To all appearances he was uncanny Rudra, the fierce god, because he burns, because he is fiery, because he devours flesh, blood, and marrow (cf. *MBh*.7.173.98).

Appearing as a wild hunter, his proper form on earth, he was feared and avoided, while sanctity emanated from his naked body, below the snakes and animal skins that he had slung around him. Because he was outside the pale of the other gods, he wanted to justify the attitudes of those who thought to demean him. He reinforced whatever was thought despicable in him; he made himself resemble the way in which he appeared to those securely established by the standards of their own position. He made himself the butt of their aversion, bringing to their notice exactly what they were capable of seeing in him. His was an asceticism that by intensifying his abject condition clarified his detachment, while outwardly its state of exultancy appeared as madness. It was a closely fitted mask by which he asserted his freedom from any standard by which those who saw the Wild God would dare to judge him. Had he been man, pride might have corroded his antics. Despised and rejected, he would low like a bull—his vehicle that would carry him through millennia of worship—he would laugh and dance as though mad. He drew to his appearance and riveted on it baffled attention; he offered himself as a spectacle that cut through the prejudices and the limitations of his detractors. Though he transcended their understanding, he fascinated them. The gods of the *Ṛg Veda* who witnessed the primordial scene made of it a work of art in which the other face of the fierce Archer was revealed to them. In the primordial upheaval itself they saw the cosmogonic order that their creative mind obeyed; they made a poem, an audible form of their vision, and out of that substance they shaped the other side of Rudra: Vāstoṣpati, the Lord of the Dwelling, the guardian of sacred ordinance.

Paśupati and Vāstoṣpati are two aspects of Rudra, opposed and complementary, part of the inscrutable physiognomy of Rudra / Śiva. Extending the human metaphor to his body, it was half fire, like the sun, flame, and lightning, and half Soma, like the moon (cf. *MBh*.7.173.95); and also half male, half female, right and left. In him polarities coexist; it could not be otherwise. Should the one cancel out the other, at that very moment creation itself would cease to exist, and

God would have lost his body, the world. Even so, the polarity of the being of Lord Rudra is not completely described, for the Wild Hunter was his form of outgoing action that was willed and directed. Under the golden raiments wrapped round the loins of the Lord—manifesting in a cosmic night—was the *ūrdhvaliṅga* of the yogi (Ch. VII.2). It was the ascetic's, the yogi's, special cognizance. The hunter who practiced the yoga of archery withdrew in *samādhi* and returned into his self, where he was at one with his Self.

He was alone, unborn, like the Uncreate. When he defied understanding he wanted to be despised. Fascinated by the horror of his abjectness, those who disregarded him were drawn to him. Though his real name should not be uttered, he had a hundred names to which he answered. They were part of his identity, but did not define him.

He even had more forms than names; his forms were beyond number, for he lived in all beings—he was their life, its operative cause. Life, self-contained, was held within him. He did not engender life. While Rudra remained *one*, he was his own plural, the Rudras. The Rudras were everywhere.

In the primordial dawn, as Rudra sent his arrow to its target, Time had intervened on the scene of Rudra's nascent cosmos. Before Rudra had recognized his antagonist, Time had entered Rudra's presence. As Kāla / Time, Rudra raced along. He was the movement itself of life, its breath, drawn by its momentum to outlive its forms that as Kāla / Death he defined. Rudra left even Time and Death behind, transcending them as Bhairava. When Rudra faced, and became, Time, his direction was hitherward, into, through, and out of, creation. Once, however, moved by pity for living beings doomed to die, he cooperated with Brahmā and, resorting to his yoga nature, let its calm flow into the current of time, so that life would rest and rise again in a new wave. Rudra then acted as the Healer, though the palliative of recurrent lives and deaths was not the remedy he would dispense by his own will. At that time he helped Brahmā out of a difficult situation into which the Creator had put himself and the creatures created by him. Rudra reserved *his* remedy for those who were strong enough to receive it. It would give them cessation of all sorrow, would free them from the misery of *karma*, would place them out of time and into the realization of ultimate reality in which they would be joined with Rudra.

In the first dawn of the creation of man Rudra released his arrow. His burning energy went along with it, pierced and became embedded in Prajāpati, and Rudra became Prajāpati's son (Ch. V.1). By this paradox, Rudra was to be born into the cosmos that was to be his own. When he had entered manifestation, he had neither mother nor father; now Prajāpati, the Lord of Generation, became his father. Sitting on his lap, the infant of cosmic dimension demanded to be given his names and to be established throughout the realm of his world. The cosmos became the embodiment of Rudra. Though he no longer appeared as a wild hunter, he retained his insignia, the bow and the arrow. Thence, Rudra's being unfolded in the cosmos, and the cosmos became his visible presence. He existed before creation and before time; he exists now and will continue to exist in the future; nothing ever exists apart from him (*AUp*.2 and commentary). The long-haired muni shared this knowledge. He drank with Rudra from the same cup.

The myths of Śiva have many levels. They have to be entered all at the same time, or else the total, multiple perspective of each is lost sight of. Crazed beggar, savior, necrophiliac, voluptuary, ascetic, he is each wholly on the plane where he acts, while on another plane he is Sadāśiva, the eternal Śiva, who lays out his presence in his five faces, of which the fifth, invisible in principle, is part of the *pañcamukha liṅga*, Śiva's concrete, monumental symbol.

With the thrust of his flaming arrow, Rudra's hot energy (*tejas*) entered and was embedded in the Lord of Generation. "Prajāpati saw in himself gold. He generated that gold." It grew and became Mahādeva, the Great God (Ch. V.1.b). An enthusiastic visionary, a Vrātya, evoked and beheld this scene. The gold that the Vrātya had seen first in Prajāpati and then, immediately, in front of the Lord of Generation was, according to another account, held in Prajāpati's hands. It had the shape of a bowl and the dimensions of an arrow's flight. In his golden bowl Prajāpati's seed by second generation was gathered. His sons had shed it on seeing his daughter, their sister. From it the Archer arose in cosmic size. He held a thousand arrows. He had a thousand heads. He filled the Universe, yet he was an infant—he clasped his father, demanding to be given a name. Full-fledged in his cosmic power, he had arisen from Prajāpati's golden bowl, the womb as it were of the Lord of Generation, the material cause of the universe.

Given his names and freed from the sin of his unforgotten past, Rudra was invested by his father with the cosmos and became the cosmos. He moved within it and exceeded it. "Puruṣa is this entire world, what has been and what will be and he is the lord of deathlessness" (*RV*.10.90.2).[3] Vedic Puruṣa held no arrows in his thousand hands, and let himself be offered by the gods as the sacrificial offering which they sacrificed into creation. Rudra, the thousand-eyed Puruṣa with his thousand arrows, was born to release them into the world of men, gods, and demons—at Dakṣa's sacrifice, or against Tripura. It was with the glance of fire from his third eye that he burnt to ashes Kāma, the archer Desire. Serpents were wreathed around Śiva meditating in a Himālayan cave, where Kāma attacked the Great God. Serpents protected Śiva; he wore serpents as amulets, ornaments, and his sacred thread. They were coiled around him, as Vṛtra, most ancient of all serpents, had lain coiled around the mountain. Jointly Vṛtra and the mountain guarded the Uncreate—before Indra's creation. It is enjoined in the *Gṛhya Sūtras*, the texts on domestic ritual, that one should make offerings to Rudra in a place where there are snakes (cf. *ĀGS*.4.8.27-28; cf. *HGS*.1.16.10). The ritual, of common practice, invoked Rudra to protect one from the dangerous, poisonous snakes, among whom he lived. The connection of Rudra and the serpents was felt in daily life. It had overtones not necessarily audible to everyone and not always present. To this day, a *liṅga*, over which a serpent rises with hood expanded, may be seen in worship in many a Śaiva household. The truth about Śiva comes from many levels, from Vedic intuitions, or the devotion of jungle folk, and from those below and outside the brahmin elite. The gods of the latter, to begin with, were at odds with Rudra; they did not let him share the sacrificial offerings, and he had his own priests who sacrificed to him (*VāP*.30.112, 113, 119). The serpents, in the polyvalence of their meaning, cling to Rudra, the healer, who knows how to control them (*TS*.4.5.1.2); they shed their skins as symbols of renewal. Rudra alone could swallow the poison that Vāsuki, the serpent king, had spat into the ocean; it beautified Rudra's throat, made it gleam blue, the color of the peacock—enemy of the serpents. He wore the mark of the serpent's poison as an ornament, as if a serpent had kissed him on that spot. "Shining with jewels or with glistening snakes, wearing an elephant hide or silk,

[3] Cf. *Ṛg Veda Saṃhitā (RV)*, tr. K. F. Geldner, 1951, 3:287.

with skulls or the moon as his diadem, no one can comprehend Śiva, who takes all forms" (*KS*.5.78). "His nature at once transcends and includes all the polarities of the living world."[4]

Cooperating opposites within Śiva's boundless orbit—or alternatives such as snakes and jewels—would also reverse their meaning. What is poison or death to the ignorant is bliss or release to the knowing. From the beginning, the phallic shape of the Śiva *liṅga*, standing erect, negated its function as an organ of procreation. It was an *ūrdhvaliṅga*, conveying by its erect shape that the seed was channeled upward, not ejected for the sake of generation, but was reversed in its course, retained and absorbed for regeneration. The *mukhaliṅga*, the face *liṅga*, a visual paradox in its unified shape of phallus and face, conveyed that the seed stirred sexually was controlled, rediverted, and absorbed mentally, and was a symbol of the metaphysical-ontological reality of Śiva.

With the "birth of Rudra" from Prajāpati's seed the God entered the cosmos, the world of his dispensation, and he became the cosmos. It was the first act in his play of manifestation. Man in the flesh had not yet come to be when Brahmā, the Creator, in a successive aeon, continued Prajāpati's work. The creation of human beings was Brahmā's self-assigned task. According to Śaiva tradition, he created Rudra to help him, for he had not been successful. Out of Brahmā's frustration, out of the anger of his mind, Rudra was born anew; and Brahmā, desperate to the point of perverse vindictiveness, charged Rudra, his ascetic, mind-born son, with the creation of mortals. Brahmā had not forgotten what Rudra had done to the procreating Father, nor had Prajāpati, from whose anger and tears, according to one account (Ch. V.1.b), Rudra had been born. By whatever mode Rudra had become the son of Prajāpati, it was a birth by bodily filiation, whether it took place from within Prajāpati's body that had held the gold, the god to be, or by indirection from Prajāpati's seed, or by Prajāpati's tears that fell on Manyu, his anger.

In his next birth and the second act of his play, Rudra was born from the mind or breath of Brahmā, the Creator; Rudra asserted and maintained his asceticism, his aversion to procreation in his triple birth from Brahmā's mind. He became Sthāṇu, the Pillar; he castrated himself, and, finally, sprang, an androgyne in shape, from

[4] H. Zimmer, *Myths and Symbols in Indian Art and Civilization*, 1946, pp. 125-126.

Brahmā's furrowed brow. Sthāṇu, the Pillar, was Śiva's most cogent form of protest against Brahmā's command to create mortals. Śiva's castration—after he emerged from the water or in the Deodar forest—gave transcosmic significance to the severed *liṅga* and established its worship on earth. Finally, in the form of Ardhanārīśvara, Lord Śiva was born from Brahmā's mind in a prognostic form of humanity, an integer of man and woman, though, as god Śiva's, the ascetic's, own shape he was precluded from sexual union by the hieratic bilateral frontality of the biune shape. This was as far as the Lord of Yoga would let himself be born from Brahmā. Born as Ardhanārīśvara, he followed, however, Brahmā's command and divided himself, allowing the Great Goddess to proceed from and return into his self. Thereafter, degree by degree, the Great Goddess allowed herself to be born from Dakṣa of the lineage of Brahmā. She was the idea of woman, but in order to fulfill her role in Śiva's play, she assumed the character of the headstrong yet fallible bride-to-be of Śiva, whose childless wife she was destined to become.

Throughout his two marriages, to Satī and to Pārvatī, Śiva the Lord of Yoga did not engender a child in the womb of the Great Goddess.[5] Though his frightful potency on one occasion persisted in the lap of Pārvatī for a thousand years of the gods, and made him oblivious of the world and his obligation to it, he remained self-contained and did not shed his seed. He was the Lord of Yoga. Pārvatī had desired Śiva because he was primarily a yogi. His fearsome appearance only enhanced the attraction she felt for him. Still, when the gods, for the well-being of the world, felt it necessary to interrupt the seemingly endless love making of Śiva—who being a yogi did not stop—while her womb remained empty, she cursed the gods who had interrupted their intercourse as well as all the goddesses to be barren. Pārvatī's curse and the childlessness of the gods were a final sequel to the events in the primordial morning. When Śiva's seed fell at last, it was an offering into the Fire.

Śiva and Pārvatī have been celebrated in art and poetry, forming as

[5] Besides Pārvatī / Umā and Satī, of whom only the Purāṇas tell, Durgā Kātyāyanī (Sāyaṇa on *TĀ*.10.1) is another name of the consort of Rudra. In one instance Mīḍhūṣī, a cow consort of Īśāna in the shape of a bull, takes part in the Śūlagava sacrifice along with Īśāna as a bull and their calf (S. K. Bhattacharji, *The Indian Theogony*, p. 142). Rudra's relation with the Pṛśni cow is of a special nature (*RV*.2.34.2.10; 5.52.16; 5.60.5; 6.66.3). See Ch. VII n. 15 and Ch. VIII n. 7.

they do the most accessible aspect of the Great God, which he offered in his play. O'Flaherty, in her book *Asceticism and Eroticism in the Mythology of Śiva*, gives full insight into their relation.

Both aspects, the ascetic and the erotic, were united in the symbol of the *liṅga*. Its ambiguously abstract and concrete shape was the pivot to which ontology gave its terms and ritual its service. To this monumental symbol of manifestation the embodiments of *mantra* attached themselves in facial terms. Time, Kāla, also found its identity in four of the faces in which Śiva's fivefold presence was made manifest. Kāla, whose face is as frightening as Death's, is as black as cosmic night. Kāla means black, and Kāla, the god who is one with Śiva, is a mythical equivalent of Śiva to whom *tamas* belongs in the cosmic texture. *Tamas*, the descending tendency, corresponds to the destructive quality of time. Just before the first cosmic dawn there was nothing but darkness (*tamas*). That darkness was Rudra (cf. *MaUp*.5.2). The darkness before manifestation spread with the fall of the Asuras into the netherworld, or, according to the mythical terms of another cosmogony, it lay all around Ā-bhu in the precosmic flood (*RV*.10.129.3). Beyond that darkness is Śiva's transcendency (*ŚUp*.4.18). Cosmogonically and *in* manifestation, *tamas*, darkness, was part of the triple design of the fabric of the cosmos. *Tamas*, the dark strand of existence, belongs to Rudra. It was interwoven with the other two *guṇas* represented by Brahmā and Viṣṇu.

Mythical time, a mode of the "eternal now"; contingent time that carries death; the time of grace, which Brahmā and Śiva conjointly granted to Death, the compassionate goddess, where activity and rest would follow one another like flood and tide, like waking and sleeping in recurrent rhythm: each manifestation of time was gathered in and overcome by the Ender of Time, transcendental Śiva, eternity.

Śiva did not create his cosmos: he pervaded this domain of his that Prajāpati had given him together with his names. These represented aspects of his being, facets of his totality meant to be seen in their coherence, though each would seem to stand or act on its own. Or one might see the many aspects of Śiva in succession. The *Ocean of Story*, the *Kathāsaritsāgara*, tells of a Śiva *liṅga* in the heavenly abode of Śiva, called Siddhīśvara, where Śiva was always present. The *liṅga* of Śiva "exhibits in succession all his forms" (*KSS*.115.110-15).[6]

The sequence of all of Śiva's forms on one constant ground, a the-

[6] *Kathāsaritsāgara (KSS)*, tr. C. H. Tawney and ed. N. M. Penzer, 1968, 8:152.

ophany displayed in time, was different from the central presence of Śiva simultaneously with his four faces in the four directions on a *pañcamukha liṅga*. An actual or mental rite of circumambulation would not lose sight of the center, while the parts would be seen from different angles.

An analogous method of seeing Śiva is to consider the several versions of a myth to be like the stations of a mentally performed rite of circumambulation, in which the total meaning shows itself together with its gradual changes. The skull fantasy of the *Skānda Purāṇa* (Ch. IX.6) sprouted from Brahmā's decapitation and, while the skulls went on multiplying, they brought into focus Śiva's exclusion from, and his subsequent less than half-hearted admission to, the sacrifice.

The above distortion of the Bhairava myth was due to a partial and narrow view. In another myth, the several versions of the reciprocal relation of Brahmā's and Śiva's fifth head ranged over half a circle of viewpoints (Ch. IX.1). A full round, however, was made when in yet another myth the antelope, Rudra's victim in the primordial morning, was hymned as Śiva himself: "Obeisance to the God in the form of a deer (or antelope), the lord of the deer."[7] This eulogy of Paśupati / Śiva further praised the god who had the form of an animal (*paśu*), who destroyed the snares (*pāśa*) of *māyā* that bind the *paśu*, and who played with the *paśu*. The eulogy of Śiva, the antelope, ended with an obeisance to the Lord who assumed the form of an animal and roamed at will with the Pramathas in a sacred forest: "Obeisance to the God who is the seed of the world's salvation."[8] The antelope, animal form of Prajāpati, had become the animal (*paśu*) form of Śiva *and* of the creature (*paśu*).

The *paśu*, the sentient being, freed from its fetters (*pāśa*) no longer knows itself as separate from Śiva, while the *paśu*, ensnared by the world and its riches, may not be aware that Śiva is in him. King Candraśekhara and his queen Tārāvatī, unknown to themselves, were incarnations of Śiva and Pārvatī. It was only under great stress that they became aware of their divine nature—for a moment only—then they returned to their day-to-day consciousness as mortals.[9]

[7] A. S. Gupta, "Eulogy of Paśupati Śiva," 1975, p. 101, translation of a passage from *Skānda Purāṇa*. While *mṛga* denotes both antelope or deer, the words used here are *hariṇa* (verse 5), which again denotes deer or antelope, and *mṛga* (verse 6), p. 100.

[8] *Ibid.*

[9] The story is summarized in W. D. O'Flaherty, *Asceticism and Eroticism in the Mythology of Śiva*, pp. 206-207. The full story is told in *KP* 48, 49, 50, 51.

Śiva and Pārvatī live in every being. Śiva is born anew in every child. When Śuciṣmatī, the wife of a sage, wanted a son like Maheśvara, and her husband, with this wish in mind, worshiped the Vīreśvara *liṅga* in Vārāṇasī, a boy appeared above the *liṅga* and Śiva fulfilled the desire of the sage and his wife. Śiva himself assumed the name of Gṛhapati, "lord of the house," and let himself be born as Śuciṣmatī's son. The legend, told in the *Skānda Purāṇa*, was represented in many images in eastern India of about the tenth century A.D. that showed the newborn child lying close to its beautiful mother on an elegant bed. The right hand of the infant is raised in the gesture of granting freedom from fear.[10]

Śiva conceived by the wife of a brahmin sage assumed the name Gṛhapati, lord of the house. It was his proper name, for the gods, in the beginning, had conceived and formed him as Vāstoṣpati, the Lord of the Dwelling. Gṛhapati, the child, an incarnation of Śiva, could have repeated the words from the hymn attributed to Śaṅkara: "My Self is you . . . my breaths your servants, my body your home."[11] The body as the house of God is the microcosmic equivalent of the *vāstu*. Vāstoṣpati, lord of the *vāstu*, was given form in the *raudra brahman*, the archetypal wonder work of the gods, of which the arts in this world are to be understood as an imitation (cf. *AB*.6.27; Ch. I.2).

Śiva is present in the world of man. Paśupati, the Lord of Animals, frees from his fetters the "animal," unregenerate man tied to his ego and its passions, and he frees this man, the "social animal," from the fetters of conventions. Rudra prepared the fire seed of creation for the Father, and it is he who implants it in man for the creation of works of art, in imitation of the archetypal wonder works of the gods.

The unnamed God of the primordial scene was a wild hunter. The *Śatarudriya* hymn rendered homage to Rudra, the archer (*TS*.4.5.1), and to the makers of arrows, to the potters, smiths, and fishermen (*TS*.4.5.4), to those of low social standing and also to those of no social standing, the robber, thief, and cheat, and also to the dogs (*TS*.4.5.3, 4).[12] Śiva appeared as a beggar, a homeless ascetic, or also a workman.

[10] Cf. R. D. Trivedi, "Mother and Child Sculptures Representing the Gṛhapati Form of Śiva," 1970, p. 143, citing *Skānda Purāṇa*.

[11] *Śivamānasapūja* in *Subodhastotrasaṃgraha*, ed. P. G. Goswami, 1962, verse 4, p. 13.

[12] Although the dog of the Dog Star (Ch. II.4) has no equal in the later myth of Śiva, in South Indian images of the later Cola period, the dog figures conspicuously in images of Bhairava (T. A. Gopinatha Rao, *Elements of Hindu Iconography*, vol. 2, part 1, p. 178, pl. 41). It must also not be forgotten that thirty million dogs were born, like Vīra-

A South Indian legend tells of an old woman who was bid by a Pandyan king to repair a dam. She was not up to the task. In her distress, she worshiped her Lord, Sundareśa, the "Beautiful Lord," Śiva. A workman appeared on the spot carrying a basket and a spade. With one stroke he repaired the dam. He was Śiva. The king built a splendid temple of Lord Sundareśa, who to this day is worshiped in the Great Temple at Madura, and is taken in procession in a golden basket with a golden spade.[13]

From the primordial dawn to this day, Śiva is present in the cosmos. From that morning time (Kāla) came to be. What happened then left its image in the sky. Rudra overcame time as Mahākāla, he became Bhairava in his breakthrough from Time into Timelessness. If Śiva of a thousand and more names and forms is evoked as one of them, he necessarily is also its opposite, the cruel kind God. He encompasses the orbit of the mind, which thinks in pairs of opposites. All of them are His in manifestation and even beyond, for he includes the ultimate pair: creation and the Uncreate. He is their Consciousness.

The Great Yogi carries within himself the consciousness of the Uncreate, the Absolute. In meditation he withdraws within himself, he returns to the Uncreate. Opening his "sun and moon" eyes, he sees himself in every thing that exists. He is Aṣṭamūrti, Existence itself. Śiva Aṣṭamūrti is Existence. Śiva, the Great Yogi, is the consciousness of Existence and of the Uncreate.

2. Viṣṇu and Śiva

While Brahmā was inextricably part of the pattern of Rudra's myth, Viṣṇu's role was supportive and subsidiary. Viṣṇu was assigned Śiva's left half in the image of Śiva called Harihara following the conception of the image of Ardhanārīśvara. However, this unified image was surpassed when it was said that Śiva was Viṣṇu and Viṣṇu was Śiva (*BNārP*.14.214).

This is told mythically as well as explicitly in the story of Arjuna's contest with a Kirāta, a wild hunter (Ch. IX.1). The Kirāta, the wild hunter who, unknown to Arjuna, was Śiva, after a fierce contest of

---

bhadra himself, of Śiva's hair (Ch. X.A.2.a). Furthermore, Saramā, the dog mother of the sun, moon, and Sirius, offered herself also to be a mother of Kārttikeya (S. Kramrisch, "The Indian Great Goddess," p. 262); cf. Ch. IX n. 27.

[13] B. N. Sharma, *Festivals of India*, 1978, p. 107.

their powers, knocked the heroic Arjuna senseless (*MBh*.3.40.50-51). Pleased with Arjuna's prowess, Śiva revealed himself to his devotee (*MBh*.3.40.52-54). Śiva had put him to the test so that Arjuna could prove his worth and be given by Śiva the Pāśupata weapon. Arjuna then saw Śiva in his glory, the Cause of all Causes, and he praised Mahādeva, "Honor to Śiva in the form of Viṣṇu and Viṣṇu in the form of Śiva, to the Destroyer of Dakṣa's sacrifice, to Harirudra!" (*MBh*.3.40. insert no. 174, lines 1-6, after verse 57).

In the opposite spirit, the myth of Śiva as Śarabha (cf. *ŚP*.3.10.4) tells of Viṣṇu in his incarnation as man-lion (Narasiṃha). Narasiṃha disembowelled the demon Hiraṇya-kaśipu, "Gold-Cloth," who had not only harassed the gods but who hated his own son, Prahlāda, a devotee of Viṣṇu. Although the demon was killed, the fury of Narasiṃha persisted (*ŚP*.3.10.15-25). He threatened to annihilate the universe (*ŚP*.3.11.27), and thought himself to be Kāla, death, the cause of universal destruction (*ŚP*.3.11.35). Śiva, who is Mahākāla, the Death of death (*ŚP*.3.11.59), like a four-legged bird dug his claws into Narasiṃha and lifted him up. The man-lion lost his power, and Śiva / Vīrabhadra put an end to Narasiṃha's life (*ŚP*.3.12.7-22). Vīrabhadra peeled off the skin of the man-lion, and Śiva since then has worn this hide (*ŚP*.3.12.35-36). Myths of this kind and their images tell less about Śiva than about the sympathies or antipathies of his followers and their struggle for power. Iconography endowed Śarabha with eight legs—four of them like a lion's and resting on the ground, and four long, clawed legs turned upward—a body that is half man, half lion, and two wings, which represent Kālī and Durgā.[14] Śarabha looked as if the Śiva bird had taken to itself the shape of the man-lion, beautified significantly by the bird's wings, symbolizing Śiva's *śaktis* or female powers. In one (unpublished) painting, the figures of the goddesses are inscribed in Śiva / Śarabha's golden wings; serpents wriggle and writhe on and around the lion's body, tail, and golden wings; the beaked head of Śarabha is surmounted by a mighty serpent. In the unknown painter's vision, the shape of the man-lion had been absorbed in Śarabha's shape, and their synthesis was guarded all over by serpents. The myth of Śarabha stirred the memory of the ancient image of the serpents surrounding a sacred center—and a tendentious fable acquired hallowed meaning. Śarabha occupies a very narrow

[14] T. A. Gopinatha Rao, *Elements of Hindu Iconography*, vol. 2, part 1, pp. 172-73.

facet of the totality that is Rudra / Śiva. Even so, the image of the bird-man-lion was invested with the power of the god that brought to life, in the work of an unknown painter of the eighteenth century, the ambience of the god with its serpents and the Ganges flowing from the golden locks of the demoniac bird-man-lion's head.

Śiva frequently acts more like a demon than a god. He retained his Asura hood in creation, when other gods had left being Asuras and other Asuras had become demons. It was proper for Śiva to meet Kāvya Uśanas on more than one occasion, for this Asura priest officiated for the gods as well as the demons, though not at the same time. The knowledge of resuscitation of the dead was Kāvya Uśanas's secret; according to some, however, it was Śiva who possessed its magic power. It was peripheral to his being.

Śiva should be thought of in a fourfold manner, and perceived as the cause of existence, existence itself, the cause of liberation, and release (*LP*.1.28.23). As the cause of existence, Śiva had prepared the seed of existence for the Lord of Generation, and was born as existence from the Lord of Generation. As the cause of liberation and release, Śiva was a yogi holding within himself the power of life, the power of creativity. As the Lord of Yoga he causes the transformation of the vitally creative power into mental creativity and the interiorized objectivity of detachment that leads to Release. He, who showed himself as the Wild Hunter, excluded from their company by the other gods, a frenzied beggar who walked and danced his way into freedom from his sin, found Release. The "passion" of Śiva / Bhairava, the erotic attachment of the ascetic god, intensified by his togetherness with his own seductive and exteriorized female power, and his burning of Kāma were different ways toward the liberation of which he himself was the cause. In more than one form was Lord Mahādeva the way and cause of Release. The *Ṛg Veda* (*RV*.2.33.3) invoked him: "O Rudra, creation's most glorious in glory, mightiest of the mighty, . . . lead us safely beyond distress."[15]

To the ignorant he showed himself in their fear, and they saw the horror of the god; those who knew him saw the god in his grace—he was Śiva who gave them peace. In whichever way he was seen, his laughter spread from transcendency over his inscrutable face, or it resounded loudly, liberatingly in the cosmic night from the *liṅga*

[15] *Ṛg Veda Saṃhitā (RV)*, tr. K. F. Geldner, 1951, 1:317.

wreathed in flames. It showed and made audible his freedom. Or Śiva dances. He does not *play* the role of a dancer. "Śiva's dance is only the dance rendering of himself. . . ."[16] His dance complements his *tapas*. Both are forms of the creative fire, the one turned inward in trance, the other turned outward in ecstasy.

Once, at the beginning of the rainy season, as the *Skānda Purāṇa* relates, all the gods came to Mount Mandara to see Śiva dance for the pleasure of the goddess. Śiva had observed *brahmacarya* and he was in a happy mood (*SkP*.6.254.8-14). All the musical instruments arrived in thousands. Śiva was surrounded by his gaṇas and demonic troops of *piśācas* and *bhūtas*. Then all the Rāgas, the Melodies, came. Śiva had created them by thinking of them. They came from the *cakras*, the centers of Śiva's subtle body (*SkP*.6.254.18-45). The gods played on their instruments as Śiva took on his form of Mahānaṭa, the cosmic dancer. Five-headed, ten-armed, ash-smeared, emerald-crested, wearing garlands and armlets, his radiant body expanded through the three worlds; the mountain resounded with the beat of Śiva's feet, the earth swayed rhythmically (*SkP*.6.254.46-56, 62). Pārvatī then praised Śiva, and Śiva let her occupy the left half of his body, which is known to belong to Viṣṇu (*SkP*.6.254.70-88). Śiva had a skull in his hand, half of his neck was marked blue by the poison that he had swallowed at the Churning of the Ocean, half of his garland was strung with skulls, the matted hair carried the crescent moon, he was clad in animal skins. The other side was Gaurī's. On one side was the bull, on the other a fish (*SkP*.6.254.89-92).[17] Brahmā and the other gods saw this marvelous configuration and praised Śiva with the words, "He who is Śiva is Viṣṇu, he who is Viṣṇu is Sadāśiva" (*SkP*.6.254.100). The words of the gods stated the same truth that had come from Arjuna's mouth when Śiva, passing as a wild hunter, revealed himself. Brahmā's equation, however, was not quite correct. He equated Lord Viṣṇu with Lord Sadāśiva, Śiva's highest aspect as manifest deity (cf. *VDh*.3.48.6).

In Vaiṣṇava elation, the *Skānda Purāṇa's* account of Śiva's cosmic dance in the rainy season assigns precedence to Viṣṇu over the goddess in being Śiva's left half. The goddess, on the other hand, by the grace of Śiva was allowed to occupy Viṣṇu's half of Śiva's body. Such

[16] C. Sivaramamurti, *Naṭarāja in Art, Thought and Literature*, p. 4.

[17] The fish as emblem of the goddess figures in embroideries (*kantha*) of Bengal of the nineteenth century.

reshufflings of mythical positions, though they are games played by sectarian interests, add a flavor of their own to the ongoing myth of Śiva. They do not seem to have disturbed the melodies that had emanated from Śiva's subtle body just before the Goddess took her own place in Ardhanārīśvara's shape.

3. Śiva's Dance

In the *Kūrma Purāṇa*, Śiva says of himself, "I am the originator, the god abiding in supreme bliss. I, the yogi, dance eternally" (*KūP*.2.4.33). "Having said this, the Lord of Yogis, the Supreme God, danced, showing his formidable, supreme reality" (*KūP*.2.5.1). In the spotless sky the yogis saw him dancing, the Great God who is Lord of all beings, whose *māyā* is all that is here, and who activates the universe (*KūP*.2.5.2-4). They saw in the sky Rudra, the Great Liberator, who loves his devotees and liberates them from ignorance (*KūP*.2.5.7). They saw the Great God full of energy dancing with Viṣṇu in the clear sky (*KūP*.2.5.2). In his dance Rudra and Viṣṇu became one, Viṣṇu becoming the left half of Lord Rudra (*KūP*. 2.5.18, 20). The *celestial* dance of Śiva the yogi was seen only by yogis and sages (*KūP*.2.5.3-4), whereas the whole cosmos was the scene of Śiva's dance. At the end of time, he dances the awesome Tāṇḍava. The stamping of his foot, the gyrations of his body, his flailing arms toss the mountains into the air; the ocean rises, the stars are lashed and scattered by Śiva's matted hair. In order to save the world, Śiva in his perverse power dances the world out of existence (*MSt*.16; *HV*.1.46),[18] wildly laughing (cf. *MD*.58), scattering ashes from his body (*KS*.5.79) so that the world may be renewed. This is the Tāṇḍava dance of Śiva, as Kāla-Mahākāla, the Destroyer, Destroyer of destruction. But, from his flowing hair the rivers will flow again into existence (cf. *LP*.1.43.32-39; *SP*.57.72-82), and the rays of sun and moon will be seen again for what they are, the hair of Śiva (*MBh*.7.173, note 92, insert no. 1470, lines 1-2).

The dance in the sky before the eyes of the yogis and sages, the cosmic dance, and the dance of destruction-creation have the universe for their stage. Another dance, the Ānanda Tāṇḍava, Śiva's "dance of bliss in the hall of consciousness,"[19] is Śiva's dance within

[18] C. Sivaramamurti, *Naṭarāja in Art, Thought and Literature*, p. 385.

[19] *Ibid*., p. 24, quoting Thāyumānavar.

the heart of man. There Naṭarāja, the lord of dancers, dancing, shows his fivefold activity, the expression of his divine totality. His dancing limbs convey by their movements and symbols the fivefold action of creation, maintenance, dissolution, veiling-unveiling, and liberation. Naṭarāja dances the cosmos into existence, upholds its existence, and dances it out of existence. The Lord veils existence with illusion so that it is seen as real, and, dancing, he removes the veil. The raised leg of the dancer shows the liberating freedom of his dance, the drum raised by the right hand sounds the note of creation, the flame in the left hand flickers in the change brought about by destruction, the right hand grants freedom from fear, the fear of repeated births and deaths, and assures the maintenance of life. The dancer's foot is firmly planted on the infant shape of the demon Amnesia, the Apasmāra Puruṣa, and accentuates the vertical, cosmic axis of the god's body.[20] The movement of the dancer around this axis, self-enclosed in balanced gyration, is encircled by flames.

The South Indian bronze image of Naṭarāja in its explicit, yet contained, form equals in its perfection the static shape of the *liṅga* with its encapsulated power. Sivaramamurti cites a panegyric of late date from Chidambaram, the sacred center of Naṭarāja's worship. The hymn, called Tatvāryāstava,[21] celebrates the "foremost of the hunters," who "dances in the company of his beloved in the . . . forest of Tillai trees, . . . causing the waves of sentience to tremor and scintillate. . . . As he dances, he appears in the immaculate lotus of the heart. . . ."[22] In the verbal sophistication of the panegyric the memory of the Hunter is fresh. The dance of this Hunter, "in the immaculate lotus of the heart" is by the same dancer who as yogi danced for yogis and sages only.

Śiva dances for the Goddess special Tāṇḍava dances for her three forms as Umā, Gaurī, and Kālikā. His dance as a beggar for Pārvatī's hand delighted Menā. He danced the Tāṇḍava before Tripura and after he killed the elephant demon, in the red glow of the setting sun,

[20] Cf. T. A. Gopinatha Rao, *Elements of Hindu Iconography*, vol. 2, part 1, pp. 231-50; A. K. Coomaraswamy, *The Dance of Śiva*, 1953, passim. Some of the most outstanding images of Śiva Naṭarāja are reproduced in *Lalit Kalā*, vol. 5 (1959), pl. 26 from Śivapuram; C. Sivaramamurti, *South Indian Bronzes*, pl. 23 in the Bṛhadīśvara Temple, Tanjavur; pl. 24 from Tiruvalangadu in the Madras Museum; pl. 26 in the Kumandarkoil, Pudukkottai.

[21] C. Sivaramamurti, *Naṭarāja in Art, Thought and Literature*, p. 131.

[22] *Ibid.*, p. 132.

blood dripping from the elephant's hide (cf. *MD*.36). He danced his mad, erotic dance (*LP*.1.31.30), rising to supreme glory—and accompanied by Viṣṇu—in the Deodar forest (*KūP*.2.37.20); he danced in the evening, after the destruction of Dakṣa's sacrifice (*NŚ*.4.234); as Bhairava, he danced on leaving Viṣṇu's house, and again when the skull fell from his hand in Vārāṇasī; he dances on the cremation ground where the funerary pyres abound and keep warm the earth scattered with corpses. He danced in the battle with Andhaka (*VmP*.43.69-76), Lord Kālāgni Rudra danced holding Andhaka aloft, impaled on the trident (*KūP*.1.15.184; *SP*.29.25-27). Andhaka himself danced when he was born, and after he had become Bhṛṅgī; Gaṇeśa, Kārttikeya, and the Goddess dance, and the Mothers whose chorus Śiva leads, playing on the *vīṇā*. Śiva's gaṇas dance; there is no end to Śiva's dance, it disperses his *tejas*, his fiery energy and glory in his world.

On one occasion Śiva did not dance. At that time the whole universe had begun to dance, nothing could resist the dance of Ṛṣi Maṅkaṇaka in his elation. He danced with the joy of discovery when his hand was cut by a blade of *kuśa* grass and plant sap flowed from his wound instead of blood. This miracle filled the ṛṣi with excessive joy and pride unbecoming to an ascetic. Śiva, at the request of the gods, put a stop to the commotion. He stood in front of the ṛṣi, struck his own thumb with his finger, and ashes fell from the wound. Ashamed, the sage danced no more.[23] In another version of the myth, Śiva, having shamed the ṛṣi by the calm flow of ashes, danced, assuming cosmic dimension, and revealed himself to the ṛṣi as Time and Death and the impeller of all (Ch. IX.4).

In between his dances Śiva stayed in different residences. He had come from the north and preferred to live in secluded caves in the Himālayan mountains. There the yogi and the wild, uncanny god felt at home. Indeed, they both were Rudra and the north was Rudra's quarter.[24] In that direction he was worshiped. All the other gods were worshiped in the eastern direction, where the sun rises. In fact, he was homeless. Satī, his bride, found it difficult to adjust to her husband's, the yogi's, way of life. Pārvatī, the daughter of the Mountain, was more confirmed in her asceticism. It filled her with holy fire whether

[23] Cf. W. D. O'Flaherty, *Hindu Myths: A Sourcebook Translated from the Sanskrit*, pp. 173-74.

[24] A. A. Macdonell, *Vedic Mythology*, p. 76.

Śiva chose to stay in palace or mountain solitude. Frequently Śiva stayed in charnel grounds, and his mansion, in *ākāśa* above the burning ground in Vārāṇasī, was a place he never forsook. Only yogis and sages could see the mansion where Śiva stayed. Śiva built for himself another mansion high above the Pole Star. It "remains suspended in the sky solely through the strength of his asceticism" (*BVP*.1.25.1-2).[25] When Śiva steps out of his mansion in the cosmic north, the empyrean, he expounds, under the shady branches of his fig tree (*ŚP*.2.2.40.35-37), music, yoga, gnosis, and all the arts and sciences to the sages.

[25] *Brahmavaivarta Purāṇa (BVP)*, tr. R. N. Sen, 1920-22, part I, p. 71.

APPENDIX
THE GREAT CAVE TEMPLE OF ŚIVA ON THE ISLAND OF ELEPHANTA

Entry into the presence of Śiva was given form in his Great Cave Temple on the island of Elephanta.* Hewn out of the rock in the middle of the sixth century A.D.,[1] wide pillared entrances in the east, west, and north lead into the interior (c. 130 ft. by 130 ft.). But for these light-filled entrances, the temple has no exterior. It is a cave made into a hall (*maṇḍapa*) by arrays of pillars and vertical limits that support a flat ceiling and the weight of the hill above it. The vertical limits of the temple are in the south and at the four corners of the *maṇḍapa* (see floor plan). The southern vertical limit, the largest "wall" exposure of the cave temple, is recessed from the *maṇḍapa* by an *ardhamaṇḍapa*, a pillared vestibule that opens into the *maṇḍapa*. In the north, and opposite the *ardhamaṇḍapa*, a pillared portico (*mukhamaṇḍapa*) leads into the hall of the Great Cave Temple. The vertical limits are carved from the mass of the rock. Hollowed out, they are chapels, caves within the solid matrix of the rock, opening into the large interior of the total cave temple. "Architectural" mouldings and pilasters are their carved frames.

Within the pillared main hall, toward the western entrance, the

* Because of the very damaged condition of some of the sculptures in Cave I, the "Great Cave Temple," only sections of these sculptures have been chosen for reproduction. Some of the sculptures are shown from different angles in more than one plate in order to reproduce their sculptural quality. For overall illustrations see pls. 3-5, 13; and C. Sivaramamurti, *The Art of India*, p. 332, figs. 194, 195; p. 342, fig. 262; p. 362, figs. 377-380. Also, H. Zimmer, *Art of Indian Asia*, vol. II, pls. 248-265; M. Neff, "Elephanta, III, IV," 1960, pp. 31-55; P. Chandra, *A Guide to the Elephanta Caves*, 1957.

[1] Elephanta is a small island in the harbor of Bombay. Hiranand Sastri and R. Parimoo, *A Guide to Elephanta: A New Light on its Significance in Indian Sculpture*, 1978, p. 1, suggests "about the fifth or sixth century as the date of the caves at Elephanta"; C. Sivaramamurti, *Art of India*, p. 426, suggests a fifth-century date. W. M. Spink, "Jogeshwari: A Brief Analysis," 1978, assigns the great Cave to the mid-sixth Century, A. de Lippe, *Indian Medieval Sculpture*, p. 8, suggests the seventh century.

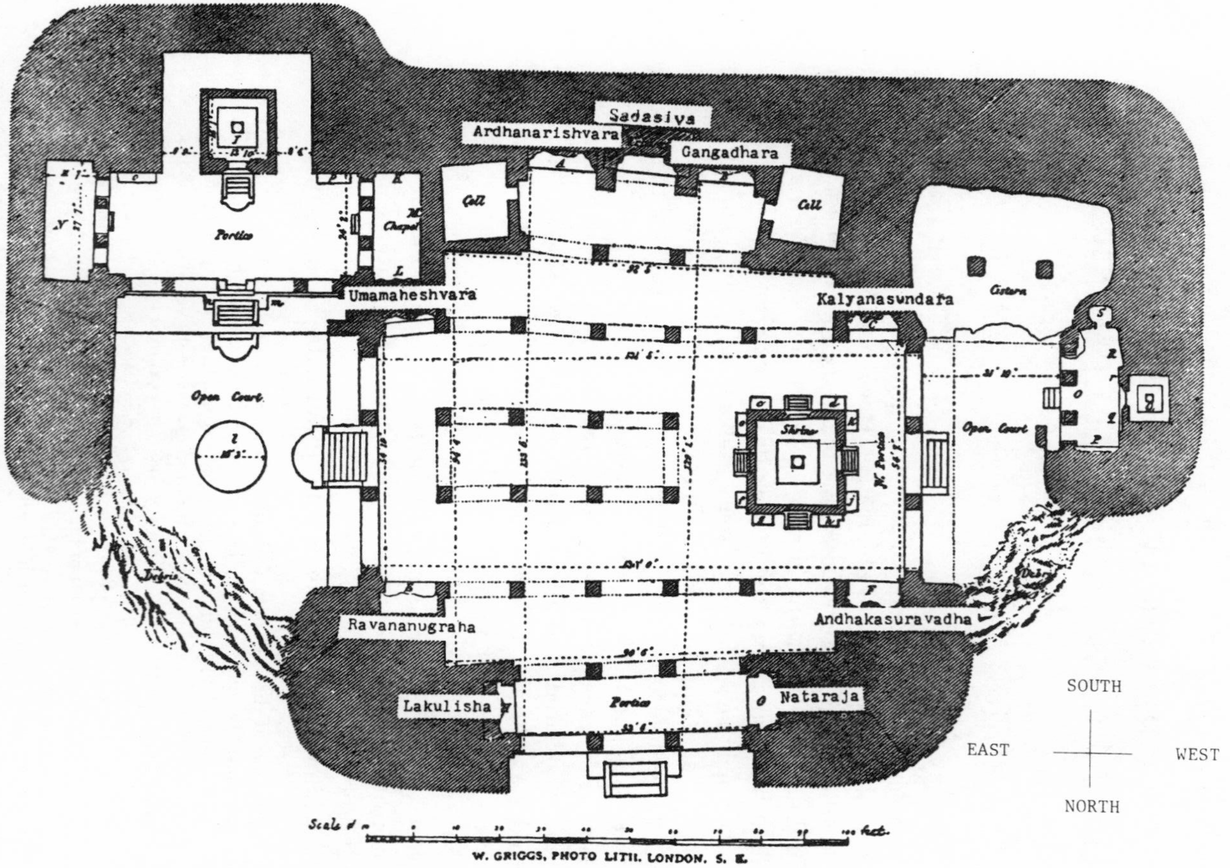

FLOOR PLAN, Elephanta Cave Temple

stark planes of a cubical cella form the walls of the innermost sanctuary (*garbhagṛha*, or "womb-house") of the cave temple (Pl. 1). They open on each of the four sides of this cubical *garbhagṛha*. Steps lead up to the open doorways. They frame the *mūlavigraha*, the nuclear form, the *liṅga*, rising in the center of the square innermost sanctuary (Pl. 2).[2] Figures of celestial guardians (*dvārapāla*), eight in all, extending nearly from floor to ceiling, flank the doors. Carved almost in the round, their calm, impassive figures project into the pillared temple hall. The pillars, plain four-sided prisms in the lower half, rise above with gently swelling ribbed shafts whose broad, circular capitals seem to cushion the pressure of the rock which they support. The pillars are aligned in columniations from east to west, leading to the *garbhagṛha*, around which they form an ambulatory. At the same time, the lines of pillars create another axis from north to south, to the recessed southern limit with its three chapels, that of Sadāśiva in the center, flanked by the chapels of Śiva Ardhanārīśvara and Śiva Gaṅgādhara (Pls. 3-5). The cave temple is double-focused: on the *mūlavigraha*, the *liṅga* in the stern cubical innermost sanctuary in the west (Pl. 2); and on the sculpture of Sadāśiva, the iconic form of a *pañcamukha liṅga*, ensconced deep in the rock in a cubical recess in the middle of the southern limit of the cave temple (Pl. 4). The other vertical limits of the temple hall are at its corners and in the portico in the north; in both, they are chapels within rectangular frames, hollowed out from the mass of the rock. The "architectural" framework functions like the front of a showcase. It sets off the individual sanctuaries embedded in the matrix of the rock.

As the *liṅga* is enclosed within its shrine, the *garbhagṛha*, the latter, together with the *liṅga*, is surrounded by the chapels of the entire temple hall. They communicate Śiva's presence, embodied as it is in the totality of this temple cave in which the unmanifest Śiva is enshrined in the innermost sanctuary.

The unmanifest Śiva, in utter transcendency, dwells in the *liṅga*. Thence, myth tells, he manifested and revealed himself to the doubting gods, Brahmā and Viṣṇu (Ch. VII.2). Or the face of Śiva is seen contiguous with the abstract *liṅga* shape (*ekamukha liṅga*);[3] or the four visible faces of Śiva are wreathed around the *liṅga* forming a *pañca-*

[2] The material of the *liṅga* is a stone different from that of the cave temple.

[3] S. Kramrisch, *The Art of India*, 1965, pl. 46, *ekamukha liṅga*, Udayagiri, ca. A.D. 400.

mukha liṅga.[4] The four faces of Śiva are those of Tatpuruṣa / Mahādeva, Aghora / Bhairava, Vāmadeva / Umā and Sadyojāta / Nandin.[5] *Ekamukha* and *pañcamukha liṅgas* had been carved and worshiped for centuries before the sculptures of Śiva as *liṅga* and image were carved in Elephanta. The Sadāśiva image in Elephanta integrates three of the visible faces of Śiva (Pl. 4). The three heads, each heightened by its crown, coalesce, their tripartite bulk letting the central face with its crown exceed the others. It rises like the high, domed cylinder of the *liṅga* symbol. Although it has only three faces, the Sadāśiva image in Elephanta is a kind of *pañcamukha liṅga*, emerging from the dark depth of the rock. The fourth face, at the back of the frontal face of Tatpuruṣa / Mahādeva, cannot be seen, as the colossal sculpture, within the darkness of its chamber, is cut out of the rock at the southern limit of the temple cave. It confronts the devotee with three of its heads rising from one broad bust and base. The fifth face—in transcendency—is beyond the sight of mortals and has not been carved.[6]

The four heads when carved on a free-standing *pañcamukha liṅga*, according to the texts (Ch. VII.5), are associated each with one of the four directions. Tatpuruṣa / Mahādeva, according to the texts, should face east. The plan of the temple cave of Elephanta, however, assigns to Sadāśiva the central and dominant position on the south wall, and Tatpuruṣa / Mahādeva, in Elephanta, faces north.[7] Iconology had to yield to technical necessity. Position and orientation of the temple were dictated by the shape of the rock from which its large hall was excavated. In planning the sculptural display, the total meaning—of which the temple cave was to be the shape—and the natural conditions of the site were the determining factors.

The central, deep recess of the south wall of the cave temple enshrines Sadāśiva within stark and straight planes. They encase the co-

[4] *Ibid.*, pl. 108, *pañcamukha liṅga*, Nachna-Kuthara, sixth century.

[5] S. Kramrisch, "The Image of Mahādeva in the Cave Temple on Elephanta Island," 1946, pp. 4-8. Mahādeva refers only to the head in the middle of the three heads shown in Elephanta of the five-faced Sadāśiva. The middle head with its high crown suggests a *liṅga* shape. Later iconography shows the five heads with one anthropomorphic body (B. N. Sharma, *Iconography of Sadāśiva*, pp. 1-31, frontispiece; and pls. 8, 10, etc.).

[6] B. N. Sharma, *Iconography of Sadāśiva*, pl. 2. The fifth "invisible" face is, however, actually carved on a *liṅga* from Bhīṭā near Allahabad, of the first to second centuries B.C.; *ibid.*, pl. 1. T. A. Gopinatha Rao, vol. 27, part 1, p. 1. *Somaśambhupaddhati (SŚp)*, tr. and ed. H. Brunner-Lachaux, part I, 1963, pp. 176-83; n. 2, pp. 178, 180. The above eleventh-century text gives a clear account of the relation of *mantra* and *mūrti* of Sadāśiva, and of the anthropomorphic image, the latter serving as a support of meditation.

[7] K. Kumar, "A Dhyāna Yoga Maheśamūrti," p. 107.

lossal paramount image (h. 20 ft. 7 in.) of the cave temple. Its faces emerge in the farthest depth of the temple cave, the darkness of the recess lit by the uncertain chiaroscuro of the cave, or the warm glow of oil lamps.

Tatpuruṣa's face contains the fullness of absolute knowledge that *is* peace. The now-damaged eyelids are lowered to let its bliss touch weighty, closed lips, relaxed in meditation. They guard the inscrutable state in which Mahādeva, the Great God, dwells (Pls. 6, 7). The face has no other definition than the sharp intersections of its bounding planes. They meet in wide curves, in the front view, a vessel of quiddity (Pls. 4, 6), and in sharp angles of the profile (Pl. 9). These are cut as if by one stroke of a trenchant tool sensitized by its contact with the rock, transforming it into the likeness of God.

Sacred composure smoothes Mahādeva's broad forehead. It is crowned by a symphony of jewelry, rising in cascades of filigree ornaments around the radiating strands of hair piled high, symbols of generative power contained in the *jaṭāmukuṭa* of the lord of ascetics (Pl. 4). His left hand holds in front of the chest a "citron" (*mātuliṅga*), a fruit rich in seeds. A wide and intricately chiselled torque and a bead string rest on the chest, surround the triple curve of the broad neck, and accentuate the *liṅga* pillar shape of Mahādeva's crowned head. The necklace also fastens to this central theme of the image the lateral heads, set off in profile from Tatpuruṣa / Mahādeva in their midst.

On the right of Mahādeva's face (Pl. 6), wriggling serpent locks and raised serpent hoods interspersed with manifold flowers and tender leaves lead to a staring skull, the crown jewel of the coiffure, piled high above Aghora / Bhairava's face. On the left of Mahādeva's crown, by contrast, rows of small cork-screw curls, surmounted by swags and swirling curves frame and crown Vāmadeva / Umā's countenance. The rich textures of the coiffures and crowns of the lateral profile heads conceived in the round and facing east and west form a foil for Mahādeva's head. Motifs and rhythms of the coiffures convey, as much as their faces, the nature of each of these aspects of Śiva.

In Bhairava's face, the vaulting planes that compose Mahādeva's face are contracted in bulges charged with energy. His irascible profile is turned toward a serpent[8] that rears from out of Bhairava's hand and faces, a threatening symbol of death, the baneful eye of the dread god. His moustache, as if twisted by rage, cuts across the full, carnal

[8] For the serpent not seen in Pls. 4, 6, see P. Chandra, *A Guide to the Elephanta Caves*, pl. 12.

cheek. Above the furled brow of the fearful god the sunken-eyed skull stares into nothingness.

On the left of Mahādeva, Umā's contemplation makes unfold a lotus flower held in her hand (Pls. 10, 4, 6). Absorbed within her own being, the Goddess communicates with the flower raised shoulder high. Vāmadeva, the Mantra and beauteous deity on Mahādeva's left, is indeed the Great Goddess, Umā (Ch. VII.5). Even though her features resemble those of Mahādeva, they do not convey Śiva's quiddity as Tatpuruṣa. They communicate his grace by her charm. Right and left of Mahādeva's "face of eternity," the contorted virile visage of Bhairava and the dreaming femininity of Umā represent the mystery of the coexistence of the absolute together with the fundamental pair of opposites of male and female as they exist in God.[9] This meaning underlies the three-faced image in Elephanta. It was described in the *Viṣṇudharmottara Purāṇa* (*VDhP*.3.48.1-7).

Doubly recessed by "pilasters" and pedestal, the mystery of Sadāśiva's image occupies the central chapel in the southern limit of the *maṇḍapa*. No room is left in that deep bay for anything besides the darkness around the image. In front of each "pilaster" or "offset," the figure of a guardian of the threshold is accompanied by a gaṇa. These *dvārapāla* figures, relaxed in their stance and more animated than those that guard the *liṅga* shrine, are attuned to the presence of Sadāśiva; they are images of empathy, and their faces, though with expressions reduced to human terms of feeling, still resemble Mahādeva's face. Their lips gently touch, and serpents are their ornaments.

The mouldings of the wide base of Sadāśiva's image are continued along the square platform, the base of each *dvārapāla*, linking architecturally these foreposts to the main image that they flank—separate from, and yet connected with, the bays or recesses beyond the pilasters.

These chapels, on either side of Sadāśiva's sanctuary, celebrate Śiva Ardhanārīśvara, the androgyne god (Pls. 3, 11, 12) and Śiva Gaṅgādhara (Pls. 5, 13), the support of Gaṅgā, the river. Each of these images is the main figure in a grotto that fills its bay in a manner peculiar to Elephanta.

In the grotto in which Ardhanārīśvara is made manifest leaning on his bull, their gigantic ensemble dominates the scene (Pl. 3). The

[9] H. Zummer, *Myths and Symbols in Indian Art and Civilization*, p. 137.

crowned androgyne god towers over the many figures of the composition. Set forth from the back of the chapel, he appears in their midst in a space as if between heavy, billowing curtains drawn apart so as to reveal the asymmetry of his androgyne shape (Pls. 3, 11, 12). Ardhanārīśvara in a leisurely way leans on Nandin's accommodating shape. The dome of Ardhanārīśvara's breast, the amplitude of the left female hip, appear even larger than they are by the *tribhaṅga* or triply bent stance of the figure. The tilt of Ardhanārīśvara's head with its high crown is unaffected by the wide-flung, curving bulk of the hip; the lowered foremost arm of the goddess passes along it. With this long, extended arm, Ardhanārīśvara communicates his being to the assembled gods whose figures seem to crowd into, fill, and make up the grotto (Pls. 11, 12).

The emphasis on the left half of Ardhanārīśvara's body by the slant of the pendant arm, is compensated on the right by the main arm of the god bending to rest on Nandin's shape; god and animal form one visual unit. Its apex touches Ardhanārīśvara's brow. The biunity of Ardhanārīśvara's body admits, in this sculptural composition, the figure of Nandin as a supplement to Śiva's shape. Nandin belongs to Śiva; in more than one sense does the bull convey Śiva. In the grotto, the epiphany of Śiva is comprised of the Goddess and the bull, as well.

Ardhanārīśvara's four arms radiating from the shoulders hold at bay the onrush of jubilant gods who come to hail the epiphany. Ardhanārīśvara remains aloof; the hands of his raised upper arms are turned inward. The goddess holds a mirror in which is reflected the god's being, while his lowered lids and slightly parted lips seem to presage a knowledge of every pain (Pl. 11). The paradoxical reality of compassionate detachment expressed in the face of the god is a physiognomical equivalent to the symbol of the mirror; it catches the reflex of the god's face. The face does not look into the mirror. The mirror is a symbol and restatement of Śiva's being. Centuries later, a hymn by Abhinavagupta[10] praises Śiva himself as the mirror of undifferentiated consciousness. In Śiva, light of consciousness, everything is reflected. The objects seen in the mirror are neither separate from each other nor from the mirror. They constitute a whole that cannot be dissociated. The undifferentiated consciousness of the Lord and the multiple reflections coexist.

[10] L. Silburn, tr., *Hymnes de Abhinavagupta*, 1970, pp. 32-36.

An oblong nimbus separates the god's epiphany from the depth of the grotto which is full of figures of celestials who seem to be arriving from right and left. Right and left do not extend in one plane with the ground in front of which Ardhanārīśvara is stationed. Rather, they form the sides of the bay and are perpendicular to the ground of his image. The sides extend forward. The multitude of figures, standing, seated, flying, emerges from these lateral grounds toward the epiphany of Ardhanārīśvara's image standing in their midst in full front view. The emerging figures are arranged in tiers (Pl. 3).

The entire scene is not a high relief in the accepted sense, that is, carved with reference to its ground. It is conceived with reference to three grounds, whence the figures have come, and which enclose the interior of the grotto in which Ardhanārīśvara manifests. From the lateral grounds—somewhere in the depth of the rock—the multitudes of celestials make their appearance. All of them are turned toward the main group of Ardhanārīśvara with Nandin. It is stationed in an interior brought about by the figures as they emerge in high relief from their respective grounds toward the central group. The unified form resulting from a relief conceived as emerging from three "grounds" or ideational limits, perpendicular to each other somewhere deep in the rock, may be called the grotto form of relief. From out of these lateral grounds the figures emerge in different degrees of vehemence and visibility. Those at the bottom of the grotto appear to have stationed themselves on the floor of the grotto: Kārttikeya, Śiva's son, on the right proper of the god; two female figures, possibly Jayā and Vijayā, "ladies in waiting" of the Goddess, to her left. These divinities occupy the lowermost part of the composition and are the largest among the divine host. They reach to the height of the hip of the figure of the goddess and to Nandin's hump. Above them, the god Brahmā on his lotus, carried by flying *haṃsas*, and Indra on his elephant are conspicuous figures, emerging from the matrix of the rock on the proper right of Ardhanārīśvara; but even more dynamic is the figure of Viṣṇu, to the left of the Goddess. He rides on impetuous, large-winged Garuḍa (Pl. 11), bursting out of the rock amid hosts of celestials, flying up toward Ardhanārīśvara. The flight of the approaching gods on their vehicles occupies the second horizontal register of the grotto composition. The figures in this register seem to be coming forth or to have emerged from within the rock on both sides of the grotto, and to advance and turn toward Ardhanārīśvara; and above them, in the third tier, celestials, no longer supported by their animal vehicles, fly by the power of their own elation.[11] Exultantly, the long-limbed bodies of these celestials soar in mighty gusts from right and left, respectively, toward Ardhanārīśvara. They form a canopy around the god's head. While most of their approaching figures fly on clouds and are carved in the main plane of the relief, others among their host emerge perpendicular to it, from their cloud bank, on either side of the god's high nimbus.

The "grotto relief" conceived with reference to these intersecting grounds, discharging, as it were, their figures into a unified space created and bounded by them, climaxes a trend established in Indian art, that is, the coming forth of the figures from out of their ground into the space of the relief. This could be seen in Sanchi, of the first century B.C., in a relief on the south gate, and later in the Mahāyāna cave paintings in Ajanta (second half of the fifth century A.D.).[12] There the figures, modeled by means of painting, seem to advance from the depth of the painting toward the spectator.

The illusion created by painting the figures emerging from the depth of the painting toward the spectator, as also the emergence of relief figures from their ground—the rock—have their analogy in the *Sāṁkhya* concept of *vyaktāvyakta*, the "manifest-unmanifest," a state of transition from the one to the other, implying the latter in the former. The particular use of this mode of visualization was put into the service of Śaiva themes in Elephanta, where the emergence of the figures is not from one ground only, but simultaneously from three grounds. The *līlās* of the Great God inspired this special employment of the "dimension of forthcoming." Hosts of figures, all comparatively small in scale, surround the figure of Śiva in his grottos in Elephanta, just as hosts of Rudras and gaṇas swarmed around Śiva, from the *Śatarudriya* hymn to the *Purāṇas*.

Whereas figureless, straight planes encase Sadāśiva's image, each of the *līlās* or playful manifestations of Śiva is bodied forth in a grotto of its own that has no sharp edges. The carved figures in their density make up its confines. The large central group of Ardhanārīśvara is set forth from the ground in front of which its majesty is displayed; the

[11] Pairs of flying celestials were carved on bracket capitals in the latest caves of Ajanta; cf. W. M. Spink, *Ajanta to Ellora*, 1967, fig. 18, a bracket capital, Cave II.

[12] S. Kramrisch, *Indian Sculpture*, pp. 30-32, fig. 33; and *A Survey of Painting in the Deccan*, 1937, pp. 51, 64, and *passim*.

lateral figures emerge from their respective ground.[13] The rock seems to discharge its contents in the sculptural shapes of the gods that form Ardhanārīśvara's grotto. Their impact seems to come from within the rock and their emergence to acquire figured shape. Propelled from their ground by the sculptor's creative dynamism, their postures are oriented toward Ardhanārīśvara. Having come to see and celebrate his manifestation, their ranks are ordered in three horizontal tiers: the lowest, with large standing figures; the middle, with the gods seated on their vehicles or thrones; and the uppermost register, in which long-limbed wingless celestials, flying in droves, approach Ardhanārīśvara's crowned majesty (Pl. 3).

The *liṅga* enshrined in the *garbhagṛha* and framed by the austere geometry of the door openings, and the image of Sadāśiva, similarly encased by straight walls, offer a dramatic contrast to the manifestations of Śiva in grotto-like chapels (Pl. 2).

The grotto of Ardhanārīśvara to the left of Sadāśiva's recess has its counterpart in the relief of Śiva Gaṅgādhara on the right of the colossal Sadāśiva sculpture (Pl. 5). In this grotto relief, which has the descent from heaven of the river (goddess) Gaṅgā for its subject, the gods take part in a cosmic event, the descent of Gaṅgā, the celestial river, from heaven to earth and into the netherworld. Gaṅgā, sister of Pārvatī and her rival, is seen from her triple bust upward, a diminutive shape above Śiva's crown. She comes down with flying garments (Pl. 5) and tops as if she were an additional coronet Śiva's *jaṭāmukuṭa*. Greeted by the long-limbed flying gods, she accentuates and forms the peak of the aureole or *prabhāmaṇḍala*-like extent of Śiva's ambience. Pārvatī, to his left, is assigned her place in a rectangular extension of Śiva's arched setting. Between the two large figures of god and goddess a small squat gaṇa intervenes. His face is turned up beseechingly, expectantly, toward Śiva. To the right proper of Śiva kneels the heroic and devout figure of King Bhagīratha; his three-quarter back view expresses both these qualities of Sagara's scion, whose austerities brought Gaṅgā down from heaven with such force, it is said, that her

[13] W. M. Spink, "Elephanta, Relationships with Ajanta and Ellora," describes the Elephanta compositoins as "being cut out of the surrounding matrix 'in a niche-like space,'" and links them with the wall paintings of Ajanta. Re the "direction of forthcoming" in these paintings, cf. S. Kramrisch, *A Survey of Painting in the Deccan*, pp. 31-32, 51, 62.

impact would have rent the earth. To save the earth Śiva caught Gaṅgā in his matted hair (Pls. 5, 13).

In the sculpture in Elephanta, however, Śiva in his grace appears to have stilled her impetuousness, offering his matted hair, piled high on his head, for her to rest on, while allowing himself to be rapt in a shower of blissfulness, his body swaying like Kuṭilā / Gaṅgā herself, the curvaceous one. While Śiva lowers his head, turned away from Pārvatī, he holds out his upper left arm toward her, thereby bridging the distance that separates them. Her body sways in the opposite direction from that of Śiva. The dehanchement of her left hip, akin to that of Ardhanārīśvara, is becoming to Pārvatī's womanly shape. And she seems to be flooded away from Śiva, reciprocating his swaying away from her, rapt as he is in the cosmic delight of Gaṅgā's descent. However, Śiva and Pārvatī are not only connected by Śiva's arm reaching out to her, and by their divine coquetry, but also by the rhythm of the formal tie in which the sculptor holds them in his composition. Their swaying away is enhanced by the projected hip of each. By their postures that space them away from each other—by these very postures, they are tied together in two sweeping curves of the composition that exceed their figures. The two curves intersect above the two figures and come close at the bottom.[14] The creative translation, in terms of visual art, of the play and tensions that separate and unite Śiva and Pārvatī is accompanied by the expression of Pārvatī's face. Waiting, enchantment, knowingness of the situation, and consciousness of her own seductiveness are conveyed by the figure of Pārvatī, resting within herself, tending away from, and drawn back toward Śiva (Pls. 13-15).[15]

While the triptych of the deeply recessed chapel of Sadāśiva flanked by the grotto reliefs of Ardhanārīśvara and Gaṅgādhara dominates the temple hall, further grottoes, carved out of the limiting

[14] The same observation has been made by Ratan Parimoo in Hiranand Sastri and R. Parimoo, *A Guide to Elephanta: A New Light on its Significance in Indian Sculpture*, p. 78.

[15] Pl. 5, in its left upper corner shows flying celestials on their scalloped clouds, the large male figure partly referable to the main plane of the relief and partly to the lateral plane at an angle of ninety degrees. The small female flying figure on his left, and floating behind the male, impetuous celestial, as also the celestial ṛṣis above her, are carved with reference to the lateral ground. Pls. 5, 13, on the right side, clearly show the angle formed by the lateral wall, the figure of Viṣṇu on Garuḍa, and the main ground of the grotto on which the figures of Śiva and Pārvatī are displayed.

"walls" and situated to either side of the three entrances, arrest and attune to Śiva's *līlās* the devotee's circumambulation around the *liṅga* shrine.[16] Turning to the right in order to circumambulate the *liṅga* shrine, the chapel or grotto celebrating Śiva's marriage to Pārvatī (Kalyāṇa-Sundaramūrti) is on the devotee's left, flanking the west side of the *liṅga* shrine and the west entrance of the ambulatory (Pls. 16-18).

The wedding of the Great God and the Great Goddess, as seen by the sculptor of Elephanta, does not take place in the palace of King Parvata, as the *Purāṇas* tell us. In the Elephanta relief, King Parvata ushers the bride toward Śiva, and Brahmā officiates as priest in the grotto formed by the gods present at the wedding (Pls. 16-18).[17] Śiva, the bridegroom, is lithe, young, and calm. His divinity ascends from his face to the high pile of the ascetic god's hair in front of the high oval of his halo that rises from the noble shoulders of a body of superhuman tenderness. It is a transubstantiated body, the subtle body, that yoga has formed and that the artist has made visible. It is in this, their subtle body, that the gods are made visible in Elephanta. It resembles the human shape, but is free from the contingencies of its mortal frame. It is the shape of an inward awareness of the body gained through yoga experience.[18]

The main right arm of the god is bent in the direction of Pārvatī. She is small and suffused by emotion. It wells up in the curves of her shy body. What difference between its yielding stillness and the sweeping elegance of Pārvatī, Śiva's wife (Pls. 13, 16)! Her face is inclined, as is Śiva's face, in sweet surrender, which her lips savor and her lowered eyelids acknowledge. A cadence of inwardness links God and Goddess as they clasp hands (now missing).

Though the figures of Śiva's wedding and Śivakalyāṇa Sundara are badly damaged, the composition in the grotto can be seen to conform with the principles followed in the lateral chapels of the Sadāśiva triptych, even though the second tier of the grotto is not occupied by celestials on their *vāhanas* or vehicles, but by the upper half of the main figures at the wedding. Bringing a large water vessel, Candra the

[16] Cf. H. Rau, *Reflections of Indian Art*, 1976, pp. 74-88, re structural plan, stylistic design, and sequence of the chapels.

[17] Remarks about the iconography of this scene by R. Sen-Gupta, "The Panels of Kalyāṇa Sundaramụrti at Ellora," 1960, pp. 14-18; also P. R. Srinivasan and R. Sen-Gupta, *Lalitkalā* 9 (1961), 62-63 in a review of the above article and its reply.

[18] Re the "subtle body" and transubstantiation in Indian art, cf. S. Kramrisch, *Indian Sculpture*, pp. 62-65.

Moon enters the grotto from its side on the right proper of Pārvatī, allowing Parvatarāja to usher in the bride, his daughter, toward Śiva.[19] King Parvata's bulky figure, in three-quarter front view, lays his hand like a blessing on his daughter's arm as he gives her away to Śiva. The group of Candra the Moon—not seen in the plates—King Parvata the Mountain, and the daughter of the Mountain proceeds as if it had come from out of the side of the grotto toward the middle and front, where Śiva and Pārvatī are being joined in marriage.[20]

The main action in the grotto is on Śiva's right proper. The left side, more static in its structure, comprises the squatting figure of Brahmā—the priest at the marriage—tending the fire, the tall figure of Viṣṇu, and others. The flying hosts on their cloud banks of the topmost register graze Śiva's halo and the heads of the protagonists. These are placed in dynamic asymmetry in which the figure of Śiva does not occupy the middle of the relief, but allows the smaller figure of Pārvatī a large share of the grotto for her retinue to make their entry into the grotto under a cloud bank of flying celestials. The latter meets at the very top of the relief, in a point above Śiva's head, the flight of the gods that halts on the other side of Śiva's aureole. In this high point two compositional arcs have also come to meet: one, rising from Śiva's left foot, ascends over the head of Brahmā; the other curves upward from Pārvatī's right foot and touches her right shoulder. The pointed arch formed by the two curves encloses the union of Śiva and Pārvatī, just as the "mandorla" of intersecting compositional curves held together the seeming estrangement of God and Goddess in the Gaṅgādhara chapel.

Proceeding further in the ambulatory along the west side of the *liṅga* shrine, the chapel of Śiva's wedding is seen to be opposite the recess that encloses the scene of Śiva killing the demon Andhaka (Andhakāsuravadha) (Pls. 19, 20). The ambulatory west of the *liṅga* shrine functions at the same time as portico of the west entrance into the temple. Śiva in his serenity, the celestial bridegroom, and Śiva in his furor, the demon slayer—the love of god and the terror of god—are both present to the devotee who enters the temple from the west.

[19] Plates 16 and 17 show part of the large water vessel held by Candra, whereas the figures of Brahmā and Viṣṇu are not shown.

[20] A group of figures, part of a larger composition carved in the Buddhist cave of Lonad, is closely related in treatment to the wedding scene of Elephanta; cf. R. v. Leyden, "The Buddhist Cave at Lonad," 1947, figs. 3 and 5.

The chapels reveal the two natures of Śiva as the *Maitrāyaṇi Saṃhitā* had evoked them (Ch. I.2): Śiva the gracious and auspicious, and Śiva the formidable and cruel. He is shown in both his natures to the right and the left of the *liṅga* shrine. The faces of Aghora / Bhairava and Vāmadeva / Umā are, similarly, to the right and left of Tatpuruṣa / Mahādeva's face (Pls. 4, 6).

Ardhanārīśvara, Gaṅgādhara, and Sundaramūrti are epiphanies of Śiva, the gracious god whose totality comprises his male and female natures. Withdrawal into his being, compassion, delight, and peace are cast over the divine countenance according to the specific *līlā* and its resolution of the male-female concomitance that each of these manifestations has for its theme—Ardhanārīśvara: biunity of the male and the female in God, undivided in his towering shape; Gaṅgādhara: god and goddess, separate figures, moving away from and drawn toward each other; Sundaramūrti: the joining in marriage of Śiva and Pārvatī. These themes were given form by one master who envisioned the grotto as their setting. He realized his vision in the Ardhanārīśvara chapel, and it stayed with him in the other two chapels (Pls. 3, 11; 5, 13; 16, 17).

Though Pārvatī's role in the myth of Andhaka is fundamental, she does not seem to have been a major figure in its sculptural presentation in Elephanta. Her figure and also those in the lowermost panel and on the right are practically destroyed. Now, Śiva alone, dancing in his furor of destruction, carries the scene. In the chapel of the frantic god, the grotto is practically blotted out by a large, plain, concave rectangular shape—the hide of the elephant demon Nīla whom Śiva had overcome by dancing him to his death, before Śiva transfixed Andhaka by his lance or trident (Pls. 19, 20).[21] By his two hindmost arms, whose mutilated stems branch off from the god's shoulders, he has raised the flayed elephant's skin like a wind-inflated cloak. Śiva's hands have gripped the edge of the skin, and it takes the shape of an elegant horizontal rim that marks the upper boundary of the raging god's concave backdrop. Only to Śiva / Bhairava's left proper, where the hollow elephant hide ends behind Andhaka's impaled body, can the lateral parts of the grotto be seen—though not in Plates 19 and 20—with its multitude of staggered figures. The long-limbed flying

[21] Cf. T. A. Gopinatha Rao, *Elements of Hindu Iconography*, vol. 1, part 2, p. 379.

gods and other celestials of the top register are relegated above the straight edge of Śiva's bleak "cave"; they form an outer border of hovering, gliding rhythms flanking a group of gaṇas and other celestials, ṛṣis, who worship a rock sanctuary. To the right proper of Śiva, the rectangular, concave recess formed by the elephant hide appears cut short by the mighty sword held upright and ready to strike, in the second right hand of the eight-armed god.

From his shoulders, a cloudburst of arms shoots off, propelling his body toward Andhaka's diminutive, impaled figure. The long shaft of the trident from whose tip Andhaka's body dangles crossed the raging god's chest. It must have been held in the same way as in a relief of the same scene from the Daśāvatāra cave (Cave 15) of Ellora. The body of Śiva lunges forward while vaulting upward, carved in the round against the curved plane of the elephant hide, its background. Abounding in exuberant power, the figure is modeled naturalistically; its dynamism is one of bodily innervation as much as of artistic form. Breath-inflated chest and abdomen, delicately modeled breast, the smooth, full cheeks rounded over high cheekbones, and a gaping, panting mouth exposing fangs, tongue lolling and eyes bulging under contracted brows—these are self-contained but coherent shapes, their effect heightened by their juxtaposition with the god's *jaṭāmukuṭa*, detailed in each of its dainty single motifs: the volumetric skull ornament, the piled-up coiffure, a sum of single small patterns, the neat precision of their array intensifying by contrast the leering horror of the god's countenance. Aghora / Bhairava's face (Pls. 4, 6), by comparison, exudes a sense of well-being in the strong flesh of its monumental stasis.

The immediacy of the god's breathing, immaculately groomed, body is communicated to the thrust of his arm, arching from behind his shoulders (Pl. 19) and the firm clasp of his hands. The second right arm does not merely hold a sword, it wields the weapon that slayed the elephant demon, whereas the corresponding left hand catches in a bowl the blood dripping from Andhaka's impaled body so that it may not fall on the earth and produce new demons. The goddess Yogeśvarī, issued from Śiva in this context, as a rule has this task assigned to her.

Possibly a master other than the sculptor of the triptych and the grottos of Sundaramūrti; Naṭarāja, and Yogīśvara / Lakulīśa (Pls. 1-

18; 21-25) created the sculpture of Śiva killing Andhaka. Although not represented by work in other chapels, two broken images[22] from Elephanta may be attributed to this particular trend within the sculptures of Elephanta.

The chapels near the eastern entrance to the cave temple are now battered and blurred. They lack the grandeur of conception of the other compositions. The two recesses, right and left of the eastern entrance, one showing Rāvaṇa shaking Kailāsa, and the other depicting Śiva in his Himālayan cave accompanied by Pārvatī, seated near him, are replete with layers of rock and cloud banks arrayed horizontally. Unlike the grotto compositions, each of these very high reliefs is carved with reference to one ground only. In this they conform with the style of the earlier reliefs of the Yogeśvarī cave temple near Bombay.[23] They look forward to the three horizontal registers of the grotto compositions, the uppermost zone teeming with cloud banks, diminutive *liṅga* shrines, long-limbed flying celestials, and other motifs of the grotto sculptures. The panels near the east entrance predate the miracle of the creation of the other sculptures in the Great Cave Temple.

The chapels at the northern entrance, oriented as they are toward the interior of the *mukhamaṇḍapa* or portico, admit to or dismiss the devotee from Śiva's presence in the cave temple. The chapel dedicated to Śiva Yogīśvara / Lakulīśa (Pl. 21) faces that of Śiva Naṭarāja (Pl. 25). Śiva is the primordial yogi, the guardian of creative energy, master of the discipline of its preservation, and also master and teacher of all the other arts that capture and give form audibly and visibly to the realization of ultimate reality. Incarnated in Lakulīśa,[24] the Great Yogi is shown absorbed in meditation, his powerful body taut with the breath of life (*prāṇa*) that sustains creation (Pl. 21). He is seated cross-legged in hieratic symmetry on an open lotus. Wide-pet-

[22] Now in the Prince of Wales Museum, Bombay, illustrated in P. Chandra, *A Guide to the Elephanta Caves*, pls. 26, 27. The images are preserved only in their lower halves. It is the image of Durgā in particular whose volumetric, palpable fleshiness offers the strongest contrast with the respective portion of Ardhanārīśvara's image, while the other image, representing Śiva with Pārvatī and a gaṇa similarly contrasts with the figure of Pārvatī (Pls. 13, 14). The tremulous contour of the pudgy limbs of the figures of the Śiva-Pārvatī fragment is absent from any of the figures of the grotto reliefs. Their contours are firm, their shapes comparatively "abstract."

[23] W. M. Spink, "Jogeshwari: A Brief Analysis," pp. 1-35, pls. I-VI.

[24] Cf. K. C. Panigrahi, "Sculptural Representations of Lakulīśa and Other Pāśupata Teachers," 1960, pp. 635-43.

alled, the lotus has unfolded in its rocky setting, on a long stalk, straight as a pillar, a symbol of the cosmic pillar that traverses and holds together the universe. A Nāga or serpent god on either side worships the pillar emerging from the watery netherworld. In the Great Yogi's grotto the congeries of figures advancing from the sides are being kept at bay from Yogīśvara's immobile seat on top of the cosmic lotus (the lower part is not included in Pl. 21).

The grotto of the epiphany of the Great Yogi incarnated as Lakulīśa is set back from the front of the chapel on a high platform leveled from out of rock boulders. Within the grotto of the lord of yogis, the two throngs of flying celestials stop short, having come to the orbit of Yogīśvara's effulgence, the high nimbus rising from his shoulders.

Śiva as Lakulīśa is at the same time the cosmic yogi enthroned in meditation on the lotus of *ākāśa* above the world pillar, worshiped by serpents in an image akin to that of the Buddha similarly represented.[25] The heroic body of Śiva, however, unlike that of the Buddha image, expands with the might of the breath held in the powerful chest vaulting forward. It sustains the imperious verticality of Śiva's body, and carries erect the full oval face of the Great Yogi in meditation. Virile, disciplined, and effortless, the image is lord over all the gods whose figures make up the vibrancy around the immobile Lord of Yoga manifest in his grotto. The destroyed sculpture gives only a blurred suggestion of the original effect of that lord and teacher, the yogi whose eternal conquest of selfhood is celebrated in this cave, the Great Yogi whose breath is life itself within the stillness of his heroic body. He is the "lord of the cave" (Guheśvara).[26] In sculptures (Elephanta), architecture (Kandariya Mahādeva Temple, eleventh-century Khajuraho),[27] paintings,[28] and hymns (by Allama Prabhu),[29] Śiva

[25] The theme of the World Pillar as shown in Elephanta is seen in Buddhist sculptures; cf. A. K. Coomaraswamy, *Elements of Buddhist Iconography*, 1935, pp. 53, 54, pl. VII, "Buddha Preaching to Bodhisattvas on Mt. Gṛdhrakūṭa" (Karli).

[26] A. K. Ramanujan, tr. *Speaking of Śiva*, pp. 144, 149-51, 153-61, 164, 166, 168 in his translations of Allama Prabhu's hymns.

[27] Kandariya means "of the cave." The name of the eleventh-century Kandariya Mahādeva Temple means "The Great God of the Cave"; cf. S. Kramrisch, "Liṅga," 1977, p. 365 n.; J. Filliozat, "Les images d'un jeu de Śiva à Khajuraho," 1961, p. 284 n. 10.

[28] In paintings from the Panjab hills of the eighteenth to nineteenth centuries, particularly from Mandi (in the style of Sajnu) (cf. W. G. Archer, *Indian Paintings from the Panjab Hills*, vol. I, p. 365, vol. II, pl. 60), and also in paintings from Garhwal, Śiva with his family is shown in a cave.

[29] See Appendix n. 26.

is the lord of caves; he resides in caves (cf. *LP*.1.86.4-5; *ŚP*.2.5.44, 39-40, 58).

In the wedding scene, the figure of Śiva was that of an ethereal adolescent, the transubstantiated body composed of sentiency. As slayer of the demon Andhaka, Śiva's body in lionlike nobility was an instrument that even the God's wildest fury left exquisite.

In the chapel opposite the image of Yogīśvara / Lakulīśa, however, the total being of Śiva as Naṭarāja, the lord of dancers, imbues his movement (Pls. 22-24). The grave gyration of the dance takes into itself the space in which Śiva dances and which surrounds him. Amplitude and distortion of the full-bodied shape comprise an apparent weightlessness; vehement energy soars, stilled by its own impetus. The face of Śiva, lord of dancers, more than any other of Śiva's faces as carved in Elephanta, resembles that of Tatpuruṣa. Naṭarāja's face is that of the quiddity of the dance. In it the Supreme Śiva manifests (cf. *KūP*.2.5.1-7).

The eight-armed figure of Śiva holds in one of his right hands an axe with a long staff. A serpent coiled round it rears its head toward Śiva. The staff is inclined to the right, parallel in its decisive line to the tilt of Śiva's head. The fourth left arm, raised and bent at the elbow, holds in its hand a folded cloth, gathered to unveil—or ready to veil—the orbit of Śiva's dance. It is the veil of *māyā*. Withdrawing it, Lord Śiva at will reveals his presence, the only reality; or he covers it by the intricate texture of the fabric of which the world of the senses is woven. In Naṭarāja's chapel, the flight of the celestials has dwindled and condensed into clusters reminiscent of bracket capitals on which the ceiling of the cave seems to rest. The throng of the gods on the right and left of Naṭarāja is held spellbound. They seem to have halted, each of his own accord: the tall figure of Kārttikeya (Pl. 25), his son holding his staff, joyfully leaping Gaṇeśa, Pārvatī's son above him, and the two celestial ṛṣis above him—all on the extreme proper right of Śiva; while Pārvatī is on the left, with Indra above her. These figures facing forward rather than toward Śiva are part of his epiphany, rather than building up the grotto in which the god manifests.[30] The floating weightlessness of the amplitude of the body as much as the calm of intersecting planes of the dance-entranced face show the god at rest in the rhythm of his movement by which he dances the world into and out of existence.

[30] Cf. C. Sivaramamurti, *The Art of India*, p. 362, fig. 379.

The most cogent array of the celestial host arriving to celebrate the presence of Śiva was seen to have congregated in Ardhanārīśvara's epiphany (Pl. 3). Jubilantly the figures make and fill the grotto of the compassionate lord. In the Gaṅgādhara chapel, the disposition of the rejoicing gods is schematized; it is modified in the nuptials of Śiva and Pārvatī. Reduced in number and more sparsely set, the attendant gods and ṛṣis witness Śiva's dance or the *samādhi* of the lord of yogis. In these two chapels of the *mukhamaṇḍapa*, the immovable stasis of the lord of yogis faces the eternal movement of the lord of dancers. States of self-trance and entrancement are bodied forth in the sculptures of Elephanta. They are part of a total work of art, Śiva's Great Cave Temple.

Never before and never after has a sculptural modality such as the "grotto" directly issued from a realization of Śiva, surrounded by the other gods manifesting in his world. Never before and never after has the transcendental reality that is Śiva imbued the ontological symbol of his cosmos, the *Pañcamukha liṅga*, so as to become the form of the triune head of Sadāśiva as carved in the depth of the cave.

A precursor to, or near contemporary with, the sculptural quality of the triptych and the Sundaramūrti chapel of Elephanta is a colossal stele, possibly of Śiva "Saptasvaramaya," Śiva as embodiment of the seven principal musical notes.[31] In weightless ponderosity the standing figures of Śiva rise, a triple pillar soaring; they issue fourfold from the central pillar, each figure, each "note," sounded in clear perfection, in symphonic ascent and radiation above the supporting orchestra of gaṇas at the bottom of the stele. The "Saptasvaramaya" image of Śiva, Śiva as the seven musical sounds—the music of the spheres—unique in its iconography and form, is another work of Śiva realization to which a surpassingly great sculptor has given form. The image is still in worship in Parel, a suburb of Bombay.

The style of these supreme works of art belongs to the region of the Konkan around Bombay, which enjoyed the patronage of the Kalacuri dynasty, who were devotees of Śiva.[32]

The Śaiva sculptures executed in the Konkan under the patronage of the Kalacuri dynasty were preceded by and owed much to Bud-

[31] Śiva "Saptasvaramaya," detail, see L. Frederic, *The Art of India*, p. 165, pl. 133; C. Sivaramamurti, *The Art of India*, p. 176; A. de Lippe, *Indian Medieval Sculpture*, pl. 7. A vial is held in the left hand of (apparently) each of the seven figures. This aspect of Śiva has as yet not been accounted for iconographically.

[32] Cf. W. M. Spink, "Jogeshwari: A Brief Analysis," pp. 3-6, 16.

dhist cave sculpture of the Deccan under Vākāṭaka patronage. This is seen in the Śaiva cave of Yogeśvarī in Amboli, near Bombay, which predates Elephanta. Soon the placid and somewhat staid character of the Vākāṭaka style influenced sculpture, as seen in the Yogeśvarī cave; but also the creative quality of this style to express by the subtlest modeling, the deepest devotion, as in the Buddhist rock-cut Cave Three, Aurangadad, became informed with dynamic grandeur and the capacity for conveying the superhuman reality that is Śiva.

The urge to give form to the realization of Śiva was supported by qualities peculiar to western Indian sculpture commingling with those of the Vākāṭaka tradition. These were a fulsome, if stolid weightiness manifest already in Kanheri (near Bombay) in the second century A.D.,[33] and a naturalism, stimulated by the Indian renaissance of Hellenistic memories. The fusion of these two components brought about figures of western Indian sculpture like those from Samalaji and other sites in Gujarat and Rajasthan.[34] They combine volumetric opulence with a facile "classical" charm. In some of the sculptures of the Yogeśvarī cave temple, as well as of Elephanta, a forcefully and naturalistically modeled body of palpable "fleshiness" was given to images such as those of Harihara (Yogeśvarī) and Durgā (Elephanta).[35] With these resources at their command, the sculptors of the Konkan fused the several components into a style having a new authority, ready to serve a new vision. Full-bodied, throbbing with elemental energies, controlled and calm in a superhuman way, of weightless gravity are the figures that communicate the presence of Śiva to the cave temple at Elephanta.

The Kalacuri school of sculpture, beginning in the Yogeśvarī cave and reaching its climax in Elephanta, continued to create rock-cut Śaiva temples in Ellora. Mythic reliefs of heroic dimension and narrative intent celebrate in the Rāmeśvara cave (Cave 21) at Ellora scenes like the "Austerities of Pārvatī" (Pl. 26), carved shortly after Elephanta, that is, in the second half of the sixth century. The master sculptor of the Rāmeśvara cave, although having taken note of the

[33] Cf. A. K. Coomaraswamy, *History of Indian and Indonesian Art*, pl. XXXI, fig. 135. Also see Zimmer, *Art of Indian Asia*, vol. II, pl. 85.

[34] Cf. U. P. Shah, *Sculptures from Samalaji and Roda*, 1960, pls. 25, 42.

[35] W. M. Spink, "Jogeshwari: A Brief Analysis," pl. VI, fig. 31; and P. Chandra, *A Guide to the Elephanta Caves* (see above, n. 22).

grottos of Elephanta, ordered the relief in sequences of pure and simple shapes. The figures seem to advance from the ground of the relief in a choreography of closely set columnar shapes attuned to the calmness of suspended emotion in which the scene is set.

The panel representing the "Austerities of Pārvatī," follows the version of the myth narrated in the *Vārāha Purāṇa* (*VrP*.22.4-26), which differs from that of the *Śiva Purāṇa* according to which Śiva in the guise of an old ascetic tries to dissuade Pārvatī from winning Śiva to be her husband, pointing out the horror of Śiva the ascetic. Hearing Pārvatī praise Śiva in his true and ultimate being, the ascetic reveals himself as Śiva (Ch. X.B.2.c). The old ascetic put to the test Pārvatī's knowledge of Śiva, the Supreme Reality (*ŚP*.2.3.26-28). According to the *Vārāha Purāṇa*, however, Śiva in the disguise of an old *brahmacārin* came to disturb Pārvatī's austerities in order to test the *tapas* and compassion of the Great Goddess (*VrP*.22.4-26).

In the relief of the Rāmeśvara cave, Pārvatī, straight as a pillar and next to an "architectural" pillar, stands in the midst of four burning fires, only two being visible, in front of rocks. A fifth fire, that of the sun—not shown in the relief—scorches her, the ardor of whose *tapas* is greater than that of the fires in whose midst she stands. She counts the beads of her rosary unaware of the young ascetic (rather than an old beggar) who has approached her, holding out his hand. Pārvatī, disturbed in her meditation on Śiva, asks the beggar to go to bathe in the lotus pond nearby and return for his meal. In the pond a *makara* catches hold of the mendicant's leg. He cries out, and Pārvatī, abandoning her meditation and also her scruples of touching the beggar, goes to his aid. She clasps his right arm with her left hand and raises the mendicant—who is Śiva himself—from the monster's mouth. In the relief, the large and crowned figure of the god towers above that of the beggar rescued by Pārvatī's hand—her left hand, not her right that avoids pollution, but her left hand that is nearer to her heart. Solemnly she stands to Śiva's right, his bride-to-be.

By her compassion, greater than her obedience to propriety, greater even than her asceticism, the Great Goddess wins Śiva. The relief tells the story, joining in continuous narration two groups, that is, its two significant moments: on the left, the ascetic Pārvatī, her attendant, and the beggar; on the right, once more Pārvatī, grown in stature, the beggar, and Śiva. The figures betray no emotion. Like pillars they mark the progress of the story. It begins with Pārvatī, the *tapasvinī*, and ends with Śiva, the Great God, with Pārvatī, the Great Goddess, at his side. Rocks in low relief rise behind them.

The sculptural restraint and solemn lyricism, the measured movements and dispassionate faces of the postlike figures grouped in dense interlocking contiguity, have hardly more than one component in common with the sculptures of Elephanta. It is the underlying ponderosity of western Indian sculpture that asserts itself, particularly in the figures of Pārvatī and in that of crowned Śiva on the extreme right of the panel. The style in which the sculptor made his vision come true is not imbued with a realization of Śiva. Rather, it is an enchanted rendering of a Śaiva theme to which the sculptor brought his training and dedication.

In a different vein and with all the resources of the school at his command, the sculptor of the image of Vārāhī (Pl. 27), one of the seven mothers whose images occupy a wall of the Rāmeśvara cave, made the usually boar-faced goddess an embodiment of capricious hauteur and sensitive elegance. This high-brow Vārāhī bewitches the viewer and subjects him to her charm. The charm of Pārvatī in Elephanta (Pls. 14, 15, 18) on the other hand, is an efflorescence of her being. More ancient than the group of the mothers who, with Yogeśvarī, came to Śiva's assistance and intercepted the blood dripping from impaled Andhaka, is their sacred number seven (*RV*.1.141.2; 1.146.1; 2.5.2; 3.6.2; 4.42.8; 9.102.4). Images of these seven who embodied bad qualities but were the active powers (*śakti*) of the great gods, were carved in Elephanta (east wing),[36] as also in the Rāmeśvara cave. While their standing figures in the former are largely defaced, their seated images in the Rāmeśvara cave are graced by the alluring and unapproachable ambiguous beauty of Vārāhī, the Śakti of Viṣṇu in his boar incarnation.

The Rāmeśvara cave represents the ability of the Kalaçuri artist to infuse the figures of Śaiva themes with responses that were in the artist and to which the artist, whether himself a devotee of Śiva or not, creatively gave form. At the other end of creative achievement, the sculptures of the nearly contemporary Dhumar Lena cave (Ellora, Cave 29), in megalomaniac emulation of Elephanta, are inflated shapes void of the meaning that their iconography connotes.

[36] See Hiranand Sastri and R. Parimoo, *A Guide to Elephanta*, pl. 15.

Continued creative impact of Elephanta on Ellora was, however, provided for by the image of Naṭarāja. The image of the dancing god in the Daśāvatāra cave (Cave 15, mid-eighth century) (Pl. 28), about two centuries later than Elephanta, shows the dancing body of the god move in the opposite direction from that of the Elephanta sculpture. Body and limbs are elongated, the body languorous and attenuated. Here the stylishness of another, namely, the western Cālukyan school of art, has assuaged the once formidable repose in movement of the image. To the three walls of the recess in which this large figure is inscribed cling the figures of a few assembled gods. The conception of the grotto is only residually valid here. The dancing figure fills, and one of its arms even exceeds, the recess in which it is displayed.[37] Compared to Elephanta, the dance has less vehemence and also less stillness. A posture sustained by the limbs of the dancing god rather than filled by his total being exceeds the bay. The subsidiary figures form an accompaniment and an audience; they identify the scene in which they are inscribed, they do not bring it about by their own dynamic participation, though an acute linear fluidity pervades the languor of the composition.

Finally, in the Laṅkeśvara cave of the Kailāsa complex of sanctuaries (Cave 16, later part, eighth century) (Pl. 29),[38] Śiva the great dancer is seen flinging himself into the plane of the relief by a torsion of hips which places the left leg from back to front and to the right with such superhuman élan that the movement of the right leg, bent in an obtuse angle, allows the lunging body to soar forward with the arms raised laterally, bent upward as a scale that balances above a slim torso the elongated head in three-quarter front view along with the backward tilt of its high coiffure. The multitude of arms branching off from the elbows leaves the shoulders unencumbered, and the hands, as far as they have not been broken off, are alive with the movements of birds in flight.

Verve and balance of this Tāṇḍava dance are enhanced by baroque fluttering scarves, festoons swinging from the crown, and a number of style elements absorbed from the several schools of art that had

[37] For the entire "grotto" relief, see L. Frederic, *The Art of India*, p. 162, pl. 129. The left raised arm, only part of which can be seen in Pl. 28, extends the diagonal thrust of the figure's movement from the bent right knee upward to the top of the bay, where it is cut short by the ceiling of the bay.

[38] Cf. H. Zimmer, *Art of Indian Asia*, vol. II, p1. 223.

succeeded the Kalacuri style of Ellora.[39] Not part of a grotto, the figures of flying gods on either side at the top establish here the foreground of the celestial spectacle. Two gaṇas have found room between the wide-apart feet of the dancer. The grotto formed by the figures of the gods and in which Śiva dances and manifests variously in Elephanta has dissolved, and its figures, in several vestigial groups, cling to the wall of a rectangular stage.

It was only after another two hundred years, from the tenth into the thirteenth century, that Śiva's Ānanda Tāṇḍava was created—this time in South India, in the round, in glorious bronze images enshrined in sanctuaries of their own.

The grotto composition created in Elephanta may be considered a specifically Śaiva form of sculpture carved in the living rock. Another type of rock-cut relief was employed in Ellora on the inner face of the entrance to the Kailāsa temple. It shows Śiva the Archer as Tripurāntaka, the Destroyer of the triple city of the demons (Pl. 30). Śiva, from his chariot drawn by four swift horses, the Vedas, flying through the air, discharges his arrow and destroys by one single shot the rule of the demons in the three worlds (Ch. XI.3.b). His bow arches over the god's slim body, a taut curve of energy sweeping upward and including the high crown of the god in its sweep. The entire scene is meant to be seen taking place in the air through which the horses are flying. The miracle of the swiftly flying arrow was the theme of the sculptor. The four Veda-horses convey it by their flight, carved on a rock-cut wall at a right angle to the plane that is the ground of the archer in his chariot. Impassive Brahmā is the charioteer and Viṣṇu, in bull shape, confidently rests in front of him. Śiva, the archer, a figure of trim Pallava style shape, and the four Veda-horses are forms of one pointed energy cutting across the air, here presented by the space held between two walls intersecting at a right angle. Śiva's bow, curving from one wall to the other, holds in its arc victor and victim, the latter of diminutive shape, limbs spread out flying, falling to his doom. His defeat parallels Śiva's victory. Above Śiva's bow more demons tumble along the wall of defeat. The flying, long-limbed celestials of Elephanta come to mind.

The architectural moldings of the chariot on one wall and the rectangular niche cut out to accommodate the horses on the other are

[39] For a perceptive analysis and characterization, see D. C. Chatham, "Stylistic Sources and Relationships of the Kailāsa Temple in Ellora," 1977.

contrivances, each of which emphasizes its own wall and singles out the space between them as part of the total composition. The continuity of the scene, represented on two adjacent intersecting walls, was taken up in the Kailāsa temple in Ellora nearly a thousand years after the excavation from the living rock of the Buddhist Vihāra at Bhaja in the Konkan.[40] There, a throng of demoniac figures carved in low relief seems to have seeped out of one wall and its density continues on the adjacent wall at a right angle, making this part of the courtyard a corner charged with mythical content. Irrespective of the difference in style, the rock, under the hand of the sculptor, allowed itself to be treated as a continuous relief around the corner.

Sculpture in the rock, different from architecture and its structural framework, allows myths to be conveyed in a visual form suggested to the sculptor by the mass of the rock itself. Continuity of relief around a corner includes the space between the perpendicular walls as part of the artistic whole, and is one of the two creative forms of rock sculpture. The other is the grotto. Its space is mytho-sculptural; it is the mode in which Śiva manifested in Elephanta.

A counter example to the mytho-sculptural quality of the Tripurāntaka carving in the gate wall of the court of the Kailāsa temple is a rectangular panel of Śiva Tripurāntaka (Pl. 31) carved in low relief in a narrow corridor of the Kailāsa temple, in yet another, the Rāṣṭrakūṭa style, proper to Ellora of the eighth century, confining within its limits the martial vigor of Śiva's attack on the "triple city."

The timeless state of being of Śiva pervaded the sculptures of Elephanta, even though a particular myth at its significant moment was the theme. In a very large sculpture of the Kailāsa temple (latter part of the eighth century) the myth is housed in a cave setting of architectural quality. The theme is "Śiva shows his grace to Rāvaṇa" (Pl. 32), as the demon king is about to uproot Śiva's mountain.[41] The event is staged in a hieratically composed grotto where rocks resembling architectural moldings in the lower part of the composition frame the deep cavity of Rāvaṇa's earth-shaking enterprise. Its futility is demonstrated by the order in Śiva's Himālayan residence, a grotto idyll recessed above Rāvaṇa's dark station. On a high throne of rocks enlivened with gaṇas, Śiva and Pārvatī tower above two guardians whose

[40] H. Zimmer, *Art of Indian Asia*, vol. II, pls. 40, 41.

[41] Cf. T. A. Gopinatha Rao, *Elements of Hindu Iconography*, vol. 2, part 1, p. 217; and B. N. Sharma, "Rāvaṇa Lifting Mount Kailāsa in Indian Art," 1973, p. 327.

quietly seated figures occupy each a niche of its own, flanking Śiva's throne of rock boulders. Pārvatī's lithe shape reclines against Śiva, and she clasps the left arm of her lord. His subtly delicate shape is averted from her in a posture of ease, with his right arm raised, balancing his battle axe with his fingers, while the toe of his left foot, by merely touching the ground, stabilizes the quaking mountain. Deeper in the grotto, unnoticed by the divine couple, a female attendant rushes into a further recess of the cave. Her fleeing back view, the face turned toward Pārvatī, gives the only indication of imminent danger. Diminutive figures of worshiping celestials on craglike, scalloped clouds, descended from the impetuously flying celestial hosts of Elephanta, form here, as they did before, a baldachin of Śiva's cave. A rationalized composition disposing its figures with courtly tact and tenderness creates a tableau of Śiva in his well-ordered mountain residence. Rāvaṇa's futile attempt at shaking the mountain will be pardoned, as is anticipated by the clear symmetries of this grotto idyll, a late descendant of Elephanta's pristine artistic power of rendering Śiva's presence.

GLOSSARY

Ābhu	the primordial life potential, the life germ
Adbhuta	*see* Agni
Āḍi	a demon
Aditi	the "Boundless," daughter and mother of Dakṣa; the mother of the gods, the mother of the world, the sovereign "mother"
Āditya(s)	the sons of Aditi; solar divinities
Aghora	the "Non-Frightful"; one of the five *mantras* that constitute the body of Śiva. Aghora is represented by the frightful face of Bhairava
Agni	*adbhuta*, the celestial fire; *gṛhapati*, the household fire; Fire
ahaṁkāra	the individuating principle; egoity
Ahi Budhnya	the Serpent of the Deep
Aiyanār	*see Śāstā*
Aja Ekapād	the Uncreate "One Foot" or the Goat One Foot
Ajagāva	the bow of Śiva; the southern portion of the path of the sun
ākāśa	ether or space, the first element of manifestation, pervading all other elements
Alakā	the city of Kubera, god of wealth, situated north of Śiva's residence Kailāsa
amṛta	the water of life and drink of immortality
Aṁśumat	grandson of King Sagara, discovered the ashes of the King's sixty thousand sons
Ananta	"Endless"; the Cosmic Serpent
Anasūyā	wife of sage Atri, one of the seven sages; renowned for her chastity
Andhaka	"Blind"; a demon; *see also* Bhṛṅgi
Aṅgiras (es)	the fire-born ṛṣis; a class of higher beings, with Agni as their head
Apasmāra Puruṣa	the demon "without memory"
Appar	a South Indian Śaiva saint
Apsaras	a celestial water nymph
Arantuka	a *yakṣa* (q.v.) (of Kurukṣetra)
ardhamaṇḍapa	a "half-hall," the architectural space between the hall and the sanctuary proper of a temple

Ardhanārīśvara	"the Lord whose Half is Woman"; Śiva, the androgyne
Arjuna	the "bright" son of Indra; the most prominent of the five Pāṇḍava brothers of the *Mahābhārata*. He and his brothers went into exile after Yudiṣṭhira, the oldest brother, lost the kingdom to the Kauravas by gambling. Arjuna went on a pilgrimage in order to obtain from Śiva celestial weapons in the war against the Kauravas. On his pilgrimage he encountered and fought with a Kirāta (q.v.) who was Śiva
arka	a white, flowering, small tree (*Calatropis Gigantea*)
artha	prosperity; one of the four aims of life, the others being *dharma*, righteousness, that is, fulfillment of one's duties according to one's station; *kāma*, fulfillment of the needs of love and sexual desire; and fourth and ultimate, *mokṣa*, release from all the other aims—total liberation
Arundhatī	wife of sage Vasiṣṭha, model of conjugal fidelity; one of the Pleiades (Cassiopeia)
āsana	a seat; a particular posture or mode of sitting in the practice of yoga
Aśani	Lightning; one of the eight names given by his father to Rudra at his birth
Aṣṭamūrti	Śiva as the totality of manifestation
asu	life, breath
aśuddha tattva	(*see tattva*); the "impure category" includes the twenty-four categories (*tattva*) from *prakṛti* (cosmic substance) to "earth," that is, the world of duality which is impure according to Kashmiri Śaivism
Asura (s)	the Godhead; the great pristine gods; Varuṇa, Agni, Soma in particular; a demon
Aśvatthāman	a commander of the Kauravas
Aśvin (s)	celestial charioteers; sons of the Sun and Saraṇyū, the "rushing one" in the shape of a mare; physicians of the gods
ātman	the life principle; the self
Atri	a sage (*see* Anasūyā)
AUM	the seed of all *mantras* (thought-forms); the three letters are the equivalents of the three *guṇas*, they represent Brahmā, Viṣṇu, and Śiva. The *mantra* leads to liberation
avatar	descent; incarnation of a deity
Avimukta	Vārāṇasī, or a *tīrtha* in or near Vārāṇasī, "not left" by Śiva

avyakta	non-manifest; cosmic substance not as yet having entered manifestation (*see prakṛti*)
Bāhīkas	a people of the Western Panjab (?)
Bhaga	an Āditya
Bhagīratha	a king descended from Sagara. Śiva, moved by his austerities, let the Gaṅgā descend from heaven to earth and the netherworld in order to purify the ashes of King Sagara's sons
Bhairava	Śiva's form of terror and transcendency
Bhairavas	sixty-four terrible lesser manifestations of Śiva (such as Ghaṇṭākarṇa)
bhakta	a devotee full of love for his god
Bhaṅgāśvana	a king
Bhārgava	a descendant of Bhṛgu, that is, Kāvya Uśanas (cf. Śukra)
Bhava	existence; one of the eight names of Rudra given by his father
Bhikṣāṭana	Śiva as the supreme beggar
Bhīma	the Terrible; one of the eight names of Śiva given by his father
Bhogavatī	"the Voluptuous"; the capital of the Nāgas in Pātāla
Bhogya	Śiva's "City of Enjoyment"
Bhṛgu	a sage arisen from the fire of Prajāpati's lake of sperm; one of the seven sages
Bhṛṅgi	the skeleton form of the demon Andhaka
bhūta	a "being"; a sense particular, that is, an object of the five senses according to Sāṅkhya; a spirit in the retinue of Śiva
bodhicitta	"mind of enlightenment"; semen virile (a term of Tantric Sandhābhāṣā or "intentional language"
Brahmā	the god Brahmā, the Creator
brahmacārin	the celibate Veda student
brahmacarya	the state of being a brahmacārin; continence
brahmahatyā	the fury embodying the sin of murdering a brahmin
brahman	formation, sacred formula, rune; supreme reality
Brāhmaṇa	the portion of the Veda or revelation (*śruti*) treating of the origin and giving explanations of the various sacrifices and the employment of the hymns at the sacrifices (*see* Veda)
Brahmapura	the "City of Brahman"; the heart
Brahmaśiras	"Head of Brahmā"; a particular "weapon" or *mantra*

brahmin	a member of the priestly or first caste
Bṛhaspati	the priest among the gods
Budha	the planet Mercury, son of the Moon; married Ilā
Caitra	a lunar month (March-April)
cakra	a subtle center of energy within the human body
Cakravartin	a universal monarch of the outer or inner world
Cāmuṇḍā	a fearful goddess sprung from the Great Goddess (Durgā)
Caṇḍā	"Fierce"; a name of the Goddess Durgā
Candra	the moon
Candraśekhara	Śiva having the moon as his crest; also name of an incarnation of Śiva
cit	consciousness
Cyavana	a sage, rejuvenated by the Aśvins
Daitya(s)	demon(s) (descended from Diti)
Ḍākinī	a female ghoul
Dakṣa	"Dexterous"; a form of the Creator; father of Satī; son of Brahmā
dakṣiṇā	a present given to brahmins at the completion of a rite
Dakṣiṇāmūrti	a form of the Śiva image facing south (*dakṣiṇa*); Śiva as teacher of yoga, gnosis, music, and as giving exposition to the sciences
Dānava(s)	demon(s) (descended from Dānu)
Dānu	the mother of Vṛtra
Devī	the Great Goddess
Dhanvantari	the physician of the gods, arisen at the Churning of the Ocean
dharma	cosmic order, righteousness, that is, discharge of one's duties according to one's station
Dhruva	the pole star
Diti	a daughter of Dakṣa and mother of the Daityas
Droṇa (*MBh*)	commander-in-chief of the Kauravas; father of Aśvatthāman
Durgā	"the Unconquerable"; the Great Goddess
Dvāpara Yuga	*see* yuga
dvārapāla	guardian of the door
Ekavrātya	the Sole Vrātya; a manifestation of Śiva (*see vrātya*)
gaṇa(s)	spirit attendant(s) of Śiva; their host
Gaṇapati	Gaṇeśa, leader of *gaṇas*, elephant-headed son of Pārvatī (and Śiva)

Gandhamādana	"intoxicating with fragrance"; a mountain resort associated with Mount Meru
Gandharva	celestial guardian of Soma, of the flowing supernal light
Gāṇḍīva	the bow of Arjuna
Gaṅgā	the Goddess and sacred river Ganges
Gaṅgādhara	Śiva, supporting Gaṅgā on his head
Gaṅgādvāra	"Ganges-Gate," the sacred site where the Ganges descends from the Himālaya to the plains (now called Hardvar)
garbhagṛha	"womb chamber"; the innermost sanctuary of a temple
Garuḍa	the "sun-bird"; the vehicle (*vāhana*) of Viṣṇu
Gaurī	"Of Light Golden Complexion"; a name of Pārvatī
Gāyatrī	a Vedic meter; a most sacred *mantra* of the *Ṛg Veda*; wife of Brahmā
Ghaṇṭākarṇa	*see* Bhairava
Girīśa	"Mountain Lord"; a name of Śiva
Gṛhapati	"Lord of the House"; an incarnation of Śiva (cf. Agni)
Guheśvara	"Lord of the Cave"; a name of Śiva
Guhyaka(s)	"the Hidden Ones," gnomes or spirits forming the retinue of Kubera; guardians of hidden treasure
guṇa(s)	"strand"; the three constituents of *prakṛti*: *sattva*, illuminating, cohesive tendency; *tamas*, "darkness" disruptive tendency; *rajas*, revolving, activating tendency
Halāhala	the poison that arose from the Churning of the Ocean (*see kālakūṭa*)
Hanumān	a monkey chief; ally of Rāma
Hara	"the Ravisher"; a name of Śiva
Hari	"the Golden-Brown"; a name of Viṣṇu
Harihara	the god whose left half is Viṣṇu, whose right half is Śiva
Himavat	Himālaya, the "abode of snow"; the mountain range; father of Pārvatī (*see* Parvata)
Hiraṇyagarbha	The "Golden Germ," or "Golden Womb"; an epithet of Prajāpati, Brahmā.
Hiraṇyakaśipu	"Gold Cloth," a demon
Hiraṇyākṣa	"Gold Eye," a demon
Hiraṇyapura	"the Golden City"; capital of the demons
icchā śakti	*see śakti*

Ila	a king of the lunar race
Ilā	Ila transformed into a woman
Indra	the Creator God of the aeon prior to that of Rudra Paśupati; king of the gods
indriya (s)	sense powers; the five capacities of cognition and the five capacities of action
Īśāna	"the Ruler," a name of Śiva; the name of one of the five *mantras* or "Five Brahmans"
Īśvara	the Lord
Jalandhara	a demon king
Jātaka	"birth story"; a story relating an incident of a former birth of the Buddha
jaṭāmukuṭa	high crown of matted hair, particularly worn by images of Śiva (and Brahmā)
Jayā	lady-in-waiting of Pārvatī
Jīmūtavāhana	"Who Has a Cloud as His Vehicle"; a name of Śiva
jīva	the principle of life in man, the microcosm
jñāna	gnosis; the knowledge derived from meditation on the supreme spirit
jñāna śakti	*see śakti*; the power of knowledge
Jvarahareśvara	"The Lord Who Seizes with Fever Heat"; a form of Śiva
Kailāsa	Śiva's Himālayan mountain residence
Kaivalya	complete detachment, absorption in the supreme spirit
Kāla	time; death
Kālabhairava	Bhairava having overcome time and death
Kālāgni	the Fire of Doomsday
Kālakāla	*see* Mahākāla
Kālakūṭa	the world poison (time)
Kālanemi	a Rākṣasa (q.v.)
Kālī	"Black"; a name of Devī
Kali Yuga	*see* yuga
kalpa	a day of Brahmā, equal to one thousand mahāyugas, or 4,320 million years of mortals
Kalyāṇa Sundaramūrti	the "happy, beautiful embodiment"; the representation of Śiva and Pārvatī's wedding
Kāma	the god of desire, Eros
Kamalākṣa	"Lotus Eye," a demon, son of Tāraka
Kandariya	"Of the Cave"; name of a Śiva temple of the eleventh century at Khajuraho

Kaṅkāla mūrti	Śiva / Bhairava carrying the skeleton of Viṣvaksena (q.v.)
kapāla	a beggar's bowl made of a skull
Kapālamocana	"releasing from the skull bowl"; a site in Vārāṇasī
kapālin	the carrier of a skull bowl
kaparda	"shell"-like coiffure of matted hair, particularly of Śiva
kapardin	the wearer of a *kaparda*, particularly Śiva
Kapila	a sage who reduced to ashes the sixty thousand sons of King Sagara
Kardama	a Prajāpati or Progenitor
karma	"action," the law of consequences of past actions, good or bad, on one's future
Kārttikeya	"of the Kṛttikās" or Pleiades. They nursed Kārttikeya, the son of Śiva
Kauṣṭubha	a jewel that appeared at the Churning of the Ocean, worn by Viṣṇu or Kṛṣṇa
Kāvya Uśanas	a priest of the Asuras and demons; a seer (*see* Śukra)
Kāyāvatāra	the present-day village of Karvan, where Śiva became incarnate as the *brahmacārin* Lakulin by entering a corpse in a cremation ground
Keśin	"Long Hair"; an ascetic who drank poison with Rudra from one cup
Ketaki	a flower of the Ketaka tree (*Pandamus odoratissimus*)
Kirāta	name of a mountain tribe; name of Śiva disguised as a Kirāta
Kīrttimukha	"Face of Glory"; a creature issued from Śiva's anger. Bid by Śiva to devour its own body, it was left with its leonine head only, the *kīrttimukha*
Kratu	"the Sacrifice"; a progenitor, one of the seven sages
krīyā śakti	the power of action (*see śakti*)
Kṛśānu	a celestial archer; a Gandharva (s.v.)
Kṛṣṇa	"Black"; an avatar of Viṣṇu, prince of Dvāraka, the charioteer of Arjuna. On the eve of the great war of the *Mahābhārata*, he related to Arjuna the *Bhagavad Gītā*, the Song of the Lord
Kṛta Yuga	*see* yuga
Kṛttikā(s)	the Pleiades; presided over by Agni, wives of the seven sages
kṣatriya	a member of the warrior or second caste, the first caste being that of the *Brāhmaṇas* (brahmins)
Kṣetrajña	"The Knower of the Field"; *see* Puruṣa

Kṣetrapāla	the guardian of the field
Kubera	"Ugly Body"; god of riches; King of Yakṣas
Kumāra	"The Boy"; Rudra after having received his eight names; also a name of Kārttikeya
Kumbhāṇḍa(s)	"Pot-Testicles"; a group of imps, attendants of Rudra
Kuṇḍalinī	the power of consciousness, Śiva's divine power, lying coiled and asleep at the bottom of the subtle body of the microcosm; awakened by the yogi, it ascends through the *cakras* and reunites with Śiva in the thousand-petalled lotus at the apex of the head
Kurukṣetra	"Field of the Kurus"; a plain near Delhi where the battle of the Kurus and the Pāṇḍavas was fought (cf. the *Mahābhārata*)
Kuṭilā	"The Curvaceous," i.e., Gaṅgā
Lakulin	an incarnation of Śiva (*see* Kāyāvatāra)
Lakulīśa	the founder or systematizer of the Pāśupata sect (first half second century A.D.); also Lakulin
laya	dissolution
līlā	the play of the Lord; his manifestations
liṅga	sign; the phallus; the symbol of Śiva; *ūrdhvaliṅga*, the erect *liṅga* indicating continence and the ascent of the semen within the body; *ekamukha liṅga*, one-faced *liṅga*; *pañcamukha liṅga*, five-faced *liṅga*
liṅga śarīra	the "subtle body," comprising *mahat*, *ahaṁkāra*, *manas*, *indriyas*, and *tanmātras*; the invisible carrier of the principle of life
Liṅgāyat	a member of the Liṅgāyat sect that arose in the twelfth century in the Kannaḍa-speaking districts of Maisur (South India)
Macakruka	a *yakṣa* (of Kurukṣetra)
Madhyamā Vāc	*see vāc*
Mahābhārata	the Epic of the great war of the Bhāratas
mahābhūta(s)	the five sense particulars; space, air, fire, water, earth
Mahādeva	the Great God; Śiva
Mahākāla	Śiva as Time beyond time
Mahāpuruṣa	the Buddha as *mahāpuruṣa*, supernal man, is marked by specific and supernatural signs (*lakṣaṇa*)
mahat	*mahātattva*, the first produce of cosmic substance (*prakṛti*)

Maheśvara	the Great Lord; Śiva
makara	the foremost monster of the deep, a symplegma of crocodile, elephant, etc.
manas	the principle of cognition
Mandākinī	"Gently Flowing"; the river Ganges in heaven
maṇḍala	a symmetrical polygon; a diagram used in invoking a divinity; a magical symbolical rendering of the universe, awakening the consciousness of man's identity with the Universal Consciousness
maṇḍapa	the hall in front of the sanctuary of a temple
Mandara	the mountain used by gods and demons as the churning stick at the Churning of the Ocean
Maṇibhadra	chief of the *yakṣas*
Maṇigrīva	a son of Kubera (q.v.)
Maṅkaṇaka	a ṛṣi
mantra	"thought instrument"; representation of a deity through basic sounds; sacred evocation, incantation
Mantramūrti	Śiva embodied by *mantras*
Manu	"Man"; one of fourteen mythical rulers of the earth, progenitors, each ruling for the fourteenth part of a Kalpa. Manu-Svayambhuva, the first Manu; Manu-Cākṣuṣa, the sixth Manu; Manu-Vaivasvata, the seventh Manu
manvantara	*see* Manu: 306,720,000 years
Manyu	"Wrath"; a name of Rudra
Mārgaśīrṣa	(also Mṛgaśiras); the "Head of the Antelope"; the constellation Orion; Prajāpati
Māriṣa	Mother of Dakṣa, born as Kṣatriya and son of the ten Pracetasas
Mārkaṇḍeya	a young sage and devotee (*bhakta*) of Śiva.
Marut(s)	son(s) of Rudra and the Pṛśni cow (q.v.). They are seven in number. Their names are each a composite with *vāyu* (wind)
Mātṛkā(s)	the Mothers; groups of female potencies, as consorts of the great gods, as planetary powers, as evil powers
mātuliṅga	a citron; a fruit rich in seed
Maya	master architect of the demons (Daityas)
māyā	illusion; the veiling power of *prakṛti* that results in phenomenal appearance
Medhatithi	a ṛṣi
Menā	mother of Pārvatī
Meru	the mountain in the center of the earth
Mohinī	"The Enchantress"; the female form assumed by Viṣṇu

mokṣa	release; total liberation
Mṛga	the antelope; Prajāpati
Mṛgaśiras	*see* Mārgaśīrṣa
Mṛgavyādha	the Hunter of the Antelope; Rudra; the Dog Star (Sirius)
Mṛtyu	Death
Mūjavat	name of a mountain (where reed grass grows)
mukhaliṅga	"face *liṅga*"; a *liṅga* having one, four, or five faces attached
mukhamaṇḍapa	portico
muni	ascetic, sage
muñja	reed grass
Nābhānediṣṭha	a Vedic seer and poet; son of Manu (q.v.)
Nāga	serpent divinity
Nakṣatra	an asterism in the moon's path; a lunar mansion
Namuci	an Asura beheaded by Indra
Nandin	"Joy"; Śiva's bull, his *vāhana*; his doorkeeper and chief of *gaṇas*
Nandīsvara	Śiva as Lord of Nandin; a name of Nandin
Nara	*see* Nārāyaṇa
Nārada	A ṛṣi
Naraka	Hell
Narasiṁha	the "man-lion" incarnation of Viṣṇu
Nārāyaṇa	Nara-Nārāyaṇa, two ṛṣis; Arjuna and Viṣṇu were their incarnations. Nara means man; Nārāyaṇa is a name of Viṣṇu
Naṭarāja	Śiva as Lord of Dancers
Nīla	"Dark Blue"; a demon in elephant shape, killed by Śiva, whose skin Śiva wears
Nīlakaṇṭha	Śiva of the blue throat, having swallowed *kālakūṭa* (q.v.)
nirvāṇa	extinction, final liberation
niṣkala	without parts; impartite
nivṛtti	withdrawal (from the world); cessation of action
Padma Kalpa	*see* kalpa
pañcabrahmans	Śiva's five *mantras*, beginning with Sadyojāta
Pañcajanya	the five classes of beings; the conch of Viṣṇu, one of the four essential cognizances of his image
Pāñcālika	a *yakṣa* of the Pañcāla country in the Panjab
pañcamukha liṅga	*see liṅga*
Pāṇḍava(s)	the descendants of Paṇḍu; the Great War of the *Mahābhārata* was fought between the Pāṇḍavas and the Kauravas

paṇi(s)	"Misers"; demons witholding the sun
Paramaśiva	the supreme transcendent Śiva; the Godhead
Parameśvara	Śiva, the Supreme Lord
parāśakti	*see śakti*
parā vāc	*see vāc*
pāriṣadas	*gaṇas* (q.v.); animal-faced
Parvata	"the Mountain"; father of Pārvatī
Pārvatī	the Great Goddess; wife of Śiva
pāśa	snare, fetter
paśu	cattle; animal; a being bound by spiritual nescience
Paśupati	Lord of Animals; Rudra
paśyantī vāc	*see vāc*
Pātāla	the netherworld
Pināka	Śiva's bow
piśāca(s)	"flesh-Eaters"; goblins; attendants of Kubera
Pitāmaha	grandfather; an epithet of Brahmā
pitṛ(s)	forefathers, manes
prabhāmaṇḍala	circle of light; aureole
Pracetasa(s)	the ten Pracetasas; progenitors; their wife is Māriṣa (q.v.)
pradhāna	*prakṛti* (q.v.)
Prahlāda	a demon (Daitya); son of Hiraṇyakaśipu; a devotee of Viṣṇu
Prajāpati	the Lord of Generation, lord of creatures; the Creator
prakṛti	cosmic substance; the uncaused cause of phenomenal existence
pralaya	dissolution; destruction of the cosmos at the end of a kalpa
Pramatha(s)	"Churn-Spirits"; attendants of Śiva
prāṇa	breath, vital energy
prāṇava	the sacred sound or syllable Om (*AUM*), the chief seed *mantra* (q.v.)
prāśitra	the "fore-offering"; the priest's, i.e., Brahman's portion of the sacrifice
Prasūti	a daughter of Manu and wife of Dakṣa
pravṛtti	the opposite of *nivṛtti*; activity
Prayāga	the site of the confluence of the rivers Ganges and Yamunā; the present city of Allahabad
preta	a ghost
Pṛśni	the "mottled," primordial, androgyne cow
Purāṇa(s)	eighteen main compendia of Hindu myths; dating in the main from the third to the fourteenth centuries of the present era

Purūravas	son of Budha and Ilā
Puruṣa	Cosmic Man; Cosmic Spirit; the ultimate principle
Pūṣan	the "nourishing" god who guards the paths of sun, stars, and man; the redeemer
Puṣkara	a *tīrtha* near Ajmer (Rajasthan)
Puṣya	an asterism; the eighth lunar mansion (*see* Tiṣya)
Rāgiṇī	"The Red"; a sister of Pārvatī
Rāhu	a demon (Daitya) who devours sun or moon, causing eclipses; the ascending node
rajas	*see guṇa*
rākṣasa	a type of demon one should "guard against"
Rāma	the seventh incarnation of Viṣṇu, at the end of the Tretā Yuga (*see* yuga)
Rasātala	one of the seven regions of the netherworld (*see pātāla*)
Rati	sexual pleasure; the wife of Kāma
Rātri	the goddess Night
Rāvaṇa	"Screaming"; a Rākṣasa, demon king of Ceylon
Ṛbhu(s)	the craftsmen among the gods; originally they were mortals
Ṛg Veda	the most ancient of the four Vedas; the most sacred book of the Hindus
ṛkṣa	a bear; the constellation of the Great Bear; the seven sages (ṛṣis)
Rohiṇī	the consort-daughter of Prajāpati: the antelope; the star Aldebaran
ṛṣi	a seer, sage
ṛta	right; divine law
Rudra	the Wild God
Sadāśiva	the "eternal Śiva"; the third category (*tattva*) in the ontology from transcendency into matter, the beginning awareness of *aham-idam* ("I am this"); of subject and object according to Kashmiri Śaivism
Sādhyas	a class of lesser celestials, the personified Vedic rites and hymns
Sadvidyā	"True Knowledge"; the fifth category (*tattva*) of *aham-idam* ("I am this"), without emphasis either on the subject (*aham*) or the object (*idam*)
Sadyojāta	the first of the five *pañca brahmāṇi, mantras* of Śiva
Sagara	"With Poison"; name of a king of the solar race

whose 60,000 sons were reduced to ashes by the sage Kapila

Śaiva — pertaining to Śiva

sakala — "with parts," contingent, in contrast to *niṣkala* (q.v.)

Śākambharī — a goddess (*yakṣiṇī*?) who subsisted on plants for a thousand years in the reckoning of the gods

Śākinī(s) — demonesses in the retinue of Durgā

śakti — (from *śak*, to be able); energy; the active power of deity regarded as the consort of a god. *Śakti-tattva*, the second category (*tattva*), the dynamic aspect of consciousness in Kashmiri Śaivism; *ādi śakti*, the primordial *śakti*; *kriyā śakti*, the ability to act; *parāśakti*, transcendental *śakti*

śāktika śarīra — the body of pure energy (cf. *liṅga śarīra*)

samādhi — the final stage in the practice of yoga in which the practitioner, in deep meditation, becomes one with the object of meditation and attains *mokṣa*

Śambhu — "Causing Happiness"; a name of Śiva

Sāṁkhya — one of the six ways of "looking"; (*darśana*), i.e., one of the six systems of Hindu philosophy. It enumerates the principles (*tattva*) of which Puruṣa and Prakṛti are the cause

Sāṁnihatya — a *tīrtha*

Saṁvartaka — a cloud of doomsday

sannyāsin — one who completely renounces the world; an ascetic

Sanaiścara — Saturn, "the Slow Moving"

Sandhyā — twilight; daughter of Brahmā, i.e., Uṣas, the "Dawn"

Sañjīvanī Vidyā — the spell for reviving the dead

Śaṅkara — "Conferring Happiness"; a name of Śiva. Cf. Śaṅkarācārya, philosopher and poet

Saptasārasvata — a *tīrtha*

Saptavadhri — a ṛṣi imprisoned in a tree and freed by the Aśvins

Śarabha — Śiva in the form of an animal symplegma victorious over Viṣṇu Narasiṁha, the man-lion

Saramā — the messenger bitch of Indra; mother of the celestial "dogs": sun, moon, and the Dog Star

Sarameya — the luminaries; the sons of Saramā

Sarasvatī — a river; wife of Brahmā

Śarva — Śiva, the cruel archer

Śāstā / Aiyanār — son of Śiva and Viṣṇu; a divinity of the Tamils of South India

sat — the existent

Śatarudriya	the hymn of a hundred praises of Rudra in the *Yajurveda*
Śatarūpā	"The Hundred Formed"; the first woman; daughter and wife of Brahmā
Satī	the Great Goddess in one of her forms; daughter of Dakṣa and wife of Śiva
sattva	*see guṇa*
Savitṛ	the impeller; the unifying power of the sun
Savitrī	wife of Brahmā
siddha	a perfected being characterized by supernatural faculties
siddhi	a superhuman power or faculty
Siddhīśvara	a name of Śiva, lord of *siddhis*
śikhara	the superstructure of the *garbhagṛha* (q.v.) of a North Indian temple
śirascakra	halo, nimbus
Sītā	"Furrow"; the wife of Rāma
Śiva	"The Kind"; in post-Vedic texts, Śiva or Rudra (q.v.) designates the Great God
Śivā	Pārvatī (q.v.) as wife of Śiva
Skanda	Kārttikeya (q.v.), a son of Śiva
smṛti	"what is remembered"; tradition
Soma	a drink; a plant; the elixir of immortality
Somāskandamūrti	the image of Śiva with Umā and Skanda
Śrī	the goddess Luck
śruti	"what is heard"; revelation
Sthāṇu	"the Pillar"; a name of Śiva
sthūla śarīra	the gross, i.e., physical body (in contrast to *liṅga śarīra*)
Suciśmatī	the mother of Śiva incarnated as Gṛhapati
sudarśana cakra	Viṣṇu's wheel emblem
Śukra	"The Seed," the planet Venus *see* Kāvya Uśanas
sūkṣma śarīra	the subtle body (*see liṅga śarīra*)
Śūlagava	the "spit ox" sacrifice
Sunda	a demon (Daitya)
Sundaramūrti	"The Beautiful Embodiment"; designation of Śiva as a bridegroom; also name of a South Indian Śaiva saint
śūnyatā	the absolute void, absolute nonexistence
Svahā	"The Oblation"; wife of Agni
svastika	a symbol of good luck, a cross, its arms of equal length extended to equal length at right angles
Svayambhū	"The Self-Existent"; a name of Brahmā
Svāyambhuva	name of the first Manu (q.v.)
Śveta	"White"; a devotee (*bhakta*) of Śiva

tad-ekam	"that one" (*see ābhu*)
Takṣaka	"Cutter"; a chief serpent in Pātāla (q.v.)
tamas	*see guṇa*
Tāṇḍava	Śiva's violent dance after the destruction of the world
Taṇḍi	a ṛṣi
tanmātra(s)	the subtle supersensible elements, i.e., the essence of sound, touch, form, flavor, and odor, perceived only through gross objects
Tantra	a body of religious texts and teaching that puts systematic emphasis on the identity of the absolute and the phenomenal world when filtered through the experience of *sādhanā* (spiritual exercise) (*see* A. Bharati, *The Tantric Tradition*, p. 18). The Tantras are said to have been revealed by Śiva
tapas	the "heat of asceticism" (O'Flaherty, *Asceticism*, p. 324)
tapasvinī	a woman practicing *tapas*
Tāraka	"Star"; a demon for whose destruction Kārttikeya (q.v.) was miraculously born
Tārakākṣa	"Star Eye"; a demon, son of Tāraka
Tarantuka	a *yakṣa* of Kurukṣetra
Tāravatī	wife of Candraśekhara (q.v.); an incarnation of Pārvatī
Tatpuruṣa	one of the five *mantras* (*pañcabrahmans*, q.v.) of Śiva
tattva	"thatness"; category, principle
tejas	fiery splendor, fiery energy
Tilottamā	an *apsaras*
timi	a fabulous fish
tīrtha	a ford, a holy place of pilgrimage
Tiṣya	a name of Rudra; an asterism, the eighth lunar mansion (*see* Puṣya)
Tretā Yuga	*see* yuga
Tripathagā	the River Ganges flowing in three realms of heaven, earth, and the netherworld
Tripura	the triple city of the demons
Tripurāntaka	Śiva, the Destroyer of the triple city
Trita	"The Third"; precursor of Indra. Trita Aptya, dwelling far off in the unknown
Tryambaka	"Having Three Mothers"; an epithet of Rudra
Tvaṣṭṛ	a primordial creator god *per artem* and *per generationem*; Father of Indra

ucchiṣṭa	the remainder
Umā-Maheśvara(mūrti)	an iconographical type of the image of Śiva together with Pārvatī, the goddess seated on Maheśvara's lap
Umā-Sahita Candraśekhara(mūrti)	the image of Śiva Candraśekhara together with Pārvatī; God and Goddess are standing
Upamanyu	son of Ṛṣi Vyāghrapādya (Tiger Foot), who heard from his mother of Śiva in his several forms; Upamanyu afterward recited to Kṛṣṇa the thousand names of Śiva
ūrdhvaliṅga	*see liṅga*
ūrdhvaretas	the semen held, ascending and absorbed within the body
Ūrva	the submarine fire
Uśanas	*see* Kāvya Uśanas
Uṣas	the Dawn; primordial cosmic dawn; daughter and consort of the Father
vāc	speech. *madhyamā vāc*, middle, i.e., subtle speech; *parā vāc*, casual speech; *paśyantī vāc*, "mental" speech (creative thought is "a seeing"); *vaikharī vāc*, articulate speech
Vaḍavā	a mare; the submarine fire
vaikharī vāc	*see vāc*
Vaivasvata Manvantara	*see manvantara*; Manu
vajra	thunderbolt; the weapon of Indra
Vālakhilya(s)	pygmy sages sprung from Prajāpati
Vāmadeva	one of the five *mantras* of Śiva (*see pañcabrahmans*)
Varāha	Viṣṇu's avatar as a boar
Varāha kalpa	the present kalpa (q.v.)
Vārāhī	*śakti* of Varāha; a Mātṛkā (q.v.)
Varuṇa	All-encompassing; (*see* Asura); god of truth and retribution, and cosmic order; king of gods; subsequently an Āditya; god of the waters
Vasanta	spring and its divine personification
vaṣaṭ	an exclamation, "May Agni conduct the offering to the gods," uttered by the priest (*hotṛ*) at the end of the sacrificial verse, when the oblation is thrown into the fire
Vasiṣṭha	one of the seven sages; his wife is Arundhatī
Vāstoṣpati	Lord of the *vāstu* (q.v.); Rudra
vāstu	site; sacrificial site; dwelling; house
vāstu-maṇḍala	the *maṇḍala* (q.v.) or ideational plan of a site or building

Vasu(s)	a group of eight deities dwelling on earth and in its fire, space, and wind; in the sky they are the sun, the stars, and the moon
vāta	*see vāyu*
vāyu	the wind and its god
Veda(s)	sacred knowledge, revelation (see *śruti*); the *Ṛg Veda*, the most ancient of the four *Vedas* (ca. 1200 B.C.), and the most sacred book of the Hindus. Each *Veda* (*Ṛg Veda, Sāma Veda, Yajur Veda*, and *Atharva Veda*) has its own *Brāhmaṇa* or *Brāhmaṇas*
Vidyunmālin	"Lightning-Wreathed"; a demon, son of Tāraka
vīṇā	the Indian lute
Vīṇādhara	"Holding a Lute"; Śiva as teacher of music
Vinayaka(s)	"Far leading"; designation of a class of gaṇas (q.v.) or *bhūtas*; also designates Gaṇeśa
Vindhya	A mountain range between northern India and the Deccan
Vīrabhadra	"Foremost Hero"; a fierce emanation of Śiva
Virāj	"Far Ruling"; the personification of the primordial plan or prefiguration of the cosmos
Vīraka	"Little Hero"; a gaṇa (q.v.)
Vīraśaiva	a sect (*see* Liṅgāyat)
Virinī	wife of Dakṣa
Viṣāpaharaṇamūrti	"Poison-Destroying"; the name of the image of Śiva having swallowed the poison *kālakūṭa* (q.v.)
Viṣṇu	"Striding Widely over the Peaks of the Earth"; the Preserver of the cosmos; the second god in the trinity with Brahmā the Creator and Śiva, who is assigned the role of the Destroyer
Viṣṇu-Hayagrīva	"Horse-Neck"; an avatar of Viṣṇu, half horse, half man or having a horse's head for the purpose of destroying a *rākṣasa* (q.v.) of the same name
viśuddha cakra	*cakra* (q.v.) of great purity; situated in the throat region, the fifth of the centers or "lotuses"
Viśvakarman	"The All Maker," i.e., Prajāpati or Tvaṣṭṛ as the creator *per artem*; subsequently the master architect of the gods
Viṣvaksena	"Army of the Universe"; the doorkeeper of Viṣṇu's mansion
Viśvarūpa	"Omniform"; a name of Tvaṣṭṛ (q.v.) and maker of all forms. As Tvaṣṭṛ-Savitṛ (q.v.), Viśvarūpa, he shapes, impels, and vivifies all form. Viśvarūpa is also Tvaṣṭṛ's son, a demon
Viśvedeva	belonging to all the gods; originally a class of nine gods

Vivasvat	"The Radiant"; represents all that is luminous in heaven and on earth
Vrātya	an ascetic belonging to an unorthodox order (cf. Ekavrātya)
Vṛndā	"The Sacred Basil Plant"; name of the wife of the demon king Jalandhara
Vṛṣabhavāhana	"Having the Bull for His Conveyance"; the name of an image of Śiva showing him and the bull
Vṛtra	"The Restrainer"; the cosmic serpent demon who had withheld the waters from flowing into creation; he offered resistance to Indra, who slew him
Vyākhyāna Dakṣiṇāmūrti	the image of Śiva giving exposition to the sciences (*see* Dakṣiṇāmūrti)
Yajur Veda	contains sacrificial formulae to be pronounced by the priest (*adhvaryu*) who performs the manual part of the sacrifice (Cf. A. Basham, *The Wonder That Was India*, p. 232; also s.v. *Veda*)
yakṣa	a sudden luminous apparition; a supernatural being attendant on Kubera; guardian of a territorial region
Yama	"Twin"; god of the dead
yoga	the method of reintegration by ascetic discipline of body, mind, and senses, leading through concentration and meditation to *samādhi* (q.v.), the condition in which total release, *mokṣa* (q.v.) is obtained from worldly existence
yoganidrā	a state, half contemplation and half sleep
yogi, yogin	a practitioner of yoga
yoginī	a female practitioner of yoga; the female partner in the fulfillment of a tantric rite
yoni	the female organ of generation
yuga	a world age; there are four world ages, called Kṛta, Tretā, Dvāpara, and Kali yuga. Their total duration is 4,320 years of the gods, i.e., a *mahāyuga* or one "great yuga" (q.v.). One thousand *mahāyugas* make a *kalpa* (q.v.). Duration and quality of the yugas decrease proportionately from the *Kṛta yuga*, the perfect age, to the *Kali yuga*

ABBREVIATIONS OF SERIAL PUBLICATIONS AND PERIODICALS

A	*Anthropos*
AA	*Artibus Asiae*
AARP	*Art and Archaeology Research Papers*
ABORI	*Annals of the Bhandarkar Oriental Research Institute*
AJP	*American Journal of Philology*
AKM	*Abhandlungen für die Kunde des Morgenlandes*
AO	*Acta Orientalia*
ArO	*Archiv Orientální*
Arts As	*Arts Asiatiques*
ĀSS	*Ānandāśrama Sanskrit Series*
BEFEO	*Bulletin de l'École Française d'Extrême Orient*
BI	*Bibliotheca Indica*
BSOAS	*Bulletin of the School of Oriental and African Studies*
ERE	*Encyclopedia of Religion and Ethics*
GOS	*Gaekwad's Oriental Series*
HOS	*Harvard Oriental Series*
HR	*History of Religions*
HTR	*Harvard Theological Review*
IA	*Indian Antiquary*
IC	*Indian Culture*
IHQ	*Indian Historical Quarterly*
JAOS	*Journal of the American Oriental Society*
JASB	*Journal of the Asiatic Society of Bengal*
JIH	*Journal of Indian History*
JISOA	*Journal of the Indian Society of Oriental Art*
JOIB	*Journal of the Oriental Institute, Baroda*
JRAS	*Journal of the Royal Asiatic Society*
JRASB	*Journal of the Royal Asiatic Society of Bengal*
KM	*Kāvyamālā*
KSS	*Kāśī Sanskrit Series*
RASI	*Report, Archaeological Survey of India*
RHR	*Revue d'Histoire de Religion*
SBE	*Sacred Books of the East*

SBH	*Sacred Books of the Hindus*
TSS	*Trivandrum Sanskrit Series*
WZKM	*Wiener Zeitschrift zur Kunde des Morgenlandes*
WZKSO	*Wiener Zeitschrift zur Kunde von Süd Ost Asien*
ZDMG	*Zeitschrift der Deutschen Morgenländischen Gesellschaft*

BIBLIOGRAPHY

Texts and Translations

AB — *Aitareya Brāhmaṇa*. Edited and translated by Martin Haug. 2 vols. Bombay, 1863.

———. *Rigveda Brāhmaṇas: The Aitareya and Kauṣītaki Brāhmaṇas of the Rigveda*. Translated by Arthur Berriedale Keith. *HOS* 25. Cambridge, Mass., 1920.

ĀGS — *Āśvalāyana Gṛhyasūtra*. Edited by Adolf Friedrich Stenzler. *AKM* 3.4. 1864.

———. Translated into German by Adolf Friedrich Stenzler. *AKM* 4.1. 1865.

AP — *Agni Purāṇa*. Edited by Āchārya Baladeva Upādhyāya. *KSS* 174. Vārāṇasī, 1966.

———. Translated by Manmatha Nath Dutt. 2 vols. Calcutta, 1903-1904.

ĀpŚS — *Āpastamba Śrautasūtra*. With the commentaries of Dhūrtaswāmi and Rāmāgnicit. Edited by Vidwan T. T. Srinivasagopalacharya. Vol. 2. Oriental Research Institute Publications, Sanskrit Series, 93. Mysore, 1953.

AUp — *Atharvaśira Upaniṣad*. In *The Śaiva Upaniṣads*. With the commentary of Śrī Upaniṣad-Brahma-Yogin. Edited by A. Mahadeva Sastri. Adyar Library Series 9. Reprint of 1st ed. Adyar, 1950.

———. *The Śaiva Upaniṣads*. Translated by T. R. Srinivasa Ayyangar and edited by G. Srinivasa Murti. Adyar Library Series 85. Adyar, 1953.

AV — *Atharva Veda Saṃhitā*. Edited by R. Roth and W. D. Whitney. Berlin, 1856.

———. With the commentary of Sāyaṇa. Edited by Shankar Pāndurang Pandit. 4 vols. Bombay, 1895-1898.

———. Translated by Ralph T. H. Griffith. 2 vols. Benares, 1895-1896.

———. Translated by William Dwight Whitney. 2 vols. *HOS* 7-8. Reprint of 1st ed. Delhi, 1962.

———. Translated by Maurice Bloomfield. *SBE* 42. Reprint of 1st ed. Delhi, 1964.

Note: Abbreviations given in the left-hand column indicate the particular edition used unless stated otherwise in the text; translations are cited by author and title.

BD	*Bṛhaddevatā* attributed to Śaunaka. Edited and translated by Arthur Anthony Macdonell. 2 vols. *HOS* 5-6. Reprint of 1st ed. Delhi, 1965.
BDP	*Bṛhaddharma Purāṇa*. Edited by Haraprasād Shāstri. *BI* 120. Calcutta, 1889.
BhP	*Bhāgavata Purāṇa*. With the commentary of Śrīdhara. Edited by Pāṇḍeya Rāmateja Śāstrī. Vārāṇasī, 1962.
	———. Translated by N. Raghunathan. 2 vols. Madras, 1976.
BhvP	*Bhaviṣya Purāṇa*. Bombay, 1910.
BNārP	*Bṛhannāradīya Purāṇa*. Edited by Hṛshīkeśa Śāstrī. *BI* 107. Calcutta, 1891.
BP	*Brahmāṇḍa Purāṇa*. Edited by J. L. Shastri. Delhi, 1973.
BrP	*Brahma Purāṇa*. Edited by Nārāyaṇa Āpṭe. *ĀSS* 28. Poona, 1895.
BṛUp	*Bṛhadāraṇyaka Upaniṣad*. With the commentary of Madhva. Edited and translated by Śriśa Chandra Vasu, with the assistance of Rāmākṣya Bhattāchārya. *SBH* 14. Reprint of 1st ed. New York, 1974.
	———. In *The Thirteen Principal Upanishads*. Translated by Robert Ernest Hume. Reprint of 2nd ed. Oxford, 1951.
BŚS	*Baudhāyana Śrautasūtra*. Edited by W. Caland. 3 vols. *BI* 163. Calcutta, 1904-1924.
BVP	*Brahmavaivarta Purāṇa*. Edited by Jīvānanda Vidyāsāgara. 2 vols. Calcutta, 1888.
	———. Translated by Rajendra Nath Sen. 2 parts. *SBH* 24. Allahabad, 1920-1922.
ChUp	*Chāndogya Upaniṣad*. With the commentary of Madhva. Edited and translated by Śriśa Chandra Vasu. *SBH* 3, *The Upaniṣads* Part II, Reprint of 1st ed. New York, 1974.
	———. Translated by R. E. Hume in *The Thirteen Principal Upanishads. See Bṛhadāraṇyaka Upaniṣad (BrUp).*
CUp	*Cūlikā Upaniṣad*. In *The Atharvaṇa Upaniṣads*. With the commentary of Nārāyaṇa. Edited by Rāmamaya Tarkaratna. BI 76. Calcutta, 1872.
DBhP	*Devībhāgavata Purāṇa*. With the commentary of the editor. Edited by Pāṇḍeya Rāmateja Śāstrī. 2nd ed. Vārāṇasī, 1965.
	———. Translated by Swami Vijñānananda. *SBH* 26. Reprint of 1st ed. New York, 1974.
DMUp	*Dakṣiṇāmūrti Upaniṣad*. In *The Śaiva Upaniṣads. See Artharvaśira Upaniṣad (AUp).*
DN	*Dīgha Nikāya*. Vol. II edited by T. W. Rhys Davids and J. Estlin Carpenter. London, 1903; Vol. III edited by J. Estlin Carpenter. London, 1911.
	———. *Dialogues of the Buddha*. Translated by T. W. and

C.A.F. Rhys Davids. Part III. *Sacred Books of the Buddhists* 4. London, 1921.

DStotra — *Dakṣiṇāmūrtistotra*. In *Subodhastotrasaṃgraha*. Edited by P. Pāṇḍuraṅga Gaṇeśa Gosvāmī. Poona, 1962.

GB — *Gopatha Brāhmaṇa*. Edited by Rajendra Lal Mitra. *BI* 69. Reprint of 1st ed. Delhi, 1972.

GGS — *Gobhilīya Gṛhyasūtra*. With a commentary by the editor. Edited by Chandrakānta Tarkālaṅkāra. 2 vols. *BI* 73. Calcutta, 1880.

GS — *Gorakṣa Saṃhitā*. Edited by Camanalāla Gautama. Bareli, 1974.

H — *Harivaṃśa*. Edited by Parashuram Lakshman Vaidya. Vol. 1, Text. Poona, 1969.

HGS — *Hiraṇyakeśi Gṛhyasūtra*. With extracts from the commentary of Mātṛdatta. Edited by J. Kirste. Vienna, 1889.

HV — *Haravijaya* of Rājānaka Ratnākara. With the commentary of Rājānaka Alaka. Edited by Durgāprasād and Kāśīnāth Pāṇḍurang Parab. *KM* 22. Bombay, 1890.

HYP — *Haṭhayogapradīpikā* of Svātmārāma. With two commentaries. Reprint of 1st ed. Bombay, 1962.

ĪPad — *Īśānaśivagurudevapaddhati* of Īśānaśivagurudevamiśra. Edited by T. Gaṇapati Śāstrī. 4 vols. *TSS* 69, 72, 77, 83. Trivandrum, 1920-1925.

Jātaka — *Jātaka*. With commentary. Edited by V. Fausboll. Vol. III. Reprint of 1st ed. London, 1963.

———. *The Jātakas or Stories of the Buddha's Birth*. Translated by E. B. Cowell. Reprint of 1895-1907 ed. 6 vols. in 3. London, 1973.

JB — *Jaiminīya Brāhmaṇa*. Edited by Raghu Vira and Lokesh Chandra. Sarasvatī-Vihāra Series 31. Nagpur, 1954.

JUp — *Jābāli Upaniṣad*. Translated by T. R. Srinivasa Ayyangar in *The Śaiva Upaniṣads. See Atharvaśira Upaniṣad (AUp).*

KāS — *Kāṭhaka Saṃhitā*. Edited by Leopold von Schroeder. 3 vols. Leipzig, 1900-1910.

KB — *Kauṣītaki Brāhmaṇa*. Edited by B. Lindner. Vol. 1, Text. Jena, 1887.

———. Translated by A. B. Keith. *See Aitareya Brāhmaṇa (AB).*

KBUp — *Kauṣītakibrāhmaṇa Upaniṣad*. With the commentary of Śaṅkarānanda. Edited and translated by E. B. Cowell. Chowkhamba Sanskrit Series 64. Vārāṇasī, 1968.

———. Translated by R. E. Hume in *The Thirteen Principal Upanishads. See Bṛhadāraṇyaka Upaniṣad (BrUp).*

KP — *Kālikā Purāṇa*. Edited by Srī Biśwanārāyan Śāstrī. Jaikrishnadas-Krishnadas Pracyavidya Granthamala 5. Vārāṇasī, 1972.

KS — *Kumārasaṃbhava* of Kālidāsa. With the commentary of Mallinātha. Edited and translated by M. R. Kale. 6th ed. Delhi, 1967.

KSS — *Kathāsaritsāgara*. Edited by Jagadīśalālaśāstrī (= J. L. Shastri). Delhi, 1970.

———. *The Ocean of Story*. Translated by C. H. Tawney and edited by N. M. Penzer. 10 vols. Reprint of 2nd ed. Delhi, 1968.

KŚS — *Kātyāyana Śrautasūtra*. With extracts from the commentaries of Karka and Yājñikadeva. Part III of the White Yajurveda. Edited by Albrecht Weber. London, 1859.

KUp — *Kena Upaniṣad*. In *Īśa, Kena, Kaṭha, Praśna, Muṇḍaka and Māṇḍukya Upaniṣads*. Edited by B. D. Basu. *SBH* 1. 2nd ed. Allahabad, 1911.

———. *Studies in the First Six Upanisads; and the Īśa and Kena Upaniṣads*. With the commentary of Saṅkara. Translated by Śriśa Chandra Vidyārnava. *SBH* 22.1. Reprint of 1st ed. New York, 1974.

———. Translated by R. E. Hume in *The Thirteen Principal Upanishads. See Bṛhadāraṇyaka Upaniṣad (BrUp).*

KūP — *Kūrma Purāṇa*. Edited by Anand Swarup Gupta. Varanasi, 1971.

———. Edited by Anand Swarup Gupta, translated by Ahibhushan Bhattacharya (Part I) and Satkari Mukherji, Virendra Kumar Varma, and Ganga Sagar Rai (Part II). Varanasi, 1972.

LP — *Liṅga Purāna*. Edited by Jīvānanda Vidyāsāgara. Calcutta, 1885.

———. Translated by "A Board of Scholars" and edited by J. L. Shastri. 2 vols. Ancient Indian Tradition and Mythology Series 5-6. Delhi, 1973.

M — *Mānava Dharmaśāstra*. Edited by Julius Jolly. London, 1887.

———. *The Laws of Manu*. Translated by Georg Bühler. *SBE* 25. Reprint of 1st ed. New York, 1969.

MāP — *Mārkaṇḍeya Purāṇa*. Translated by F. Eden Pargiter. *BI* 125. Calcutta, 1904.

MaUp — *Maitrī (Maitrāyaṇīya) Upaniṣad*. With the commentary of Rāmatīrtha. Edited and translated by E. B. Cowell. *BI* 42. London, 1870.

———. Translated by R. E. Hume in *The Thirteen Principal Upanishads. See Bṛhadāraṇyaka Upaniṣad (BrUp).*

MāUp — *Māṇḍukya Upaniṣad. See Kena Upaniṣad (KUp).*

MBh — *Mahābhārata*. Edited by Vishnu S. Sukthankar, et al. 19 vols. Poona, 1933-1959.

———. *Mahābhārata with Nīlakaṇṭha's Commentary*. Edited by Kṛṣṇa Śāstrī Gurjar. 7 vols. Bombay, 1888-1890.

———. Translated by J.A.B. van Buitenen. 3 vols (Books 1-5). Chicago, 1973-1978.

———. Translated by P. C. Roy. 13 vols. Calcutta, 1883-1896.

MD *Meghadūta* of Kālidāsa. Edited by Sushil Kumar De. 2nd ed. Delhi, 1970.

———. Translated by Leonard Nathan. Berkeley, 1976.

MP *Matsya Purāṇa*. Edited by Nārāyaṇa Āpṭe. *ĀSS* 54. Poona, 1907.

———. Translated by "A Taluqdar of Oudh." *SBH* 17. Allahabad, 1916.

MS *Maitrāyaṇī Saṃhitā*. Edited by Leopold von Schroeder. 4 vols. Leipzig, 1881-1886.

MŚS *Mānava Śrautasūtra*. Edited by Friedrich Knauer. 3 parts. St. Petersburg, 1900-1903.

———. Translated by Jeannette M. van Gelder. Śata-Piṭaka Series 27. New Delhi, 1963.

MSt *Mahimnastava. The Mahimnastava or Praise of Śiva's Greatness*. Translated and edited by W. Norman Brown. American Institute of Indian Studies Publication 1. Poona, 1965.

MUp *Muṇḍaka Upaniṣad*. Edited by Johannes Hertel. Indo-Iranische Quellen und Forschungen 3. Leipzig, 1924.

———. Translated by R. E. Hume in *The Thirteen Principal Upanishads. See Bṛhadāraṇyaka Upaniṣad (BṛUp).*

N *Nirukta. The Nighaṇṭu and the Nirukta*. Edited and translated by Lakshman Sarup. Reprint of 1st ed. Delhi, 1967.

NŚ *Nāṭyaśāstra* of Bharata Muni. Edited by Śivadatta and Kāśināth Pāṇḍurang Parab. *KM* 42. Bombay, 1894.

———. Translated by Manomohan Ghosh. Vol. I, 2nd ed. Calcutta, 1967; Vol. II, *BI* 272, Calcutta, 1961.

PBUp *Pañcabrahma Upaniṣad.* Translated by T.R.S. Ayyangar in *The Saiva Upaniṣads. See Atharvaśira Upaniṣad (AUp).*

PGS *Pāraskara Gṛhyasūtra*. Edited by Adolf Friedrich Stenzler. *AKM* 6.2. 1876.

———. Translated into German by Adolf Friedrich Stenzler. *AKM* 6.4. 1878.

PP *Padma Purāṇa.* Edited by Viśvanātha Nārāyaṇa Maṇḍalika. 4 vols. *ĀSS* extra Vol. 1. Poona, 1893-1894.

PS *Pāśupata Sūtras.* With the Pañcārthabhāṣya of Kauṇḍinya. Edited by R. Ananthakrishna Sastri. *TSS* 143. Trivandrum, 1940.

———. Translated by Haripada Chakraborti. Calcutta, 1970.

R *Rāmāyaṇa* of Valmīki. Edited by G. H. Bhatt, et al. Baroda, 1960-1975.

R — *Rāmāyaṇa* of Valmīki. Translated by Hari Prasad Shastri. 3 vols. 2nd ed. London, 1957-1962.

RHUp — *Rudrahṛdaya Upaniṣad*. In *The Śaiva Upaniṣads*. *See Atharvaśira Upaniṣad (AUp)*

RV — *Ṛg Veda Saṃhitā*. With the commentary of Sāyaṇa. Edited by F. Max Müller. 6 vols. London, 1849-1874.

———. Edited by Theodor Aufrecht. 2 vols. 3rd ed. Berlin, 1955.

———. Translated by Manmatha Nath Dutt. Calcutta, 1906.

———. *Der Rig Veda*. Translated by Karl Friedrich Geldner. 3 vols. *HOS* 33-35. Cambridge, Mass., 1951.

———. Translated into German by Hermann Grassmann. 2 vols. Leipzig, 1876-1877.

———. Translated by Ralph T. H. Griffith. Reprint of 2nd ed. Delhi, 1973.

———. Translated by H. H. Wilson. 7 vols. Reprint of 1st ed. Delhi, 1977.

ŚB — *Śatapatha Brāhmaṇa*. In the *Mādhyandina Śākhā*. With extracts from the commentaries of Sāyaṇa, Harisvāmin, and Dvivedagaṅgā (Part II of the White Yajurveda). Edited by Albrecht Weber. London, 1855.

———. Translated by Julius Eggeling. 5 vols. *SBE* 12, 26, 41, 43, 44. Reprint of 1st ed. Delhi, 1963.

SDS — *Sarvadarśanasaṃgraha* of Mādhava. Edited by Jīvānanda Vidyāsāgara. 2nd ed. Calcutta, 1889.

———. Translated by E. B. Cowell and A. E. Gough. 3rd ed. London, 1908.

ŚGS — *Śāṅkhāyana Gṛhyasūtra*. Edited by Hermann Oldenberg. Indische Studien 15. 1878, pp. 1-166.

SkP — *Skānda Purāṇa*. Bombay, 1910.

SP — *Saura Purāṇa*. Edited by Kaśinātha Śāstrī Lele. *ĀSS* 18. Poona, 1889.

———. Translated into German by Wilhelm Jahn. Strassburg, 1908.

ŚP — *Śiva Purāṇa*. Edited by Jvālāprasāda Miśra. Bombay, 1965.

———. Translated by "A Board of Scholars" and edited by J. L. Shastri. 4 vols. Ancient Indian Tradition and Mythology Series 1-4. Delhi, 1973.

ŚP, JS
ŚP, DhS — *Śiva Purāṇa*. With the commentary of Paṇḍita Rājarām Śāstrī. Containing the *Jñānasaṃhitā (JS)* and *Dharmasaṃhitā (DhS)*. Edited by Ganapata Krishnaji. Bombay, 1884.

ŚRa — *Śilparatna* of Śrī Kumāra. Edited by T. Ganapati Śāstrī (Vol. I) and K. Sāmbaśiva Śāstrī (Vol. II). *TSS* 75, 98. Trivandrum, 1922-1929.

SRSu *Samarāṅgaṇa Sūtradhāra* of Mahārājādhirāja Bhoja. Edited by T. Ganapati Śāstrī and Vasudevan Saran Agrawala. *GOS* 25. Baroda, 1966.

SS *Sūtasaṃhitā*. With the commentary of Mādhava. Edited by Vāsudeva Śāstri Paṇaśīkara. Part I. *ĀSS* 25. Poona, 1893.

ŚS *Śivasaṃhitā*. Edited and translated by Śriśa Chandra Vasu. 2nd ed. New Delhi, 1975.

SSi *Sūryasiddhānta*. With the exposition of Raṅganātha. Edited by Fitz Edward Hall. *BI* 25. Calcutta, 1859.

———. Translated by Ebenezer Burgess. *JAOS* 6 (1860), 141-498.

SŚp *Somaśambhupaddhati*. Translated into French and edited by Hélène Brunner-Lachaux. Part I. Publications de l'Institut Français d'Indologie 25. Pondicherry, 1963.

ŚŚS *Śāṅkhāyana Śrautasūtra*. With the commentaries of Varadattasuta Ānartīya and Govinda. Edited by Alfred Hillebrandt. 4 vols. *BI* 99. Calcutta, 1888-1899.

Subh *Subhāṣitaratnakoṣa* of Vidyākara. Edited by D. D. Kosambi and V. V. Gokhale. *HOS* 42. Cambridge, Mass., 1957.

———. Translated by Daniel H. H. Ingalls. *HOS* 44. Cambridge, Mass., 1965.

ŚUp *Śvetāśvatara Upaniṣad*. Edited and translated by Siddheshvar Varma Shastri. *SBH* 18.2. Reprint of 1st ed. New York, 1974.

———. Translated by R. E. Hume in *The Thirteen Principal Upanishads. See Bṛhadāraṇyaka Upaniṣad (BṛUp).*

Sānkhyakārika of Īśvara Krsna. Edited and translated by S. S. Suryanarayana Sastri. Madras University Philosophical Series 3. Reprint of 2nd ed. Madras, 1973.

Śāradātilaka of Laksmanadeśikendra. With the commentary Padārthādarśa of Raghavabhatta. Edited by Mukunda Jha Bakshi. *KSS* 107. Vārānasī, 1963.

Śivamānaspūjā. In *Subodhastotrasaṃgraha*. Edited by P. Pāṇḍuraṅga Gaṇeśa Gosvāmī. Poona, 1962.

TĀ *Taittirīya Āraṇyaka*. With the commentary of Sāyaṇa. Edited by Bābā Śāstrī Phaḍke. 2 parts. *ĀSS* 36. Poona, 1897-1898.

TB *Taittirīya Brāhmaṇa*. With the commentary of Sāyaṇa. Edited by Nārāyaṇa Śāstrī Goḍabole. 3 parts. *ĀSS* 37. Poona, 1898.

TmB *Tāṇḍya Mahābrāhmaṇa*. With the commentary of Sāyaṇa. Edited by Ānandachandra Vedāntavāgīśa. 2 vols. *BI* 62. Calcutta, 1870-1874.

TS *Taittirīya Saṃhitā*. Edited by Albrecht Weber. Indische Studien 11 (1871), 12 (1872).

———. Translated by Arthur Berriedale Keith. *HOS* 18-19. Cambridge, Mass., 1914.

TUp — *Taittirīya Upaniṣad*. With the commentaries of Ānandagiri and Śaṅkarānanda. Edited by Vāmanaśāstrī Islāmpurkar. *ĀSS* 12. 2nd ed. Poona, 1897.

———. Translated by R. E. Hume in *The Thirteen Principal Upanishads*. *See Bṛhadāraṇyaka Upaniṣad (BṛUp)*.

VāP — *Vāyu Purāṇa*. Edited by Nārāyaṇa Āpṭe. *ASS* 49. Poona, 1905.

VDhP — *Viṣṇudharmottara Purāṇa*. Third Khaṇḍa. Edited by Priyabola Shah. *GOS* CXXX. Baroda, 1958.

———. Part III. Translated by Stella Kramrisch. 2nd ed. Calcutta, 1928.

VmP
VmP, SM — *Vāmana Purāṇa*. Containing the *Saromāhātmya*. Edited by Anand Swarup Gupta and translated by Satyamsu Mohan Mukhopadhyaya, Ahibhushan Bhattacharya, N. C. Nath, and V. K. Verma. Vārāṇāsī, 1968.

VP — *Viṣṇu Purāṇa*. Edited by Śrīmunilāla Gupta. Gorakhpur, 1967.

———. Translated by H. H. Wilson. Reprint of 1st ed. Calcutta, 1961.

VrP — *Varāha Purāṇa*. Bombay, 1902.

VS — *Vājasaneyi Saṃhitā* in the *Mādhyandina* and the *Kāṇva Śākhā*. With the commentary of Mahīdhara (Part I of the White Yajurveda). Edited by Albrecht Weber. London, 1852.

VVi — *Vāstuvidyā*. With the commentary of M. R. Ry. K. Mahādeva Śāstrī. Edited by L. A. Ravi Varmā. *TSS* 142. Trivandrum, 1940.

Yāj — *Yājñavalkya Dharmaśāstra*. Edited and translated into German by Adolf Friedrich Stenzler. London, 1849.

YUp — *Yogatattva Upaniṣad*. In *The Yoga Upanisads*. With the commentary of Śrī Upaniṣad Brahmayogin. Edited by A. Mahadeva Sastri. Adyar Library Series 6. Reprint of 1st ed. Adyar, 1968.

Secondary Sources

Adiceam, Marguerite E. "De quelques images d'Aiya Nār-Śāstā." *Arts As* 34 (1978): 87-104.

———. *Contribution à l'étude d'Aiyanār-Śāstā*. Publications de l'Institut Français d'Indologie, No. 32. Pondicherry, 1967.

———. "Les images de Śiva dans l'Inde du Sud: II; Bhairava." *Arts As*, 11 (1965): 23-44. "III, Bhikṣāṭana," "IV, Kaṇkāla Mūrti." *Arts As* 12 (1965): 83-112. "V, Harihara." *Arts As* 13 (1966): 83-98. "VI, Ardhanārīśvara." *Arts As* 17 (1968): 143-72. "VII, Vṛṣavāhanamūrti." *Arts As* 19 (1969): 85-106. "VIII, Kevala," "IX, Umāsahita," "X, Āliṅgana-Candraśekharamūrti." *Arts As* 21 (1970): 41-70. "XI, Pāśupatamūrti." *Arts As* 24 (1971): 23-50. "XII, Sukhāsana," "XIII, Umāsahitasukhāsana," "XIV, Umāmaāheśvaramūrti." *Arts As* 28 (1973): 63-101. "XV, Gaṅgādharamūrti." *Arts As* 32 (1976): 99-138.

Agrawala, Vasudeva Sharana. *India as Known to Pāṇini*. Lucknow, 1953.

———. *Matsya Purāṇa—A Study*. Vārāṇasī, 1963.

———. *Śiva Mahādeva*. Vārāṇasī, 1966.

Apte, V. M. "From the Rigvedic Rudra to Purāṇic Śiva." *Saugor University Journal* 6 (1957): 81-85.

Apte, V. S. *The Practical Sanskrit-English Dictionary*. Poona, Vol. 1, 1957; Vol. 2, 1958; Vol. 3, 1959.

Arbman, Ernst. *Rudra*. Untersuchungen zum Altindischen Glauben und Kultus. Uppsala, 1922.

Archer, W. G. *Indian Paintings from the Panjab Hills*. Vols. 1 and 2. London, 1973.

———. *The Vertical Man*. London, 1947.

Ashton, Sir Leigh, ed. *The Art of India and Pakistan*. London, 1949.

Banerjea, Jitendra Nath. *The Development of Hindu Iconography*. 2nd ed., Calcutta, 1956.

———. "The Phallic Emblem in Ancient and Medieval India." *JISOA* 3 (June 1935): 36-44.

Banerjee, R. D. *The Eastern Indian School of Medieval Sculpture. RASI*, New Imperial Series 47. Delhi, 1933.

Barrett, Douglas. *Early Cola Bronzes*. Bombay, 1965.

Basham, A. L. *The Wonder That Was India*. New York, 1954.

Bergaigne, Abel. *La Religion védique*. 4 vols. Paris. 1963.

Bhandarkar, R. G. *Vaiṣṇavism, Śaivism and Minor Religious Systems*. Reprint of 1913 ed., Vārāṇasī, 1965.

Bharati, Agehananda. *The Tantric Tradition*. London, 1970.

Bhattacharji, S. *The Indian Theogony*. Cambridge, 1970.

———. "Rudra from the Vedas to the Mahābhārata." *ABORI* 41 (1960): 85-128.

Bhave, S. S. *The Soma Hymns of the Ṛg Veda*. 3 vols. Baroda, 1957, 1960, 1962.

Biardeau, Madeleine. "Études de mythologie hindoue, III, IV, V." *BEFEO*, 58 (1971), 63 (1976), 65 (1978).

Biswas, D. K. "Sūrya and Śiva." *IHQ* 24 (1948): 142-47.

Blair, C. *Heat in the Rig Veda and Atharva Veda*. American Oriental Society, Publication No. 45. Cambridge, Mass., 1961.

Bloomfield, Maurice. "Contributions to the Interpretation of the Veda." *AJP* 12 (1891): 414-43.

———. "On Jalāṣah, Jalāṣabheṣajah, Jalāṣam and Jālāṣam." *AJP* 12 (1891): 425-29.

———. "The Two Dogs of Yama in a New Role." *JAOS* 15 (1893): 163-72.

———. *A Vedic Concordance. HOS* 10. Reprint, Delhi, 1964.

Böhtlingk, O., and R. Roth. *Sanskrit Wörterbuch*. 7 vols. St. Petersburg, 1855-1875.

Boetzelaer, J. M. van, tr. Sureśvara's *Taittirīyopaniṣadbhāṣyavārtikam*. Leiden, 1971.

Boner, Alice, and Sadāśiva Rath Śarmā, with Rajendra Prasād Dās. *New Light on the Sun Temple at Koṇārka*. Vārāṇasī, 1972.
Brown, W. Norman. "Proselyting the Asuras." *JAOS* 39 (1919): 100-103.
———. "The Rigvedic Equivalent for Hell." *JAOS* 61 (1941): 76-80.
———. "The Sources and Nature of *puruṣa* in the Puruṣasūkta (*Rigveda* 10.91)." *JAOS* 51 (1931): 108-18.
———. "Theories of Creation in the Rig Veda." *JAOS* 85 (1965): 23-34.
Bühler, Georg. *The Sacred Laws of the Aryas as Taught in the Schools of Apastamba, Gautama, Vasiṣṭha and Baudhāyana. SBE* 2, 14. Delhi. 1965.
Butterworth, E.A.S. *The Tree at the Navel of the Earth*. Berlin, 1970.
Chandra, Pramod. *A Guide to the Elephanta Caves*. Bombay, 1957.
Charpentier, Jarl. "Über Rudra-Śiva." *WZKM* 23 (1909): 151-79.
Chatham, Doris C. "Stylistic Sources and Relationships of the Kailāsa Temple in Ellora." Ph.D. dissertation, University of California, Berkeley, 1977.
Chattopadhyaya, Sudhakar. *The Evolution of Theistic Sects in Ancient India*. Calcutta, 1962.
Chaudhuri, N. "Liṅga Worship in the Mahābhārata." *IHQ* 24 (1948): 269-92.
Chaudhuri, Nanimadhab. "Rudra-Śiva as an Agricultural Deity." *IHQ* 15 (1939): 183-96.
Choudhury, R. *Vrātyas in Ancient India*. Vārāṇasī, 1964.
Church, C. D. "The Myth of the Four Yugas in the Sanskrit Purāṇas." *Purāṇa* 16:1 (1974): 5-25.
———. "The Purāṇic Myth of the Four Yugas." *Purāṇa* 13:2 (1971): 151-59.
Churchill, J. *A Collection of Voyages and Travels*. London, 1752.
Clark, T. W. "Evolution of Hinduism in Medieval Bengali Literature: Śiva, Caṇḍī, Manasā." *BSOAS* 17 (1955): 503-18.
Coomaraswamy, A. K. "Angel and Titan, an Essay on Vedic Ontology." *JAOS* 55 (1935), 373-419.
———. *Coomaraswamy*. I, *Selected Papers: Traditional Art and Symbolism*, edited by R. Lipsey; II, *Selected Papers: Metaphysics*, edited by R. Lipsey; III, *His Life and Work*, by R. Lipsey. Bollingen Series LXXXIX. Princeton, 1977.
———. *The Dance of Śiva*. New York, 1953.
———. *The Darker Side of Dawn*. Smithsonian Miscellaneous Publications 94. Washingotn, D.C., 1935.
———. *Elements of Buddhist Iconography*. Cambridge, Mass., 1935.
———. *History of Indian and Indonesian Art*. Reprint of 1927 ed., New York, 1965.
———. "The Mystery of Mahādeva." *Indian Arts and Letters* 6 (1932), 10-13.
———. *Time and Eternity*. *AA* Monograph Series 8. Ascona, 1947.
———. *Yakṣas*. 2 vols. Washington, D.C., 1928, 1931.
———. "The Yakṣa of the Vedas and Upaniṣads." *Quarterly Journal of the Mythical Society* 28 (1938).
Crooke, William. "Folktales from Northern India." *IA* 25 (1906), 142-50.
———. *The Popular Religion and Folklore of North India*. 2 vols. 2nd ed., London, 1896.

Curtis, J.W.V. *Motivations of Temple Architecture in Śaiva Siddhānta*. Madras, n.d.

Daly, C. D. *Hindu Mythologie und Kastrations-komplex, eine psycho-analytische Studie*. Reprint from *Imago* 13 (1927). Vienna, 1927.

Dandekar, R. N. "Aspects of Agni Mythology." *JOIB* 11 (1961-1962), 347-70.

———. "Rudra in the Veda." *Journal of the University of Poona*, 1953, pp. 94-148.

Dange, S. A. *Legends in the Mahābhārata*. New Delhi, 1969.

———. "Prajāpati and His Daughter." *Purāṇa* 5:1 (1963), 39-46.

Daniélou, Alain. *Hindu Polytheism*. Bollingen Series LXXIII. New York, 1964.

Darian, S. G. *The Ganges in Myth and History*. Honolulu, 1978.

Dasgupta, S. N. *A History of Indian Philosophy*. 5 vols. Cambridge, 1922-1955.

Deppert, Joachim. *Rudras Geburt: Systematische Untersuchungen zum Inzest in der Mythologie der Brāhmaṇas*. Wiesbaden, 1977.

Desai, Devangana. *Erotic Sculpture in India: A Socio-Cultural Study*. New Delhi, 1970.

Dessigane, R., and P. Z. Pattabiramin. *La légende de Skanda selon le Kāñchipurāṇam tamoul et l'iconographie*. Publication de l'Institut Français d'Indologie 31. Pondicherry, 1967.

——— and J. Filliozat. *La légende des jeux de Çiva á Madurai (Hālāsyamāhātmya)*. Publication de l'Institut Français d'Indologie 19. 2 vols. Pondicherry, 1960.

———, P. Z. Pattabiramin, and J. Filliozat. *Les légendes çivaites de Kāñcipuram*. Publications de l'Institut Français d'Indologie 27. Pondicherry, 1964.

Deussen, P. *Sechzig Upaniṣads des Veda*. Reprint, Darmstadt, 1964.

Devanandan, P. D. *The Concept of Māyā*. London, 1950.

Devasenapathi, V. A. *Śaiva Siddhānta*. Madras University Philosophical Series 7. Reprint of 1960 ed. Madras, 1966.

Devasthali, G. V. *Religion and Mythology of the Brāhmaṇas*. Poona, 1965.

Dhaky, M. A. "The 'Ākāśaliṅga' Finial," *AA* 36:4 (1974), 307-15.

Dhavamony, Mariasusai. *Love of God, According to Śaiva Siddhānta*. Oxford, 1971.

Diehl, Carl Gustav. *Instrument and Purpose: Studies on Rites and Rituals in South India*. Lund, 1956.

Dikshitar, V. R. Ramachandra. *The Matsya Purāṇa: A Study*. Madras, 1935.

———. *The Purāṇa Index*. 3 vols. Madras, Vol. 1, 1951; Vol. II, 1952; Vol. III, 1955.

Dimmitt, Cornelia, and J.A.B. van Buitenen, eds. *Classical Hindu Mythology*. Philadelphia, 1978.

Divanji, R. C. "The Maheśvara Cult and Its Offshoots." *JASB* 30: 2 (1955).

Douglas, Mary. "The Meaning of Myth, with Special Reference to 'La geste d'Asdiwal.' " In E. R. Leach, *The Structural Study of Myth and Totemism*. Association of Social Anthropologists, Monograph 5. London, 1967, pp. 49-70.

Dowson, J. *A Classical Dictionary of Hindu Mythology and Religion*. 6th ed. London, 1928.

Dubois, Abbé J. A. *Hindu Manners, Customs and Ceremonies*. Translated and edited by Henry K. Beauchamp. London, 1816; 3rd ed., Oxford, 1959.

Dumézil, G. *Mythe et Épopée*. Paris, 1968.

Dumont, Louis. "A Structural Definition of a Folk Deity of Tamil Nad: Aiyanar, the Lord." *Contributions to Indian Sociology* 3 (July 1959), 75-87.

———. "World Renunciation in Indian Religion." *Contributions to Indian Sociology* 4 (April 1960), 33-62.

Dumont, Paul E. *L'Aśvamedha: description du sacrifice du cheval*. Paris, 1927.

Durkheim, Emil. *Les formes élémentaires de la vie religieuse*. 2nd ed., Paris, 1925.

Edgerton, F. "The Fountain of Youth." *JAOS* 26 (1905), 1-67.

———. "The Meaning of Sāṅkhya and Yoga." *AJP* 45 (1924), 1-46.

Eliade, Mircea. *Images and Symbols*. New York, 1952.

———. *Mephistopheles and the Androgyne: Studies in Religious Myth and Symbol*. New York, 1965.

———. "Methodological Remarks on the Study of Religious Symbolism." In *HR. Essays in Methodology*, edited by Mircea Eliade and J. M. Kitagawa. Chicago, 1959, pp. 86-107.

———. *Myth and Reality*. Chicago, 1964.

———. *The Sacred and the Profane: The Nature of Religion*. New York, 1959.

———. "Spirit, Light, and Seed." *HR* 11:1 (1971), 1-30.

———. *Traité d'histoire des religions*. Paris, 1953.

———. *Yoga: Immortality and Freedom*. Translated from the French by Willard R. Trask. Bollingen Series LVI. New York, 1958.

Eliot, Sir Charles. *Hinduism and Buddhism*. 3 vols. London, 1921.

Fairservis, W. A., Jr. *Excavations at Allahdino*. Papers of the Allahdino Expedition 1. New York, 1976.

———. *The Roots of Ancient India*. 2nd ed., New York, 1971.

Farquhar, John Nicol. *An Outline of the Religious Literature of India*. Oxford, 1920.

Fausboll, Viggo. *Indian Mythology in Outline, According to the Mahābhārata*. London, 1903.

———, ed. *The Jātaka, Together with its Commentary, Being Tales of the Anterior Births of Gotama Buddha*. Vol. 3. 1st ed. 1883; London, 1963.

Fergusson, James. *Tree and Serpent Worship*. London, 1868.

Filliozat, Jean. "Les images de Śiva dans l'Inde de Sud: I, L'image de l'origine du liṅga (liṅgodbhavamūrti)." *Arts As* 8 (1961), 43-56.

Frazer, R. W. "Śaivism." *ERE* 11. New York, 1951, 91-96.

Frederic, Louis. *The Art of India*. New York, n.d.

Gangadharan, N. "Garuḍa Purāṇa: A Study." *Purāṇa* 13 (July 1971), 105-67.

Geldner, Karl F. *Zur Kosmogonie des Rigveda mit besonderer Berücksichtigung des Liedes 10, 129*. Marburg, 1908.

Getty, Alice. *Gaṇeśa: A Monograph on the Elephant-faced God*. Oxford, 1936.

Ghosh, A. "Śiva: His Pre-Aryan Origin." *IC* 2 (1936), 763-67.

Ghosh, Oroon. *The Dance of Shiva and Other Tales from India*. New York, 1965.

Ghurye, G. S. *Indian Sādhus*. Bombay, 1953.

Goldman, Robert. *Myth and Meta Myth: The Bhārgava Cycle of the Mahābhārata*. New York, 1976.
Gonda, Jan. *Change and Continuity in Indian Religion*. The Hague, 1965.
———. "Einige Mitteilungen über das Altjavanische Brahmāṇḍa Purāṇa." *AO* 11 (1933), 218-59.
———. *Notes on Brahman*. Utrecht, 1950.
———. *Die Religionen Indiens*. 3 vols. Stuttgart, 1963.
Gopinatha Rao, T. A. *Elements of Hindu Iconography*. 2 vols., 4 parts. Reprint of 1914 ed. New York, 1968.
Grassmann, Hermann. *Wörterbuch zum Rigveda*. Wiesbaden, 1964.
Gregoire, H.; R. Goossens; and M. Mathieu. *Asklepios, Apollon Smintheus et Rudra*. Brussels, 1949.
Grousset, René. *The Civilization of India*. Translated by Catherine Alison Phillips. New York, 1931.
Gubernatis, A. de. *Zoological Mythology*. 2 vols. London, 1872.
Gupta, Anand Swarup. "Eulogy of Paśupati Śiva." *Purāṇa* 17:2 (1975), 100-105.
Gupta, Shakti M. *Plant Myths and Traditions in India*. Leiden, 1971.
Hackin, J. *Asiatic Mythology*. London, 1932.
Harle, J. C. *Gupta Sculpture: Indian Sculpture of the Fourth to the Sixth Centuries, A.D.* Oxford, 1974.
Hartland, Edwin Sidney. *Primitive Paternity: The Myth of Supernatural Birth in Relation to the History of the Family*. London, 1909.
Hastings, James, ed. *Encyclopedia of Religion and Ethics*. 13 vols. Edinburgh, 1908-1926.
Hauer, Jakob Wilhelm. *Die Anfänge der Yogapraxis im Alten Indien*. Berlin, 1932.
———. *Der Yoga als Heilsweg nach den indischen Quellen dargestellt*. Stuttgart, 1932.
———. *Der Vrātya: Untersuchungen über die nichtbrahmanische Religion Altindiens*. Stuttgart, 1927.
Hazra, R. C. *Studies in the Purāṇic Records on Hindu Rites and Customs*. 2nd ed. Delhi, 1975.
———. *Studies in the Upapurāṇas*. I, *Saura and Vaiṣṇava Upapurāṇas;* II, *Śākta and Non-Sectarian Upapurāṇas*. Calcutta Sanskrit College Research Series 2 and 22. Calcutta, 1958, 1963.
Heesterman, J. C. "Brahmin, Ritual and Renouncer." *WZKSO* 8 (1964), 1-31.
———. "The Case of the Severed Head." *WZKSO* 11 (1967), 22-43.
———. "Vrātya and Sacrifice." *IIJ* 6 (1962), 1-37.
Henry, V. *La magie dans l'Inde antique*. Paris, 1909.
Hillebrandt, A. *Ritual-Literatur, Vedische Opfer und Zauber*. Grundriss der Indo-Arischen Philologie und Altertumskunde 3: 2. Strassburg, 1897.
———. *Vedische Mythologie*. 2 vols. Breslau, 1927.
Hiltebeitel, A. "The Indus Valley 'Proto-Śiva' Reexamined through Reflections on the Goddess, the Buffalo and the Symbolism of *Vāhanas*." *A* 73 (1978), 767-97.

Hiltebeitel, A. *The Ritual of Battle: Krishna in the Mahābhārata*. Ithaca, 1976.

Hirananda Sastri and Ratan Parimoo. *A Guide to Elephanta: A New Light on its Significance in Indian Sculpture.*. Reprint of 1934 ed. by Hiranand Sastri. New Delhi, 1978.

Hoens, Dirk Jan. *Śānti: A Contribution to Ancient Indian Religious Terminology*. The Hague, 1951.

Hopkins, Edward Washburn. *Epic Mythology*. Encyclopedia of Indo-Aryan Research, edited by Georg Bühler. 3:I.B. Strassbourg, 1951.

———. "The Fountain of Youth." *JAOS* 26 (1905), 1-67.

———. *The Religions of India*. Boston, 1895.

Hume, Robert Ernest, tr. *The Thirteen Principal Upanishads*. Reprint of 1931 revised ed. Madras, 1951.

Huntington, R. "Avatārs and Yugas: Purāṇic Cosmology." *Purāṇa* 6 (1964), 7-39.

Ingalls, Daniel H. H., tr. *An Anthology of Sanskrit Court Poetry; Vidyākara's Subhāṣitaratnakoṣa. HOS* 44. Cambridge, Mass., 1965.

———. "Cynics and Pāśupatas: The Seeking of Dishonor." *HTR* 55 (1962), 281-98.

———. "Dharma and Moksha." *Philosophy East and West* 7 (April-July 1957), 41-48.

Jacobi, Hermann, "Brahmanism." *ERE* 2:799-813.

———. "Nochmals das Alter des Veda." *ZDMG* 50 (1896), 69-83.

———. "On the Ambiguity of Vedic Culture." *JRAS*, 1909, pp. 721-26.

———. "Der Vedische Kalender und das Alter des Veda." *ZDMG* 49 (1895), 218-30.

Jahn, Wilhelm. "Die Legende vom Devadāruvana." *ZDMG* 69 (1915), 529-57; 70 (1916), 301-20; 71 (1917), 167-208.

Jesudasan, C., and Hepzibah Jesudasan. *A History of Tamil Literature*. Calcutta, 1961.

Jolly, Julius. "Expiation and Atonement (Hindu)." *ERE* 5:659.

Joshi, N. P. *Catalogue of the Brahmanical Sculptures in the State Museum, Lucknow*. Part I. Lucknow, 1972.

———. "A Unique Figure of Śiva from Musanagar." *Bulletin of Museums and Archaeology in Uttar Pradesh*. Vol. 3. Lucknow, 1969.

Kane, P. V. *History of Dharmaśāstra*. 5 vols. 2nd ed. Poona, 1968-1975.

Kantawala, S. G. *Cultural History of the Matsya Purāṇa*. Baroda, 1964.

Keith, Arthur Berriedale. *Indian Mythology*. Vol. 6, Part I, of *The Mythology of All Races*, edited by L. H. Grey. Boston, 1917.

———. *The Religion and Philosophy of the Vedas and Upanishads. HOS* 31-32. Cambridge, Mass., 1925.

———. *The Sāṁkhya System.* Calcutta and London, 1918.

———. "The Saturnalia and the Mahāvrata." *JRAS* 35 (1915), 133-38.

———. "Some Modern Theories of Religion and the Veda." *JRAS* 29 (1907), 929-49.

Kirfel, Willibald. *Die fünf Elemente, insbesondere Wasser und Feuer*. Beiträge zur Sprach-und Kulturgeschichte des Orients 4. Walldorf-Hessen, 1951.

———. "Śiva und Dionysos." *Zeitschrift für Ethnologie* 78 (1953), 83-90.

———. *Die Kosmographie der Inder*. Bonn and Leipzig, 1920.

Kittel, F. *Über den Ursprung des Lingakultus in Indien*. Mangalore, 1876.

Knipe, D. M. *In the Image of Fire*. Delhi, 1975.

Kosambi, D. D. *An Introduction to the Study of Indian History*. Bombay, 1956.

Kramrisch, Stella. *The Art of India*. London, 1965.

———. *The Hindu Temple*. 2 vols. Reprint of Calcutta 1946 ed. Delhi, 1977.

———. "The Image of Mahādeva in the Cave Temple on Elephanta Island." *Ancient India* 2 (1946), 4-8.

———. "The Indian Great Goddess." *HR* 14 (1975), 235-65.

———. *Indian Sculpture*. London, 1933.

———. "Liṅga." *Beiträge zur Indienforschung*. Ernst Waldschmidt zum 80, Geburtstag Gewidmet, Museum für Indische Kunst. Berlin, 1977.

———. "The Mahāvīra Vessel and the Plant Pūtika." *JAOS* 95 (April-June 1975), 222-35.

———. "Pūṣan." *JAOS* 81 (1961), 104-22.

———. "Śiva the Archer." *Deutsche Indologentagung 1971*. Wiesbaden, 1973, pp. 140-50.

———. *A Survey of Painting in the Deccan*. London, 1937.

Krishna Shastri, H. *South Indian Images of Gods and Goddesses*. Madras, 1916.

Kuhn, Adalbert, *Mythologische Studien*. I, *Die Herabkunft des Feuers und des Göttertranks*. Gütersloh, 1886.

Kulke, H. *Cidambaramāhātmya*. Wiesbaden, 1970.

Kumar, Krishna. "A Dhyāna-Yoga Maheśamūrti, and Some Reflections on the Iconography of the Maheśamūrti-Images." *AA* 37:1/2 (1975), 105-20.

Lal, Kanwar. *The Cult of Desire: An Interpretation of the Erotic Sculpture of India*. 2nd ed. London, 1967.

Leach, Edmund R. "Genesis as Myth." In *Genesis as Myth and Other Essays*. London, 1969, pp. 7-23.

———. *The Structural Study of Myth and Totemism*. Association of Social Anthropologists Monograph 5. London, 1967.

Leeson, Francis. *Kāma Shilpa: A Study of Indian Sculptures Depicting Love in Action*. Bombay, 1962.

Leeuw, Gerardus Van der. *Religion in Essence and Manifestations*. Reprint of London, 1938 ed. New York, 1963.

Lévi, Sylvain. *La doctrine du sacrifice dans les Brāhmaṇas*. 2nd ed. Bibliothèque de l'Ecole des Hautes Études, Sciences Religieuses 73. Paris, 1966.

Lévi-Strauss, Claude. *The Raw and the Cooked, Introduction to a Science of Mythology: 1*. New York, 1969.

———. *Structural Anthopology*. New York, 1963.

———. "The Structural Study of Myth." In T. A. Sebeok, ed., *Myth: A Symposium*. Bloomington, 1958, pp. 81-106.

Leyden, R. v. "The Buddhist Cave at Lonad." *JISOA* 15 (1947), pp. 84-88.

Liebert, Goesta. *Iconographic Dictionary of the Indian Religions*. Leiden, 1976.

Lippe, A. de. *Indian Medieval Sculpture*. Oxford, 1978.

Lommel, H. *Altbrahmanische Legenden*. Stuttgart, 1964.

Lommel, H. "Soma." *Forschungen und Fortschritte*, 11:2 (1935), 21.

———, tr. *Die Yäšt's des Awesta*. Quellen der Religions-geschichte 6, 15. Göttingen, 1927.

Long, J. G. "Life Out of Death: A Structural Analysis of the Myth of the Churning of the Ocean of Milk." In Bardwell Smith, ed., *Hinduism: New Essays in the History of Religion*. Leiden, 1975.

———. "Śiva as Promulgator of Traditional Learning and Patron Deity of the Fine Arts." *ABORI* 52 (1972), 67-80.

———. "Visions of Terror and Bliss." Ph.D. dissertation, University of Chicago, 1970.

Lorenzen, David N. *The Kāpālikas and Kālāmukhas: Two Lost Śaivite Sects*. Berkeley, 1972.

Lüders, Heinrich. *Varuṇa*. 2 vols. Göttingen, 1951, 1959.

Macdonnell, Arthur Anthony. *Hymns from the Rigveda (Selected and Metrically Translated)*. Reprint, New Delhi, 1966.

———. "Mythological Studies in the Rig Veda." *JRAS* 35 (1893), 419-96.

———. *Vedic Mythology*. Grundriss der Indo-Arischen Philologie und Altertumskunde 3:1A. Strasbourg, 1897.

———, with Arthur Berriedale Keith. *Vedic Index of Names and Subjects*. 2 vols. Reprint of 1912 ed., Vārāṇasī, 1967.

Machek, V. "Origin of the Gods Rudra and Pūṣan." *ArO* 22 (1954), 544-62.

Mackay, E.J.H. *Further Excavations at Mohenjo-Daro*. New Delhi, 1937.

MacMunn, Sir George. *The Religions and Hidden Cults of India*. London, 1931.

Mahadevan, T.M.P. *Outlines of Hinduism*. Bombay, 1956.

Majumdar, R. C., and A. D. Pusalker, eds. *History and Culture of the Indian People*. 10 vols. London and Bombay, 1951-1969.

Mallman, M. Th. de. *Les enseignements iconographiques de l'Agni Purāṇa*. Paris, 1965.

Marshall, Sir John. *Mohenjo-Daro and the Indus Civilization*. 3 vols. London, 1931.

Martin, E. Osborn. *The Gods of India*. London, 1913.

Matthews, G. *Sivanana-Bodham*. Oxford, 1948.

Maxwell, T. S. "Transformation Aspects of Hindu Myth and Iconology: Viśvarūpa." *AARP* 4 (December 1973), 59-79.

Mayrhofer, M. *Concise Etymological Sanskrit Dictionary*. 3 vols. Heidelberg, 1953, 1963, 1976.

———. "Der Gottesname Rudra." *ZDMG* 103 (1953), 140-50.

Mazumdar, B. C. "Phallus Worship in the Mahābhārata." *JRAS* 27 (1907), 337-39.

McCormack, William. "On Lingayat Culture." In A. K. Ramanujan, tr., *Speaking of Śiva*. Baltimore, 1973, pp. 175-87.

Meinhard, Heinrich. "Beiträge zur Kenntnis des Śivaismus nach den Purāṇas. Baessler Archiv 12. Thesis, Bonn, 1928.

Meyer, Conrad Ferdinand. *Huttens Letzte Tage, Eine Dichtung*. 8th ed. Leipzig, 1891.

Meyer, Johann Jakob. *Sexual Life in Ancient India*. New York, 1930.

———. *Trilogie Altindischer Mächte und Feste der Vegetation*. Zurich, 1937.
Miles, A. *Land of the Lingam*. London, 1933.
Moeller, Volker. *Symbolik des Hinduismus und des Jainismus*. Stuttgart, 1974.
Monier-Williams, Sir Monier. *Brahmanism and Hinduism*. London, 1891.
———. *Religious Thought and Life in India.* I, *Vedism, Brahmanism and Hinduism*. London, 1885.
Moor, Edward. *Śrī Sarvadevasabhā. The Hindu Pantheon.* Reprint. London, 1810.
Muir, J. *Original Sanskrit Texts*. Vol. 4. Reprint of 1873 ed. New Delhi, 1976.
———. *Original Sanskrit Texts on the Origin and History of the People of India, Their Religion and Institutions*. 5 vols. London, 1868-1874.
Mukhopadhyaya, B. "The Tripura Episode in Sanskrit Literature." *J. Ganganath Jha Research Institute* 7:4 (1950), 371-95.
Müller, F. Max, tr. *Vedic Hymns*. Part I. *SBE* 32. Reprint of 1891 Oxford ed. Delhi, 1964.
Narayan, R. K. *Gods, Demons and Others*. New York, 1964.
Narayana Ayyar, C. V., *Origin and Early History of Śaivism in South India*. Madras, 1936.
Nathan, Leonard, tr. *The Transport of Love: The Meghadūta of Kālidāsa*. Berkeley, 1976.
Neff, Muriel. "Elephanta, III, IV." *Marg* 13 (1960), 31-55.
Nivedita, Sister (Margaret E. Noble), and Ananda K. Coomaraswamy. *Myths of the Hindus and Buddhists*. London, 1913.
O'Flaherty, Wendy Doniger. *Asceticism and Eroticism in the Mythology of Śiva*. London, 1973.
———. "Asceticism and Sexuality in the Mythology of Śiva." *HR* 8 (May 1969), 300-37; *HR* 9 (August 1969), 1-41.
———. *Hindu Myths: A Sourcebook Translated from the Sanskrit*. Baltimore, 1975.
———. "The Hindu Symbolism of Cows, Bulls, Stallions and Mares." *AARP* 8 (1975), pp. 1-7.
———. "The Origin of Heresy in Hindu Mythology." *HR* 10 (May 1971), 271-333.
———. *The Origins of Evil in Hindu Mythology*. Berkeley, 1976.
———. "The Submarine Mare in the Mythology of Śiva." *JRAS*, 1971, pp. 9-27.
———. "The Symbolism of Ashes in the Mythology of Śiva." *Purāṇa* 13 (1971), 26-35.
———. "The Symbolism of the Third Eye of Śiva in the Purāṇas." *Purāṇa* 11 (July 1969), 273-84.
Ogibenin, B. L. *Structure d'un mythe védique: le mythe cosmogonic dans le Ṛg Veda*. The Hague, 1973.
———. *Sur le symbolisme du type chamanique dans le Ṛgveda*. Tartu, 1968.
Oldenberg, H. *Die Religion des Veda*. Stuttgart, 1923.
———. "Der Vedische Kalender und das Alter des Veda." *ZDMG* 48 (1894), 629-48.
Oman, John Campbell. *The Mystics, Ascetics and Saints of India*. London, 1903.

Oppert, Gustav. *On the Original Inhabitants of Bharatavarsha or India*. London, 1893.

Otto, R. *The Idea of the Holy*. Reprint of revised ed., London, 1929. Oxford, 1958.

Pal, Pratapaditya. *Bronzes of Kashmir*. New York, 1975.

———. "A Kushān Indra and Some Related Sculptures." *Oriental Art* 25 (Summer 1979), 212-26.

———. *The Sensuous Immortals: A Selection of Sculptures from the Pan-Asian Collection*. Los Angeles, 1978.

———. *Nepal, Where the Gods Are Young*. New York, 1975.

Panigrahi, K. D. "Sculptural Presentations of Lakulīśa and Other Pāśupata Teachers." *JIH* 38:3 (1960), 635-43.

Pathak, M.V.S. *History of Śaiva Cults in North India*. Vārāṇasī, 1960.

Pattabiramin, P. Z. "Notes d'iconographie dravidienne: II. Ardhanārīśvaramūrti. III. Jvarahareśvara ou Jvaradeva. IV. Candraśekharamūrti." *Arts As* 6 (1959), 13-32.

———. "Notes d'iconographie dravidienne: Ekapadatrimūrti." *Arts As* 5 (1958), 303-306.

———. "Statues en bronze de Tripurātaṇḍavam ou Tripurāntakamūrti et de son epouse Pārvatī à Kulapadu (sud de l'Inde)." *Arts As* 3 (1956), 293-95.

Piggott, Stuart. *Pre-Historic India*. London, 1952.

Polo, Marco. *The Book of Ser Marco Polo*. Translated and edited by Sir Henry Yule. 3rd ed. 2 vols. London, 1903.

Pott, P. H. *Yoga and Yantra: Their Interrelationship and Their Significance for Indian Archaeology*. Leiden, 1946. Koninlijk Institut voor Taal-Land-en Volkenkunde, Translation Series 8, The Hague, 1966.

Pusalker, A. D. *Studies in the Epics and Purāṇas of India*. Bombay, 1955.

Radhakrishnan, S. *Indian Philosophy*. 2 vols. New York, 1927.

Raghavan, V. "Tamil Versions of the Purāṇas." *Purāṇa* 2 (1960), 223-46.

Ramanujan, A. K. *Speaking of Śiva*. Baltimore, 1973.

Rao, M. Raja. "The Astronomical Background of Vedic Rudra and Purāṇic Śiva." *Bharatiya Vidyā* 13 (1952).

Rao, T.A.G. *See* Gopinatha Rao, T. A.

Rau, Heimo. *Reflections on Indian Art*. Bombay, 1976.

Rawson, P. *The Art of Tantra*. London, 1973.

———. *Tantra*. London, 1971.

Regnaud, P. "Les origines du myth d'Aurva." *RHR* 23 (1891), 308-15.

Renou, Louis, tr. *Hymnes et prières du Veda*. Paris, 1938.

———. *Religion of Ancient India*. London, 1953.

———. "Sur la notion de 'brahman.' " *JA* 237 (1949).

———. *Vocabulaire du rituel védique*. Paris, 1954.

———, and J. Filliozat. *L'Inde classique*. 2 vols. Paris, 1947, 1953.

Rhode, J. G. *Über Religiöse Bildung, Mythologie und Philosophie der Hindus*. Leipzig, 1827.

Rivett-Carnac, J. G. "The Snake Symbol in India, Especially in Connection with the Worship of Śiva." *JRASB* 48 (1879).

Rivière, Juan Roger. "The Problem of Gaṇeśa in the Purāṇas." *Purāṇa* 4:1 (1962), 96-102.

Robinson, Marguerite S., and L. E. Joiner. "An Experiment in the Structural Study of Myth." *Contributions to Indian Sociology* N.S. 2 (1968), 1-37.

Rosenfield, John M. *The Dynastic Arts of the Kushans*. Berkeley, 1967.

Ruben, W. *Eisenschmiede und Daemonen in Indien*. Supplement to Internationales Archiv für Ethnographie 37. Leiden, 1939.

Ryder, A. W. *Die Ṛbhu's im Ṛgveda*. Inaugural dissertation, Gütersloh, 1901.

Santillana, G. de, and H. von Dechend. *Hamlet's Mill*. Boston, 1968.

Sarkar, B. K. *The Folk Element in Hindu Culture*. London, 1917.

Scharbau, C. A. *Die Idee der Schöpfung in der Vedischen Literatur*. Stuttgart, 1932.

Scherer, Anton. *Gestirnnamen Bei Den Indogermanischen Völkern*. Heidelberg, 1953.

Schneider, U. *Der Somaraub des Manu*. Wiesbaden, 1971.

Schroeder, L. von. *Mysterium und Mimus im Rig Veda*. Leipzig, 1908.

Sebeok, Thomas A. *Myth: A Symposium*. Bloomington, 1958.

Sen-Gupta, R. "The Panels of Kalyāṇa Sundaramūrti at Ellora." *Lalitkalā* 7 (1960), 14-18.

Shah, U. P. *Sculptures from Samalaji and Roda*. Baroda, 1960.

Sharma, Brijendra Nath. *Festivals of India*. New Delhi, 1978.

———. *Iconography of Sadāśiva*. New Delhi, 1976.

———. "Rāvaṇa Lifting Mount Kailāsa in Indian Art." *East and West* 23 (1973), 327-38.

Shivpadasundaram, P. *The Śaiva School of Hinduism*. London, 1934.

Sieg, Emil. *Die Sagenstoffe des Ṛgveda und die Indische Itihāsatradition*. Stuttgart, 1902.

Silburn, Lilian, tr. *Hymnes de Abhinavagupta, Traduits et Commentés*. Paris, 1970.

Sircar, Dines Chandra. "The Sākta Pīṭhas." *JRASB*, Letters 14:1 (1948), 1-108.

Sivaramamurti, C. *The Art of India*. New York, 1977.

———. *Gaṅgā*. New Delhi, 1976.

———. *Naṭarāja in Art, Thought and Literature*. New Delhi, 1976.

———. *Śatarudrīya: Vibhūti of Śiva's Iconography*. New Delhi, 1976.

———. *South Indian Bronzes*. New Delhi, 1963.

———. *South Indian Painting*. New Delhi, 1968.

Sörensen, S. *An Index to the Names in the Mahābhārata and A Concordance of the Bombay and Calcutta editions and P. C. Roy's Translations*. Reprint of 1904 ed. Delhi, 1963.

Spink, Walter M. "Elephanta, Relationships with Ajanta and Ellora." In *Memorial Volume of Dr. Moti Chandra*. Bombay, forthcoming.

———. "Jogeshwari: A Brief Analysis." *JISOA*, Moti Chandra Commemoration Volume, No. 1 (1978), 1-35.

———. *Ajanta to Ellora*. Bombay, 1967.

Spratt, P. *Hindu Culture and Personality: A Psychoanalytic Study*. Bombay, 1960.

Srinivasan, Doris. "The Religious Significance of Multiple Bodily Parts to Denote the Divine Findings from the Rig Veda." *Asiatische Studien (Études Asiatiques)* 29:2 (1975), 137-79.

Srinivasan, Doris. "The So-Called Proto-Śiva Seal from Mohenjo-Daro: An Iconological Assessment." *Archives of Asian Art* 29 (1975-1976), 47-58.

Srinivasan, K. R. *Bronzes of South India*. Madras, 1963.

Stietencron, H. von. "Bhairava." *ZDMG* Supplement I, Vorträge, Teil 3 (1969) 863-71.

———. *Gaṅgā und Yamunā; zur symbolischen Bedeutung der Flussgöttinnen an Indischen Tempeln*. Wiesbaden, 1972.

Suryanarayana Sastri, S. S., "The Philosophy of Śaivism." In H. Bhattacharyya, ed., *The Cultural Heritage of India* 3. 2nd ed. Calcutta, 1953, pp. 387-99.

Thieme, P. "Brahman." *ZDMG* 102 (1952), 91-129.

Thomas, P. *Epics, Myths and Legends of India*. 5th ed. Bombay, 1958.

———. *Hindu Religion, Customs and Manners*. Bombay, 1960.

———. *Kāma Kalpa: The Hindu Ritual of Love*. 11th ed. Bombay, 1959.

Tilak, B. G. *The Orion or Researches into the Antiquity of the Vedas*. Reprint of 1893 Bombay ed. 4th ed., Poona, 1955.

Trivedi, R. D. "Mother and Child Sculptures Representing the Gṛhapati Form of Śiva." *East and West* 24 (1970).

Tucci, G. *The Theory and Practice of the Maṇḍala*. London, 1961.

Vaidya, Parashuram Lakshman. *The Harivaṃśa* 2, Appendices. Poona, 1971.

Vats, Madho Sarup. *Excavations at Harappa* 1. Reprint of 1940 ed. New Delhi, 1974.

Venkataramanayya, N. *Rudra-Śiva*. Madras, 1941.

Volchok, B. Ya. "Protoindiiskie paralleli k mifu o Skande." Institut Etnografii, Akademii Nauk, SSSR, *Proto-Indica*, 1972, pp. 305-12.

———. "Towards an Interpretation of Proto-Indian Pictures." *Journal of Tamil Studies* 2 (May 1970), 29-53.

Wallis, H. W. *The Cosmology of the Ṛg Veda*. Edinburgh, 1887.

Wayman, Alex. "Contributions Regarding the Thirty-two Characteristics of the Great Person." *Liebenthal Festschrift, Sino-Indian Studies*. 5:3 and 4 (May 1957), 234-60.

Weber, Albrecht. *Indische Streifen*. Berlin, 1868-1870.

———. *Die Vedischen Nachrichten von den naxatra (Mondstationen)*. Berlin, 1860.

Wheeler, Sir Mortimer. *The Indus Civilisation*. 3rd ed. Cambridge, 1958.

Whitney, William Dwight. "On the Jaiminīya or Talavakara Brāhmaṇa." *Proceedings of the American Oriental Society*, 1883, pp. cxlii-cxliv.

Wilkins, W. J. *Hindu Mythology, Vedic and Purāṇic*. Calcutta, 1900.

Wilson, Horace Hayman. "Analysis of the Purāṇas." *JRASB* 1 (1832), 81-86, 217-33, 431-42, 535-43.

———. "Essays on the Purāṇas." *JRASB* 5 (1839), 61-73, 298-313.

———. *Essays on the Religion of the Hindus*. 2 vols. London, 1864.

Winternitz, Moriz. *A History of Indian Literature*. I, *Introduction, Veda, National Epics, Purāṇas, and Tantras*. 2nd ed. Calcutta, 1963.

Woodroffe, Sir John George (Arthur Avalon). *Śakti and Śākta, Essays and Addresses on the Śākta Tantraśāstras*. Madras, 1959.

Zaehner, Robert Charles. *Hinduism*. Oxford, 1962.

———. "Sexual Symbolism in the Śvetāśvatara Upanishad." In *Myths and Symbols, Studies in Honor of Mircea Eliade*, edited by J. M. Kitagawa and Charles Long. Chicago, 1969, pp. 209-15.

Ziegenbalg, Bartholomaeus. *Genealogy of the South Indian Gods*. Madras, 1869.

Zimmer, H. *Art of Indian Asia*. Bollingen Series XXXIX. 2 vols. New York, 1955.

———. *Māyā, der Indische Mythos*. Zürich, 1952.

———. *Myths and Symbols in Indian Art and Civilization*. Bollingen Series VI. New York, 1946.

INDEX OF THEMES

The Flight of the Arrow

THE ARCHER

Rudra, Wild Hunter, 8, 71, 83, 424, 425, 434
Rudra, Wild Hunter and ascetic; Wild Hunter, Lord of Yoga, 16, 21, 38, 232, 329, 354, 424
Śarva, name of Rudra as Archer, 15, 35, 48, 64, 74, 103, 107, 331
Rudra, the Fire, the Archer, the Avenger, Guardian of the Uncreate, 16, 25, 30, 63, 77, 78, 83, 102, 103, 124, 232, 240, 406, 421, 423
Rudra's primordial shot, 4, 6, 29, 31, 60, 232
Rudra pierces Prajāpati, the sacrifice, 326
Rudra is made Paśupati, "Lord of Animals" by Prajāpati and the gods; His shape of horror given by the gods, 6, 9, 21, 30, 53, 58, 59, 98, 99, 252, 253, 330, 405
Rudra is made Paśupati before Tripura, 405, 412
Rudra (at Dakṣa's sacrifice) pierces heart of embodied sacrifice, the antelope; Rudra pursues fleeing antelope to the sky, 328, 329, 330
Rudra excluded from the sacrifice after he pierced Prajāpati, 58-60, 326, 327
Rudra pierces the sacrifice because the gods excluded him from the sacrifice, 65, 327
Archers in all directions (*see* Ekavrātya), 94
Birth of Rudra as Cosmic Archer (from Prajāpati's golden bowl), 103, 106
Kṛśānu, the Archer, guardian of Soma, 27, 37, 38, 40, 79, 124, 343, 413
Rudra, the cause of the sanctifying power of the antelope skin, 338
Re-enactment of Rudra's piercing Prajāpati: Śiva severs Brahmā's fifth head; Śiva cuts off Dakṣa's head, 255, 259, 325
Rudra as Kirāta, 258
Kāma: tests arrows directing them against Brahmā; his victim. His ultimate target: Śiva, the Archer, 219, 252, 304, 305, 320

THE ARROW

Rudra's arrow flies against copulating Father, Prajāpati, the antelope, at the beginning of time; arrow remains in wound, 31, 39, 218, 418, 420
Arrow speeds along time; flight of arrow, 99, 124, 271, 424
Rudra's arrows flit across the universe, 49, 74
Pierced part of Prajāpati caused havoc amongst the gods, they were deprived of their creativity, 31, 59, 326, 327, 420, 424
Spot pierced by arrow, first part of offering; Arrow cut out when anger of gods subsided, 31, 59, 326-328
Prajāpati's golden bowl from which Rudra is born as Puruṣa with a thousand arrows, its measure: an arrow's flight, 101
The arrows: of Śarva; of Manyu, 49, 103
Kṛśānu's arrow; serpents, 28
Upasad rite, an arrow, 405, 415
Arrow and healing plant in hand of Rudra, 39

LIBRARY OF CONGRESS CATALOGING IN PUBLICATION DATA

Kramrisch, Stella, 1898-
The presence of Śiva.

Bibliography: p.
Includes index.
1. Śiva (Hindu deity)—Art. 2. Sculpture, Hindu—India—Elephanta Island. 3. Cave temples—India—Elephanta Island. 4. Sculpture, Hindu—India—Ellora. 5. Cave temples—India—Ellora. I. Title.
NB1007.S67K7 704.9'48945211 80-8558
ISBN 0-691-03964-X
ISBN 0-691-10115-9 (lim. pbk. ed.)

PLATES

ELEPHANTA

PLATE 1. Interior of the Great Cave Temple along the east-west axis leading to the innermost sanctuary (*garbhagṛha*)

PLATE 2. Entrance to *garbhagṛha* and *liṅga*

PLATE 3. The south of the cave: Ardhanārīśvara

PLATE 4. The south of the cave: Sadāśiva

PLATE 5. The south of the cave: Gaṅgādhara

PLATE 6. Heads of Sadāśiva (detail of Plate 4)

PLATE 7. The central face: Mahādeva (cf. Plate 6)

PLATE 8. Mahādeva, profile

PLATE 9. Mahādeva, profile

PLATE 10. Umā (cf. Plates 4 and 6)

PLATE 11. Ardhanārīśvara (cf. Plate 3)

PLATE 12. Ardhanārīśvara (detail of Plate 11)

PLATE 13. Gaṅgādhara

PLATE 14. Pārvatī (detail of Plate 13)

PLATE 15. Pārvatī (detail of Plate 13)

PLATE 16. Kalyāṇa-Sundaramūrti

PLATE 17. Kalyāṇa-Sundaramūrti (detail of Plate 16)

PLATE 18. Kalyāṇa-Sundaramūrti (detail of Plate 16)

PLATE 19. Andhakāsura vadha

PLATE 20. Andhakāsura vadha

Plate 21. Yogīśvara/Lakulīśa

PLATE 22. Naṭarāja

PLATE 23. Naṭarāja (detail of Plate 22)

PLATE 24. Naṭarāja (detail of Plate 22)

PLATE 25. Kārttikeya (detail not included in Plates 22-24)

ELLORA

PLATE 26. The Austerities of Pārvatī (Rāmeśvara Cave Temple)

PLATE 27. Vārāhī (detail of Saptamātṛkā sculpture, Rāmeśvara Cave Temple)

PLATE 28. Śiva dancing (Daśāvatār Cave Temple)

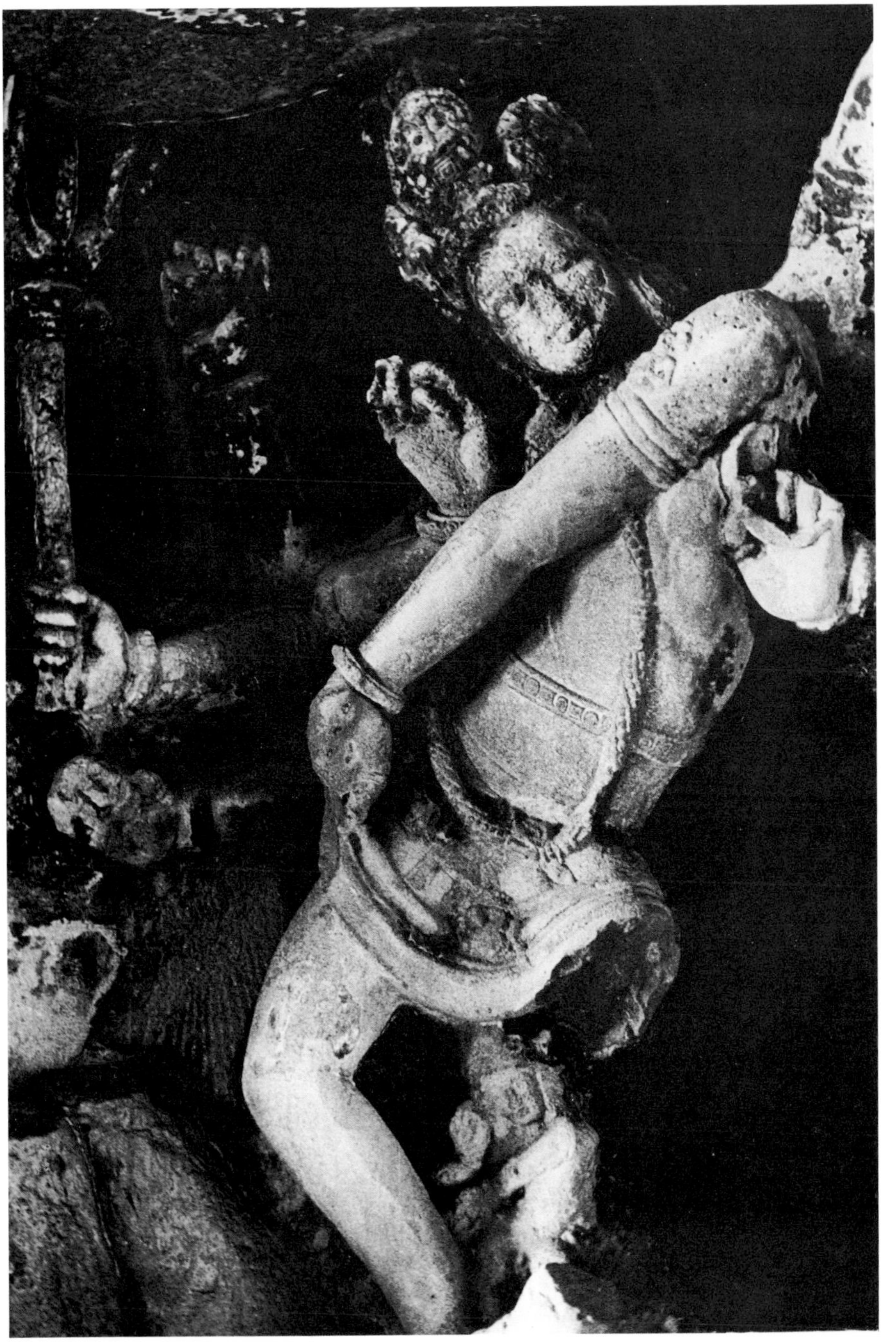

PLATE 29. Śiva dancing (Laṅkeśvara Cave Temple)

PLATE 30. Tripurāntaka (Kailāsa Temple; on inner face of entrance into the court)

PLATE 31. Tripurāntaka (Kailāsa Temple; in corridor)